Political Thought

Michael Rosen studied philosophy and social science at Oxford and at the University of Frankfurt. He has taught philosophy at Oxford, Harvard and University College London. His writings include *Hegel's Dialectic and its Criticism* (Cambridge University Press, 1982) and *On Voluntary Servitude: False Consciousness and the Theory of Ideology* (Polity Press, 1996). He is currently Fellow and Tutor in Philosophy at Lincoln College, Oxford.

Jonathan Wolff is Reader in Philosophy, University College, London and was Founding Director of the Philosophy Programme in the University of London School of Advanced Study. His publications include *Robert Nozick: Property, Justice and the Minimal State* (Polity Press, 1991) and *An Introduction to Political Philosophy* (Oxford University Press, 1996) and he is Editor of The Proceedings of the Aristotelian Society.

OXFORD **READERS**

The Oxford Readers series represents a unique resource which brings together extracts of texts from a wide variety of sources, primary and secondary, on a wide range of inderdisciplinary topics.

OXFORD **READERS**

Political Thought

Edited by Michael Rosen *and* Jonathan Wolff
with the assistance of Catriona McKinnon

OXFORD
UNIVERSITY PRESS

OXFORD
UNIVERSITY PRESS

Great Clarendon Street, Oxford OX2 6DP

Oxford University Press is a department of the University of Oxford.
It furthers the University's objective of excellence in research, scholarship,
and education by publishing worldwide in

Oxford New York

Auckland Cape Town Dar es Salaam Hong Kong Karachi
Kuala Lumpur Madrid Melbourne Mexico City Nairobi
New Delhi Taipei Toronto Shanghai

With offices in

Argentina Austria Brazil Chile Czech Republic France Greece
Guatemala Hungary Italy Japan Poland Portugal Singapore
South Korea Switzerland Thailand Turkey Ukraine Vietnam

Published in the United States
by Oxford University Press Inc., New York

Introductions, selection, and editorial matter © Michael Rosen and Jonathan Wolff 1999

British Library Cataloguing in Publication Data
Data available

Library of Congress Cataloging in Publication Data
Political thought/edited by Michael Rosen and Jonathan Wolff with
the assistance of Catriona McKinnon.
p. cm.—(Oxford readers)
Includes bibliographical references.
1. Political science—Philosophy. I. Rosen, Michael. II. Wolff,
Jonathan. III. McKinnon, Catriona. IV. Series.
JA66 P647 1999
320´.01—dc21 99–21005

ISBN 978-0-19-289278-2

Typeset in Dante
by Cambrian Typesetters, Frimley, Surrey
Printed and bound by
CPI Group (UK) Ltd, Croydon, CR0 4YY

To Leah and Max

Preface

Political thought extends over a vast domain and no anthology, however generously conceived, could present more than a very small fraction of it. For this, then, we make no apology, but the reader is entitled to be given some sense of the principles on which our inevitably ruthless selection was made. We own up to three biases which, we recognize, not everyone will share.

The first is towards continuity. We have presented a diversity of thinkers as addressing, over the centuries, a range of broadly characterized, but recognizably continuous, issues. This is not to pretend, of course, that the positions taken towards those issues have themselves been stable—on the contrary, we hope that the anthology will illustrate how radically attitudes to many fundamental political questions have changed—or that the thinkers of the past did not also concern themselves with issues and problems that now seem very foreign to us. Even so, to treat texts in this way is to cut oneself off from those layers of significance that can only be revealed by a proper appreciation of their historical context. An anthology with a different purpose might have presented the same authors very differently.

Our second bias is towards argument. We have selected not only striking and significant positions taken in relation to political issues but looked for arguments to support them. To do so is to suppose that political discourse involves more than stirring rhetoric or appeals to self-interest. That the latter play a great role it would, of course, be foolish to deny, but argument too, if less spectacularly, plays its part, we believe, and we have allowed our selections to favour those who back up their views with evidence and reasoning.

Finally, we must confess to a certain bias towards issues of contemporary relevance. So, for instance, we have looked at what ancient authors had to say about the proper place of women in society rather than the justification of slavery, not because the authors themselves would have regarded the former question as any more interesting or important than the latter but, quite simply, because it is contentious for us in a way that (we hope) the question of slavery is not. Of course, issues come and go in surprising ways and so we have tried to be inclusive rather than narrow in our selection. Nevertheless, although many of the authors represented here are of timeless value, this is an anthology that does, to some extent, reflect the preoccupations of its own time. We hope that, in consequence, readers will find that the questions it addresses are ones whose importance they can easily recognize and that the arguments contained in it will help them to broaden and sharpen their own views on the subject.

We have listened to (and sometimes taken) advice from many people, including three anonymous readers for Oxford University Press. We are grateful to them. We owe a particular debt to Catriona McKinnon, who took on the job of tracking down our selections and providing a first edit for the great majority of them. We also thank (if slightly ruefully) George Miller of Oxford University Press for setting us on the path that led to this book.

London   M.R.
1999   J.W.

Contents

III. Democracy and Its Difficulties

IV. Liberty and Rights

V. Economic Justice

VI. Justice between Groups

VII. Alternatives to Liberalism

VIII. Progress and Civilization

Appendix: Fundamental Political Documents

Political Thought

Introduction

In *The Social Contract* Rousseau remarks that he will 'take men as they are, and institutions as they may be'. This resonant phrase communicates both a sense of realism and a sense of optimism. It is an inspiring call to design the best society for human beings, but for human beings as we know them to be, rather than as—in our fantasies—we hope they might possibly become. Critics may wonder whether Rousseau really did obey this constraint in his own work, but that is not the issue for us now. Rather, this simple remark opens up for us many of the central issues to be encountered in this Reader.

Let us start with the obvious question: what are men, or rather, human beings, like? (One of the questions to be raised in Section I is whether political thought has ignored, misperceived, or otherwise mistreated, women.) If we are to take human beings as they are, first we have to know what they are. Rousseau has his own complex view; namely that man in the state of nature is innocent, and that the evil to be found in society is social in origin. We will look at Rousseau's view, as well as the opposed view of Hobbes and Locke, in Section I, where selections from these three towering figures of modern political philosophy first appear.

Thus there is disagreement about what human beings are like, or, to put this another way, disagreement about human nature. Are human beings naturally greedy and selfish, naturally compassionate, or both, or neither? This leads on to a second question: how can we know what they are like? What materials can we draw on to justify one account of human nature over another? Is there actual evidence in favour of any particular view, or are differing accounts based on mere prejudice or—to put it more kindly—speculation?

Rousseau assumes that he knows what human nature is and he implies that there are limits to how much it might change: why else should he insist on taking 'men as they are'? This is a major assumption, for is it so obvious—is it even true?—that human nature is fixed? Many have thought that if conditions on earth became properly fit for human beings then human beings will learn new ways of behaving and new forms of enjoyment. The thought is that we are constrained by social conditions. Change the social conditions and we will change too. The selection from Robert Owen in Section I is the boldest statement of such a view, but we can find more subtle versions of it in the writings of Marx, Engels, and Kropotkin also printed here.

In saying that he will 'take institutions as they may be' Rousseau is clearly making some very different assumptions about institutions; most notably about their potential for change. But first, what does Rousseau mean by 'institutions'? The most obvious examples of institutions are the forms and mechanisms of government: the bodies and processes which make, execute, and enforce the laws. We can also include religious organizations, economic structures, schools, universities, hospitals, and, in general, all the ways in which human beings as collectives organize themselves for whatever purposes. Rousseau's assumption—and on the face of it a very plausible one—is that we can organize ourselves in a huge variety of ways. We can have liberal laws or authoritarian ones; we can have a single dominant religion, religious pluralism, or no religion at all; we can have a free market or a government-regulated economy. The list of possibilities appears almost endless.

No doubt everyone has some views about which, among these alternatives, are the best, or, at least, are better than others. But what does it mean to say that one option is *better* than another? Better for whom, and in what respects? And—that question again—how can we know? Our experience is always limited, so how can we judge alternatives we have never faced? Indeed, what is judgement anyway? Are 'value judgements' no more than assertions of subjective preferences, as we are sometimes told, or can we find objective moral standards? Interestingly most of the thinkers represented here seem simply to have assumed that argument in moral and political matters is as secure and firmly grounded as any area of inquiry. The extreme opposite view, that appeal to values is a sophisticated form of empty rhetoric, makes its appearance here in the selection from Nietzsche in Section VII.

To return to the main theme, though, even if we are convinced that there are many possible alternative ways of organizing our societies, how can we assure ourselves they are alternatives for *us*? There are many subtle difficulties here. Perhaps it is already too late to bring about the best possible world. For example, we will probably never recreate a world in which no one has the knowledge of how to make nuclear weapons. But, more generally, there is a real question of how much human societies can achieve by will or choice. Can human societies expect to achieve what they aim at, or is the social world so complex as to be, like the weather, largely beyond deliberate human control? We have an important question here. Even if we can know that one organization of society—one possible set of institutions—is preferable to all others, it remains to be seen whether we can bring it into existence. Popper, in Section VIII, claims that any attempt to bring about large-scale change by means of a rational plan is bound to lead to tyranny.

Sceptics will say, then, that we have far less control over human institutions than Rousseau assumes. Of course no one will deny that we can make at least some changes; we can pass new laws or repeal old ones, for example. However it could be said that such changes are relatively superficial and two separate lines of argument could be made. First, it may be claimed that human institutions change much less than we might think: consider, for example, the fact that religion, or market trading, or the family, seem to have survived even the most systematic attempts to suppress them. Hayek, in Section V, expressed doubt that we will ever to be able to live without some form of market and price structure for long. Second, it will be said by some that, although fundamental changes take place in society over time, these are not brought about by deliberate human action. One may, like Hegel, or Marx in Section VIII, see a pattern to underlying change, or, alternatively, believe that such changes come about largely through chance. There are, then, many ways of questioning whether human beings are able to bring about changes in their institutions through choice. This is not to say that Rousseau's assumption that we have some measure of control is false; rather the point is that this is not the only view of the matter.

We should also note another feature of the opening remark from Rousseau; that it counter-poses the individual and society. It asks how society can be arranged so as to be best for the individuals who make it up. This reveals the further assumption that the primary object of concern is the individual; his or her rights, liberties, well-being, or flourishing. Policies should be judged in terms of their impact on individuals. This 'individualist' assumption goes so deep in the western liberal tradition that it is hard to recognize it even as an assumption. However it is not the only possible view. It could be argued that we should be concerned, above all, to preserve culture, or high art, or the true religion, and the effect on individuals of doing so is at best a secondary consideration. Although it may be hard to find examples of such views supported by reasons for them, more moderate versions—in which the culture or collective goods are valued in addition to the individuals who produce them—can be seen in very different ways in writers such as T. S. Eliot and Michael Sandel in Section VII.

Finally, a question of a different sort. We began with Rousseau's statement that he will take human beings as they are, and institutions as they may be, and we have brought out some of the assumptions that lie behind this thought. But what we have not yet done is ask why take human beings and their institutions at all. Why did he embark on this line of inquiry? What was the nature of his project and what did he hope to achieve? Rousseau attempted to provide a blueprint—or at least an outline—of the good society. Why did he and others set out on such projects (or warn of the folly of doing so)?

One possibility is that political thinkers are motivated simply by the search for truth. A good number of the writers selected here—and we can include Plato, Aristotle, Hobbes, Locke, Hume, Rousseau, Kant, Hegel, and Mill—would be on anyone's list of the most important philosophers in the western tradition. Just as they sought the truth on the ultimate questions of metaphysics and epistemology so, one might imagine, they sought the truth about the question of the good society.

No doubt there is something of this motivation in some cases but there is surely more to be said to explain why people have been moved to write about fundamental political issues. Many of the writers here are driven, at least in part, by a sense of wasted potential: that if only the right steps were taken, many, or even all, of us could have better lives. Many political thinkers take a tragic view of current societies; our societies thwart human potential for no good reason. Changing our laws, our religions, our political institutions, or our economic structures will unlock the sources of real human fulfilment. Such writers are inspired by what they see as a grave deficiency in the world around us. The perceived deficiency and its supposed solution may vary, but their general project has the same type of inspiration.

We should not assume, though, that all political thinkers fit this mould. A smaller, but still significant, group take their task to be quite different. In reaction to those who point out how much better things could be, if only . . ., these other theorists warn us against the dangerous naivety of the first group. The world is not so simple, they say. Attempted improvements often backfire; our goals may not even be coherent; and if we try too hard to reach them we may do untold damage. We should, so say these thinkers, such as Edmund Burke in Section VII, learn to value and appreciate what we have, rather than risk it in the name of utopia.

Whatever the message, whether optimistic or pessimistic for the future, whether bitter or proud about the present, political thinkers share engagement and commitment. In this Reader we have selected a wide range of voices and views on a wide range of problems and questions. No Reader of this type could reasonably claim to be comprehensive—it must be more like a scrapbook of snapshots and sketches than a map. But what we hope to communicate is a sense of the living tradition of political thought, where thinkers from the present age debate with thinkers from the past, and other thinkers from the past reply. What links them all is a sense of the importance of the task on which they are engaged.

Section I

Human Nature

INTRODUCTION

Every human being alive today is the subject of some state or other. A statement like this is bound to lead to anyone of a philosophical temperament reaching for a counter-example. Isn't there a reclusive millionaire somewhere, sitting out on his own island? And aren't there hermits, survivalists, and even tribal peoples who refuse to accept the authority of any state? But whether or not these are genuine counter-examples—probably not—the scarcity of plausible candidates alone makes the main point. Human beings, for whatever reasons, have a strong tendency to organize themselves into societies, and these societies contain the type of power structures which will tend to qualify them as states.

In the next section we will look at what the state is, and whether it might be justified. Here our primary task is to consider the related question of whether we can conceive of human beings living without a state, or other organized power structure. Is it possible? Might it even be preferable to how things are now? This is the question of what life would be like in 'the state of nature'. Reflection on this question goes hand in hand with reflection on human nature. Aristotle, in the first selection here, argues that the state and human beings are made for each other: the good human life is simply not possible without the state.

Hobbes reaches a similar conclusion, if for different reasons, famously and graphically arguing that life in the state of nature is 'solitary, poor, nasty, brutish and short'. The state of nature, argues Hobbes, is a place where it is too dangerous to respect the moral law, and people cannot be criticized for doing whatever they feel necessary—in competition with others—for their own preservation. Locke presents a moderate view: the state of nature, although 'inconvenient', is governed by a law of nature which commands people to preserve each other as well as themselves. This law generates natural rights, and Locke argues that individuals in the state of nature even have the right to punish those who violate the natural rights of others. Locke is keen to argue that the state of nature need not be a state of war.

Montesquieu agrees with Hobbes that individuals in the state of nature would be highly fearful of each other, but argues that this will tend to keep them apart, rather than provide a motive for attack. War, Montesquieu concludes, happens only once the state of nature has passed and people have

formed themselves into societies. Rousseau, typically, is contemptuous of earlier philosophers' attempts to give a true picture of the life of the 'savage', and,
with some justice, accuses his predecessors of projecting their experience of
human beings, softened and corrupted by civilized society, back on to the state
of nature. Rousseau paints a picture of a human being as a member of the animal kingdom: an animal with the wits and skill to flourish, but one with instincts for survival and compassion, in contrast to Hobbes's calculator of
self-interest or Locke's possessor and enforcer of natural rights.

There are, of course, ways of talking about human nature which do not require one to imagine a state of nature, and the selections from Robert Owen
provide an example. Owen asserted the extreme materialist thesis that the character of any human being is entirely determined by that being's circumstances.
Change the circumstances and you will change the person. We have included
texts where Owen lays out his view, as well as an illustration of how he thought
it might usefully be applied through the use of the device of a 'silent monitor'.
Karl Marx and Friedrich Engels, though influenced to a degree by Owen, believed that his view was simplistic. In contrast they emphasize the capacity of
human beings to change themselves and their social relations through their productive activity, in their social interaction with material nature.

In the first of two selections Darwin explains how nature selects those or-
ganisms with competitive advantages over others, while in the second he argues
that even though acting according to a high moral standard does not aid an individual, a group in which moral standards exist will win in competition with a
group which has no such standards. Finally, the anarchist, Kropotkin, in opposition to Hobbes as well as to Darwin, seeks to convince us of the cooperative
nature of all animal species, human beings among them.

We remarked earlier that reflection on the state of nature goes hand in hand
with reflection about human nature. And this leads to the second part of this
section. Is there a difference between male nature and female nature? If so,
should this—should anything—rationally exclude women from participation
in the political process, as has been the case for the great part of human history?
In addition to lacking the right to vote or stand for office, women have, at various times and places, lacked the right to hold private property, to enter various
professions, or even to receive a university degree. Things are improving, of
course, but no doubt forms of discrimination exist that we don't even recognize
yet.

The selection from Plato provides one common view of the social place of
men and women: that both men and women can perform all social functions,
but aside from such 'trivial' matters as weaving and cooking, men tend to be
much better than women. Nevertheless, an exceptional woman can compete
on equal terms. Aristotle provides an equally common opposing view: that
men and women have their own special functions, and are each supreme in
their own sphere. Rousseau pursues a similar theme in greater detail, dwelling

on the delicate power relations that are likely to develop between a demanding male and a cunning female.

Mary Wollstonecraft takes the discussion in a new direction, arguing that in order to become full citizens women must lose their financial and social dependence on men, while John Stuart Mill argues that the fact of such dependence means that no one knows woman's true nature: that is, how they would act if they were not bowed into submission. Mill agrees with Plato that women should be encouraged to compete with men. He is less convinced, though, that they will generally tend to lose out in competition.

The trend of the thought of Wollstonecraft and Mill is to argue that the apparent differences between men and women are much less significant than is commonly believed. Interestingly, though, recent feminist theory quite often attempts to demonstrate that there are some very important sexual differences that can play a role in political theory, and perhaps even political practice. Carol Gilligan argues that men and women often exhibit different patterns of moral reasoning, and this colours their perception of the world. Alison Jaggar takes this a step further, claiming that women's oppression gives them a more insightful standpoint from which to view society. Where men and women's perceptions of society differ, she claims, those of women are to be preferred.

I.a. The Natural State of Mankind

ARISTOTLE

1 The State Exists by Nature

Now in this as in other fields we shall get the best view of things if we look at their natural growth from their beginnings. First, those which are incapable of existing without each other must unite as a pair. For example, (*a*) male and female, for breeding (and this not from choice; rather, as in the other animals too and in plants, the urge to leave behind another such as one is oneself is natural); (*b*) that which naturally rules and that which is ruled, for preservation. For that which can use its intellect to look ahead is by nature ruler and by nature master, while that which has the bodily strength to labour is ruled, and is by nature a slave. Hence master and slave benefit from the same thing.

So it is by nature that a distinction has been made between female and slave. For nature produces nothing skimpily (like the Delphic knife that smiths make), but one thing for one purpose; for every tool will be made best if it subserves not many tasks but one. Non-Greeks, however, assign to female and slave the same status. This is because they do not have that which naturally rules: their association comes to be that of a male slave and a female slave. Hence, as the poets say, 'It is proper that Greeks should rule non-Greeks', on the assumption that non-Greek and slave are by nature identical.

Thus it was from these two associations that a household first arose, and Hesiod was right in his poetry when he said, 'first of all a house and a wife and an ox to draw the plough.' (The ox is the poor man's slave.) So the association formed according to nature for the satisfaction of the purposes of every day is a household, the members of which Charondas calls 'bread-fellows', and Epimenides the Cretan 'stable-companions'.

The first association, from several households, for the satisfaction of other than daily purposes, is a village. The village seems to be by nature in the highest degree, as a colony of a household—children and grandchildren, whom some people call 'homogalactic'. This is why states were at first ruled by kings (as are the nations to this day): they were formed from persons who were under kingly rule. For every household is under the kingly rule of its most senior member; so too the colonies, because of the kinship. This is what is mentioned in Homer: 'Each one lays down the law to children and wives.' For they were scattered; and that is how they dwelt in ancient times. For this reason the gods too are said by everyone to be governed by a king—namely because men themselves were originally ruled by kings and some are so still. Men model the gods' forms on themselves, and similarly their way of life too.

The complete association, from several villages, is the state, which at once reaches the limit of total self-sufficiency, so to say. Whereas it comes into existence for the sake of life, it exists for the sake of the good life. Therefore every state exists by nature, since the first associations did too. For this association is their end, and nature is an end; for whatever each thing is in character when its coming into existence has been completed, that is what we call the nature of each thing—of a man, for instance, or a horse or a house. Moreover the aim, i.e. the end, is best; and self-sufficiency is both end and best.

These considerations make it clear, then, that the state is one of those things which exist by nature, and that man is by nature an animal fit for a state. Anyone who by his nature and not by ill-luck has no state is either a wretch or superhuman; he is also like the man condemned by Homer as having 'no brotherhood, no law, no hearth'; for he is at once such by nature and keen to go to war, being isolated like a piece in a game of *pettoi*.

[From *Politics Books I and II*, trans. with a commentary by Trevor J. Saunders (Clarendon Press, Oxford, 1995), 2–3.]

THOMAS HOBBES

2 The Misery of the Natural Condition of Mankind

Nature hath made men so equal, in the faculties of the body, and mind; as that though there be found one man sometimes manifestly stronger in body, or of quicker mind than another; yet when all is reckoned together, the difference between man, and man, is not so considerable, as that one man can thereupon claim to himself any benefit, to which another may not pretend, as well as he. For as to the strength of body, the weakest has strength enough to kill the strongest, either by secret machination, or by confederacy with others, that are in the same danger with himself.

And as to the faculties of the mind, (setting aside the arts grounded upon words, and especially that skill of proceeding upon general, and infallible rules, called science; which very few have, and but in few things; as being not a native faculty, born with us; nor attained (as prudence,) while we look after somewhat else,) I find yet a greater equality amongst men, than that of strength. For prudence, is but experience; which equal time, equally bestows on all men, in those things they equally apply themselves unto. That which may perhaps make such equality incredible, is but a vain conceit of one's own wisdom, which almost all men think they have in a greater degree, than the vulgar; that is, than all men but themselves, and a few others, whom by fame, or for concurring with themselves, they approve. For such is the nature of men, that howsoever they may acknowledge many others to be more witty, or more eloquent, or more learned; yet they will hardly believe there be many so wise as themselves; for they see their own wit at hand, and other men's at a distance. But this proveth rather that men are in that point equal, than unequal. For there is not ordinarily a greater sign of the equal distribution of any thing, than that every man is contented with his share.

From this equality of ability, ariseth equality of hope in the attaining of our ends. And therefore if any two men desire the same thing, which nevertheless they cannot both enjoy, they become enemies; and in the way to their end, (which is principally their own conservation, and sometimes their delectation only,) endeavour to destroy, or subdue one another. And from hence it comes to pass, that where an invader hath no more to fear, than another man's single power; if one plant, sow, build, or possess a convenient seat, others may probably be expected to come prepared with forces united, to dispossess, and deprive him, not only of the fruit of his labour, but also of his life, or liberty. And the invader again is in the like danger of another.

And from this diffidence of one another, there is no way for any man to secure himself, so reasonable, as anticipation; that is, by force, or wiles, to master the persons of all men he can, so long, till he see no other power great enough to endanger him: and this is no more than his own conservation requireth, and is generally allowed. Also because there be some, that taking pleasure in contemplating their own power in the acts of conquest, which they pursue farther than their security requires; if others, that otherwise would be glad to be at ease within modest bounds, should not by invasion increase their power, they would not be able, long time, by standing only on their defence, to subsist. And by consequence, such augmentation of dominion over men, being necessary to a man's conservation, it ought to be allowed him.

Again, men have no pleasure, (but on the contrary a great deal of grief) in keeping company, where there is no power able to over-awe them all. For every man looketh that his companion should value him, at the same rate he sets upon himself: and upon all signs of contempt, or undervaluing, naturally endeavours, as far as he dares (which amongst them that have no common power to keep them quiet, is far enough to make them destroy each other,) to extort a greater value from his contemners, by damage; and from others, by the example.

So that in the nature of man, we find three principal causes of quarrel. First, competition; secondly, diffidence; thirdly, glory.

The first, maketh men invade for gain; the second, for safety; and the third, for reputation. The first use violence, to make themselves masters of other men's persons, wives, children, and cattle; the second, to defend them; the third, for trifles, as a word, a smile, a different opinion, and any other sign of undervalue, either direct in their persons, or by reflection in their kindred, their friends, their nation, their profession, or their name.

Hereby it is manifest, that during the time men live without a common power to keep them all in awe, they are in that condition which is called war;

and such a war, as is of every man, against every man. For WAR, consisteth not in battle only, or the act of fighting; but in a tract of time, wherein the will to contend by battle is sufficiently known: and therefore the notion of *time*, is to be considered in the nature of war; as it is in the nature of weather. For as the nature of foul weather, lieth not in a shower or two of rain; but in an inclination thereto of many days together: so the nature of war, consisteth not in actual fighting; but in the known disposition thereto, during all the time there is no assurance to the contrary. All other time is PEACE.

Whatsoever therefore is consequent to a time of war, where every man is enemy to every man; the same is consequent to the time, wherein men live without other security, than what their own strength, and their own invention shall furnish them withal. In such condition, there is no place for industry; because the fruit thereof is uncertain: and consequently no culture of the earth; no navigation, nor use of the commodities that may be imported by sea; no commodious building; no instruments of moving, and removing such things as require much force; no knowledge of the face of the earth; no account of time; no arts; no letters; no society; and which is worst of all, continual fear, and danger of violent death; and the life of man, solitary, poor, nasty, brutish, and short.

It may seem strange to some man, that has not well weighed these things; that nature should thus dissociate, and render men apt to invade, and destroy one another: and he may therefore, not trusting to this inference, made from the passions, desire perhaps to have the same confirmed by experience. Let him therefore consider with himself, when taking a journey, he arms himself, and seeks to go well accompanied; when going to sleep, he locks his doors; when even in his house he locks his chests; and this when he knows there be laws, and public officers, armed, to revenge all injuries shall be done him; what opinion he has of his fellow-subjects, when he rides armed; of his fellow citizens, when he locks his doors; and of his children, and servants, when he locks his chests. Does he not there as much accuse mankind by his actions, as I do by my words? But neither of us accuse man's nature in it. The desires, and other passions of man, are in themselves no sin. No more are the actions, that proceed from those passions, till they know a law that forbids them: which till laws be made they cannot know: nor can any law be made, till they have agreed upon the person that shall make it.

It may peradventure be thought, there was never such a time, nor condition of war as this; and I believe it was never generally so, over all the world: but there are many places, where they live so now. For the savage people in many places of America, except the government of small families, the concord whereof dependeth on natural lust, have no government at all; and live at this day in that brutish manner, as I said before. Howsoever, it may be perceived what manner of life there would be, where there were no common power to fear; by the manner of life, which men that have formerly lived under a peaceful government, use to degenerate into, in a civil war.

But though there had never been any time, wherein particular men were in a condition of war one against another; yet in all times, kings, and persons of sovereign authority, because of their independency, are in continual jealousies, and in the state and posture of gladiators; having their weapons pointing, and their eyes fixed on one another; that is, their forts, garrisons, and guns upon the frontiers of their kingdoms; and continual spies upon their neighbours; which is a posture of war. But because they uphold thereby, the industry of their subjects; there does not follow from it, that misery, which accompanies the liberty of particular men.

To this war of every man against every man, this also is consequent; that nothing can be unjust. The notions of right and wrong, justice and injustice have there no place. Where there is no common power, there is no law: where no law, no injustice. Force, and fraud, are in war the two cardinal virtues. Justice, and injustice are none of the faculties neither of the body, nor mind. If they were, they might be in a man that were alone in the world, as well as his senses, and passions. They are qualities, that relate to men in society, not in solitude. It is consequent also to the same condition, that there be no propriety, no dominion, no *mine* and *thine* distinct; but only that to be every man's, that he can get; and for so long, as he can keep it. And thus much for the ill condition, which man by mere nature is actually placed in; though with a possibility to come out of it, consisting partly in the passions, partly in his reason.

The passions that incline men to peace, are fear of death; desire of such things as are necessary to commodious living; and a hope by their industry to obtain them. And reason suggesteth convenient articles of peace, upon which men may be drawn to agreement. These articles, are they, which otherwise are called the Laws of Nature.

[From *Leviathan*, ed. with introd. by J. C. A. Gaskin (Oxford University Press, Oxford, 1996), 82–6. First published 1651.]

JOHN LOCKE

3   The State of Nature and the State of War

To understand political power aright, and derive it from its original, we must consider what estate all men are naturally in, and that is, a state of perfect freedom to order their actions, and dispose of their possessions and persons as they think fit, within the bounds of the law of Nature, without asking leave or depending upon the will of any other man.

A state also of equality, wherein all the power and jurisdiction is reciprocal, no one having more than another, there being nothing more evident than that creatures of the same species and rank, promiscuously born to all the same advantages of Nature, and the use of the same faculties, should also be equal one amongst another, without subordination or subjection, unless the lord and master of them all should, by any manifest declaration of his will, set one above another, and confer on him, by an evident and clear appointment, an undoubted right to dominion and sovereignty. [. . .]

But though this be a state of liberty, yet it is not a state of licence; though man in that state have an uncontrollable liberty to dispose of his person or possessions, yet he has not liberty to destroy himself, or so much as any creature in his possession, but where some nobler use than its bare preservation calls for it. The state of Nature has a law of Nature to govern it, which obliges every one, and reason, which is that law, teaches all mankind who will but consult it, that being all equal and independent, no one ought to harm another in his life, health, liberty or possessions; for men being all the workmanship of one omnipotent and infinitely wise Maker; all the servants of one sovereign Master, sent into the world by His order and about His business; they are His property, whose workmanship they are made to last during His, not one another's pleasure. And, being furnished with like faculties, sharing all in one community of Nature, there cannot be supposed any such subordination among us that may authorise us to destroy one another, as if we were made for one another's uses, as the inferior ranks of creatures are for ours. Every one as he is bound to preserve himself, and not to quit his station wilfully, so by the like reason, when his own preservation comes not in competition, ought he as much as he can to preserve the rest of mankind, and not unless it be to do justice on an offender, take away or impair the life, or what tends to the preservation of the life, the liberty, health, limb, or goods of another.

And that all men may be restrained from invading others' rights, and from doing hurt to one another, and the law of Nature be observed, which willeth the peace and preservation of all mankind, the execution of the law of Nature is in that state put into every man's hands, whereby every one has a right to punish the transgressors of that law to such a degree as may hinder its violation. For the law of Nature would, as all other laws that concern men in this world, be in vain if there were nobody that in the state of Nature had a power to execute that law, and thereby preserve the innocent and restrain offenders; and if any one in the state of Nature may punish another for any evil he has done, every one may do so. For in that state of perfect equality, where naturally there is no superiority of jurisdiction of one over another, what any may do in prosecution of that law, every one must needs have a right to do.

And thus, in the state of Nature, one man comes by a power over another, but yet no absolute or arbitrary power to use a criminal, when he has got him in his hands, according to the passionate heats or boundless extravagancy of his own will, but only to retribute to him so far as calm reason and conscience dictate, what is proportionate to his transgression, which is so much as may serve for reparation and restraint. For these two are the only reasons why one man may lawfully do harm to another, which is that we call punishment. In transgressing the law of Nature, the offender declares himself to live by another rule than that of reason and common equity, which is that measure God has set to the actions of men for their mutual security, and so he becomes dangerous to mankind; the tie which is to secure them from injury and violence being slighted and broken by him, which being a trespass against the whole species, and the peace and safety of it, provided for by the law of Nature, every man upon this score, by the right he hath to preserve mankind in general, may restrain, or where it is necessary, destroy things noxious to them, and so may bring such evil on any one who hath transgressed that law, as may make him repent the doing of it, and thereby deter him, and, by his example, others from doing the like mischief. And in this case, and upon this ground, every man hath a right to punish the offender, and be executioner of the law of Nature.

I doubt not but this will seem a very strange doctrine to some men; but before they condemn it, I desire them to resolve me by what right any prince or state can put to death or punish an alien for any crime he commits in their country? It is certain their laws, by virtue of any sanction they receive from the promulgated will of the legislature, reach not a stranger. They speak not to him, nor, if they did, is he bound to hearken to them. The legislative authority by which they are in force over the subjects of that commonwealth hath no power over him. Those who have the supreme power of making laws in England, France, or Holland are, to an Indian, but like the rest of the world—men without authority. And therefore, if by the law of Nature every man hath not a power to punish offences against it, as he soberly judges the case to require, I see not how the magistrates of any community can punish an alien of another country, since, in reference to him, they can have no more power than what every man naturally may have over another. [. . .]

From these two distinct rights (the one of punishing the crime, for restraint and preventing the like offence, which right of punishing is in everybody, the other of taking reparation, which belongs only to the injured party) comes it to pass that the magistrate, who by being magistrate hath the common right of punishing put into his hands, can often, where the public good demands not the execution of the law, remit the punishment of criminal offences by his own authority, but yet cannot remit the satisfaction due to any private man for the damage he has received. That he who hath suffered the damage has a right to demand in his own name, and he alone can remit. The damnified person has this power of appropriating to himself the goods or service of the offender by right of self-preservation, as every man has a power to punish the crime to prevent its being committed again, by the right he has of preserving all mankind, and doing all reasonable things he can in order to that end. And thus it is that every man in the state of Nature has a power to kill a murderer, both to deter others from doing the like injury (which no reparation can compensate) by the example of the punishment that attends it from everybody, and also to secure men from the attempts of a criminal who, having renounced reason, the common rule and measure God hath given to mankind, hath, by the unjust violence and slaughter he hath committed upon one, declared war against all mankind, and therefore may be destroyed as a lion or a tiger, one of those wild savage beasts with whom men can have no society nor security. And upon this is grounded that great law of Nature, 'Whoso sheddeth man's blood, by man shall his blood be shed.' And Cain was so fully convinced that every one had a right to destroy such a criminal, that, after the murder of his brother, he cries out, 'Every one that findeth me shall slay me,' so plain was it writ in the hearts of all mankind.

By the same reason may a man in the state of Nature punish the lesser breaches of that law, it will, perhaps, be demanded, with death? I answer: Each transgression may be punished to that degree, and with so much severity, as will suffice to make it an ill bargain to the offender, give him cause to repent, and terrify others from doing the like. Every offence that can be committed in the state of Nature may, in the state of Nature, be also punished equally, and as far forth, as it may, in a commonwealth. For though it would be beside my present purpose to enter here into the particulars of the law of Nature, or its measures of punishment, yet it is certain there is such a law, and that too as intelligible and plain to a rational creature and a studier of that law as the positive laws of commonwealths, nay, possibly plainer; as much as reason is easier to be understood than the fancies and intricate contrivances of men, following contrary and hidden interests put into words; for truly so are a great part of the municipal laws of countries, which are only so far right as they are founded on the law of Nature, by which they are to be regulated and interpreted.

To this strange doctrine—viz., That in the state of Nature every one has the executive power of the law of Nature—I doubt not but it will be objected that it is unreasonable for men to be judges in their own cases, that self-love will make men partial to themselves and their friends; and, on the other side, ill-nature, passion, and revenge will carry them too far in punishing others, and hence nothing but confusion and disorder will follow, and that therefore God hath certainly appointed government to restrain the partiality and violence of men. I easily grant that civil government is the proper remedy for the inconveniences of the state of Nature, which must certainly be great where men may be judges in their own case, since it is easy to be imagined that he who was so unjust as to do his brother an injury will scarce be so just as to condemn himself for it. But I shall desire those who make this objection to remember that absolute monarchs are but men; and if government is to be the remedy of those evils which necessarily follow from men being judges in their own cases, and the state of Nature is therefore not to be endured, I desire to know what kind of government that is, and how much better it is than the state of Nature, where one man commanding a multitude has the liberty to be judge in his own case, and may do to all his subjects whatever he pleases without the least question or control of those who execute his pleasure? and in whatsoever he doth, whether led by reason, mistake, or passion, must be submitted to? which men in the state of Nature are not bound to do one to another. And if he that judges, judges amiss in his own or any other case, he is answerable for it to the rest of mankind.

It is often asked as a mighty objection, where are, or ever were, there any men in such a state of Nature? To which it may suffice as an answer at present, that since all princes and rulers of 'independent' governments all through the world are in a state of Nature, it is plain the world never was, nor never will be, without numbers of men in that state. I have named all governors of 'independent' communities, whether they are, or are not, in league with others; for it is not every compact that puts an end to the state of Nature between men, but only this one of agreeing together mutually to enter into one community, and make one body politic; other promises and compacts men may make one with another, and yet still be in the state of Nature. The promises and bargains for truck, etc., between the two men in Soldania, in or between a Swiss and an Indian, in the woods of America, are binding to them, though they are perfectly in a state of Nature in reference to one another for truth, and keeping of faith belongs to men as men, and not as members of society. [. . .]

And here we have the plain difference between the state of Nature and the state of war, which however some men have confounded, are as far distant as a state of peace, goodwill, mutual assistance, and preservation; and a state of enmity, malice, violence and mutual destruction are one from another. Men living together according to reason without a common superior on earth, with authority to judge between them, is properly the state of Nature. But force, or a declared design of force upon the person of another, where there is no common superior on earth to appeal to for relief, is the state of war; and it is the want of such an appeal gives a man the right of war even against an aggressor, though he be in society and a fellow-subject.

[From *Two Treatises of Civil Government*, ed. W. S. Carpenter (J. M. Dent, London, 1924 (1962 repr.)), 118–21, 123–4, 126. First published 1690.]

BARON DE MONTESQUIEU

4   **Fear and Peace**

Man, as a physical being, is like other bodies governed by invariable laws. As an intelligent being, he incessantly transgresses the laws established by God, and changes those of his own instituting. He is left to his private direction, though a limited being, and subject, like all finite intelligences, to ignorance and error: even his imperfect knowledge he loses; and as a sensible creature, he is hurried away by a thousand impetuous passions. Such a being might every instant forget his Creator; God has therefore reminded him of his duty by the laws of religion. Such a being is liable every moment to forget himself; philosophy has provided against this by the laws of morality. Formed to live in society, he might forget his fellow-creatures; legislators have, therefore, by political and civil laws, confined him to his duty.

Antecedent to the above-mentioned laws are those of nature, so called, because they derive their force entirely from our frame and existence. In order to have a perfect knowledge of these laws, we must consider man before the establishment of society: the laws received in such a state would be those of nature.

The law which, impressing on our minds the idea of a Creator, inclines us towards Him, is the first in importance, though not in order, of natural laws. Man in a state of nature would have the faculty of knowing, before he had acquired any knowledge. Plain it is that his first ideas would not be of a speculative nature; he would think of the preservation of his being, before he would investigate its origin. Such a man would feel nothing in himself at first but impotency and weakness; his fears and apprehensions would be excessive; as appears from instances (were there any necessity of proving it) of savages found in forests, trembling at the motion of a leaf, and flying from every shadow.

In this state every man, instead of being sensible of his equality, would fancy himself inferior. There would, therefore, be no danger of their attacking one another; peace would be the first law of nature.

The natural impulse or desire which Hobbes attributes to mankind of subduing one another is far from being well founded. The idea of empire and dominion is so complex, and depends on so many other notions, that it could never be the first which occurred to the human understanding.

Hobbes inquires, 'For what reason go men armed, and have locks and keys to fasten their doors, if they be not naturally in a state of war?' But is it not obvious that he attributes to mankind before the establishment of society what can happen but in consequence of this establishment, which furnishes them with motives for hostile attacks and self-defence?

Next to a sense of his weakness man would soon find that of his wants. Hence another law of nature would prompt him to seek for nourishment.

Fear, I have observed, would induce men to shun one another; but the marks of this fear being reciprocal, would soon engage them to associate. Besides, this association would quickly follow from the very pleasure one animal feels at the approach of another of the same species. Again, the attraction arising from the difference of sexes would enhance this pleasure, and the natural inclination they have for each other would form a third law.

Besides the sense or instinct which man possesses in common with brutes, he has the advantage of acquired knowledge; and thence arises a second tie, which brutes have not. Mankind have, therefore, a new motive of uniting; and a fourth law of nature results from the desire of living in society.

As soon as man enters into a state of society he loses the sense of his weakness; equality ceases, and then commences the state of war.

[From Charles Louis de Secondat, Baron de Montesquieu, *The Spirit of the Laws*, trans. Thomas Nugent, with an Introduction by Franz Neumann (Hafner Press, New York, Collier Macmillan, London, 1949), 3–5. First published 1748.]

JEAN-JACQUES ROUSSEAU
....

5 The Noble Savage

The philosophers, who have inquired into the foundations of society, have all felt the necessity of going back to a state of nature; but not one of them has got there. Some of them have not hesitated to ascribe to man, in such a state, the idea of just and unjust, without troubling themselves to show that he must be possessed of such an idea, or that it could be of any use to him. [. . .]

We should beware, therefore, of confounding the savage man with the men we have daily before our eyes. Nature treats all the animals left to her care with a predilection that seems to show how jealous she is of that right. The horse, the cat, the bull, and even the ass are generally of greater stature, and always more robust, and have more vigour, strength, and courage, when they run wild in the forests than when bred in the stall. By becoming domesticated, they lose half these advantages; and it seems as if all our care to feed and treat them well serves only to deprave them. It is thus with man also: as he becomes sociable and a slave, he grows weak, timid, and servile; his effeminate way of life totally enervates his strength and courage. To this it may be added that there is still a greater difference between savage and civilized man than between wild and tame beasts; for men and brutes having been treated alike by nature, the several conveniences in which men indulge themselves still more than they do their beasts, are so many additional causes of their deeper degeneracy.

It is not therefore so great a misfortunate to these primitive men, nor so great an obstacle to their preservation, that they go naked, have no dwellings, and lack all the superfluities which we think so necessary. If their skins are not covered with hair, they have no need of such covering in warm climates; and, in cold countries, they soon learn to appropriate the skins of the beasts they have overcome. If they have but two legs to run with, they have two arms to defend themselves with, and provide for their wants. Their children are slowly and with difficulty taught to walk; but their mothers are able to carry them with ease; an advantage which other animals lack, as the mother, if pursued, is forced either to abandon her young, or to regulate her pace by theirs. Unless, in short, we suppose a singular and fortuitous concurrence of circumstances of which I shall speak later, and which could well never come about, it is plain in every state of the case, that the man who first made himself clothes or a dwelling was furnishing himself with things not at all necessary; for he had till then done without them, and there is no reason why he should not have been able to put up in manhood with the same kind of life as had been his in infancy. [. . .]

Whatever moralists may hold, the human understanding is greatly indebted to the passions, which, it is universally allowed, are also much indebted to the understanding. It is by the activity of the passions that our reason is improved; for we desire knowledge only because we wish to enjoy; and it is impossible to conceive any reason why a person who has neither fears nor desires should give himself the trouble of reasoning. The passions, again, originate in our wants, and their progress depends on that of our knowledge; for we cannot desire or fear anything, except from the idea we have of it, or from the simple impulse of nature. Now savage man, being destitute of every species of enlightenment, can have no passions save those of the latter kind: his desires never go beyond his physical wants. The only goods he recognizes in the universe are food, a female, and sleep: the only evils he fears are pain and hunger. I say pain, and not death: for no animal can know what it is to die; the knowledge of death and its terrors being one of the first acquisitions made by man in departing from an animal state. [. . .]

It appears, at first view, that men in a state of nature, having no moral relations or determinate obligations one with another, could not be either good or bad, virtuous or vicious; unless we take these terms in a physical sense, and call, in an individual, those qualities vices which may be injurious to his preservation, and those virtues which contribute to it; in which case, he would have to be accounted most virtuous, who put least check on the pure impulses of nature. But without deviating from the ordinary sense of the words, it will be proper to suspend the judgment we might be led to form on such a state, and be on our guard against our prejudices, till we have weighted the matter in the scales of impartiality, and seen whether virtues or vices preponderate among civilized men: and whether their virtues do them more good than their vices do harm; till we have discovered whether the progress of the sciences sufficiently indemnifies them for the mischiefs they do one another, in proportion as they are better informed of the good they ought to do; or whether they would not be, on the whole, in a much happier condition if they had nothing to fear or to hope from any one, than as they are, subjected to universal dependence, and obliged to take everything from those who engage to give them nothing in return.

Above all, let us not conclude, with Hobbes, that because man has no idea of goodness, he must be naturally wicked; that he is vicious because he does not know virtue; that he always refuses to do his fellow-creatures services which he does not think they have a right to demand; or that by virtue of the right he justly claims to all he needs, he foolishly imagines himself the sole proprietor of the whole universe. Hobbes had seen clearly the defects of all the modern definitions of natural right: but the consequences which he deduces from his own show that he understands it in an equally false sense. In reasoning on the principles he lays down, he ought to have said that the state of nature, being that in which the care for our own preservation is the least prejudicial to that of others, was consequently the best calculated to promote peace, and the most suitable for mankind. He does say the exact opposite, in consequence of having improperly admitted, as a part of savage man's care for self-preservation, the gratification of a multitude of passions which are the work of society, and have made laws necessary. A bad man, he says, is a robust child. But it remains to be proved whether man in a state of nature is this robust child: and, should we grant that he is, what would he infer? Why truly, that if this man, when robust and strong, were dependent on others as he is when feeble, there is no extravagance he would not be guilty of; that he would beat his mother when she was too slow in giving him her breast; that he would strangle one of his younger brothers, if he should be troublesome to him, or bite the leg of another, if he put him to any inconvenience. But that man in the state of nature is both strong and dependent involves two contrary suppositions. Man is weak when he is dependent, and is his own master before he comes to be strong. Hobbes did not reflect that the same cause, which prevents a savage from making use of his reason, as our jurists hold, prevents him also from abusing his faculties, as Hobbes himself allows; so that it may be justly said that savages are not bad merely because they do not know what it is to be good: for it is neither the development of the understanding nor the restraint of law that hinders them from doing ill; but the peacefulness of their passions, and their ignorance of vice: *tanto plus in illis proficit vitiorum ignoratio, quam in his cognitio virtutis.* There is another principle which has escaped Hobbes; which, having been bestowed on mankind, to moderate, on certain occasions, the impetuosity of *amour-propre*, or, before its birth, the desire of self-preservation, tempers the ardour with which he pursues his own welfare, by an innate repugnance at seeing a fellow-creature suffer. I think I need not fear contradiction in holding man to be possessed of the only natural virtue, which could not be denied him by the most violent detractor of human virtue. I am speaking of compassion, which is a disposition suitable to creatures so weak and subject to so many evils as we certainly are: by so much the more universal and useful to mankind, as it comes before any kind of reflection; and at the same time so natural, that the very brutes themselves sometimes give evident proofs of it. Not to mention the tenderness of mothers for their offspring and the perils they encounter to save them from danger, it is well known that horses show a reluctance to trample on living bodies. One animal never passes by the dead body of another of its species without disquiet: some even give their fellows a sort of burial; while the mournful lowings of the cattle when they enter the slaughter-house show the impressions made on them by the horrible spectacle which meets them. [. . .]

Such is the pure emotion of nature, prior to all kinds of reflection! Such is the force of natural compassion, which the greatest depravity of morals has as yet hardly been able to destroy! [. . .]

Let us conclude then that man in a state of nature, wandering up and down the forests, without industry, without speech, and without home, an equal stranger to war and to all ties, neither standing in need of his fellow-creatures nor having any desire to hurt them, and perhaps even not distinguishing them one from another; let us conclude that, being self-sufficient and subject to so few passions, he could have no feelings or knowledge but such as befitted his situation; that he felt only his actual necessities, and disregarded everything he did not think himself immediately concerned to notice, and that his understanding made no greater progress than his vanity. If by accident he made any discovery, he was the less able to communicate it to others, as he did not know even his own children. Every art would necessarily perish with its inventor, where there was no kind of education among men, and generations succeeded generations without the least advance; when, all setting out from the same point, centuries must have elapsed in the barbarism of the first ages; when the race was already old, and man remained a child.

[From *A Discourse on the Origin of Inequality*, in *The Social Contract and Discourses*, trans. and introd. G. D. H. Cole (J. M. Dent, London, 1973), 50, 57–8, 61, 71–4, 79–80. First published 1755.]

6   Man's Character is Formed for Him

From the earliest ages it has been the practice of the world to act on the supposition that each individual man forms his own character, and that therefore he is accountable for all his sentiments and habits, and consequently merits reward for some and punishment for others. Every system which has been established among men has been founded on these erroneous principles. When, however, they shall be brought to the test of fair examination, they will be found not only unsupported, but in direct opposition to all experience, and to the evidence of our senses.

This is not a slight mistake, which involves only trivial consequences; it is a fundamental error of the highest possible magnitude, it enters into all our proceedings regarding man from his infancy; and it will be found to be the true and sole origin of evil. It generates and perpetuates ignorance, hatred and revenge, where, without such error, only intelligence, confidence, and kindness would exist. It has hitherto been the Evil Genius of the world. It severs man from man throughout the various regions of the earth; and it makes enemies of those who, but for this gross error, would have enjoyed each other's kind offices and sincere friendship. It is, in short, an error which carries misery in all its consequences.

This error cannot much longer exist; for every day will make it more evident *that the character of man is, without a single exception, always formed for him; and that it may be, and is, chiefly created by his predecessors that they give him, or may give him, his ideas and habits, which are the powers that govern and direct his conduct. Man, therefore, never did, nor is it possible that he ever can, form his own character.*

The knowledge of this important fact has not been derived from any of the wild and heated speculations of an ardent and ungoverned imagination; on the contrary, it proceeds from a long and patient study of the theory and practice of human nature, under many varied circumstances; and it will be found to be a deduction drawn from such a multiplicity of facts, as to afford the most complete demonstration.

Every society which now exists, as well as every society history records, has been formed and governed on a belief in the notions, assumed as *first principles*:

First—That it is in the power of every individual to form his own character.

Hence the various systems called by the name of religion, codes of law and punishments. Hence also the angry passions entertained by individuals and nations towards each other.

Second—That the affections are at the command of the individual.

Hence insincerity and degradation of character. Hence the miseries of domestic life, and more than one half of the crimes of mankind.

Third—That it is necessary that a large portion of mankind should exist in ignorance and poverty, in order to secure the remaining part such a degree of happiness as they now enjoy.

Hence a system of counteraction in the pursuits of man, a general opposition among individuals to the interests of each other, and the necessary effects of such a system—ignorance, poverty, and vice.

Facts prove, however—

First—that character is universally formed *for*, and not *by* the individual.

Second—That *any* habits and sentiments may be given to mankind.

Third—That the affections are *not* under the control of the individual.

Fourth—That every individual may be trained to produce far more than he can consume, while there is a sufficiency of soil left for him to cultivate.

Fifth—That nature has provided means by which populations may be at all times maintained in the proper state to give the greatest happiness to every individual, without one check of vice or misery.

Sixth—That any community may be arranged, on a due combination of the foregoing principles, in such a manner, as not only to withdraw vice, poverty, and, in a great degree, misery, from the world; but also to place *every* individual under such circumstances in which he shall enjoy more permanent happiness than can be given to *any* individual under the principles which have hitherto regulated society.

Seventh—That all the assumed fundamental principles on which society has hitherto been founded are erroneous, and may be demonstrated to be contrary to fact. And—

Eighth—That the change which would follow the abandonment of these erroneous maxims which bring misery to the world, and the adoption of principles of truth, unfolding a system which shall remove and for ever exclude that misery, may be effected without the slightest injury to any human being. [. . .]

How much longer shall we continue to allow generation after generation to be taught crime from their infancy, and when so taught, hunt them like beasts of the forests, until they are entangled beyond escape in the toils and nets of the law? When, if the circumstances of those poor unpitied sufferers had been reversed with those who are even surrounded with the pomp and dignity of justice, these latter would have been at the bar of the culprit, and the former would have been at the judgement seat.

Had the present Judges of these realms been born and educated among the poor and profligate of St Giles, or some similar situation, is it not certain, inasmuch as they possess native energies and abilities, that ere this they would have been at the head of their *then* profession, and, in consequence of that superiority and proficiency, would already have suffered imprisonment, transportation or death? Can we for a moment hesitate to decide, that if some of those men whom the laws dispensed by the present Judges have doomed to suffer capital punishments, had been born, trained and circumstanced as these Judges were born, trained and circumstanced, that some of those who had so suffered would have been the identical individuals who would have passed the same awful sentences on the present highly esteemed dignitaries of the law. [. . .]

I was greatly averse to punishments, and much preferred as far as possible simple means to render punishment unnecessary, as it is always unjust to the individual. To prevent punishment by the overlooker and masters of departments who had been accustomed to whip and strap the young people, and who often from ignorance abused their authority, I invented what the people soon called a telegraph.

This consisted of a four-sided piece of wood, about two inches long, and one broad, each side coloured—one side black, another blue, the third yellow, and the fourth white, tapered at the top, and finished with wire eyes, to hang upon a hook with either side to the front. One of these was suspended in a conspicuous place near to each of the persons employed, and the colour at the front told the conduct of the individual during the preceding day, to four degrees by comparison. Bad, denoted by black, indifferent by blue, good by yellow and excellent by white.

This was the preventer of punishment. There was no beating—no abusive language. I passed daily through all the rooms, and the workers observed me always to look at these telegraphs—and when black I merely looked at the person and then at the colour—but never said a word to one of them by way of blame. And if any one thought the inferior colour was not deserved by him as given, it was desired that complaint should be made to me. But this seldom occurred. Now this simple device and silent monitor began to show its effects upon the character of the workers. At first a large proportion daily were black and blue, few yellow and scarcely any white. Gradually the black were changed for blue, the blues for yellow, and the yellows for white. And for many years the permanent daily conduct of a very large number of those who were employed, deserved and had No. 1 placed as their character on the books of the establishment. Soon after the adoption of this telegraph I could at once see by the expression of the countenance what was the colour which was shown. As there were four colours there were four different expressions of countenance most evident to me as I passed along the rooms.

Never perhaps in the history of the human race has so simple a device created in so short a period so much order, virtue, goodness, and happiness, out of so much ignorance, error, and misery.

[Note by A. L. Morton: It is often said that in this, and other ways, Owen treated his work-people as if they were children. There is some truth in this, but it must be remembered that a large proportion of them were children. And it was always with children that Owen was most successful.]

[From A. L. Morton, *The Life and Ideas of Robert Owen* (International Publishers, New York, and Lawrence & Wishart, London, 1962 and 1969), 73–6, 81–2, 98–9. First published 1813, 1816, 1857.]

KARL MARX AND FRIEDRICH ENGELS

7   Man as a Productive Being

The premises from which we begin are not arbitrary ones, not dogmas, but real premises from which abstraction can only be made in the imagination. They are the real individuals, their activity and the material conditions under which they live, both those which they find already existing and those produced by their activity. These premises can thus be verified in a purely empirical way.

The first premise of all human history is, of course, the existence of living human individuals. Thus the first fact to be established is the physical organisation of these individuals and their consequent relation to the rest of nature. Of course, we cannot here go either into the actual physical nature of man, or into the natural conditions in which man finds himself—geological, orohydrographical, climatic and so on. The writing of history must always set out from these natural bases and their modification in the course of history through the action of men.

Men can be distinguished from animals by consciousness, by religion or anything else you like. They themselves begin to distinguish themselves from animals as soon as they begin to *produce* their means of subsistence, a step which is conditioned by their physical organisation. By producing their means of subsistence men are indirectly producing their actual material life.

The way in which men produce their means of subsistence depends first of all on the nature of the actual means of subsistence they find in existence and have to reproduce. This mode of production must not be considered simply as being the production of the physical existence of the individuals. Rather it is a definite form of activity of these individuals, a definite form of expressing their life, a definite *mode of life* on their part. As individuals express their life, so they are. What they are, therefore, coincides with their production, both with *what* they produce and with *how* they produce. The nature of individuals thus depends on the material conditions determining their production. [. . .]

The fact is, therefore, that definite individuals who are productively active in a definite way enter into these definite social and political relations. Empirical observation must in each separate instance bring out empirically, and without any mystification and speculation, the connection of the social and political structure with production. The social structure and the State are continually evolving out of the life process of definite individuals, but of individuals, not as they may appear in their own or other people's imagination, but as they *really* are; i.e. as they operate, produce materially, and hence as they work under definite material limits, presuppositions and conditions independent of their will. [. . .]

This method of approach is not devoid of premises. It starts out from the real premises and does not abandon them for a moment. Its premises are men, not in any fantastic isolation and rigidity, but in their actual, empirically perceptible process of development under definite conditions. As soon as this active life-process is described, history ceases to be a collection of dead facts as it is with the empiricists (themselves still abstract), or an imagined activity of imagined subjects, as with the idealists.

Where speculation ends—in real life—there real, positive science begins: the representation of the practical activity, of the practical process of development of men. Empty talk about consciousness ceases, and real knowledge has to take its place. When reality is depicted, philosophy as an independent branch of knowledge loses its medium of existence. At the best its place can only be taken by a summing-up of the most general results, abstractions which arise from the observation of the historical development of men. Viewed apart from real history, these abstractions have in themselves no value whatsoever. They can only serve to facilitate the arrangement of historical material, to indicate the sequence of its separate strata. But they by no means afford a recipe or schema, as does philosophy, for neatly trimming the epochs of history. On the contrary, our difficulties begin only when we set about the observation and the arrangement—the real depiction—of our historical material, whether of a past epoch or of the present. The removal of these difficulties is governed by premises which it is quite impossible to state here, but which only the study of the actual life-process and the activity of the individuals of each epoch will make evident. [. . .]

Language is as old as consciousness, language *is* practical consciousness that exists also for other men, and for that reason alone it really exists for me personally as well; language, like consciousness, only arises from the need, the necessity, of intercourse with other men. Where there exists a relationship, it exists for me: the animal does not enter into *'relations'* with anything, it does not enter into any relation at all. For the animal, its relation to others does not exist as a relation. Consciousness is, therefore, from the very beginning a social product, and remains so as long as men exist at all. Consciousness is at first, of course, merely consciousness concerning the *immediate* sensuous environment and consciousness of the limited connection with other persons and things outside the individual who is growing self-conscious. At the same time it is consciousness of nature, which first appears to men as a completely alien, all-powerful and unassailable force, with which men's relations are purely animal and by which they are overawed like beasts; it is thus a purely animal consciousness of nature (natural religion) just because nature is as yet hardly modified historically. (We see here immediately: this natural religion or this particular relation of men to nature is determined by the form of society and vice versa. Here, as everywhere, the identity of nature and man appears in such a way that the restricted relation of men to nature determines their restricted relation to one another, and their restricted relation to one another determines men's restricted relation to nature.) On the other hand, man's consciousness of the necessity of associating with the individuals around him is the beginning of the consciousness that he is living in society at all. This beginning is as animal as social life itself at this stage. It is mere herd-consciousness, and at this point man is only distinguished from sheep by the fact that with him consciousness takes the place of instinct or that his instinct is a conscious one. This sheep-like or tribal consciousness receives its further development and extension through increased productivity, the increase of needs, and, what is fundamental to both of these, the increase of population. With these there develops the division of labour, which was originally nothing but the division of labour in the sexual act, then that division of labour which develops spontaneously or 'naturally' by virtue of natural predisposition (e.g. physical strength), needs, accidents, etc. etc.

[From *The German Ideology*, ed. and introd. C. J. Arthur (Lawrence & Wishart, London, 1970), 42, 46–8, 50–1. Written 1845–6.]

CHARLES DARWIN

8   Natural Selection

We have reason to believe that a change in the conditions of life, by specially acting on the reproductive system, causes or increases variability; and in the foregoing case the conditions of life are supposed to have undergone a change, and this would manifestly be favourable to natural selection, by giving a better chance of profitable variations occurring; and unless profitable variations do occur, natural selection can do nothing. Not that, as I believe, any extreme amount of variability is necessary; as man can certainly produce great results by adding up in any given direction mere individual differences, so could Nature, but far more easily, from having incomparably longer time at her disposal. Nor do I believe that any great physical change, as of climate, or any unusual degree of isolation to check immigration, is actually necessary to produce new and un-occupied places for natural selection to fill up by modifying and improving some of the varying inhabitants. For as all the inhabitants of each country are struggling together with nicely balanced forces, extremely slight modifications in the structure or habits of one inhabitant would often give it an advantage over others; and still further modifications of the same kind would often still further increase the advantage. No country can be named in which all the native inhabitants are now so perfectly adapted to each other and to the physical con-ditions under which they live, that none of them could anyhow be improved; for in all countries, the natives have been so far conquered by naturalised pro-ductions, that they have allowed foreigners to take firm possession of the land. And as foreigners have thus everywhere beaten some of the natives, we may safely conclude that the natives might have been modified with advantage, so as to have better resisted such intruders.

As man can produce and certainly has produced a great result by his me-thodical and unconscious means of selection, what may not Nature effect? Man can act only on external and visible characters: Nature cares nothing for ap-pearances, except in so far as they may be useful to any being. She can act on every internal organ, on every shade of constitutional difference, on the whole machinery of life. Man selects only for his own good; Nature only for that of the being which she tends. Every selected character is fully exercised by her; and the being is placed under well-suited conditions of life. Man keeps the natives of many climates in the same country; he seldom exercises each selected character in some peculiar and fitting manner; he feeds a long and a short beaked pigeon on the same food; he does not exercise a long-backed or long-legged quadruped in any peculiar manner; he exposes sheep with long and short wool to the same climate. He does not allow the most vigorous males to struggle for the females. He does not rigidly destroy all inferior animals, but protects during each vary-ing season, as far as lies in his power, all his productions. He often begins his se-lection by some half-monstrous form; or at least by some modification prominent enough to catch his eye, or to be plainly useful to him. Under nature, the slightest difference of structure or constitution may well turn the nicely-balanced scale in the struggle for life, and so be preserved. How fleeting are the wishes and efforts of man! how short his time! and consequently how poor will his products be, compared with those accumulated by Nature during whole geological periods. Can we wonder, then, that Nature's productions should be far 'truer' in character than man's productions; that they should be infinitely better adapted to the most complex conditions of life, and should plainly bear the stamp of far higher workmanship?

It may metaphorically be said that natural selection is daily and hourly scrutinising, throughout the world, every variation, even the slightest; rejecting that which is bad, preserving and adding up all that is good; silently and insensibly working, whenever and wherever opportunity offers, at the improvement of each organic being in relation to its organic and inorganic conditions of life. We see nothing of these slow changes in progress, until the hand of time has marked the long lapse of ages, and then so imperfect is our view into long past geological ages, that we only see that the forms of life are now different from what they formerly were.

[From *The Origin of Species*, ed. with introd. by Gillian Beer (Oxford University Press, Oxford, 1996), 68–70. First published 1859.]

CHARLES DARWIN

9 The Advantage of Morality

It must not be forgotten that although a high standard of morality gives but a slight or no advantage to each individual man and his children over the other men of the same tribe, yet that an advancement in the standard of morality and an increase in the number of well-endowed men will certainly give an immense advantage to one tribe over another. There can be no doubt that a tribe including many members who, from possessing in a high degree the spirit of patriotism, fidelity, obedience, courage, and sympathy, were always ready to give aid to each other and to sacrifice themselves for the common good, would be victorious over most other tribes; and this would be natural selection.

[From *The Descent of Man and Selection in Relation to Sex* (John Murray, London, 1871), i. 166.]

PETER KROPOTKIN

10 Mutual Aid

Happily enough, competition is not the rule either in the animal world or in mankind. It is limited among animals to exceptional periods, and natural selection finds better fields for its activity. Better conditions are created by the *elimination of competition* by means of mutual aid and mutual support. In the great struggle for life—for the greatest possible fullness and intensity of life with the least waste of energy—natural selection continually seeks out the ways precisely for avoiding competition as much as possible. The ants combine in nests and nations; they pile up their stores, they rear their cattle—and thus avoid competition; and natural selection picks out of the ants' family the species which know best how to avoid competition, with its unavoidably deleterious consequences. Most of our birds slowly move southwards as the winter comes, or gather in numberless societies and undertake long journeys—and thus avoid competition. Many rodents fall asleep when the time comes that competition should set in; while other rodents store food for the winter, and gather in large villages for obtaining the necessary protection when at work. The reindeer, when the lichens are dry in the interior of the continent, migrate towards the sea. Buffaloes cross an immense continent in order to find plenty of food. And the beavers, when they grow numerous on a river, divide into two parties, and go, the old ones down the river, and the young ones up the river—and avoid competition. And when animals can neither fall asleep, nor migrate, nor lay in stores, nor themselves grow their food like the ants, they do what the titmouse does, and what Wallace (*Darwinism*, ch. v.) has so charmingly described: they resort to new kinds of food—and thus, again, avoid competition.

'Don't compete!—competition is always injurious to the species, and you have plenty of resources to avoid it!' That is the *tendency* of nature, not always realized in full, but always present. That is the watchword which comes to us from the bush, the forest, the river, the ocean. 'Therefore combine—practise mutual aid! That is the surest means for giving to each and to all the greatest safety, the best guarantee of existence and progress, bodily, intellectual, and moral.' That is what Nature teaches us; and that is what all those animals which have attained the highest position in their respective classes have done. That is also what man—the most primitive man—has been doing; and that is why man has reached the position upon which we stand now [. . .]

Though a good deal of warfare goes on between different classes of animals, or different species, or even different tribes of the same species, peace and mutual support are the rule within the tribe or the species; and that those species which best know how to combine, and to avoid competition, have the best chances of survival and of a further progressive development. They prosper, while the unsociable species decay.

It is evident that it would be quite contrary to all that we know of nature if men were an exception to so general a rule: if a creature so defenceless as man was at his beginnings should have found his protection and his way to progress, not in mutual support, like other animals, but in a reckless competition for personal advantages, with no regard to the interests of the species. To a mind accustomed to the idea of unity in nature, such a proposition appears utterly indefensible. And yet, improbable and unphilosophical as it is, it has never found a lack of supporters. There always were writers who took a pessimistic view of mankind. They knew it, more or less superficially, through their own limited experience; they knew of history what the annalists, always watchful of wars, cruelty, and oppression, told of it, and little more besides; and they concluded that mankind is nothing but a loose aggregation of beings, always ready to fight with each other, and only prevented from so doing by the intervention of some authority.

Hobbes took that position; and while some of his eighteenth-century followers endeavoured to prove that at no epoch of its existence—not even in its most primitive condition—mankind lived in a state of perpetual warfare; that men have been sociable even in 'the state of nature,' and that want of knowledge, rather than the natural bad inclinations of man, brought humanity to all the horrors of its early historical life,—his idea was, on the contrary, that the so-called 'state of nature' was nothing but a permanent fight between individuals, accidentally huddled together by the mere caprice of their bestial existence. True, that science has made some progress since Hobbes's time, and that we have safer ground to stand upon than the speculations of Hobbes or Rousseau. But the Hobbesian philosophy has plenty of admirers still; and we have had of late quite a school of writers who, taking possession of Darwin's terminology rather than of his leading ideas, made of it an argument in favour of Hobbes's views upon primitive man, and even succeeded in giving them a scientific appearance. Huxley, as is known, took the lead of that school, and in a paper written in 1888 he represented primitive men as a sort of tigers or lions, deprived of all ethical conceptions, fighting out the struggle for existence to its bitter end, and living a life of 'continual free fight'; to quote his own words—'beyond the limited and temporary relations of the family, the Hobbesian war of each against all was the normal state of existence.'

It has been remarked more than once that the chief error of Hobbes, and the eighteenth-century philosophers as well, was to imagine that mankind began its life in the shape of small straggling families, something like the 'limited and temporary' families of the bigger carnivores, while in reality it is now positively known that such was *not* the case. Of course, we have no direct evidence as to the modes of life of the first man-like beings. We are not yet settled even as to the time of their first appearance, geologists being inclined at present to see their traces in the pliocene, or even the miocene, deposits of the Tertiary period. But we have the indirect method which permits us to throw some light even upon that remote antiquity. A most careful investigation into the social institutions of the lowest races has been carried on during the last forty years, and it has revealed among the present institutions of primitive folk some traces of still older institutions which have long disappeared, but nevertheless left unmistakable traces of their previous existence. [. . .] And that science has established beyond any doubt that mankind did *not* begin its life in the shape of small isolated families.

Far from being a primitive form of organization, the family is a very late product of human evolution. As far as we can go back in the palæo-ethnology of mankind, we find men living in societies—in tribes similar to those of the highest mammals; and an extremely slow and long evolution was required to bring these societies to the gentile, or clan organization, which, in its turn, had to undergo another, also very long evolution, before the first germs of family, polygamous or monogamous, could appear. Societies, bands, or tribes—not families—were thus the primitive form of organization of mankind and its earliest ancestors. That is what ethnology has come to after its painstaking researches. And in so doing it simply came to what might have been foreseen by the zoologist. None of the higher mammals, save a few carnivores and a few undoubtedly-decaying species of apes (orang-outangs and gorillas), live in small families, isolatedly straggling in the woods. All others live in societies. And Darwin so well understood that isolately-living apes never could have developed into man-like beings, that he was inclined to consider man as descended from some comparatively weak *but social species*, like the chimpanzee, rather than from some stronger but unsociable species, like the gorilla. Zoology and palæo-ethnology are thus agreed in considering that the band, not the family, was the earliest form of social life. The first human societies simply were a further development of those societies which constitute the very essence of life of the higher animals.

[From *Mutual Aid*, introd. George Woodcock (Black Rose Books, Montreal, 1989), 74–80.
First published 1910.]

I.b. Man's Nature and Woman's Nature

11 **Women as Weaker Partners**

'Then is there anything men do at which they aren't far better in all these respects than women? We need not waste time over exceptions like weaving and cooking, at which women are thought to be experts, and get badly laughed at if men do them better.'

'It's quite true,' he replied, 'that in general the one sex is much better at everything than the other. A good many women are better than a good many men at a good many things. But the general rule is as you stated it.'

'There is therefore no function in society which is peculiar to woman as woman or man as man; natural abilities are similarly distributed in each sex, and it is natural for women to share all occupations with men, though in all women will be the weaker partners.'

'Agreed.'

'Are we therefore to confine all occupations to men only?'

'How can we?'

'Obviously we can't; for we are agreed, I think, that one woman may have a natural ability for medicine or music, another not.'

'Yes.'

'And one may be athletic, another not; one be good at soldiering, another not.'

'I think so.'

'Then may a woman not be philosophic or unphilosophic, high-spirited or spiritless?'

'She may.'

'Then there will also be some women fitted to be Guardians: for these qualities, you will remember, were those for which we picked our men Guardians.'

'Yes, they were.'

'So men and women have the same natural capacity for Guardianship, save in so far as woman is the weaker of the two.'

'That is clear.'

'We must therefore pick suitable women to share the life and duties of Guardian with men; they are capable of it and the natures of both are alike.'

'Yes.'

'And like natures should have like employment, shouldn't they?'

'Yes.'

'We come back again, then, to our former agreement that it is natural that our Guardians' wives should share their intellectual and physical training.'

'There's no doubt about it.'

'So what we proposed was no impossible day-dream; it was entirely natural, and it is our present practice which now seems unnatural.'

'It looks like it.'

'Well, set out to discover whether our proposals were possible, but also whether they were the best that could be made. We have shown them to be possible; we must go on to satisfy ourselves that they are best.'

'Yes, we clearly must.'

'To turn a woman into a Guardian we presumably need the same education as we need to turn a man into one, as it will operate on the same nature in both.'

'True.'

'There's another point I'd like your opinion on.'

'What is it?'

'Do you think some men are better than others? Or are all equally good?'

'They certainly aren't all equally good!'

'Then in our imaginary state which will produce the better men—the education which we have prescribed for the Guardians or the training our shoemakers get?'

'It's absurd to ask.'

'All right. So the Guardians will be the best citizens?'

'Far the best.'

'Then won't the women Guardians be the best women?'

'Much the best again.'

'And is there anything better for a state than to produce men and women of the best possible kind?'

'No.'

'But that is the result of the education we have described.'

'Of course it is.'

'So the arrangements we proposed are not only possible but also the best our state could have.'

'Yes.'

'Our women Guardians must strip for exercise, then—their character will be all the clothes they need. They must play their part in war and in all other duties of a Guardian, which will be their sole occupation; only, as they are the weaker sex, we must give them a lighter share of these duties than men. And any man who laughs at women who, for these excellent reasons, exercise themselves naked is, as Pindar says, 'picking the unripe fruit of laughter'—he does not know what he is laughing at or what he is doing. For it will always be the best of sayings that what benefits us is good, what harms us bad.'

'I agree entirely.'

[From *The Republic*, trans. with introd. by H. D. P. Lee (Penguin, Harmondsworth, 1955, 209–11.]

12 Separate Spheres

The skill of household management proved to have three parts, one being the skill of a master, next that of a father, and a third marital. For he rules over wife and children, over both as free persons, but not with the same style of rule: over a wife he rules in the manner of a statesman, over children in that of a king; for by nature the male is more fitted to be in command than the female, unless conditions in some respect contravene nature; and the elder and fully grown is more fitted than the younger and underdeveloped. Now in most cases of rule by statesmen there is an interchange of the role of ruler and ruled, since they tend to be equal by nature and not to differ at all. (Nevertheless, while one is ruling and the other is being ruled, the former seeks to have a distinction made in outward dignity in style of address, and in honours, as for example in what Amasis said about his foot-basin.) But that is the permanent relationship of male to female.

But there is a kind of rule which rules over free men of the same stock. This is what we hold political rule to be. The ruler must learn it by being ruled, squadron-leading by being led, generalship by being generalled, colonelcy and captaincy likewise. Hence it is also a good saying that only those who have been ruled can rule well. While good ruling is distinct from good obeying, the good citizen must possess the knowledge and the ability both to obey and to rule; and the goodness of a citizen consists in understanding the government of free men in both directions. Both of them belong to the good man, even if the temperance and justice of a ruler are different.

It is also plain that even the goodness of the free subject, for example his justice, will not be always the same, but will take different forms according as he is ruling or being ruled. Similarly, the temperance and courage of a man are different from those of a woman. A man would seem cowardly if he were no braver than a brave woman; and a woman would seem talkative if she were no more decorous than the good man. The household management of a man is also distinct from that of a woman, his business being to get and hers to keep.

[From *Politics Books I and II*, trans. with a commentary by Trevor J. Saunders (Clarendon Press, Oxford, 1995), 18; *Politics Books III and IV*, trans. with introd. and comments by Richard Robinson (Clarendon Press, Oxford, 1995), 13.

13   The Likeness and Unlikeness of the Sexes

But for her sex, a woman is a man; she has the same organs, the same needs, the same faculties. The machine is the same in its construction; its parts, its working, and its appearance are similar. Regard it as you will the difference is only in degree.

Yet where sex is concerned man and woman are unlike; each is the complement of the other; the difficulty in comparing them lies in our inability to decide, in either case, what is a matter of sex, and what is not. General differences present themselves to the comparative anatomist and even to the superficial observer; they seem not to be a matter of sex; yet they are really sex differences, though the connection eludes our observation. How far such differences may extend we cannot tell; all we know for certain is that where man and woman are alike we have to do with the characteristics of the species; where they are unlike, we have to do with the characteristics of sex. Considered from these two standpoints, we find so many instances of likeness and unlikeness that it is perhaps one of the greatest of marvels how nature has contrived to make two beings so like and yet so different.

These resemblances and differences must have an influence on the moral nature; this inference is obvious, and it is confirmed by experience; it shows the vanity of the disputes as to the superiority or the equality of the sexes; as if each sex, pursuing the path marked out for it by nature, were not more perfect in that very divergence than if it more closely resembled the other. A perfect man and a perfect woman should no more be alike in mind than in face, and perfection admits of neither less nor more.

In the union of the sexes each alike contributes to the common end, but in different ways. From this diversity springs the first difference which may be observed between man and woman in their moral relations. The man should be strong and active; the woman should be weak and passive; the one must have both the power and the will; it is enough that the other should offer little resistance.

When this principle is admitted, it follows that woman is specially made for man's delight. If man in his turn ought to be pleasing in her eyes, the necessity is less urgent, his virtue is in his strength, he pleases because he is strong. I grant you this is not the law of love, but it is the law of nature, which is older than love itself.

If woman is made to please and to be in subjection to man, she ought to make herself pleasing in his eyes and not provoke him to anger; her strength is in her charms, by their means she should compel him to discover and use his strength. The surest way of arousing this strength is to make it necessary by resistance. Thus pride comes to the help of desire and each exults in the other's victory.

This is the origin of attack and defence, of the boldness of one sex and the timidity of the other, and even of the shame and modesty with which nature has armed the weak for the conquest of the strong. [. . .]

The Most High has deigned to do honour to mankind; he has endowed man with boundless passions, together with a law to guide them, so that man may be alike free and self-controlled; though swayed by these passions man is endowed with reason by which to control them. Woman is also endowed with boundless passions; God has given her modesty to restrain them. Moreover, he has given to both a present reward for the right use of their powers, in the delight which springs from that right use of them, i.e., the taste for right conduct established as the law of our behaviour. To my mind this is far higher than the instinct of the beasts [. . .]

Thus the different constitution of the two sexes leads us to a third conclusion, that the stronger party seems to be master, but is as a matter of fact dependent on the weaker, and that, not by any foolish custom of gallantry, nor yet by the magnanimity of the protector, but by an inexorable law of nature. For nature has endowed woman with a power of stimulating man's passions in excess of man's power of satisfying those passions, and has thus made him dependent on her goodwill, and compelled him in his turn to endeavour to please her, so that she may be willing to yield to his superior strength. Is it weakness which yields to force, or is it voluntary self-surrender? This uncertainty constitutes the chief charm of the man's victory, and the woman is usually cunning enough to leave him in doubt. In this respect the woman's mind exactly resembles her body; far from being ashamed of her weakness, she is proud of it; her soft muscles offer no resistance, she professes that she cannot lift the lightest weight; she would be ashamed to be strong. And why? Not only to gain an appearance of refinement; she is too clever for that; she is providing herself beforehand with excuses, with the right to be weak if she chooses.

The experience we have gained through our vices has considerably modified the views held in older times; we rarely hear of violence for which there is so little occasion that it would hardly be credited. Yet such stories are common enough among the Jews and ancient Greeks; for such views belong to the simplicity of nature, and have only been uprooted by our profligacy. If fewer deeds of violence are quoted in our days, it is not that men are more temperate, but because they are less credulous, and a complaint which would have been believed among a simple people would only excite laughter among ourselves; therefore silence is the better course. There is a law in Deuteronomy, under which the outraged maiden was punished, along with her assailant, if the crime were committed in a town; but if in the country or in a lonely place, the latter alone was punished. 'For,' says the law, 'the maiden cried for help, and there was none to hear.' From this merciful interpretation of the law, girls learnt not to let themselves be surprised in lonely places.

This change in public opinion has had a perceptible effect on our morals. It has produced our modern gallantry. Men have found that their pleasures depend, more than they expected, on the goodwill of the fair sex, and have secured this goodwill by attentions which have had their reward.

See how we find ourselves led unconsciously from the physical to the moral constitution, how from the grosser union of the sexes spring the sweet laws of love. Woman reigns, not by the will of man, but by the decrees of nature herself; she had the power long before she showed it. That same Hercules who proposed to violate all the fifty daughters of Thespis was compelled to spin at the feet of Omphale, and Samson, the strong man, was less strong than Delilah. This power cannot be taken from woman; it is hers by right; she would have lost it long ago, were it possible.

[From *Émile*, trans. Barbara Foxley (Dent, London, 1911), 321–5. First published 1780.]

MARY WOLLSTONECRAFT

14   The Rights of Women

The preposterous distinctions of rank, which render civilization a curse, by dividing the world between voluptuous tyrants, and cunning envious dependents, corrupt, almost equally, every class of people, because respectability is not attached to the discharge of the relative duties of life, but to the station, and when the duties are not fulfiled the affections cannot gain sufficient strength to fortify the virtue of which they are the natural reward. Still there are some loopholes out of which a man may creep, and dare to think and act for himself; but for a woman it is an herculean task, because she has difficulties peculiar to her sex to overcome, which require almost superhuman powers.

A truly benevolent legislator always endeavours to make it the interest of each individual to be virtuous; and thus private virtue becoming the cement of public happiness, an orderly whole is consolidated by the tendency of all the parts towards a common centre. But, the private or public virtue of woman is very problematical; for Rousseau, and a numerous list of male writers, insist that she should all her life be subjected to a severe restraint, that of propriety. Why subject her to propriety—blind propriety, if she be capable of acting from a nobler spring, if she be an heir of immortality? Is sugar always to be produced by vital blood? Is one half of the human species, like the poor African slaves, to be subject to prejudices that brutalize them, when principles would be a surer guard, only to sweeten the cup of man? Is not this indirectly to deny woman reason? For a gift is a mockery, if it be unfit for use.

Women are, in common with men, rendered weak and luxurious by the relaxing pleasures which wealth procures; but added to this they are made slaves to their persons, and must render them alluring that man may lend them his reason to guide their tottering steps aright. Or should they be ambitious, they must govern their tyrants by sinister tricks, for without rights there cannot be any incumbent duties. The laws respecting woman make an absurd unit of a man and his wife; and then, by the easy transition of only considering him as responsible, she is reduced to a mere cypher.

The being who discharges the duties of its station is independent; and, speaking of women at large, their first duty is to themselves as rational creatures, and the next, in point of importance, as citizens, is that, which includes so many, of a mother. The rank in life which dispenses with their fulfiling this duty, necessarily degrades them by making them mere dolls. Or, should they turn to something more important than merely fitting drapery upon a smooth block, their minds are only occupied by some soft platonic attachment; or, the actual management of an intrigue may keep their thoughts in motion; for when they neglect domestic duties, they have it not in their power to take the field and march and counter-march like soldiers, or wrangle in the senate to keep their faculties from rusting. [. . .]

But, to render here really virtuous and useful, [a woman] must not, if she discharge her civil duties, want, individually, the protection of civil laws, she must not be dependent on her husband's bounty for her subsistence during his life, or support after his death—for how can a being be generous who has nothing of its own? or, virtuous, who is not free? The wife, in the present state of things, who is faithful to her husband, and neither suckles nor educates her children, scarcely deserves the name of a wife, and has no right to that of a citizen. But take away natural rights, and duties become null.

[From *A Vindication of the Rights of Women*, ed. Carol Poston (Norton, New York, 1975), 144–6. First published 1792.]

JOHN STUART MILL

15   **The Subjection of Women**

Standing on the ground of common sense and the constitution of the human mind, I deny that any one knows, or can know, the nature of the two sexes, as long as they have only been seen in their present relation to one another. If men had ever been found in society without women, or women without men, or if there had been a society of men and women in which the women were not under the control of the men, something might have been positively known about the mental and moral differences which may be inherent in the nature of each. What is now called the nature of women is an eminently artificial thing—the result of forced repression in some directions, unnatural stimulation in others. It may be asserted without scruple, that no other class of dependents have had their character so entirely distorted from its natural proportions by their relation with their masters; for, if conquered and slave races have been, in some respects, more forcibly repressed, whatever in them has not been crushed down by an iron heel has generally been let alone, and if left with any liberty of development, it has developed itself according to its own laws; but in the case of women, a hot-house and stove cultivation has always been carried on of some of the capabilities of their nature, for the benefit and pleasure of their masters. Then, because certain products of the general vital force sprout luxuriantly and reach a great development in this heated atmosphere and under this active nurture and watering, while other shoots from the same root, which are left outside in the wintry air, with ice purposely heaped all round them, have a stunted growth, and some are burnt off with fire and disappear; men, with that inability to recognise their own work which distinguishes the unanalytic mind, indolently believe that the tree grows of itself in the way they have made it grow, and that it would die if one half of it were not kept in a vapour bath and the other half in the snow.

Of all difficulties which impede the progress of thought, and the formation of well-grounded opinions on life and social arrangements, the greatest is now the unspeakable ignorance and inattention of mankind in respect to the influences which form human character. Whatever any portion of the human species now are, or seem to be, such, it is supposed, they have a natural tendency to be: even when the most elementary knowledge of the circumstances in which they have been placed, clearly points out the causes that made them what they are. Because a cottier deeply in arrears to his landlord is not industrious, there are people who think that the Irish are naturally idle. Because constitutions can be overthrown when the authorities appointed to execute them turn their arms against them, there are people who think the French incapable of free government. Because the Greeks cheated the Turks, and the Turks only plundered the Greeks, there are persons who think that the Turks are naturally more sincere: and because women, as is often said, care nothing about politics except their personalities, it is supposed that the general good is naturally less interesting to women than to men. History, which is now so much better understood than formerly, teaches another lesson: if only by showing the extraordinary susceptibility of human nature to external influences, and the extreme variableness of those of its manifestations which are supposed to be most universal and uniform. But in history, as in travelling, men usually see only what they already had in their own minds; and few learn much from history, who do not bring much with them to its study.

Hence, in regard to that most difficult question, what are the natural differences between the two sexes—a subject on which it is impossible in the present state of society to obtain complete and correct knowledge—while almost everybody dogmatises upon it, almost all neglect and make light of the only means by which any partial insight can be obtained into it. This is, an analytic study of the most important department of psychology, the laws of the influence of circumstances on character. For, however great and apparently ineradicable the moral and intellectual differences between men and women might be, the evidence of their being natural differences could only be negative. Those only could be inferred to be natural which could not possibly be artificial—the residuum, after deducting every characteristic of either sex which can admit of being explained from education or external circumstances. The profoundest knowledge of the laws of the formation of character is indispensable to entitle any one to affirm even that there is any difference, much more what the difference is, between the two sexes considered as moral and rational beings; and since no one, as yet, has that knowledge, (for there is hardly any subject which, in proportion to its importance, has been so little studied), no one is thus far entitled to any positive opinion on the subject. Conjectures are all that can at present be made; conjectures more or less probable, according as more or less authorised by such knowledge as we yet have of the laws of psychology, as applied to the formation of character. [. . .]

One thing we may be certain of—that what is contrary to women's nature to do, they never will be made to do by simply giving their nature free play. The anxiety of mankind to interfere in behalf of nature, for fear lest nature should not succeed in effecting its purpose, is an altogether unnecessary solicitude. What women by nature cannot do, it is quite superfluous to forbid them from doing. What they can do, but not so well as the men who are their competitors, competition suffices to exclude them from; since nobody asks for protective duties and bounties in favour of women; it is only asked that the present bounties and protective duties in favour of men should be recalled. If women have a greater natural inclination for some things than for others, there is no need of laws or social inculcation to make the majority of them do the former in preference to the later. Whatever women's services are most wanted for, the free play of competition will hold out the strongest inducements to them to undertake. And, as the words imply, they are most wanted for the things for which they are most fit; by the apportionment of which to them, the collective faculties of the two sexes can be applied on the whole with the greatest sum of valuable result. [. . .]

On the other point which is involved in the just equality of women, their admissibility to all the functions and occupations hitherto retained as the monopoly of the stronger sex, I should anticipate no difficulty in convincing any one who has gone with me on the subject of the equality of women in the family. I believe that there disabilities elsewhere are only clung to in order to maintain their subordination in domestic life; because the generality of the male sex cannot yet tolerate the idea of living with an equal. Were it not for that, I think that almost every one, in the existing state of opinion in politics and political economy, would admit the injustice of excluding half the human race from the greater number of lucrative occupations, and from almost all high social functions; ordaining from their birth either that they are not, and cannot by any possibility become, fit for employments which are legally open to the stupidest and basest of the other sex, or else that however fit they may be, those employments shall be interdicted to them, in order to be preserved for the inclusive benefit of males. In the last two centuries, when (which was seldom the case) any reason beyond the mere existence of the fact was thought to be required to justify the disabilities of women, people seldom assigned as a reason their inferior mental capacity; which, in times when there was a real trial of personal faculties (from which all women were not excluded) in the struggles of public life, no one really believed in. The reason given in those days was not women's unfitness, but the interest of society, by which was meant the interest of men: just as the *raison d'état*, meaning the convenience of the government, and the support of existing authority, was deemed a sufficient explanation and excuse for the most flagitious crimes. In the present day, power holds a smoother language, and whomsoever it oppresses, always pretends to do so for their own good: accordingly, when anything is forbidden to women, it is thought necessary to say, and desirable to believe, that they are incapable of doing it, and that they depart from their real path of success and happiness when they aspire to it. But to make this reason plausible (I do not say valid), those by whom it is urged must be prepared to carry it to a much greater length than any one ventures to do in the face of present experience. It is not sufficient to maintain that women on the average are less gifted than men on the average, with certain of the higher mental faculties, or that a smaller number of women than of men are fit for occupations and functions of the highest intellectual character. It is necessary to maintain that no women at all are fit for them, and that the most eminent women are inferior in mental faculties to the most mediocre of the men on whom those functions at present devolve. For if the performance of the function is decided either by competition, or by any mode of choice which secures regard to the public interest, there needs be no apprehension that any important employments will fall into the hands of women inferior to average men, or to the average of their male competitors. The only result would be that there would be fewer women than men in such employments; a result certain to happen in any case, if only from the preference always likely to be felt by the majority of women for the one vocation in which there is nobody to compete with them. Now, the most determined depreciator of women will not venture to deny, that when we add the experience of recent times to that of ages past, women, and not a few merely, but many women, have proved themselves capable of everything, perhaps without a single exception, which is done by men, and of doing it successfully and creditably. The utmost that can be said is, that there are many things which none of them have succeeded in doing as well as they have been done by some men—many in which they have not reached the very highest rank. But there are extremely few, dependent only on mental faculties, in which they have not attained the rank next to the highest. Is not this enough, and much more than enough, to make it a tyranny to them, and a detriment to society, that they should not be allowed to compete with men for the exercise of these functions? Is it not a mere truism to say, that such functions are often filled by men far less fit for them than numbers of women, and who would be beaten by women in any fair field of competition? What difference does it make that there may be men somewhere, fully employed about other things, who may be still better qualified for the things in question than these women? Does not this take place in all competitions? Is there so great a superfluity of men fit for high duties, that society can afford to reject the service of any competent person? Are we so certain of always finding a man made to our hands for any duty or function of social importance which falls vacant, that we lose nothing by putting a ban upon one-half of mankind, and refusing beforehand to make their faculties available, however distinguished they may be? And even if we could do without them, would it be consistent with justice to refuse to them their fair share of honour and distinction, or to deny to them the equal moral right of all human beings to choose their occupation (short of injury to others) according to their own preferences, at their own risk? Nor is the injustice confined to them: it is shared by those who are in a position to benefit by their services. To ordain that any kind of persons shall not be physicians, or shall not be advocates, or shall not be members of parliament, is to injure not them only, but all who employ physicians or advocates, or elect members of parliament, and who are deprived of the stimulating effect of greater competition on the exertions of the competitors, as well as restricted to a narrower range of individual choice.

[From *The Subjection of Women*, in *On Liberty and The Subjection of Women*, with introd. by Jane O'Grady (Wordsworth Editions, Ware, 1996), 136–8, 141–2, 164–6. First published 1869.]

CAROL GILLIGAN

16 In a Different Voice

In 1914, with his essay 'On Narcissism,' Freud swallows his distaste at the thought of 'abandoning observation for barren theoretical controversy' and extends his map of the psychological domain. Tracing the development of the capacity to love, which he equates with maturity and psychic health, he locates its origins in the contrast between love for the mother and love for the self. But in thus dividing the world of love into narcissism and 'object' relationships, he finds that while men's development becomes clearer, women's becomes increasingly opaque. The problem arises because the contrast between mother and self yields two different images of relationships. Relying on the imagery of men's lives in charting the course of human growth, Freud is unable to trace in women the development of relationships, morality, or a clear sense of self. This difficulty in fitting the logic of his theory to women's experience leads him in the end to set women apart, marking their relationships, like their sexual life, as 'a "dark continent" for psychology'.

Thus the problem of interpretation that shadows the understanding of women's development arises from the differences observed in their experience of relationships. To Freud, though living surrounded by women and otherwise seeing so much and so well, women's relationships seemed increasingly mysterious, difficult to discern, and hard to describe. While this mystery indicates how theory can blind observation, it also suggests that development in women is masked by a particular conception of human relationships. Since the imagery of relationships shapes the narrative of human development, the inclusion of women, by changing that imagery, implies a change in the entire account.

The shift in imagery that creates the problem in interpreting women's development is elucidated by the moral judgments of two eleven-year-old children, a boy and a girl, who see, in the same dilemma, two very different moral problems. While current theory brightly illuminates the line and the logic of the boy's thought, it casts scant light on that of the girl. The choice of a girl whose moral judgments elude existing categories of developmental assessment is meant to highlight the issue of interpretation rather than to exemplify sex differences per se. Adding a new line of interpretation, based on the imagery of the girl's thought, makes it possible not only to see development where previously development was not discerned but also to consider differences in the understanding of relationships without scaling these differences from better to worse.

The two children were in the same sixth-grade class at school and were participants in the rights and responsibilities study, designed to explore different conceptions of morality and self. The sample selected for this study was chosen to focus the variables of gender and age while maximizing developmental potential by holding constant, at a high level, the factors of intelligence, education, and social class that have been associated with moral development, at least as measured by existing scales. The two children in question, Amy and Jake, were both bright and articulate and, at least in their eleven-year-old aspirations, resisted easy categories of sex-role stereotyping, since Amy aspired to become a scientist while Jake preferred English to math. Yet their moral judgments seem initially to confirm familiar notions about differences between the sexes, suggesting that the edge girls have on moral development during the early school years gives way at puberty with the ascendance of formal logical thought in boys.

The dilemma that these eleven-year-olds were asked to resolve was one in the series devised by Kohlberg to measure moral development in adolescence by presenting a conflict between moral norms and exploring the logic of its resolution. In this particular dilemma, a man named Heinz considers whether or not to steal a drug which he cannot afford to buy in order to save the life of his wife. In the standard format of Kohlberg's interviewing procedure, the description of the dilemma itself—Heinz's predicament, the wife's disease, the druggist's refusal to lower his price—is followed by the question, 'Should Heinz steal the drug?' The reasons for and against stealing are then explored through a series of questions that vary and extend the parameters of the dilemma in a way designed to reveal the underlying structure of moral thought.

Jake, at eleven, is clear from the outset that Heinz should steal the drug. Constructing the dilemma, as Kohlberg did, as a conflict between the values of property and life, he discerns the logical priority of life and uses that logic to justify his choice:

For one thing, a human life is worth more than money, and if the druggist only makes $1,000, he is still going to live, but if Heinz doesn't steal the drug, his wife is going to die. (*Why is life worth more than money?*) Because the druggist can get a thousand dollars later from rich people with cancer, but Heinz can't get his wife again. (*Why not?*) Because people are all different and so you couldn't get Heinz's wife again.

Asked whether Heinz should steal the drug if he does not love his wife, Jake replies that he should, saying that not only is there 'a difference between hating and killing,' but also, if Heinz were caught, 'the judge would probably think it was the right thing to do,' Asked about the fact that, in stealing, Heinz would be breaking the law, he says that 'the laws have mistakes, and you can't go writing up a law for everything that you can imagine.'

Thus, while taking the law into account and recognizing its function in maintaining social order (the judge, Jake says, 'should give Heinz the lightest possible sentence'), he also sees the law as man-made and therefore subject to error and change. Yet his judgment that Heinz should steal the drug, like his view of the law as having mistakes, rests on the assumption of agreement, a societal consensus around moral values that allows one to know and expect others to recognize what is 'the right thing to do.'

Fascinated by the power of logic, this eleven-year-old boy locates truth in math, which, he says, is 'the only thing that is totally logical.' Considering the moral dilemma to be 'sort of like a math problem with humans,' he sets it up as an equation and proceeds to work out the solution. Since his solution is rationally derived, he assumes that anyone following reason would arrive at the same conclusion and thus that a judge would also consider stealing to be the right thing for Heinz to do. Yet he is also aware of the limits of logic. Asked whether there is a right answer to moral problems, Jake replies that 'there can only be right and wrong in judgment,' since the parameters of action are variable and complex. Illustrating how actions undertaken with the best of intentions can eventuate in the most disastrous of consequences, he says, 'like if you give an old lady your seat on the trolley, if you are in a trolley crash and that seat goes through the window, it might be that reason that the old lady dies.'

Theories of developmental psychology illuminate well the position of this child, standing at the juncture of childhood and adolescence, at what Piaget describes as the pinnacle of childhood intelligence, and beginning through thought to discover a wider universe of possibility. The moment of preadolescence is caught by the conjunction of formal operational thought with a description of self still anchored in the factual parameters of his childhood world—his age, his town, his father's occupation, the substance of his likes, dislikes, and beliefs. Yet as his self-description radiates the self-confidence of a child who has arrived, in Erikson's terms, at a favorable balance of industry over inferiority—competent, sure of himself, and knowing well the rules of the game—so his emergent capacity for formal thought, his ability to think about thinking and to reason things out in a logical way, frees him from dependence on authority and allows him to find solutions to problems by himself.

This emergent autonomy follows the trajectory that Kohlberg's six stages of moral development trace, a three-level progression from an egocentric understanding of fairness based on individual need (stages one and two), to a conception of fairness anchored in the shared conventions of societal agreement (stages three and four), and finally to a principled understanding of fairness that rests on the free-standing logic of equality and reciprocity (stages five and six). While this boy's judgments at eleven are scored as conventional on Kohlberg's scale, a mixture of stages three and four, his ability to bring deductive logic to bear on the solution of moral dilemma, to differentiate morality from law, and to see how laws can be considered to have mistakes points toward the principled conception of justice that Kohlberg equates with moral maturity.

In contrast, Amy's response to the dilemma conveys a very different impression, an image of development stunted by a failure of logic, an inability to think for herself. Asked if Heinz should steal the drug, she replies in a way that seems evasive and unsure:

Well, I don't think so. I think there might be other ways besides stealing it, like if he could borrow the money or make a loan or something, but he really shouldn't steal the drug—but his wife shouldn't die either.

Asked why he should not steal the drug, she considers neither property nor law but rather the effect that theft could have on the relationship between Heinz and his wife:

If he stole the drug, he might save his wife then, but if he did, he might have to go to jail, and then his wife might get sicker again, and he couldn't get more of the drug, and it might not be good. So, they should really just talk it out and find some other way to make the money.

Seeing in the dilemma not a math problem with humans but a narrative of relationships that extends over time, Amy envisions the wife's continuing need for her husband and the husband's continuing concern for his wife and seeks to respond to the druggist's need in a way that would sustain rather than sever connection. Just as she ties the wife's survival to the preservation of relationships, so she considers the value of the wife's life in a context of relationships, saying that it would be wrong to let her die because, 'if she died, it hurts a lot of people and it hurts her.' Since Amy's moral judgment is grounded in the belief that, 'if somebody has something that would keep somebody alive, then it's not right not to give it to them,' she considers the problem in the dilemma to arise not from the druggist's assertion of rights but from his failure of response.

As the interviewer proceeds with the series of questions that follow from Kohlberg's construction of the dilemma, Amy's answers remain essentially unchanged, the various probes serving neither to elucidate nor to modify her initial response. Whether or not Heinz loves his wife, he still shouldn't steal or let her die; if it were a stranger dying instead, Amy says that 'if the stranger didn't have anybody near or anyone she knew,' then Heinz should try to save her life, but he should not steal the drug. But as the interviewer conveys through the repetition of questions that the answers she gave were not heard or not right, Amy's confidence begins to diminish, and her replies become more constrained and unsure. Asked again why Heinz should not steal the drug, she simply repeats, 'Because it's not right.' Asked again to explain why, she states again that theft would not be a good solution, adding lamely, 'if he took it, he might not know how to give it to his wife, and so his wife might still die.' Failing to see the dilemma as a self-contained problem in moral logic, she does not discern the internal structure of its resolution; as she constructs the problem differently herself, Kohlberg's conception completely evades her.

Instead, seeing a world comprised of relationships rather than of people standing alone, a world that coheres through human connection rather than through systems of rules, she finds the puzzle in the dilemma to lie in the failure of the druggist to respond to the wife. Saying that 'it is not right for someone to die when their life could be saved,' she assumes that if the druggist were to see the consequences of his refusal to lower his price, he would realize that 'he should just give it to the wife and then have the husband pay back the money later.' Thus she considers the solution to the dilemma to lie in making the wife's condition more salient to the druggist or, that failing, in appealing to others who are in a position to help.

[From *In a Different Voice* (Harvard University Press, Cambridge, Mass., 1982), 24–9.]

17 Socialist Feminism and the Standpoint of Women

The socialist feminist theory of human nature is structurally identical with that of traditional Marxism and so, consequently, is the structure of its epistemology. Like both traditional Marxists and radical feminists, socialist feminists view knowledge as a social and practical construct and they believe that conceptual frameworks are shaped and limited by their social origins. They believe that, in any historical period, the prevailing world view will reflect the interests and values of the dominant class. Consequently, they recognize that the establishment of a less mystified and more reliable world view will require not only scientific struggle and intellectual argument but also the overthrow of the prevailing system of social relations.

Where social feminist differs from traditional Marxist epistemology is in its assertion that the special social or class position of women gives them a special epistemological standpoint which makes possible a view of the world that is more reliable and less distorted than that available either to capitalist or to working-class men. Socialist feminists believe, therefore, that a primary condition for the adequacy of a feminist theory, indeed for the adequacy of any theory, is that it should represent the world from the standpoint of women. A number of theorists are working to develop this insight, although they do not all use the terminology of women's standpoint or even mean quite the same thing by it when they do. These theorists include Elizabeth Fee, Jane Flax, Sandra Harding, Nancy Hartsock, Evelyn Fox Keller and Dorothy Smith.

Both liberal and Marxist epistemologists consider that, in order to arrive at an adequate representation of reality, it is important to begin from the proper standpoint. Within liberal epistemology, the proper standpoint is the standpoint of the neutral, disinterested observer, a so-called Archimedean standpoint somewhere outside the reality that is being observed. Marxist epistemology, by contrast, recognizes that there is no such standpoint: that all systems of conceptualization reflect certain social interests and values. In a society where the production of knowledge is controlled by a certain class, the knowledge produced will reflect the interests and values of that class. In other words, in class societies the prevailing knowledge and science interpret reality from the standpoint of the ruling class. Because the ruling class has an interest in concealing the way in which it dominates and exploits the rest of the population, the interpretation of reality that it presents will be distorted in characteristic ways. In particular, the suffering of the subordinate classes will be ignored, redescribed as enjoyment or justified as freely chosen, deserved or inevitable.

Because their class position insulates them from the suffering of the oppressed, many members of the ruling class are likely to be convinced by their own ideology; either they fail to perceive the suffering of the oppressed or they believe that it is freely chosen, deserved or inevitable. They experience the current organization of society as basically satisfactory and so they accept the interpretation of reality that justifies that system of organization. They encounter little in their daily lives that conflicts with that interpretation. Oppressed groups, by contrast, suffer directly from the system that oppresses them. Sometimes the ruling ideology succeeds in duping them into partial denial of their pain or into accepting it temporarily but the pervasiveness, intensity and relentlessness of their suffering constantly push oppressed groups toward a realization that something is wrong with the prevailing social order. Their pain provides them with a motivation for finding out what is wrong, for criticizing accepted interpretations of reality and for developing new and less distorted ways of understanding the world. These new systems of conceptualization will reflect the interests and values of the oppressed groups and so constitute a representation of reality from an alternative to the dominant standpoint.

The standpoint of the oppressed is not just different from that of the ruling class; it is also epistemologically advantageous. It provides the basis for a view of reality that is more impartial than that of the ruling class and also more comprehensive. It is more impartial because it comes closer to representing the interests of society as a whole; whereas the standpoint of the ruling class reflects the interests only of one section of the population, the standpoint of the oppressed represents the interests of the totality in that historical period. Moreover, whereas the condition of the oppressed groups is visible only dimly to the ruling class, the oppressed are able to see more clearly the ruled as well as the rulers and the relation between them. Thus, the standpoint of the oppressed includes and is able to explain the standpoint of the ruling class.

The political economy of socialist feminism establishes that, in contemporary society, women suffer a special form of exploitation and oppression. Socialist feminist epistemologists argue that this distinctive social or class position provides women with a distinctive epistemological standpoint. From this standpoint, it is possible to gain a less biased and more comprehensive view of reality than that provided either by established bourgeois science or by the male-dominated leftist alternatives to it. An adequate understanding of reality must be undertaken from the standpoint of women. As socialist feminists conceive it, however, the standpoint of women is not expressed directly in women's naive and unreflective world view. We have seen earlier that socialist feminists recognize that women's perceptions of reality are distorted both by male-dominant ideology and by the male-dominated structure of everyday life. The standpoint of women, therefore, is not something that can be discovered through a survey of women's existing beliefs and attitudes—although such a survey should identify certain commonalities that might be incorporated eventually into a systematic representation of the world from women's perspective. Instead, the standpoint of women is discovered through a collective process of political and scientific struggle. The distinctive social experience of women generates insights that are incompatible with men's interpretations of reality and these insights provide clues to how reality might be interpreted from the standpoint of women. The validity of these insights, however, must be tested in political struggle and developed into a systematic representation of reality that is not distorted in ways that promote the interests of men above those of women.

Considerable work still needs to be done in elaborating the concept of women's standpoint. A number of arguments used to establish it are still speculative and require further development and investigation. Even so, the concept of women's standpoint promises to provide an important criterion for evaluating the adequacy of feminist theory. It is supported by a variety of arguments: by psychological research, which demonstrates that women's perceptions of reality are in fact different from those of men; by psychoanalytic theory, which offers an explanation of those differences in terms of the different infant experiences of girls and boys; by investigations in the sociology of knowledge, which link the distinctive social experience of women with distinctively feminine ways of perceiving the world; and by feminist critiques of existing knowledge, which reveal how prevailing systems of conceptualization are biased because they invalidate women's interests and promote the interests and values of the men who created them. Of course, the epistemological superiority of women's standpoint will be demonstrated conclusively only through a distinctively feminist reconstruction of reality in which women's interests are not subordinated to those of men. This reconstruction must be practical as well as theoretical.

[From, *Feminist Politics and Human Nature* (Rowman & Littlefield, Atlantic Highlands, NJ, 1983), 369–71.]

Section II

The Justification of the State

INTRODUCTION

What is the state? Can its existence be justified? Are there, in any case, moral limits to what the state may ask us to do? The first pair of selections here—Locke and Weber—address the question of the definition of the state. Locke makes the point that political power is the right to make laws and punish those who disobey, while Weber adds that a state attempts to monopolize legitimate violence. This stark reminder of the state's role forces upon us the question of what could possibly justify such a threatening organization.

The idea that the authority of the state has its sources somehow in the will of the people generates the tradition of thought known as social contract theory, which is represented here by Hobbes, Locke, Rousseau, and Kant. Hobbes argues that we will remain in the state of nature—the state of war for Hobbes—until we set up a common power to protect us from each other and from external threat. This is possible only through our universal agreement: only our consent can bind us to obedience. To the obvious objection that none of us seem to have been explicitly consulted on this matter Locke argues that by enjoying the benefits of the protection of the state we tacitly consent to its authority. Only express consent can make someone a full member, but we all give our tacit consent whether or not we expressly consent. Rousseau is especially concerned to argue that if the state is constituted in the right way then not only is our full human nature awakened under such conditions (an echo of Aristotle) but, somehow, we remain as free as we were before. Kant's contribution is to answer the suspicion that, as the idea of a social contract is a complete fiction, it can have no moral or political force. His point is that the idea of a social contract has an important role even if no contract exists. He puts forward what has come to be seen as the hypothetical negative contract: that is, if an arrangement is such that free individuals couldn't (or at least wouldn't) have agreed to it, then it is unjust. It is here, many think, that the social contract tradition received its mature expression.

Not surprisingly the idea of the social contract has received many forms of criticism. The most formidable opponent may well be David Hume, who submits the doctrine to a barrage of criticisms, and is especially scathing of the idea of tacit consent. Bentham follows Hume's lead, arguing that utility is the real foundation both of the authority of the state and of our duty to keep promises. Hegel is equally sceptical, but from a different perspective. Given that we are all born citizens of particular states, it is entirely artificial to think that our obligations as citizens are founded on our consent. The state does not need our permission to exist; we are, in an important sense, its products. Hart is a more concessive critic. The real basis of the state's authority, he claims, is something that could easily be confused with the idea of tacit consent, but is quite distinct from it. This is what has been called the duty of fairness. I owe an obligation to obey the state because of the sacrifices made by my fellow citizens. It would be unfair for me to reap the benefits without sharing in the burdens.

All the theorists mentioned so far accept that the state, in some form or other, is morally justified. Yet this is not the universal view. Kropotkin, whose work appeared in the previous section, is an anarchist who argues against the necessity of the state. In this section we include a selection from Bakunin, who warned of what he saw as the twin evils of the bourgeois state and its authoritarian Marxist alternatives. In this extract he warns of the dangers of giving power to expert scientists. The second anarchist extract is from the contemporary theorist Robert Paul Wolff, who argues that accepting the authority of the state is incompatible with retaining one's moral autonomy.

Even those who accept the state's authority must, from time to time, question whether they should obey all its commands. Plato writes an imagined dialogue between Socrates and Crito in which Socrates, despite having been unjustly sentenced to death, argues powerfully that, at least in his particular circumstances, he should not flee the country but remain to be executed. Thoreau, equally powerfully, argues that if one's government is engaged in gross injustice—in his case the injustice of permitting slavery—the only place for the person with moral scruples is in jail for civil disobedience. The point is emphasized by Martin Luther King's moving *Letter from Birmingham Jail*, and the section closes with John Rawls's attempt to set out the definition of civil disobedience and the conditions which might justify it.

II.a. What is the State?

18 Political Power

I think it may not be amiss to set down what I take to be political power. That the power of a magistrate over a subject may be distinguished from that of a father over his children, a master over his servant, a husband over his wife, and a lord over his slave. All which distinct powers happening sometimes together in the same man, if he be considered under these different relations, it may help us to distinguish these powers one from another, and show the difference betwixt a ruler of a commonwealth, a father of a family, and a captain of a galley.

Political power, then, I take to be a right of making laws, with penalties of death, and consequently all less penalties for the regulating and preserving of property, and of employing the force of the community in the execution of such laws, and in the defence of the commonwealth from foreign injury, and all this only for the public good.

[From *Two Treatises of Civil Government*, ed. W. S. Carpenter (J. M. Dent, London, 1924 (1962 repr.)), 118. First published 1690.]

MAX WEBER

19 The State and Coercion

What is a 'state'? Sociologically, the state cannot be defined in terms of its ends. There is scarcely any task that some political association has not taken in hand, and there is no task that one could say has always been exclusive and peculiar to those associations which are designated as political ones: today the state, or historically, those associations which have been the predecessors of the modern state. Ultimately, one can define the modern state sociologically only in terms of the specific means peculiar to it, as to every political association, namely, the use of physical force.

'Every state is founded on force,' said Trotsky at Brest-Litovsk. That is indeed right. If no social institutions existed which knew the use of violence, then the concept of 'state' would be eliminated, and a condition would emerge that could be designated as 'anarchy,' in the specific sense of this word. Of course, force is certainly not the normal or the only means of the state—nobody says that—but force is a means specific to the state. Today the relation between the state and violence is an especially intimate one. In the past, the most varied institutions—beginning with the sib—have known the use of physical force as quite normal. Today, however, we have to say that a state is a human community that (successfully) claims the *monopoly of the legitimate use of physical force* within a given territory. Note that 'territory' is one of the characteristics of the state. Specifically, at the present time, the right to use physical force is ascribed to other institutions or to individuals only to the extent to which the state permits it. The state is considered the sole source of the 'right' to use violence. Hence, 'politics' for us means striving to share power or striving to influence the distribution of power, either among states or among groups within a state.

This corresponds essentially to ordinary usage. When a question is said to be a 'political' question, when a cabinet minister or an official is said to be a 'political' official, or when a decision is said to be 'politically' determined, what is always meant is that interests in the distribution, maintenance, or transfer of power are decisive for answering the questions and determining the decision or the official's sphere of activity. He who is active in politics strives for power either as a means in serving other aims, ideal or egoistic, or as 'power for power's sake,' that is, in order to enjoy the prestige-feeling that power gives.

Like the political institutions historically preceding it, the state is a relation of men dominating men, a relation supported by means of legitimate (i.e. considered to be legitimate) violence. If the state is to exist, the dominated must obey the authority claimed by the powers that be.

[From 'Politics as a Vocation' in *Max Weber*, trans. and ed. H. H. Gerth and C. Wright Mills (Routledge & Kegan Paul, London, 1948), 77–8. First published 1919.]

II.b. The Social Contract

20 Creating Leviathan

And because the condition of man, (as hath been declared in the precedent chapter) is a condition of war of every one against every one; in which case every one is governed by his own reason; and there is nothing he can make use of, that may not be a help unto him, in preserving his life against his enemies; it followeth, that in such a condition, every man has a right to every thing; even to one another's body. And therefore, as long as this natural right of every man to every thing endureth, there can be no security to any man, (how strong or wise soever he be,) of living out the time, which nature ordinarily alloweth men to live. And consequently it is a precept, or general rule of reason, *that every man, ought to endeavour peace, as far as he has hope of obtaining it; and when he cannot obtain it, that he may seek, and use, all helps, and advantages of war.* The first branch of which rule, containeth the first, and fundamental law of nature; which is, *to seek peace, and follow it.* The second, the sum of the right of nature; which is, *by all means we can, to defend ourselves.*

From this fundamental law of nature, by which men are commanded to endeavour peace, is derived this second law; *that a man be willing, when others are so too, as far-forth, as for peace, and defence of himself he shall think it necessary, to lay down this right to all things; and be contented with so much liberty against other men, as he would allow other men against himself.* For as long as every man holdeth this right, of doing any thing he liketh; so long are all men in the condition of war. But if other men will not lay down their right, as well as he; then there is no reason for any one, to divest himself of his: for that were to expose himself to prey, (which no man is bound to) rather than to dispose himself to peace. This is that law of the Gospel; *whatsoever you require that others should do to you, that do ye to them.* And that law of all men, *quod tibi fieri non vis, alteri ne feceris.*

To *lay down* a man's *right* to any thing, is to *divest* himself of the *liberty*, of hindering another of the benefit of his own right to the same. For he that renounceth, or passeth away his right, giveth not to any other man a right which he had not before; because there is nothing to which every man had not right by nature: but only standeth out of his way, that he may enjoy his own original right, without hindrance from him; not without hindrance from another. So that the effect which redoundeth to one man, by another man's defect of right, is but so much diminution of impediments to the use of his own right original. [. . .]

The mutual transferring of right, is that which men call CONTRACT.

Signs of contract, are either *express*, or by *inference*. Express are words spoken with understanding of what they signify: and such words are either of the time *present*, or *past*; as, *I give, I grant, I have given, I have granted, I will that this be yours*: or of the future; as, *I will give, I will grant*: which words of the future are called PROMISE.

Signs by inference, are sometimes the consequence of words; sometimes the consequence of silence; sometimes the consequence of actions; sometimes the consequence of forbearing an action: and generally a sign by inference, of any contract, is whatsoever sufficiently argues the will of the contractor. [. . .]

If a covenant be made, wherein neither of the parties perform presently, but trust one another; in the condition of mere nature, (which is a condition of war of every man against every man,) upon any reasonable suspicion, it is void: but if there be a common power set over them both, with right and force sufficient to compel performance, it is not void. For he that performeth first, has no assurance the other will perform after; because the bonds of words are too weak to bridle men's ambition, avarice, anger, and other passions, without the fear of some coercive power; which in the condition of mere nature, where all men are equal, and judges of the justness of their own fears, cannot possibly be supposed. And therefore he which performeth first, does but betray himself to his enemy; contrary to the right (he can never abandon) of defending his life, and means of living.

But in a civil estate, where there is a power set up to constrain those that would otherwise violate their faith, that fear is no more reasonable; and for that cause, he which by the covenant is to perform first, is obliged so to do. [. . .]

It is true, that certain living creatures, as bees, and ants, live sociably one with another, (which are therefore by Aristotle numbered amongst political creatures;) and yet have no other direction, than their particular judgments and appetites; not speech, whereby one of them can signify to another, what he thinks expedient for the common benefit: and therefore some man may perhaps desire to know, why mankind cannot do the same. To which I answer,

First, that men are continually in competition for honour and dignity, which these creatures are not; and consequently amongst men there ariseth on that ground, envy and hatred, and finally war; but amongst these not so.

Secondly, that amongst these creatures, the common good differeth not from the private; and being by nature inclined to their private, they procure thereby the common benefit. But man, whose joy consisteth in comparing himself with other men, can relish nothing but what is eminent.

Thirdly, that these creatures, having not (as man) the use of reason, do not see, nor think they see any fault, in the administration of their common business: whereas amongst men, there are very many, that think themselves wiser, and abler to govern the public, better than the rest; and these strive to reform and innovate, one this way, another that way; and thereby bring it into distraction and civil war.

Fourthly, that these creatures, though they have some use of voice, in making known to one another their desires, and other affections; yet they want that art of words, by which some men can represent to others, that which is good, in the likeness of evil; and evil, in the likeness of good; and augment, or diminish the apparent greatness of good and evil; discontenting men, and troubling their peace at their pleasure.

Fifthly, irrational creatures cannot distinguish between *injury*, and *damage*; and therefore as long as they be at ease, they are not offended with their fellows: whereas man is then most troublesome, when he is most at ease: for then it is that he loves to shew his wisdom, and control the actions of them that govern the commonwealth.

Lastly, the agreement of these creatures is natural; that of men, is by covenant only, which is artificial: and therefore it is no wonder if there be somewhat else required (besides covenant) to make their agreement constant and lasting; which is a common power, to keep them in awe, and to direct their actions to the common benefit.

The only way to erect such a common power, as may be able to defend them from the invasion of foreigners, and the injuries of one another, and thereby to secure them in such sort, as that by their own industry, and by the fruits of the earth, they may nourish themselves and live contentedly; is, to confer all their power and strength upon one man, or upon one assembly of men, that may reduce all their wills, by plurality of voices, unto one will [. . .]

This done, the multitude so united in one person, is called a COMMONWEALTH, in Latin CIVITAS. There is the generation of that great LEVIATHAN, or rather (to speak more reverently) of that *Mortal God*, to which we owe under the *Immortal God*, our peace and defence. For by this authority, given him by every particular man in the commonwealth, he hath the use of so much power and strength conferred on him, that by terror thereof, he is enabled to conform the wills of them all, to peace at home, and mutual aid against their enemies abroad. And in him consisteth the essence of the commonwealth; which (to define it,) is *one person, of whose acts a great multitude, by mutual covenants one with another, have made themselves every one the author, to the end he may use the strength and means of them all, as he shall think expedient, for their peace and common defence.*

And he that carrieth this person, is called SOVEREIGN, and said to have *sovereign power*; and every one besides, his SUBJECT.

The attaining to the sovereign power, is by two ways. One, by natural force; as when a man maketh his children, to submit themselves, and their children to his government, as being able to destroy them if they refuse; or by war subdueth his enemies to his will, giving them their lives on that condition. The other, is when men agree amongst themselves, to submit to some man, or assembly of men, voluntarily, on confidence to be protected by him against all others. This latter, may be called a political commonwealth, or commonwealth by *institution*; and the former, a commonwealth by *acquisition*.

[From *Leviathan*, ed. with introd. by J. C. A. Gaskin (Oxford University Press, Oxford, 1996), 86–7, 89, 91, 113–15. First published 1651.]

21   Express and Tacit Consent

Men being, as has been said, by nature all free, equal, and independent, no one can be put out of this estate and subjected to the political power of another without his own consent, which is done by agreeing with other men, to join and unite into a community for their comfortable, safe, and peaceable living, one amongst another, in a secure enjoyment of their properties, and a greater security against any that are not of it. This any number of men may do, because it injures not the freedom of the rest; they are left, as they were, in the liberty of the state of Nature. When any number of men have so consented to make one community or government, they are thereby presently incorporated, and make one body politic, wherein the majority have a right to act and conclude the rest.

For, when any number of men have, by the consent of every individual, made a community, they have thereby made that community one body, with a power to act as one body, which is only by the will and determination of the majority. For that which acts any community, being only the consent of the individuals of it, and it being one body, must move one way, it is necessary the body should move that way whither the greater force carries it, which is the consent of the majority, or else it is impossible it should act or continue one body, one community, which the consent of every individual that united into it agreed that it should; and so every one is bound by that consent to be concluded by the majority. And therefore we see that in assemblies empowered to act by positive laws where no number is set by that positive law which empowers them, the act of the majority passes for the act of the whole, and of course determines as having, by the law of Nature and reason, the power of the whole.

And thus every man, by consenting with others to make one body politic under one government, puts himself under an obligation to every one of that society to submit to the determination of the majority, and to be concluded by it; or else this original compact, whereby he with others incorporates into one society, would signify nothing, and be no compact if he be left free and under no other ties than he was in before in the state of Nature. For what appearance would there be of any compact? What new engagement if he were no farther tied by any decrees of the society than he himself fit and did actually consent to? This would be still as great a liberty as he himself had before his compact, or any one else in the state of Nature, who may submit himself and consent to any acts of it if he thinks fit.

For if the consent of the majority shall not in reason be received as the act of the whole, and conclude every individual, nothing but the consent of every individual can make anything to be the act of the whole, which, considering the infirmities of health and advocations of business, which in a number though much less than that of a commonwealth, will necessarily keep many away from the public assembly; and the variety of opinions and contrariety of interests which unavoidably happen in all collections of men, it is next impossible ever to be had. And, therefore, if coming into society be upon such terms, it will be only like Cato's coming into the theatre, *tantum ut exiret*. Such a constitution as this would make the mighty leviathan of a shorter duration than the feeblest creatures, and not let it outlast the day it was born in, which cannot be supposed till we think that rational creatures should desire and constitute societies only to be dissolved. For where the majority cannot conclude the rest, there they cannot act as one body, and consequently will be immediately dissolved again.

Whosoever, therefore, out of a state of Nature unite into a community, must be understood to give up all the power necessary to the ends for which they unite into society to the majority of the community, unless they expressly agreed in any number greater than the majority. And this is done by barely agreeing to unite into one political society, which is all the compact that is, or needs be, between the individuals that enter into or make up a commonwealth. And thus, that which begins and actually constitutes any political society is nothing but the consent of any number of freemen capable of majority, to unite and incorporate into such a society. And this is that, and that only, which did or could give beginning to any lawful government in the world. [. . .]

Every man being, as has been showed, naturally free, and nothing being able to put him into subjection to any earthly power, but only his own consent, it is to be considered what shall be understood to be a sufficient declaration of a man's consent to make him subject to the laws of any government. There is a common distinction of an express and a tacit consent, which will concern our present case. Nobody doubts but an express consent of any man, entering into any society, makes him a perfect member of that society, a subject of that government. The difficulty is, what ought to be looked upon as a tacit consent, and how far it binds—*i.e.*, how far any one shall be looked on to have consented, and thereby submitted to any government, where he has made no expressions of it at all. And to this I say, that every man that hath any possession or enjoyment of any part of the dominions of any government doth hereby give his tacit consent, and is as far forth obliged to obedience to the laws of that government, during such enjoyment, as any one under it, whether this his possession be of land to him and his heirs for ever, or a lodging only for a week; or whether it be barely travelling freely on the highway; and, in effect, it reaches as far as the very being of any one within the territories of that government.

To understand this the better, it is fit to consider that every man when he at first incorporates himself into any commonwealth, he, by his uniting himself thereunto, annexes also, and submits to the community those possessions which he has, or shall acquire, that do not already belong to any other government. For it would be a direct contradiction for any one to enter into society with others for the securing and regulating of property, and yet to suppose his land, whose property is to be regulated by the laws of the society, should be exempt from the jurisdiction of that government to which he himself, and the property of the land is a subject. By the same act, therefore, whereby any one unites his person, which was before free, to any commonwealth, by the same he unites his possessions, which were before free, to it also; and they become, both of them, person and possession, subject to the government and dominion of that commonwealth as long as it hath a being. Whoever therefore, from thenceforth, by inheritance, purchases permission, or otherwise enjoys any part of the land so annexed to, and under the government of that commonwealth, must take it with the condition it is under—that is, of submitting to the government of the commonwealth, under whose jurisdiction it is, as far forth as any subject of it.

But since the government has a direct jurisdiction only over the land and reaches the possessor of it (before he has actually incorporated himself in the society) only as he dwells upon and enjoys that, the obligation any one is under by virtue of such enjoyment to submit to the government begins and ends with the enjoyment; so that whenever the owner, who has given nothing but such a tacit consent to the government will, by donation, sale or otherwise, quit the said possession, he is at liberty to go and incorporate himself into any other commonwealth, or agree with others to begin a new one *in vacuis locis*, in any part of the world they can find free and unpossessed; whereas he that has once, by actual agreement and any express declaration, given his consent to be of any commonweal, is perpetually and indispensably obliged to be, and remain unalterably a subject to it, and can never be again in the liberty of the state of Nature, unless by any calamity the government he was under comes to be dissolved.

But submitting to the laws of any country, living quietly and enjoying privileges and protection under them, makes not a man a member of that society; it is only a local protection and homage due to and from all those who, not being in a state of war, come within the territories belonging to any government, to all parts whereof the force of its law extends. But this no more makes a man a member of that society, a perpetual subject of that commonwealth, than it would make a man a subject to another in whose family he found it convenient to abide for some time, though, whilst he continued in it, he were obliged to comply with the laws and submit to the government he found there. And thus we see that foreigners, by living all their lives under another government, and enjoying the privileges and protection of it, though they are bound, even in conscience, to submit to its administration as far forth as any denizen, yet do not thereby come to be subjects or members of that commonwealth. Nothing can make any man so but his actually entering into it by positive engagement and express promise and compact. This is that which, I think, concerning the beginning of political societies, and that consent which makes any one a member of any commonwealth.

[From *Two Treatises of Civil Government*, ed. W. S. Carpenter (J. M. Dent, London, 1924 (1962 repr.)), 164–6, 177–9. First published 1690.]

22 Natural Freedom and the Freedom of the Citizen

Man is born free; and everywhere he is in chains. One thinks himself the master of others, and still remains a greater slave than they. How did this change come about? I do not know. What can make it legitimate? That question I think I can answer. [. . .]

I suppose men to have reached the point at which the obstacles in the way of their preservation in the state of nature show their power of resistance to be greater than the resources at the disposal of each individual for his maintenance in that state. That primitive condition can then subsist no longer; and the human race would perish unless it changed its manner of existence.

But, as men cannot engender new forces, but only unite and direct existing ones, they have no other means of preserving themselves than the formation, by aggregation, of a sum of forces great enough to overcome the resistance. These they have to bring into play by means of a single motive power, and cause to act in concert.

This sum of forces can arise only where several persons come together: but, as the force and liberty of each man are the chief instruments of his self-preservation, how can he pledge them without harming his own interests, and neglecting the care he owes to himself? This difficulty, in its bearing on my present subject, may be stated in the following terms:

'The problem is to find a form of association which will defend and protect with the whole common force the person and goods of each associate, and in which each, while uniting himself with all, may still obey himself alone, and remain as free as before.' This is the fundamental problem of which the social contract provides the solution.

The clauses of this contract are so determined by the nature of the act that the slightest modification would make them vain and ineffective; so that, although they have perhaps never been formally set forth, they are everywhere the same and everywhere tacitly admitted and recognized, until, on the violation of the social compact, each regains his original rights and resumes his natural liberty, while losing the conventional liberty in favour of which he renounced it.

These clauses, properly understood, may be reduced to one—the total alienation of each associate, together with all his rights, to the whole community; for, in the first place, as each gives himself absolutely, the conditions are the same for all; and, this being so, no one has any interest in making them burdensome to others.

Moreover, the alienation being without reserve, the union is as perfect as it can be, and no associate has anything more to demand: for, if the individuals retained certain rights, as there would be no common superior to decide between them and the public, each, being on one point his own judge, would ask to be so on all; the state of nature would thus continue, and the association would necessarily become inoperative or tyrannical.

Finally, each man, in giving himself to all, gives himself to nobody; and as there is no associate over which he does not acquire the same right as he yields others over himself, he gains an equivalent for everything he loses, and an increase of force for the preservation of what he has.

If then we discard from the social compact what is not of its essence, we shall find that it reduces itself to the following terms:

'Each of us puts his person and all his power in common under the supreme direction of the general will, and, in our corporate capacity, we receive each member as an indivisible part of the whole.'

At once, in place of the individual personality of each contracting party, this act of association creates a corporate and collective body, composed of as many members as the assembly contains voters, and receiving from this act its unity, its common identity, its life, and its will. This public person, so formed by the union of all other persons, formerly took the name of *city*, and now takes that of *Republic* or *body politic*; it is called by its members *State* when passive, *Sovereign* when active, and *Power* when compared with others like itself. Those who associated in it take collectively the name of *people*, and severally are called *citizens*, as sharing in the sovereign authority, and *subjects*, as being under the laws of the State. But these terms are often confused and taken one for another: it is enough to know how to distinguish them when they are being used with precision. [. . .]

The passage from the state of nature to the civil state produces a very remarkable change in man, by substituting justice for instinct in his conduct, and giving his actions the morality they had formerly lacked. Then only, when the voice of duty takes the place of physical impulses and right of appetite, does man, who so far had considered only himself, find that he is forced to act on different principles, and to consult his reason before listening to his inclinations. Although, in this state, he deprives himself of some advantages which he got from nature, he gains in return others so great, his faculties are so stimulated and developed, his ideas so extended, his feelings so ennobled, and his whole soul so uplifted, that, did not the abuses of this new condition often degrade him below that which he left, he would be bound to bless continually the happy moment which took him from it for ever, and, instead of a stupid and unimaginative animal, made him an intelligent being and a man.

[From *The Social Contract*, in *The Social Contract and Discourses*, trans. and introd. G. D. H. Cole (J. M. Dent, London, 1973), 181, 190–3, 195–6. First published 1762.]

This, then, is an *original contract* by means of which a civil and thus completely lawful constitution and commonwealth can alone be established. But we need by no means assume that this contract (*contractus originarius* or *pactum sociale*), based on a coalition of the wills of all private individuals in a nation to form a common, public will for the purposes of rightful legislation, actually exists as a *fact*, for it cannot possibly be so. Such an assumption would mean that we would first have to prove from history that some nation, whose rights and obligations have been passed down to us, did in fact perform such an act, and handed down some authentic record or legal instrument, orally or in writing, before we could regard ourselves as bound by a pre-existing civil constitution. It is in fact merely an *idea* of reason, which nonetheless has undoubted practical reality; for it can oblige every legislator to frame his laws in such a way that they could have been produced by the united will of a whole nation, and to regard each subject, in so far as he can claim citizenship, as if he had consented within the general will. This is the test of the rightfulness of every public law. For if the law is such that a whole people could not *possibly* agree to it (for example, if it stated that a certain class of *subjects* must be privileged as a hereditary *ruling class*), it is unjust; but if it is at least *possible* that a people could agree to it, it is our duty to consider the law as just, even if the people is at present in such a position or attitude of mind that it would probably refuse its consent if it were consulted. But this restriction obviously applies only to the judgement of the legislator, not to that of the subject. Thus if a people, under some existing legislation, were asked to make a judgment which in all probability would prejudice its happiness, what should it do? Should the people not oppose the measure? The only possible answer is that they can do nothing but obey. For we are not concerned here with any happiness which the subject might expect to derive from the institutions or administration of the commonwealth, but primarily with the rights which would thereby be secured for everyone. And this is the highest principle from which all maxims relating to the commonwealth must begin, and which cannot be qualified by any other principles. No generally valid principle of legislation can be based on happiness. For both the current circumstances and the highly conflicting and variable illusions as to what happiness is (and no-one can prescribe to others how they should attain it) make all fixed principles impossible, so that happiness alone can never be a suitable principle of legislation. The doctrine that *salus publica suprema civitatis lex est* retains its value and authority undiminished; but the public welfare which demands *first* consideration lies precisely in that legal constitution which guarantees everyone his freedom within the law, so that each remains free to seek his happiness in whatever way he thinks best, so long as he does not violate the lawful freedom and rights of his fellow subjects at large. If the supreme power makes laws which are primarily directed towards happiness (the affluence of the citizens, increased population etc.), this cannot be regarded as the end for which a civil constitution was established, but only as a means of *securing the rightful state*, especially against external enemies of the people. The head of state must be authorised to judge for himself whether such measures are necessary for the commonwealth's prosperity, which is required to maintain its strength and stability both internally and against external enemies. The aim is not, as it were, to make the people happy against its will, but only to ensure its continued existence as a commonwealth. The legislator may indeed err in judging whether or not the measures he adopts are *prudent*, but not in deciding whether or not the law harmonises with the principle of right. For he has ready to hand as an infallible *a priori* standard the idea of an original contract, and he need not wait for experience to show whether the means are suitable, as would be necessary if they were based on the principle of happiness. For so long as it is not self-contradictory to say that an entire people could agree to such a law, however painful it might seem, then the law is in harmony with right. But if a public law is beyond reproach (i.e. *irreprehensible*) with respect to right, it carries with it the authority to coerce those to whom it applies, and conversely, it forbids them to resist the will of the legislator by violent means. In other words, the power of the state to put the law into effect is also *irresistible*, and no rightfully established commonwealth can exist without a force of this kind to suppress all internal resistance. For such resistance would be dictated by a maxim which, if it became general, would destroy the whole civil constitution and put an end to the only state in which men can possess rights.

[From *On the Common Saying 'This may be true in theory, but it does not apply in practice'*, in *Kant: Political Writings*, ed. Hans Reiss, trans. H. B. Nisbet (Cambridge University Press, Cambridge, 1970, 1991), 79–81. First published 1793.]

II.c. Against the Social Contract

DAVID HUME

24 **The Irrelevance of Consent**

When we consider how nearly equal all men are in their bodily force, and even in their mental powers and faculties, till cultivated by education; we must necessarily allow, that nothing but their own consent could, at first, associate them together, and subject them to any authority. The people, if we trace government to its first origin in the woods and desarts, are the source of all power and jurisdiction, and voluntarily, for the sake of peace and order, abandoned their native liberty, and received laws from their equal and companion. The conditions, upon which they were willing to submit, were either expressed, or were so clear and obvious, that it might well be esteemed superfluous to express them. If this, then, be meant by the *original contract*, it cannot be denied, that all government is, at first, founded on a contract, and that the most ancient rude combinations of mankind were formed chiefly by that principle. In vain, are we asked in what records this charter of our liberties is registered. It was not written on parchment, nor yet on leaves or barks of trees. It preceded the use of writing and all the other civilized arts of life. But we trace it plainly in the nature of man, and in the equality, or something approaching equality, which we find in all the individuals of that species. The force, which now prevails, and which is founded on fleets and armies, is plainly political, and derived from authority, the effect of established government. A man's natural force consists only in the vigour of his limbs, and the firmness of his courage; which could never subject multitudes to the command of one. Nothing but their own consent, and their sense of the advantages resulting from peace and order, could have had that influence.

Yet even this consent was long very imperfect, and could not be the basis of a regular administration. [. . .]

Almost all the governments, which exist at present, or of which there remains any record in story, have been founded originally, either on usurpation or conquest, or both, without any pretence of a fair consent, or voluntary subjection of the people. When an artful and bold man is placed at the head of an army or faction, it is often easy for him, by employing, sometimes violence, sometimes false pretences, to establish his dominion over a people a hundred times more numerous than his partizans. He allows no such open communication, that his enemies can know, with certainty, their number or force. He gives them no leisure to assemble together in a body to oppose him. Even all those,

who are the instruments of his usurpation, may wish his fall; but their ignorance of each other's intention keeps them in awe, and is the sole cause of his security. By such arts as these, many governments have been established; and this
is all the *original contract*, which they have to boast of. [. . .]

My intention here is not to exclude the consent of the people from being one
just foundation of government where it has place. It is surely the best and most
sacred of any. I only pretend, that it has very seldom had place in any degree, and
never almost in its full extent. And that therefore some other foundation of government must also be admitted. [. . .]

Should it be said, that, by living under the dominion of a prince, which one
might leave, every individual has given a *tacit* consent to his authority, and
promised him obedience; it may be answered, that such an implied consent can
only have place, where a man imagines, that the matter depends on his choice.
But where he thinks (as all mankind do who are born under established governments) that by his birth he owes allegiance to a certain prince or certain
form of government; it would be absurd to infer a consent or choice, which he
expressly, in this case, renounces and disclaims.

Can we seriously say, that a poor peasant or artizan has a free choice to leave
his country, when he knows no foreign language or manners, and lives from day
to day, by the small wages which he acquires? We may as well assert, that a man,
by remaining in a vessel, freely consents to the dominion of the master; though
he was carried on board while asleep, and must leap into the ocean, and perish,
the moment he leaves her. [. . .]

The truest *tacit* consent of this kind, that is ever observed, is when a foreigner
settles in any country, and is beforehand acquainted with the prince, and government, and laws, to which he must submit: Yet is his allegiance, though more
voluntary, much less expected or depended on, than that of a natural born subject. On the contrary, his native prince still asserts a claim to him. And if he punish not the renegade, when he seizes him in war with his new prince's
commission; this clemency is not founded on the municipal law, which in all
countries condemns the prisoner; but on the consent of princes, who have
agreed to this indulgence, in order to prevent reprisals.

Did one generation of men go off the stage at once, and another succeed, as
is the case with silk-worms and butterflies, the new race, if they had sense
enough to choose their government, which surely is never the case with men,
might voluntarily, and by general consent, establish their own form of civil
polity, without any regard to the laws or precedents, which prevailed among
their ancestors. But as human society is in perpetual flux, one man every hour
going out of the world, another coming into it, it is necessary, in order to preserve stability in government, that the new brood should conform themselves
to the established constitution, and nearly follow the path which their fathers,
treading in the footsteps of theirs, had marked out to them. Some innovations
must necessarily have place in every human institution, and it is happy where

the enlightened genius of the age give these a direction to the side of reason, liberty, and justice: but violent innovations no individual is entitled to make: they are even dangerous to be attempted by the legislature: more ill than good is ever to be expected from them: and if history affords examples to the contrary, they are not to be drawn into precedent, and are only to be regarded as proofs, that the science of politics affords few rules, which will not admit of some exception, and which may not sometimes be controlled by fortune and accident. The violent innovations in the reign of HENRY VIII. proceeded from an imperious monarch, seconded by the appearance of legislative authority: Those in the reign of CHARLES I. were derived from faction and fanaticism; and both of them have proved happy in the issue: But even the former were long the source of many disorders, and still more dangers; and if the measures of allegiance were to be taken from the latter, a total anarchy must have place in human society, and a final period at once be put to every government. [. . .]

What necessity, therefore, is there to found the duty of *allegiance* or obedience to magistrates on that of *fidelity* or a regard to promises, and to suppose, that it is the consent of each individual, which subjects him to government; when it appears, that both allegiance and fidelity stand precisely on the same foundation, and are both submitted to by mankind, on account of the apparent interests and necessities of human society? We are bound to obey our sovereign, it is said; because we have given a tacit promise to that purpose. But why are we bound to observe our promise? It must here be asserted, that the commerce and intercourse of mankind, which are of such mighty advantage, can have no security where men pay no regard to their engagements. In like manner, may it be said, that men could not live at all in society, at least in a civilized society, without laws and magistrates and judges, to prevent the encroachments of the strong upon the weak, of the violent upon the just and equitable. The obligation to allegiance being of like force and authority with the obligation to fidelity, we gain nothing by resolving the one into the other. The general interests or necessities of society are sufficient to establish both.

If the reason be asked of that obedience, which we are bound to pay to government, I readily answer, *because society could not otherwise subsist*: And this answer is clear and intelligible to all mankind. Your answer is, *because we should keep our word*. But besides, that no body, till trained in a philosophical system, can either comprehend or relish this answer: Besides this, I say, you find yourself embarrassed, when it is asked, *why we are bound to keep our word?* Nor can you give any answer, but what would, immediately, without any circuit, have accounted for our obligation to allegiance.

[From 'Of the Original Contract', in *Essays Moral, Political and Literary*, ed. Eugene F. Miller (Liberty Press, Indianapolis, 1985), 467–8, 471, 474, 475–7, 480–1. First published 1748.]

25 Utility as the True Foundation

For what *reason* is it, that men *ought* to keep their promises? The moment any intelligible reason is given, it is this: that it is for the *advantage* of society they should keep them; and if they do not, that, as far as *punishment* will go, they should be *made* to keep them. It is for the advantage of the whole number that the promises of each individual should be kept: and, rather than they should not be kept, that such individuals as fail to keep them should be punished. If it be asked, how this appears? the answer is at hand:—Such is the benefit to gain, and mischief to avoid, by keeping them, as much more than compensates the mischief of so much punishment as is requisite to oblige men to it. Whether the dependence of *benefit* and *mischief* (that is, of *pleasure* and *pain*) upon men's conduct in this behalf, be as here stated, is a question of *fact*, to be decided, in the same manner that all other questions of fact are to be decided, by testimony, observation, and experience.

This then, and no other, being the *reason* why men should be made to keep their promises, viz. that it is for the advantage of society that they should, is a reason that may as well be given at once, why *Kings*, on the one hand, in governing, should in general keep within established Laws, and (to speak universally) abstain from all such measures as tend to the unhappiness of their subjects: and, on the other hand, why *subjects* should obey Kings as long as they so conduct themselves, and no longer; why they should obey in short *so long as the probable mischiefs of obedience are less than the probable mischiefs of resistance:* why, in a word, taking the whole body together, it is their *duty* to obey, just so long as it is their *interest*, and no longer. This being the case, what need of saying of the one, that he PROMISED so to *govern*; of the other, that they PROMISED so to *obey*, when the fact is otherwise? [. . .]

One experiment there is, by which every reflecting man may satisfy himself, I think, beyond a doubt, that it is the consideration of *utility*, and no other, that, secretly but unavoidably, has governed his judgment upon all these matters. The experiment is easy and decisive. [. . .] Suppose the King to promise that he would govern his subjects *not* according to Law; *not* in the view to promote their happiness:—would this be binding upon *him*? Suppose the people to promise they would obey him *at all events*, let him govern as he will; let him govern to their destruction. Would this be binding upon *them*? Suppose the constant and universal effect of an observance of promises were to produce *mischief*, would it *then* be men's *duty* to observe them? Would it *then* be *right* to make Laws, and apply punishment to *oblige* men to observe them?

[From *A Fragment on Government*, in *A Comment on the Commentaries and A Fragment on Government*, ed. J. H. Burns and H. L. A. Hart (Athlone Press, London, 1977), 444–5. First published 1776.]

26   The Priority of the State over the Individual

The two contracting parties are related to each other as *immediate* self-subsistent persons. Therefore (α) contract arises from the arbitrary will. (β) The identical will which is brought into existence by the contract is only one *posited* by the parties, and so is only a will shared in common and not an absolutely universal will. (γ) The object about which a contract is made is a single external thing, since it is only things of that kind which the parties' purely arbitrary will has it in its power to alienate.

To subsume marriage under the concept of contract is thus quite impossible; this subsumption—though shameful is the only word for it—is propounded in Kant's *Philosophy of Law*. It is equally far from the truth to ground the nature of the state on the contractual relation, whether the state is supposed to be a contract of all with all, or of all with the monarch and the government.

The intrusion of this contractual relation, and relationships concerning private property generally, into the relation between the individual and the state has been productive of the greatest confusion in both constitutional law and public life. Just as at one time political rights and duties were considered and maintained to be an unqualified private property of particular individuals, something contrasted with the right of the monarch and the state, so also in more recent times the rights of the monarch and the state have been regarded as the subjects of a contract and as grounded in contract, as something embodying merely a common will and resulting from the arbitrariness of parties united into a state. However different these two points of view may be, they have this in common, that they have transferred the characteristics of private property into a sphere of a quite different and higher nature. [. . .]

It has recently become very fashionable to regard the state as a contract of all with all. Everyone makes a contract with the monarch, so the argument runs, and he again with his subjects. This point of view arises from thinking superficially of a mere unity of different wills. In contract, however, there are two identical wills who are both persons and wish to remain property-owners. Thus contract springs from a person's arbitrary will, an origin which marriage too has in common with contract. But the case is quite different with the state; it does not lie with an individual's arbitrary will to separate himself from the state, because we are already citizens of the state by birth. The rational end of man is life in the state, and if there is no state there, reason at once demands that one be founded. Permission to enter a state or leave it must be given by the state; this then is not a matter which depends on an individual's arbitrary will and therefore the state does not rest on contract, for contract presupposes arbitrariness. It is false to to maintain that the foundation of the state is something at the option of all its members. It is nearer the truth to say that it is absolutely necessary for every individual to be a citizen. The great advance of the state in modern times is that nowadays all the citizens have one and the same end, an absolute and permanent end; it is no longer open to individuals, as it was in the Middle Ages, to make private stipulations in connexion with it.

[From *Philosophy of Right*, trans. T. M. Knox (Clarendon Press, Oxford, 1952), 58–9, 242. First published 1821.]

H. L. A. HART

27 The Principle of Fairness

When rights arise out of special transactions between individuals or out of some special relationship in which they stand to each other, both the persons who have the right and those who have the corresponding obligation are limited to the parties to the special transaction or relationship. I call such rights special rights to distinguish them from those moral rights which are thought of as rights against (i.e., as imposing obligations upon) everyone, such as those that are asserted when some unjustified interference is made or threatened. [. . .]

Special rights are not only those created by the deliberate choice of the party on whom the obligation falls, as they are when they are accorded or spring from promises, and not all obligations to other persons are deliberately incurred, though I think it is true of all special rights that they arise from previous voluntary actions. A third very important source of special rights and obligations which we recognize in many spheres of life is what may be termed mutuality of restrictions, and I think political obligation is intelligible only if we see what precisely this is and how it differs from the other right-creating transactions (consent, promising) to which philosophers have assimilated it. In its bare schematic outline it is this: when a number of persons conduct any joint enterprise according to rules and thus restrict their liberty, those who have submitted to these restrictions when required have a right to a similar submission from those who have benefited by their submission. The rules may provide that officials should have authority to enforce obedience and make further rules, and this will create a structure of legal rights and duties, but the moral obligation to obey the rules in such circumstances is *due to* the co-operating members of the society, and they have the correlative moral right to obedience. In social situations of this sort (of which political society is the most complex example) the obligation to obey the rules is something distinct from whatever other moral reasons there may be for obedience in terms of good consequences (e.g., the prevention of suffering); the obligation is due to the co-operating members of the society as such and not because they are human beings on whom it would be wrong to inflict suffering. The utilitarian explanation of political obligation fails to take account of this feature of the situation both in its simple version that the obligation exists because and only if the direct consequences of a particular act of disobedience are worse than obedience, and also in its more sophisticated version that the obligation exists even when this is not so, if disobedience increases the probability that the law in question or other laws will be disobeyed on other occasions when the direct consequences of obedience are better than those of disobedience.

Of course to say that there is such a moral obligation upon those who have benefited by the submission of other members of society to restrictive rules to obey these rules in their turn does not entail either that this is the only kind of moral reason for obedience or that there can be no cases where disobedience will be morally justified. There is no contradiction or other impropriety in saying 'I have an obligation to do X, someone has a right to ask me to, but I now see I ought not to do it'. It will in painful situations sometimes be the lesser of two moral evils to disregard what really are people's rights and not perform our obligations to them. This seems to me particularly obvious from the case of promises: I may promise to do something and thereby incur an obligation just because that is one way in which obligations (to be distinguished from other forms of moral reasons for acting) are created; reflection may show that it would in the circumstances be wrong to keep this promise because of the suffering it might cause, and we can express this by saying '*I ought not* to do it though *I have an obligation to him* to do it' just because the italicized expressions are not synonyms but come from different dimensions of morality. The attempt to explain this situation by saying that our real obligation here is to avoid the suffering and that there is only a prima facie obligation to keep the promise seems to me to confuse two quite different kinds of moral reason, and in practice such a terminology obscures the precise character of what is at stake when 'for some greater good' we infringe people's rights or do not perform our obligations to them.

The social-contract theorists rightly fastened on the fact that the obligation to obey the law is not merely a special case of benevolence (direct or indirect), but something which arises between members of a particular political society out of their mutual relationship. Their mistake was to identify *this* right-creating situation of mutual restrictions with the paradigm case of promising; there are of course important similarities, and these are just the points which all special rights have in common, viz., that they arise out of special relationships between human beings and not out of the character of the action to be done or its effects.

[From 'Are there any natural rights?', *Philosophical Review*, 64 (1955), repr. in *Political Philosophy*, ed. Anthony Quinton (Oxford University Press, Oxford, 1967), 60–3.]

II.d. The Anarchist Response

28 Science and the People

The living, concretely rational method of science is to proceed from the real fact to the idea that encompasses it, expresses it, and thereby explains it. In the practical world it is the movement from social life to the most rational possible organization of it, in accordance with the specifications, conditions, needs, and more or less passionate demands of social life itself.

That is the broad popular method, the method of real and total liberation, accessible to anyone and therefore truly popular. It is the method of the *anarchist* social revolution, which arises spontaneously within the people and destroys everything that opposes the broad flow of popular life so as to create new forms of free social organization out of the very depths of the people's existence.

The metaphysicians' method is entirely different. By 'metaphysicians' we mean not just the followers of Hegel's doctrines, few of whom are left in the world, but also positivists and in general all the present-day worshippers of the goddess science; all those who by one means or another (if only by a very diligent but necessarily always imperfect study of the past and present) have created for themselves an ideal social organization into which, like new Procrustes, they want to force the life of future generations whatever the cost; in short, all those who, instead of regarding thought or science as one of the necessary manifestations of natural and social life, take such a narrow view of that poor life that they see in it only the practical manifestation of their own thought and their own always imperfect science.

Metaphysicians or positivists, all these knights of science and thought, in the name of which they consider themselves ordained to prescribe the laws of life, are reactionaries, conscious or unconscious. This is very easy to prove.

We are not speaking of metaphysics in general, with which only a few individuals occupied themselves even in those periods when it flourished most brilliantly. Even today, science in the broad sense of the term, serious science that is at all worthy of the name, is accessible only to a very insignificant minority. For example, out of 80 million inhabitants of Russia, how many serious scholars do we have? People who talk about science may number in the thousands, but there are barely a few hundred who are truly knowledgeable about it. If science is to prescribe the laws of life, however, then the great majority of mankind, millions of people, must be governed by one or two hundred scholars. In fact, the number is much smaller, for it is not just any science that renders an individual capable of governing society but the science of sciences, the crown of all the sciences—sociology, which presumes in the fortunate scholar a prior sound knowledge of all other sciences. Are there many such scholars even in the whole of Europe, let alone in Russia? Perhaps twenty or thirty! And those twenty or thirty scholars are to govern the entire world! Can you imagine a despotism more preposterous or abominable than that?

In the first place, those thirty scholars will most likely quarrel among themselves, and if they do unite it will be to the detriment of all mankind. By his very nature a scholar is disposed to intellectual and moral depravity of every kind, but his principal vice is to exalt his own knowledge and intellect and scorn all the ignorant. Let him govern, and he will become the most unbearable tyrant, for scholarly pride is repulsive, offensive, and more oppressive than any other. To be the slaves of pedants—what a fate for mankind! Give them free rein, and they will start performing the same experiments on human society that for the sake of science they now perform on rabbits, cats, and dogs.

We will esteem scholars according to their merits, but for the salvation of their intellect and morality they must not be given any social privileges or accorded any other right than the common one of freedom to propagate their convictions, ideas, and knowledge. Power should no more be given to them than to anyone else, for anyone who is invested with power by an invariable social law will inevitably become the oppressor and exploiter of society.

It will be said that science will not always be the property of only a few people; the time will come when it will be accessible to each and every individual. Well, that time is still far off, and a great many social upheavals will have to be carried out before it begins. Until it does, who will consent to put his fate in the hands of scholars, in the hands of priests of science? Why bother, then, to wrest it from the hands of Christian priests?

It seems to us that anyone who imagines that after the social revolution all will be equally learned is profoundly mistaken. Science as such, then as now, will remain one of the numerous social specializations, the sole difference being that once classes have been abolished this specialization, which is accessible today only to members of the privileged classes, will become accessible to any individual with the vocation and desire to devote himself to it, though not at the expense of general manual labor, which will be obligatory for everyone.

Only general scientific education will become common property, particularly a familiarity with scientific method as a way of thinking, that is, of generalizing facts and drawing more or less correct conclusions from them. But there will always be very few encyclopedic minds, and, therefore, learned sociologists. Woe to mankind if thought ever became the source and sole guide of life, if science and learning began to govern society. Life would dry up, and human society would be turned into a dumb and servile herd. The government of life by science could have no other result than to turn all mankind into fools.

We revolutionary anarchists are proponents of universal popular education, liberation, and the broad development of social life, and hence are enemies of the state and of any form of statehood. By contrast to all metaphysicians, positivists, and scholarly or unscholarly worshippers of the goddess science, we maintain that natural and social life always precedes thought (which is merely one of its functions) but is never its result. Life develops out of its own inexhaustible depths by means of a succession of diverse facts, not a succession of abstract reflections; the latter, always produced by life but never producing it, like milestones merely indicate its direction and the different phases of its spontaneous and self-generated development.

In keeping with this conviction, we have neither the intention nor the least desire to impose on our own people or on any other an ideal social organization that we have drawn from books or thought up on our own. In the belief that the masses bear all the elements of their future organizational norms in their own more or less historically evolved instincts, in their everyday needs and their conscious and unconscious desires, we seek that ideal within the people themselves. Since every state power, every government, by its nature and by its position stands outside the people and above them, and must invariably try to subject them to rules and objectives which are alien to them, we declare ourselves the enemies of every government and every state power, the enemies of state organization of any kind. We believe that the people can be happy and free only when they create their own life, organizing themselves from below upward by means of independent and completely free associations, subject to no official tutelage but open to the free and diverse influences of individuals and parties.

Those are the convictions of social revolutionaries, and for them we are called anarchists. We do not object to this term because we are in fact the enemies of all power, knowing that power corrupts those invested with it just as much as those compelled to submit to it. Under its pernicious influence the former become ambitious and avaricious despots, exploiters of society for their own personal or class advantage, and the latter become slaves.

Idealists of every stripe, metaphysicians, positivists, defenders of the predominance of science over life, and doctrinaire revolutionaries—all of them with identical ardor though different arguments uphold the idea of the state and of state power. *With perfect logic* (in their own terms), they regard it as the sole salvation of society. I say *with perfect logic* because once they have adopted the position—utterly false, in our view—that thought precedes life, that abstract theory precedes social practice, and that sociology must therefore be the point of departure for social upheavals and reconstructions, they necessarily conclude that since thought, theory, and science, at least for the present, are the property of a very few individuals, those few must be the directors of social life. They must be not only the instigators but the managers of all popular movements, and on the morrow of the revolution a new social organization must be created not by the free union of popular associations, communes, districts, and provinces from below upward, in conformity with popular needs and instincts, but solely by means of the dictatorial power of this learned minority, which supposedly expresses the will of all the people.

[From *Statism and Anarchy*, trans. and ed. Marshall S. Shatz (Cambridge University Press, Cambridge, 1990), 133–6. First published 1873.]

ROBERT PAUL WOLFF

29 **The Conflict of Autonomy and Authority**

That men accede to claims of supreme authority is plain. That men *ought* to accede to claims of supreme authority is not so obvious. Our first question must therefore be, Under what conditions and for what reasons does one man have supreme authority over another? The same question can be restated, Under what conditions can a state (understood normatively) exist? [. . .]

The fundamental assumption of moral philosophy is that men are responsible for their actions. [. . .]

Taking responsibility for one's actions means making the final decisions about what one should do. For the autonomous man, there is no such thing, strictly speaking, as a *command*. If someone in my environment is issuing what are intended as commands, and if he or others expect those commands to be obeyed, that fact will be taken account of in my deliberations. I may decide that I ought to do what that person is commanding me to do, and it may even be that his issuing the command is the factor in the situation which makes it desirable for me to do so. For example, if I am on a sinking ship and the captain is giving orders for manning the lifeboats, and if everyone else is obeying the captain *because he is the captain*, I may decide that under the circumstances I had better do what he says, since the confusion caused by disobeying him would be generally harmful. But insofar as I make such a decision, I am not *obeying his command*; that is, I am not acknowledging him as having authority over me. I would make the same decision, for exactly the same reasons, if one of the passengers had started to issue 'orders' and had, in the confusion, come to be obeyed. [. . .]

The defining mark of the state is authority, the right to rule. The primary obligation of man is autonomy, the refusal to be ruled. It would seem, then, that there can be no resolution of the conflict between the autonomy of the individual and the putative authority of the state. Insofar as a man fulfills his obligation to make himself the author of his decisions, he will resist the state's claim to have authority over him. That is to say, he will deny that he has a duty to obey the laws of the state *simply because they are the laws*. In that sense, it would seem that anarchism is the only political doctrine consistent with the virtue of autonomy.

Now, of course, an anarchist may grant the necessity of *complying* with the law under certain circumstances or for the time being. He may ever doubt that there is any real prospect of eliminating the state as a human institution. But he will never view the commands of the state as *legitimate*, as having a binding moral force. In a sense, we might characterize the anarchist as a man without a country, for despite the ties which bind him to the land of his childhood, he stands in precisely the same moral relationship to 'his' government as he does to the government of any other country in which he might happen to be staying for a time. When I take a vacation in Great Britain, I obey its laws, both because of prudential self-interest and because of the obvious moral considerations concerning the value of order, the general good consequences of preserving a system of property, and so forth. On my return to the United States, I have a sense of reentering *my* country, and if I think about the matter at all, I imagine myself to stand in a different and more intimate relation to American laws. They have been promulgated by *my* government, and I therefore have a special obligation to obey them. But the anarchist tells me that my feeling is purely sentimental and has no objective moral basis. All authority is equally illegitimate, although of course not therefore equally worthy or unworthy of support, and my obedience to American laws, if I am to be morally autonomous, must proceed from the same considerations which determine me abroad.

The dilemma which we have posed can be succinctly expressed in terms of the concept of a *de jure* state. If all men have a continuing obligation to achieve the highest degree of autonomy possible, then there would appear to be no state whose subjects have a moral obligation to obey its commands. Hence, the concept of a *de jure* legitimate state would appear to be vacuous, and philosophical anarchism would seem to be the only reasonable political belief for an enlightened man.

[From *In Defence of Anarchism* (Harper & Row, New York, 1970), 8, 12, 15–16, 18–19.]

II.e. Civil Disobedience

30 The Duty of Obedience

Socrates: Look at it in this way. Suppose that while we were preparing to run away from her (or however one should describe it) the Laws and Constitution of Athens were to come and confront us and ask this question: 'Now, Socrates, what are you proposing to do? Can you deny that by this act which you are contemplating you intend, so far as you have the power, to destroy us, the Laws, and the whole State as well? Do you imagine that a city can continue to exist and not be turned upside down, if the legal judgements which are pronounced in it have no force but are nullified and destroyed by private persons?' [. . .] Shall we say 'Yes, I do intend to destroy the laws, because the State wronged me by passing a faulty judgement at my trial'? Is this to be our answer, or what?

Crito: What you have just said, by all means, Socrates.

Socrates: Then what supposing the Laws say 'Was there provision for this in the agreement between you and us, Socrates? Or did you undertake to abide by whatever judgements the State pronounced?' [. . .] Come now, what charge do you bring against us and the State, that you are trying to destroy us? Did we not give you life in the first place? Was it not through us that your father married your mother and begot you? Tell us, have you any complaint against those of us Laws that deal with marriage?' 'No, none', I should say. 'Well, have you any against the laws which deal with children's upbringing and education, such as you had yourself? Are you not grateful to those of us Laws which were instituted for this end, for requiring your father to give you a cultural and physical education?' 'Yes', I should say. 'Very good. Then since you have been born and brought up and educated, can you deny, in the first place, that you were our child and servant, both you and your ancestors? And if this is so, do you imagine that what is right for us is equally right for you, and that whatever we try to do to you, you are justified in retaliating? You did not have equality of rights with your father, or your employer (supposing that you had had one), to enable you to retaliate; you were not allowed to answer back when you were scolded or to hit back when you were beaten, or to do a great many other things of the same kind. Do you expect to have such license against your country and its laws that if we try to put you to death in the belief that it is right to do so, you on your part will try your hardest to destroy your country and us its Laws in return? And will you, the true devotee of goodness, claim that you are justified in doing so? Are you so wise as to have forgotten that compared with your mother and father and all the rest of your ancestors your country is something far more precious, more venerable, more sacred, and held in greater honour both among gods and among all reasonable men? Do you not realize that you are even more bound to respect and placate the anger of your country than your father's anger? that if you cannot persuade your country you must do whatever it orders, and patiently submit to any punishment that it imposes, whether it be flogging or imprisonment? [. . .]' What shall we say to this, Crito?—that what the Laws say is true, or not?

Crito: Yes, I think so.

Socrates: 'Consider, then, Socrates,' the Laws would probably continue, 'whether it is also true for us to say that what you are now trying to do to us is not right. Although we have brought you into the world and reared you and educated you, and given you and all your fellow-citizens a share in all the good things at our disposal, nevertheless by the very fact of granting our permission we openly proclaim this principle: that any Athenian, on attaining to manhood and seeing for himself the political organization of the State and us its Laws, is permitted, if he is not satisfied with us, to take his property and go away wherever he likes. If any of you chooses to go to one of our colonies, supposing that he should not be satisfied with us and the State, or to emigrate to any other country, not one of us Laws hinders or prevents him from going away wherever he likes, without any loss of property. On the other hand, if any one of you stands his ground when he can see how we administer justice and the rest of our public organization, we hold that by so doing he has in fact undertaken to do anything that we tell him; and we maintain that anyone who disobeys is guilty of doing wrong on three separate counts: first because we are his parents, and secondly because we are his guardians; and thirdly because, after promising obedience, he is neither obeying us nor persuading us to change our decision if we are at fault in any way; and although all our orders are in the form of proposals, not of savage commands, and we give him the choice of either persuading us or doing what we say, he is actually doing neither. [. . .]'

There are very few people in Athens who have entered into this agreement with them as explicitly as I have. They would say 'Socrates, we have substantial evidence that you are satisfied with us and with the State. You would not have been so exceptionally reluctant to cross the borders of your country if you had not been exceptionally attached to it. You have never left the city to attend a festival or for any other purpose, except on some military expedition; you have never travelled abroad as other people do, and you have never felt the impulse to acquaint yourself with another country or constitution; you have been content with us and with our city. You have definitely chosen us, and undertaken to observe us in all your activities as a citizen; and as the crowning proof that you are satisfied with our city, you have begotten children in it. Furthermore, even at the time of your trial you could have proposed the penalty of banishment, if you had chosen to do so; that is, you could have done then with the sanction of the State what you are now trying to do without it. But whereas at that time you made a noble show of indifference if you had to die, and in fact preferred death, as you said, to banishment, now you show no respect for your earlier professions, and no regard for us, the Laws, whom you are trying to destroy; you are behaving like the lowest type of menial, trying to run away in spite of the contracts and undertakings by which you agreed to live as a member of our State. Now first answer this question: Are we or are we not speaking the truth when we say that you have undertaken, in deed if not in word, to live your life as a citizen in obedience to us?' What are we to say to that, Crito? Are we not bound to admit it?

Crito: We cannot help it, Socrates.

Socrates: 'It is a fact, then,' they would say, 'that you are breaking covenants and undertakings made with us, although you made them under no compulsion or misunderstanding, and were not compelled to decide in a limited time; you had seventy years in which you could have left the country, if you were not satisfied with us or felt that the agreements were unfair. You did not choose Sparta or Crete—your favourite models of good government—or any other Greek or foreign state; you could not have absented yourself from the city less if you had been lame or blind or decrepit in some other way. It is quite obvious that you stand by yourself above all other Athenians in your affection for this city and for us its Laws;—who would care for a city without laws? And now, after all this, are you not going to stand by your agreement? Yes, you are, Socrates, if you will take our advice; and then you will at least escape being laughed at for leaving the city. [. . .] Incidentally you will confirm the opinion of the jurors who tried you that they gave a correct verdict; a destroyer of laws might very well be supposed to have a destructive influence upon young and foolish human beings. [. . .]

'Socrates; be advised by us your guardians, and do not think more of your children or of your life or of anything else than you think of what is right; so that when you enter the next world you may have all this to plead in your defence before the authorities there. It seems clear that if you do this thing, neither you nor any of your friends will be the better for it or be more upright or have a cleaner conscience here in this world, nor will it be better for you when you reach the next. As it is, you will leave this place, when you do, as the victim of a wrong done not by us, the Laws, but by your fellowmen. But if you leave in that dishonourable way, returning wrong for wrong and evil for evil, breaking your agreements and covenants with us, and injuring those whom you least ought to injure—yourself, your friends, your country, and us—then you will have to face our anger in your lifetime, and in that place beyond when the laws of the other world know that you have tried, so far as you could, to destroy even us their brothers, they will not receive you with a kindly welcome. Do not take Crito's advice, but follow ours.'

That, my dear friend Crito, I do assure you, is what I seem to hear them saying, just as a mystic seems to hear the strains of music; and the sound of their arguments rings so loudly in my head that I cannot hear the other side. I warn you that, as my opinion stands at present, it will be useless to urge a different view. However, if you think that you will do any good by it, say what you like.

Crito: No, Socrates, I have nothing to say.

Socrates: Then give it up, Crito, and let us follow this course, since God points out the way.

[From *Crito*, in *The Last Days of Socrates*, trans. Hugh Tredennick (Penguin, Harmondsworth, 1954), 89–96.]

HENRY DAVID THOREAU

31 The Duty of Disobedience

I heartily accept the motto,—'That government is best which governs least;' and I should like to see it acted up to more rapidly and systematically. Carried out, it finally amounts to this, which also I believe,—'That government is best which governs not at all;' and when men are prepared for it, that will be the kind of government which they will have. Government is at best but an expedient; but most governments are usually, and all governments are sometimes, inexpedient. The objections which have been brought against a standing army, and they are many and weighty, and deserve to prevail, may also at last be brought against a standing government. The standing army is only an arm of the standing government.

After all, the practical reason why, when the power is once in the hands of the people, a majority are permitted, and for a long period continue, to rule, is not because they are most likely to be in the right, nor because this seems fairest to the minority, but because they are physically the strongest. But a government in which the majority rule in all cases cannot be based on justice, even as far as men understand it. Can there not be a government in which majorities do not virtually decide right and wrong, but conscience?—in which majorities decide only those questions to which the rule of expediency is applicable? Must the citizen ever for a moment, or in the least degree, resign his conscience to the legislator? Why has every man a conscience, then? I think that we should be men first, and subjects afterward. It is not desirable to cultivate a respect for the law, so much as for the right. The only obligation which I have a right to assume, is to do at any time what I think right. It is truly enough said, that a corporation has no conscience; but a corporation of conscientious men is a corporation *with* a conscience. [. . .]

How does it become a man to behave toward this American government today? I answer that he cannot without disgrace be associated with it. I cannot for any instant recognize that political organization as *my* government which is the *slave's* government also.

All men recognize the right of revolution; that is, the right to refuse allegiance to and to resist the government, when its tyranny or its inefficiency are great and unendurable. But almost all say that such is not the case now. But such was the case, they think, in the Revolution of '75. If one were to tell me that this was a bad government because it taxed certain foreign commodities brought to its ports, it is most probable that I should not make an ado about it, for I can do without them: all machines have their friction; and possibly this does enough good to counterbalance the evil. At any rate, it is a great evil to make a stir about it. But when the friction comes to have its machine, and oppression and robbery are organized, I say, let us not have such a machine any longer. In other words, when a sixth of the population of a nation which has undertaken to be the refuge of liberty are slaves, and a whole country is unjustly overrun and conquered by a foreign army, and subjected to military law, I think that it is not too soon for honest men to rebel and revolutionize. What makes this duty the more urgent is the fact, that the country so overrun is not our own, but ours is the invading army.

Paley, a common authority with many on moral questions, in his chapter on the 'Duty of Submission to Civil Government,' resolves all civil obligation into expediency; and he proceeds to say, 'that so long as the interest of the whole society requires it, that is, so long as the established government cannot be resisted or changed without public inconveniency, it is the will of God, that the established government be obeyed, and no longer.'—'This principle being admitted, the justice of every particular case of resistance is reduced to a computation of the quantity of the danger and grievance on the one side, and of the probability and expense of redressing it on the other.' Of this, he says, every man shall judge for himself. But Paley appears never to have contemplated those cases to which the rule of expediency does not apply, in which a people, as well as an individual, must do justice, cost what it may. If I have unjustly wrested a plank from a drowning man, I must restore it to him though I drown myself. This, according to Paley, would be inconvenient. But he that would save his life, in such a case, shall lose it. This people must cease to hold slaves, and to make war on Mexico, though it cost them their existence as a people. [. . .]

Under a government which imprisons any unjustly, the true place for a just man is also a prison. The proper place to-day, the only place which Massachusetts has provided for her freer and less desponding spirits, is in her prisons, to be put out and locked out of the State by her own act, as they have already put themselves out by their principles. It is there that the fugitive slave, and the Mexican prisoner on parole, and the Indian come to plead the wrongs of his race, should find them; on that separate but more free and honorable ground, where the State places those who are not *with* her but *against* her,—the only house in a slave-state in which a free man can abide with honor. [. . .]

The authority of government, even such as I am willing to submit to,—for I will cheerfully obey those who know and can do better than I, and in many things even those who neither know nor can do so well,—is still an impure one: to be strictly just, it must have the sanction and consent of the governed. It can have no pure right over my person and property but what I concede to it. The progress from an absolute to a limited monarchy, from a limited monarchy to a democracy, is a progress toward a true respect for the individual. Even the Chinese philosopher was wise enough to regard the individual as the basis of the empire. Is a democracy, such as we know it, the last improvement possible in government? Is it not possible to take a step further towards recognizing and organizing the rights of man? There will never be a really free and enlightened State until the State comes to recognize the individual as a higher and independent power, from which all its own power and authority are derived and treats him accordingly. I please myself with imagining a State at last which can afford to be just to all men and to treat the individual with respect as a neighbor; which even would not think it inconsistent with its own repose, if a few were to live aloof from it, not meddling with it, nor embraced by it, who fulfilled all the duties of neighbors and fellow-men. A State which bore this kind of fruit and suffered it to drop off as fast as it ripened, would prepare the way for a still more perfect and glorious State, which also I have imagined, but not yet anywhere seen.

[From *On the Duty of Civil Disobedience*, in *Walden and On the Duty of Civil Disobedience* (New American Library, New York, 1980), 222–3, 224–5, 230–1, 240. First published 1854.]

MARTIN LUTHER KING

32 An Unjust Law is No Law

My friends, I must say to you that we have not made a single gain in civil rights without determined legal and non-violent pressure. History is the long and tragic story of the fact that privileged groups seldom give up their privileges voluntarily. Individuals may see the moral light and voluntarily give up their unjust posture; but as Reinhold Niebuhr has reminded us, groups are more immoral than individuals.

We know through painful experience that freedom is never voluntarily given by the oppressor; it must be demanded by the oppressed. Frankly, I have never yet engaged in a direct action movement that was 'well timed,' according to the timetable of those who have not suffered unduly from the disease of segregation. For years now I have heard the words 'Wait!' It rings in the ear of every Negro with a piercing familiarity. This 'Wait' has almost always meant 'Never'. It has been a tranquilizing thalidomide, relieving the emotional stress for a moment, only to give birth to an ill-formed infant of frustration. We must come to see with the distinguished jurist of yesterday that 'justice too long delayed is justice denied.' We have waited for more than three hundred and forty years for our constitutional and god-given rights. The nations of Asia and Africa are moving with jet-like speed toward the goal of political independence, and we still creep at horse-and-buggy pace toward the gaining of a cup of coffee at a lunch counter. I guess it is easy for those who have never felt the stinging darts of segregation to say, 'Wait'. But when you have seen vicious mobs lynch your mothers and fathers at will and drown your sisters and brothers at whim; when you have seen hate-filled policemen curse, kick, brutalize and even kill your black brothers and sisters with impunity; when you see the vast majority of your twenty million Negro brothers smothering in an air-tight cage of poverty in the midst of an affluent society; when you suddenly find your tongue twisted and your speech stammering as you seek to explain to your six-year-old daughter why she can't go to the public amusement park that has just been advertised on television, and see tears welling up in her little eyes when she is told that Funtown is closed to colored children, and see the depressing clouds of inferiority begin to form in her little mental sky, and see her begin to distort her little personality by unconsciously developing a bitterness toward white people; when you have to concoct an answer for a five-year-old son asking in agonizing pathos: 'Daddy, why do white people treat colored people so mean?'; when you take a cross-country drive and find it necessary to sleep night after night in the uncomfortable corners of your automobile because no motel will accept you; when you are humiliated day in and day out by nagging signs reading 'white' and 'colored'; when your first name becomes 'nigger' and your middle name becomes 'boy' (however old you are) and your last name becomes 'John', and when your wife and mother are never given the respected title 'Mrs'; when you are harried by day and haunted at night by the fact that you are a Negro, living constantly at tip-toe stance never quite knowing what to expect next, and plagued with inner fears and outer resentments; when you are forever fighting a degenerating sense of 'nobodiness'; then you will understand why we find it difficult to wait. There comes a time when the cup of endurance runs over, and men are no longer willing to be plunged into an abyss of injustice where they experience the blackness of corroding despair. I hope, sirs, you can understand our legitimate and unavoidable impatience.

You express a great deal of anxiety over our willingness to break laws. This is certainly a legitimate concern. Since we so diligently urge people to obey the Supreme Court's decision of 1954 outlawing segregation in the public schools, it is rather strange and paradoxical to find us consciously breaking laws. One may well ask, 'How can you advocate breaking some laws and obeying others?' The answer is found in the fact that there are two types of laws: There are *just* and there are *unjust* laws. I would agree with Saint Augustine that 'An unjust law is no law at all.'

Now what is the difference between the two? How does one determine when a law is just or unjust? A just law is a man-made code that squares with the moral law or the law of God. An unjust law is a code that is out of harmony with the moral law. To put it in the terms of Saint Thomas Aquinas, an unjust law is a human law that is not rooted in eternal and natural law. Any law that uplifts human personality is just. Any law that degrades human personality is unjust. All segregation statutes are unjust because segregation distorts the soul and damages the personality. It gives the segregator a false sense of superiority, and the segregated a false sense of inferiority. To use the words of Martin Buber, the great Jewish philosopher, segregation substitutes an 'I-it' relationship for the 'I-thou' relationship, and ends up relegating persons to the status of things. So segregation is not only politically, economically and sociologically unsound, but it is morally wrong and sinful. Paul Tillich has said that sin is separation. Isn't segregation an existential expression of man's tragic separation, an expression of his awful estrangement, his terrible sinfulness? So I can urge men to disobey segregation ordinances because they are morally wrong. [. . .]

I hope you can see the distinction I am trying to point out. In no sense do I advocate evading or defying the law as the rabid segregationist would do. This would lead to anarchy. One who breaks an unjust law must do it *openly, lovingly* (not hatefully as the white mothers did in New Orleans when they were seen on television screaming 'nigger, nigger, nigger'), and with a willingness to accept the penalty. I submit that an individual who breaks a law that conscience tells him is unjust, and willingly accepts the penalty by staying in jail to arouse the conscience of the community over its injustice, is in reality expressing the very highest respect for law.

[From Letter from Birmingham City Jail, in Civil Disobedience in Focus, ed. Hugo Bedau
(Routledge, London, 1991), 71–4. First published 1963.]

JOHN RAWLS

33 Civil Disobedience

A constitutional theory of civil disobedience has three parts. First, it defines this kind of dissent and separates it from other forms of opposition to democratic authority. These range from legal demonstrations and infractions of law designed to raise test cases before the courts to militant action and organized resistance. A theory specifies the place of civil disobedience in this spectrum of possibilities. Next, it sets out the grounds of civil disobedience and the conditions under which such action is justified in a (more or less) just democratic regime. And finally, a theory should explain the role of civil disobedience within a constitutional system and account for the appropriateness of this mode of protest within a free society. [. . .]

I shall begin by defining civil disobedience as a public, nonviolent, conscientious yet political act contrary to law usually done with the aim of bringing about a change in the law or policies of the government. By acting in this way one addresses the sense of justice of the majority of the community and declares that in one's considered opinion the principles of social cooperation among free and equal men are not being respected. A preliminary gloss on this definition is that it does not require that the civilly disobedient act breach the same law that is being protested. It allows for what some have called indirect as well as direct civil disobedience. And this as a definition should do, as there are sometimes strong reasons for not infringing on the law or policy held to be unjust. Instead, one may disobey traffic ordinances or laws of trespass as a way of presenting one's case. Thus, if the government enacts a vague and harsh statute against treason, it would not be appropriate to commit treason as a way of objecting to it, and in any event, the penalty might be far more than one should reasonably be ready to accept. In other cases there is no way to violate the government's policy directly, as when it concerns foreign affairs, or affects another part of the country. A second gloss is that the civilly disobedient act is indeed thought to be contrary to law, at least in the sense that those engaged in it are not simply presenting a test case for a constitutional decision; they are prepared to oppose the statute even if it should be upheld. [. . .]

It should also be noted that civil disobedience is a political act not only in the sense that it is addressed to the majority that holds political power, but also because it is an act guided and justified by political principles, that is, by the principles of justice which regulate the constitution and social institutions generally. In justifying civil disobedience one does not appeal to principles of personal morality or to religious doctrines, though these may coincide with and support one's claims; and it goes without saying that civil disobedience cannot be grounded solely on group or self-interest. Instead one invokes the commonly shared conception of justice that underlies the political order. [. . .]

A further point is that civil disobedience is a public act. Not only is it addressed to public principles, it is done in public. It is engaged in openly with fair notice; it is not covert or secretive. One may compare it to public speech, and being a form of address, an expression of profound and conscientious political conviction, it takes place in the public forum. For this reason, among others, civil disobedience is nonviolent. It tries to avoid the use of violence, especially against persons, not from the abhorrence of the use of force in principle, but because it is a final expression of one's case. To engage in violent acts likely to injure and to hurt is incompatible with civil disobedience as a mode of address. [. . .]

Civil disobedience is nonviolent for another reason. It expresses disobedience to law within the limits of fidelity to law, although it is at the outer edge thereof. The law is broken, but fidelity to law is expressed by the public and nonviolent nature of the act, by the willingness to accept the legal consequences of one's conduct. This fidelity to law helps to establish to the majority that the act is indeed politically conscientious and sincere, and that it is intended to address the public's sense of justice. [. . .]

With these various distinctions in mind, I shall consider the circumstances under which civil disobedience is justified. [. . .]

The first point concerns the kinds of wrongs that are appropriate objects of civil disobedience. Now if one views such disobedience as a political act addressed to the sense of justice of the community, then it seems reasonable, other things equal, to limit it to instances of substantial and clear injustice, and preferably to those which block in the way to removing other injustices. For this reason there is a presumption in favor of restricting civil disobedience to serious infringements of the first principle of justice, the principle of equal liberty, and to blatant violations of the second part of the second principle, the principle of fair equality of opportunity. [. . .]

A further condition for civil disobedience is the following. We may suppose that the normal appeals to the political majority have already been made in good faith and that they have failed. The legal means of redress have proved to no avail. Thus, for example, the existing political parties have shown themselves indifferent to the claims of the minority or have proved unwilling to accommodate them. Attempts to have the laws repealed have been ignored and legal protests and demonstrations have had no success. Since civil disobedience is a last resort, we should be sure that it is necessary. Note that it has not been said, however, that legal means have been exhausted. At any rate, further normal appeals can be repeated; free speech is always possible. But if past actions have shown the majority immovable or apathetic, further attempts may reasonably be thought fruitless, and a second condition for justified civil disobedience is met. This condition is, however, a presumption. Some cases may be so extreme that there may be no duty to use first only legal means of political opposition. [. . .]

The third and last condition I shall discuss can be rather complicated. It arises from the fact that while the two preceding conditions are often sufficient to justify civil disobedience, this is not always the case. In certain circumstances the natural duty of justice may require a certain restraint. We can see this as follows. If a certain minority is justified in engaging in civil disobedience, then any other minority in relevantly similar circumstances is likewise justified. Using the two previous conditions as the criteria of relevantly similar circumstances, we can say that, other things equal, two minorities are similarly justified in resorting to civil disobedience if they have suffered for the same length of time from the same degree of injustice and if their equally sincere and normal political appeals have likewise been to no avail. It is, conceivable, however, even if it is unlikely, that there should be many groups with an equally sound case (in the sense just defined) for being civilly disobedient; but that, if they were all to act in this way, serious disorder would follow which might well undermine the efficacy of the just constitution. [. . .]

Certainly the situation envisaged is a special one, and it is quite possible that these sorts of considerations will not be a bar to justified civil disobedience.

There are not likely to be many groups similarly entitled to engage in this form of dissent while at the same time recognizing a duty to a just constitution. [. . .]

Suppose that in the light of the three conditions, one has a right to appeal one's case by civil disobedience. [. . .] There is still, of course, the question whether it is wise or prudent to exercise this right. [. . .] Since civil disobedience is a mode of address taking place in the public forum, care must be taken to see that it is understood. Thus the exercise of the right to civil disobedience should, like any other right, be rationally framed to advance one's ends or the ends of those one wishes to assist.

[John Rawls, *A Theory of Justice* (Clarendon Press, Oxford, 1972), 363–7, 371–6.]

Section III

Democracy and Its Difficulties

INTRODUCTION

What sort of government should we have? What structures of power should there be, and how should our rulers be appointed? In the contemporary world the common assumption is that only a democratic government, in which rulers are subject to periodic election, can be fully legitimate. Furthermore, a state should be governed by a framework of settled, publicly known law which can be changed only by following certain well-laid-out procedures.

Given our current devotion to the idea of 'rule by the people' it comes as something of a surprise to realize how recent a development this has been. Although some Ancient Greek states were democratic (if we leave aside the point that women, slaves, and non-citizens were excluded from the franchise) for the following 2,000 years or so there was hardly a democratic government to be seen. Only in the twentieth century did democracy come to be almost universally regarded as the only form of legitimate rule.

One of the most powerful arguments against democracy—written by someone who had experienced democracy in the Ancient World—was given by Plato. In its essentials Plato's argument is that the ability to rule is a rare skill which, like any form of genuine expertise, needs both talent and extensive training. Given this, it is as irrational to let the people, the rabble, have any say in how they are to be governed as it would be to let the passengers navigate a ship at sea. Frederick the Great, writing 2,000 years later, sets out some of the advantages and duties of the 'enlightened despot', as he sees them.

Against this background it was necessary for political theorists to explain with as much clarity as they could why exactly we should value democracy to such a degree that we should prefer it even to the most enlightened and benevolent form of despotism. Rousseau sets out a form of democracy as providing the conditions under which we can come to know the 'general will', although even Rousseau admits that there must be limits to how democratic we can make any state. Kant emphasizes the values of freedom and equality, and the role they must play in a just constitution, while Mill brings out the point that even for the ordinary citizen, engaging in democratic politics has an 'improving' effect: it requires individuals to take on a wider view, considering many matters he or she would not ordinarily encounter in daily business. Finally, in this section, John Rawls presents his view that majority rule is the best way of achieving just and efficient legislation, and is also compatible with the freedom and equality of the citizens.

It would be wrong, though, to give the impression that there is agreement on the nature of democracy. Here we include two selections which argue that the type of political systems we have grown accustomed to fail to be truly democratic. Lenin argues that liberal democracy is a screen which hides the exploitation and domination of the masses, while Carole Pateman argues that democracy must also extend to the workplace—where most people spend the great part of their day— before we can be said to live under democratic conditions.

A different type of criticism of democracy tries to temper our enthusiasm not so much by arguing that we are not democratic enough, as by pointing out that democracy can go wrong, even dangerously so. Aristotle reminds us that even a democracy needs a stable system of law. Democracy can become the arbitrary dictatorship of the many: mob rule. De Tocqueville, in similar spirit, argues that democracy creates the possibility of a new form of tyranny, the tyranny of the majority. Madison warns of the danger of faction, by which he means a group, large or small, whose interests do not reflect the general interest, and who attempt to subvert the democratic system for their own purposes.

In the following section two writers explore the tendency of modern democracies to create bureaucratic organization around themselves. For Weber the interest of this observation is that it creates a type of tension in democratic practice, as the bureaucracy created by democracy will have a tendency to impede and choke off the democratic process. Pareto argues that however democratic a society may claim to be, it will inevitably be ruled by a powerful elite or oligarchy.

In the final section we include two selections which introduce the idea of the separation of powers: the thought that to avoid despotism we need to ensure that those people who make the laws do not also enforce them. Locke sets out the doctrine in abstract principle, while Montesquieu provides a somewhat different classification and sets out his own view of which groups among the citizens are best equipped to wield the different powers, if liberty is to be preserved.

34 | **Ruling as a Skill**

'Tell me, this doctor in the precise sense you have just been talking about, is he a business-man or a medical practitioner? I mean the man who really is a doctor.'

'A medical practitioner.'

'And a ship's captain? Is he a member of the crew or in command of it?'

'In command.'

'For it would I take it be wrong to take account of his mere presence on board to call him a member of the crew. For he is not captain by virtue of being on board, but because of his professional skill and command of the crew.'

'True.' [. . .]

'Suppose, for example, that you were to ask me whether the body were self-sufficient, with no needs beyond itself, I should answer "It certainly has needs. That is the reason why medicine has been discovered, because the body has its defects and these need curing; medical skill was, in fact, acquired to look after the interests of the body." Would that be a correct answer, do you think?'

'It would.'

'Then is the science or art of medicine itself defective? Does it or any other skilled activity need anything to complete it? I mean as the eyes need sight and the ears hearing, so they also need an art to look to their interests and provide them with what they need in this respect. But is it a characteristic of skilled activity as such to be defective, so that each activity needs another to look after its interests, and this one another, and so *ad infinitum*? Or does each look after its own interest? Is it not rather true that each has no need either of its own or another's supervision to check its faults and watch its interests? For there is no fault or flaw in any science or art, nor is it its business to seek the interest of anything but its subject matter; each is faultless and flawless and right, so long as it is entirely and precisely what it is. And it is in your precise sense that I want you to tell me if I am right.'

'You are right,' he said. [. . .]

'Then it follows that the doctor *qua* doctor prescribes with a view not to his own interest but that of his patient. For we agreed that a doctor in the precise sense controlled the body and was not in business for profit, did we not?'

He assented.

'And did we not also agree that a ship's captain in the precise sense controlled the crew but was not one of them? So that a captain in this sense will not give his orders with his own interest in view, but that of the crew which he controls.'

He agreed reluctantly.

'And therefore, my dear Thrasymachus,' I concluded, 'no ruler of any kind, *qua* ruler, exercises his authority, whatever its sphere, with his own interest in view, but that of the subject of his skill. It is his subject and his subject's proper interest to which he looks in all he says and does.' [. . .]

'Suppose the following to be the state of affairs on board a ship or ships. The captain is larger and stronger than any of the crew, but a bit deaf and short-sighted, and doesn't know much about navigation. The crew are all quarrelling with each other about how to navigate the ship, each thinking he ought to be at the helm; they know no navigation and cannot say that anyone ever taught it them, or that they spent any time studying it; indeed they say it can't be taught and are ready to murder anyone who says it can. They spend all their time milling round the captain and trying to get him to give them the wheel. If one faction is more successful than another, their rivals may kill them and throw them overboard, lay out the honest captain with drugs or drink, take control of the ship, help themselves to what's on board, and behave as if they were on a drunken pleasure-cruise. Finally, they reserve their admiration for the man who knows how to lend a hand in controlling the captain by force or fraud; they praise his seamanship and navigation and knowledge of the sea and condemn everyone else as useless. They have no idea that the true navigator must study the seasons of the year, the sky, the stars, the winds and other professional subjects, if he is to be really fit to control a ship; and they think that it's quite impossible to acquire professional skill in navigation (quite apart from whether they want it exercised) and that there's no such thing as an art of navigation. In these circumstances aren't the sailors on any such ship bound to regard the true navigator as a gossip and a star-gazer, of no use to them at all?'

'Yes, they are,' Adeimantus agreed.

'I think you probably understand, without any explanation, that my illustration is intended to show the present attitude of society towards the true philosopher.'

'Yes, I understand.'

'Then you must tell it to anyone who is surprised that society does not value its philosophers, and try, first, to convince him that it would be far more surprising if it did.'

'I will,' he said. [. . .]

'Our next subject, I suppose, is democracy. When we know how it originates, and what it is like, we can again identify and pass judgement on the corresponding individual.'

'That would be consistent with the procedure we've been following.'

'Then doesn't oligarchy change into democracy because of lack of restraint in the pursuit of its objective of getting as rich as possible?' [. . .]

'When a person's unhealthy, it takes very little to upset him and make him ill; there may even be an internal cause for disorder. The same is true of an unhealthy society. It will fall into sickness and dissension at the slightest external provocation, when one party or the other calls in help from a neighbouring oligarchy or democracy; while sometimes faction fights will start without any external stimulus at all.'

'Very true.'

'Then democracy originates when the poor win, kill or exile their opponents, and give the rest equal rights and opportunities of office, appointment to office being as a rule by lot.'

'Yes,' he agreed, 'that is how a democracy is established, whether it's done by force of arms or by frightening its opponents into retreat.'

'What sort of a society will it be?' I asked, 'and how will it be run? The answer, obviously, will show us the character of the democratic man.' [. . .]

'It's a shop in which he'd find plenty of models on show.'

'Then in democracy,' I went on, 'there's no compulsion either to exercise authority if you are capable of it, or to submit to authority if you don't want to; you needn't fight if there's a war, or you can wage a private war in peacetime if you don't like peace; and if there's any law that debars you from political or judicial office, you will none the less take either if they come your way. It's a wonderfully pleasant way of carrying on in the short run, isn't it?' [. . .]

'Let's go back to the question how the democratic man originates from the oligarchic. This generally happens when a young man, brought up in the narrow economical way we have described, gets a taste of the drones' honey and gets into wild and dangerous company, where he can be provided with every variety and refinement of pleasure, with the result that his internal oligarchy starts turning into a democracy.'

'That's bound to happen.'

'In society the change took place when one party brought in sympathizers from outside to help it. Will the change in our young men be brought about when one or other type of desire in him gets assistance from similar passions outside him?'

'Yes, certainly.' [. . .]

'In the end they capture the seat of government, having discovered that the young man's mind is devoid of knowledge, principle and truth, the most effective safeguards the mind of man can be blessed with.'

'Far the most effective.'

'The vacant place is filled instead by an invasion of pretentious fallacies, and back he goes to live with the Lotus-eaters. If his family send help to the economical element in him, the pretentious invaders shut the gates of the citadel, and will not admit it; nor will they listen to the individual representations of old and trusted friends. They make themselves masters by force, they call shame silliness and drive it into disgrace and exile; they call self-control cowardice and expel it with abuse; and they call on a lot of useless desires to help them banish economy and moderation, which they regard as provincial parsimony.'

'All very true.' [. . .]

'If anyone tells him that some pleasures, because they spring from good desires, are to be encouraged and approved, and others, springing from evil desires, to be disciplined and controlled, he won't listen or open his doors to the truth, but shakes his head and says all pleasures are equal and should have equal rights.'

'Yes, that's just what he does.'

'In fact,' I said, 'he lives for the pleasure of the moment. One day it's wine, women, and song, the next bread and water; one day it's hard physical training, the next indolence and ease, and then a period of philosophic study. Next he takes to politics and is always on his feet saying or doing whatever comes into his head. Sometimes all his ambitions are military, sometimes they are all directed to success in business. There's no order or restraint in his life, and he reckons his way of living is pleasant, free and happy.'

'A very good description of one who believes in liberty and equality,' he commented.

'Yes,' I said, 'and I think that the versatility of the individual, and the attractiveness of his combination of diverse characteristics, match the variety of the democratic society. It's a life which many men and women would envy, it has so many possibilities.'

'It has indeed.'

'This, then, is the individual corresponding to the democratic society, and we can fairly call him the democratic man.'

'Agreed.'

[From *The Republic*, trans. with introd. by H. D. P. Lee (Penguin, Harmondsworth, 1955), 69–71, 249–50, 327, 329, 330, 332, 333, 334.]

FREDERICK THE GREAT
....

35   **The Enlightened Despot**

With respect to the true monarchical government, it is the best or the worst of all others, accordingly as it is administered.

We have remarked that men granted pre-eminence to one of their equals, in expectation that he should do them certain services. These services consisted in the maintenance of the laws; a strict execution of justice; an employment of his whole powers to prevent any corruption of manners; and defending the state against its enemies. It is the duty of this magistrate to pay attention to agriculture; it should be his care that provisions for the nation should be in abundance, and that commerce and industry should be encouraged. He is a perpetual sentinel, who must watch the acts and the conduct of the enemies of the state. His foresight and prudence should form timely alliances, which should be made with those who might most conduce to the interest of the association. [. . .]

The sovereign is attached by indissoluble ties to the body of the state; hence it follows that he, by repercussions, is sensible of all the ills which afflict his subjects; and the people, in like manner, suffer from the misfortunes which affect their sovereign. There is but one general good, which is that of the state. If the monarch lose his provinces, he is no longer able as formerly to assist his subjects. If misfortune has obliged him to contract debts, they must be liquidated by the poor citizens; and, in return, if the people are not numerous, and if they are oppressed by poverty, the sovereign is destitute of all resource. These are truths so incontestable that there is no need to insist on them further.

I once more repeat, the sovereign represents the state; he and his people form but one body, which can only be happy as far as it is united by concord. The prince is to the nation he governs what the head is to the man; it is his duty to see, think, and act for the whole community, that he may procure it every advantage of which it is capable. If it be intended that a monarchical should excel a republican government, sentence is pronounced on the sovereign. He must be active, possess integrity, and collect his whole powers, that he may be able to run the career he has commenced. Here follow my ideas concerning his duties. [. . .]

In order that he may never depart from his duties, the prince ought often to recollect that he himself is but a man, like the least of his subjects. If he be the first general, the first minister of the realm, it is not that he should remain the shadow of authority, but that he should fulfil the duties of such titles. He is only the first servant of the state, who is obliged to act with probity and prudence; and to remain as totally disinterested as if he were each moment liable to render an account of his administrations to his fellow citizens.

Thus he is culpable, if he be prodigal of the money of the people, dispersing the produce of the taxes in luxury, pomp, or licentiousness. It is for him to watch over morals, which are the guardians of the laws, and to improve the national education, and not pervert it by ill examples. One of the most important objects is the preservation of good morals, in all their purity; to which the sovereign may greatly contribute, by distinguishing and rewarding those citizens who have performed virtuous actions, and testifying his contempt for such as are so depraved as not to blush at their own disorders. The prince ought highly to disapprove of every dishonest act, and refuse distinctions to men who are incorrigible. [. . .]

As the sovereign is properly the head of a family of citizens, the father of his people, he ought on all occasions to be the last refuge of the unfortunate; to be the parent of the orphan, and the husband of the widow; to have as much pity for the lowest wretch as for the greatest courtier; and to shed his benefactions over those who, deprived of all other aid, can only find succor in his benevolence.

[From *Essay on Forms of Government*, in *The Portable Enlightenment Reader*, ed. Isaac Kramnick (Penguin, Harmondsworth, 1995), 452, 454, 458, 459. First published 1777.]

III.b. Democratic Ideals

36 **The General Will**

Sovereignty, for the same reason as makes it inalienable, is indivisible; for will either is, or is not, general; it is the will either of the body of the people, or only of a part of it. In the first case, the will, when declared, is an act of Sovereignty and constitutes law: in the second, it is merely a particular will, or act of magistracy—at the most a decree. [. . .]

It follows from what has gone before that the general will is always upright and always tends to the public advantage; but it does not follow that the deliberations of the people always have the same rectitude. Our will is always for our own good, but we do not always see what that is; the people is never corrupted, but it is often deceived, and on such occasions only does it seem to will what is bad.

There is often a great deal of difference between the will of all and the general will; the latter considers only the common interest, while the former takes private interest into account, and is no more than a sum of particular wills: but take away from these same wills the pluses and minuses that cancel one another, and the general will remains as the sum of the differences.

If, when the people, being furnished with adequate information, held its deliberations, the citizens had no communication one with another, the grand total of the small differences would always give the general will, and the decision would always be good. But when intrigues arise, and partial associations are formed at the expense of the great association, the will of each of these associations becomes general in relation to its members, while it remains particular in relation to the State: it may then be said that there are no longer as many votes as there are men, but only as many as there are associations. The differences become less numerous and give a less general result. Lastly, when one of these associations is so great as to prevail over all the rest, the result is no longer a sum of small differences, but a single difference; in this case there is no longer a general will, and the opinion which prevails is purely particular.

It is therefore essential, if the general will is to be able to make itself known, that there should be no partial society in the state and that each citizen should express only his own opinion.

If we take the term in the strict sense, there never has been a real democracy, and there never will be. It is against the natural order for the many to govern and the few to be governed. It is unimaginable that the people should remain continually assembled to devote their time to public affairs, and it is clear that they cannot set up commissions for that purpose without the form of administration being changed.

In fact, I can confidently lay down as a principle that, when the functions of government are shared by several tribunals, the less numerous sooner or later acquire the greatest authority, if only because they are in a position to expedite affairs, and power thus naturally comes into their hands.

Besides, how many conditions that are difficult to unite does such a government presuppose! First, a very small State, where the people can readily be got together and where each citizen can with ease know all the rest; secondly, great simplicity of manners, to prevent business from multiplying and raising thorny problems; next, a large measure of equality in rank and fortune, without which equality of rights and authority cannot long subsist; lastly, little or no luxury— for luxury either comes of riches or makes them necessary; it corrupts at once rich and poor, the rich by possession and the poor by covetousness; it sells the country to softness and vanity, and takes away from the State all its citizens, to make them slaves one to another, and one and all to public opinion. [. . .]

Were there a people of gods, their government would be democratic. So perfect a government is not for men.

[From *The Social Contract*, in *The Social Contract and Discourses*, trans. and introd. G. D. H. Cole (J. M. Dent, London, 1973), 200–1, 203–4, 239–40. First published 1762.]

IMMANUEL KANT

37 **Freedom and Equality**

Man's *freedom* as a human being, as a principle for the constitution of a commonwealth, can be expressed in the following formula. No-one can compel me to be happy in accordance with his conception of the welfare of others, for each may seek his happiness in whatever way he sees fit, so long as he does not infringe upon the freedom of others to pursue a similar end which can be reconciled with the freedom of everyone else within a workable general law—i.e. he must accord to others the same right as he enjoys himself. A government might be established on the principle of benevolence towards the people, like that of a father towards his children. Under such a *paternal government* (*imperium paternale*), the subjects, as immature children who cannot distinguish what is truly useful or harmful to themselves, would be obliged to behave purely passively and to rely upon the judgement of the head of state as to how they *ought* to be happy, and upon his kindness in willing their happiness at all. Such a government is the greatest conceivable *despotism*, i.e. a constitution which suspends the entire freedom of its subjects, who thenceforth have no rights whatsoever. The only conceivable government for men who are capable of possessing rights, even if the ruler is benevolent, is not a *paternal* but a *patriotic* government (*imperium non paternale, sed patrioticum*). A *patriotic* attitude is one where everyone in the state, not excepting its head, regards the commonwealth as a maternal womb, or the land as the paternal ground from which he himself sprang and which he must leave to his descendants as a treasured pledge. Each regards himself as authorised to protect the rights of the commonwealth by laws of the general will, but not to submit it to his personal use at his own absolute pleasure. This right of freedom belongs to each member of the commonwealth as a human being, in so far as each is a being capable of possessing rights.

Man's *equality* as a subject might be formulated as follows. Each member of the commonwealth has rights of coercion in relation to all the others, except in relation to the head of state. For he alone is not a member of the commonwealth, but its creator or preserver, and he alone is authorised to coerce others without being subject to any coercive law himself. But all who are subject to laws are the subjects of a state, and are thus subject to the right of coercion along with all other members of the commonwealth; the only exception is a single person (in either the physical or the moral sense of the word), the head of state, through whom alone the rightful coercion of all others can be exercised. For if he too could be coerced, he would not be the head of state, and the hierarchy of subordination would ascend infinitely. But if there were two persons exempt from coercion, neither would be subject to coercive laws, and neither could do to the other anything contrary to right, which is impossible.

This uniform equality of human beings as subjects of a state is, however, perfectly consistent with the utmost inequality of the mass in the degree of its possessions, whether these take the form of physical or mental superiority over others, or of fortuitous external property and of particular rights (of which there may be many) with respect to others. Thus the welfare of the one depends very much on the will of the other (the poor depending on the rich), the one must obey the other (as the child its parents or the wife her husband), the one serves (the labourer) while the other pays, etc. Nevertheless, they are all equal as subjects *before the law*, which, as the pronouncement of the general will, can only be single in form, and which concerns the form of right and not the material or object in relation to which I possess rights. For no-one can coerce anyone else other than through the public law and its executor, the head of state, while everyone else can resist the others in the same way and to the same degree. No-one, however, can lose this authority to coerce others and to have rights towards them except through committing a crime. And no-one can voluntarily renounce his rights by a contract or legal transaction to the effect that he has no rights but only duties, for such a contract would deprive him of the right to make a contract, and would thus invalidate the one he had already made.

[From *On the Common Saying 'This may be true in theory, but it does not apply in practice'*, in *Kant: Political Writings*, ed. Hans Reiss, trans. H. B. Nisbet (Cambridge University Press, Cambridge, 1970, 1991), 74–5. First published 1793.]

It is not sufficiently considered how little there is in most men's ordinary life to give any largeness either to their conceptions or to their sentiments. Their work is a routine; not a labour of love, but of self-interest in the most elementary form, the satisfaction of daily wants; neither the thing done, nor the process of doing it, introduces the mind to thoughts or feelings extending beyond individuals; if instructive books are within their reach, there is no stimulus to read them; and in most cases the individual has no access to any person of cultivation much superior to his own. Giving him something to do for the public, supplies, in a measure, all these deficiencies. If circumstances allow the amount of public duty assigned him to be considerable, it makes him an educated man. Notwithstanding the defects of the social system and moral ideas of antiquity, the practice of the diecastery and the ecclesia raised the intellectual standard of an average Athenian citizen far beyond anything of which there is yet an example in any other mass of men, ancient or modern. The proofs of this are apparent in every page of our great historian of Greece; but we need scarcely look further than to the high quality of the addresses which their great orators deemed best calculated to act with effect on their understanding and will. A benefit of the same kind, though far less in degree, is produced on Englishmen of the lower middle class by their liability to be placed on juries and to serve parish offices; which, though it does not occur to so many, nor is so continuous, nor introduces them to so great a variety of elevated considerations, as to admit of comparison with the public education which every citizen of Athens obtained from her democratic institutions, must make them nevertheless very different beings, in range of ideas and development of faculties, from those who have done nothing in their lives but drive a quill, or sell goods over a counter. Still more salutary is the moral part of the instruction afforded by the participation of the private citizen, if even rarely, in public functions. He is called upon, while so engaged, to weigh interests not his own; to be guided, in case of conflicting claims, by another rule than his private partialities; to apply, at every turn, principles and maxims which have for their reason of existence the common good: and he usually finds associated with him in the same work minds more familiarised than his own with these ideas and operations, whose study it will be to supply reasons to his understanding, and stimulation to his feeling for the general interest. He is made to feel himself one of the public, and whatever is for their benefit to be for his benefit. Where this school of public spirit does not exist, scarcely any sense is entertained that private persons, in no eminent social situation, owe any duties to society, except to obey the laws and submit to the government. There is no unselfish sentiment of identification with the public. Every thought or feeling, either of interest or of duty, is absorbed in the individual and in the family. The man never thinks of any collective interest, of any objects to be pursued jointly with others, but only in competition with them, and in some measure at their expense. A neighbour, not being an ally or an associate, since he is never engaged in any common under-taking for joint benefit, is therefore only a rival. Thus even private morality suf-fers, while public is actually extinct. Were this the universal and only possible state of things, the utmost aspirations of the lawgiver or the moralist could only stretch to make the bulk of the community a flock of sheep innocently nibbling the grass side by side.

From these accumulated considerations it is evident that the only govern-ment which can fully satisfy all the exigencies of the social state is one in which the whole people participate; that any participation, even in the smallest public function, is useful; that the participation should everywhere be as great as the general degree of improvement of the community will allow; and that nothing less can be ultimately desirable than the admission of all to a share in the sover-eign power of the state. But since all cannot, in a community exceeding a single small town, participate personally in any but some very minor portions of the public business, it follows that the ideal type of a perfect government must be representative.

[From *Considerations on Representative Government*, in *Utilitarianism, On Liberty and Considerations on Representative Government*, ed. H. B. Acton (Dent, London, 1972), 216–18. First published 1861.]

JOHN RAWLS

39 Majority Rule

The procedure of majority rule, however it is defined and circumscribed, has a subordinate place as a procedural device. The justification for it rests squarely on the political ends that the constitution is designed to achieve, and therefore on the two principles of justice. I have assumed that some form of majority rule is justified as the best available way of insuring just and effective legislation. It is compatible with equal liberty and possesses a certain naturalness; for if minor-ity rule is allowed, there is no obvious criterion to select which one is to decide and equality is violated. A fundamental part of the majority principle is that the procedure should satisfy the conditions of background justice. In this case these conditions are those of political liberty—freedom of speech and assembly, free-dom to take part in public affairs and to influence by constitutional means the course of legislation—and the guarantee of the fair value of these freedoms. When this background is absent, the first principle of justice is not satisfied; yet even when it is present, there is no assurance that just legislation will be en-acted.

There is nothing to the view, then, that what the majority wills is right. In fact, none of the traditional conceptions of justice have held this doctrine, maintaining always that the outcome of the voting is subject to political principles. Although in given circumstances it is justified that the majority (suitably defined and circumscribed) has the constitutional right to make law, this does not imply that the laws enacted are just. The dispute of substance about majority rule concerns how it is best defined and whether constitutional constraints are effective and reasonable devices for strengthening the overall balance of justice. These limitations may often be used by entrenched minorities to preserve their illicit advantages. This question is one of political judgment and does not belong to the theory of justice. It suffices to note that while citizens normally submit their conduct to democratic authority, that is, recognize the outcome of a vote as establishing a binding rule, other things equal, they do not submit their judgment to it.

I now wish to take up the place of the principle of majority rule in the ideal procedure that forms a part of the theory of justice. A just constitution is defined as a constitution that would be agreed upon by rational delegates in a constitutional convention who are guided by the two principles of justice. When we justify a constitution, we present considerations to show that it would be adopted under these conditions. Similarly, just laws and policies are those that would be enacted by rational legislators at the legislative stage who are constrained by a just constitution and who are conscientiously trying to follow the principles of justice as their standard. When we criticize laws and policies we try to show that they would not be chosen under this ideal procedure. Now since even rational legislators would often reach different conclusions, there is a necessity for a vote under ideal conditions. The restrictions on information will not guarantee agreement, since the tendencies of the general social facts will often be ambiguous and difficult to assess.

A law or policy is sufficiently just, or at least not unjust, if when we try to imagine how the ideal procedure would work out, we conclude that most persons taking part in this procedure and carrying out its stipulations would favor that law or policy. In the ideal procedure, the decision reached is not a compromise, a bargain struck between opposing parties trying to advance their ends. The legislative discussion must be conceived not as a contest between interests, but as an attempt to find the best policy as defined by the principles of justice. I suppose, then, as part of the theory of justice, that an impartial legislator's only desire is to make the correct decision in this regard, given the general facts known to him. He is to vote solely according to his judgment. The outcome of the vote gives an estimate of what is most in line with the conception of justice.

If we ask how likely it is that the majority opinion will be correct, it is evident that the ideal procedure bears a certain analogy to the statistical problem of pooling the views of a group of experts to arrive at a best judgment. Here the experts are rational legislators able to take an objective perspective because they are impartial. The suggestion goes back to Condorcet that if the likelihood of a correct judgment on the part of the representative legislator is greater than that of an incorrect one, the probability that the majority vote is correct increases as the likelihood of a correct decision by the representative legislator increases. Thus we might be tempted to suppose that if many rational persons were to try to simulate the conditions of the ideal procedure and conducted their reasoning and discussion accordingly, a large majority anyway would be almost certainly right. This would be a mistake. We must not only be sure that there is a greater chance of a correct than of an incorrect judgment on the part of the representative legislator, but it is also clear that the votes of different persons are not independent. Since their views will be influenced by the course of the discussion, the simpler sorts of probabilistic reasoning do not apply.

Nevertheless, we normally assume that an ideally conducted discussion among many persons is more likely to arrive at the correct conclusion (by a vote if necessary) than the deliberations of any one of them by himself. Why should this be so? In everyday life the exchange of opinion with others checks our partiality and widens our perspective; we are made to see things from their standpoint and the limits of our vision are brought home to us. But in the ideal process the veil of ignorance means that the legislators are already impartial. The benefits from discussion lie in the fact that even representative legislators are limited in knowledge and the ability to reason. No one of them knows everything the others know, or can make all the same inferences that they can draw in concert. Discussion is a way of combining information and enlarging the range of arguments. At least in the course of time, the effects of common deliberation seem bound to improve matters.

[From *A Theory of Justice* (Clarendon Press, Oxford, 1972), 356–9.]

III.c. True and False Democracy

V. I. LENIN

40 Bourgeois and Proletarian Democracy

If we are not to mock at common sense and history, it is obvious that we cannot speak of 'pure democracy' so long as different *classes* exist; we can only speak of *class* democracy. (Be it said in parenthesis that 'pure democracy' is not only an *ignorant* phrase, revealing a lack of understanding both of the class struggle and of the nature of the state, but also a thrice-empty phrase, since in communist society democracy will *wither away* in the process of changing and becoming a habit, but will never be 'pure' democracy.)

'Pure democracy' is the mendacious phrase of a liberal who wants to fool the workers. History knows of bourgeois democracy which takes the place of feudalism, and of proletarian democracy which takes the place of bourgeois democracy. [. . .]

Bourgeois democracy, although a great historical advance in comparison with medievalism, always remains, and under capitalism cannot but remain, restricted, truncated, false and hypocritical, a paradise for the rich and a snare and a deception for the exploited, for the poor. [. . .]

Take the fundamental laws of modern states, take their administration, take the right of assembly, freedom of the press, or 'equality of all citizens before the law,' and you will see at every step evidence of the hypocrisy of bourgeois democracy with which every honest and class-conscious worker is familiar. There is not a single state, however democratic, which has no loopholes or reservations in its constitution guaranteeing the bourgeoisie the possibility of dispatching troops against the workers, of proclaiming martial law, and so forth, in case of a 'violation of public order,' and actually in case the exploited class 'violates' its position of slavery and tries to behave in a nonslavish manner. [. . .]

Even in the most democratic bourgeois state the oppressed masses at every step encounter the crying contradiction between the *formal* equality proclaimed by the 'democracy' of the capitalists and the thousands of *real* limitations and subterfuges which turn the proletarians into *wage slaves*. It is precisely this contradiction that is opening the eyes of the masses to the rottenness, mendacity and hypocrisy of capitalism. It is this contradiction that the agitators and propagandists of Socialism are constantly exposing to the masses, *in order to prepare* them for revolution! [. . .]

Proletarian democracy, of which Soviet government is one of the forms, has brought a development and expansion of democracy hitherto unprecedented in the world, precisely for the vast majority of the population, for the exploited and toiling people. [. . .]

The toiling masses are *barred* from participation in bourgeois parliaments (which *never decide* important questions under bourgeois democracy; they are decided by the stock exchange and the banks) by thousands of obstacles, and the workers know and feel, see and realize perfectly well that the bourgeois parliaments are institutions *alien* to them, *instruments for the oppression* of the proletarians by the bourgeoisie, institutions of a hostile class, of the exploiting minority. [. . .]

Proletarian democracy is *a million times* more democratic than any bourgeois democracy; Soviet power is a million times more democratic than the most democratic bourgeois republic.

To fail to see this one must either deliberately serve the bourgeoisie, or be politically as dead as a doornail, unable to see real life from behind the dusty pages of bourgeois books, be thoroughly imbued with bourgeois-democratic prejudices, and thereby objectively convert himself into a lackey of the bourgeoisie.

[From *The Proletarian Revolution and the Renegade Kautsky* (Foreign Languages Press, Peking, 1965), 19, 20, 22, 24, 25, 26, 27. First published 1918.]

CAROLE PATEMAN

41 Participatory Democracy

The theory of participatory democracy is built round the central assertion that individuals and their institutions cannot be considered in isolation from one another. The existence of representative institutions at national level is not sufficient for democracy; for maximum participation by all the people at that level socialisation, or 'social training', for democracy must take place in other spheres in order that the necessary individual attitudes and psychological qualities can be developed. This development takes place through the process of participation itself. The major function of participation in the theory of participatory democracy is therefore an educative one, educative in the very widest sense, including both the psychological aspect and the gaining of practice in democratic skills and procedures. Thus there is no special problem about the stability of a participatory system; it is self-sustaining through the educative impact of the participatory process. Participation develops and fosters the very qualities necessary for it; the more individuals participate the better able they become to do so. Subsidiary hypotheses about participation are that it has an integrative effect and that it aids the acceptance of collective decisions.

Therefore, for a democratic polity to exist it is necessary for a participatory society to exist, i.e. a society where all political systems have been democratised and socialisation through participation can take place in all areas. The most important area is industry; most individuals spend a great deal of their lifetime at work and the business of the workplace provides an education in the management of collective affairs that it is difficult to parallel elsewhere. The second aspect of the theory of participatory democracy is that spheres such as industry should be seen as political systems in their own right, offering areas of participation additional to the national level. If individuals are to exercise the maximum amount of control over their own lives and environment then authority structures in these areas must be so organised that they can participate in decision making. A further reason for the central place of industry in the theory relates to the substantive measure of economic equality required to give the individual the independence and security necessary for (equal) participation; the democratising of industrial authority structures, abolishing the permanent distinction between 'managers' and 'men' would mean a large step toward meeting this condition.

The contemporary and participatory theories of democracy can be contrasted on every point of substance, including the characterisation of 'democracy' itself and the definition of 'political', which in the participatory theory is not confined to the usual national or local government sphere. Again, in the participatory theory 'participation' refers to (equal) participation in the making of decisions, and 'political equality' refers to equality of power in determining the outcome of decisions, a very different definition from that in the contemporary theory. Finally, the justification for a democratic system in the participatory theory of democracy rests primarily on the human results that accrue from the participatory process. One might characterise the participatory model as one where maximum input (participation) is required and where output includes not just policies (decisions) but also the development of the social and political capacities of each individual, so that there is 'feedback' from output to input.

[From *Participation and Democratic Theory* (Cambridge University Press, Cambridge, 1970), 42–3.]

III.d. Dangers in Democracy

ARISTOTLE

42 Rule of the People and Rule of Law

Another kind of democracy is where the mass is sovereign and not the law. This kind arises when decrees are sovereign instead of the law; and this happens because of the demagogues. In law-abiding democracies the demagogue does not arise; on the contrary, the best of the citizens preside. But where the laws are not sovereign, there demagogues arise. This is because the demos becomes a monarch, one person composed of many; for the many are sovereign not as individuals but all together.

When Homer says that to have many chiefs is not good, it is obscure whether he means this kind of constitution, or that where there are several individual rulers. Anyhow, this kind of demos, not being ruled by law, seeks to act like the sole ruler that it is. It becomes despotic; and flatterers are held in honour. Such a demos is the analogue of tyranny among the monarchies. They both have the same character. They are both despotic towards the better persons. The decrees of the one are like the edicts of the other. The demagogue and the flatterer are the same and analogous. Each attain their greatest power with each, the flatterers with the tyrants and the demagogues with this kind of demos. It is they who, by referring everything to the demos, cause decrees to be sovereign instead of laws. For they grow great through the demos being sovereign over everything and their being sovereign over the opinion of the demos, because the mass believes them. Furthermore, persons who are accusing the governors say that the demos ought to decide; the demos gladly accepts the challenge; and so the whole government is undermined.

It would seem reasonable to object that this kind of democracy is not a constitution at all, on the ground that where laws do not rule there is no constitution. The law should rule over all general matters, the officers over particulars; and that should be considered a constitution. It clearly follows that, if democracy is one of the constitutions, such a state of affairs as this, in which everything is settled by decrees, is not really a democracy at all, since no decree can be general.

[From *Politics Books III and IV*, trans. with introd. and comments by Richard Robinson
(Clarendon Press, Oxford, 1995), 79–81.]

43 The Danger of Faction

By a faction I understand a number of citizens, whether amounting to a majority or minority of the whole, who are united and actuated by some common impulse of passion, or of interest, adverse to the rights of other citizens, or to the permanent and aggregate interests of the community.

There are two methods of curing the mischiefs of faction: the one, by removing its causes; the other, by controlling its effects.

There are again two methods of removing the causes of faction: the one, by destroying the liberty which is essential to its existence; the other, by giving to every citizen the same opinions, the same passions, and the same interests.

It could never be more truly said than of the first remedy that it was worse than the disease. Liberty is to faction what air is to fire, an aliment without which it instantly expires. But it could not be a less folly to abolish liberty, which is essential to political life, because it nourishes faction than it would be to wish the annihilation of air, which is essential to animal life, because it imparts to fire its destructive agency.

The second expedient is as impracticable as the first would be unwise. As long as the reason of man continues fallible, and he is at liberty to exercise it, different opinions will be formed. As long as the connection subsists between his reason and his self-love, his opinions and his passions will have a reciprocal influence on each other; and the former will be objects to which the latter will attach themselves. [. . .]

The inference to which we are brought is that the *causes* of faction cannot be removed and that relief is only to be sought in the means of controlling its *effects*.

If a faction consists of less than a majority, relief is supplied by the republican principle, which enables the majority to defeat its sinister views by regular vote. It may clog the administration, it may convulse the society; but it will be unable to execute and mask its violence under the forms of the Constitution. When a majority is included in a faction, the form of popular government, on the other hand, enables it to sacrifice to its ruling passion or interest both the public good and the rights of other citizens. To secure the public good and private rights against the danger of such a faction, and at the same time to preserve the spirit and the form of popular government, is then the great object to which our inquiries are directed. Let me add that it is the great desideratum by which alone this form of government can be rescued from the opprobrium under which it has so long labored and be recommended to the esteem and adoption of mankind.

By what means is this object attainable? Evidently by one of two only. Either the existence of the same passion or interest in a majority at the same time must be prevented, or the majority, having such coexistent passion or interest, must be rendered, by their number and local situation, unable to concert and carry into effect schemes of oppression. If the impulse and the opportunity be suffered to coincide, we well know that neither moral nor religious motives can be relied on as an adequate control. They are not found to be such on the injustice and violence of individuals, and lose their efficacy in proportion to the number combined together, that is, in proportion as their efficacy becomes needful.

From this view of the subject it may be concluded that a pure democracy, by which I mean a society consisting of a small number of citizens, who assemble and administer the government in person, can admit of no cure for the mischiefs of faction. A common passion or interest will, in almost every case, be felt by a majority of the whole; a communication and concert results from the form of government itself; and there is nothing to check the inducements to sacrifice the weaker party or an obnoxious individual. Hence it is that such democracies have ever been spectacles of turbulence and contention; have ever been found incompatible with personal security or the rights of property; and have in general been as short in their lives as they have been violent in their deaths. Theoretic politicians, who have patronized this species of government, have erroneously supposed that by reducing mankind to perfect equality in their political rights, they would at the same time be perfectly equalized and assimilated in their possessions, their opinions, and their passions.

A republic, by which I mean a government in which the scheme of representation takes place, opens a different prospect and promises the cure for which we are seeking. Let us examine the points in which it varies from pure democracy, and we shall comprehend both the nature of the cure and the efficacy which it must derive from the Union.

The two great points of difference between a democracy and a republic are: first, the delegation of the government, in the latter, to a small number of citizens elected by the rest; secondly, the greater number of citizens and greater sphere of country over which the latter may be extended.

The effect of the first difference is, on the one hand, to refine and enlarge the public view by passing them through the medium of a chosen body of citizens, whose wisdom may best discern the true interest of their country and whose patriotism and love of justice will be least likely to sacrifice it to temporary or partial considerations. Under such a regulation it may well happen that the public voice, pronounced by the representatives of the people, will be more consonant to the public good than if pronounced by the people themselves, convened for the purpose. On the other hand, the effect may be inverted. Men of factious tempers, of local prejudices, or of sinister designs, may, by intrigue, by corruption, or by other means, first obtain the suffrages, and then betray the interests of the people. The question resulting is, whether small or extensive republics are most favorable to the election of proper guardians of the public weal; and it is clearly decided in favor of the latter by two obvious considerations.

In the first place it is to be remarked that however small the republic may be the representatives must be raised to a certain number in order to guard against the cabals of a few; and that however large it may be they must be limited to a certain number in order to guard against the confusion of a multitude. [. . .]

In the next place, as each representative will be chosen by a greater number of citizens in the large than in the small republic, it will be more difficult for unworthy candidates to practise with success the vicious arts by which elections are too often carried; and the suffrages of the people being more free, will be more likely to center on men who possess the most attractive merit and the most diffusive and established characters. [. . .]

The other point of difference is the greater number of citizens and extent of territory which may be brought within the compass of republican than of democratic government; and it is this circumstance principally which renders factious combinations less to be dreaded in the former than in the latter. The smaller the society, the fewer probably will be the distinct parties and interests composing it; the fewer the distinct parties and interests, the more frequently will a majority be found of the same party; and the smaller the number of individuals composing a majority, and the smaller the compass within which they are placed, the more easily will they concert and execute their plans of oppression. Extend the sphere and you take in a greater variety of parties and interests; you make it less probable that a majority of the whole will have a common motive to invade the rights of other citizens; or if such a common motive exists, it will be more difficult for all who feel it to discover their own strength and to act in unison with each other. [. . .]

Hence, it clearly appears that the same advantage which a republic has over a democracy in controlling the effects of faction is enjoyed by a large over a small republic.

[From Federalist Paper No. 10, in Alexander Hamilton, James Madison, and John Jay, *The Federalist Papers* (New American Library, New York, 1961), 78–83. First published 1788.]

ALEXIS DE TOCQUEVILLE

44 **Tyranny of the Majority**

I hold it to be an impious and detestable maxim that, politically speaking, the people have a right to do anything; and yet I have asserted that all authority originates in the will of the majority. Am I, then, in contradiction with myself?

A general law, which bears the name of justice, has been made and sanctioned, not only by a majority of this or that people, but by a majority of mankind. The rights of every people are therefore confined within the limits of what is just. A nation may be considered as a jury which is empowered to represent society at large and to apply justice, which is its law. Ought such a jury, which represents society, to have more power than the society itself whose laws it executes?

When I refuse to obey an unjust law, I do not contest the right of the majority to command, but I simply appeal from the sovereignty of the people to the sovereignty of mankind. Some have not feared to assert that a people can never outstep the boundaries of justice and reason in those affairs which are peculiarly its own; and that consequently full power may be given to the majority by which it is represented. But this is the language of a slave.

A majority taken collectively is only an individual, whose opinions, and frequently whose interests, are opposed to those of another individual, who is styled a minority. If it be admitted that a man possessing absolute power may misuse that power by wronging his adversaries, why should not a majority be liable to the same reproach? Men do not change their characters by uniting with one another; nor does their patience in the presence of obstacles increase with their strength. For my own part, I cannot believe it; the power to do everything, which I should refuse to one of my equals, I will never grant to any number of them. [. . .]

Unlimited power is in itself a bad and dangerous thing. Human beings are not competent to exercise it with discretion. God alone can be omnipotent, because his wisdom and his justice are always equal to his power. There is no power on earth so worthy of honor in itself or clothed with rights so sacred that I would admit its uncontrolled and all-predominant authority. When I see that the right and the means of absolute command are conferred on any power whatever, be it called a people or a king, an aristocracy or a democracy, a monarchy or a republic, I say there is the germ of tyranny, and I seek to live elsewhere, under other laws.

In my opinion, the main evil of the present democratic institutions of the United States does not arise, as is often asserted in Europe, from their weakness, but from their irresistible strength. I am not so much alarmed at the excessive liberty which reigns in that country as at the inadequate securities which one finds there against tyranny.

When an individual or a party is wronged in the United States, to whom can he apply for redress? If to public opinion, public opinion constitutes the majority; if to the legislature, it represents the majority and implicitly obeys it; if to the executive power, it is appointed by the majority and serves as a passive tool in its hands. The public force consists of the majority under arms; the jury is the majority invested with the right of hearing judicial cases; and in certain states even the judges are elected by the majority. However iniquitous or absurd the measure of which you complain, you must submit to it as well as you can.

[From *Democracy in America*, vol. i (Vintage Books, New York, 1945), 269–71. First published 1835.]

III.e. Democracy and Bureaucracy

MAX WEBER
....
45 **Bureaucratic Administration**

Bureaucratic organization has usually come into power on the basis of a leveling of economic and social differences. This leveling has been at least relative, and has concerned the significance of social and economic differences for the assumption of administrative functions.

Bureaucracy inevitably accompanies modern *mass democracy* in contrast to the democratic self-government of small homogeneous units. This results from the characteristic principle of bureaucracy: the abstract regularity of the execution of authority, which is a result of the demand for 'equality before the law' in the personal and functional sense—hence, of the horror of 'privilege,' and the principled rejection of doing business 'from case to case.' Such regularity also follows from the social preconditions of the origin of bureaucracies. The nonbureaucratic administration of any large social structure rests in some way upon the fact that existing social, material, or honorific preferences and ranks are connected with administrative functions and duties. This usually means that a direct or indirect economic exploitation or a 'social' exploitation of position, which every sort of administrative activity gives to its bearers, is equivalent to the assumption of administrative functions.

Bureaucratization and democratization within the administration of the state therefore signify and increase the case expenditures of the public treasury. And this is the case in spite of the fact that bureaucratic administration is usually more 'economical' in character than other forms of administration. Until recent times—at least from the point of view of the treasury—the cheapest way of satisfying the need for administration was to leave almost the entire local administration and lower judicature to the landlords of Eastern Prussia. The same fact applies to the administration of sheriffs in England. Mass democracy makes a clean sweep of the feudal, patrimonial, and—at least in intent—the plutocratic privileges in administration. Unavoidably it puts paid professional labour in place of the historically inherited avocational administration by notables.

This not only applies to structures of the state. For it is no accident that in their own organizations, the democratic mass parties have completely broken with traditional notable rule based upon personal relationships and personal esteem. Yet such personal structures frequently continue among the old conservative as well as the old liberal parties. Democratic mass parties are bureaucratically organized under the leadership of party officials, professional party and trade union secretaries, et cetera. In Germany, for instance, this has happened in the Social Democratic party and in the agrarian mass-movement; and in England, for the first time, in the caucus democracy of Gladstone-Chamberlain, which was originally organized in Birmingham and since the 1870s has spread. In the United States, both parties since Jackson's administration have developed bureaucratically. In France, however, attempts to organize disciplined political parties on the basis of an election system that would compel bureaucratic organization have repeatedly failed. The resistance of local circles of notables against the ultimately unavoidable bureaucratization of the parties, which would encompass the entire country and break their influence, could not be overcome. Every advance of the simple election techniques, for instance the system of proportional elections, which calculates with figures, means a strict and inter-local bureaucratic organization of the parties and therewith an increasing domination of party bureaucracy and discipline, as well as the elimination of the local circles of notables—at least this holds for great states.

The progress of bureaucratization in the state administration itself is a parallel phenomenon of democracy, as is quite obvious in France, North America, and now in England. Of course one must always remember that the term 'democratization' can be misleading. The *demos* itself, in the sense of an inarticulate mass, never 'governs' larger associations; rather, it is governed, and its existence only changes the way in which the executive leaders are selected and the measure of influence which the *demos*, or better, which social circles from its midst are able to exert upon the content and the direction of administrative activities by supplementing what is called 'public opinion.' 'Democratization,' in the sense here intended, does not necessarily mean an increasingly active share of the governed in the authority of the social structure. This may be a result of democratization, but it is not necessarily the case.

We must expressly recall at this point that the political concept of democracy, deduced from the 'equal rights' of the governed, includes these postulates: (1) prevention of the development of a closed status group of officials in the interest of a universal accessibility of office, and (2) minimization of the authority of officialdom in the interest of expanding the sphere of influence of 'public opinion' as far as practicable. Hence, wherever possible, political democracy strives to shorten the term of office by election and recall and by not binding the candidate to a special expertness. Thereby democracy inevitably comes into conflict with the bureaucratic tendencies which, by its fight against notable rule, democracy has produced. The generally loose term 'democratization' cannot be used here, in so far as it is understood to mean the minimization of the civil servants' ruling power in favour of the greatest possible 'direct' rule of the *demos*, which in practice means the respective party leaders of the *demos*. The most decisive thing here—indeed it is rather exclusively so—is the *leveling of the governed* in opposition to the ruling and bureaucratically articulated group, which in its turn may occupy a quite autocratic position, both in fact and in form.

[From 'Bureaucracy' in *From Max Weber*, trans. and ed. H. H. Gerth and C. Wright Mills (Routledge & Kegan Paul, London, 1948), 224–6.]

VILFREDO PARETO

46 Rule by Oligarchy

All governments use force, and all assert that they are founded on reason. In fact, whether universal suffrage prevails or not, it is always an oligarchy that governs, finding ways to give to the 'will of the people' that expression which the few desire, from the 'royal law' that bestowed the *imperium* on the Roman Emperors down to the votes of a legislative majority elected in one way or another, from the plebiscite that gave the empire to Napoleon III down to the universal suffrage that is shrewdly bought, steered and manipulated by our 'speculators'. Who is this new god called Universal Suffrage? He is no more exactly definable, no less shrouded in mystery, no less beyond the pale of reality, than the hosts of other divinities; nor are there fewer and less patent contradictions in his theology than in theirs. Worshippers of Universal Suffrage are not led by their god. It is they who lead him—and by the nose, determining the forms in which he must manifest himself. Oftentimes, proclaiming the sanctity of 'majority rule', they resist 'majority rule' by obstructionist tactics, even though they form but small minorities, and burning incense to the goddess Reason, they in no wise disdain, in certain cases, alliances with Chicanery, Fraud and Corruption.

Substantially such derivations express the sentiments felt by people who have climbed into the saddle and are willing to stay there—along with the far more general sentiment that social stability is a good thing. If, the moment a group, large or small, ceased to be satisfied with certain norms established in the community of which it is a part, it flew to arms to abolish them, organized society would fall to pieces. Social stability is so beneficial a thing that to maintain it it is well worth while to enlist the aid of fantastic ideals and this or that theology— among the others, the theology of universal suffrage—and be resigned to putting up with certain actual disadvantages. Before it becomes advisable to disturb the public peace, such disadvantages must have grown very very serious; and since human beings are effectively guided not by the sceptical reasonings of science but by 'living faiths' expressed in ideals, theories such as the divine right of kings, the legitimacy of oligarchies, of 'the people', of 'majorities', of legislative assemblies and other such things, may be useful within certain limits, and have in fact proved to be, however absurd they may be from the scientific standpoint.

Theories designed to justify the use of force by the governed are almost always combined with theories condemning the use of force by the public authority. A few dreamers reject the use of force in general, on whatever side; but their theories either have no influence at all or else serve merely to weaken resistance on the part of people in power, so clearing the field for violence on the part of the governed. In view of that we may confine ourselves to considering such theories, in general, in the combined form.

No great number of theories are required to rouse to resistance and to the use of force people who are, or think they are, oppressed. The derivations therefore are chiefly designed to incline people who would otherwise be neutral in the struggle to condemn resistance on the part of the governing powers, and so to make their resistance less vigorous; or at a venture, to persuade the rulers themselves in that sense, a thing, for that matter, that is not likely to have any great success in our day save with those whose spinal columns have utterly rotted from the bane of humanitarianism. A few centuries ago some results might have been achieved in our Western countries by working with religious derivations upon sincere Christians; and, in other countries, by working upon firm believers with derivations of the religion prevailing in the given case. Since humanitarianism is a religion, like the Christian, the Moslem, or any other, we may say, in general, that one may sometimes secure the aid of neutrals and weaken resistance on the part of people in power by using derivations of the religion, whatever it may be, in which they sincerely believe. But since derivations readily lend themselves to proving the pro and the contra, that device is often of scant effect even when it is not a mere mask for interests.

[From *Mind and Society* (Dover, New York, 1963), 1476–8. First published 1917–18.]

JOHN LOCKE

47 Legislative, Executive, and Federative Powers

The legislative power is that which has a right to direct how the force of the commonwealth shall be employed for preserving the community and the members of it. Because those laws which are constantly to be executed, and whose force is always to continue, may be made in a little time, therefore there is no need that the legislative should be always in being, not having always business to do. And because it may be too great temptation to human frailty, apt to grasp at power, for the same persons who have the power of making laws to have also in their hands the power to execute them, whereby they may exempt themselves from obedience to the laws they make, and suit the law, both in its making and execution, to their own private advantage, and thereby come to have a distinct interest from the rest of the community, contrary to the end of society and government. Therefore in well-ordered commonwealths, where the good of the whole is so considered as it ought, the legislative power is put into the hands of divers persons who, duly assembled, have by themselves, or jointly with others, a power to make laws, which when they have done, being separated again, they are themselves subject to the laws they have made; which is a new and near tie upon them to take care that they make them for the public good.

But because the laws that are at once, and in a short time made, have a constant and lasting force, and need a perpetual execution, or an attendance thereunto, therefore it is necessary there should be a power always in being which should see to the execution of the laws that are made, and remain in force. And thus the legislative and executive power come often to be separated.

There is another power in every commonwealth which one may call natural, because it is that which answers to the power every man naturally had before he entered into society. For though in a commonwealth the members of it are distinct persons, still, in reference to one another, and, as such, are governed by the laws of the society, yet, in reference to the rest of mankind, they make one body, which is, as every member of it before was, still in the state of Nature with the rest of mankind, so that the controversies that happen between any man of the society with those that are out of it are managed by the public, and an injury done to a member of their body engages the whole in the reparation of it. So that under this consideration the whole community is one body in the state of Nature in respect of all other states or persons out of its community.

This, therefore, contains the power of war and peace, leagues and alliances, and all the transactions with all persons and communities without the commonwealth, and may be called federative if any one pleases. So the thing be understood, I am indifferent as to the name.

These two powers, executive and federative, though they be really distinct in themselves, yet one comprehending the execution of the municipal laws of the society within itself upon all that are parts of it, the other the management of the security and interest of the public without with all those that it may receive benefit or damage from, yet they are always almost united. And though this federative power in the well or ill management of it be of great moment to the commonwealth, yet it is much less capable to be directed by antecedent, standing, positive laws than the executive, and so must necessarily be left to the prudence and wisdom of those whose hands it is in, to be managed for the public good. For the laws that concern subjects one amongst another, being to direct their actions, may well enough precede them. But what is to be done in reference to foreigners depending much upon their actions, and the variation of designs and interests, must be left in great part to the prudence of those who have this power committed to them, to be managed by the best of their skill for the advantage of the commonwealth.

Though, as I said, the executive and federative power of every community be really distinct in themselves, yet they are hardly to be separated and placed at the same time in the hands of distinct persons. For both of them requiring the force of the society for their exercise, it is almost impracticable to place the force of the commonwealth in distinct and not subordinate hands, or that the executive and federative power should be placed in persons that might act separately, whereby the force of the public would be under different commands, which would be apt some time or other to cause disorder and ruin.

Though in a constituted commonwealth standing upon its own basis and acting according to its own nature—that is, acting for the preservation of the community, there can be but one supreme power, which is the legislative, to which all the rest are and must be subordinate, yet the legislative being only a fiduciary power to act for certain ends, there remains still in the people a supreme power to remove or alter the legislative, when they find the legislative act contrary to the trust reposed in them. For all power given with trust for the attaining an end being limited by that end, whenever that end is manifestly neglected or opposed, the trust must necessarily be forfeited, and the power devolve into the hands of those that gave it, who may place it anew where they shall think best for their safety and security. And thus the community perpetually retains a supreme power of saving themselves from the attempts and designs of anybody, even of their legislators, whenever they shall be so foolish or so wicked as to lay and carry on designs against the liberties and properties of the subject. For no man or society of men having a power to deliver up their preservation, or consequently the means of it, to the absolute will and arbitrary dominion of another, whenever any one shall go about to bring them into such a slavish condition, they will always have a right to preserve what they have not a power to part with, and to rid themselves of those who invade this fundamental, sacred, and unalterable law of self-preservation for which they entered into society. And thus the community may be said in this respect to be always the supreme power, but not as considered under any form of government, because this power of the people can never take place till the government be dissolved.

[From *Two Treatises of Civil Government*, ed. W. S. Carpenter (J. M. Dent, London, 1924 (1962 repr.)), 190–3. First published 1690.]

BARON DE MONTESQUIEU

48 The Ideal Constitution

In every government there are three sorts of power: the legislative; the executive in respect to things dependent on the law of nations; and the executive in regard to matters that depend on the civil law.

By virtue of the first, the prince or magistrate enacts temporary or perpetual laws, and amends or abrogates those that have been already enacted. By the second, he makes peace or war, sends or receives embassies, establishes the public security, and provides against invasions. By the third, he punishes criminals, or determines the disputes that arise between individuals. The latter we shall call the judiciary power, and the other simply the executive power of the state. [. . .]

When the legislative and executive powers are united in the same person, or in the same body of magistrates, there can be no liberty; because apprehensions may arise, lest the same monarch or senate should enact tyrannical laws, to execute them in a tyrannical manner.

Again, there is no liberty, if the judiciary power be not separated from the legislative and executive. Were it joined with the legislative, the life and liberty of the subject would be exposed to arbitrary control; for the judge would be then the legislator. Were it joined to the executive power, the judge might behave with violence and oppression. [. . .]

One great fault there was in most of the ancient republics, that the people had a right to active resolutions, such as require some execution, a thing of which they are absolutely incapable. They ought to have no share in the government but for the choosing of representatives, which is within their reach. For though few can tell the exact degree of men's capacities, yet there are none but are capable of knowing in general whether the person they choose is better qualified than most of his neighbors.

Neither ought the representative body to be chosen for the executive part of government, for which it is not so fit; but for the enacting of laws, or to see whether the laws in being are duly executed, a thing suited to their abilities, and which none indeed but themselves can properly perform.

In such a state there are always persons distinguished by their birth, riches, or honors: but were they to be confounded with the common people, and to have only the weight of a single vote like the rest, the common liberty would be their slavery, and they would have no interest in supporting it, as most of the popular resolutions would be against them. The share they have, therefore, in the legislature ought to be proportioned to their other advantages in the state; which happens only when they form a body that has a right to check the licentiousness of the people, as the people have a right to oppose any encroachment of theirs.

The legislative power is therefore committed to the body of the nobles, and to that which represents the people, each having their assemblies and deliberations apart, each their separate views and interests.

Of the three powers above mentioned, the judiciary is in some measure next to nothing: there remain, therefore, only two; and as these have need of a regulating power to moderate them, the part of the legislative body composed of the nobility is extremely proper for this purpose.

The body of the nobility ought to be hereditary. In the first place it is so in its own nature; and in the next there must be a considerable interest to preserve its privileges—privileges that in themselves are obnoxious to popular envy, and of course in a free state are always in danger.

But as a hereditary power might be tempted to pursue its own particular interests, and forget those of the people, it is proper that where a singular advantage may be gained by corrupting the nobility, as in the laws relating to the supplies, they should have no other share in the legislation than the power of rejecting, and not that of resolving.

By the power of resolving I mean the right of ordaining by their own authority, or of amending what has been ordained by others. By the power of rejecting I would be understood to mean the right of annulling a resolution taken by another; which was the power of the tribunes at Rome. And though the person possessed of the privilege of rejecting may likewise have the right of approving, yet this approbation passes for no more than a declaration, that he intends to make no use of his privilege of rejecting, and is derived from that very privilege.

The executive power ought to be in the hands of a monarch, because this branch of government, having need of despatch, is better administered by one than by many: on the other hand, whatever depends on the legislative power is oftentimes better regulated by many than by a single person.

But if there were no monarch, and the executive power should be committed to a certain number of persons selected from the legislative body, there would be an end then of liberty; by reason the two powers would be united, as the same persons would sometimes possess, and would be always able to possess a share in both.

[From Charles Louis de Secondat, Baron de Montesquieu, *The Spirit of the Laws*, trans. Thomas Nugent, with an Introduction by Franz Neumann. (Hafner Press, New York; Collier Macmillan, London, 1949), 151–2, 155–6. First published 1748.]

Section IV

Liberty and Rights

INTRODUCTION

Democracy, we saw in the last section, carries with it the possibility of the tyranny of the majority. Unless they receive protection, the rights and liberties of the citizen are under threat. But what is liberty and what are rights? What rights and liberties do we properly have? These are the questions we explore in this section.

We start with Constant, who contrasts the liberties of the ancients with the liberties of the moderns. In Constant's view ancient liberty was a matter of participation in the collective political life, whereas for the moderns, liberty is peaceful independence. The theme is taken up by Isaiah Berlin, who contrasts two concepts of liberty: the negative liberty of non-interference and the positive liberty of achieving a form of self-mastery. Berlin warns of the dangers of the idea of positive liberty, for it seems, so he argues, to lead to the possibility that individuals can be oppressed in the name of their 'true goals', and thus, in Rousseau's notorious expression, can be 'forced to be free'. Charles Taylor, by contrast argues that the notion of freedom as non-interference is inadequate. Whether a restriction renders us unfree depends, at least to a degree, on how much it interferes with what we hold important, given our goals and purposes. This means, he argues, that we cannot avoid valuing positive freedom. The question of whether we have a right to liberty is taken up by Ronald Dworkin. He concedes that we may have rights to many particular liberties, but he argues that we cannot defend the notion of a right to liberty in general.

The following section takes up the question of the relation between liberty and the law, by providing selections from two famous exchanges. The first, in the nineteenth century is Mill's defence of his 'one simple principle', that the only reason one can justifiably interfere with the liberty of anyone is to prevent that person from harming another. In reply Stephen argues that Mill has not properly thought through the appalling consequences of implementing such a principle. In the twentieth century, in reflecting upon the Wolfenden report, which among other things led to the legalisation of male homosexuality in Britain, Lord Devlin argues that one of the functions of law is to uphold common moral standards, even at some cost to liberty. Hart, in response, argues that the moral standards of a society are constantly shifting, and such change can be necessary to the preservation of society.

Toleration has long been one of the primary liberal virtues, and for this reason we include a number of selections on toleration and free expression. Locke, who was particularly concerned with religious freedom, argues that not only does the state have no right to interfere with religious belief, it would be unable to do so even if it wanted to. While outward pressure can affect what you say you believe, it cannot change your real beliefs. T. M. Scanlon argues that the state must recognize individual rights to free expression, for the very source of the state's power depends on the autonomy of the individual, which in turn requires freedom of expression. However it is not always so clear what might count as exceeding the bounds of legitimate expression. Jeremy Waldron considers the Rushdie affair, in which the author Salman Rushdie was placed under the threat of assassination for his work *The Satanic Verses*, which was considered blasphemous by many Muslims. Finally the feminist lawyer Catharine MacKinnon argues that insisting on complete freedom of speech can undermine equality.

The requirements of citizenship is our next topic: this relates back to the questions of ancient liberty and positive liberty. Is liberty really a matter of being left alone to do what one wants, or does it require engagement in some way in public life? In other words must a free person also be an active citizen? This was certainly the view of Pericles, in his inspiring account of Athenian democracy, as recorded by Thucydides. Aristotle is concerned with a slightly different question, arguing that it is possible to be a good citizen, yet not a good man. Machiavelli decries the way in which people in the modern world have learnt to become weak and humble, compared to the ancients, and De Tocqueville takes up the theme, detailing the new forms of servitude which have replaced despotism and tyranny. Finally Quentin Skinner, in arguing that the republican idea of political liberty entails that without the state we cannot be free, draws together many of the threads of the debates about liberty and citizenship.

We turn next to the vexed question of the nature and scope of rights. Many political theorists simply take it on trust that we have rights; accordingly some of the most striking writing on this topic is by those who are sceptical about this claim, at least in any straightforward sense. Bentham, commenting on the *Declaration of Rights of Man and Citizen* (reprinted here in the Appendix) presents the case against natural rights with great rhetorical power. Marx, with reference to the same document, argues that the rights of man go no further than providing a screen and protection for individual egoism. Two contemporary writers, in their different ways, reassert the case for rights. Nozick presents the view of rights as 'side-constraints', by which he means that they are not to be balanced against other factors in moral decision-making, but take priority, while Dworkin connects the notion of a right to the ideas of dignity and equality.

There are, nevertheless, circumstances under which we think it is permissible to treat people in a way that would normally be considered a violation of their rights. The most obvious example, perhaps, is that of punishment, and in the final section we look at how it might be justified. Two leading, competing, theories are deterrence and retribution. According to deterrence theory, we are justified in punishing an individual when doing so would deter others from breaking the law in the future. Mill, somewhat surprisingly perhaps for a liberal theorist, argues in favour of capital punishment on the twin grounds of deterrence, and humanity to the criminal. Hart tries to recover the notion of responsibility from the idea of deterrence, while in the final selection Nozick mounts a powerful attack upon deterrence theories of punishment, in favour of retribution.

IV.a. What is Liberty?

BENJAMIN CONSTANT

49 **The Liberty of the Ancients and the Liberty of the Moderns**

First ask yourselves, Gentlemen, what an Englishman, a Frenchman, and a citizen of the United States of America understand today by the word 'liberty'.

For each of them it is the right to be subjected only to the laws, and to be neither arrested, detained, put to death or maltreated in any way by the arbitrary will of one or more individuals. It is the right of everyone to express their opinion, choose a profession and practise it, to dispose of property, and even to abuse it; to come and go without permission, and without having to account for their motives or undertakings. It is everyone's right to associate with other individuals, either to discuss their interests, or to profess the religion which they and their associates prefer, or even simply to occupy their days or hours in a way which is most compatible with their inclinations or whims. Finally it is everyone's right to exercise some influence on the administration of the government, either by electing all or particular officials, or through representations, petitions, demands to which the authorities are more or less compelled to pay heed. Now compare this liberty with that of the ancients.

The latter consisted in exercising collectively, but directly, several parts of the complete sovereignty; in deliberating, in the public square, over war and peace; in forming alliances with foreign governments; in voting laws, in pronouncing judgements; in examining the accounts, the acts, the stewardship of the magistrates; in calling them to appear in front of the assembled people, in accusing, condemning or absolving them. But if this was what the ancients called liberty, they admitted as compatible with this collective freedom the complete subjection of the individual to the authority of the community. [. . .]

We can no longer enjoy the liberty of the ancients, which consisted in an active and constant participation in collective power. Our freedom must consist of peaceful enjoyment and private independence. The share which in antiquity everyone held in national sovereignty was by no means an abstract presumption as it is in our own day. The will of each individual had real influence: the exercise of this will was a vivid and repeated pleasure. Consequently the ancients were ready to make many a sacrifice to preserve their political rights and their share in the administration of the state. Everybody, feeling with pride all that his suffrage was worth, found in this awareness of his personal importance a great compensation.

This compensation no longer exists for us today. Lost in the multitude, the individual can almost never perceive the influence he exercises. Never does his will impress itself upon the whole; nothing confirms in his eyes his own cooperation. [...]

It follows that we must be far more attached than the ancients to our individual independence. For the ancients when they sacrificed that independence to their political rights, sacrificed less to obtain more; while in making the same sacrifice, we would give more to obtain less.

The aim of the ancients was the sharing of social power among the citizens of the same fatherland: this is what they called liberty. The aim of the moderns is the enjoyment of security in private pleasures; and they call liberty the guarantees accorded by institutions to these pleasures. [...]

Individual liberty, I repeat, is the true modern liberty. Political liberty is its guarantee, consequently political liberty is indispensable. But to ask the peoples of our day to sacrifice, like those of the past, the whole of their individual liberty to political liberty, is the surest means of detaching them from the former and, once this result has been achieved, it would be only too easy to deprive them of the latter. [...]

For from the fact that modern liberty differs from ancient liberty, it follows that it is also threatened by a different sort of danger.

The danger of ancient liberty was that men, exclusively concerned with securing their share of social power, might attach too little value to individual rights and enjoyments.

The danger of modern liberty is that, absorbed in the enjoyment of our private independence, and in the pursuit of our particular interests, we should surrender our right to share in political power too easily.

The holders of authority are only too anxious to encourage us to do so. They are so ready to spare us all sort of troubles, except those of obeying and paying! They will say to us: what, in the end, is the aim of your efforts, the motive of your labours, the object of all your hopes? Is it not happiness? Well, leave this happiness to us and we shall give it to you. No, Sirs, we must not leave it to them. No matter how touching such a tender commitment may be, let us ask the authorities to keep within their limits. Let them confine themselves to being just. We shall assume the responsibility of being happy for ourselves. [...]

Political liberty, by submitting to all the citizens, without exception, the care and assessment of their most sacred interests, enlarges their spirit, ennobles their thoughts, and establishes among them a kind of intellectual equality which forms the glory and power of a people.

[From *Political Writings*, trans. and ed. Biancamaria Fontana (Cambridge University Press, Cambridge, 1988), 310–11, 316–17, 323, 326, 327. First published 1820.]

I am normally said to be free to the degree to which no man or body of men interferes with my activity. Political liberty in this sense is simply the area within which a man can act unobstructed by others. If I am prevented by others from doing what I could otherwise do, I am to that degree unfree; and if this area is contracted by other men beyond a certain minimum, I can be described as being coerced, or, it may be, enslaved. Coercion is not, however, a term that covers every form of of inability. If I say that I am unable to jump more than ten feet in the air, or cannot read because I am blind, or cannot understand the darker pages of Hegel, it would be eccentric to say that I am to that degree enslaved or coerced. Coercion implies the deliberate interference of other human beings within the area in which I could otherwise act. You lack political liberty or freedom only if you are prevented from attaining a goal by human beings. Mere incapacity to attain a goal is not lack of political freedom. [. . .]

This is what the classical English political philosophers meant when they used this word. They disagreed about how wide the area could or should be. They supposed that it could not, as things were, be unlimited, because if it were, it would entail a state in which all men could boundlessly interfere with all other men; and this kind of 'natural' freedom would lead to social chaos in which men's minimum needs would not be satisfied; or else the liberties of the weak would be suppressed by the strong. Because they perceived that human purposes and activities do not automatically harmonize with one another, and because (whatever their official doctrines) they put high value on other goals, such as justice, or happiness, or culture, or security, or varying degrees of equality, they were prepared to curtail freedom in the interests of other values and, indeed, of freedom itself. For, without this, it was impossible to create the kind of association that they thought desirable. Consequently, it is assumed by these thinkers that the area of men's free action must be limited by law. But equally it is assumed, especially by such libertarians as Locke and Mill in England, and Constant and Tocqueville in France, that there ought to exist a certain minimum area of personal freedom which must on no account be violated; for if it is overstepped, the individual will find himself in an area too narrow for even that minimum development of his natural faculties which alone makes it possible to pursue, and even to conceive, the various ends which men hold good or right or sacred. It follows that a frontier must be drawn between the area of private life and that of public authority. Where it is to be drawn is a matter of argument, indeed of haggling. Men are largely interdependent, and no man's activity is so completely private as never to obstruct the lives of others in any way. 'Freedom for the pike is death for the minnows'; the liberty of some must depend on the restraint of others. 'Freedom for an Oxford don', others have been known to add, 'is a very different thing from freedom for an Egyptian peasant.'

What troubles the consciences of Western liberals is not, I think, the belief that the freedom that men seek differs according to their social or economic conditions, but that the minority who possess it have gained it by exploiting, or, at least, averting their gaze from, the vast majority who do not. They believe, with good reason, that if individual liberty is an ultimate end for human beings, none should be deprived of it by others; least of all that some should enjoy it at the expense of others. Equality of liberty; not to treat others as I should not wish them to treat me; repayment of my debt to those who alone have made possible my liberty or prosperity or enlightenment; justice, in its simplest and most universal sense—these are the foundations of liberal morality. Liberty is not the only goal of men. I can, like the Russian critic Belinsky, say that if others are to be deprived of it—if my brothers are to remain in poverty, squalor, and chains—then I do not want it for myself, I reject it with both hands and infinitely prefer to share their fate. But nothing is gained by a confusion of terms. To avoid glaring inequality or widespread misery I am ready to sacrifice some, or all, of my freedom: I may do so willingly and freely: but it is freedom that I am giving up for the sake of justice or equality or the love of my fellow men. I should be guilt-stricken, and rightly so, if I were not, in some circumstances, ready to make this sacrifice. But a sacrifice is not an increase in what is being sacrificed, namely freedom, however great the moral need or the compensation for it. Everything is what it is: liberty is liberty, not equality or fairness or justice or culture, or human happiness or a quiet conscience. If the liberty of myself or my class or nation depends on the misery of a number of other human beings, the system which promotes this is unjust and immoral. But if I curtail or lose my freedom, in order to lessen the shame of such inequality, and do not thereby materially increase the individual liberty of others, an absolute loss of liberty occurs.

Liberty in this sense is principally concerned with the area of control, not with its source. Just as a democracy may, in fact, deprive the individual citizen of a great many liberties which he might have in some other form of society, so it is perfectly conceivable that a liberal-minded despot would allow his subjects a large measure of personal freedom. The despot who leaves his subjects a wide area of liberty may be unjust, or encourage the wildest inequalities, care little for order, or virtue, or knowledge; but provided he does not curb their liberty, or at least curbs it less than many other régimes, he meets with Mill's specification. Freedom in this sense is not, at any rate logically, connected with democracy or self-government. Self-government may, on the whole, provide a better guarantee of the preservation of civil liberties than other régimes, and has been defended as such by libertarians. But there is no necessary connexion between individual liberty and democratic rule. The answer to the question

'Who governs me?' is logically distinct from the question 'How far does government interfere with me?' It is in this difference that the great contrast between the two concepts of negative and positive liberty, in the end, consists. [...]

The 'positive' sense of the word 'liberty' derives from the wish on the part of the individual to be his own master. I wish my life and decisions to depend on myself, not on external forces of whatever kind. I wish to be the instrument of my own, not of other men's, acts of will. I wish to be a subject, not an object; to be moved by reasons, by conscious purposes, which are my own, not by causes which affect me, as it were, from outside. I wish to be somebody, not nobody; a doer—deciding, not being decided for, self-directed and not acted upon by external nature or by other men as if I were a thing, or an animal, or a slave incapable of playing a human role, that is, of conceiving goals and policies of my own and realizing them. This is at least part of what I mean when I say that I am rational, and that it is my reason that distinguishes me as a human being from the rest of the world. I wish, above all, to be conscious of myself as a thinking, willing, active being, bearing responsibility for my choices and able to explain them by references to my own ideas and purposes. I feel free to the degree that I believe this to be true, and enslaved to the degree that I am made to realize that it is not.

The freedom which consists in being one's own master, and the freedom which consists in not being prevented from choosing as I do by other men, may, on the face of it, seem concepts at no great logical distance from each other— no more than negative and positive ways of saying much the same thing. Yet the 'positive' and 'negative' notions of freedom historically developed in divergent directions not always by logical reputable steps, until, in the end, they came into direct conflict with each other.

One way of making this clear is in terms of the independent momentum which the, initially perhaps quite harmless, metaphor of self-mastery acquired. 'I am my own master'; 'I am slave to no man'; but may I not (as Platonists or Hegelians tend to say) be a slave to nature? Or to my own 'unbridled' passions? Are these not so many species of the identical genus 'slave'—some political or legal, others moral or spiritual? Have not men had the experience of liberating themselves from spiritual slavery, or slavery to nature, and do they not in the course of it become aware, on the one hand, of a self which dominates, and, on the other, of something in them which is brought to heel? This dominant self is then variously identified with reason, with my 'higher nature', with the self which calculates and aims at what will satisfy it in the long run, with my 'real', or 'ideal', or 'autonomous' self, or with my self 'at its best'; which is then contrasted with irrational impulse, uncontrolled desires, my 'lower' nature, the pursuit of immediate pleasures, my 'empirical' or 'heteronomous' self, swept by every gust of desire and passion, needing to be rigidly disciplined if it is ever to rise to the full height of its 'real' nature.

Presently the two selves may be represented as divided by an even larger gap: the real self may be conceived as something wider than the individual (as the term is normally understood), as a social 'whole' of which the individual is an element or aspect: a tribe, a race, a church, a state, the great society of the living and the dead and the yet unborn. This entity is then identified as being the 'true' self which, by imposing its collective, or 'organic', single will upon its recalcitrant 'members', achieves its own, and therefore their, 'higher' freedom. The perils of using organic metaphors to justify the coercion of some men by others in order to raise them to a 'higher' level of freedom have often been pointed out. But what gives such plausibility as it has to this kind of language is that we recognize that it is possible, and at times justifiable, to coerce men in the name of some goal (let us say, justice or public health) which they would, if they were more enlightened, themselves pursue, but do not, because they are blind or ignorant or corrupt. This renders it easy for me to conceive of myself as coercing others for their own sake, in their, not my, interest. I am then claiming that I know what they truly need better than they know it themselves. What, at most, this entails is that they would not resist me if they were rational and as wise as I and understood their interests as I do. But I may go on to claim a good deal more than this. I may declare that they are actually aiming at what in their benighted state they consciously resist, because there exists within them an occult entity—their latent rational will, or their 'true' purpose—and that this entity, although it is belied by all that they overtly feel and do and say, is their 'real' self, of which the poor empirical self in space and time may know nothing or little; and that this inner spirit is the only self that deserves to have its wishes taken into account. Once I take this view, I am in a position to ignore the actual wishes of men or societies, to bully, oppress, torture them in the name, and on behalf, of their 'real' selves, in the secure knowledge that whatever is the true goal of man (happiness, performance of duty, wisdom, a just society, self-fulfilment) must be identical with his freedom—the free choice of his 'true', albeit often submerged and inarticulate, self.

   This paradox has been often exposed. It is one thing to say that I know what is good for X, while he himself does not; and even to ignore his wishes for its— and his—sake; and a very different one to say that he has *eo ipso* chosen it, not indeed consciously, not as he seems in everyday life, but in his role as a rational self which his empirical self may not know—the 'real' self which discerns the good, and cannot help choosing it once it is revealed. This monstrous impersonation, which consists in equating what X would choose if he were something he is not, or at least not yet, with what X actually seeks and chooses, is at the heart of all political theories of self-realization. It is one thing to say that I may be coerced for my own good which I am too blind to see: this may, on occasion, be for my benefit; indeed it may enlarge the scope of my liberty. It is another to say that if it is my good, then I am not being coerced, for I have willed it, whether I know this or not, and am free (or 'truly' free) even while my poor earthly body and foolish mind bitterly reject it, and struggle against those who seek however benevolently to impose it, with the greatest desperation. [. . .]

Recent history has made it only too clear that the issue is not merely academic.

[From 'Two Concepts of Liberty', in *Four Essays on Liberty* (Oxford University Press, Oxford, 1969), 122, 123–5, 129–34.]

CHARLES TAYLOR

51   In Defence of Positive Freedom

Consider the following diabolical defence of Albania as a free country. We recognise that religion has been abolished in Albania, whereas it hasn't in Britain. But on the other hand there are probably far fewer traffic lights per head in Tirana than in London. (I haven't checked for myself, but this is a very plausible assumption.) Suppose an apologist for Albanian Socialism were nevertheless to claim that this country was freer than Britain, because the number of acts restricted was far smaller. After all, only a minority of Londoners practise some religion in public places, but all have to negotiate their way through traffic. Those who do practise a religion generally do so on one day of the week, while they are held up at traffic lights every day. In sheer quantitative terms, the number of acts restricted by traffic lights must be greater than that restricted by a ban on public religious practice. So if Britain is considered a free society, why not Albania?

So the application even of our negative notion of freedom requires a background conception of what is significant, according to which some restrictions are seen to be without relevance for freedom altogether, and others are judged as being of greater and lesser importance. So some discrimination among motivations seems essential to our concept of freedom. A minute's reflection shows why this must be so. Freedom is important to us because we are purposive beings. But then there must be distinctions in the significance of different kinds of freedom based on the distinction in the significance of different purposes. [. . .]

This creates some embarrassment for the crude negative theory, but it can cope with it by simply adding a recognition that we make judgements of significance. Its central claim that freedom just is the absence of external obstacles seems untouched, as also its view of freedom as an opportunity-concept. It is just that we now have to admit that not all opportunities are equal.

But there is more trouble in store for the crude view when we examine further what these qualitative discriminations are based on. What lies behind our judging certain purposes/feelings as more significant than others? One might think that there was room here again for another quantitative theory; that the more significant purposes are those we want more. But this account is either vacuous or false.

It is true but vacuous if we take wanting more just to mean being more significant. It is false as soon as we try to give wanting more an independent criterion, such as, for instance, the urgency or force of a desire, or the prevalence of one desire over another, because it is a matter of the most banal experience that the purposes we know to be more significant are not always those which we desire with the greatest urgency to encompass, nor the ones that actually always win out in cases of conflict of desires.

When we reflect on this kind of significance, we come up against what I have called elsewhere the fact of strong evaluation, the fact that we human subjects are not only subjects of first-order desires, but of second-order desires, desires about desires. We experience our desires and purposes as qualitatively discriminated, as higher or lower, noble or base, integrated or fragmented, significant or trivial, good and bad. [. . .]

But then the question arises whether this fact of strong evaluation doesn't have other consequences for our notion of freedom, than just that it permits us to rank freedoms in importance. Is freedom not at stake when we find ourselves carried away by a less significant goal to override a highly significant one? Or when we are led to act out of a motive we consider bad or despicable?

The answer is that we sometimes do speak in this way. Suppose I have some irrational fear, which is preventing me from doing something I very much want to do. Say the fear of public speaking is preventing me from taking up a career that I should find very fulfilling, and that I should be quite good at, if I could just get over this 'hang-up'. It is clear that we experience this fear as an obstacle, and that we feel we are less than we would be if we could overcome it. [. . .]

My irrational fear, my being quite distressed by discomfort, my spite—these are all things which I can easily see myself losing without any loss whatsoever to what I am. This is why I can see them as obstacles to my purposes, and hence to my freedom, even though they are in a sense unquestionably desires and feelings of mine. [. . .]

The whole notion of our identity, whereby we recognise that some goals, desires, allegiances are central to what we are, while others are not or are less so, can make sense only against a background of desires and feelings which are not brute, but what I shall call import-attributing, to invent a term of art for the occasion. [. . .]

But once we admit that our feelings are import-attributing, then we admit the possibility of error, or false appreciation. And indeed, we have to admit a kind of false appreciation which the agent himself detects in order to make sense of the cases where we experience our own desires as fetters. How can we exclude in principle that there may be other false appreciations which the agent does not detect? That he may be profoundly in error, that is, have a very distorted sense of his fundamental purposes? Who can say that such people can't exist? All cases are, of course, controversial; but I should nominate Charles Manson and Andreas Baader for this category, among others. I pick them out as people with a strong sense of some purposes and goals as incomparably more fundamental than others, or at least with a propensity to act the having such a sense so as to take in even themselves a good part of the time, but whose sense of fundamental purpose was shot through with confusion and error. And once we recognise such extreme cases, how avoid admitting that many of the rest of mankind can suffer to a lesser degree from the same disabilities? [. . .]

Once we see that we make distinctions of degree and significance in freedoms depending on the significance of the purpose fettered / enabled, how can we deny that it makes a difference to the degree of freedom not only whether one of my basic purposes is frustrated by my own desires but also whether I have grievously misidentified this purpose? The only way to avoid this would be to hold that there is no such thing as getting it wrong, that your basic purpose is just what you feel it to be. But there is such a thing as getting it wrong, as we have seen, and the very distinctions of significance depend on this fact.

But if this is so, then the crude negative view of freedom, the Hobbesian definition, is untenable. Freedom can't just be the absence of external obstacles, for there may also be internal ones. And nor may the internal obstacles be just confined to those that the subject identifies as such, so that he is the final arbiter; for he may be profoundly mistaken about his purposes and about what he wants to repudiate. And if so, he is less capable of freedom in the meaningful sense of the word. Hence we cannot maintain the incorrigibility of the subject's judgements about his freedom, or rule out second-guessing, as we put it above. And at the same time, we are forced to abandon the pure opportunity-concept of freedom.

[From 'What's wrong with negative liberty?', in *The Idea of Freedom*, ed. Alan Ryan (Oxford University Press, Oxford, 1979), 183–6, 188, 191, 192–3.]

RONALD DWORKIN

52 No Right to Liberty

Do we have a right to liberty? Thomas Jefferson thought so, and since his day the right to liberty has received more play than the competing rights he mentioned to life and the pursuit of happiness. Liberty gave its name to the most influential political movement of the last century, and many of those who now despise liberals do so on the ground that they are not sufficiently libertarian. Of course, almost everyone concedes that the right to liberty is not the only political right, and that therefore claims to freedom must be limited, for example, by restraints that protect the security or property of others. Nevertheless the consensus in favor of some right to liberty is a vast one, though it is, as I shall argue, misguided. [. . .]

If freedom to choose one's schools, or employees, or neighborhood is simply something that we all want, like air conditioning or lobsters, then we are not entitled to hang on to these freedoms in the face of what we concede to be the rights of others to an equal share of respect and resources. But if we can say, not simply that we want these freedoms, but that we are ourselves entitled to them, then we have established at least a basis for demanding a compromise. [. . .]

It seems to me absurd to suppose that men and women have any general right to liberty at all, at least as liberty has traditionally been conceived by its champions.

I have in mind the traditional definition of liberty as the absence of constraints placed by a government upon what a man might do if he wants to. [. . .] This conception of liberty as license is neutral amongst the various activities a man might pursue, the various roads he might wish to walk. It diminishes a man's liberty when we prevent him from talking or making love as he wishes, but it also diminishes his liberty when we prevent him from murdering or defaming others. These latter constraints may be justifiable, but only because they are compromises necessary to protect the liberty or security of others, and not because they do not, in themselves, infringe the independent value of liberty. [. . .]

The term 'right' is used in politics and philosophy in many different senses. In order sensibly to ask whether we have a right to liberty in the neutral sense, we must fix on some one meaning of 'right'. It would not be difficult to find a sense of that term in which we could say with some confidence that men have a right to liberty. We might say, for example, that someone has a right to liberty if it is in his interest to have liberty, that is, if he either wants it or if it would be good for him to have it. In this sense, I would be prepared to concede that citizens have a right to liberty. But in this sense I would also have to concede that they have a right, at least generally, to vanilla ice cream. My concession about liberty, moreover, would have very little value in political debate. I should want to claim, for example, that people have a right to equality in a much stronger sense, that they do not simply want equality but that they are entitled to it, and I would therefore not recognize the claim that some men and women want liberty as requiring any compromise in the efforts that I believe are necessary to give other men and women the equality to which they are entitled. [. . .]

A successful claim of right, in the strong sense I described, has this consequence. If someone has a right to something, then it is wrong for the government to deny it to him even though it would be in the general interest to do so. [. . .]

I do not think that the right to liberty would come to very much, or have much power in political argument, if it relied on any sense of the right any weaker than that. If we settle on this concept of a right, however, then it seems plain that there exists no general right to liberty as such. I have no political right to drive up Lexington Avenue. If the government chooses to make Lexington

Avenue one-way down town, it is a sufficient justification that this would be in the general interest, and it would be ridiculous for me to argue that for some reason it would nevertheless be wrong. The vast bulk of the laws which diminish my liberty are justified on utilitarian grounds, as being in the general interest or for the general welfare; if, as Bentham supposes, each of these laws diminishes my liberty, they nevertheless do not take away from me any thing that I have a right to have. It will not do, in the one-way street case, to say that although I have a right to drive up Lexington Avenue, nevertheless the government for special reasons is justified in overriding that right. That seems silly because the government needs no special justification—but only a justification—for this sort of legislation. So I can have a political right to liberty, such that every act of constraint diminishes or infringes that right, only in such a weak sense of right that the so called right to liberty is not competitive with strong rights, like the right to equality, at all. In any strong sense of right, which would be competitive with the right to equality, there exists no general right to liberty at all. [. . .]

The idea of a right to liberty is a misconceived concept that does a dis-service to political thought in at least two ways. First, the idea creates a false sense of a necessary conflict between liberty and other values when social regulation, like the busing program, is proposed. Second, the idea provides too easy an answer to the question of why we regard certain kinds of restraints, like the restraint on free speech or the exercise of religion, as especially unjust. The idea of a right to liberty allows us to say that these constraints are unjust because they have a special impact on liberty as such.

[From 'What rights do we have?', in *Taking Rights Seriously* (Duckworth, London, 1977, 1978), 266–9, 271.]

IV.b. Law and Morality

JOHN STUART MILL

53 **One Simple Principle**

The object of this Essay is to assert one very simple principle, as entitled to govern absolutely the dealings of society with the individual in the way of compulsion and control, whether the means used be physical force in the form of legal penalties, or the moral coercion of public opinion. That principle is, that the sole end for which mankind are warranted, individually or collectively, in interfering with the liberty of action of any of their number, is self-protection. That the only purpose for which power can be rightfully exercised over any member of a civilised community, against his will, is to prevent harm to others. His own good, either physical or moral, is not a sufficient warrant. He cannot rightfully be compelled to do or forbear because it will be better for him to do so, because it will make him happier, because, in the opinions of others, to do so would be wise, or even right. These are good reasons for remonstrating with him, or reasoning with him, or persuading him, or entreating him, but not for compelling him, or visiting him with any evil in case he do otherwise. To justify that, the conduct from which it is desired to deter him must be calculated to produce evil to some one else. The only part of the conduct of any one, for which he is amenable to society, is that which concerns others. In the part which merely concerns himself, his independence is, of right, absolute. Over himself, over his own body and mind, the individual is sovereign. [. . .]

If any one does an act hurtful to others, there is a *prima facie* case for punishing him, by law, or, where legal penalties are not safely applicable, by general disapprobation. There are also many positive acts for the benefit of others, which he may rightfully be compelled to perform; such as to give evidence in a court of justice; to bear his fair share in the common defence, or in any other joint work necessary to the interest of the society of which he enjoys the protection; and to perform certain acts of individual beneficence, such as saving a fellow-creature's life, or interposing to protect the defenceless against ill-usage, things which whenever it is obviously a man's duty to do, he may rightfully be made responsible to society for not doing. [. . .]

But there is a sphere of action in which society, as distinguished from the individual, has, if any, only an indirect interest; comprehending all that portion of a person's life and conduct which affects only himself, or if it also affects others, only with their free, voluntary, and undeceived consent and participation. When I say only himself, I mean directly, and in the first instance; for whatever affects himself, may affect others through himself; and the objection which may be grounded on this contingency, will receive consideration in the sequel. This, then, is the appropriate region of human liberty. It comprises, first, the inward domain of consciousness; demanding liberty of conscience in the most comprehensive sense; liberty of thought and feeling; absolute freedom of opinion and sentiment on all subjects, practical or speculative, scientific, moral, or theological. The liberty of expressing and publishing opinions may seem to fall under a different principle, since it belongs to that part of the conduct of an individual which concerns other people; but, being almost of as much importance as the liberty of thought itself, and resting in great part on the same reasons, is practically inseparable from it. Secondly, the principle requires liberty of tastes and pursuits; of framing the plan of our life to suit our own character; of doing as we like, subject to such consequences as may follow: without impediment from our fellow-creatures, so long as what we do does not harm them, even though they should think our conduct foolish, perverse, or wrong. Thirdly, from this liberty of each individual, follows the liberty, within the same limits, of combination among individuals; freedom to unite, for any purpose not involving harm to others: the persons combining being supposed to be of full age, and not forced or deceived.

No society in which these liberties are not, on the whole, respected, is free, whatever may be its form of government; and none is completely free in which they do not exist absolute and unqualified.

[From *On Liberty*, in *Utilitarianism, On Liberty and Considerations on Representative Government*, ed. H. B. Acton (Dent, London, 1972), 72–5. First published 1859.]

JAMES FITZJAMES STEPHEN

54   The Consequences of Liberty

So far I have considered the theoretical grounds of Mr Mill's principle and its practical application to liberty of thought and discussion. I now proceed to consider its application to morals. It may be well to restate it for fear that I may appear to be arguing with an imaginary opponent. 'The object of this essay is to assert one very simple principle as entitled to govern absolutely all the dealings of society with the individual in the way of compulsion and control, whether the means used be physical force or the moral coercion of public opinion. That principle is, that the sole end for which mankind are warranted, individually or collectively, in interfering with the liberty of action of any of their number is self-protection.' A little further on we are told that 'from the liberty of each individual follows the liberty within the same limits of combination among individuals—freedom to unite for any purpose not involving harm to others.'

The following consequences would flow legitimately from this principle. A number of persons form themselves into an association for the purpose of countenancing each other in the practice of seducing women, and giving the widest possible extension to the theory that adultery is a good thing. They carry out these objects by organizing a system for the publication and circulation of lascivious novels and pamphlets calculated to inflame the passions of the young and inexperienced. The law of England would treat this as a crime. It would call such books obscene libels, and a combination for such a purpose a conspiracy. Mr Mill, apparently, would not only regard this as wrong, but he would regard it as an act of persecution if the newspapers were to excite public indignation against the parties concerned by language going one step beyond the calmest discussion of the expediency of such an 'experiment in living.' Such an association would be impossible in this country, because if the law of the land did not deal with it, lynch law infallibly would. This Mr Mill ought in consistency to regard as a lamentable proof of our bigotry and want of acquaintance with the true principles of liberty.

The manner in which he discusses an illustration closely analogous to this, and in which he attempts to answer an objection which must suggest itself to every one, throws the strongest possible light on the value of his own theory. His illustration is as follows: 'Fornication must be tolerated and so must gambling; but should a person be free to be a pimp or to keep a gambling house?' He puts the arguments on each side without drawing any conclusion, and the strongest of them are as follows:

On the side of toleration it may be said that if the principles which we have hitherto defended are true, society has no business *as* society to decide anything to be wrong which concerns only the individual; that it cannot go beyond persuasion, and that one person should be as free to persuade as another to dissuade. In opposition to this it may be contended that, although the public or the State are not warranted in authoritatively deciding for purposes of repression or punishment that such or such conduct affecting only the interests of the individual is good or bad, they are fully justified in assuming, if they regard it as bad, that its being so or not is at least a disputable question; that this being supposed they cannot be acting wrongly in endeavouring to exclude the influence of solicitations which are not disinterested, of instigators who cannot possibly be impartial, who have a direct personal interest on one side, and that the side which the State believes to be wrong and who confessedly promote it for personal objects only.

There is a kind of ingenuity which carries its own refutation on its face. How can the State or the public be competent to determine any question whatever if it is not competent to decide that gross vice is a bad thing? I do not think the State ought to stand bandying compliments with pimps. 'Without offence to your better judgment, dear sir, and without presuming to set up my opinion against yours, I beg to observe that I am entitled for certain purposes to treat the question whether your views of life are right as one which admits of two opinions. I am far from expressing absolute condemnation of an experiment in living from which I dissent (I am sure that mere dissent will not offend a person of your liberality of sentiment), but still I am compelled to observe that you are not altogether unbiassed by personal considerations in the choice of the course of life which you have adopted (no doubt for reasons which appear to you satisfactory, though they do not convince me). I venture, accordingly, though with the greatest deference, to call upon you not to exercise your profession; at least I am not indisposed to think that I may, upon full consideration, feel myself compelled to do so.' My feeling is that if society gets its grip on the collar of such a fellow it should say to him, 'You dirty rascal, it may be a question whether you should be suffered to remain in your native filth untouched, or whether my opinion about you should be printed by the lash on your bare back. That question will be determined without the smallest reference to your wishes or feelings; but as to the nature of my opinion about you, there can be no question at all.' [. . .]

It is surely a simple matter of fact that every human creature is deeply interested not only in the conduct, but in the thoughts, feelings, and opinions of millions of persons who stand in no other assignable relation to him than that of being his fellow-creatures. A great writer who makes a mistake in his speculations may mislead multitudes whom he has never seen. The strong metaphor that we are all members one of another is little more than the expression of a fact. A man would no more be a man if he was alone in the world than a hand would be a hand without the rest of the body.

I will now turn to the manner in which Mr Mill deals with the objection just stated, and I must observe by the way that nothing proves his candour and honesty so clearly as the force with which he states objections to which he has no, or very weak, answers to make. His answer is twofold. He first admits that where 'by conduct of this sort' (i.e. self-regarding vices) 'a person is led to violate a distinct and assignable obligation to any other person or persons, the case is taken out of the self-regarding class, and becomes amenable to moral disapprobation in the proper sense of the term. If, for example, a man through intemperance . . . becomes unable to pay his debts, . . . he is deservedly reprobated, and might be justly punished, but it is for the breach of duty . . . to his creditors, not for his extravagance.' A party of people get drunk together at a public-house. Public opinion ought to stigmatize those only who could not afford it. The rest are 'trying an experiment in living' which happens to suit their taste, and no one else has anything to say to it.

There is no principle on which the cases in which Mr Mill admits the justice of legal punishment can be distinguished from those in which he denies it. The principle is that private vices which are injurious to others may justly be punished, if the injury be specific and the persons injured distinctly assignable, but not otherwise. If the question were as to the possibility in most cases of drawing an indictment against such persons I should agree with him. Criminal law is an extremely rough engine, and must be worked with great caution; but it is one thing to point out a practical difficulty which limits the application of a principle and quite another to refute the principle itself. Mr Mill's proviso deserves attention in considering the question whether a given act should be punished by law, but he applies it to 'the moral coercion of public opinion,' as well as to legal coercion, and to this the practical difficulty which he points out does not apply. A set of young noblemen of great fortune and hereditary influence, the representatives of ancient names, the natural leaders of the society of large districts, pass their whole time and employ all their means in gross debauchery. Such people are far more injurious to society than common pickpockets, but Mr Mill says that if any one having the opportunity of making them ashamed of themselves uses it in order to coerce them into decency, he sins against liberty, unless their example does assignable harm to specific people. It might be right to say, 'You, the Duke of A, by extravagantly keeping four mistresses—to wit, B and C in London, and D and E in Paris—set an example which induced your friend F to elope with Mrs G at——on——, and you are a great blackguard for your pains, and all the more because you are a duke.' It could never be right to say, 'You, the Duke of A, are scandalously immoral and ought to be made to smart for it, though the law cannot touch you.' The distinction is more likely to be overlooked than to be misunderstood.

[From *Liberty, Equality, Fraternity*, ed. R. J. White (Cambridge University Press, Cambridge, 2nd edn., 1967), 135–41. First published 1874.]

PATRICK DEVLIN

55 The Enforcement of Morals

The criminal law of England has from the very first concerned itself with moral principles. A simple way of testing this point is to consider the attitude which the crminal law adopts towards consent.

Subject to certain exceptions inherent in the nature of particular crimes, the criminal law has never permitted consent of the victim to be used as a defence. In rape, for example, consent negatives an essential element. But consent of the victim is no defence to a charge of murder. It is not a defence to any form of assault that the victim thought his punishment well deserved and submitted to it; to make a good defence the accused must prove that the law gave him the right to chastise and that he exercised it reasonably. Likewise, the victim may not forgive the aggressor and require the prosecution to desist; the right to enter a *nolle prosequi* belongs to the Attorney-General alone.

Now, if the law existed for the protection of the individual, there would be no reason why he should avail himself of it if he did not want it. The reason why a man may not consent to the commission of an offence against himself beforehand or forgive it afterwards is because it is an offence against society. It is not that society is physically injured; that would be impossible. Nor indeed any individual be shocked, corrupted, or exploited; everything may be done in private. Nor can it be explained on the practical ground that a violent man is a potential danger to others in the community who have therefore a direct interest in his apprehension and punishment as being necessary to their own protection. That would be true of a man whom the victim is prepared to forgive but not of one who gets his consent first; a murderer who acts only upon the consent, and maybe the request, of his victim is no menace to others, but he does threaten one of the great moral principles upon which society is based, that is, the sanctity of human life. There is only one explanation of what has hitherto been accepted as the basis of the criminal law and that is that there are certain standards of behaviour or moral principles which society requires to be observed; and the breach of them is an offence not merely against the person who is injured but against society as a whole.

Thus, if the criminal law were to be reformed so as to eliminate from it everything that was not designed to preserve order and decency or to protect citizens (including the protection of youth from corruption), it would overturn a fundamental principle. It would also end a number of specific crimes. Euthanasia or the killing of another at his own request, suicide, attempted suicide and suicide pacts, duelling, abortion, incest between brother and sister, are all acts which can be done in private and without offence to others and need not involve the corruption or exploitation of others. Many people think that the law on some of these subjects is in need of reform, but no one hitherto has gone so far as to suggest that they should all be left outside the criminal law as matters of private morality. They can be brought within it only as a matter of moral principle. It must be remembered also that although there is much immorality that is not punished by the law, there is none that is condoned by the law. The law will not allow its processes to be used by those engaged in immorality of any sort. For example, a house may not be let for immoral purposes; the lease is invalid and would not be enforced. But if what goes on inside there is a matter of private morality and not the law's business, why does the law inquire into it at all?

I think it is clear that the criminal law as we know it is based upon moral principle. In a number of crimes its function is simply to enforce a moral principle and nothing else. The law, both criminal and civil, claims to be able to speak about morality and immorality generally. Where does it get its authority to do this and how does it settle the moral principles which it enforces? Undoubtedly, as a matter of history, it derived both from Christian teaching. But I think that the strict logician is right when he says that the law can no longer rely on doctrines in which citizens are entitled to disbelieve. It is necessary therefore to look for some other source. [. . .]

The fact that a majority of people may disapprove of a practice does not of itself make it a matter for society as a whole. Nine men out of ten may disapprove of what the tenth man is doing and still say that it is not their business. There is a case for a collective judgement (as distinct from a large number of individual opinions which sensible people may even refrain from pronouncing at all if it is upon somebody else's private affairs) only if society is affected. Without a collective judgement there can be no case at all for intervention. Let me take as an illustration the Englishman's attitude to religion as it is now and as it has been in the past. His attitude now is that a man's religion is his private affair; he may think of another man's religion that it is right or wrong, true or untrue, but not that it is good or bad. In earlier times that was not so; a man was denied the right to practise what was thought of as heresy, and heresy was thought of as destructive of society. [. . .]

What makes a society of any sort is community of ideas, not only political ideas but also ideas about the way its members should behave and govern their lives; these latter ideas are its morals. Every society has a moral structure as well as a political one: or rather, since that might suggest two independent systems, I should say that the structure of every society is made up both of politics and morals. [. . .]

The institution of marriage is a good example for my purpose because it bridges the division, if there is one, between politics and morals. Marriage is part of the structure of our society and it is also the basis of a moral code which condemns fornication and adultery. The institution of marriage would be gravely threatened if individual judgements were permitted about the morality of adultery; on these points there must be a public morality. But public morality is not to be confined to those moral principles which support institutions such as marriage. People do not think of monogamy as something which has to be supported because our society has chosen to organize itself upon it; they think of it as something that is good in itself and offering a good way of life and that it is for that reason that our society has adopted it. Society means a community of ideas; without shared ideas on politics, morals, and ethics no society can exist. Each one of us has ideas about what is good and what is evil; they cannot be kept private from the society in which we live. If men and women try to create a society in which there is no fundamental agreement about good and evil they will fail; if, having based it on common agreement, the agreement goes, the society will disintegrate. For society is not something that is kept together physically; it is held by the invisible bonds of common thought. If the bonds were too far relaxed the members would drift apart. A common morality is part of the bondage. The bondage is part of the price of society; and mankind, which needs society, must pay its price. [. . .]

The suppression of vice is as much the law's business as the suppression of subversive activities; it is no more possible to define a sphere of private morality than it is to define one of private subversive activity. It is wrong to talk of private morality or of the law not being concerned with immorality as such or to try to set rigid bounds to the part which the law may play in the suppression of vice. There are no theoretical limits to the power of the State to legislate against treason and sedition, and likewise I think there can be no theoretical limits to legislation against immorality. You may argue that if a man's sins affect only himself it cannot be the concern of society. If he chooses to get drunk every night in the privacy of his own home, is any one except himself the worse for it? But suppose a quarter or a half of the population got drunk every night, what sort of society would it be? You cannot set a theoretical limit to the number of people who can get drunk before society is entitled to legislate against drunkenness.

> [From 'Morals and the Criminal Law', in *The Enforcement of Morals* (Oxford University Press, Oxford, 1965), 6–10, 13–14. First published 1959 in *Proceedings of the British Academy*.]

H. L. A. HART

56 The Changing Sense of Morality

When we turn to the positive grounds held to justify the legal enforcement of morality it is important to distinguish a moderate and an extreme thesis, though critics of Mill have sometimes moved from one to the other without marking the transition. Lord Devlin seems to me to maintain, for most of his essay, the moderate thesis.

According to the moderate thesis, a shared morality is the cement of society; without it there would be aggregates of individuals but no society. 'A recognized morality' is, in Lord Devlin's words, 'as necessary to society's existence as a recognized government,' and though a particular act of immorality may not harm or endanger or corrupt others nor, when done in private, either shock or give offence to others, this does not conclude the matter. For we must not view conduct in isolation from its effect on the moral code: if we remember this, we can see that one who is 'no menace to others' nonetheless may by his immoral conduct 'threaten one of the great moral principles on which society is based.' In this sense the breach of moral principle is an offence 'against society as a whole,' and society may use the law to preserve its morality as it uses it to safeguard anything else essential to its existence. This is why 'the suppression of vice is as much the law's business as the suppression of subversive activities.' [. . .]

Lord Devlin appears to defend the moderate thesis. I say 'appears' because, though he says that society has the right to enforce a morality as such on the ground that a shared morality is essential to society's existence, it is not at all clear that for him the statement that immorality jeopardizes or weakens society is a statement of empirical fact. It seems sometimes to be an *a priori* assumption, and sometimes a necessary truth and a very odd one. The most important indication that this is so is that, apart from one vague reference to 'history' showing that 'the loosening of moral bonds is often the first stage of disintegration,' no evidence is produced to show that deviation from accepted sexual morality, even by adults in private, is something which, like treason, threatens the existence of society. No reputable historian has maintained this thesis, and there is indeed much evidence against it. As a proposition of fact it is entitled to no more respect than the Emperor Justinian's statement that homosexuality was the cause of earthquakes. Lord Devlin's belief in it, and his apparent indifference to the question of evidence, are at points traceable to an undiscussed assumption. This is that all morality—sexual morality together with the morality that forbids acts injurious to others such as killing, stealing, and dishonesty—forms a single seamless web, so that those who deviate from any part are likely or perhaps bound to deviate from the whole. It is of course clear (and one of the oldest insights of political theory) that society could not exist without a morality which mirrored and supplemented the law's proscription of conduct injurious to others. But there is again no evidence to support, and much to refute, the theory that those who deviate from conventional sexual morality are in other ways hostile to society.

There seems, however, to be central to Lord Devlin's thought something more interesting, though no more convincing, than the conception of social morality as a seamless web. For he appears to move from the acceptable proposition that *some* shared morality is essential to the existence of any society to the unacceptable proposition that a society is identical with its morality as that is at any given moment of its history, so that a change in its morality is tantamount to the destruction of a society. The former proposition might be even accepted as a necessary rather than an empirical truth depending on a quite plausible definition of society as a body of men who hold certain moral views in common. But the latter proposition is absurd. Taken strictly, it would prevent us saying that the morality of a given society had changed, and would compel us instead to say that one society had disappeared and another one taken its place. But it is only on this absurd criterion of what it is for the same society to continue to exist that it could be asserted without evidence that any deviation from a society's shared morality threatens its existence.

It is clear that only this tacit identification of a society with its shared morality supports Lord Devlin's denial that there could be such a thing as private immorality and his comparison of sexual immorality, even when it takes place 'in private,' with treason. No doubt it is true that if deviations from conventional sexual morality are tolerated by the law and come to be known, the conventional morality might change in a permissive direction, though this does not seem to be the case with homosexuality in those European countries where it is not punishable by law. But even if the conventional morality did so change, the society in question would not have been destroyed or 'subverted.' We should compare such a development not to the violent overthrow of government but to a peaceful constitutional change in its form, consistent not only with the preservation of a society but with its advance.

[From *Law Liberty and Morality* (Oxford University Press, Oxford, 1963), 48–52.]

JOHN LOCKE

57 **The Futility of Intolerance**

The Toleration of those that differ from others in Matters of Religion, is so agreeable to the Gospel of Jesus Christ, and to the genuine Reason of Mankind, that it seems monstrous for Men to be so blind, as not to perceive the Necessity and Advantage of it, in so clear a Light. I will not here tax the Pride and Ambition of some, the Passion and uncharitable Zeal of others. These are Faults from which Humane Affairs can perhaps scarce ever be perfectly freed; but yet such as no body will bear the plain Imputation of, without covering them with some specious Colour; and so pretend to Commendation, whilst they are carried away by their own irregular Passions. But however, that some may not colour their Spirit of Persecution and unchristian Cruelty with a Pretence of Care of the Publick Weal, and Observation of the Laws; and that others, under pretence of Religion, may not seek Impunity for their Libertinism and Licentiousness; in a word, that none may impose either upon himself or others, by the Pretences of Loyalty and Obedience to the Prince, or of Tenderness and Sincerity in the Worship of God; I esteem it above all things necessary to distinguish exactly the Business of Civil Government from that of Religion, and to settle the just Bounds that lie between the one and the other. If this be not done, there can be no end put to the Controversies that will be always arising, between those that have, or at least pretend to have, on the one side, a Concernment for the Interest of Mens Souls, and on the other side, a Care of the Commonwealth.

The Commonwealth seems to me to be a Society of Men constituted only for the procuring, preserving, and advancing of their own *Civil Interests*.

Civil Interests I call Life, Liberty, Health, and Indolency of Body; and the Possession of outward things, such as Money, Lands, Houses, Furniture, and the like.

It is the Duty of the Civil Magistrate, by the impartial Execution of equal Laws, to secure unto all the People in general, and to every one of his Subjects in particular, the just Possession of these things belonging to this Life. If any one presume to violate the Laws of Publick Justice and Equity, established for the Preservation of those things, his Presumption is to be check'd by the fear of Punishment, consisting of the Deprivation or Diminution of those Civil Interests, or Goods, which otherwise he might and ought to enjoy. But seeing no Man does willingly suffer himself to be punished by the Deprivation of any part of his Goods, and much less of his Liberty or Life, therefore is the Magistrate armed with the Force and Strength of all his Subjects, in order to the punishment of those that violate any other Man's Rights.

Now that the whole Jurisdiction of the Magistrate reaches only to these Civil Concernments; and that all Civil Power, Right and Dominion, is bounded and confined to the only care of promoting these things; and that it neither can nor ought in any manner to be extended to the Salvation of Souls, these following Considerations seem unto me abundantly to demonstrate.

First, Because the Care of Souls is not committed to the Civil Magistrate, any more than to other Men. It is not committed unto him, I say, by God; because it appears not that God has ever given any such Authority to one Man over another, as to compel any one to his Religion. Nor can any such Power be vested in the Magistrate by the *consent of the People*; because no man can so far abandon the care of his own Salvation, as blindly to leave it to the choice of any other, whether Prince or Subject, to prescribe to him what Faith or Worship he shall embrace. For no Man can, if he would, conform his Faith to the Dictates of another. All the Life and Power of true Religion consists in the inward and full persuasion of the mind; and Faith is not Faith without believing. Whatever Profession we make, to whatever outward Worship we conform, if we are not fully satisfied in our own mind that the one is true, and the other well pleasing unto God, such Profession and such Practice, far from being any furtherance, are indeed great Obstacles to our Salvation. For in this manner, instead of expiating other Sins by the exercise of Religion, I say in offering thus unto God Almighty such a Worship as we esteem to be displeasing unto him, we add unto the number of our other sins, those also of Hypocrisie, and Contempt of his Divine Majesty.

In the second place. The care of Souls cannot belong to the Civil Magistrate, because his Power consists only in outward force; but true and saving Religion consists in the inward persuasion of the Mind, without which nothing can be acceptable to God. And such is the nature of the Understanding, that it cannot be compell'd to the belief of any thing by outward force. Confiscation of Estate, Imprisonment, Torments, nothing of that nature can have any such Efficacy as to make Men change the inward Judgment that they have framed of things.

It may indeed be alleged, that the Magistrate may make use of Arguments, and thereby draw the Heterodox into the way of Truth, and procure their Salvation. I grant it; but this is common to him with other Men. In teaching, instructing, and redressing the Erroneous by Reason, he may certainly do what becomes any good Man to do. Magistracy does not oblige him to put off either Humanity or Christianity. But it is one thing to persuade, another to command; one thing to press with Arguments, another with Penalties. This Civil Power alone has a right to do; to the other Good-will is Authority enough. Every Man has Commission to admonish, exhort, convince another of Error, and by reasoning to draw him into Truth: but to give Laws, receive Obedience, and compel with the Sword, belongs to none but the Magistrate. And upon this ground

I affirm, that the Magistrate's Power extends not to the establishing of any Articles of Faith, or Forms of Worship, by the force of his Laws. For Laws are of no force at all without Penalties, and Penalties in this case are absolutely impertinent; because they are not proper to convince the mind. [. . .]

In the third place. The care of the Salvation of Mens Souls cannot belong to the Magistrate; because, though the rigour of Laws and the force of Penalties were capable to convince and change Mens minds, yet would not that help at all to the Salvation of their Souls. For there being but one Truth, one way to Heaven; what Hopes is there that more Men would be led into it, if they had no Rule but the Religion of the Court, and were put under a necessity to quit the Light of their own Reason, and oppose the Dictates of their own Consciences, and blindly to resign up themselves to the Will of their Governors, and to the Religion, which either Ignorance, Ambition, or Superstition had chanced to establish in the Countries where they were born? In the variety and contradiction of Opinions in Religion, wherein the Princes of the World are as much divided as in their Secular Interests, the narrow way would be much straitned; one Country alone would be in the right, and all the rest of the World put under an obligation of following their Princes in the ways that lead to Destruction; and that which heightens the absurdity, and very ill suits the Notion of a Deity, Men would owe their eternal Happiness or Misery to the places of their Nativity. [. . .]

The principal Consideration, and which absolutely determines this Controversie, is this. Although the Magistrates Opinion in Religion be sound, and the way that he appoints be truly Evangelical, yet if I be not thoroughly persuaded thereof in my own mind, there will be no safety for me in following it. No way whatsoever that I shall walk in, against the Dictates of my Conscience, will ever bring me to the Mansions of the Blessed. I may grow rich by an Art that I take not delight in; I may be cured of some Disease by Remedies that I have not Faith in; but I cannot be saved by a Religion that I distrust, and by a Worship that I abhor. It is in vain for an Unbeliever to take up the outward shew of another mans Profession. Faith only, and inward Sincerity, are the things that procure acceptance with God. The most likely and most approved Remedy can have no effect upon the Patient, if his Stomach reject it as soon taken. And you will in vain cram a Medicine down a sick mans Throat, which his particular Constitution will be sure to turn into Poison. In a word. Whatsoever may be doubtful in Religion, yet this at least is certain, that no Religion, which I believe not to be true, can be either true, or profitable unto me. In vain therefore do Princes compel their Subjects to come into their Church-communion, under pretence of saving their Souls. If they believe, they will come of their own accord; if they believe not, their coming will nothing avail them. How great soever, in fine, may be the pretence of Good-will, and Charity, and concern for the Salvation of mens Souls, men cannot be forced to be saved whether they will or no. And therefore, when all is done, they must be left to their own Consciences. [. . .]

That we may draw towards a Conclusion. The *Sum of all* we drive at is, *That every Man may enjoy the same Rights that are granted to others.* Is it permitted to worship God in the *Roman* manner? Let it be permitted to do it in the *Geneva* Form also. Is it permitted to speak *Latin* in the Market-place? Let those that have a mind to it, be permitted to do it also in the Church. Is it lawful for any man in his own House, to kneel, stand, sit, or use any other Posture; and to cloath himself in White or Black, in short or in long Garments? Let it not be made unlawful to eat Bread, drink Wine, or wash with Water, in the Church. In a Word: Whatsoever things are left free by Law in the common occasions of Life, let them remain free unto every Church in Divine Worship. Let no Mans Life, or Body, or House, or Estate, suffer any manner of Prejudice upon these Accounts.

[From John Locke, *A Letter Concerning Toleration*, ed. James Tully (Hackett, Indianapolis, 1983), 25–8, 38, 53. First published 1689.]

THOMAS SCANLON

58 Free Expression and the Authority of the State

If I were to say to you, an adult in full possession of your faculties, 'What you ought to do is rob a bank', and you were subsequently to act on this advice, I could not be held legally responsible for your act, nor could my act legitimately be made a separate crime. This remains true if I supplement my advice with a battery of arguments about why banks should be robbed or even about why a certain bank in particular should be robbed and why you in particular are entitled to rob it. It might become false—what I did might legitimately be made a crime—if certain further conditions held: for example, if you were a child, or so weak-minded as to be legally incompetent, and I knew this or ought to have known it; or if you were my subordinate in some organization and what I said to you was not advice but an order, backed by the discipline of the group; or if I went on to make further contributions to your act, such as aiding you in preparations or providing you with tools or giving you crucial information about the bank.

The explanation for these differences seems to me to be this. A person who acts on reasons he has acquired from another's act of expression acts on what *he* has come to believe and has judged to be a sufficient basis for action. The contribution to the genesis of his action made by the act of expression is, so to speak, superseded by the agent's own judgment. This is not true of the contribution made by an accomplice, or by a person who knowingly provides the agent with tools (the key to the bank) or with technical information (the combination of the safe) which he uses to achieve his ends. Nor would it be true of my contribution to your act if, instead of providing you with reasons for thinking bank robbery a good thing, I issued orders or commands backed by threats, thus changing your circumstances so as to make it a (comparatively) good thing for you to do. [. . .]

I will now state the principle of freedom of expression which was promised at the beginning of this section. The principle, which seems to me to be a natural extension of the thesis Mill defends in Chapter II of *On Liberty*, and which I will therefore call the Millian Principle, is the following:

There are certain harms which, although they would not occur but for certain acts of expression, nonetheless cannot be taken as part of a justification for legal restrictions on these acts. These harms are: (a) harms to certain individuals which consist in their coming to have false beliefs as a result of those acts of expression; (b) harmful consequences of acts performed as a result of those acts of expression, where the connection between the acts of expression and the subsequent harmful acts consist merely in the fact that the act of expression led the agents to believe (or increased their tendency to believe) these acts to be worth performing. [. . .]

I will defend the Millian Principle by showing it to be a consequence of the view that the powers of a state are limited to those that citizens could recognize while still regarding themselves as equal, autonomous, rational agents. Since the sense of autonomy to which I will appeal is extremely weak, this seems to me to constitute a strong defence of the Millian Principle as an exceptionless restriction on governmental authority.

To regard himself as autonomous in the sense I have in mind a person must see himself as sovereign in deciding what to believe and in weighing competing reasons for action. He must apply to these tasks his own canons of rationality, and must recognize the need to defend his beliefs and decisions in accordance with these canons. This does not mean, of course, that he must be perfectly rational, even by his own standard of rationality, or that his standard of rationality must be exactly ours. [. . .] For present purposes what will be important is this. An autonomous person cannot accept without independent consideration the judgment of others as to what he should believe or what he should do. He may rely on the judgment of others, but when he does so he must be prepared to advance independent reasons for thinking their judgment likely to be correct, and to weigh the evidential value of their opinion against contrary evidence. [. . .]

An autonomous man may, if he believes the appropriate arguments, believe that the state has a distinctive right to command him. That is, he may believe that (within certain limits, perhaps) the fact that the law requires a certain action provides him with a very strong reason for performing that action, a reason which is quite independent of the consequences, for him or others, of his performing it or refraining. How strong this reason is—what, if anything, could override it—will depend on his view of the arguments for obedience to law. [. . .]

Thus, while it is not obviously inconsistent with being autonomous to recognize a special obligation to obey the commands of the state, there are limits on the *kind* of obligation which autonomous citizens could recognize. In particular, they could not regard themselves as being under an 'obligation' to believe the decrees of the state to be correct, nor could they concede to the state the right to have its decrees obeyed without deliberation. The Millian Principle can be seen as a refinement of these limitations.

The apparent irrationality of the doctrine of freedom of expression derives from its apparent conflict with the principle that it is the prerogative of a state—indeed, part of its duty to its citizens—to decide when the threat of certain harms is great enough to warrant legal action, and when it is, to make laws adequate to meet this threat. [. . .] The Millian Principle specifies two ways in which this prerogative must be limited if the state is to be acceptable to autonomous subjects. The argument for the first part of the principle is as follows.

The harm of coming to have false beliefs is not one that an autonomous man could allow the state to protect him against through restrictions on expression. For a law to provide such protection it would have to be in effect and deterring potential misleaders while the potentially misled remained susceptible to persuasion by them. In order to be protected by such a law a person would thus have to concede to the state the right to decide that certain views were false and, once it had so decided, to prevent him from hearing them advocated even if he might wish to. The conflict between doing this and remaining autonomous would be direct if a person who authorized the state to protect him in this way necessarily also bound himself to accept the state's judgment about which views were false. [. . .]

The argument for the second half of the Millian Principle is parallel to this one. What must be argued against is the view that the state, once it has declared certain conduct to be illegal, may when necessary move to prevent that conduct by outlawing its advocacy. The conflict between this thesis and the autonomy of citizens is, just as in the previous case, slightly oblique. Conceding to the state the right to use this means to secure compliance with its laws does not immediately involve conceding to it the right to require citizens to believe that what the law says ought not to be done ought not to be done. None the less, it is a concession that autonomous citizens could not make, since it gives the state the right to deprive citizens of the grounds for arriving at an independent judgment as to whether the law should be obeyed.

[From 'A Theory of Freedom of Expression', *Philosophy and Public Affairs*, 1 (1972) 212–13, 215–18.]

To appeal to another for toleration is to invoke some value we both share. It is to say that something like knowledge, or freedom, or security, or even the bare possibility of a decent life for all will be imperiled unless we find a modus vivendi. But we cannot make that plea if we have no interests in common, or if all our interests are colored differently by our rival faiths and outlooks. If someone is convinced that life is literally not worth living, truth not worth seeking, or freedom not worth exercising in the company of the infidel, there is no foothold for argument.

Even if we have that foothold of common interest, it gets us only half the way. There is no evading the fact that lives erected on this common basis may differ profoundly in faith, meaning, and aspiration. Some are devout Muslims, some are Jews, some are Hindus, some are Catholics, some are Christian fundamentalists, some are fervent atheists, some are just trying to make it through their lives. What respect is due to those differences? How gingerly must we treat one another's religious sensibilities? Rushdie's critics say that he should have dealt more delicately, more seriously with the themes that he raised, or else avoided them altogether. What are we to say about that?

Toleration, mutual respect, live-and-let-live, can be conceived in different ways. On what we might call a one-dimensional account, toleration involves leaving people entirely alone with their faith and sensibilities. We are all to take care not to say anything that criticizes or cuts across the religious convictions of anyone else. If you believe that Jesus is the Son of God, who am I to contradict you? If I am the fool who says that there is no God, you must be equally circumspect. And both of us must take care not to say anything that treads on the sensibilities of someone who believes that it is the Koran that is the Word Incarnate.

But faith cannot be sealed off in this way. The religions of the world make *rival* claims about the nature and being of God and the meaning of human life. It is not possible for me to avoid criticizing the tenets of your faith without stifling my own. So mutual respect cannot possibly require us to refrain from criticism, if only because criticism of other sects is implicit already in the affirmations of any creed.

A second kind of toleration concedes this, and adds a dimension of debate. Criticism and discussion between rival faiths is fine and unavoidable, but two-dimensional toleration insists that it must be serious, earnest and respectful in its character. If I disagree with you about the existence of God, I may put forward my arguments, but I must do so in a way that is circumspect and inoffensive, taking full account of the fact that your religious beliefs are not just your *views*, but convictions which go to the core or essence of your being. I must be sensitive to the role these beliefs play in your life, and not deal with them lightly, sarcastically, or insultingly.

According to this model, *The Satanic Verses* went wrong, not in saying things against Islam, but in the offensive tone that it took. Rushdie spun fantasies, told ribald jokes, rehearsed heresies, used obscene language to make the points he wanted to make. He mocked the sacred, instead of asking us soberly to reconsider some doctrine.

Two-dimensional toleration would seem to combine the values of truth seeking—which John Stuart Mill made so much of in his essay *On Liberty*—with a principle of respect. It leaves room for debate, but it eschews mockery, offence, and insult. Above all it enables us to understand notions like sacrilege and blasphemy not as ideals internal to any religion, but as principles embodying what we owe to one another as humans, in respect for deeply held convictions.

But as soon as we say that, we begin to see the fallacy of two-dimensional toleration. What is serious and what is offensive, what is sober and what is mockery—these are not neutral ideas. They come as part of the package, and different religions define them in different ways. In some rabbinical traditions, theological debate proceeds through the telling of jokes. Some Muslim sects regard it as an unspeakable affront if a woman participates in religious discussion, no matter how sober her tone. For a long time in the Christian west, it was regarded as a capital mockery of the Almighty if one not in holy orders dared to debate the ways of God with man. This is exactly what we should expect; the demeanor with which religious disputation is to be conducted is itself an issue on which religious views are taken. It is bound up with the fact that faith addresses the deepest issues of truth, value, and knowledge. There is nothing necessarily privileged about the norms of civility that we call moral seriousness, and indeed requiring religious controversy to observe the ponderous debating rules of a Midwestern Rotary Club may be the worst, not the best, of both worlds.

By the same token, it is fatuous to think that there is a way of running a multicultural society without disturbance or offence. When Mill made his argument for free discussion, the disturbance of complacency and the shaking of faith were positive values in the debate. It is hard to see how free expression could do its work if it remained psychologically innocuous. In any case, there are some who hold their beliefs so devoutly that even the most sober and respectful criticism would count as a mortal insult to their personality. Some are so devout that the mere presence of the ungodly is more than they can bear. If the questions are as important as they seem, then distress at others' answers is part of the price of addressing them. Sensitivity is not trumps in this game; the stakes are already too high for that.

It would be different if religious faith were like a certain sort of posture or state of being, so that the seriousness with which one held oneself were not to be mocked by anyone else. But religious commitments have content: they address issues that have significance not only for one believer, but at least potentially for everyone. Is there a God? What is God like? What are His (or Her) purposes with us? What are we like? Why is there evil? These questions matter; nothing is more important. It cannot be that one person's style of answering (or even the style of a billion believers) precludes others from addressing the questions in the style that seems appropriate to them.

We are pushed, then, toward three-dimensional toleration. Persons and peoples must leave one another free to address the deep questions of religion and philosophy the best way they can, with all the resources they have at their disposal. In the modern world, that may mean the the whole kaleidoscope of literary technique—fantasy, irony, poetry, word-play, and the speculative juggling of ideas—is unleashed on what many regard as the holy, the good, the immaculate, and the indubitable.

How could it be otherwise? Either the issues are important or they are not. If they are, we know that they strain our resources of psyche and intellect. They drive us to the limits of linear disputation and beyond, for they address the edgy, the shy, the disturbing, the frightening, the knowable, and the unthinkable. The religions of the world make their claims, tell their stories, and consecrate their symbols, and all that goes out into the world too, as public property, as part of the cultural and psychological furniture which we cannot respectfully tiptoe around in our endeavour to make sense of our being. We have to do what we can with the questions, and make what we can of the answers that have been drummed into us.

It is sometimes said tritely that secular humanism is a religion like any other. The grain of truth in that view is that the issues the great religions address are implicitly issues for all of us. But if that's the case, the great religions cannot lay down the terms on which those issues are dealt with. For example, we all cast about for an understanding of ourselves, our bodies, and the intense experience of our sexuality. We find in our culture tales of pure and holy men, like Mohammed, and even the claim that God has taken human form, flesh and blood, in the person of Jesus Christ. Now incarnation itself is not a straightforward idea, and it beggars belief to say we are required to think about it without dealing edgily with the question of Christ's sexuality. In general, our view of the body is so bound up with what we are taught about holiness that we cannot prohibit the association of the sacred and the sexual in our attempt to come to terms with ourselves. Some may be able to hold the two apart, but their piety cannot clinch the issue of how others are to deal with this experience.

By the same token, we all cast about for an understanding of evil in the world. There is disease, there are great crimes, children are killed in their millions, the heavens are silent, and there seems no sense in it. We know the great religions address the issue shyly and indirectly, with a cornucopia of images and stories. Satan lays a wager with God that Job, a good and holy man, can be brought by misfortune to curse Him to His face—a story which, if it were not already in the Bible, might have earned its publisher a firebomb or two. The point is not a cute *tu quoque*: it is that no one even within the religious traditions thinks this can be addressed without the full range of fantastic and poetical technique. Once again, respect for the sensitivities of some cannot in conscience be used to limit the means available to others to come to terms with the problem of evil. It is already too important for that.

Three-dimensional toleration is not an easy ideal to live with. Things that seem sacred to some will in the hands of others be played with, joked about, taken seriously, taken lightly, sworn at, fantasized upon, juggled, dreamed about backward, sung about, and mixed up with all sorts of stuff. This is what happens in *The Satanic Verses*. It is not a solemn theological disquisition, and it is not to be defended as such. Nor is it to be defended as a work of art that just happens to include some regrettable passages. Like all modern literature, it is a way of trying to make sense of human experience. It touches on some problems that Islam addresses, and it invokes images and narratives with which Islam has colored Rushdie's world. It does so playfully and kaleidoscopically, but that doesn't mean that the themes matter less to the author than they do to the millions of the faithful.

It may be too late to make a case for Salman Rushdie's freedom from terror and the threat of assassination. But if we make a plea for others like him in the world, it must be on this high ground—that the great themes of religion matter too much to be closeted by the sensitivity of those who are counted as the pious. There is no other way we can live together and respect each other's grappling with life.

[From 'Rushdie and Religion', in *Liberal Rights* (Cambridge University Press, Cambridge, 1993), 137–42. Originally published in *Times Literary Supplement*, 10–16 March 1989, pp. 248 and 260.]

CATHARINE MACKINNON

60 Only Words

The law of equality and the law of freedom of speech are on a collision course. Free speech protections have developed worldwide without taking seriously the problems of social inequality or the need for substantive legal equality. The tension between equality and speech stands out particularly in the United States, where both rights have been highly developed but each out of sight of the other.

Originally, the US Constitution contained no equality guarantee to serve as context, expansion joint, handmaiden, counterbalance or co-equal goal to the speech guarantee. Yet its modern doctrine of speech dates from considerably after the entrenchment of equality in the Fourteenth Amendment, and still the

First Amendment has been interpreted, with a few exceptions, as if the Fourteenth were not there. In Europe, equality and speech have been equally present in the European Convention from the beginning, but they have not noticed each other yet, or at least have left no visible marks of engagement.

In the United States, the law of freedom of expression has grown as if a commitment to speech were no part of a commitment to equality and as if a commitment to equality had no implications for the law of speech. It is as if the Civil War, the upheaval that produced the Reconstruction Amendments, did not move the ground under the expressive freedom, setting new limits and mandating new extensions, perhaps even demanding reconstruction of the speech right itself. The version of equality that *has* become part of First Amendment law has been negative—equally keeping law from regulating one forum or view as another—and formal—speech protected for one group or interest is equally protected for others. It is, in other words, largely redundant. The subprovince of the First Amendment that resonates in equal protection is simply an unbiased extension of precedent and the rule of law—a narrow equality supporting a shallow speech. Fourteenth Amendment equality, for its part, has grown as if equality could be achieved while the First Amendment protects the speech of inequality, meaning whenever inequality takes an expressive form, and without considering equal access to speech as central to any equality agenda.

Although it is worst in the United States, nowhere in the world is the law of speech systematically sensitive to the damage done to social equality by expressive means or to the fact that some people get a lot more speech than others. In the absence of these recognitions, the power of those who have speech has become more and more exclusive, coercive, and violent as it has become more and more legally protected. Understanding that there is a relationship between these two issues—the less speech you have, the more the speech of those who have it keeps you unequal; the more the speech of the dominant is protected, the more dominant they become and the less the subordinated are heard from—is virtually nonexistent. [. . .]

Because society is made of language, distinguishing talk about inferiority from verbal imposition of inferiority may be complicated at the edges, but it is clear enough at the centre with sexual and racial harassment, pornography, and hate propaganda. At the very least, when equality is taken seriously in expressive settings, such practices are not constitutionally insulated from regulation on the ground that the ideas they express cannot be regarded as false. Attempts to address them would not be prohibited—as they were in rejecting the Indianapolis pornography ordinance, for example—on the ground that, in taking a position in favor of equality, such attempts assume that the idea of human equality is true. The legal equality guarantee has already decided that. There is no requirement that the state remain neutral as between equality and inequality—quite the contrary. Equality is a 'compelling state interest' that can already outweigh First Amendment rights in certain settings. In other words, expressive means of practicing inequality can be prohibited.

This is not the place to spell out in detail all the policy implications of such a view. Suffice it to say that those who wish to keep materials that promote inequality from being imposed on students—such as academic books purporting to document women's biological inferiority to men, or arguments that slavery of Africans should return, or that the Fourteenth Amendment equality should be repealed, or that reports of rape are routinely fabricated—especially without critical commentary, should not be legally precluded from trying on the grounds that the ideas contained in them cannot be assumed false. No teacher should be forced to teach falsehoods as if they must be considered provisionally true, just because bigots who have managed to get published have made their lies part of a debate. Teachers who wish to teach such materials should be prepared to explain what they are doing to avoid creating a hostile learning environment and to provide all students the equal benefit of an education. Wherever equality is mandated, racial and sexual epithets, vilification, and abuse should be able to be prohibited, unprotected by guarantees of free speech. In the United States, for example, the current legal distinction between screaming 'go kill that nigger' and advocating the view that African–Americans should be eliminated from parts of the country needs to be seriously reconsidered, if real equality is ever to be achieved, as does the current line worldwide that separates what is done to make pornography from what are termed the materials themselves.

Pornography, under current conditions, is largely its own context. Many believe that in settings that encourage critical distance, its showing does not damage women as much as it sensitizes views to the damage it does to women. My experience, as well as all the information available, makes me think that it is naive to believe that anything other words can do is as powerful as what pornography itself does. At the very least, pornography should never be imposed on a viewer who does not choose—then and there, without pressure of any kind— to be exposed to it. Tom Emerson said a long time ago that imposing what he called 'erotic material' on individuals against their will is a form of action that 'has all the characteristics of a physical assault'. Equality on campuses, in workplaces, everywhere, would be promoted if such assaults were actionable. Why any woman should have to attend school in a setting stacked against her equality by the showing of pornography—especially when authoritatively permitted by those who are legally obligated to take her equality seriously—is a question that those who support its showing should have to answer. The answer is not that she should have to wait for the resulting abuse or leave.

Where is all this leading? To a new model for freedom of expression in which the free speech position no longer supports social dominance, as it does now; in which free speech does not most readily protect the activities of Nazis, Klansmen, and pornographers, while doing nothing for their victims, as it does now;

in which defending free speech is not speaking on behalf of a large pile of money in the hands of a small group of people, as it is now. In this new model, principle will be defined in terms of specific experiences, the particularity of history, substantively rather than abstractly. It will notice who is being hurt and never forget who they are. The state will have as great a role in providing relief from injury to equality through speech and in giving equal access to speech, as it now has in disciplining its power to intervene in that speech which manages to get expressed.

In a society in which equality is a fact, not merely a word, words of racial or sexual assault and humiliation will be nonsense syllables. Sex between people and things, human beings and pieces of paper, real men and unreal women, will be a turn-off. Artifacts of these abuses will reside under glass in museums next to the dinosaur skeletons. When this day comes, silence will be neither an act of power, as it is now for those who hide behind it, nor an experience of imposed powerlessness, as it is now for those who are submerged in it, but a context of repose into which thought can expand, an invitation that gives speech its shape, an opening to a new conversation.

[From *Only Words* (Harvard University Press, Cambridge, Mass., 1993), 51–2, 75–8.]

IV.d. Virtue and Citizenship

61 The Democratic Citizen

'Let me say that our system of government does not copy the institutions of our neighbours. It is more the case of our being a model to others, than of our imitating anyone else. Our constitution is called a democracy because power is in the hands not of a minority but of the whole people. When it is a question of settling private disputes, everyone is equal before the law; when it is a question of putting one person before another in positions of public responsibility, what counts is not membership of a particular class, but the actual ability which the man possesses. No one, so long as he has it in him to be of service to the state, is kept in political obscurity because of poverty. And, just as our political life is free and open, so is our day-to-day life in our relations with each other. We do not get into a state with our next-door neighbour if he enjoys himself in his own way, nor do we give him the kind of black looks which, though they do no real harm, still do hurt people's feelings. We are free and tolerant in our private lives; but in public affairs we keep to the law. This is because it commands our deep respect.

'We give our obedience to those whom we put in positions of authority, and we obey the laws themselves, especially those which are for the protection of the oppressed, and those unwritten laws which it is an acknowledged shame to break. [. . .]

'Our love of what is beautiful does not lead to extravagance; our love of the things of the mind does not make us soft. We regard wealth as something to be properly used, rather than as something to boast about. As for poverty, no one need be ashamed to admit it: the real shame is in not taking practical measures to escape from it. Here each individual is interested not only in his own affairs but in the affairs of the state as well: even those who are mostly occupied with their own business are extremely well-informed on general politics—this is a peculiarity of ours: we do not say that a man who takes no interest in politics is a man who minds his own business; we say that he has no business here at all. We Athenians, in our own persons, take our decisions on policy or submit them to proper discussions: for we do not think that there is an incompatibility between words and deeds; the worst thing is to rush into action before the consequences have been properly debated. And this is another point where we differ from other people. We are capable at the same time of taking risks and of estimating them beforehand. Others are brave out of ignorance; and, when they stop to think, they begin to fear. But the man who can most truly be accounted brave is he who best knows the meaning of what is sweet in life and of what is terrible, and then goes out undeterred to meet what is to come.

'Again, in questions of general good feeling there is a great contrast between us and most other people. We make friends by doing good to others, not by receiving good from them. This makes our friendship all the more reliable, since we want to keep alive the gratitude of those who are in our debt by showing continued good-will to them: whereas the feelings of one who owes us something lack the same enthusiasm, since he knows that, when he repays our kindness, it will be more like paying back a debt than giving something spontaneously. We are unique in this. When we do kindnesses to others, we do not do them out of any calculations of profit or loss: we do them without afterthought, relying on our free liberality. Taking everything together then, I declare that our city is an education to Greece, and I declare that in my opinion each single one of our citizens, in all the manifold aspects of life, is able to show himself the rightful lord and owner of his own person, and do this, moreover, with exceptional grace and exceptional versatility.

[From Pericles' Funeral Oration, in Thucydides, *History of the Peloponnesian War*, trans. Rex Warner with introd. by M. I. Finley, (Penguin, Harmondsworth, 1972), 145, 147–8.]

ARISTOTLE

62   The Requirements of Citizenship

Connected with these matters is the following question: are we to say that the goodness of a good man and a good citizen are the same, or not? If this ought to be examined, we must first get some outline of the goodness of the citizen. We say, then, that the citizen, like the sailor, is one of the partners in a society. Sailors are unlike each other in capacity: one is an oarsman, another a helmsman, another a bowman, and others have other such names;but it is clear that, while the most precise account of each one's goodness will be peculiar to himself, there will also be some common account fitting them all alike. The safety of the voyage is the business of them all, for each of the sailors aims at that. Similarly the citizens, though unlike each other, have the safety of the society as their business; and their society is the constitution. Hence the goodness of the citizen must be relative to the constitution; and, since there are several kinds of constitution, there clearly cannot be one single goodness of the good citizen, namely perfect goodness. But the good man, we say, has one single goodness, namely perfect goodness. Plainly, therefore, it is possible to be a good citizen and yet not possess the goodness of a good man.

One can go into the same argument by raising the question in another way, namely with regard to the best constitution. For, if it is impossible for a city to consist entirely of good men, it is nevertheless necessary that each should do his own job well, and do it out of goodness; but, since it is impossible for the citizens to be all alike, there would not be one single goodness of a citizen and a good man. This is because the goodness of the good citizen must belong to them all (only so can the city be the best), whereas the goodness of the good man cannot do so, since the citizens in the good city cannot all be good men.

Moreover, the city consists of unlike members. As an animal consists of soul and body, and a soul of reason and desire, and a household of man and woman, and a proprietorship of master and slave, so a city consists of all these and of other unlike forms in addition. Necessarily, therefore, the goodness of all the citizens is no more identical than is that of the leader and the sideman in a chorus.

That it is not always the same is plain from these considerations. But will there be anyone in whom the goodness of a citizen and the goodness of a man do coincide? We say that the good ruler is also a good and wise man, but that the citizen need not be wise. Some say that the very upbringing of a ruler is different. The sons of kings appear to be brought up on the arts of riding and war. And Euripides says:

> No subtleties for me . . .,
> But what a city needs . . .,

implying that a ruler has a special upbringing. If then the goodness of a good ruler is identical with that of a good man, while the subject also is a citizen, the goodness of a man would be identical with that of a certain citizen but not with that of every citizen. The goodness of a ruler and of a citizen are not the same. Perhaps this is why Jason said he was hungry when not a tyrant: he did not know how to be a private man.

Furthermore, we praise the power to rule and to obey, and it seems that the goodness of an approved citizen consists in being able both to rule and to obey well. If therefore we make the goodness of the man to consist in ruling, but that of the citizen in both, the two would not be equally praiseworthy. Since then there are occasions when they seem different, and ruler and subject should not learn the same things, while the citizen should know and share in both, the consequence becomes clear. [. . .]

One problem concerning the citizen remains: Is it really the case that the citizen is he who has the right to take part in the government, or should we call workmen also citizens?

If we are to include these persons also, who have no part in governing, such goodness cannot belong to every citizen, this man being a citizen. But, if such a person is not a citizen, in what class are we to put him? He is not a resident foreigner, nor a stranger.

Can we not say that there is no absurdity here? He is in the same position as slaves and freedmen. It is certain that we must not call citizens all those without whom there would be no city. Even children are not citizens in the same way as adults. Adults are citizens simply; but children are only hypothetically so. They are citizens, but imperfect ones.

In ancient times the working class was slave or foreign in some places, which is why most of them are so today; and the best city will not make a workman a citizen. If, however, he too is a citizen, then we must say that the goodness we spoke of does not belong to every citizen, nor to every free man, but only to those who are released from necessary services. Those who provide necessary services for one man are slaves. Those who do it for the community are workmen and labourers.

[From *Politics Books III and IV*, trans. with introd. and comments by Richard Robinson (Clarendon Press, Oxford, 1995), 10–12, 15–16.]

NICCOLO MACHIAVELLI

63   The Servility of the Moderns

If one asks oneself how it comes about that the peoples of old were more fond of liberty than they are today, I think the answer is that it is due to the same cause that makes men today less bold than they used to be; and this is due, I think, to the difference between our education and that of bygone times, which is based on the difference between our religion and the religion of those days. For our religion, having taught us the truth and the true way of life, leads us to ascribe less esteem to worldly honour. Hence the gentiles, who held it in high esteem and looked upon it as their highest good, displayed in their actions more ferocity than we do. This is evidenced by many of their institutions. To begin with, compare the magnificence of their sacrifices with the humility that characterizes ours. The ceremonial in ours is delicate rather than imposing, and there is no display of ferocity or courage. Their ceremonies lacked neither pomp nor magnificence, but, conjoined with this, were sacrificial acts in which there was much shedding of blood and much ferocity; and in them great numbers of animals were killed. Such spectacles, because terrible, caused men to become like them. Besides, the old religion did not beatify men unless they were replete with worldly glory: army commanders, for instance, and rulers of republics. Our religion has glorified humble and contemplative men, rather than men of action. It has assigned as man's highest good humility, abnegation, and contempt for mundane things, whereas the other identified it with magnanimity, bodily strength, and everything else that conduces to make men very bold. And, if our religion demands that in you there be strength, what it asks for is strength to suffer rather than strength to do bold things.

This pattern of life, therefore, appears to have made the world weak, and to have handed it over as a prey to the wicked, who run it successfully and securely since they are well aware that the generality of men, with paradise for their goal, consider how best to bear, rather than how best to avenge, their injuries. But, though it looks as if the world were become effeminate and as if heaven were powerless, this undoubtedly is due rather to the pusillanimity of those who have interpreted our religion in terms of *laissez faire*, not in terms of *virtù*. For, had they born in mind that religion permits us to exalt and defend the fatherland, they would have seen that it also wishes us to love and honour it, and to train ourselves to be such that we may defend it.

This kind of education, then, and these grave misinterpretations account for the fact that we see in the world fewer republics than there used to be of old, and that, consequently, in peoples we do not find the same love of liberty as there then was.

> [From *The Discourses*, translation copyright Routledge 1950 (Penguin, Harmondsworth, 1970), 276–9. Written around 1513.]

ALEXIS DE TOCQUEVILLE

64 The Nature of Modern Servitude

Democratic governments may become violent and even cruel at certain periods of extreme effervescence or of great danger, but these crises will be rare and brief. When I consider the petty passions of our contemporaries, the mildness of their manners, the extent of their education, the purity of their religion, the gentleness of their morality, their regular and industrious habits, and the restraint which they almost all observe in their vices no less than in their virtues, I have no fear that they will meet with tyranny in their rules, but rather with guardians.

I think, then, that the species of oppression by which democratic nations are menaced is unlike anything that ever before existed in the world; our contemporaries will find no prototype of it in their memories. I seek in vain for an expression that will accurately convey the whole of the idea I have formed of it; the old words *despotism* and *tyranny* are inappropriate: the thing itself is new, and since I cannot name, I must attempt to defend it.

I seek to trace the novel features under which despotism may appear in the world. The first thing that strikes the observation is an innumerable multitude of men, all equal and alike, incessantly endeavoring to procure the petty and paltry pleasures with which they glut their lives. Each of them, living apart, is as a stranger to the fate of all the rest; his children and his private friends constitute to him the whole of mankind. As for the rest of his fellow citizens, he is close to them, but does not see them; he touches them, but he does not feel them; he exists only in himself and for himself alone; and if his kindred still remain to him, he may be said at any rate to have lost his country.

Above this race of men stands an immense and tutelary power, which takes upon itself alone to secure their gratifications and to watch over their fate. That power is absolute, minute, regular, provident, and mild. It would be like the authority of a parent if, like that authority, its object was to prepare men for manhood; but it seeks, on the contrary, to keep them in perpetual childhood: it is well content that the people should rejoice, provided they think of nothing but rejoicing. For their happiness such a government willingly labors, but it chooses to be the sole agent and the only arbiter of that happiness; it provides for their security, foresees and supplies their necessities, facilitates their pleasures, manages their principal concerns, directs their industry, regulates the descent of property, and subdivides their inheritances: what remains, but to spare them all the care of thinking and all the trouble of living?

Thus it every day renders the exercise of the free agency of man less useful and less frequent; it circumscribes the will within a narrower range and gradually robs a man of all the uses of himself. The principle of equality has prepared men for these things; it has predisposed men to endure them and often to look on them as benefits.

After having thus successively taken each member of the community in its powerful grasp and fashioned him at will, the supreme power then extends its arm over the whole community. It covers the surface of society with a network of small complicated rules, minute and uniform, through which the most original minds and the most energetic characters cannot penetrate, to rise above the crowd. The will of man is not shattered, but softened, bent, and guided; men are seldom forced by it to act, but they are constantly restrained from acting. Such a power does not destroy, but it prevents existence; it does not tyrannize, but it compresses, enervates, extinguishes, and stupefies a people, till each nation is reduced to nothing better than a flock of timid and industrious animals, of which the government is the shepherd.

I have always thought that servitude of the regular, quiet, and gentle kind which I have just described might be combined more easily than is commonly believed with some of the outward forms of freedom, and that it might even establish itself under the wing of the sovereignty of the people.

Our contemporaries are constantly excited by two conflicting passions: they want to be led, and they wish to remain free. As they cannot destroy either the one or the other of these contrary propensities, they strive to satisfy them both at once. They devise a sole, tutelary, and all-powerful form of government, but elected by the people. They combine the principle of centralization and that of popular sovereignty; this gives them a respite: they console themselves for being in tutelage by the reflection that they have chosen their own guardians. Every man allows himself to be put in leading-strings, because he sees that it is not a person or a class of persons, but the people at large who hold the end of his chain.

[From *Democracy in America*, vol. ii (Vintage Books, New York, 1945), 335–7. First published 1835.]

65 The Republican Ideal of Political Liberty

I

'The crucial moral opposition', Alasdair MacIntyre has recently claimed, 'is be-tween liberal individualism in some version or other and the Aristotelian tradi-tion in some version or other.'[1] Part of the significance of the republican tradition analysed in this book lies in suggesting that this is a false dichotomy. I should like to end by underlining this point, seeking to do so by way of concen-trating on the 'republican' theory of political liberty. I want in particular to focus on two distinctively 'republican' claims about liberty which are apt to be dismissed as paradoxical or merely confused, but which ought I think to be seen as constituting a challenge to our received views on the subject.[2]

First a word about what I mean by speaking, as I have just done, about our re-ceived views on political liberty. I have in mind the fact that, in recent discus-sions of the concept among analytical philosophers, one conclusion has been reached which commands a remarkably wide measure of assent. It can best be expressed in the formula originally introduced into the argument by Jeremy Bentham and recently made famous by Isaiah Berlin.[3] The suggestion is that the idea of political liberty is essentially a negative one. The presence of liberty is al-ways marked by the absence of something else; specifically, by the absence of some element of constraint which inhibits an agent from being able to act in pursuit of his or her chosen ends, from being able to pursue different options, or at least from being able to choose between alternatives.[4]

Hobbes bequeathed a classic statement of this point of view—one that is still repeatedly invoked—in his chapter 'Of the Liberty of Subjects' in *Leviathan*. He begins by assuring us, with typical briskness, that 'liberty or freedom signifieth (properly) the absence of opposition'—and signifies nothing more.[5] Locke makes the same point in the *Essay*, where he speaks with even greater confi-dence. 'Liberty, 'tis plain, consists in a power to do or not to do; to do or forbear doing as we will. This cannot be denied'.[6]

Among contemporary analytical philosophers, this basic contention has generally been unpacked into two propositions, the formulation of which ap-pears in many cases to reflect the influence of Gerald MacCallum's classic paper on negative and positive freedom.[7] The first states that there is only one coher-ent way of thinking about political liberty, that of treating the concept nega-tively as the absence of impediments to the pursuit of one's chosen ends.[8] The other proposition states that all such talk about negative liberty can in turn be shown, often despite appearances, to reduce to the discussion of one particular triadic relationship between agents, constraints, and ends. All debates about lib-erty are thus held to consist in effect of disputes either about who are to count as agents, or what are to count as constraints, or what range of things an agent must be free to do, be, or become (or not be or become) in order to count as being at liberty.[9]

I now turn to the two claims about political liberty which, in the light of these assumptions, are apt to be stigmatised as confused. The first connects freedom with self-government, and in consequence links the idea of personal liberty, in a seemingly paradoxical way, with that of public service. The thesis, as Charles Taylor has recently expressed it, is that we can only be free within a 'society of a certain canonical form, incorporating true self-government'.[10] If we wish to assure our own individual liberty, it follows that we must devote ourselves as wholeheartedly as possible to a life of public service, and thus to the cultivation of the civic virtues required for participating most effectively in political life. The attainment of our fullest liberty, in short, presupposes our recognition of the fact that only certain determinate ends are rational for us to pursue.[11]

The other and related thesis states that we may have to be forced to be free, and thus connects the idea of individual liberty, in an even more blatantly paradoxical fashion, with the concepts of coercion and constraint. The assumption underlying this further step in the argument is that we may sometimes fail to remember—or may altogether fail to grasp—that the performance of our public duties is indispensable to the maintenance of our own liberty. If it is nevertheless true that freedom depends on service, and hence on our willingness to cultivate the civic virtues, it follows that we may have to be coerced into virtue and thereby constrained into upholding a liberty which, left to ourselves, we would have undermined.

II

Among contemporary theorists of liberty who have criticised these arguments, we need to distinguish two different lines of attack. One of these I shall consider in the present section, the other I shall turn to discuss in section III.

The most unyielding retort has been that, since the negative analysis of liberty is the only coherent one, and since the two contentions I have isolated are incompatible with any such analysis, it follows that they cannot be embodied in any satisfactory account of social freedom at all.

We already find Hobbes taking this view of the alleged relationship between social freedom and public service in the course of his highly influential attack on Renaissance republicanism in *Leviathan*. In Chapter 21 he tells us with scorn about the Lucchese, who have 'written on the turrets of the city of Lucca in great characters, at this day, the word LIBERTAS', in spite of the fact that the constitution of their small-scale city-republic placed heavy demands upon their public-spiritedness.[12] To Hobbes, for whom liberty (as we have seen) simply means absence of interference, it seems obvious that the maximising of our social freedom must depend upon our capacity to maximise the area within which we can claim 'immunity from the service of the commonwealth'.[13] So it seems to him merely absurd of the Lucchese to proclaim their liberty in circumstances in which such services are so stringently exacted. Hobbes' modern sympathisers regularly make the same point. As Oppenheim puts it, for example, in his recent book *Political Concepts*, the claim that we can speak of 'freedom of participation in the political process' is simply confused.[14] Freedom presupposes the absence of any such obligation or constraints. So this 'so-called freedom of participation does not relate to freedom in any sense'.[15]

We find the same line of argument advanced even more frequently in the case of the other claim I am considering: that our freedom may have to be the fruit of our being coerced. Consider, for example, how Raphael handles this suggestion in his *Problems of Political Philosophy*. He simply reiterates the contention that 'when we speak of having or not having liberty or freedom in a political context, we are referring to freedom of action or social freedom, i.e., the absence of restraint or compulsion by human agency, including compulsion by the State'.[16] To suggest, therefore, that 'compulsion by the State can make a man more free' is not merely to state a paradoxical conclusion; it is to present an 'extraordinary view' that simply consists of confusing two polar opposites, freedom and constraint.[17] Again, Oppenheim makes the same point. Since freedom consists in the absence of constraint, to suggest that someone might be 'forced to be free' is no longer to speak of freedom at all but 'its opposite'.[18]

What are we to think of this first line of attack, culminating as it does in the suggestion that, as Oppenheim expresses it, neither of the arguments I have isolated 'relate to freedom in any sense'?

It seems to me that this conclusion relies on dismissing, far too readily, a different tradition of thought about social freedom which, at this point in my argument, it becomes important briefly to lay out.

The tradition I have in mind is essentially the Aristotelian one, which may be said to be founded on two distinctive and highly influential premises. The first, developed in various subsequent systems of naturalistic ethics, claims that we are moral beings with certain characteristically human purposes. The second, later taken up in particular by scholastic political philosophy, adds that the human animal is *naturale sociale et politicum*, and thus that our purposes must be essentially social in character.[19] The view of human freedom to which these assumptions give rise is thus a 'positive' one. We can only be said to be fully or genuinely at liberty, according to this account, if we actually engage in just those activities which are most conducive to *eudaimonia* or 'human flourishing', and may therefore be said to embody our deepest human purposes.

I have no wish to defend the truth of these premises. I merely wish to underline what the above account already makes clear: that if they are granted, a positive theory of liberty flows from them without the least paradox or incoherence.

This has two important implications for my present argument. One is that the basic claim advanced by the theorists of negative liberty I have so far been considering would appear to be false. They have argued that all coherent theories of liberty must have a certain triadic structure. But the theory of social freedom I have just stated, although perfectly coherent if we grant its premises, has a strongly contrasting shape.[20]

The contrast can be readily spelled out. The structure within which MacCallum and his numerous followers insist on analysing all claims about social freedom is such that they make it a sufficient condition of an agent's being at liberty that he or she should be unconstrained from pursuing some particular option, or at least from choosing between alternatives. Freedom, in the terminology Charles Taylor has recently introduced, becomes a pure opportunity concept.[21] I am already free if I have the opportunity to act, whether or not I happen to make use of that opportunity. By contrast, the positive theory I have just laid out makes it a necessary condition of an agent's being fully or truly at liberty that he or she should actually engage in the pursuit of certain determinate ends. Freedom, to invoke Taylor's terminology once more, is viewed not as an opportunity but as an exercise concept.[22] I am only in the fullest sense in possession of my liberty if I actually exercise the capacities and pursue the goals that serve to realise my most distinctively human purposes.

The other implication of this positive analysis is even more important for my present argument. According to the negative theories I have so far considered, the two claims I began by isolating can safely be dismissed as misunderstandings of the concept of liberty.[23] According to some, indeed, they are far worse than misunderstandings; they are 'patent sophisms' that are really designed, in consequence of sinister ideological commitments, to convert social freedom 'into something very different, if not its opposite'.[24] Once we recognise, however, that the positive view of liberty stemming from the thesis of naturalism is a perfectly coherent one, we are bound to view these claims in a quite different light.

There ceases, in the first place, to be any self-evident reason for impugning the motives of those who have defended them.[25] Belief in the idea of 'human flourishing' and its accompanying vision of social freedom arises at a far deeper level than that of mere ideological debate. It arises as an attempt to answer one of the central questions in moral philosophy, the question whether it is rational to be moral. The suggested answer is that it is in fact rational, the reason being that we have an interest in morality, the reason for this in turn being the fact that we are moral agents committed by our very natures to certain normative ends. We may wish to claim that this theory of human nature is false. But we can hardly claim to know a priori that it could never in principle be sincerely held.

We can carry this argument a stage further, moreover, if we revert to the particular brand of Thomist and Aristotelian naturalism I have singled out. Suppose for the sake of argument we accept both its distinctive premises: not only that human nature embodies certain moral purposes, but that these purposes are essentially social in character as well. If we do so, the two claims I began by isolating not only cease to look confused; they both begin to look highly plausible.

Consider first the alleged connection between freedom and public service. We are supposing that human nature has an essence, and that this is social and political in character. But this makes it almost truistic to suggest that we may need to establish one particular form of political association—thereafter devoting ourselves to serving and sustaining it—if we wish to realise our own natures and hence our fullest liberty. For the form of association we shall need to maintain will of course be just that form in which our freedom to be our true selves is capable of being realised as completely as possible.

Finally, consider the paradox that connects this idea of freedom with constraint. If we need to serve a certain sort of society in order to become most fully ourselves, we can certainly imagine tensions arising between our apparent interests and the duties we need to discharge if our true natures, and hence our fullest liberty, are both to be realised. But in those circumstances we can scarcely call it paradoxical—though we may certainly find it disturbing—if we are told what Rousseau tells us so forcefully in *The Social Contract*: that if anyone regards 'what he owes to the common cause as a gratuitous contribution, the loss of which would be less painful for others than the payment is onerous for him', then he must be 'forced to be free', coerced into enjoying a liberty he will otherwise allow to degenerate into servitude.[26]

III

I now turn to assess the other standpoint from which my two opening claims about liberty have commonly been dismissed. The theorists I now wish to discuss have recognised that there may well be more than one coherent way of thinking about the idea of political liberty. Sometimes they have even suggested, in line with the formula used in Isaiah Berlin's classic essay, that there may be more than one coherent *concept* of liberty.[27] As a result, they have sometimes explicitly stated that there may be theories of liberty within which the two seemingly paradoxical contentions I have singled out no longer appear to be paradoxical at all. As Berlin himself emphasises, for example, several 'positive' theories of freedom, religious as well as political, seem readily able to encompass the suggestion that people may have to act 'in certain self-improving ways, which they could be coerced to do' if there is to be any prospect of realising their fullest or truest liberty.[28]

When such writers express doubts about the two claims I am considering, therefore, their thesis is not that they are incapable of being accommodated within any coherent theory of liberty. It is only that they are incapable of being accommodated within any coherent theory of negative liberty—any theory in which the idea of liberty itself is equated with the mere absence of impediments to the realisation of one's chosen ends. To put the argument in the form in which my opening quotation from MacIntyre appears to advance it, the suggestion is that the two claims I began by isolating can *only* be rendered coherent within an essentially Aristotelian structure of thought.

This appears, for example, to be Isaiah Berlin's view of the matter in his 'Two Concepts of Liberty'. Citing Cranmer's epigram 'Whose service is perfect freedom', Berlin allows that such an ideal, perhaps even coupled with a demand for coercion in its name, might conceivably form part of a theory of freedom 'without thereby rendering the word "freedom" wholly meaningless'. His objection is merely that, as he adds, 'all this has little to do with' the idea of negative liberty as someone like John Stuart Mill would ordinarily understand it.[29]

Considering the same question from the opposite angle, so to speak, Charles Taylor appears to reach the same conclusion in his essay, 'What's wrong with negative liberty'. It is only because liberty is *not* a mere opportunity concept, he argues, that we need to confront the two paradoxes I have isolated, asking ourselves whether our liberty is 'realisable only within a certain form of society', and whether this commits us 'to justifying the excesses of totalitarian oppression in the name of liberty'.[30] Taylor's final reason, indeed, for treating the strictly negative view of liberty as an impoverished one is that, if we restrict ourselves to such an understanding of the concept, these troubling but unavoidable questions do not arise.[31]

What are we to think of this second line of argument, culminating in the suggestion that the two claims I am considering, whatever else may be said about them, have no place in any ordinary theory of negative liberty? This brings me to the main point I am concerned to bring out. For it seems to me that this conclusion depends on ignoring another whole tradition of social thought, the Renaissance republican tradition. [...] The view of social freedom to which this tradition gave rise is one that has largely been overlooked in recent philosophical debate. But it seems well worth trying to restore it to view, for the effect of doing so will be to show us, I believe, that the two paradoxes I have isolated can in fact be accommodated within an ordinary theory of negative liberty. It is to this task of exposition, accordingly, that I now turn, albeit in an unavoidably promissory and overschematic style.[32]

Within the classical republican tradition, the discussion of political liberty was generally embedded in an analysis of what it means to speak of living in a 'free state'. [...] This approach was largely derived from Roman moral philosophy, and especially from those writers whose greatest admiration had been reserved for the doomed Roman republic: Livy, Sallust, and above all Cicero. Within modern political theory, their line of argument was first taken up in Renaissance Italy as a means of defending the traditional liberties of the city-republics against the rising tyranny of the *signori* and the secular powers of the Church. Many theorists espoused the republican cause at this formative stage in

its development, but the greatest among those who did so, [...], was undoubtedly Machiavelli in his *Discorsi* on the first ten books of Livy's *History of Rome*.
Later we find a similar defence of 'free states' being mounted—with acknowl-
edgements to Machiavelli's influence—by James Harrington and other English
republicans of the seventeenth century, among whom, [...], John Milton must
undoubtedly be numbered. Still later, we find something of the same outlook—
again owing much to Machiavelli's inspiration—among the opponents of absolutism in eighteenth-century France. [...] many elements of the theory recur in
a mutated form in Montesquieu's account of republican virtue in *De L'esprit des
Lois*.

By this time, however, the ideals of classical republicanism had largely
been swallowed up by the rising tide of contractarian political thought. If we
wish to investigate the heyday of classical republicanism, accordingly, we
need to turn back to the period with which this book has mainly been concerned, the period before the concept of individual rights attained that hege-
mony which it has never subsequently lost. We need, that is, to turn back to
the moral and political philosophy of the Renaissance, as well as to the
Roman republican writers on whom the Renaissance theorists placed such
overwhelming weight. It is from these sources, therefore, that I shall mainly
draw my picture of the republican ideal of liberty, and it is from Machiavelli's
Discorsi—perhaps the most compelling presentation of the case—that I shall
mainly cite.[33]

IV

I have said that the classical republicans were mainly concerned to celebrate
what Marchamont Nedham later described in a resounding title as 'the excel-
lency of a free state'. It will be best to begin, therefore, by asking what they had
in mind when they predicated liberty of entire communities. To grasp the answer, we need only recall that these writers take the metaphor of the body
politic as seriously as possible. A political body, no less than a natural one, is said
to be at liberty if and only if it is not subject to external constraint. Like a free
person, a free state is one that is able to act according to its own will, in pursuit
of its own chosen ends. It is a community, that is, in which the will of the citizens, the general will of the body politic, chooses and determines whatever
ends are pursued by the community as a whole. As Machiavelli expresses the
point at the beginning of his *Discorsi*, free states are those 'which are far from all
external servitude, and are able to govern themselves according to their own
will'.[34]

There are two principal benefits, according to these theorists, which we can
only hope to enjoy with any degree of assurance if we live as members of free
states. One is civic greatness and wealth. Sallust had laid it down in his *Catiline*
(7.1) that Rome only became great as a result of throwing off the tyranny of her

kings, and the same sentiment was endlessly echoed, [as I have tried to show in chapter 6,] by later exponents of classical republican thought. Machiavelli also insists, for example, that 'it is easy to understand the affection that people feel for living in liberty, for experience shows that no cities have ever grown in power or wealth except those which have been established as free states'.[35]

But there is another and even greater gift that free states are alone capable of bequeathing with any confidence to their citizens. This is personal liberty, understood in the ordinary sense to mean that each citizen remains free from any elements of constraint (especially those which arise from personal dependence and servitude) and in consequence remains free to pursue his own chosen ends. As Machiavelli insists in a highly emphatic passage at the start of Book II of the *Discorsi*, it is only 'in lands and provinces which live as free states' that individual citizens can hope 'to live without fear that their patrimony will be taken away from them, knowing not merely that they are born as free citizens and not as slaves, but that they can hope to rise by their abilities to become leaders of their communities'.[36]

It is important to add that, by contrast with the Aristotelian assumptions about *eudaimonia* that pervade scholastic political philosophy, the writers I am considering never suggest that there are certain specific goals we need to realise in order to count as being fully or truly in possession of our liberty. Rather they emphasise that different classes of people will always have varying dispositions, and will in consequence value their liberty as the means to attain varying ends. As Machiavelli explains, some people place a high value on the pursuit of honour, glory, and power: 'they will want their liberty in order to be able to dominate others'.[37] But other people merely want to be left to their own devices, free to pursue their own family and professional lives: 'they want liberty in order to be able to live in security'.[38] To be free, in short, is simply to be unconstrained from pursuing whatever goals we may happen to set ourselves.

How then can we hope to set up and maintain a free state, thereby preventing our own individual liberty from degenerating into servitude? This is clearly the pivotal question, and by way of answering it the writers I am considering advance the distinctive claim that entitles them to be treated as a separate school of thought. A free state, they argue, must constitutionally speaking be what Livy and Sallust and Cicero had all described and celebrated as a *res publica*.

We need to exercise some care in assessing what this means, however, for it would certainly be an oversimplification to suppose that what they have in mind is necessarily a republic in the modern sense. [As Professor Maihofer makes clear in chapter 14,] what the republicans take themselves to be describing is any set of constitutional arrangements under which it might justifiably be claimed that the *res* (the government) genuinely reflects the will and promotes the good of the *publica* (the community as a whole). Whether a *res publica* has to take the form of a self-governing republic is not therefore an empty definitional question, as modern usage suggests, but rather a matter for earnest enquiry and debate. It is true, however, that most of the writers I have cited remain sceptical about the possibility that an individual or even a governing class could ever hope to remain sufficiently disinterested to equate their own will with the general will, and thereby act to promote the good of the community at all times. So they generally conclude that, if we wish to set up a *res publica*, it will be best to set up a republic as opposed to any kind of principality or monarchical rule.

The central contention of the theory I am examining is thus that a self-governing republic is the only type of regime under which a community can hope to attain greatness at the same time as guaranteeing its citizens their individual liberty. This is Machiavelli's usual view, Harrington's consistent view, and the view that Milton eventually came to accept.[39] But if this is so, we very much need to know how this particular form of government can in practice be established and kept in existence. For it turns out that each one of us has a strong personal interest in understanding how this can best be done.

The writers I am considering all respond, in effect, with a one-word answer. A self-governing republic can only be kept in being, they reply, if its citizens cultivate that crucial quality which Cicero had described as *virtus*, which the Italian theorists later rendered as *virtù*, and which the English republicans translated as civic virtue or public-spiritedness. The term is thus used to denote the range of capacities that each one of us as a citizen most needs to possess: the capacities that enable us willingly to serve the common good, thereby to uphold the freedom of our community, and in consequence to ensure its rise to greatness as well as our own individual liberty.

But what *are* these capacities? First of all, we need to possess the courage and determination to defend our community against the threat of conquest and enslavement by external enemies. A body-politic, no less than a natural body, which entrusts itself to be defended by someone else is exposing itself gratuitously to the loss of its liberty and even its life. For no one else can be expected to care as much for our own life and liberty as we care ourselves. Once we are conquered, moreover, we shall find ourselves serving the ends of our new masters rather than being able to pursue our own purposes. It follows that a willingness to cultivate the martial virtues, and to place them in the service of our community, must be indispensable to the preservation of our own individual liberty as well as the independence of our native land.[40]

We also need to have enough prudence and other civic qualities to play an active and effective role in public life. To allow the political decisions of a body-politic to be determined by the will of anyone other than the entire membership of the body itself is, as in the case of a natural body, to run the gratuitous risk that the behaviour of the body in question will be directed to the attainment not of its own ends, but merely the ends of those who have managed to gain control of it. It follows that, in order to avoid such servitude, and hence to ensure our own individual liberty, we must all cultivate the political virtues and devote ourselves wholeheartedly to a life of public service.[41]

This strenuous view of citizenship gives rise to a grave difficulty, however, as the classical republican theorists readily admit. Each of us needs courage to help defend our community and prudence to take part in its government. But no one can be relied on consistently to display these cardinal virtues. On the contrary, as Machiavelli repeatedly emphasises, we are generally reluctant to cultivate the qualities that enable us to serve the common good. Rather we tend to be 'corrupt', a term of art the republican theorists habitually use to denote our natural tendency to ignore the claims of our community as soon as they seem to conflict with the pursuit of our own immediate advantage.[42]

To be corrupt, however, is to forget—or fail to grasp—something which it is profoundly in our interests to remember: that if we wish to enjoy as much freedom as we can hope to attain within political society, there is good reason for us to act in the first instance as virtuous citizens, placing the common good above the pursuit of any individual or factional ends. Corruption, in short, is simply a failure of rationality, an inability to recognise that our own liberty depends on committing ourselves to a life of virtue and public service. And the consequence of our habitual tendency to forget or misunderstand this vital piece of practical reasoning is therefore that we regularly tend to defeat our own purposes. As Machiavelli puts it, we often think we are acting to maximise our own liberty when we are really shouting, 'Long live our own ruin'.[43]

For the republican writers, accordingly, the deepest question of statecraft is one that recent theorists of liberty have supposed it pointless to ask. Contemporary theories of social freedom, analysing the concept of individual liberty in terms of 'background' rights, have come to rely heavily on the doctrine of the invisible hand. If we all pursue our own enlightened self-interest, we are assured, the outcome will in fact be the greatest good of the community as a whole.[44] From the point of view of the republican tradition, however, this is simply another way of describing corruption, the overcoming of which is said to be a necessary condition of maximising our own individual liberty. For the republican writers, accordingly, the deepest and most troubling question still remains: how can naturally self-interested citizens be persuaded to act virtuously, such that they can hope to maximise a freedom which, left to themselves, they will infallibly throw away?

The answer at first sounds familiar: the republican writers place all their faith in the coercive powers of the law. Machiavelli, for example, puts the point graphically in the course of analysing the Roman republican constitution in Book I of his *Discorsi*. 'It is hunger and poverty that make men industrious', he declares, 'and it is the laws that make them good.'[45]

The account the republican writers give, however, of the relationship between law and liberty stands in strong contrast with the more familiar account to be found in contractarian political thought. To Hobbes, for example, or to Locke, the law preserves our liberty essentially by coercing other people. It prevents them from interfering with my acknowledged rights, helps me to draw around myself a circle within which they may not trespass, and prevents me at the same time from interfering with their freedom in just the same way. To a theorist such as Machiavelli, by contrast, the law preserves our liberty not merely by coercing others, but also by directly coercing each one of us into acting in a particular way. The law is also used, that is, to force us out of our habitual patterns of self-interested behaviour, to force us into discharging the full range of our civic duties, and thereby to ensure that the free state on which our own liberty depends is itself maintained free of servitude.

The justifications offered by the classical republican writers for the coercion that law brings with it also stand in marked contrast to those we find in contractarian or even in classical utilitarian thought. For Hobbes or for Locke, our freedom is a natural possession, a property of ourselves. The law's claim to limit its exercise can only be justified if it can be shown that, were the law to be withdrawn, the effect would not in fact be a greater liberty, but rather a diminution of the security with which our existing liberty is enjoyed. For a writer like Machiavelli, however, the justification of law is nothing to do with the protection of individual rights, a concept that makes no appearance in the *Discorsi* at all. The main justification for its exercise is that, by coercing people into acting in such a way as to uphold the institutions of a free state, the law creates and preserves a degree of individual liberty which, in its absence, would promptly collapse into absolute servitude.

[From 'The Republican Ideal of Political Liberty', in G. Bock, Q. Skinner, and M. Viroli (eds.), *Machiavelli and Republicanism* (Cambridge University Press, Cambridge, 1990), 293–305.]

IV.e. Rights

JEREMY BENTHAM

66   Nonsense on Stilts

We know what it is for men to live without government—and living without government, to live without rights: we know what it is for men to live without government, for we see instances of such a way of life—we see it in many savage nations, or rather races of mankind; for instance, among the savages of New South Wales, whose way of living is so well known to us: no habit of obedience, and thence no government—no government, and thence no laws—no laws, and thence no such things as rights—no security—no property:—liberty, as against regular controul, the controul of laws and government—perfect; but as against all irregular controul, the mandates of stronger individuals, none. In this state, at a time earlier than the commencement of history—in this same state, judging from analogy, we, the inhabitants of the part of the globe we call Europe, were;—no government, consequently no rights: no rights, consequently no property—no legal security—no legal liberty: security not more than belongs to beasts—forecast and sense of insecurity keener—consequently in point of happiness below the level of the brutal race.

In proportion to the want of happiness resulting from the want of rights, a reason exists for wishing that there were such things as rights. But reasons for wishing there were such things as rights, are not rights;—a reason for wishing that a certain right were established, is not that right—want is no supply—hunger is not bread.

That which has no existence cannot be destroyed—that which cannot be destroyed cannot require anything to preserve it from destruction. *Natural rights* is simple nonsense: natural and imprescriptible rights, rhetorical nonsense,—nonsense upon stilts. But this rhetorical nonsense ends in the old strain of mischievous nonsense: for immediately a list of these pretended natural rights is given, and those are so expressed as to present to view legal rights. And of these rights, whatever they are, there is not, it seems, any one of which any government *can*, upon any occasion whatever, abrogate the smallest particle. [. . .]

I know of no natural rights except what are created by general utility: and even in that sense it were much better the word were never heard of. All such language is at any rate false: all such language is either pernicious, or at the best an improper and fallacious way of indicating what is true.

In starting this topic or rather this expression I am full well aware what a deluge of nonsense I am treading up. But as this sort of nonsense is not one of the readiest of arguments, but perhaps the most formidable opponent which a useful and rational proposal can have to struggle with, I know not how to get altogether clear of mentioning it: but what I do say of it shall be as little and as short as possible.

Relations have a natural right to succeed to one: and as no one can say where this right ends, this is as much as to say that it ends no where. To set bounds to the right of succession any where is therefore to violate natural rights. But a law by which any natural right is violated is a grievance and an act of tyranny: and tyranny ought to be risen up against and resisted: the right of resistance to oppression is one of these natural rights which are indefeasible and have not been given up and cannot be, &c. &c. &c.

To this head of argument I have two answers. One is that it is mere nonsense: to say nothing of its being such mischievous nonsense—a topic which is not to the present purpose.

The other is that it is inconsistent nonsense: in as much as, if it be intelligible and just, it does not apply with any greater force against the arrangement here proposed to be made than against every other arrangement that can be named, actual or possible.

First then it is stark nonsense: it is a contradiction in terms.

Of a natural right who has any idea? I, for my part, I have none: a natural right is a round square,—an incorporeal body. What a legal right is I know. I know how it was made. I know what it means when made. To me a right and a legal right are the same thing, for I know no other. Right and law are correlative terms: as much so as son and father. Right is with me the child of law: from different operations of the law result different sorts of rights. A natural right is a son that never had a father. By natural right is meant a sort of a thing which is to have the effect of law, which is to have an effect paramount to that of law, but which subsists not only without law, but against law: and its characteristic property, as well as sole and constant use, is the being the everlasting and irreconcilable enemy of law. As scissors were invented to cut up cloth, so were natural rights invented to cut up law, and legal rights. A natural right is a species of cold heat, a sort of dry moisture, a kind of resplendent darkness.

[From *Anarchical Fallacies* and *Supply without Burthen*, in *Nonsense upon Stilts* ed. Jeremy Waldron (Methuen, London, 1987), 53, 72–3. Written 1796.]

KARL MARX
....

67 The Rights of Egoistic Man

The first point we should note is that the so-called *rights of man*, as distinct from the *rights of the citizen*, are quite simply the rights of the *member of civil society*, i.e. of egoistic man, of man separated from other men and from the community. Consider the most radical constitution, the Constitution of 1793:

Declaration of the Rights of Man and of the Citizen.

Article 2. 'These rights, etc. (the natural and imprescriptible rights) are: equality, liberty, security, property.'

What is liberty?

Article 6. 'Liberty is the power which belongs to man to do anything that does not harm the rights of others', or according to the Declaration of the Rights of Man of 1791: 'Liberty consists in being able to do anything which does not harm others.'

Liberty is therefore the right to do and perform everything which does not harm others. The limits within which each individual can move *without* harming others are determined by law, just as the boundary between two fields is determined by a stake. The liberty we are here dealing with is that of man as an isolated monad who is withdrawn into himself. Why does Bauer say that the Jew is incapable of acquiring the rights of man?

'As long as he is a Jew the restricted nature which makes him a Jew will inevitably gain the ascendancy over the human nature which should join him as a man to other men; the effect will be to separate him from non-Jews.'

But the right of man to freedom is not based on the association of man with man but rather on the separation of man from man. It is the *right* of this separation, the right of the *restricted* individual, restricted to himself.

The practical application of the right of man to freedom is the right of man to *private property.*

What is the right of man to private property?

Article 16 (Constitution of 1793): 'The right of *property* is that right which belongs to each citizen to enjoy and dispose *at will* of his goods, his revenues and the fruit of his work and industry.'

The right to private property is therefore the right to enjoy and dispose of one's resources as one wills, without regard for other men and independently of society: the right of self-interest. The individual freedom mentioned above, together with this application of it, forms the foundation of civil society. It leads each man to see in other men not the *realization* but the *limitation* of his own freedom. But above all it proclaims the right of man 'to enjoy and dispose *at will* of his goods, his revenues and the fruit of his work and industry'.

There remain the other rights of man, equality and security.

Equality, here in its non-political sense, simply means equal access to liberty as described above, namely that each man is equally considered to be a self-sufficient monad. The Constitution of 1795 defines the concept of this equality, in keeping with this meaning, as follows:

Article 3 (Constitution of 1795): 'Equality consists in the fact that the law is the same for everyone, whether it protects or whether it punishes.'

And security?

Article 8 (Constitution of 1793): 'Security consists in the protection accorded by society to each of its members for the conservation of his person, his rights and his property.'

Security is the supreme social concept of civil society, the concept of *police*, the concept that the whole of society is there only to guarantee each of its members the conservation of his person, his rights and his property. In this sense Hegel calls civil society 'the state of need and of reason'.

The concept of security does not enable civil society to rise above its egoism. On the contrary, security is the *guarantee* of its egoism.

Therefore not one of the so-called rights of man goes beyond egoistic man, man as a member of civil society, namely an individual withdrawn into himself, his private interest and his private desires and separated from the community. In the rights of man it is not man who appears as a species-being; on the contrary, species-life itself, society, appears as a framework extraneous to the individuals, as a limitation of their original independence. The only bond which holds them together is natural necessity, need and private interest, the conservation of their property and their egoistic persons.

It is a curious thing that a people which is just beginning to free itself, to tear down all the barriers between the different sections of the people and to found a political community, that such a people should solemnly proclaim the rights of egoistic man, separated from his fellow men and from the community (Declaration of 1791), and even repeat this proclamation at a time when only the most heroic devotion can save the nation and is for that reason pressingly required, at a time when the sacrifice of all the interests of civil society becomes the order of the day and egoism must be punished as a crime. (*Declaration of the Rights of Man*, etc., 1793.) This fact appears even more curious when we observe that citizenship, the *political community*, is reduced by the political emancipators to a mere *means* for the conservation of these so-called rights of man and that the citizen is therefore proclaimed the servant of egoistic man; that the sphere in which man behaves as a communal being [*Gemeinwesen*] is degraded to a level below the sphere in which he behaves as a partial being, and finally that it is man as *bourgeois*, i.e. as a member of civil society, and not man as citizen who is taken as the *real* and *authentic* man.

'The *goal* of all *political association* is the *conservation* of the natural and imprescriptible rights of man' (*Declaration of the Rights of Man* etc., 1791, Article 2). 'Government is instituted in order to guarantee man the enjoyment of his natural and imprescriptible rights' (*Declaration* etc., 1793, Article 1).

Thus even during the ardour of its youth, urged on to new heights by the pressure of circumstances, political life declares itself to be a mere *means* whose goal is the life of civil society.

[From 'On the Jewish Question', in *Early Writings*, ed. L. Colletti, trans. Rodney Livingstone and Gregor Benton (Penguin, Harmondsworth, 1975), 229–31. First published 1843.]

68 Rights as Side-Constraints

It is often thought that what is wrong with utilitarianism [...] is its too narrow conception of good. Utilitarianism doesn't, it is said, properly take rights and their nonviolation into account; it instead leaves them a derivative status. Many of the counterexample cases to utilitarianism fit under this objection, for example, punishing an innocent man to save a neighborhood from a vengeful rampage. But a theory may include in a primary way the nonviolation of rights, yet include it in the wrong place and the wrong manner. For suppose some condition about minimizing the total (weighted) amounts of violations of rights is built into the desirable end state to be achieved. We then would have something like a 'utilitarianism of rights'; violations of rights (to be *minimized*) merely would replace the total happiness as the relevant end state in the utilitarian structure. (Note that we do not hold the nonviolation of our rights as our sole greatest good or even rank it first lexicographically to exclude trade-offs, if there is some desirable society we should choose to inhabit even though in it some rights of ours sometimes are violated, rather than move to a desert island where we could survive alone.) This still would require us to violate someone's rights when doing so minimizes the total (weighted) amount of the violation of rights in the society. For example, violating someone's rights might deflect others from *their* intended action of gravely violating rights, or might remove their motive for doing so, or might divert their attention, and so on. A mob rampaging through a part of town killing and burning *will* violate the rights of those living there. Therefore, someone might try to justify his punishing another *he* knows to be innocent of a crime that enraged a mob, on the grounds that punishing this innocent person would help to avoid even greater violations of rights by others, and so would lead to a minimum weighted score for rights violations in the society.

In contrast to incorporating rights into the end state to be achieved, one might place them as side constraints upon the actions to be done: don't violate constraints C. The rights of others determine the constraints upon your actions. (A *goal-directed* view with constraints added would be: among those acts available to you that don't violate constraints C, act so as to maximize goal G. Here, the rights of others would constrain your goal-directed behavior. I do not mean to imply that the correct moral view includes mandatory goals that must be pursued, even within the constraints.) This view differs from one that tries to build the side constraints C *into* the goal G. The side-constraint view forbids you to violate these moral constraints in the pursuit of your goals; whereas the view whose objective is to minimize the violation of these rights allows you to violate the rights (the constraints) in order to lessen their total violation in the society. [...]

Isn't it *irrational* to accept a side constraint C, rather than a view that directs minimizing the violations of C? (The latter view treats C as a condition rather than a constraint.) If nonviolation of C is so important, shouldn't that be the goal? How can a concern for the nonviolation of C lead to the refusal to violate C even when this would prevent other more extensive violations of C? What is the rationale for placing the nonviolation of rights as a side constraint upon action instead of including it solely as a goal of one's actions?

Side constraints upon action reflect the underlying Kantian principle that individuals are ends and not merely means; they may not be sacrificed or used for the achieving of other ends without their consent. Individuals are inviolable. More should be said to illuminate this talk of ends and means. Consider a prime example of a means, a tool. There is no side constraint on how we may use a tool, other than the moral constraints on how we may use it upon others. There are procedures to be followed to preserve it for future use ('don't leave it out in the rain'), and there are more and less efficient ways of using it. But there is no limit on what we may do to it to best achieve our goals. Now imagine that there was an overrideable constraint C on some tool's use. For example, the tool might have been lent to you only on the condition that C not be violated unless the gain from doing so was above a certain specified amount, or unless it was necessary to achieve a certain specified goal. Here the object is not *completely* your tool, for use according to your wish or whim. But it is a tool nevertheless, even with regard to the overrideable constraint. If we add constraints on its use that may not be overridden, then the object may not be used as a tool *in those ways*. *In those respects*, it is not a tool at all. Can one add enough constraints so that an object cannot be used as a tool at all, in *any* respect?

Can behavior toward a person be constrained so that he is not to be used for any end except as he chooses? This is an impossibly stringent condition if it requires everyone who provides us with a good to approve positively of every use to which we wish to put it. Even the requirement that he merely should not object to any use we plan would seriously curtail bilateral exchange, not to mention sequences of such exchanges. It is sufficient that the other party stands to gain enough from the exchange so that he is willing to go through with it, even though he objects to one or more of the uses to which you shall put the good. Under such conditions, the other party is not being used solely as a means, in that respect. Another party, however, who would not choose to interact with you if he knew of the uses to which you *intend* to put his actions or good, *is* being used as a means, even if he receives enough to choose (in his ignorance) to interact with you. ('All along, you were just *using* me' can be said by someone who chose to interact only because he was ignorant of another's goals and of the uses to which he himself would be put.) Is it morally incumbent upon someone to reveal his intended uses of an interaction if he has good reason to believe the other would refuse to interact if he knew? Is he *using* the other person, if he does not reveal this? And what of the cases where the other does not choose to be of use at all? In getting pleasure from seeing an attractive person go by, does one use the other solely as a means? Does someone so use an object of sexual fantasies? These and related questions raise very interesting issues for moral philosophy; but not, I think, for political philosophy.

Political philosophy is concerned only with *certain* ways that persons may not use others; primarily, physically aggressing against them. A specific side constraint upon action toward others expresses the fact that others may not be used in the specific ways the side constraint excludes. Side constraints express the inviolability of others, in the ways they specify. These modes of inviolability are expressed by the following injunction: 'Don't use people in specified ways.' An end-state view, on the other hand, would express the view that people are ends and not merely means (if it chooses to express this view at all), by a different injunction: 'Minimize the use in specified ways of persons as means.' Following this precept itself may involve using someone as a means in one of the ways specified. Had Kant held this view, he would have given the second formula of the categorical imperative as, 'So act as to minimize the use of humanity simply as a means,' rather than the one he actually used: 'Act in such a way that you always treat humanity, whether in your own person or in the person of any other, never simply as a means, but always at the same time as an end.'

Side constraints express the inviolability of other persons. But why may not one violate persons for the greater social good? Individually, we each sometimes choose to undergo some pain or sacrifice for a greater benefit or to avoid a greater harm: we go to the dentist to avoid worse suffering later; we do some unpleasant work for its results; some persons diet to improve their health or looks; some save money to support themselves when they are older. In each case, some cost is borne for the sake of the greater overall good. Why not, *similarly*, hold that some persons have to bear some costs that benefit other persons more, for the sake of the overall social good? But there is no *social entity* with a good that undergoes some sacrifice for its own good. There are only individual people, different individual people, with their own individual lives. Using one of these people for the benefit of others, uses him and benefits the others. Nothing more. What happens is that something is done to him for the sake of others. Talk of an overall social good covers this up. (Intentionally?) To use a person in this way does not sufficiently respect and take account of the fact that he is a separate person, that his is the only life he has. *He* does not get some overbalancing good from his sacrifice, and no one is entitled to force this upon him—least of all a state or government that claims his allegiance (as other individuals do not) and that therefore scrupulously must be *neutral* between its citizens.

The moral side constraints upon what we may do, I claim, reflect the fact of our separate existences. They reflect the fact that no moral balancing act can take place among us; there is no moral outweighing of one of our lives by others so as to lead to a greater overall *social* good. There is no justified sacrifice of some of us for others. This root idea, namely, that there are different individuals with separate lives and so no one may be sacrificed for others, underlies the existence of moral side constraints, but it also, I believe, leads to a libertarian side constraint that prohibits aggression against another.

[From *Anarchy, State, and Utopia* (Basic Books, New York, 1974), 28–33.]

RONALD DWORKIN

 69 **Taking Rights Seriously**

The institution of rights against the Government is not a gift of God, or an ancient ritual, or a national sport. It is a complex and troublesome practice that makes the Government's job of securing the general benefit more difficult and more expensive, and it would be a frivolous and wrongful practice unless it served some point. Anyone who professes to take rights seriously, and who praises our Government for respecting them, must have some sense of what that point is. He must accept, at the minimum, one or both of two important ideas. The first is the vague but powerful idea of human dignity. This idea, associated with Kant, but defended by philosophers of different schools, supposes that there are ways of treating a man that are inconsistent with recognizing him as a full member of the human community, and holds that such treatment is profoundly unjust.

The second is the more familiar idea of political equality. This supposes that the weaker members of a political community are entitled to the same concern and respect of their government as the more powerful members have secured for themselves, so that if some men have freedom of decision whatever the effect on the general good, then all men must have the same freedom. I do not want to defend or elaborate these ideas here, but only to insist that anyone who claims that citizens have rights must accept ideas very close to these.

It makes sense to say that a man has a fundamental right against the Government, in the strong sense, like free speech, if that right is necessary to protect his dignity, or his standing as equally entitled to concern and respect, or some other personal value of like consequence. It does not make sense otherwise.

So if rights make sense at all, then the invasion of a relatively important right must be a very serious matter. It means treating a man as less than a man, or as less worthy of concern than other men. The institution of rights rests on the conviction that this is a grave injustice, and that it is worth paying the incremental cost in social policy or efficiency that is necessary to prevent it. But then it must be wrong to say that inflating rights is as serious as invading them. If the

Government errs on the side of the individual, then it simply pays a little more in social efficiency than it has to pay; it pays a little more, that is, of the same coin that it has already decided must be spent. But if it errs against the individual it inflicts an insult upon him that, on its own reckoning, it is worth a great deal of that coin to avoid. [. . .]

[From 'Taking Rights Seriously', in *Taking Rights Seriously* (Duckworth, London, 1977, 1978), 198–9.]

JOHN STUART MILL

70 In Favour of Capital Punishment

When there has been brought home to any one, by conclusive evidence, the greatest crime known to the law; and when the attendant circumstances suggest no palliation of the guilt, no hope that the culprit may even yet not be unworthy to live among mankind, nothing to make it probable that the crime was an exception to his general character rather than a consequence of it, then I confess it appears to me that to deprive the criminal of the life of which he has proved himself to be unworthy—solemnly to blot him out from the fellowship of mankind and from the catalogue of the living—is the most appropriate, as it is certainly the most impressive, mode in which society can attach to so great a crime the penal consequences which for the security of life it is indispensable to annex to it. I defend this penalty, when confined to atrocious cases, on the very ground on which it is commonly attacked—on that of humanity to the criminal; as beyond comparison the least cruel mode in which it is possible adequately to deter from the crime. If, in our horror of inflicting death, we endeavour to devise some punishment for the living criminal which shall act on the human mind with a deterrent force at all comparable to that of death, we are driven to inflictions less severe indeed in appearance, and therefore less efficacious, but far more cruel in reality. Few, I think, would venture to propose, as a punishment for aggravated murder, less than imprisonment with hard labour for life; that is the fate to which a murderer would be consigned by the mercy which shrinks from putting him to death. But has it been sufficiently considered what sort of a mercy this is, and what kind of life it leaves to him? If, indeed, the punishment is not really inflicted—if it becomes the sham which a few years ago such punishments were rapidly becoming—then, indeed, its adoption would be almost tantamount to giving up the attempt to repress murder altogether. [. . .]

What comparison can there really be, in point of severity, between consigning a man to the short pang of a rapid death, and immuring him in a living tomb, there to linger out what may be a long life in the hardest and most monotonous toil, without any of its alleviations or rewards—debarred from all pleasant sights and sounds, and cut off from all earthly hope, except a slight mitigation of bodily restraint, or a small improvement of diet? [. . .]

Much has been said of the sanctity of human life, and the absurdity of supposing that we can teach respect for life by ourselves destroying it. But I am surprised at the employment of this argument, for it is one which might be brought against any punishment whatever. It is not human life only, not human life as such, that ought to be sacred to us, but human feelings. The human capacity of suffering is what we should cause to be respected, not the mere capacity of existing. And we may imagine somebody asking how we can teach people not to inflict suffering by ourselves inflicting it? But to this I should answer—all of us would answer—that to deter by suffering from inflicting suffering is not only possible, but the very purpose of penal justice. Does fining a criminal show want of respect for property, or imprisoning him, for personal freedom? Just as unreasonable is it to think that to take the life of a man who has taken that of another is to show want of regard for human life. We show, on the contrary, most emphatically our regard for it, by the adoption of a rule that he who violates that right in another forfeits it for himself, and that while no other crime that he can commit deprives him of his right to live, this shall.

[From 'Speech in Favour of Capital Punishment', in *Applied Ethics*, ed. Peter Singer (Oxford University Press, Oxford, 1986), 98–9, 102. First published 1868.]

H. L. A. HART

71   Punishment and Responsibility

Here I wish to reconsider the assumption, which seems to me to be very widespread, that only within the framework of a theory which sees punishment in a retributive or denunciatory light does the doctrine of responsibility make sense. There is, I believe, at this point something to defend, a moral position which ought not to be evacuated as if the decay of retributive ideas had made it untenable. There are values quite distinct from those of retributive punishment which the system of responsibility does maintain, and which remain of great importance even if our aims in punishing are the forward-looking aims of social protection. Perhaps there is something stale and outmoded in the terms in which we tend to discuss the morality of punishment—as if we were forced to choose between retribution and an Erewhon where we never raise the question 'could he help it?' What is needed is a reinterpretation of the notions of desert and responsibility, and fresh accounts of the importance of the principle that a voluntary act should normally be required as a condition of liability to punishment. Such a reinterpretation would not stress, as our legal moralists do, the importance of judgments of degrees of wickedness about which there is far less agreement than they suppose. Instead it would stress the much more nearly universal ideas of fairness or justice and of the value of individual liberty.

Thus a primary vindication of the principle of responsibility could rest on the simple idea that unless a man has the capacity and a fair opportunity or chance to adjust his behaviour to the law its penalties ought not to be applied to him. Even if we punish men not as wicked but as nuisances, this is something we should still respect. Such a doctrine of fair opportunity would not only provide a rationale for most of the existing excuses which the law admits in its doctrine of *mens rea* but it could also function as a critical principle to demand more from the law than it gives. That is, in its light we might question English law's general adherence to the doctrine that ignorance of the law does not excuse and in its light we might press further objections to strict liability.

But more could be said by way of reinterpretation of the principle of responsibility. Its importance emerges afresh if for the moment we imagine that we had eliminated this principle and changed to a system in which all liability was strict. What should we lose? Among other things, we should lose the ability which the present system in some degree guarantees to us, to predict and plan the future course of our lives within the coercive framework of the law. For the system which makes liability to the law's sanctions dependent upon a voluntary act not only maximizes the power of the individual to determine by his choice his future fate; it also maximizes his power to identify in advance the space which will be left open to him free from the law's interference. Whereas a system from which responsibility was eliminated so that he was liable for what he did by mistake or accident would leave each individual not only less able to exclude the future interference by the law with his life, but also less able to foresee the times of the law's interference.

Thirdly, there is this. At present the law which makes liability to punishment depend on a voluntary act calls for the exercise of powers of self-control but not for complete success in conforming to law. It is illuminating to look at the various excuses which the law admits, like accident or mistake, as ways of rewarding self-restraint. In effect the law says that even if things go wrong, as they do when mistakes are made or accidents occur, a man whose choices are right and who has done his best to keep the law will not suffer. If we contrast this system with one in which men were conditioned to obey the law by psychological or other means, or one in which they were liable to punishment or 'treatment' whether they had voluntarily offended or not, it is plain that our system takes a risk which these alternative systems do not. Our system does not interfere till harm has been done and has been proved to have been done with the appropriate *mens rea*. But the risk that is here taken is not taken for nothing. It is the price we pay for general recognition that a man's fate should depend upon his choice and this is to foster the prime social virtue of self-restraint.

Underlying these separate points there is I think a more important general principle. Human society is a society of persons; and persons do not view themselves or each other merely as so many bodies moving in ways which are sometimes harmful and have to be prevented or altered. Instead persons interpret each other's movements as manifestations of intention and choices, and these subjective factors are often more important to their social relations than the movements by which they are manifested or their effects. If one person hits another, the person struck does not think of the other as just a cause of pain to him; for it is of crucial importance to him whether the blow was deliberate or involuntary. If the blow was light but deliberate, it has a significance for the person struck quite different from an accidental much heavier blow. No doubt the moral judgments to be passed are among the things affected by this crucial distinction; but this is perhaps the least important thing so affected. If you strike me, the judgment that the blow was deliberate will elicit fear, indignation, anger, resentment: these are not voluntary responses; but the same judgment will enter into deliberations about my future voluntary conduct towards you and will colour all my social relations with you. Shall I be your friend or enemy? Offer soothing words? Or return the blow? All this will be different if the blow is not voluntary. This is how human nature in human society actually is and as yet we have no power to alter it. The bearing of this fundamental fact on the law is this. If as our legal moralists maintain it is important for the law to reflect common judgments of morality, it is surely even more important that it should in general reflect in its judgments on human conduct distinctions which not only underlay morality, but pervade the whole of our social life. This it would fail to do if it treated men merely as alterable, predictable, curable or manipulable things.

For these reasons then I think there will be a place for the principle of responsibility even when retributive and denunciatory ideas of punishment are dead. But it is important to be realistic: to be aware of the social costs of making the control of anti-social behaviour dependent on this principle and to recognize cases where the benefits secured by it are minimal.

[From *Punishment and Responsibility* (Oxford University Press, Oxford, 1968), 180–3.]

ROBERT NOZICK

72   Where Deterrence Theory Goes Wrong

Two contrasting questions delimit our present concern:

1. Why is any action ever prohibited, rather than allowed, provided its victims are compensated?
2. Why not prohibit all crossings of the moral boundary that the party impinged upon did not first consent to? Why ever permit anyone to cross another's boundary without prior consent?

Our first question is too broad. For a system allowing acts *A* provided compensation is paid must prohibit at least the joint act of doing *A* and refusing to pay compensation. To narrow the issue, let us suppose there exist easy means to collect assessed compensation. Compensation is easily collected, once it is known who owes it. But those who cross another's protected boundary sometimes escape without revealing their identity. Merely to require (upon detection, apprehension, and determination of guilt) compensation of the victim might be insufficient to deter someone from an action. Why wouldn't he attempt continually to get away with it, to gain without paying compensation? True, if apprehended and judged guilty, he would be required to pay the costs of detecting, apprehending, and trying him; perhaps these possible additional costs would be sufficiently great to deter him. But they might not be. So one might be led to prohibit doing certain acts without paying compensation, and to impose penalties upon those who refuse to pay compensation or who fail to identify themselves as the crossers of certain boundaries.

A person's option of crossing a boundary is constituted by a $(1 - p)$ chance of gain G from the act, where p is the probability he is apprehended, combined with the probability p of paying various costs of the act. These costs are first, the compensation to the victim over and above returning whatever transferable thing may be left from the ill-gotten gains, which we shall label C. In addition, since any nonremovable benefit from carrying out the act (for example, pleasure over fond memories) also will be exactly counterbalanced so as to leave none net, we may ignore it in what follows. Other costs are the psychological, social, and emotional costs of being apprehended, placed on trial, and so on (call them D); and the financial costs (call them E) of the processes of apprehension and trial which he must pay since they were produced by his attempt to evade paying compensation. Prospects for deterrence look dim if the expected costs of a boundary crossing are less than its expected gain; that is, if $p \times (C + D + E)$ is less than $(1 - p) \times G$. (Nevertheless, a person may refrain from a boundary crossing because he has something better to do, an option available to him with even higher expected utility.) If apprehension is imperfect, though inexpensive, additional penalties may be needed to deter crimes. (Attempts to evade paying compensation then would be made prohibited acts.)

Such considerations pose difficulties for retributive theories that set, on retributive grounds, an *upper limit* to the penalty that may be inflicted upon a person. Let us suppose (on such theories) that R, the retribution deserved, equals $r \times H$; where H is a measure of the seriousness of the harm of the act, and r (ranging between 0 and 1 inclusive) indicates the person's degree of responsibility for H. (We pass over the delicate issue of whether H represents the harm intended or the harm done or some function of both of these; or whether this varies with the type of case.) When others will know that $r = 1$, they will believe that $R = H$. A person deciding whether to perform some harmful action then faces a probability $(1 - p)$ of gain G, and a probability p of paying out $(C + D + E + R)$. Usually (though not always) the gain from a boundary crossing is close to the loss or harm it inflicts on the other party; R will be somewhere in the neighborhood of G. But when p is small, or R is, $p + (C + D + E + R)$ may be less than $(1 - p) \times G$, often leaving no deterrence.

Retributive theory seems to allow failures of deterrence. Deterrence theorists (though they wouldn't choose to) would be in a position to gloat at retributivists' squirming over this, if they themselves possessed another theory. But 'the penalty for a crime should be the minimal one necessary to deter commission of it' provides no guidance until we're told *how much* commission of it is to be deterred. If all commission is to be deterred, so that the crime is eliminated, the penalty will be set unacceptably high. If only one instance of the crime is to be deterred, so that there is merely less of the crime than there would be with no penalty at all, the penalty will be unacceptably low and will lead to almost zero deterrence. Where in between is the goal and penalty to be set? Deterrence theorists of the utilitarian sort would suggest (something like) setting the penalty P for a crime at the least point where any penalty for the crime greater than P would lead to more additional unhappiness inflicted in punishment than would be saved to the (potential) victims of the crimes deterred by the additional increment in punishment.

This utilitarian suggestion equates the unhappiness the criminal's punishment causes him with the unhappiness a crime causes its victim. It gives these two unhappinesses the same weight in calculating a social optimum. So the utilitarian would refuse to raise the penalty for a crime, even though the greater penalty (well below any retributive upper limit) would deter more crimes, so long as it increases the unhappiness of those penalized more, even slightly, than it diminishes the unhappiness of those it saves from being victimized by the crime, and of those it deters and saves from punishment. (Will the utilitarian at least always select, between two amounts of penalty that equally maximize the total happiness, the option that minimizes the unhappiness of the victims?) Constructing counterexamples to this bizarre view is left as an exercise for the reader. Utilitarian deterrence 'theory' could avoid this consequence, it seems, only by giving lesser weight to the punished party's unhappiness. One would suppose that considerations of desert, which deterrence theorists had thought avoidable if not incoherent, would play a role here; one would suppose this if one weren't bewildered at how to proceed, even using such considerations, in assigning the 'proper' weight to different persons' (un)happiness. The retributive theorist, on the other hand, *doesn't* have to say that a felon's happiness is less important than his victim's. For the retributivist does not view determining the proper punishment as a task of weighing and weighting and allocating happiness at all.

[From *Anarchy, State, and Utopia* (Basic Books, New York, 1974), 59–62.]

Section V

Economic Justice

INTRODUCTION

Questions of economic justice have always been of central concern to political thinkers. Most obviously, many seek to establish whether or not we live in a world where economic goods are justly distributed. Do some people have too much wealth, or too little? Are there fair returns for effort, or are some exploited while others unjustly prosper? This section starts by looking at one of the most fundamental issues: whether or not there should be rights to private property. Although we often take it for granted that people can be the rightful owners of things, it is far less clear how this belief is to be justified. After all, anything that any individual owns is likely to be made from things that, ultimately, no one owned. How can things pass from a state of no ownership, to an individual person's ownership?

In the first selection Locke puts forward a version of what may well be the most obvious answer: we can come to acquire goods from nature through labour. This simple idea is spelt out in several different ways by Locke, in what has come to be the most influential discussion of the right to private property in the modern western tradition. The very short selection from Rousseau, however, shows that one need not view the right to private property in entirely positive terms. This is followed by Hegel's difficult, but fascinating, discussion, in which he argues that the right to property is justified not so much in terms of labour, but by the fact that it allows one to objectify one's will, and thereby to come to self-definition.

The long selection from Herbert Spencer explains and attempts to defend his view that unrestricted private property is detrimental to liberty and has no other sound justification. It is worth noting that this particular chapter—'The Right to the Use of Earth'—was included only in the first edition of Spencer's book *Social Statics*, and was removed from later editions. In the first of two selections from Marx in Section V.a., attention is turned to money. This manuscript, which went unpublished in Marx's own life, starts by citing passages from Goethe's *Faust* and Shakespeare's *Timon of Athens*, and Marx combines literary commentary and philosophical argument to present the case that money transforms qualities into their opposite and acts as a barrier preventing people from enjoying truly human relations. In the following extract Marx famously points out how much current property ownership can ultimately be traced back to force and fraud. Freud, however, comments that abolishing private property would not have the effects hoped for by some communists: the human aggressive instinct which expresses itself in property would simply express itself in some other fashion.

Tawney returns to the original theme, the connection between labour and property, making the point that if labour is to be the proper foundation of property, then this condemns as many contemporary claims to property as it justifies. With Robert Nozick we come full circle. Although he is a contemporary defender of a strong right to private property, in this selection he skilfully points out numerous difficulties in Locke's defence, and considers some attempted modifications.

Up to this point we have been concerned largely with the question of how legitimate private property rights can be formed. A further question is how rights can be transferred from one person to another. In effect we are used to two forms of transfer, by individual sale and purchase and by government-led tax and redistribution. This raises the question of how much we should leave to the market and how much we should expect governments to do. In other words, should we prefer the free market, a planned economy, or some mix of the two?

The free market has both its friends and enemies, and here we start with perhaps the most famous defender of the market, Adam Smith, who provides a short but detailed argument that, at least in some cases, government interference in the free market is almost bound to achieve the exact opposite of what is intended. Marx, characteristically, adds a twist: the supposed freedom of the free market is experienced as something rather different by the exploited worker. The defence of the market, however, is taken forward by Hayek, who, in comparing the market to a game, explains how market prices convey information in such a way that the market will naturally produce a high level of order and efficiency. Milton and Rose Friedman add a further dimension, arguing that without economic freedom—in other words the freedom to buy and sell as one chooses—other freedoms are threatened. However the section ends with an argument from Cohen that, in the free market, those without money suffer from a lack of freedom.

The final group of selections consider the question of distributive justice. What principles should regulate the distribution of goods in the just society? Should we distribute according to need, or to merit, or should everything be left to the market? We begin with one of Aesop's fables which implicitly appeals to a principle beloved of folk wisdom: if you do not work, then you cannot expect to eat! In the first of two extracts from Aristotle, it is argued that demand provides a standard through which reciprocity is possible, and in the second he considers cases where inequalities are, and are not, appropriate ground for differential treatment.

Inequality and equality are taken up in quite a different way by the early English communist writer, Gerald Winstanley, who sets out his vision of a society without money or trade. Winstanley's position, however, is subject to withering attack by Hume, who argues that, appealing though such a regime may sound, in practice it will lead to both tyranny and severe poverty. Karl Marx, obviously unimpressed by Hume, sets out his famous principle of distribution for the communist society of the future, a society transformed by historical struggle: from each according to his abilities, to each according to his needs. The extract from Edward Bellamy's utopian novel *Looking Backward* sets out some of the imagined details of how a society operating on such principles might function.

Hayek, however, in response to the growing concern for social justice in the twentieth century, revives a version of Hume's argument, with his own twist. It is simply impossible, he claims, to run a fair and equal society. Without the market, and the inequalities it inevitably brings with it, we do not even have a standard for judging what prices different goods should have, and therefore no standard by which we can judge whether a distribution is equal or unequal.

Contemporary believers in equality, however, are prepared to accept some of the points made by Hume and Hayek, among others, to propose schemes which may be more robust. Since 1971 the discussion has been dominated by the proposal made by John Rawls, who set out what he refers to as two principles of justice. Simplified, these state that, first, each person is to have an equal right to the most extensive basic liberty; and second, that social and economic advantages are to be arranged so that they make the worst off group of people as well-off as possible. Injustice, says Rawls, is inequality that is not to the advantage of all. In opposition to Rawls, Robert Nozick sets out what he calls the 'Entitlement Theory'. What matters, according to Nozick, is not whether a distribution of resources fits some predetermined 'pattern' or other, but whether people come to hold their resources through legitimate means. If they have done so, he claims, the resulting distribution is just. Finally, we look at the contribution of Ronald Dworkin, who attempts to reconcile the demand for equality with the idea of responsibility for one's choices, arriving at a view which, in assessing whether or not a distribution is equal, takes into account the choices people have made.

V.a. Private Property

JOHN LOCKE

73 Labour as the Basis of Property

Whether we consider natural reason, which tells us that men, being once born, have a right to their preservation, and consequently to meat and drink and such other things as Nature affords for their subsistence, or 'revelation,' which gives us an account of those grants God made of the world to Adam, and to Noah and his sons, it is very clear that God, as King David says (Psalm cxv. 16), 'has given the earth to the children of men,' given it to mankind in common. But, this being supposed, it seems to some a very great difficulty how any one should ever come to have a property in anything, I will not content myself to answer, that, if it be difficult to make out 'property' upon a supposition that God gave the world to Adam and his posterity in common, it is impossible that any man but one universal monarch should have any 'property' upon a supposition that God gave the world to Adam and his heirs in succession, exclusive of all the rest of his posterity; but I shall endeavour to show how men might come to have a property in several parts of that which God gave to mankind in common, and that without any express compact of all the commoners.

God, who hath given the world to men in common, hath also given them reason to make use of it to the best advantage of life and convenience. The earth and all that is therein is given to men for the support and comfort of their being. And though all the fruits it naturally produces, and beasts it feeds, belong to mankind in common, as they are produced by the spontaneous hand of Nature, and nobody has originally a private dominion exclusive of the rest of mankind in any of them, as they are thus in their natural state, yet being given for the use of men, there must of necessity be a means to appropriate them some way or other before they can be of any use, or at all beneficial, to any particular men. The fruit or venison which nourishes the wild Indian, who knows no enclosure, and is still a tenant in common, must be his, and so his—*i.e.*, a part of him, that another can no longer have any right to it before it can do him any good for the support of his life.

Though the earth and all inferior creatures be common to all men, yet every man has a 'property' in his own 'person.' This nobody has any right to but himself. The 'labour' of his body and the 'work' of his hands, we may say, are properly his. Whatsoever, then, he removes out of the state that Nature hath provided and left it in, he hath mixed his labour with it, and joined to it something that is his own, and thereby makes it his property. It being by him removed from the common state Nature placed it in, it hath by this labour something annexed to it that excludes the common right of other men. For this 'labour' being the unquestionable property of the labourer, no man but he can have a right to what that is once joined to, at least where there is enough, and as good left in common for others.

He that is nourished by the acorns he picked up under an oak, or the apples he gathered from the trees in the wood, has certainly appropriated them to himself. Nobody can deny but the nourishment is his. I ask, then, when did they begin to be his? when he digested? or when he ate? or when he boiled? or when he brought them home? or when he picked them up? And it is plain, if the first gathering made them not his, nothing else could. That labour put a distinction between them and common. That added something to them more than Nature, the common mother of all, had done, and so they became his private right. And will any one say he had no right to those acorns or apples he thus appropriated because he had not the consent of all mankind to make them his? Was it a robbery thus to assume to himself what belonged to all in common? If such a consent as that was necessary, man had starved, notwithstanding the plenty God had given him. We see in commons, which remain so by compact, that it is the taking any part of what is common, and removing it out of the state Nature leaves it in, which begins the property, without which the common is of no use. And the taking of this or that part does not depend on the express consent of all the commoners. Thus, the grass my horse has bit, the turfs my servant has cut, and the ore I have digged in any place, where I have a right to them in common with others, become my property without the assignation or consent of anybody. The labour that was mine, removing them out of that common state they were in, hath fixed my property in them.

By making an explicit consent of every commoner necessary to any one's appropriating to himself any part of what is given in common, children or servants could not cut the meat which their father or master had provided for them in common without assigning to every one his particular part. Though the water running in the fountain be every one's, yet who can doubt but that in the pitcher is his only who drew it out? His labour hath taken it out of the hands of Nature where it was common, and belonged equally to all her children, and hath thereby appropriated it to himself.

Thus this law of reason makes the deer that Indian's who hath killed it; it is allowed to be his goods who hath bestowed his labour upon it, though, before it was the common right of every one. And amongst those who are counted the civilised part of mankind, who have made and multiplied positive laws to determine property, this original law of Nature for the beginning of property, in what was before common, still takes place, and by virtue thereof, what fish any one catches in the ocean, that great and still remaining common of mankind; or what ambergris any one takes up here is by the labour that removes it out of that common state Nature left it in, made his property who takes that pains about it.

And even amongst us, the hare that any one is hunting is thought his who pursues her during the chase. For being a beast that is still looked upon as common, and no man's private possession, whoever has employed so much labour about any of that kind as to find and pursue her has thereby removed her from the state of Nature wherein she was common, and hath begun a property.

It will, perhaps, be objected to this, that if gathering the acorns or other fruits of the earth, etc., makes a right to them, then any one may engross as much as he will. To which I answer, Not so. The same law of Nature that does by this means give us property, does also bound that property too. 'God has given us all things richly.' Is the voice of reason confirmed by inspiration? But how far has He given it us—'to enjoy'? As much as any one can make use of to any advantage of life before it spoils, so much he may by his labour fix a property in. Whatever is beyond this is more than his share, and belongs to others. Nothing was made by God for man to spoil or destroy. And thus considering the plenty of natural provisions there was a long time in the world, and the few spenders, and to how small a part of that provision the industry of one man could extend itself and engross it to the prejudice of others, especially keeping within the bounds set by reason of what might serve for his use, there could be then little room for quarrels or contentions about property so established.

But the chief matter of property being now not the fruits of the earth and the beasts that subsist on it, but the earth itself, as that which takes in and carries with it all the rest, I think it is plain that property in that too is acquired as the former. As much land as a man tills, plants, improves, cultivates, and can use the product of, so much is his property. He by his labour does, as it were, enclose it from the common. Nor will it invalidate his right to say everybody else has an equal title to it, and therefore he cannot appropriate, he cannot enclose, without the consent of all his fellow-commoners, all mankind. God, when He gave the world in common to all mankind, commanded man also to labour, and the penury of his condition required it of him. God and his reason commanded him to subdue the earth—i.e., improve it for the benefit of life and therein lay out something upon it that was his own, his labour. He that, in obedience to this command of God, subdued, tilled, and sowed any part of it, thereby annexed to it something that was his property, which another had no title to, nor could without injury take from him.

Nor was this appropriation of any parcel of land, by improving it, any prejudice to any other man, since there was still enough and as good left, and more than the yet unprovided could use. So that, in effect, there was never the less left for others because of his enclosure for himself. For he that leaves as much as another can make use of does as good as take nothing at all. Nobody could think himself injured by the drinking of another man, though he took a good draught, who had a whole river of the same water left him to quench his thirst. And the case of land and water, where there is enough of both, is perfectly the same.

God gave the world to men in common, but since He gave it them for their benefit and the greatest conveniences of life they were capable to draw from it, it cannot be supposed He meant it should always remain common and unculti- vated. He gave it to the use of the industrious and rational (and labour was to be his title to it); not to the fancy or covetousness of the quarrelsome and con- tentious. He that had as good left for his improvement as was already taken up needed not complain, ought not to meddle with what was already improved by another's labour; if he did it is plain he desired the benefit of another's pains, which he had no right to, and not the ground which God had given him, in com- mon with others, to labour on, and whereof there was as good left as that al- ready possessed, and more than he knew what to do with, or his industry could reach to. [. . .]

And thus, without supposing any private dominion and property in Adam over all the world, exclusive of all other men, which can no way be proved, nor any one's property be made out from it, but supposing the world, given as it was to the children of men in common, we see how labour could make men distinct titles to several parcels of it for their private uses, wherein there could be no doubt of right, no room for quarrel.

Nor is it so strange as, perhaps, before consideration, it may appear, that the property of labour should be able to overbalance the community of land, for it is labour indeed that puts the difference of value on everything; and let any one consider what the difference is between an acre of land planted with tobacco or sugar, sown with wheat or barley, and an acre of the same land lying in common without any husbandry upon it, and he will find that the improvement of labour makes the far greater part of the value. I think it will be but a very mod- est computation to say, that of the products of the earth useful to the life of man, nine-tenths are the effects of labour. Nay, if we will rightly estimate things as they come to our use, and cast up the several expenses about them—what in them is purely owing to Nature and what to labour—we shall find that in most of them ninety-nine hundredths are wholly to be put on the account of labour.

There cannot be a clearer demonstration of anything than several nations of the Americans are of this, who are rich in land and poor in all the comforts of life; whom Nature, having furnished as liberally as any other people with the materials of plenty—i.e., a fruitful soil, apt to produce in abundance what might serve for food, raiment, and delight; yet, for want of improving it by labour, have not one hundredth part of the conveniences we enjoy, and a king of a large and fruitful territory there feeds, lodges, and is clad worse than a day labourer in England.

[From *Two Treatises of Civil Government*, ed. W. S. Carpenter (J. M. Dent, London, 1924 (1962 repr.)), 128–33, 136. First published 1690.]

74 The Earth Belongs to Nobody

The first man who, having enclosed a piece of ground, bethought himself of saying 'This is mine', and found people simple enough to believe him, was the real founder of civil society. From how many crimes, wars, and murders, from how many horrors and misfortunes might not any one have saved mankind, by pulling up the stakes, or filling up the ditch, and crying to his fellows: 'Beware of listening to this impostor; you are undone if you once forget that the fruits of the earth belong to us all, and the earth itself to nobody.'

[From *A Discourse on the Origin of Inequality*, in *The Social Contract and Discourses*, trans. and introd. G. D. H. Cole (J. M. Dent, London, 1973), 84. First published 1755.]

G. W. F. HEGEL

75 Property as Expression

A person must translate his freedom into an external sphere in order to exist as Idea. Personality is the first, still wholly abstract, determination of the absolute and infinite will, and therefore this sphere distinct from the person, the sphere capable of embodying his freedom, is likewise determined as what is immediately different and separable from him. [. . .]

A person has as his substantive end the right of putting his will into any and every thing and thereby making it his, because it has no such end in itself and derives its destiny and soul from his will. This is the absolute right of appropriation which man has over all 'things'. [. . .]

Since my will, as the will of a person, and so as a single will, becomes objective to me in property, property acquires the character of private property; and common property of such a nature that it may be owned by separate persons acquires the character of an inherently dissoluble partnership in which the retention of my share is explicitly a matter of my arbitrary preference. [. . .]

The rationale of property is to be found not in the satisfaction of needs but in the supersession of the pure subjectivity of personality. In his property a person exists for the first time as reason. Even if my freedom is here realized first of all in an external thing, and so falsely realized, nevertheless abstract personality in its immediacy can have no other embodiment save one characterized by immediacy. [. . .]

All things may become man's property, because man is free will and consequently is absolute, while what stands over against him lacks this quality. Thus everyone has the right to make his will the thing or to make the thing his will, or in other words to destroy the thing and transform it into his own; for the thing, as externality, has no end in itself; it is not infinite self-relation but something external to itself. A living thing too (an animal) is external to itself in this way and is so far itself a thing. Only the will is the infinite, absolute in contrast with everything other than itself, while that other is on its side only relative. Thus 'to appropriate' means at bottom only to manifest the pre-eminence of my will over the thing and to prove that it is not absolute, is not an end in itself. This is made manifest when I endow the thing with some purpose not directly its own. When the living thing becomes my property, I give to it a soul other than the one it had before, I give to it my soul. The free will, therefore, is the idealism which does not take things as they are to be absolute, while realism pronounces them to be absolute, even if they only exist in the form of finitude. Even an animal has gone beyond this realist philosophy since it devours things and so proves that they are not absolutely self-subsistent.

In property my will is the will of a person; but a person is a unit and so property becomes the personality of this unitary will. Since property is the means whereby I give my will an embodiment, property must also have the character of being 'this' or 'mine'. This is the important doctrine of the necessity of private property. While the state may cancel private ownership in exceptional cases, it is nevertheless only the state that can do this; but frequently, especially in our day, private property has been re-introduced by the state. For example, many states have dissolved the monasteries, and rightly, for in the last resort no community has so good a right to property as a person has.

[From *Philosophy of Right*, trans. T. M. Knox (Clarendon Press, Oxford, 1952), 40–2, 235–6. First published 1821.]

HERBERT SPENCER

76 The Right to the Use of the Earth

Given a race of beings having like claims to pursue the objects of their desires— given a world adapted to the gratification of those desires—a world into which such beings are similarly born, and it unavoidably follows that they have equal rights to the use of this world. For if each of them 'has freedom to do all that he wills provided he infringes not the equal freedom of any other,' then each of them is free to use the earth for the satisfaction of his wants, provided he allows all others the same liberty. And conversely, it is manifest that no one, or part of them, may use the earth in such a way as to prevent the rest from similarly using it; seeing that to do this is to assume greater freedom than the rest, and consequently to break the law.

Equity, therefore, does not permit property in land. For if *one* portion of the earth's surface may justly become the possession of an individual, and may be held by him for his sole use and benefit, as a thing to which he has an exclusive right, then *other* portions of the earth's surface may be so held; and eventually the *whole* of the earth's surface may be so held; and our planet may thus lapse altogether into private hands. Observe now the dilemma to which this leads. Supposing the entire habitable globe to be so enclosed, it follows that if the landowners have a valid right to its surface, all who are not landowners, have no right at all to its surface. Hence, such can exist on the earth by sufferance only. They are all trespassers. Save by the permission of the lords of the soil, they can have no room for the soles of their feet. Nay, should the others think fit to deny them a resting-place, these landless men might equitably be expelled from the earth altogether. If, then, the assumption that land can be held as property, involves that the whole globe may become the private domain of a part of its inhabitants; and if, by consequence, the rest of its inhabitants can then exercise their faculties—can then exist even—only by consent of the landowners; it is manifest, that an exclusive possession of the soil necessitates an infringement of the law of equal freedom. For, men who cannot 'live and move and have their being' without the leave of others, cannot be equally free with those others.

Passing from the consideration of the possible, to that of the actual, we find yet further reason to deny the rectitude of property in land. It can never be pretended that the existing titles to such property are legitimate. Should any one think so, let him look in the chronicles. Violence, fraud, the prerogative of force, the claims of superior cunning—these are the sources to which those titles may be traced. The original deeds were written with the sword, rather than with the pen: not lawyers, but soldiers, were the conveyancers: blows were the current coin given in payment; and for seals, blood was used in preference to wax. Could valid claims be thus constituted? Hardly. And if not, what becomes of the pretensions of all subsequent holders of estates so obtained? Does sale or bequest generate a right where it did not previously exist? Would the original claimants be nonsuited at the bar of reason, because the thing stolen from them had changed hands? Certainly not. And if one act of transfer can give no title, can many? No: though *nothing* be multiplied for ever, it will not produce *one*. Even the law recognizes this principle. An existing holder must, if called upon, substantiate the claims of those from whom he purchased or inherited his property; and any flaw in the original parchment, even though the property should have had a score intermediate owners, quashes his right.

'But Time,' say some, 'is a great legaliser. Immemorial possession must be taken to constitute a legitimate claim. That which has been held from age to age as private property, and has been bought and sold as such, must now be considered as irrevocably belonging to individuals.' To which proposition a willing assent shall be given when its propounders can assign it a definite meaning. To do this, however, they must find satisfactory answers to such questions as—How long does it take for what was originally a *wrong* to grow into a *right*? At what rate per annum do invalid claims become valid? If a title gets perfect in a thousand years, how much more than perfect will it be in two thousand years?—and so forth. For the solution of which they will require a new calculus.

Whether it may be expedient to admit claims of a certain standing, is not the point. We have here nothing to do with considerations of conventional privilege or legislative convenience. We have simply to inquire what is the verdict given by pure equity in the matter. And this verdict enjoins a protest against every existing pretension to the individual possession of the soil; and dictates the assertion, that the right of mankind at large to the earth's surface is still valid; all deeds, customs, and laws, notwithstanding.

Not only have present land tenures an indefensible origin, but it is impossible to discover any mode in which land *can* become private property. Cultivation is commonly considered to give a legitimate title. He who has reclaimed a tract of ground from its primitive wildness, is supposed to have thereby made it his own. But if his right is disputed, by what system of logic can he vindicate it? Let us listen a moment to his pleadings.

'Hallo, you Sir,' cries the cosmopolite to some backwoodsman, smoking at the door of his shanty, 'by what authority do you take possession of these acres that you have cleared; round which you have put up a snake-fence, and on which you have built this log-house?'

'By what authority? I squatted here because there was no one to say nay—because I was as much at liberty to do so as any other man. Besides, now that I have cut down the wood, and ploughed and cropped the ground, this farm is more mine than yours, or anybody's; and I mean to keep it.'

'Ay, so you all say. But I do not yet see how you have substantiated your claim. When you came here you found the land producing trees—sugar-maples, perhaps; or may be it was covered with prairie-grass and wild strawberries. Well, instead of these, you made it yield wheat, or maize, or tobacco. Now I want to understand how, by exterminating one set of plants, and making the soil bear another set in their place, you have constituted yourself lord of this soil for all succeeding time.'

'Oh, those natural products which I destroyed were of little or no use; whereas I caused the earth to bring forth things good for food—things that help to give life and happiness.'

'Still you have not shown why such a process makes the portion of earth you have so modified yours. What is it that you have done? You have turned over the soil to a few inches in depth with a spade or a plough; you have scattered over this prepared surface a few seeds; and you have gathered the fruits which the sun, rain, and air, helped the soil to produce. Just tell me, if you please, by what magic have these acts made you sole owner of that vast mass of matter, having for its base the surface of your estate, and for its apex the centre of the globe? all of which it appears you would monopolise to yourself and your descendants for ever.'

'Well, if it isn't mine, whose is it? I have dispossessed nobody. When I crossed the Mississippi yonder, I found nothing but the silent woods. If some one else had settled here, and made this clearing, he would have had as good a right to the location as I have. I have done nothing but what any other person was at liberty to do had he come before me. Whilst they were unreclaimed, these lands belonged to all men—as much to one as to another—and they are now mine simply because I was the first to discover and improve them.'

'You say truly, when you say that "whilst they were unreclaimed these lands belonged to all men." And it is my duty to tell you that they belong to all men still; and that your "improvements" as you call them, cannot vitiate the claim of all men. You may plough and harrow, and sow and reap; you may turn over the soil as often as you like; but all your manipulations will fail to make that soil yours, which was not yours to begin with. Let me put a case. Suppose now that in the course of your wanderings you come upon an empty house, which in spite of its dilapidated state takes your fancy; suppose that with the intention of making it your abode you expend much time and trouble in repairing it—that you paint and paper, and whitewash, and at considerable cost bring it into a habitable state. Suppose further, that on some fatal day a stranger is announced, who turns out to be the heir to whom this house has been bequeathed; and that this professed heir is prepared with all the necessary proofs of his identity: what becomes of your improvements? Do they give you a valid title to the house? Do they quash the title of the original claimant?'

'No.'

'Neither then do your pioneering operations give you a valid title to this land. Neither do they quash the title of its original claimants—the human race. The world is God's bequest to mankind. All men are joint heirs to it; you amongst the number. And because you have taken up your residence on a certain part of it, and have subdued, cultivated, beautified that part—improved it as you say, you are not therefore warranted in appropriating it as entirely private property. At least if you do so, you may at any moment be justly expelled by the lawful owner—Society.'

'Well, but surely you would not eject me without making some recompense for the great additional value I have given to this tract, by reducing what was a wilderness into fertile fields. You would not turn me adrift and deprive me of all the benefit of those years of toil it has cost me to bring this spot into its present state.'

'Of course not: just as in the case of the house, you would have an equitable title to compensation from the proprietor for repairs and new fittings, so the community cannot justly take possession of this estate, without paying for all that you have done to it. This extra worth which your labour has imparted to it is fairly yours; and although you have, without leave, busied yourself in bettering what belongs to the community, yet no doubt the community will duly discharge your claim. But admitting this, is quite a different thing from recognising your right to the land itself. It may be true that you are entitled to compensation for the improvements this enclosure has received at your hands; and at the same time it may be equally true that no act, form, proceeding, or ceremony, can make this enclosure your private property.'

It does indeed at first sight seem possible for the earth to become the exclusive possession of individuals by some process of equitable distribution. 'Why,' it may be asked, 'should not men agree to a fair subdivision? If all are co-heirs, why may not the estate be equally apportioned, and each be afterwards perfect master of his own share?'

To this question it may in the first place be replied, that such a division is vetoed by the difficulty of fixing the values of respective tracts of land. Variations in productiveness, different degrees of accessibility, advantages of climate, proximity to the centres of civilization—these, and other such considerations, remove the problems out of the sphere of mere mensuration into the region of impossibility.

But, waiving this, let us inquire who are to be the allottees. Shall adult males, and all who have reached twenty-one on a specified day, be the fortunate individuals? If so, what is to be done with those who come of age on the morrow? Is it proposed that each man, woman, and child, shall have a section? If so, what becomes of all who are to be born next year? And what will be the fate of those whose fathers sell their estates and squander the proceeds? These portionless ones must constitute a class already described as having no right to a resting-place on earth—as living by the sufferance of their fellow men—as being practically serfs. And the existence of such a class is wholly at variance with the law of equal freedom.

Until therefore, we can produce a valid commission authorizing us to make this distribution—until it can be proved that God has given one charter of privileges to one generation, and another to the next—until we can demonstrate that men born after a certain date are doomed to slavery, we must consider that no such allotment is permissible.

Probably some will regard the difficulties inseparable from individual ownership of the soil, as caused by pushing to excess a doctrine applicable only within rational limits. This is a very favourite style of thinking with some. There are people who hate anything in the shape of exact conclusions; and these are of them. According to such, the right is never in either extreme, but always half way between the extremes. They are continually trying to reconcile *Yes* and *No*. Ifs, and buts, and excepts, are their delight. They have so great a faith in 'the judicious mean' that they would scarcely believe an oracle, if it uttered a full-length principle. Were you to inquire of them whether the earth turns on its axis from East to West, or from West to East, you might almost expect the reply—'A little of both,' or 'Not exactly either.' It is doubtful whether they would assent to the axiom that the whole is greater than its part, without making some qualification. They have a passion for compromises. To meet their taste, Truth must always be spiced with a little Error. They cannot conceive of a pure, definite, entire, and unlimited law. And hence, in discussions like the present, they are constantly petitioning for limitations—always wishing to abate, and modify, and moderate—ever protesting against doctrines being pursued to their ultimate consequences.

But it behoves such to recollect, that ethical truth is as exact and as peremptory as physical truth; and that in this matter of land-tenure, the verdict of morality must be distinctly *yea* or *nay*. Either men *have* a right to make the soil private property, or they *have not*. There is no medium. We must choose one of the two positions. There can be no half-and-half opinion. In the nature of things the fact must be either one way or the other.

If men *have not* such a right, we are at once delivered from the several predicaments already pointed out. If they *have* such a right, then is that right absolute, sacred, not on any pretence to be violated. If they *have* such a right, then is his Grace of Leeds justified in warning-off tourists from Ben Mac Dhui, the Duke of Atholl in closing Glen Tilt, the Duke of Buccleugh in denying sites to the Free Church, and the Duke of Sutherland in banishing the Highlanders to make room for sheep-walks. If they *have* such a right, then it would be proper for the sole proprietor of any kingdom—a Jersey or Guernsey, for example—to impose just what regulations he might choose on its inhabitants—to tell them that they should not live on his property, unless they professed a certain religion, spoke a particular language, paid him a specified reverence, adopted an authorized dress, and conformed to all other conditions he might see fit to make. If they *have* such a right, then is there truth in that tenet of the ultra-Tory school, that the landowners are the only legitimate rulers of a country—that the people at large remain in it only by the landowners' permission, and ought consequently to submit to the landowners' rule, and respect whatever institutions the landowners set up. There is no escape from these inferences. They are necessary corollaries to the theory that the earth can become individual property. And they can only be repudiated by denying that theory.

After all, nobody does implicitly believe in landlordism. We hear of estates being held under the king, that is, the State; or of their being kept in trust for the public benefit; and not that they are the inalienable possessions of their nominal owners. Moreover, we daily deny landlordism by our legislation. Is a canal, a railway, or a turnpike road to be made? we do not scruple to seize just as many acres as may be requisite; allowing the holders compensation for the capital invested. We do not wait for consent. An Act of Parliament supersedes the authority of title deeds, and serves proprietors with notices to quit, whether they will or not. Either this is equitable, or it is not. Either the public are free to resume as much of the earth's surface as they think fit, or the titles of the landowners must be considered absolute, and all national works must be postponed until lords and squires please to part with the requisite slices of their estates. If we decide that the claims of individual ownership must give way, then we imply that the right of the nation at large to the soil is supreme—that the right of private possession only exists by general consent—that general consent being withdrawn it ceases—or, in other words, that it is no right at all.

'But to what does this doctrine, that men are equally entitled to the use of the earth, lead? Must we return to the times of unenclosed wilds, and subsist on roots, berries, and game? Or are we to be left to the management of Messrs. Fourrier, Owen, Louis Blanc, and Co.?'

Neither. Such a doctrine is consistent with the highest state of civilization; may be carried out without involving a community of goods; and need cause no very serious revolution in existing arrangements. The change required would simply be a change of landlords. Separate ownerships would merge into the joint-stock ownership of the public. Instead of being in the possession of individuals, the country would be held by the great corporate body—Society. Instead of leasing his acres from an isolated proprietor, the farmer would lease them from the nation. Instead of paying his rent to the agent of Sir John or his Grace, he would pay it to an agent or deputy-agent of the community. Stewards would be public officials instead of private ones; and tenancy the only land tenure.

A state of things so ordered would be in perfect harmony with the moral law. Under it all men would be equally landlords; all men would be alike free to become tenants. A, B, C, and the rest, might compete for a vacant farm as now, and one of them might take that farm, without in any way violating the principles of pure equity. All would be equally free to bid; all would be equally free to refrain. And when the farm had been let to A, B, or C, all parties would have done that which they willed—the one in choosing to pay a given sum to his fellowmen for the use of certain lands—the others in refusing to pay that sum. Clearly, therefore, on such a system, the earth might be inclosed, occupied, and cultivated, in entire subordination to the law of equal freedom.

No doubt great difficulties must attend the resumption, by mankind at large, of their rights to the soil. The question of compensation to existing proprietors is a complicated one—one that perhaps cannot be settled in a strictly-equitable manner. Had we to deal with the parties who originally robbed the human race of its heritage, we might make short work of the matter. But, unfortunately, most of our present landowners are men who have, either mediately or immediately—either by their own acts, or by the acts of their ancestors—given for their estates, equivalents of honestly-earned wealth, believing that they were investing their savings in a legitimate manner. To justly estimate and liquidate the claims of such, is one of the most intricate problems society will one day have to solve. But with this perplexity and our extrication from it, abstract morality has no concern. Men having got themselves into the dilemma by disobedience to the law, must get out of it as well as they can; and with as little injury to the landed class as may be.

Meanwhile, we shall do well to recollect, that there are others besides the landed class to be considered. In our tender regard for the vested interests of the few, let us not forget that the rights of the many are in abeyance; and must remain so, as long as the earth is monopolized by individuals. Let us remember, too, that the injustice thus inflicted on the mass of mankind, is an injustice of the gravest nature. The fact that it is not so regarded, proves nothing. In early phases of civilization even homicide is thought lightly of. The suttees of India, together with the practice elsewhere followed of sacrificing a hecatomb of human victims at the burial of a chief, show this: and probably cannibals consider the slaughter of those whom 'the fortune of war' has made their prisoners, perfectly justifiable. It was once also universally supposed that slavery was a natural and quite legitimate institution—a condition into which some were born, and to which they ought to submit as to a Divine ordination; nay, indeed, a great proportion of mankind hold this opinion still. A higher social development, however, has generated in us a better faith, and we now to a considerable extent recognize the claims of humanity. But our civilization is only partial. It may by-and-by be perceived, that Equity utters dictates to which we have not yet listened; and men may then learn, that to deprive others of their rights to the use of the earth, is to commit a crime inferior only in wickedness to the crime of taking away their lives or personal liberties.

Briefly reviewing the argument, we see that the right of each man to the use of the earth, limited only by the like rights of his fellow-men, is immediately deducible from the law of equal freedom. We see that the maintenance of this right necessarily forbids private property in land. On examination all existing titles to such property turn out to be invalid; those founded on reclamation inclusive. It appears that not even an equal apportionment of the earth amongst its inhabitants could generate a legitimate proprietorship. We find that if pushed to its ultimate consequences, a claim to exclusive possession of the soil involves a landowning despotism. We further find that such a claim is constantly denied by the enactments of our legislature. And we find lastly, that the theory of the co-heirship of all men to the soil, is consistent with the highest civilization; and that, however difficult it may be to embody that theory in fact, Equity sternly commands it to be done.

[From *Social Statics* (Chapman, London, 1851), 114–25.]

KARL MARX

77   Money, the Universal Whore

Money, inasmuch as it possesses the *property* of being able to buy everything and appropriate all objects, is the *object* most worth possessing. The universality of this *property* is the basis of money's omnipotence; hence it is regarded as an omnipotent being . . . Money is the *pimp* between need and object, between life and man's means of life. But *that* which mediates *my* life also *mediates* the existence of other men for me. It is for me the *other* person.

> What, man! confound it, hands and feet
> And head and backside, all are yours!
> And what we take while life is sweet,
> Is that to be declared not ours?
>   Six stallions, say, I can afford,
> Is not their strength my property?
> I tear along, a sporting lord
> As if their legs belonged to me.
>   (Goethe, *Faust*—Mephistopheles)

Shakespeare in *Timon of Athens*:

> Gold? Yellow, glittering, precious gold? No, gods,
> I am no idle votarist: roots, you clear heavens!
> Thus much of this will make black, white; foul, fair;
> Wrong, right; base, noble; old, young; coward, valiant.
> . . . Why, this
> Will lug your priests and servants from your sides;
> Pluck stout men's pillows from below their heads:
> This yellow slave
> Will knit and break religions; bless th'accurst;
> Make the hoar leprosy adored; place thieves,
> And give them title, knee, and approbation,
> With senators on the bench: this is it
> That makes the wappen'd widow wed again;
> She whom the spital-house and ulcerous sores
> Would cast the gorge at, this embalms and spices
> To th' April day again. Come, damned earth,
> Thou common whore of mankind, that putt'st odds
> Among the rout of nations, I will make thee
> Do they right nature.

And later on:

> O thou sweet king-killer, and dear divorce
> 'Twixt natural son and sire! Thou bright defiler
> Of Hymen's purest bed! Thou valiant Mars!
> Thou ever young, fresh, loved and delicate wooer,
> Whose blush doth thaw the consecrated snow
> That lies on Dian's lap! Thou *visible god*,
> That solder'st close *impossibilities*,
> And mak'st them kiss! That speak'st with every tongue,
> To every purpose! O thou touch of hearts!
> Think, thy slave man rebels; and by thy virtue
> Set them into confounding odds, that beasts
> May have the world in empire!

Shakespeare paints a brilliant picture of the nature of *money*. To understand him, let us begin by expounding the passage from Goethe.

That which exists for me through the medium of *money*, that which I can pay for, i.e. which money can buy, that *am I*, the possessor of the money. The stronger the power of my money, the stronger am I. The properties of money are my, the possessor's, properties and essential powers. Therefore what I *am* and what I *can do* is by no means determined by my individuality. I *am* ugly, but I can buy the *most beautiful* woman. Which means to say that I am not *ugly*, for the effect of *ugliness*, its repelling power, is destroyed by money. As an individual, I am *lame*, but money procures me twenty-four legs. Consequently, I am not lame. I am a wicked, dishonest, unscrupulous and stupid individual, but money is respected, and also is its owner. Money is the highest good, and consequently its owner is also good. Moreover, money spares me the trouble of being dishonest, and I am therefore presumed to be honest. I am *mindless*, but if money is the *true mind* of all things, how can its owner be mindless? What is more, he can buy clever people for himself, and is not he who has power over clever people cleverer than them? Through money I can have anything the human heart desires. Do I not therefore possess all human abilities? Does not money therefore transform all my incapacities into their opposite?

If *money* is the bond which ties me to *human* life and society to me, which links me to nature and to man, is money not the bond of all *bonds*? Can it not bind and loose all bonds? Is it therefore not the universal *means of separation*? It is the true *agent of separation* and the true *cementing agent*, it is the *chemical* power of society.

Shakespeare brings out two properties of money in particular:

(1) It is the visible divinity, the transformation of all human and natural qualities into their opposites, the universal confusion and inversion of things; it brings together impossibilities.

(2) It is the universal whore, the universal pimp of men and peoples.

The inversion and confusion of all human and natural qualities, the bringing together of impossibilities, the *divine* power of money lies in its *nature* as the estranged and alienating *species-essence* of man which alienates itself by selling itself. It is the alienated *capacity* of *mankind*.

What I as a man cannot do, i.e. what all my individual powers cannot do, I can do with the help of *money*. Money therefore transforms each of these essential powers into something which it is not, into its *opposite*.

If I desire a meal or want to take the mail coach because I am not strong enough to make the journey on foot, money can procure me both the meal and the mail coach, i.e. it transfers my wishes from the realm of imagination, it translates them from their existence as thought, imagination and desires into their *sensuous*, *real* existence, from imagination into life, and from imagined being into real being. In this mediating role money is the *truly creative* power.

Demand also exists for those who have no money, but their demand is simply a figment of the imagination. For me or for any other third party it has no effect, no existence. For me it therefore remains *unreal* and *without an object*. The difference between effective demand based on money and ineffective demand based on my need, my passion, my desire, etc., is the difference between *being* and *thinking*, between a representation which merely *exists* within me and one which exists outside me as a *real object*.

If I have no money for travel, I have no *need*, i.e. no real and self-realizing need, to travel. If I have a vocation to study, but no money for it, I have *no* vocation to study, i.e. no *real, true* vocation. But if I really do not have any vocation to study, but have the will *and* the money, then I have an *effective* vocation to do so. *Money*, which is the external, universal *means* and *power*—derived not from man as man and not from human society as society—to turn *imagination into reality* and *reality into mere imagination*, similarly turns *real human and natural powers* into purely abstract representations, and therefore *imperfections* and tormenting phantoms, just as it turns *real imperfections and phantoms*—truly impotent powers which exist only in the individual's fantasy—into *real essential powers* and *abilities*. Thus characterized, money is the universal inversion of *individualities*, which it turns into their opposites and to whose qualities it attaches contradictory qualities.

Money therefore appears as an *inverting* power in relation to the individual and to those social and other bonds which claim to be *essences* in themselves. It transforms loyalty into treason, love into hate, hate into love, virtue into vice, vice into virtue, servant into master, master into servant, nonsense into reason and reason into nonsense.

Since money, as the existing and active concept of value, confounds and exchanges everything, it is the universal *confusion* and *exchange* of all things, an inverted world, the confusion and exchange of all natural and human qualities.

He who can buy courage is brave, even if he is a coward. Money is not exchanged for a particular quality, a particular thing, or for any particular one of the essential powers of man, but for the whole objective world of man and of nature. Seen from the standpoint of the person who possesses it, money exchanges every quality for every other quality and object, even if it is contradictory; it is the power which brings together impossibilities and forces contradictions to embrace.

If we assume *man* to be *man*, and his relation to the world to be a human one, then love can be exchanged only for love, trust for trust, and so on. If you wish to enjoy art you must be an artistically educated person; if you wish to exercise influence on other men you must be the sort of person who has a truly stimulating and encouraging effect on others. Each one of your relations to man— and to nature—must be a *particular expression*, corresponding to the object of your will, of your *real individual* life. If you love unrequitedly, i.e. if your love as love does not call forth love in return, if through the *vital expression* of yourself as a loving person you fail to become a *loved person*, then your love is impotent, it is a misfortune.

[From 'On Money', from *Economic and Philosophical Manuscripts*, in *Early Writings*, ed. L. Colletti, trans. by Rodney Livingstone and Gregor Benton (Penguin, Harmondsworth, 1975), 375–9. Written 1844. Embedded quotations: Goethe, *Faust*—Mephistopheles, Part I, scene iv, trans. P. Wayne (Penguin, Harmondsworth, 1949); Shakespeare, *Timon of Athens*, Act IV, scene iii.]

KARL MARX

78 The True Foundation of Private Property

Primitive accumulation plays approximately the same role in political economy as original sin does in theology. Adam bit the apple, and thereupon sin fell on the human race. Its origin is supposed to be explained when it is told as an anecdote about the past. Long, long ago there were two sorts of people; one, the diligent, intelligent and above all frugal élite; the other, lazy rascals, spending their substance, and more, in riotous living. The legend of theological original sin tells us certainly how man came to be condemned to eat his bread in the sweat of his brow; but the history of economic original sin reveals to us that there are people to whom this is by no means essential. Never mind! Thus it came to pass that the former sort accumulated wealth, and the latter sort finally had nothing to sell except their own skins. And from this original sin dates the poverty of the great majority who, despite all their labour, have up to now nothing to sell but themselves, and the wealth of the few that increases constantly, although they have long ceased to work. Such insipid childishness is every day preached to us in the defence of property. M. Thiers, for example, still repeats it with all the solemnity of a statesman to the French people, who were once so full of wit and ingenuity. But as soon as the question of property is at stake, it becomes a sacred duty to proclaim the standpoint of the nursery tale as the one thing fit for all age-groups and all stages of development. In actual history, it is a notorious fact that conquest, enslavement, robbery, murder, in short, force, play the greatest part. In the tender annals of political economy, the idyllic reigns from time immemorial. Right and 'labour' were from the beginning of time the sole means of enrichment, 'this year' of course always excepted. As a matter of fact, the methods of primitive accumulation are anything but idyllic.

[From *Capital*, vol. i, trans. Ben Fowkes (Penguin, Harmondsworth, 1976), 873–4. First published 1867.]

79 Property and Aggression

The existence of this inclination to aggression, which we can detect in ourselves and justly assume to be present in others, is the factor which disturbs our relations with our neighbour and which forces civilization into such a high expenditure (of energy). In consequence of this primary mutual hostility of human beings, civilized society is perpetually threatened with disintegration. The interest of work in common would not hold it together; instinctual passions are stronger than reasonable interests. Civilization has to use its utmost efforts in order to set limits to man's aggressive instincts and to hold the manifestations of them in check by psychical reaction-formations. Hence, therefore, the use of methods intended to incite people into identifications and aim-inhibited relationships of love, hence the restriction upon sexual life, and hence too the ideal's commandment to love one's neighbour as oneself—a commandment which is really justified by the fact that nothing else runs so strongly counter to the original nature of man. In spite of every effort, these endeavours of civilization have not so far achieved very much. It hopes to prevent the crudest excesses of brutal violence by itself assuming the right to use violence against criminals, but the law is not able to lay hold of the more cautious and refined manifestations of human aggressiveness. The time comes when each one of us has to give up as illusions the expectations which, in his youth, he pinned upon his fellow-men, and when he may learn how much difficulty and pain has been added to his life by their ill-will. At the same time, it would be unfair to reproach civilization with trying to eliminate strife and competition from human activity. These things are undoubtedly indispensable. But opposition is not necessarily enmity; it is merely misused and made an *occasion* for enmity.

The communists believe that they have found the path to deliverance from our evils. According to them, man is wholly good and is well-disposed to his neighbour; but the institution of private property has corrupted his nature. The ownership of private wealth gives the individual power, and with it the temptation to ill-treat his neighbour; while the man who is excluded from possession is bound to rebel in hostility against his oppressor. If private property were abolished, all wealth held in common, and everyone allowed to share in the enjoyment of it, ill-will and hostility would disappear among men. Since everyone's needs would be satisfied, no one would have any reason to regard another as his enemy; all would willingly undertake the work that was necessary. I have no concern with any economic criticisms of the communist system; I cannot enquire into whether the abolition of private property is expedient or advantageous. But I am able to recognize that the psychological premises on which the system is based are an untenable illusion. In abolishing private property we deprive the human love of aggression of one of its instruments, certainly a strong one, though certainly not the strongest; but we have in no way altered the differences in power and influence which are misused by aggressiveness, nor have we altered anything in its nature. Aggressiveness was not created by property. It reigned almost without limit in primitive times, when property was still very scanty, and it already shows itself in the nursery almost before property has given up its primal, anal form; it forms the basis of every relation of affection and love among people (with the single exception, perhaps, of the mother's relation to her male child). If we do away with personal rights over material wealth, there still remains prerogative in the field of sexual relationships, which is bound to become the source of the strongest dislike and the most violent hostility among men who in other respects are on an equal footing. If we were to remove this factor, too, by allowing complete freedom of sexual life and thus abolishing the family, the germ-cell of civilization, we cannot, it is true, easily foresee what new paths the development of civilization could take; but one thing we can expect, and that is that this indestructible feature of human nature will follow it there.

[From *Civilization and Its Discontents*, trans. Joan Riviere (Hogarth, London, 1930), 112–14.]

R. H. TAWNEY

80   Reaping without Sowing

Whatever may have been the historical process by which they have been established and recognized, the *rationale* of private property traditional in England is that which sees in it either the results of the personal labour of its owner, or—what is in effect the same thing—the security that each man will reap where he has sown. Locke argued that a man necessarily and legitimately becomes the owner of 'whatsoever he removes out of the state that nature hath provided,' and that 'he makes it his property' because he 'hath mixed his labour with it.' Paley derived property from the fact that 'it is the intention of God that the produce of the earth be applied to the use of man, and this intention cannot be fulfilled without establishing property.' Adam Smith, who wrote the dangerous sentence, 'Civil Government, in so far as it is instituted for the protection of property, is in reality instituted for the defence of the rich against the poor,' sometimes spoke of property as the result of usurpation—'Landlords, like other men, love to reap where they have never sowed'—but in general ascribed it to the need of offering protection to productive effort. 'If I despair of enjoying the fruits of labour,' said Bentham, repeating what were in all essentials the utilitarian arguments of Hume, 'I shall only live from day to day; I shall not undertake labours which will only benefit my enemies.' This theory passed into America, and became the foundation of the sanctity ascribed to property in *The Federalist* and implied in a long line of judicial decisions on the Fourteenth

Amendment to the Constitution. Property, it is argued, is a moral right, and not merely a legal right, because it insures that the producer will not be deprived by violence of the result of his efforts. [. . .]

Property was to be an aid to creative work, not an alternative to it. The patentee was secured protection for a new invention, in order to secure him the fruits of his own brain, but the monopolist who grew fat on the industry of others was to be put down. [. . .]

The argument has evidently more than one edge. If it justifies certain types of property, it condemns others; and in the conditions of modern industrial civilization, what it justifies is less than what it condemns. The truth is, indeed, that this theory of property, and the institutions in which it is embodied, have survived into an age in which the whole structure of society is radically different from that in which it was formulated, and which made it a valid argument, if not for all, at least for the most common and characteristic, kinds of property. It is not merely that the ownership of any substantial share in the national wealth is concentrated to-day in the hands of a few hundred thousand families, and that at the end of an age which began with an affirmation of the rights of property, proprietary rights are, in fact, far from being widely distributed. Nor is it merely that what makes property insecure to-day is not the arbitrary taxation of unconstitutional monarchies or the privileges of an idle *noblesse*, but the insatiable expansion and aggregation of property itself, which menaces with absorption all property less than the greatest, the small master, the little shopkeeper, the country bank, and has turned the mass of mankind into a proletariat working under the agents and for the profit of those who own.

The characteristic fact which differentiates most modern property from that of the pre-industrial age, and which turns against it the very reasoning by which formerly it was supported, is that in modern economic conditions ownership is not active, but passive, that to most of those who own property to-day it is not a means of work but an instrument for the acquisition of gain or the exercise of power, and that there is no guarantee that gain bears any relation to service, or power to responsibility. For property which can be regarded as a condition of the performance of function, like the tools of the craftsman, or the holding of the peasant, or the personal possessions which contribute to a life of health and efficiency, forms an insignificant proportion, as far as its value is concerned, of the property rights existing at present. In modern industrial societies the great mass of property consists, as the annual review of wealth passing at death reveals, neither of personal acquisitions such as household furniture, nor of the owner's stock-in-trade, but of rights of various kinds, such as royalties, ground-rents, and, above all, of course, shares in industrial undertakings, which yield an income irrespective of any personal service rendered by their owners. Ownership and use are normally divorced. The greater part of modern property has been attenuated to a pecuniary lien or bond on the product of industry, which carries with it a right to payment, but which is normally valued precisely because it relieves the owner from any obligation to perform a positive or constructive function. [. . .]

Hence the real analogy to many kinds of modern property is not the simple property of the small landowner or craftsman, still less the household goods and dear domestic amenities, which is what the word suggests to the guileless minds of clerks and shopkeepers, and which stampede them into displaying the ferocity of terrified sheep when the cry is raised that 'Property' is threatened. It is the feudal dues which robbed the French peasant of part of his produce till the Revolution abolished them.

[From *The Acquisitive Society* (Fontana, London, 1966), 51–2, 55, 56–8, 67. First published 1921.]

ROBERT NOZICK

81 Difficulties with Mixing Labour

Locke views property rights in an unowned object as originating through someone's mixing his labor with it. This gives rise to many questions. What are the boundaries of what labor is mixed with? If a private astronaut clears a place on Mars, has he mixed his labor with (so that he comes to own) the whole planet, the whole uninhabited universe, or just a particular plot? Which plot does an act bring under ownership? The minimal (possibly disconnected) area such that an act decreases entropy in that area, and not elsewhere? Can virgin land (for the purposes of ecological investigation by high-flying airplane) come under ownership by a Lockean process? Building a fence around a territory presumably would make one the owner of only the fence (and the land immediately underneath it).

Why does mixing one's labor with something make one the owner of it? Perhaps because one owns one's labor, and so one comes to own a previously unowned thing that becomes permeated with what one owns. Ownership seeps over into the rest. But why isn't mixing what I own with what I don't own a way of losing what I own rather than a way of gaining what I don't? If I own a can of tomato juice and spill it in the sea so that its molecules (made radioactive, so I can check this) mingle evenly throughout the sea, do I thereby come to own the sea, or have I foolishly dissipated my tomato juice? Perhaps the idea, instead, is that laboring on something improves it and makes it more valuable; and anyone is entitled to own a thing whose value he has created. (Reinforcing this, perhaps, is the view that laboring is unpleasant. If some people made things effortlessly, as the cartoon characters in *The Yellow Submarine* trail flowers in their wake, would they have lesser claim to their own products whose making didn't *cost* them anything?) Ignore the fact that laboring on something may make it less valuable (spraying pink enamel paint on a piece of driftwood that you have found). Why should one's entitlement extend to the whole object rather than just to the *added value* one's labor has produced? (Such reference to value might also serve to delimit the extent of ownership; for example, substitute 'increases the value of' for 'decreases entropy in' in the above entropy criterion.) No workable or coherent value-added property scheme has yet been devised, and any such scheme presumably would fall to objections (similar to those) that fell the theory of Henry George.

It will be implausible to view improving an object as giving full ownership to it, if the stock of unowned objects that might be improved is limited. For an object's coming under one person's ownership changes the situation of all others. Whereas previously they were at liberty (in Hohfeld's sense) to use the object, they now no longer are. This change in the situation of others (by removing their liberty to act on a previously unowned object) need not worsen their situation. If I appropriate a grain of sand from Coney Island, no one else may now do as they will with *that* grain of sand. But there are plenty of other grains of sand left for them to do the same with. Or if not grains of sand, then other things. Alternatively, the things I do with the grain of sand I appropriate might improve the position of others, counterbalancing their loss of the liberty to use that grain. The crucial point is whether appropriation of an unowned object worsens the situation of others.

Locke's proviso that there be 'enough and as good left in common for others' is meant to ensure that the situation of others is not worsened. (If this proviso is met is there any motivation for his further condition of nonwaste?) It is often said that this proviso once held but now no longer does. But there appears to be an argument for the conclusion that if the proviso no longer holds, then it cannot ever have held so as to yield permanent and inheritable property rights. Consider the first person Z for whom there is not enough and as good left to appropriate. The last person Y to appropriate left Z without his previous liberty to act on an object, and so worsened Z's situation. So Y's appropriation is not allowed under Locke's proviso. Therefore the next to last person X to appropriate left Y in a worse position, for X's act ended permissible appropriation. Therefore X's appropriation wasn't permissible. But then the appropriator two from last, W, ended permissible appropriation and so, since it worsened X's position, W's appropriation wasn't permissible. And so on back to the first person A to appropriate a permanent property right.

This argument, however, proceeds too quickly. Someone may be made worse off by another's appropriation in two ways: first, by losing the opportunity to improve his situation by a particular appropriation or any one; and second, by no longer being able to use freely (without appropriation) what he previously could. A *stringent* requirement that another not be made worse off by an appropriation would exclude the first way if nothing else counterbalances the diminution in opportunity, as well as the second. A *weaker* requirement would exclude the second way, though not the first. With the weaker requirement, we cannot zip back so quickly from Z to A, as in the above argument; for though person Z can no longer *appropriate*, there may remain some for him to *use* as before. In this case Y's appropriation would not violate the weaker Lockean condition. (With less remaining that people are at liberty to use, users might face more inconvenience, crowding, and so on; in that way the situation of others might be worsened, unless appropriation stopped far short of such a point.) It is arguable that no one legitimately can complain if the weaker provision is satisfied. However, since this is less clear than in the case of the more stringent proviso, Locke may have intended this stringent proviso by 'enough and as good' remaining, and perhaps he meant the nonwaste condition to delay the end point from which the argument zips back.

Is the situation of persons who are unable to appropriate (there being no more accessible and useful unowned objects) worsened by a system allowing appropriation and permanent property? Here enter the various familiar social considerations favoring private property: it increases the social product by putting means of production in the hands of those who can use them most efficiently (profitably); experimentation is encouraged, because with separate persons controlling resources, there is no one person or small group whom someone with a new idea must convince to try it out; private property enables people to decide on the pattern and types of risks they wish to bear, leading to specialized types of risk bearing; private property protects future persons by leading some to hold back resources from current consumption for future markets; it provides alternate sources of employment for unpopular persons who don't have to convince any one person or small group to hire them, and so on. These considerations enter a Lockean theory to support the claim that appropriation of private property satisfies the intent behind the 'enough and as good left over' proviso, *not* as a utilitarian justification of property. They enter to rebut the claim that because the proviso is violated no natural right to private property can arise by a Lockean process. The difficulty in working such an argument to show that the proviso is satisfied is in fixing the appropriate base line for comparison. Lockean appropriation makes people no worse off than they would be *how*? This question of fixing the baseline needs more detailed investigation than we are able to give it here. It would be desirable to have an estimate of the general economic importance of original appropriation in order to see how much leeway there is for differing theories of appropriation and of the location of the baseline. Perhaps this importance can be measured by the percentage of all income that is based upon untransformed raw materials and given resources (rather than upon human actions), mainly rental income representing the unimproved value of land, and the price of raw material *in situ*, and by the percentage of current wealth which represents such income in the past.

We should note that it is not only persons favoring *private* property who need a theory of how property rights legitimately originate. Those believing in collective property, for example those believing that a group of persons living in an area jointly own the territory, or its mineral resources, also must provide a theory of how such property rights arise; they must show why the persons living there have rights to determine what is done with the land and resources there that persons living elsewhere don't have (with regard to the same land and resources).

[From *Anarchy, State, and Utopia* (Basic Books, New York, 1974), 174–8.]

ADAM SMITH

82 **The Dangers of Government Interference**

The greatest and most important branch of the commerce of every nation, it has already been observed, is that which is carried on between the inhabitants of the town and those of the country. The inhabitants of the town draw from the country the rude produce which constitutes both the materials of their work and the fund of their subsistence; and they pay for this rude produce by sending back to the country a certain portion of it manufactured and prepared for immediate use. The trade which is carried on between these two different sets of people consists ultimately in a certain quantity of rude produce exchanged for a certain quantity of manufactured produce. The dearer the latter, therefore, the cheaper the former; and whatever tends in any country to raise the price of manufactured produce tends to lower that of the rude produce of the land, and thereby to discourage agriculture. The smaller the quantity of manufactured produce which any given quantity of rude produce, or, what comes to the same thing, which the price of any given quantity of rude produce is capable of purchasing, the smaller the exchangeable value of that given quantity of rude produce, the smaller the encouragement which either the landlord has to increase its quantity by improving or the farmer by cultivating the land. Whatever, besides, tends to diminish in any country the number of artificers and manufacturers, tends to diminish the home market, the most important of all markets for the rude produce of the land, and thereby still further to discourage agriculture.

These systems, therefore, which, preferring agriculture to all other employments, in order to promote it, impose restraints upon manufactures and foreign trade, act contrary to the very ends which they propose, and indirectly discourage that very species of industry which they mean to promote. They are, so far perhaps, more inconsistent than even the mercantile system. That system, by encouraging manufactures and foreign trade more than agriculture, turns a certain portion of the capital of the society from supporting a more advantageous, to support a less advantageous species of industry. But still it really and in the end encourages that species of industry which it means to promote. Those agricultural systems, on the contrary, really and in the end discourage their own favourite species of industry.

It is thus that every system which endeavours, either by extraordinary encouragements to draw towards a particular species of industry a greater share of the capital of the society than would naturally go to it, or, by extraordinary restraints, force from a particular species of industry some share of the capital which would otherwise be employed in it, is in reality subversive of the great purpose which it means to promote. It retards, instead of accelerating, the progress of society towards real wealth and greatness; and diminishes, instead of increasing, the real value of the annual produce of its land and labours.

All systems either of preference or of restraint, therefore, being thus completely taken away, the obvious and simple system of natural liberty establishes itself of its own accord. Every man, as long as he does not violate the laws of justice, is left perfectly free to pursue his own interest his own way, and to bring both his industry and capital into competition with those of any other man, or order of men. The sovereign is completely discharged from a duty, in the attempting to perform which he must always be exposed to innumerable delusions, and for the proper performance of which no human wisdom or knowledge could ever be sufficient; the duty of superintending the industry of private people and of directing it towards the employments most suitable to the interests of the society. According to the system of natural liberty, the sovereign has only three duties to attend to; three duties of great importance, indeed, but plain and intelligible to common understandings: first, the duty of protecting the society from the violence and invasion of other independent societies; secondly, the duty of protecting, as far as possible, every member of the society from the injustice or oppression of every other member of it, or the duty of establishing an exact administration of justice; and, thirdly, the duty of erecting and maintaining certain public works and certain public institutions, which it can never be for the interest of any individual, or small number of individuals, to erect and maintain; because the profit could never repay the expense to any individual or small number of individuals, though it may frequently do much more than repay it to a great society.

[From *An Inquiry into the Nature and Causes of the Wealth of Nations*, ed. Edwin Cannan (The Modern Library, New York, 1937), 649–51. First published 1776.]

83   Appearance and Reality

The sphere of circulation or commodity exchange, within whose boundaries the sale and purchase of labour-power goes on, is in fact a very Eden of the innate rights of man. It is the exclusive realm of Freedom, Equality, Property and Bentham. Freedom, because both buyer and seller of a commodity, let us say of labour-power, are determined only by their own free will. They contract as free persons, who are equal before the law. Their contract is the final result in which their joint will finds a common legal expression. Equality, because each enters into relation with the other, as with a simple owner of commodities, and they exchange equivalent for equivalent. Property, because each disposes only of what is his own. And Bentham, because each looks only to his own advantage. The only force bringing them together, and putting them into relation with each other, is the selfishness, the gain and the private interest of each. Each pays heed to himself only, and no one worries about the others. And precisely for that reason, either in accordance with the pre-established harmony of things, or under the auspices of an omniscient providence, they all work together to their mutual advantage, for the common weal, and in the common interest.

When we leave this sphere of simple circulation or the exchange of commodities, which provides the 'free-trader *vulgaris*' with his views, his concepts and the standard by which he judges the society of capital and wage-labour, a certain change takes place, or so it appears, in the physiognomy of our *dramatis personae*. He who was previously the money-owner now strides out in front as a capitalist; the possessor of labour-power follows as his worker. The one smirks self-importantly and is intent on business; the other is timid and holds back, like someone who has brought his own hide to market and now has nothing else to expect but—a tanning. [. . .]

In every stock-jobbing swindle everyone knows that some time or other the crash must come, but everyone hopes that it may fall on the head of his neighbour, after he himself has caught the shower of gold and placed it in secure hands. *Après moi le déluge!* is the watchword of every capitalist and of every capitalist nation. Capital therefore takes no account of the health and the length of life of the worker, unless society forces it to do so. Its answer to the outcry about the physical and mental degradation, the premature death, the torture of overwork, is this: Should that pain trouble us, since it increases our pleasure (profit)? But looking at these things as a whole, it is evident that this does not depend on the will, either good or bad, of the individual capitalist. Under free competition, the immanent laws of capitalist production confront the individual capitalist as a coercive force external to him.

[From *Capital*, vol. i, trans. Ben Fowkes (Penguin, Harmondsworth, 1976), 280, 380. First published 1867.]

F. A. HAYEK

84   Prices as a Code

The best way to understand how the operation of the market system leads not only to the creation of an order, but also to a great increase of the return which men receive from their efforts, is to think of it as a game. It is a wealth-creating game (and not what game theory calls a zero-sum game), that is, one that leads to an increase of the stream of goods and of the prospects of all participants to satisfy their needs, but which retains the character of a game in the sense in which the term is defined by the *Oxford English Dictionary*: 'a contest played according to rules and decided by superior skill, strength or good fortune'. That the outcome of this game for each will, because of its very character, necessarily be determined by a mixture of skill and chance will be one of the main points we must now try to make clear.

The chief cause of the wealth-creating character of the game is that the returns of the efforts of each player act as the signs which enable him to contribute to the satisfaction of needs of which he does not know, and to do so by taking advantage of conditions of which he also learns only indirectly through their being reflected in the prices of the factors of production which they use. It is thus a wealth-producing game because it supplies to each player information which enables him to provide for needs of which he has no direct knowledge and by the use of means of the existence of which without it he would have no cognizance, thus bringing about the satisfaction of a greater range of needs than would otherwise be possible. The manufacturer does not produce shoes because he knows that Jones needs them. He produces because he knows that dozens of traders will buy certain numbers at various prices because they (or rather the retailer they serve) know that thousands of Joneses, whom the manufacturer does not know, want to buy them. Similarly, a manufacturer will release resources for additional production by others by substituting, say, aluminium for magnesium in the production of his output, not because he knows of all the changes in demand and supply which on balance have made aluminium less scarce and magnesium more scarce, but because he learns the one simple fact that the price at which aluminium is offered to him has fallen relatively to the price of magnesium. Indeed, probably the most important instance of the price system bringing about the taking into account of conflicts of desires which otherwise would have been overlooked is the accounting of costs—in the interests of the community at large the most important aspect, i.e. the one most likely to benefit many other persons, and the one at which private enterprise excels but government enterprise notoriously fails.

Thus in the market order each is made by the visible gain to himself to serve needs which to him are invisible, and in order to do so to avail himself of to him unknown particular circumstances which put him in the position to satisfy these needs at as small a cost as possible in terms of other things which it is possible to produce instead. And where only a few know yet of an important new fact, the much maligned speculators will see to it that the relevant information will rapidly be spread by an appropriate change of prices. The important effect of this will of course be that all changes are currently taken account of as they become known to somebody connected with the trade, not that the adaptation to the new facts will ever be perfect.

The current prices, it must be specially noted, serve in this process as indicators of what ought to be done in the present circumstances and have no necessary relation to what has been done in the past in order to bring the current supply of any particular good on the market. For the same reason that the prices which guide the direction of the different efforts reflect events which the producer does not know, the return from his efforts will frequently be different from what he expected, and must be so if they are to guide production appropriately. The remunerations which the market determines are, as it were, not functionally related with what people *have* done, but only with what they *ought* to do. They are incentives which as a rule guide people to success, but will produce a viable order only because they often disappoint the expectations they have caused when relevant circumstances have unexpectedly changed. It is one of the chief tasks of competition to show which plans are false. The facts that full utilization of the limited information which the prices convey is usually rewarded, and that this makes it worthwhile to pay the greatest attention to them, are as important as that in the case of unforeseen changes the expectations are disappointed. The element of luck is as inseparable from the operation of the market as the element of skill.

There is no need morally to justify specific distributions (of income or wealth) which have not been brought about deliberately but are the outcome of a game that is played because it improves the chances of all. In such a game nobody 'treats' people differently and it is entirely consistent with respecting all people equally that the outcome of the game for different people is very different. It would also be as much a gamble what the effects of any one man's efforts would be worth if they were directed by a planning authority, only that not his knowledge but that of the authority would be used in determining the success or failure of his efforts.

The sum of information reflected or precipitated in the prices is wholly the product of competition, or at least of the openness of the market to anyone who has relevant information about some source of demand or supply for the good in question. Competition operates as a discovery procedure not only by giving anyone who has the opportunity to exploit special circumstances the possibility to do so profitably, but also by conveying to the other parties the information that there is some such opportunity. It is by this conveying of information in coded form that the competitive efforts of the market game secure the utilization of widely dispersed knowledge.

[From *Law, Legislation and Liberty* (Routledge, London, 1982), ii. 115–17. First published 1976.]

MILTON FRIEDMAN and ROSE FRIEDMAN

85 The Tyranny of Controls

An essential part of economic freedom is freedom to choose how to use our income: how much to spend on ourselves and on what items; how much to save and in what form; how much to give away and to whom. Currently, more than

40 percent of our income is disposed of on our behalf by government at federal, state, and local levels combined. One of us once suggested a new national holiday, 'Personal Independence Day—that day in the year when we stop working to pay the expenses of government . . . and start working to pay for the items we severally and individually choose in light of our own needs and desires.' In 1929 that holiday would have come on Abraham Lincoln's birthday, February 12; today it would come about May 30; if present trends were to continue, it would coincide with the other Independence Day, July 4, around 1988.

Of course, we have something to say about how much of our income is spent on our behalf by government. We participate in the political process that has resulted in government's spending an amount equal to more than 40 percent of our income. Majority rule is a necessary and desirable expedient. It is, however, very different from the kind of freedom you have when you shop at a supermarket. When you enter the voting booth once a year, you almost always vote for a package rather than for specific items. If you are in the majority, you will at best get both the items you favored and the ones you opposed but regarded as on balance less important. Generally, you end up with something different from what you thought you voted for. If you are in the minority, you must conform to the majority vote and wait for your turn to come. When you vote daily in the supermarket, you get precisely what you voted for, and so does everyone else. The ballot box produces conformity without unanimity; the marketplace, unanimity without conformity. That is why it is desirable to use the ballot box, so far as possible, only for those decisions where conformity is essential.

As consumers, we are not even free to choose how to spend the part of our income that is left after taxes. We are not free to buy cyclamates or laetrile, and soon, perhaps, saccharin. Our physician is not free to prescribe many drugs for us that he may regard as the most effective for our ailments, even though the drugs may be widely available abroad. We are not free to buy an automobile without seat belts, though, for the time being, we are still free to choose whether or not to buckle up.

Another essential part of economic freedom is freedom to use the resources we possess in accordance with our own values—freedom to enter any occupation, engage in any business enterprise, buy from and sell to anyone else, so long as we do so on a strictly voluntary basis and do not resort to force in order to coerce others.

Today you are not free to offer your services as a lawyer, a physician, a dentist, a plumber, a barber, a mortician, or engage in a host of other occupations, without first getting a permit or license from a government official. You are not free to work overtime at terms mutually agreeable to you and your employer, unless the terms conform to rules and regulations laid down by a government official.

You are not free to set up a bank, go into the taxicab business, or the business of selling electricity or telephone service, or running a railroad, busline, or airline, without first receiving permission from a government official.

You are not free to raise funds on the capital markets unless you fill out the numerous pages of forms the S E C requires and unless you satisfy the S E C that the prospectus you propose to issue presents such a bleak picture of your prospects that no investor in his right mind would invest in your project if he took the prospectus literally. And getting S E C approval may cost upwards of $100,000—which certainly discourages the small firms our government professes to help.

Freedom to own property is another essential part of economic freedom. And we do have widespread property ownership. Well over half of us own the homes we live in. When it comes to machines, factories, and similar means of production, the situation is very different. We refer to ourselves as a free private enterprise society, as a capitalist society. Yet in terms of the ownership of corporate enterprise, we are about 46 percent socialist. Owning 1 percent of a corporation means that you are entitled to receive 1 percent of its profits and must share 1 percent of its losses up to the full value of your stock. The 1979 federal corporate income tax is 46 percent on all income over $100,000 (reduced from 48 percent in prior years). The federal government is entitled to 46 cents out of every dollar of profit, and it shares 46 cents out of every dollar losses (provided there are some earlier profits to offset those losses). The federal government owns 46 percent of every corporation—though not in a form that entitles it to vote directly on corporate affairs.

It would take a book much longer than this one even to list in full all the restrictions on our economic freedom, let alone describe them in detail. These examples are intended simply to suggest how pervasive such restrictions have become.

Restrictions on economic freedom inevitably affect freedom in general, even such areas as freedom of speech and press.

Consider the following excerpts from a 1977 letter from Lee Grace, then executive vice-president of an oil and gas association. This is what he wrote with respect to energy legislation:

As you know, the real issue more so than the price per thousand cubic feet is the continuation of the First Amendment of the Constitution, the guarantee of freedom of speech. With increasing regulation, as big brother looks closer over our shoulder, we grow timid against speaking out for truth and our beliefs against falsehoods and wrong doings. Fear of IRS audits, bureaucratic strangulation or government harassment is a powerful weapon against freedom of speech.

In the October 31 [1977] edition of the US News & World Report, the Washington Whispers section noted that, 'Oil industry officials claim that they have received the ultimatum from Energy Secretary James Schlesinger: "Support the Administration's proposed tax on crude oil—or else face tougher regulation and a possible drive to break up the oil companies."'

His judgment is amply confirmed by the public behavior of oil officials. Tongue-lashed by Senator Henry Jackson for earning 'obscene profits,' not a single member of a group of oil industry executives answered back, or even left the room and refused to submit to further personal abuse. Oil company executives, who in private express strong opposition to the present complex structure of federal controls under which they operate or to the major extension of government intervention proposed by President Carter, make bland public statements approving the objectives of the controls.

Few businessmen regard President Carter's so-called voluntary wage and price controls as a desirable or effective way to combat inflation. Yet one businessman after another, one business organization after another, has paid lip service to the program, said nice things about it, and promised to cooperate. Only a few, like Donald Rumsfeld, former congressman, White House official, and Cabinet member, had the courage to denounce it publicly. They were joined by George Meany, the crusty octogenarian former head of the AFL-CIO.

It is entirely appropriate that people should bear a cost—if only of unpopularity and criticism—for speaking freely. However, the cost should be reasonable and not disproportionate. There should not be, in the words of a famous Supreme Court decision, 'a chilling effect' on free speech. Yet there is little doubt that currently there is such an effect on business executives.

The 'chilling effect' is not restricted to business executives. It affects all of us. We know most intimately the academic community. Many of our colleagues in economics and the natural science departments receive grants from the National Science Foundation; in the humanities, from the National Foundation for the Humanities; all those who teach in state universities get their salaries partly from the state legislatures. We believe that the National Science Foundation, the National Foundation for the Humanities, and tax subsidies to higher education are all undesirable and should be terminated. That is undoubtedly a minority view in the academic community, but the minority is much larger than anyone would gather from public statements to that effect.

The press is highly dependent on government—not only as a major source of news but in numerous other day-to-day operating matters. Consider a striking example from Great Britain. The London *Times*, a great newspaper, was prevented from publishing one day several years ago by one of its unions because of a story that it was planning to publish about the union's attempt to influence the content of the paper. Subsequently, labor disputes closed down the paper entirely. The unions in question are able to exercise this power because they have been granted special immunities by government. The National Union of Journalists in Britain is pushing for a closed shop of journalists and threatening to boycott papers that employ nonmembers of the union. All this in the country that was the source of so many of our liberties.

With respect to religious freedom, Amish farmers in the United States have had their houses and other property seized because they refused, on religious grounds, to pay Social Security taxes—and also to accept Social Security benefits. Church schools have had their students cited as truants in violation of compulsory attendance laws because their teachers did not have the requisite slips of paper certifying to their having satisfied state requirements.

Although these examples only scratch the surface, they illustrate the fundamental proposition that freedom is one whole, that anything that reduces freedom in one part of our lives is likely to affect freedom in the other parts.

Freedom cannot be absolute. We do live in an interdependent society. Some restrictions on our freedom are necessary to avoid other, still worse, restrictions. However, we have gone far beyond that point. The urgent need today is to eliminate restrictions, not add to them.

[From *Free to Choose* (Penguin, Harmondsworth, 1980), 89–94.]

G. A. COHEN

86 Poverty as Lack of Freedom

Suppose [. . .] that I want to perform an action which involves a legally prohibited use of your property. I want, let us say, to pitch a tent in your large back garden, perhaps just in order to annoy you, or perhaps for the more substantial reason that I have nowhere to live and no land of my own, but I have got hold of a tent, legitimately or otherwise. If I now try to do this thing that I want to do, the chances are that the state will intervene on your behalf. If it does, I shall suffer a constraint on my freedom. The same goes, of course, for all unpermitted uses of a piece of private property by those who do not own it, and there are always those who do not own it, since 'private ownership by one person presupposes non-ownership on the part of other persons'. But the free enterprise economy rests upon private property: in that economy you sell and buy what you respectively own and come to own. It follows that libertarians cannot complain that a socialist dispensation restricts freedom, by contrast with the dispensation that they themselves favour. [. . .]

The Right extols the freedom enjoyed by all in a liberal capitalist society. The Left complains that the freedom in question is meagre for poor people. The Right rejoins that the Left confuses freedom with resources. 'You are free to do what no one will interfere with your doing', says the Right. 'If you cannot afford to do it, that does not mean that someone will interfere with your doing it, but just that you lack the means or ability to do it. The problem the poor face is lack of ability, not lack of freedom'. The Left may then say that ability should count for as much as freedom does. The Right can then reply, to significant political effect: so *you* may think, but our priority is freedom.

In my view, the depicted right-wing stance depends upon a reified view of money. Money is unlike intelligence or physical strength, poor endowments of which do not, indeed, prejudice freedom, where freedom is understood as absence of interference. The difference between money and those endowments implies, I shall argue, that lack of money *is* (a form of) lack of freedom, in the favoured sense of freedom, where it is taken to be absence of interference.

To see this, begin by imagining a society without money, in which courses of action available to people, courses they are free to follow without interference, are laid down by the law. The law says what each sort of person, or even each particular person, may and may not do without interference, and each person is issued with a set of tickets detailing what she is allowed to do. So I may have a ticket saying that I am free to plough this piece of land, another one saying that I am free to go to that opera, or to walk across that field, while you have different tickets, with different freedoms inscribed on them.

Imagine, now, that the structure of the options written on the tickets is more complex. Each ticket lays out a disjunction of conjunctions of courses of action that I may perform. I may do A and B and C and D OR B and C and D and E OR E and F and G and A, and so on. If I try to do something not licensed by my tickets or ticket, armed force intervenes.

By hypothesis, these tickets say what my freedoms (and, consequently, my unfreedoms) are. But a sum of money is nothing but a highly generalized form of such a ticket. A sum of money is a licence to perform a disjunction of conjunctions of actions—actions, like, for example, visiting one's sister in Bristol, or taking home, and wearing, the sweater on the counter at Selfridge's.

Suppose that someone is too poor to visit her sister in Bristol. She cannot save, from week to week, enough to buy her way there. Then, as far as her freedom is concerned, this is equivalent to 'trip to Bristol' not being written on someone's ticket in the imagined non-monetary economy. The woman I have described has the capacity to go to Bristol. She can board the underground and approach the barrier which she must cross to reach the train. But she will be physically prevented from passing through it, or physically ejected from the train, or, in the other example, she will be physically stopped outside Selfridge's and the sweater will be removed. The only way that she will not be prevented from getting and using such things is by offering money for them.

To have money is to have freedom, and the assimilation of money to mental and bodily resources is a piece of unthinking fetishism, in the good old Marxist sense that it misrepresents *social relations of constraint* as *things* that people lack. In a word: money is no object.

[From 'Justice, Freedom and Market Transactions', in *Self-Ownership, Freedom and Equality* (Cambridge University Press, Cambridge, 1995), 56–9.]

V.c. Theories of Distributive Justice

AESOP

87 The Grasshopper and the Ants

One fine day in winter some ants were busy drying their store of corn, which had got rather damp during a long spell of rain. Presently up came a grasshopper and begged them to spare her a few grains, 'For,' she said, 'I'm simply starving.' The ants stopped work for a moment, though this was against their principles. 'May we ask,' said they, 'what you were doing with yourself all last summer? Why didn't you collect a store of food for the winter?' 'The fact is,' replied the grasshopper, 'I was so busy singing that I hadn't the time.' 'If you spent the summer singing,' replied the ants, 'you can't do better than spend the winter dancing.' And they chuckled and went on with their work.

['The Grasshopper and the Ants', *Aesop's Fables*, trans. V. S. Vernon Jones (Wordsworth Editions, Ware, 1994), 120.]

ARISTOTLE

88 Reciprocity

There are some who think that justice is nothing more or less than reciprocity. This was maintained, for example, by the Pythagoreans, who actually defined the just as simply 'to have done to one what one has done to another.' But simple reciprocity cannot be squared either with distributive or corrective justice, though people would like to say it was the latter, quoting the judgement of Rhadamanthus:

> If he that did has had done unto him
> That which he did, then justice will be wrought.

But they cannot be identified—there are many points of difference. For example, if a man in authority strikes somebody under him, it is wrong for the latter to return the blow. But if *he* strikes his superior officer, it is not enough that he should be struck back; he should receive some extra punishment. Again, it makes a world of difference whether consent entered into an act or not. It is true that in the give and take of mutual services this kind of justice—reciprocity of treatment—forms the bond between the parts of the process. But the *ground* of it is not equality but a proportion. It is just the feeling that, as one does, so one will be done by, that keeps a political association in being. For men regard it as their right to return evil for evil—and, if they cannot, feel they have lost their liberty—or good for good. Without some such understanding no exchange can be effected, and the link formed by the exchange is what holds the members of the association together. That is why a temple of the Graces is set up in a place where it cannot fail to be seen and remind men to repay a kindness. To make such a return is the distinguishing mark of grace, for it is our duty not merely to repay a service done, but to do one ourselves on another occasion.

This process of give and take according to the right proportion is carried out by 'diagonal conjunction'. Let me give you an illustration. A is a builder, B a shoemaker, C a house, D a shoe. It is required that the builder shall receive from the shoemaker some part of what the latter produces, giving him at the same time some part of what he produces himself. Now if they achieve, first, proportionate equality, secondly fair give and take, they will find the problem we have stated solved. But if they fail to achieve this, there will not be equality, nor will there be fairness in their dealing, and it cannot continue. For nothing prevents the product of one of the parties from being better value than that of the other, and this requires a process of reducing them to equality. It is the same with all the other arts and crafts. They would never have survived unless the active element—the producer—produced and received the same quantity and quality of products as the passive element—the recipient—gets. Each party must have something different to offer. Two doctors cannot associate for the purpose of exchanging what they have to give, but a doctor and a farmer can, and so, generally, can different types of people. Where there is not an original equality between them it has to be created. This implies that all products exchanged must be somehow comparable. It is this that has led to the introduction of money, which may be regarded as a medium of exchange, since it is a measure of everything, and so a measure of the more and the less than the mean in value, informing us, for example, how many shoes are worth one house or a fixed quantity of food. In this way we arrive at the formula: As a builder is to a shoemaker, so are *x* shoes to a house. Unless it be carried out in accordance with this formula, there can be no true exchange or association, and such reciprocity will be found impossible, if the things exchanged are not somehow reduced to equal value. To repeat what I said before, there must be one standard by which all commodities are to be measured. This standard is in fact demand; in every situation of the kind demand is the unifying factor. For if people should have different wants from what they do have, or no wants at all, there would be a different kind of exchange or none at all. By a convention which has come to be accepted, demand is expressed in the form of money, which is the reason why money is called 'currency'. For it is not a natural thing, but exists by current custom, while at the same time it is in our power to change or destroy its value.

After the products have been equalized reciprocal proportion will come into operation, so as to produce an equation: As farmer to shoemaker, so the product of the shoemaker to the product of the farmer. When they exchange their products they must reduce them to the form of a proportion, because, if they fail to do this, one or other of the two, having more than he ought, will have the advantage both in this respect and in the equivalent loss suffered by the other party to the exchange. When on the other hand they 'have their own' they are equal and can enter into an association with one another, because their case admits of such equality. But if reciprocal proportion could not be arrived at in this way, there could be no association between the parties. That it is demand, forming as it does a single standard, that holds such associations together, comes out clearly in the circumstance that, where there is no demand for an exchange of services from one or both the parties, they do not enter into association. . . . This possibility makes it necessary to introduce some means of producing equality.

[From *Nicomachean Ethics*, trans. J. A. K. Thomson (Penguin, Harmondsworth, 1953), 151–3.]

ARISTOTLE

89   Equality and Inequality

In all the sciences and arts the end is a good. Greatest and most good is the end of the most sovereign of them all, which is political ability. The political good is justice, and that is the common advantage.

All men hold that justice is some kind of equality; and up to a certain point they agree with what has been determined in our philosophical discussions on ethical matters. That is, they say that justice is a certain distribution to certain persons, and must be equal for equals. What we have to discover is equality and inequality of what sort of persons. That is difficult, and calls for political philosophy.

Perhaps someone would say that superiority in any good whatever deserves inequality in the assignment of offices, provided that in all other respects the men do not differ but are alike, on the ground that whoever differs has a different right and worth. But, if this is true, complexion and height and any good whatever will entitle those who excel in it to an excess of political rights. But is not this obviously false? That it is so is plain from the other sciences and abilities. Among fluteplayers who are equal in the art we should not give the preference of flutes to the more nobly born, because they will not play any better. We should give the superiority in instruments to him who is superior at the work. If the point is not yet clear, it will be made plain by developing it even further. If someone excelled at playing the flute, but was very inferior in birth or beauty, then, even if each of these is a greater good than fluteplaying (I mean birth and beauty), and even if their superiority as a fluteplayer, still he should be given the outstanding flutes. For the superiority must contribute to the work; but superiority in wealth and birth contribute nothing.

Furthermore, this principle would make every good comparable with every other good. For, if a certain height counted, then height in general would count, both as compared with wealth and as compared with freedom. Consequently, if one man differs from another in height more than the other differs from him in goodness, then, even if in general goodness excels height, everything would be comparable. For, plainly, if this much is better than that much, some other amount is equal thereto.

Since this is impossible, it is clear that in politics also it is reasonable not to claim office on the ground of any and every inequality. Differences in speed, for example, do not entitle a person to more political power; they get their reward in athletic competitions. The claim must be based on a difference in something that helps to constitute a city. Hence it is reasonable for the noble and free and rich to claim the honour, because the citizens must be free and have taxable property; a city could not consist entirely of needy persons, any more than of slaves. And, if those attributes are necessary, evidently justice and political goodness are necessary too. Without these, also, a city cannot go on. Or, rather, without the former, it cannot exist, and without these it cannot go on well.

[From *Politics Books III and IV*, trans. with introd. and comments by Richard Robinson (Clarendon Press, Oxford, 1995), 40–2.]

GERALD WINSTANLEY

90   **The Common Stock**

The great searching of heart in these days is to find out where true freedom lies, that the commonwealth of England might be established in peace.

Some say, 'It lies in the free use of trading, and to have all patents, licences and restraints removed'. But this is a freedom under the will of a conqueror.

Others say, 'It is true freedom to have ministers to preach, and for people to hear whom they will, without being restrained or compelled from or to any form of worship'. But this is an unsettled freedom.

Others say, 'It is true freedom to have community with all women, and to have liberty to satisfy their lusts and greedy appetites'. But this is the freedom of wanton unreasonable beasts, and tends to destruction.

Others say, 'It is true freedom that the elder brother shall be landlord of the earth, and the younger brother a servant'. And this is but a half freedom, and begets murmurings, wars and quarrels.

All these and such like are freedoms: but they lead to bondage, and are not the true foundation-freedom which settles a commonwealth in peace.

True commonwealth's freedom lies in the free enjoyment of the earth.

True freedom lies where a man receives his nourishment and preservation, and that is in the use of the earth. For as man is compounded of the four materials of the creation, fire, water, earth and air; so is he preserved by the compounded bodies of these four, which are the fruits of the earth; and he cannot live without them. For take away the free use of these and the body languishes, the spirit is brought into bondage and at length departs, and ceaseth his motional action in the body.

All that a man labours for, saith Solomon, is this, That he may enjoy the free use of the earth, with the fruits thereof. Eccles. 2.24.

Do not the ministers preach for maintenance in the earth? the lawyers plead causes to get the possessions of the earth? Doth not the soldier fight for the earth? And doth not the landlord require rent, that he may live in the fullness of the earth by the labour of his tenants?

And so, from the thief upon the highway to the king who sits upon the throne, do not everyone strive, either by force of arms or secret cheats, to get the possessions of the earth one from another, because they see their freedom lies in plenty, and their bondage lies in poverty?

Surely then, oppressing lords of manors, exacting landlords and tithe-takers, may as well say their brethren shall not breathe in the air, nor enjoy warmth in their bodies, nor have the moist waters to fall upon them in showers, unless they will pay them rent for it: as to say their brethren shall not work upon earth, nor eat the fruits thereof, unless they will hire that liberty of them. For he that takes upon him to restrain his brother from the liberty of the one, may upon the same ground restrain him from the liberty of all four, viz. fire, water, earth and air.

A man had better to have had no body than to have no food for it; therefore this restraining of the earth from brethren by brethren is oppression and bondage; but the free enjoyment thereof is true freedom.

I speak now in relation between the oppressor and the oppressed; the inward bondages I meddle not with in this place, though I am assured that, if it be rightly searched into, the inward bondages of the mind, as covetousness, pride, hypocrisy, envy, sorry, fears, desperation and madness, are all occasioned by the outward bondage that one sort of people lay upon another.

And thus far natural experience makes it good, that true freedom lies in the free enjoyment of the earth. [. . .]

That which true righteousness in my judgment calls community is this, to have the earth set free from all kingly bondage of lords of manors and oppressing landlords, which came in by conquest as a thief takes a true man's purse upon the highway, being stronger than he.

And that neither the earth, nor any fruits thereof, should be bought or sold by the inhabitants one among another, which is slavery the kingly conquerors have brought in; therefore he set his stamp upon silver, that every one should buy and sell in his name.

And though this be, yet shall not men live idle; for the earth shall be planted and reaped, and the fruits carried into barns and store-houses by the assistance of every family, according as is shewed hereafter in order.

Every man shall be brought up in trades and labours, and all trades shall be maintained with more improvement, to the enriching of the commonwealth, more than now they be under kingly power.

Every tradesman shall fetch materials, as leather, wool, flax, corn and the like, from the public store-houses, to work upon without buying and selling; and when particular works are made, as cloth, shoes, hats and the like, the tradesmen shall bring these particular works to particular shops, as it is now in practice, without buying and selling. And every family as they want such things as they cannot make, they shall go to these shops and fetch without money, even as now they fetch with money, as hereafter is shewed how in order.

If any say, 'This will nurse idleness'; I answer, this platform proves the contrary, for idle persons and beggars will be made to work.

If any say, 'This will make some men to take goods from others by violence and call it theirs, because the earth and fruits are a common stock'; I answer, the laws or rules following prevents that ignorance. For though the store-houses and public shops be commonly furnished by every family's assistance, and for every family's use, as is shewed hereafter how: yet every man's house is proper to himself, and all the furniture therein, and provision which he hath fetched from the store-houses is proper to himself; every man's wife and every woman's husband proper to themselves, and so are their children at their dispose till they come to age.

And if any other man endeavour to take away his house, furniture, food, wife or children, saying every thing is common, and so abusing the law of peace, such a one is a transgressor, and shall suffer punishment, as by the government and laws following is expressed.

For though the public store-houses be a common treasury, yet every man's particular dwelling is not common but by his consent, and the commonwealth's laws are to preserve a man's peace in his person and in his private dwelling, against the rudeness and ignorance that may arise in mankind.

[From *The Law of Freedom*, ed. Christopher Hill (Penguin, Harmondsworth, 1973), 294–6, 302–4. First published 1652.]

DAVID HUME

91 The Impossibility of Equality

We shall suppose that a creature, possessed of reason, but unacquainted with human nature, deliberates with himself what rules of justice or property would best promote public interest, and establish peace and security among mankind:

His most obvious thought would be, to assign the largest possessions to the most extensive virtue, and give every one the power of doing good, proportioned to his inclination. In a perfect theocracy, where a being, infinitely intelligent, governs by particular volitions, this rule would certainly have place, and might serve to the wisest purposes: But were mankind to execute such a law; so great is the uncertainty of merit, both from its natural obscurity, and from the self-conceit of each individual, that no determinate rule of conduct would ever result from it; and the total dissolution of society must be the immediate consequence. Fanatics may suppose, *that dominion is founded on grace*, and *that saints alone inherit the earth*; but the civil magistrate very justly puts these sublime theorists on the same footing with common robbers, and teaches them by the severest discipline, that a rule, which, in speculation, may seem the most advantageous to society, may yet be found, in practice, totally pernicious and destructive.

That there were *religious* fanatics of this kind in England, during the civil wars, we learn from history; though it is probable, that the obvious *tendency* of these principles excited such horror in mankind, as soon obliged the dangerous enthusiasts to renounce, or at least conceal their tenets. Perhaps the *levellers*, who claimed an equal distribution of property, were a kind of *political* fanatics, which arose from the religious species, and more openly avowed their pretensions; as carrying a more plausible appearance, of being practicable in themselves, as well as useful to human society.

It must, indeed, be confessed, that nature is so liberal to mankind, that, were all her presents equally divided among the species, and improved by art and industry, every individual would enjoy all the necessaries, and even most of the comforts of life; nor would ever be liable to any ills, but such as might accidentally arise from the sickly frame and constitution of his body. It must also be confessed, that, wherever we depart from this equality, we rob the poor of more satisfaction than we add to the rich, and that the slight gratification of a frivolous vanity, in one individual, frequently costs more than bread to many families, and even provinces. It may appear withal, that the rule of equality, as it would be highly *useful*, is not altogether *impracticable*; but has taken place, at least in an imperfect degree, in some republics; particularly that of Sparta; where it was attended, it is said, with the most beneficial consequences. Not to mention that the Agrarian laws, so frequently claimed in Rome, and carried into execution in many Greek cities, proceeded, all of them, from a general idea of the utility of this principle.

But historians, and even common sense, may inform us, that, however specious these ideas of *perfect* equality may seem, they are really, at bottom, *impracticable*; and were they not so, would be extremely *pernicious* to human society. Render possessions ever so equal, men's different degrees of art, care, and industry will immediately break that equality. Or if you check these virtues, you reduce society to the most extreme indigence; and instead of preventing want and beggary in a few, render it unavoidable to the whole community. The most rigorous inquisition too is requisite to watch every inequality on its first appearance; and the most severe jurisdiction, to punish and redress it. But besides, that so much authority must soon degenerate into tyranny, and be exerted with great partialities; who can possibly be possessed of it, in such a situation as is here supposed? Perfect equality of possessions, destroying all subordination, weakens extremely the authority of magistracy, and must reduce all power nearly to a level, as well as property.

[From *Enquiry Concerning the Principles of Morals, in Enquiries*, ed. L. A. Selby-Bigge, 3rd edn. (Clarendon Press, Oxford, 1975), 192–4. First published 1751.]

KARL MARX

92 From Each According to His Abilities, To Each According to His Needs

What is 'just' distribution?

Does not the bourgeoisie claim that the present system of distribution is 'just'? And given the present mode of production is it not, in fact, the only 'just' system of distribution? Are economic relations regulated by legal concepts of right or is the opposite not the case, that legal relations spring from economic ones? Do not the socialist sectarians themselves have the most varied notions of 'just' distribution?

Within the cooperative society based on common ownership of the means of production the producers do not exchange their products; similarly, the labour spent on the products no longer appears *as the value* of these products, possessed by them as a material characteristic, for now, in contrast to capitalist society, individual pieces of labour are no longer merely indirectly, but directly, a component part of the total labour. The phrase 'proceeds of labour', which even today is too ambiguous to be of any value, thus loses any meaning whatsoever.

We are dealing here with a communist society, not as it has *developed* on its own foundations, but on the contrary, just as it *emerges* from capitalist society. In every respect, economically, morally, intellectually, it is thus still stamped with the birth-marks of the old society from whose womb it has emerged. Accordingly, the individual producer gets back from society—after the deductions—exactly what he has given it. What he has given it is his individual quantum of labour. For instance, the social working day consists of the sum of the individual hours of work. The individual labour time of the individual producer thus constitutes his contribution to the social working day, his share of it. Society gives him a certificate stating that he has done such and such an amount of work (after the labour done for the communal fund has been deducted), and with this certificate he can withdraw from the social supply of means of consumption as much as costs an equivalent amount of labour. The same amount of labour he has given to society in one form, he receives back in another.

Clearly, the same principle is at work here as that which regulates the exchange of commodities as far as this is an exchange of equal values. Content and form have changed because under the new conditions no one can contribute anything except his labour and conversely nothing can pass into the ownership of individuals except individual means of consumption. The latter's distribution among individual producers, however, is governed by the same principle as the exchange of commodity equivalents: a given amount of labour in one form is exchanged for the same amount in another.

Hence *equal right* is here still—in principle—a *bourgeois right*, although principle and practice are no longer at loggerheads, while the exchange of equivalents in commodity exchange only exists *on the average* and not in the individual case.

In spite of such progress this *equal right* still constantly suffers a bourgeois limitation. The right of the producers is *proportional* to the labour they do; the equality consists in the fact that measurement is *by the same standard*, labour. One person, however, may be physically and intellectually superior to another and thus be able to do more labour in the same space of time or work for a longer period. To serve as a measure labour must therefore be determined by duration or intensity, otherwise it ceases to be a standard. This *equal* right is an unequal right for unequal labour. It does not acknowledge any class distinctions, because everyone is just a worker like everyone else, but it gives tacit recognition to a worker's individual endowment and hence productive capacity as natural privileges. *This right is thus in its content one of inequality, just like any other right.* A right can by its nature only consist in the application of an equal standard, but unequal individuals (and they would not be different individuals if they were not unequal) can only be measured by the same standard if they are looked at from the same aspect, if they are grasped from one *particular* side, e.g., if in the present case they are regarded *only as workers* and nothing else is seen in them, everything else is ignored. Further: one worker is married, another is not; one has more children than another, etc., etc. Thus, with the same work performance and hence the same share of the social consumption fund, one will in fact be receiving more than another, one will be richer than another, etc. If all these defects were to be avoided rights would have to be unequal rather than equal.

Such defects, however, are inevitable in the first phase of communist society, given the specific form in which it has emerged after prolonged birth-pangs from capitalist society. Right can never rise above the economic structure of a society and its contingent cultural development.

In a more advanced phase of communist society, when the enslaving subjugation of individuals to the division of labour, and thereby the antithesis between intellectual and physical labour, have disappeared; when labour is no longer just a means of keeping alive but has itself become a vital need; when the all-round development of individuals has also increased their productive powers and all the springs of cooperative wealth flow more abundantly—only then can society wholly cross the narrow horizon of bourgeois right and inscribe on its banner: From each according to his abilities, to each according to his needs! [. . .]

Quite apart from the points made so far, it was a mistake anyway to lay the main stress on so-called *distribution* and to make it into the central point.

The distribution of the means of consumption at any given time is merely a consequence of the distribution of the conditions of production themselves; the distribution of the latter, however, is a feature of the mode of production itself. The capitalist mode of production, for example, rests on the fact that the material conditions of production are in the hands of non-workers in the form of property in capital and land, while the masses are only in possession of their personal condition of production, labour power. If the elements of production are distributed in this way, the present distribution of the means of consumption follows automatically. If the material conditions of production were the cooperative property of the workers themselves a different distribution of the means of consumption from that of today would follow of its own accord. Vulgar socialists (and from them, in turn, a section of the democrats) have followed the bourgeois economists in their consideration and treatment of distribution as something independent of the mode of production and hence in the presentation of socialism as primarily revolving around the question of distribution. Why go back a step when the real state of affairs has been laid bare?

[From 'Critique of the Gotha Programme', trans. Joris de Bres, in *The First International and After* (Penguin, Harmondsworth, 1974), 344–8. Written 1875.]

EDWARD BELLAMY

93 Looking Backward

'How, then, do you regulate wages?' I once more asked.

Dr Leete did not reply till after several moments of meditative silence. 'I know, of course,' he finally said, 'enough of the old order of things to understand just what you mean by that question; and yet the present order is so utterly different at this point that I am a little at loss how to answer you best. You ask me how we regulate wages; I can only reply that there is no idea in the modern social economy which at all corresponds with what was meant by wages in your day.'

'I suppose you mean that you have no money to pay wages in,' said I. 'But the credit given the worker at the government storehouse answers to his wages with us. How is the amount of the credit given respectively to the workers in different lines determined? By what title does the individual claim his particular share? What is the basis of allotment?'

'His title,' replied Dr Leete, 'is his humanity. The basis of his claim is the fact that he is a man.'

'The fact that he is a man!' I repeated, incredulously. 'Do you possibly mean that all have the same share?'

'Most assuredly.'

The readers of this book never having practically known any other arrangement, or perhaps very carefully considered the historical accounts of former epochs in which a very different system prevailed, cannot be expected to appreciate the stupor of amazement into which Dr Leete's simple statement plunged me.

'You see,' he said, smiling, 'that it is not merely that we have no money to pay wages in, but, as I said, we have nothing at all answering to your idea of wages.'

By this time I had pulled myself together sufficiently to voice some of the criticisms which, man of the nineteenth century as I was, came uppermost in my mind, upon this to me astounding arrangement. 'Some men do twice the work of others!' I exclaimed. 'Are the clever workmen content with a plan that ranks them with the indifferent?'

'We leave no possible ground for any complaint of injustice,' replied Dr Leete, 'by requiring precisely the same measure of service from all.'

'How can you do that, I should like to know, when no two men's powers are the same?'

'Nothing could be simpler,' was Dr Leete's reply. 'We require of each that he shall make the same effort; that is, we demand of him the best service it is in his power to give.'

'And supposing all do the best they can,' I answered, 'the amount of the product resulting is twice greater from one man than from another.'

'Very true,' replied Dr Leete; 'but the amount of the resulting product has nothing whatever to do with the question, which is one of desert. Desert is a moral question, and the amount of the product a material quantity. It would be an extraordinary sort of logic which should try to determine a moral question by a material standard. The amount of the effort alone is pertinent to the question of desert. All men who do their best, do the same. A man's endowments, however godlike, merely fix the measure of his duty. The man of great endowments who does not do all he might, though he may do more than a man of small endowments who does his best, is deemed a less deserving worker than the latter, and dies a debtor to his fellows. The Creator sets men's tasks for them by the faculties he gives them; we simply exact their fulfillment.'

'No doubt that is very fine philosophy,' I said; 'nevertheless it seems hard that the man who produces twice as much as another, even if both do their best, should have only the same share.'

'Does it, indeed, seem so to you?' responded Dr Leete. 'Now, do you know, that seems very curious to me? The way it strikes people nowadays is, that a man who can produce twice as much as another with the same effort, instead of being rewarded for doing so, ought to be punished if he does not do so. In the nineteenth century, when a horse pulled a heavier load than a goat, I suppose you rewarded him. Now, we should have whipped him soundly if he had not, on the ground that, being much stronger, he ought to. It is singular how ethical standards change.' The doctor said this with such a twinkle in his eye that I was obliged to laugh.

'I suppose,' I said, 'that the real reason that we rewarded men for their endowments, while we considered those of horses and goats merely as fixing the service to be severally required of them, was that the animals, not being reasoning beings, naturally did the best they could, whereas men could only be induced to do so by rewarding them according to the amount of their product. That brings me to ask why, unless human nature has mightily changed in a hundred years, you are not under the same necessity.'

'We are,' replied Dr Leete. 'I don't think there has been any change in human nature in that respect since your day. It is still so constituted that special incentives in the form of prizes, and advantages to be gained, are requisite to call out the best endeavors of the average man in any direction.'

'But what inducement,' I asked, 'can a man have to put forth his best endeavors when, however much or little he accomplishes, his income remains the same? High characters may be moved by devotion to the common welfare under such a system, but does not the average man tend to rest back on his oar, reasoning that it is of no use to make a special effort, since the effort will not increase his income, nor its withholding diminish it?'

'Does it then really seem to you,' answered my companion, 'that human nature is insensible to any motives save fear of want and love of luxury, that you should expect security and equality of livelihood to leave them without possible incentives to effort? Your contemporaries did not really think so, though they might fancy they did. When it was a question of the grandest class of efforts, the most absolute self-devotion, they depended on quite other incentives. Not higher wages, but honor and the hope of men's gratitude, patriotism and the inspiration of duty, were the motives which they set before their soldiers when it was a question of dying for the nation, and never was there an age of the world when those motives did not call out what is best and noblest in men. And not only this, but when you come to analyze the love of money which was the general impulse to effort in your day, you find that the dread of want and desire of luxury was but one of several motives which the pursuit of money represented; the others, and with many the more influential, being desire of power, of social position, and reputation for ability and success. So you see that though we have abolished poverty and the fear of it, and inordinate luxury with the hope of it, we have not touched the greater part of the motives which underlay the love of money in former times, or any of those which prompted the supremer sorts of effort. The coarser motives, which no longer move us, have been replaced by higher motives wholly unknown to the mere wage earners of your age. Now that industry of whatever sort is no longer self-service, but service of the nation, patriotism, passion for humanity, impel the worker as in your day they did the soldier. The army of industry is an army, not alone by virtue of its perfect organization, but by reason also of the ardor of self-devotion which animates its members.

'But as you used to supplement the motives of patriotism with the love of glory, in order to stimulate the valor of your soldiers, so do we. Based as our industrial system is on the principle of requiring the same unit of effort from every man, that is, the best he can do, you will see that the means by which we spur the workers to do their best must be a very essential part of our scheme. With us, diligence in the national service is the sole and certain way to public repute, social distinction, and official power. The value of a man's services to society fixes his rank in it. Compared with the effect of our social arrangements on impelling men to be zealous in business, we deem the object-lessons of biting poverty and wanton luxury on which you depended a service as weak and uncertain as it was barbaric. The lust of honor even in your sordid day notoriously impelled men to more desperate effort than the love of money could.' [. . .]

'I should not fail to mention,' resumed the doctor, 'that for those too deficient in mental or bodily strength to be fairly graded with the main body of workers, we have a separate grade, unconnected with the others,—a sort of invalid corps, the members of which are provided with a light class of tasks fitted to their strength. All our sick in mind and body, all our deaf and dumb, and lame and blind and crippled, and even our insane, belong to this invalid corps, and bear its insignia. The strongest often do nearly a man's work, the feeblest, of course, nothing; but none who can do anything are willing quite to give up. In their lucid intervals, even our insane are eager to do what they can.'

'That is a pretty idea of the invalid corps,' I said. 'Even a barbarian from the nineteenth century can appreciate that. It is a very graceful way of disguising charity, and must be grateful to the feelings of its recipients.'

'Charity!' repeated Dr Leete. 'Did you suppose that we consider the incapable class we are talking of objects of charity?'

'Why, naturally,' I said, 'inasmuch as they are incapable of self-support.'

But here the doctor took me up quickly.

'Who is capable of self-support?' he demanded. 'There is no such thing in a civilized society as self-support. In a state of society so barbarous as not even to know family coöperation, each individual may possibly support himself, though even then for a part of his life only; but from the moment that men begin to live together, and constitute even the rudest sort of society, self-support becomes impossible. As men grow more civilized, and the subdivision of occupations and services is carried out, a complex mutual dependence becomes the universal rule. Every man, however solitary may seem his occupation, is a member of a vast industrial partnership, as large as the nation, as large as humanity. The necessity of mutual dependence should imply the duty and guarantee of mutual support; and that it did not in your day constituted the essential cruelty and unreason of your system.'

'That may all be so,' I replied, 'but it does not touch the case of those who are unable to contribute anything to the product of industry.'

'Surely I told you this morning, at least I thought I did,' replied Dr Leete, 'that the right of a man to maintenance at the nation's table depends on the fact that he is a man, and not on the amount of health and strength he may have, so long as he does his best.'

'You said so,' I answered, 'but I supposed the role applied only to the workers of different ability. Does it also hold of those who can do nothing at all?'

'Are they not also men?'

'I am to understand, then, that the lame, the blind, the sick, and the impotent, are as well off as the most efficient and have the same income?'

'Certainly,' was the reply.

'The idea of charity on such a scale,' I answered, 'would have made our most enthusiastic philanthropists gasp.'

'If you had a sick brother at home,' replied Dr Leete, 'unable to work, would you feed him on less dainty food, and lodge and clothe him more poorly, than yourself? More likely far, you would give him the preference; nor would you think of calling it charity. Would not the word, in that connection, fill you with indignation?'

'Of course,' I replied; 'but the cases are not parallel. There is a sense, no doubt, in which all men are brothers; but this general sort of brotherhood is not to be compared, except for rhetorical purposes, to the brotherhood of blood, either as to its sentiment or its obligations.'

'There speaks the nineteenth century!' exclaimed Dr Leete. 'Ah, Mr West, there is no doubt as to the length of time that you slept. If I were to give you, in one sentence, a key to what may seem the mysteries of our civilization as compared with that of your age, I should say that it is the fact that the solidarity of the race and the brotherhood of man, which to you were but fine phrases, are, to our thinking and feeling, ties as real and as vital as physical fraternity.

'But even setting that consideration aside, I do not see why it so surprises you that those who cannot work are conceded the full right to live on the produce of those who can. Even in your day, the duty of military service for the protection of the nation, to which our industrial service corresponds, while obligatory on those able to discharge it, did not operate to deprive of the privileges of citizenship those who were unable. They stayed at home, and were protected by those who fought, and nobody questioned their right to be, or thought less of them. So, now, the requirement of industrial service from those able to render it does not operate to deprive of the privileges of citizenship, which now implies the citizen's maintenance, him who cannot work. the worker is not a citizen because he works, but works because he is a citizen. As you recognize the duty of the strong to fight for the weak, we, now that fighting is gone by, recognize his duty to work for him.

[From *Looking Backward* (The Modern Library, New York, 1982), 65–9, 94–6. First published 1882.]

F. A. HAYEK

94   The Impossibility of Planning

As soon as the state takes upon itself the task of planning the whole economic life, the problems of the due station of the different individuals and groups must indeed inevitably become the central political problem. As the coercive power of the state will alone decide who is to have what, the only power worth having will be a share in the exercise of this directing power. There will be no economic or social questions that would not be political questions in the sense that their solution will depend exclusively on who wields the coercive power, on whose are the views that will prevail on all occasions.

I believe it was Lenin himself who introduced to Russia the famous phrase 'who, whom?'—during the early years of Soviet rule the byword in which the people summed up the universal problem of a socialist society. Who plans whom, who directs and dominates whom, who assigns to other people their station in life, and who is to have his due allotted by others? These become necessarily the central issues to be decided solely by the supreme power.

More recently an American student of politics has enlarged upon Lenin's phrase and asserted that the problem of all government is 'who gets what, when, and how?' In a way this is not untrue. That all government affects the relative position of different people and that there is under any system scarcely an aspect of our lives which may not be affected by government action, is certainly true. In so far as government does anything at all, its action will always have some effect on 'who gets what, when, and how'.

There are, however, two fundamental distinctions to be made. Firstly, particular measures may be taken without the knowledge of how they will affect particular individuals, and without aiming at such particular effects. This point we have already discussed. Secondly, it is the extent of the activities of the government which decides whether everything that any person gets at any time depends on the government, or whether its influence is confined to whether some people will get some things in some way at some time. Here lies the whole difference between a free and a totalitarian system.

The contrast between a liberal and a totally planned system is characteristically illustrated by the common complaints of Nazis and socialists of the 'artificial separations of economics and politics', and their equally common demand for the dominance of politics over economics. These phrases presumably mean not only that economic forces are now allowed to work for ends which are not part of the policy of the government, but also that economic power can be used independently of government direction and for ends of which the government may not approve. But the alternative is not merely that there would be only one power, but that this single power, the ruling group, should have control over all human ends, and particularly that it should have complete power over the position of each individual in society.

That a government which undertakes to direct economic activity will have to use its power to realise somebody's ideal of distributive justice is certain. But how can and how will it use that power? By what principles will it or ought it to be guided? Is there a definite answer to the innumerable questions of relative merits that will arise and which will have to be solved deliberately? Is there a scale of values on which reasonable people can be expected to agree, which would justify a new hierarchical order of society, and is likely to satisfy the demands for justice?

There is only one general principle, one simple rule which would indeed provide a definite answer to all these questions: equality, complete and absolute equality of all individuals in all those points which are subject to human control. If this were generally regarded as desirable (quite apart from the question whether it would be practicable, i.e., whether it would provide adequate incentives), it would give the vague idea of distributive justice a clear meaning and would give the planner definite guidance. But nothing is further from the truth than that people in general regard mechanical equality of this kind as desirable. No socialist movement which aimed at complete equality has ever gained substantial support. What socialism promised was not an absolute equal, but a more just and more equal distribution. Not equality in the absolute sense, but 'greater equality' is the only goal which is seriously aimed at.

Though these two ideals sound very similar, they are as different as possible as far as our problem is concerned. While absolute equality would clearly determine the planner's task, the desire for greater equality is merely negative, no more than an expression of dislike of the present state of affairs; and so long as we are not prepared to say that every move in the direction towards complete equality is desirable, it answers scarcely any of the questions the planner will have to decide.

This is not a quibble about words. We face here a crucial issue which the similarity of the terms used is apt to conceal. While agreement on complete equality would answer all the problems of merit the planner must answer, the formula of the approach to greater equality answers practically none. Its content is hardly more definite than the phrases 'common good' or 'social welfare'. It does not free us from the necessity of deciding in every particular instance between the merits of particular individuals or groups, and gives us no help in that decision. All it tells us in effect is to take from the rich as much as we can. But when it comes to the distribution of the spoils, the problem is the same as if the formula of 'greater equality' had never been conceived.

Most people find it difficult to admit that we do not possess moral standards which would enable us to settle these questions—if not perfectly, at least to greater general satisfaction than is done by the competitive system. Have we not all some idea of what is a 'just price' or a 'fair wage'? Can we not rely on the strong sense of fairness of the people? And even if we do not now agree fully on what is just or fair in a particular case, would popular ideas not soon consolidate into more definite standards if people were given an opportunity to see their ideals realised?

Unfortunately there is little ground for such hopes. What standards we have are derived from the competitive regime we have known, and would necessarily disappear soon after the disappearance of competition. What we mean by a just price, or a fair wage, is either the customary price or wage, the return which past experience has made people expect, or the price or wage that would exist if there were no monopolistic exploitation. The only important exception to this used to be the claim of the workers to the 'full produce of their labour', to which so much of socialist doctrine traces back. But there are few socialists to-day who believe that in a socialist society the output of each industry would be entirely shared by the workers of that industry; for this would mean that workers in industries using a great deal of capital would have a much larger income than those in industries using little capital, which most socialists would regard as very unjust. And it is now fairly generally agreed that this particular claim was based on an erroneous interpretation of the facts. But once the claim of the individual worker to the whole of 'his' product is disallowed, and the whole of the return from capital is to be divided among all workers, the problem of how to divide it raises the same basic issue.

What the 'just price' of a particular commodity or the 'fair' remuneration for a particular service is, might conceivably be determined objectively if the quantities needed were independently fixed. If these were given irrespective of cost, the planner might try to find what price or wage is necessary to bring forth this supply. But the planner must also decide how much is to be produced of each kind of goods, and in so doing he determines what will be the just price or fair wage to pay. If the planner decides that fewer architects or watch-makers are wanted and that the need can be met by those who are willing to stay in the trade at a lower remuneration, the 'fair' wage will be lower. In deciding the relative importance of the different ends, the planner also decides the relative importance of the different groups and persons. As he is not supposed to treat the people merely as a means, he must take account of these effects and consciously balance the importance of the different ends against the effects of his decision. This means, however, that he will necessarily exercise direct control over the conditions of the different people.

This applies to the relative position of individuals no less than to that of the different occupational groups. We are in general far too apt to think of incomes within a given trade or profession as more or less uniform. But the differences between the incomes, not only of the most and the least successful doctor or architect, writer or cinema actor, boxer or jockey, but also of the more and the less successful plumber or market gardener, grocer or tailor, are as great as those between the propertied and the property-less classes. And although, no doubt, there would be some attempt at standardisation by creating categories, the necessity of discrimination between individuals would remain the same, whether it were exercised by fixing their individual incomes or by allocating them to particular categories.

We need say no more about the likelihood of men in a free society submitting to such control—or about their remaining free if they submitted. On the whole question what John Stuart Mill wrote nearly a hundred years ago remains equally true to-day:

A fixed rule, like that of equality, might be acquiesced in, and so might chance, or an external necessity; but that a handful of human beings should weigh everybody in the balance, and give more to one and less to another at their sole pleasure and judgement, would not be borne unless from persons believed to be more than men, and backed by supernatural terrors.

[From *The Road to Serfdom* (Routledge & Kegan Paul, London, 1944), 80–4.]

JOHN RAWLS

95 Two Principles of Justice

I shall now state in a provisional form the two principles of justice [. . .]

First: each person is to have an equal right to the most extensive basic liberty compatible with a similar liberty for others.

Second: social and economic inequalities are to be arranged so that they are both (a) reasonably expected to be to everyone's advantage, and (b) attached to positions and offices open to all.

The basic liberties of citizens are, roughly speaking, political liberty (the right to vote and to be eligible for public office) together with freedom of speech and assembly; liberty of conscience and freedom of thought; freedom of the person along with the right to hold (personal) property; and freedom from arbitrary arrest and seizure as defined by the concept of the rule of law. These liberties are all required to be equal by the first principle, since citizens of a just society are to have the same basic rights.

The second principle applies, in the first approximation, to the distribution of income and wealth and to the design of organizations that make use of differences in authority and responsibility, or chains of command. While the distribution of wealth and income need not be equal, it must be to everyone's advantage, and at the same time, positions of authority and offices of command must be accessible to all. One applies the second principle by holding positions open, and then, subject to this constraint, arranges social and economic inequalities so that everyone benefits.

These principles are to be arranged in a serial order with the first principle prior to the second. This ordering means that a departure from the institutions of equal liberty required by the first principle cannot be justified by, or compensated for, by greater social and economic advantages. The distribution of wealth and income, and the hierarchies of authority, must be consistent with both the liberties of equal citizenship and equality of opportunity. [. . .]

It should be observed that the two principles (and this holds for all formulations) are a special case of a more general conception of justice that can be expressed as follows.

All social values—liberty and opportunity, income and wealth, and the bases of self-respect—are to be distributed equally unless an unequal distribution of any, or all, of these values is to everyone's advantage.

Injustice, then, is simply inequalities that are not to the benefit of all. [. . .]

As a first step, suppose that the basic structure of society distributes certain primary goods, that is, things that every rational man is presumed to want. These goods normally have a use whatever a person's rational plan of life. For simplicity, assume that the chief primary goods at the disposition of society are rights and liberties, powers and opportunities, income and wealth. These are the social primary goods. Other primary goods such as health and vigor, intelligence and imagination, are natural goods; although their possession is influenced by the basic structure, they are not so directly under its control. Imagine, then, a hypothetical initial arrangement in which all the social primary goods are equally distributed: everyone has similar rights and duties, and income and wealth are evenly shared. This state of affairs provides a benchmark for judging improvements. If certain inequalities of wealth and organizational powers would make everyone better off than in this hypothetical starting situation, then they accord with the general conception. [. . .]

To illustrate the difference principle, consider the distribution of income among social classes. Let us suppose that the various income groups correlate with representative individuals by reference to whose expectations we can judge the distribution. Now those starting out as members of the entrepreneurial class in property-owning democracy, say, have a better prospect than those who begin in the class of unskilled laborers. It seems likely that this will be true even when the social injustices which now exist are removed. What, then, can possibly justify this kind of initial inequality in life prospects? According to the difference principle, it is justifiable only if the difference in expectation is to the advantage of the representative man who is worse off, in this case the representative unskilled worker. The inequality in expectation is permissible only if lowering it would make the working class even more worse off. Supposedly, given the rider in the second principle concerning open positions, and the principle of liberty generally, the greater expectations allowed to entrepreneurs encourages them to do things which raise the long-term prospects of laboring class. Their better prospects act as incentives so that the economic process is more efficient, innovation proceeds at a faster pace, and so on. Eventually the resulting material benefits spread throughout the system and to the least advantaged. I shall not consider how far these things are true. The point is that something of this kind must be argued if these inequalities are to be just by the difference principle. [. . .]

In view of these remarks we may reject the contention that the injustice of institutions is always imperfect because the distribution of natural talents and the contingencies of social circumstance are unjust, and this injustice must inevitably carry over to human arrangements. Occasionally this reflection is offered as an excuse for ignoring injustice, as if the refusal to acquiesce in injustice is on a par with being unable to accept death. The natural distribution is neither just nor unjust; nor is it unjust that men are born into society at some particular position. These are simply natural facts. What is just and unjust is the way that institutions deal with these facts. Aristocratic and caste societies are unjust because they make these contingencies the ascriptive basis for belonging to more or less enclosed and privileged social classes. The basic structure of these societies incorporates the arbitrariness found in nature. But there is no necessity for men to resign themselves to these contingencies. The social system is not an unchangeable order beyond human control but a pattern of human action. In justice as fairness men agree to share one another's fate. In designing institutions they undertake to avail themselves of the accidents of nature and social circumstance only when doing so is for the common benefit. The two principles are a fair way of meeting the arbitrariness of fortune; and while no doubt imperfect in other ways, the institutions which satisfy these principles are just.

A further point is that the difference principle expresses a conception of reciprocity. It is a principle of mutual benefit. We have seen that, at least when chain connection holds, each representative man can accept the basic structure as designed to advance his interests. The social order can be justified to everyone, and in particular to those who are least favored; and in this sense it is egalitarian. But it seems necessary to consider in an intuitive way how the condition of mutual benefit is satisfied. Consider any two representative men A and B, and let B be the one who is less favored. Actually, since we are most interested in the comparison with the least favored man, let us assume that B is this individual. Now B can accept A's being better off since A's advantages have been gained in ways that improve B's prospects. If A were not allowed his better position, B would be even worse off than he is. The difficulty is to show that A has no grounds for complaint. Perhaps he is required to have less than he might since his having more would result in some loss to B. Now what can be said to the more favored man? To begin with, it is clear that the well-being of each depends on a scheme of social cooperation without which no one could have a satisfactory life. Secondly, we can ask for the willing cooperation of everyone only if the terms of the scheme are reasonable. The difference principle, then, seems to be a fair basis on which those better endowed, or more fortunate in their social circumstances, could expect others to collaborate with them when some workable arrangement is a necessary condition of the good of all. [. . .]

Perhaps some will think that the person with greater natural endowments deserves those assets and the superior character that made their development possible. Because he is more worthy in this sense, he deserves the greater advantages that he could achieve with them. This view, however, is surely incorrect. It seems to be one of the fixed points of our considered judgments that no one deserves his place in the distribution of native endowments any more than one deserves one's initial starting place in society. The assertion that a man deserves the superior character that enables him to make the effort to cultivate his abilities is equally problematic; for his character depends in large part upon fortunate family and social circumstances for which he can claim no credit. The notion of desert seems not to apply to these cases. Thus the more advantaged representative man cannot say that he deserves and therefore has a right to a scheme of cooperation in which he is permitted to acquire benefits in ways that do not contribute to the welfare of others. There is no basis for his making this claim. From the standpoint of common sense, then, the difference principle appears to be acceptable both to the more advantaged and to the less advantaged individual. Of course, none of this is strictly speaking an argument for the principle, since in a contract theory arguments are made from the point of view of the original position. But these intuitive considerations help to clarify the nature of the principle and the sense in which it is egalitarian. [. . .]

A further merit of the difference principle is that it provides an interpretation of the principle of fraternity. In comparison with liberty and equality, the idea of fraternity has had a lesser place in democratic theory. It is thought to be less specifically a political concept, not in itself defining any of the democratic rights but conveying instead certain attitudes of mind and forms of conduct without which we would lose sight of the values expressed by these rights. Or closely related to this, fraternity is held to represent a certain equality of social esteem manifest in various public conventions and in the absence of manners of deference and servility. No doubt fraternity does imply these things, as well as a sense of civic friendship and social solidarity, but so understood it expresses no definite requirement. We have yet to find a principle of justice that matches the underlying idea. The difference principle, however, does seem to correspond to a natural meaning of fraternity: namely, to the idea of not wanting to have greater advantages unless this is to the benefit of others who are less well off. The family, in its ideal conception and often in practice, is one place where the principle of maximizing the sum of advantages is rejected. Members of a family commonly do not wish to gain unless they can do so in ways that further the interests of the rest. Now wanting to act on the difference principle has precisely this consequence. Those better circumstanced are willing to have their greater advantages only under a scheme in which this works out for the benefit of the less fortunate.

[From *A Theory of Justice* (Clarendon Press, Oxford, 1972), 60–2, 78, 102–5.]

ROBERT NOZICK

96 The Entitlement Theory

Almost every suggested principle of distributive justice is patterned: to each according to his moral merit, or needs, or marginal product, or how hard he tries, or the weighted sum of the foregoing, and so on. The principle of entitlement we have sketched is not patterned. There is no one natural dimension or weighted sum or combination of a small number of natural dimensions that yields the distributions generated in accordance with the principle of entitlement. The set of holdings that results when some persons receive their marginal products, others win at gambling, others receive a share of their mate's income, others receive gifts from foundations, others receive interest on loans, others receive gifts from admirers, others receive returns on investment, others make for themselves much of what they have, others find things, and so on, will not be patterned. [. . .]

To think that the task of a theory of distributive justice is to fill in the blank in 'to each according to his——' is to be predisposed to search for a pattern; and the separate treatment of 'from each according to his——' treats production and distribution as two separate and independent issues. On an entitlement view these are *not* two separate questions. Whoever makes something, having bought or contracted for all other held resources used in the process (transferring some of his holdings for these cooperating factors), is entitled to it. The situation is *not* one of something's getting made, and there being an open question of who is to get it. Things come into the world already attached to people having entitlements over them. From the point of view of the historical entitlement conception of justice in holdings, those who start afresh to complete 'to each according to his——' treat objects as if they appeared from nowhere, out of nothing. A complete theory of justice might cover this limit case as well; perhaps here is a use for the usual conceptions of distributive justice.

So entrenched are maxims of the usual form that perhaps we should present the entitlement conception as a competitor. Ignoring acquisition and rectification, we might say:

From each according to what he chooses to do, to each according to what he makes for himself (perhaps with the contracted aid of others) and what others choose to do for him and choose to give him of what they've been given previously (under this maxim) and haven't yet expended or transferred.

This, the discerning reader will have noticed, has its defects as a slogan. So as a summary and great simplification (and not as a maxim with any independent meaning) we have:

From each as they choose, to each as they are chosen.

It is not clear how those holding alternative conceptions of distributive justice can reject the entitlement conception of justice in holdings. For suppose a distribution favored by one of these non-entitlement conceptions is realized. Let us suppose it is your favorite one and let us call this distribution D_1; perhaps everyone has an equal share, perhaps shares vary in accordance with some dimension you treasure. Now suppose that Wilt Chamberlain is greatly in demand by basketball teams, being a great gate attraction. (Also suppose contracts run only for a year, with players being free agents.) He signs the following sort of contract with a team: In each home game, twenty-five cents from the price of each ticket of admission goes to him. (We ignore the question of whether he is 'gouging' the owners, letting them look out for themselves.) The season starts, and people cheerfully attend his team's games; they buy their tickets, each time dropping a separate twenty-five cents of their admission price into a special box with Chamberlain's name on it. They are excited about seeing him play; it is worth the total admission price to them. Let us suppose that in one season one million persons attend his home games, and Wilt Chamberlain winds up with $250,000, a much larger sum than the average income and larger even than anyone else has. Is he entitled to this income? Is this new distribution D_2, unjust? If so, why? There is *no* question about whether each of the people was entitled to the control over the resources they held in D_1; because that was the distribution (your favorite) that (for the purposes of argument) we assumed was acceptable. Each of these persons *chose* to give twenty-five cents of their money to Chamberlain. They could have spent it on going to the movies, or on candy bars, or on copies of *Dissent* magazine, or of *Monthly Review*. But they all, at least one million of them, converged on giving it to Wilt Chamberlain in exchange for watching him play basketball. If D_1 was a just distribution, and people voluntarily moved from it to D_2, transferring parts of their shares they were given under D_1 (what was it for if not to do something with?), isn't D_2 also just? If the people were entitled to dispose of the resources to which they were entitled (under D_1), didn't this include their being entitled to give it to, or exchange it with, Wilt Chamberlain? Can anyone else complain on grounds of justice? Each other person already has his legitimate share under D_1. Under D_1, there is nothing that anyone has that anyone else has a claim of justice against. After someone transfers something to Wilt Chamberlain, third parties *still* have their legitimate shares; *their* shares are not changed. By what process could such a transfer among two persons give rise to a legitimate claim of distributive justice on a portion of what was transferred, by a third party who had no claim of justice on any holding of the others *before* the transfer? To cut off objections irrelevant here, we might imagine the exchanges occurring in a socialist society, after hours. After playing whatever basketball he does in his daily work, or doing whatever other daily work he does, Wilt Chamberlain decides to put in *overtime* to earn additional money. (First his work quota is set; he works time over that.) Or imagine it is a skilled juggler people like to see, who puts on shows after hours.

Why might someone work overtime in a society in which it is assumed their needs are satisfied? Perhaps because they care about things other than needs. I like to write in books that I read, and to have easy access to books for browsing at odd hours. It would be very pleasant and convenient to have the resources of Widener Library in my back yard. No society, I assume, will provide such resources close to each person who would like them as part of his regular allotment (under D_1). Thus, persons either must do without some extra things that they want, or be allowed to do something extra to get some of these things. On what basis could the inequalities that would eventuate be forbidden? Notice also that small factories would spring up in a socialist society, unless forbidden. I melt down some of my personal possessions (under D_1) and build a machine out of the material. I offer you, and others, a philosophy lecture once a week in exchange for your cranking the handle on my machine, whose products I exchange for yet other things, and so on. (The raw materials used by the machine are given to me by others who possess them under D_1, in exchange for hearing lectures.) Each person might participate to gain things over and above their allotment under D_1. Some persons even might want to leave their job in socialist industry and work full time in this private sector. I shall say something more about these issues in the next chapter. Here I wish merely to note how private property even in means of production would occur in a socialist society that did not forbid people to use as they wished some of the resources they are given under the socialist distribution D_1. The socialist society would have to forbid capitalist acts between consenting adults.

The general point illustrated by the Wilt Chamberlain example and the example of the entrepreneur in a socialist society is that no end-state principle or distributional patterned principle of justice can be continuously realized without continuous interference with people's lives. Any favored pattern would be transformed into one unfavored by the principle, by people choosing to act in various ways; for example, by people exchanging goods and services with other people, or giving things to other people, things the transferrers are entitled to under the favored distributional pattern. To maintain a pattern one must either continually interfere to stop people from transferring resources as they wish to, or continually (or periodically) interfere to take from some persons resources that others for some reason chose to transfer to them. (But if some time limit is to be set on how long people may keep resources others voluntarily transfer to them, why let them keep these resources for *any* period of time? Why not have immediate confiscation?) It might be objected that all persons voluntarily will choose to refrain from actions which would upset the pattern. This presupposes unrealistically (1) that all will most want to maintain the pattern (are those who don't, to be 'reeducated' or forced to undergo 'self-criticism'?), (2) that each can gather enough information about his own actions and the ongoing activities of others to discover which of his actions will upset the pattern, and (3) that diverse and far-flung persons can coordinate their actions to dove-tail into the pattern. Compare the manner in which the market is neutral among persons' desires, as it reflects and transmits widely scattered information via prices, and coordinates persons' activities.

[From Anarchy, State, and Utopia (Basic Books, New York, 1974), 156, 159–64.]

RONALD DWORKIN

97 Equality of Resources

Suppose a number of shipwreck survivors are washed up on a desert island which has abundant resources and no native population, and any likely rescue is many years away. These immigrants accept the principle that no one is antecedently entitled to any of these resources, but that they shall instead be divided equally among them. (They do not yet realize, let us say, that it might be wise to keep some resources as owned in common by any state they might create.) They also accept (at least provisionally) the following test of an equal division of resources, which I shall call the envy test. No division of resources is an equal division if, once the division is complete, any immigrant would prefer someone else's bundle of resources to his own bundle.

Now suppose some one immigrant is elected to achieve the division according to that principle. It is unlikely that he can succeed simply by physically dividing the resources of the island into *n* identical bundles of resources. The number of each kind of the nondivisible resources, like milking cows, might not be an exact multiple of *n*, and even in the case of divisible resources, like arable land, some land would be better than others, and some better for one use than another. [. . .]

The envy test cannot be satisfied by any simple mechanical division of resources. If any more complex division can be found that will satisfy it, many such might be found, so that the choice amongst these would be arbitrary. The same solution will by now have occurred to all readers. The divider needs some form of auction or other market procedure in order to respond to these problems. I shall describe a reasonably straightforward procedure that would seem acceptable if it could be made to work, though as I shall describe it it will be impossibly expensive of time. Suppose the divider hands each of the immigrants an equal and large number of clamshells, which are sufficiently numerous and in themselves valued by no one, to use as counters in a market of the following sort. Each distinct item on the island (not including the immigrants themselves) is listed as a lot to be sold, unless someone notifies the auctioneer (as the divider has now become) of his or her desire to bid for some part of an item, including part, for example, of some piece of land, in which case that part becomes itself a distinct lot. The auctioneer then proposes a set of prices for each lot and discovers whether that set of prices clears all markets, that is, whether there is only one purchaser at that price and all lots are sold. If not, then the auctioneer adjusts his prices until he reaches a set that does clear the markets. But the process does not stop then, because each of the immigrants remains free to change his bids even when an initially market-clearing set of prices is reached, or even to propose different lots. But let us suppose that in time even this leisurely process comes to an end, everyone declares himself satisfied, and goods are distributed accordingly.

Now the envy test will have been met. No one will envy another's set of purchases because, by hypothesis, he could have purchased that bundle with his clamshells instead of his own bundle. Nor is the choice of sets of bundles arbitrary. Many people will be able to imagine a different set of bundles meeting the no-envy test that might have been established, but the actual set of bundles has the merit that each person played, through his purchases against an initially equal stock of counters, an equal role in determining the set of bundles actually chosen. [. . .]

Equality of resources supposes that the resources devoted to each person's life should be equal. That goal needs a metric. The auction proposes what the envy test in fact assumes, that the true measure of the social resources devoted to the life of one person is fixed by asking how important, in fact, that resource is for others. It insists that the cost, measured in that way, figure in each person's sense of what is rightly his and in each person's judgment of what life he should lead, given that command of justice. [. . .]

If the auction is successful as described, then equality of resources holds for the moment among the immigrants. But perhaps only for the moment, because if they are left alone, once the auction is completed, to produce and trade as they wish, then the envy test will shortly fail. Some may be more skillful than others at producing what others want and will trade to get. Some may like to work, or to work in a way that will produce more to trade, while others like not to work or prefer to work at what will bring them less. Some will stay healthy while others fall sick, or lightning will strike the farms of others but avoid theirs. For any of these and dozens of other reasons some people will prefer the bundle others have in say, five years, to their own.

We must ask whether (or rather how far) such developments are consistent with equality of resources, and I shall begin by considering the character and impact of luck on the immigrants' post-auction fortunes. I shall distinguish, at least for the moment, between two kinds of luck. Option luck is a matter of how deliberate and calculated gambles turn out—whether someone gains or loses through accepting an isolated risk he or she should have anticipated and might have declined. Brute luck is a matter of how risks fall out that are not in that sense deliberate gambles. If I buy a stock on the exchange that rises, then my option luck is good. If I am hit by a falling meteorite whose course could not have been predicted, then my bad luck is brute (even though I could have moved just before it struck if I had any reason to know where it would strike). Obviously the difference between these two forms of luck can be represented as a matter of degree, and we may be uncertain how to describe a particular piece of bad luck. If someone develops cancer in the course of a normal life, and there is no particular decision to which we can point as a gamble risking the disease, then we will say that he has suffered brute bad luck. But if he smoked cigarettes heavily then we may prefer to say that he took an unsuccessful gamble.

Insurance, so far as it is available, provides a link between brute and option luck, because the decision to buy or reject catastrophe insurance is a calculated gamble. Of course, insurance does not erase the distinction. Someone who buys medical insurance and is hit by an unexpected meteorite still suffers brute bad luck, because he is worse off than if he had bought insurance and not needed it. But he has had better option luck than if he had not bought the insurance, because his situation is better in virtue of his not having run the gamble of refusing to insure.

Is it consistent with equality of resources that people should have different income or wealth in virtue of differing option luck? Suppose some of the immigrants plant valuable but risky crops while others play it safer, and that some of the former buy insurance against uncongenial weather while others do not. Skill will play a part in determining which of these various programs succeed, of course, and we shall consider the problems this raises later. But option luck will also play a part. Does its role threaten or invade equality of resources?

Consider, first, the differences in wealth between those who play it safe and those who gamble and succeed. Some people enjoy, while others hate, risks; but this particular difference in personality is comprehended in a more general difference between the kinds of lives that different people wish to lead. The life chosen by someone who gambles contains, as an element, the factor of risk; someone who chooses not to gamble has decided that he prefers a safer life. We have already decided that people should pay the price of the life they have decided to lead, measured in what others give up in order that they can do so. That was the point of the auction as a device to establish initial equality of resources. But the price of a safer life, measured in this way, is precisely forgoing any chance of the gains whose prospect induces others to gamble. So we have no reason to object, against the background of our earlier decisions, to a result in which those who decline to gamble have less than some of those who do not.

But we must also compare the situation of those who gamble and win with that of those who gamble and lose. We cannot say that the latter have chosen a different life and must sacrifice gains accordingly; for they have chosen the same lives as those who won. But we can say that the possibility of loss was part of the life they chose—that it was the fair price of the possibility of gain. For we might have designed our initial auction so that people could purchase (for example) lottery tickets with their clamshells. But the price of those tickets would have been some amount of other resources (fixed by the odds and the gambling preferences of others) that the shells would otherwise have bought, and which will be wholly forgone if the ticket does not win. [. . .]

Nor does the argument yet confront the case of brute bad luck. If two people lead roughly the same lives, but one goes suddenly blind, then we cannot explain the resulting differences in their incomes either by saying that one took risks that the other chose not to take, or that we could not redistribute without denying both the lives they prefer. For the accident has (we assume) nothing to do with choices in the pertinent sense. It is not necessary to the life either has chosen that he run the risk of going blind without redistribution of funds from the other. This is a fortiori so if one is born blind and the other sighted.

But the possibility of insurance provides, as I suggested, a link between the two kinds of luck. For suppose insurance against blindness is available, in the initial auction, at whatever level of coverage the policy holder chooses to buy. And also suppose that two sighted people have, at the time of the auction, equal chance of suffering an accident that will blind them, and know that they have. Now if one chooses to spend part of his initial resources for such insurance and the other does not, or if one buys more coverage than the other, then this difference will reflect their different opinions about the relative value of different forms or components of their prospective lives. It may reflect the fact that one puts more value on sight than the other. Or, differently, that one would count monetary compensation for the loss of his sight as worthless in the face of such a tragedy while the other, more practical, would fix his mind on the aids and special training that such money might buy. Or simply that one minds or values risk differently from the other, and would, for example, rather try for a brilliant life that would collapse under catastrophe than a life guarded at the cost of resources necessary to make it brilliant.

But in any case the bare idea of equality of resources, apart from any paternalistic additions, would not argue for redistribution from the person who had insured to the person who had not if, horribly, they were both blinded in the same accident. For the availability of insurance would mean that, though they had both had brute bad luck, the difference between them was a matter of option luck, and the arguments we entertained against disturbing the results of option luck under conditions of equal antecedent risk hold here as well. But then the situation cannot be different if the person who decided not to insure is the only one to be blinded. For once again the difference is a difference in option luck against a background of equal opportunity to insure or not. If neither had been blinded, the man who had insured against blindness would have been the loser. His option luck would have been bad—though it seems bizarre to put it this way—because he spent resources that, as things turned out, would have been better spent otherwise. But he would have no claim, in that event, from the man who did not insure and also survived unhurt.

So if the condition just stated were met—if everyone had an equal risk of suffering some catastrophe that would leave him or her handicapped, and everyone knew roughly what the odds were and had ample opportunity to insure—then handicaps would pose no special problem for equality of resources. But of course that condition is not met. Some people are born with handicaps, or develop them before they have either sufficient knowledge or funds to insure on their own behalf. They cannot buy insurance after the event. Even handicaps that develop later in life, against which people do have the opportunity to insure, and not randomly distributed through the population, but follow genetic tracks, so that sophisticated insurers would charge some people higher premiums for the same coverage before the event. Nevertheless the idea of a market in insurance provides a counterfactual guide through which equality of resources might face the problem of handicaps in the real world.

Suppose we can make sense of and even give a rough answer to the following question. If (contrary to fact) everyone had at the appropriate age the same risk of developing physical or mental handicaps in the future (which assumes that no one has developed these yet) but that the total number of handicaps remained what it is, how much insurance coverage against these handicaps would the average member of the community purchase? We might then say that but for (uninsurable) brute luck that has altered these equal odds, the average person would have purchased insurance at that level, and compensate those who do develop handicaps accordingly, out of some fund collected by taxation or other compulsory process but designed to match the fund that would have been provided through premiums if the odds had been equal. Those who develop handicaps will then have more resources at their command than others, but the extent of their extra resources will be fixed by the market decisions that people would supposedly have made if circumstances had been more equal than they are. [. . .]

Equality of resources, once established by the auction, and corrected to provide for handicaps, would be disturbed by production and trade. If one of the immigrants, for example, was specially proficient at producing tomatoes, he might trade his surplus for more than anyone else could acquire, in which case others would begin to envy his bundle of resources. Suppose we wished to create a society in which the division of resources would be continuously equal, in spite of different kinds and degrees of production and trade. Can we adapt our auction so as to produce such a society?

We should begin by considering a different sequence after which people would envy each other's resources, and the division might be thought no longer to be equal. Suppose all the immigrants are in fact sufficiently equal in talent at the few modes of production that the resources allow so that each could produce roughly the same goods from the same set of resources. Nevertheless they wish to lead their lives in different ways, and they in fact acquire different bundles of resources in the initial auction and use them differently thereafter. Adrian chooses resources and works them with the single-minded ambition of producing as much of what others value as possible; and so, at the end of a year, his total stock of goods is larger than anyone else's. Each of the other immigrants would now prefer Adrian's stock to his own; but by hypothesis none of them would have been willing to lead his life so as to produce them. If we look for envy at particular points in time, then each envies Adrian's resources at the end of the year, and the division is therefore not equal. But if we look at envy differently, as a matter of resources over an entire life, and we include a person's occupation as part of the bundle of his goods, then no one envies Adrian's bundle, and the distribution cannot be said to be unequal on that account.

Surely we should take the second, synoptic, point of view. Our final aim is that an equal share of resources should be devoted to the lives of each person, and we have chosen the auction as the right way to measure the value of what is made available to a person, through his decision, for that purpose. [. . .]

So we must apply the envy test diachronically: it requires that no one envy the bundle of occupation and resources at the disposal of anyone else over time, though someone may envy another's bundle at any particular time. [. . .] Would the auction produce continuing equality of resources if (as in the real world) talents for production differed sharply from person to person? Now the envy test would fail, even interpreted diachronically. Claude (who likes farming but has a black thumb) would not bid enough for farming land to take that land from Adrian. Or, if he did, he would have to settle for less in the rest of his life. But he would then envy the package of Adrian's occupation and wealth. If we interpret occupation in a manner sensitive to the joys of craft, then Adrian's occupation, which must then be described as skillful, craftsmanlike farming, is simply unavailable to Claude. If we interpret occupation in a more census-like fashion, then Claude may undertake Adrian's occupation, but he cannot have the further resources that Adrian has along with it. So if we continue to insist that the envy test is a necessary condition of equality of resources, then our initial auction will not insure continuing equality, in the real worlds of unequal talents for production. [. . .]

Though skills are different from handicaps, the difference can be understood as one of degree: we may say that someone who cannot play basketball like Wilt Chamberlain, paint like Piero, or make money like Geneen, suffers from an (especially common) handicap. This description emphasizes one aspect of skills, which is their genetic and, hence, luck component, at the expense of hiding the more intimate and reciprocal play we noticed between skills and ambitions. But it also points to one theoretical solution to the problem of identifying at least the minimum requirements of a fair redistribution policy responding to differences in skill. We may capitalize on the similarities between handicaps and relative lack of skill to propose that the level of compensation for the latter be fixed, in principle, by asking how much insurance someone would have bought, in an insurance sub-auction with initially equal resources, against the possibility of not having a particular level of some skill. [. . .]

The argument from the hypothetical insurance market contrasts two worlds. In the first those who are relatively disadvantaged by the tastes and ambitions of others, vis-à-vis their own talents to produce, are known in advance and bear the full consequences of that disadvantage. In the second the same pattern of relative disadvantage holds, but everyone has subjectively an equal antecedent chance of suffering it, and so everyone has an equal opportunity of mitigating the disadvantage by insuring against it. The argument assumes that equality prefers the second world, because it is a world in which the resources of talent are in one important sense more evenly divided. The hypothetical insurance argument aims to reproduce the consequences of the second world, as nearly as it can, in an actual world. It answers those who would do better in the first world (who include, as I said, many of those who would have more money at their disposal in the second) by the simple proposition that the second is a world that, on grounds independent of how things happen to work out for them given their tastes and ambitions, is more nearly equal in resources.

[From 'What is Equality? Part 2: Equality of Resources', *Philosophy and Public Affairs*, 10 (1981), 285–7, 289, 292–4, 296–8, 304–7, 314–15, 331.]

Section VI

Justice between Groups

INTRODUCTION

So far this Reader has looked at a number of issues concerning the relations between individuals and the state and the relations between different individuals within the state or in the state of nature. The task of this section, by contrast, is to look at the relations between states, and to look at issues of justice which arise between groups smaller than the state but large enough to be considered as some form of collective entity.

We start with peace and war and Kant's attempt to set out the conditions through which the world can live in perpetual peace. Two achievements are vital, argues Kant: the establishment of a federation of states, and world trade, which will make war against our economic interests. Cobden, too, eloquently urges the civilizing influence of trade. The concern of Michael Walzer is rather different: to examine the circumstances in which one can be justified in going to war. He argues that war can be a justified response to aggression, but no war can be just on both sides. Thomas Nagel, prompted by reflection upon the Vietnam War, argues that even in a just war there are grave limits to the sort of behaviour that can be justified.

We follow with two extracts concerning nationalism. Isaiah Berlin points out the pervasive power and depth of national sentiment; a theme carried forward by Alasdair MacIntyre, who explores the debate about the value of patriotism: is it a virtue or a vice? Affirmative action, also known as positive discrimination, is the next topic. Thomas Hill sets out the case that appropriate programmes of affirmative action can communicate a message of fairness, respect, and trust, even if, on a superficial view, they may well look unfair. Bringing together issues of nationalism and minority rights, Margalit and Raz argue that a group can have a right of national self-determination, provided it seeks self-determination for good reasons.

We turn next to justice between generations. Brian Barry reflects on the kind of moral theory one would have to hold in order to maintain the apparently natural belief that we have obligations to maintain the world's resources for the benefit of those who do not yet exist. Peter Singer's concern is with those people who do exist now, in distant lands, but are threatened by famine. Is there any good reason why the affluent should not provide aid? Do such people have less of a claim for our help than those immediately around us? Singer argues that the case for assistance can be so strong that those who do contribute barely deserve praise. Onora O'Neill develops an argument which links the issues discussed by Singer and Barry: the policy we adopt to bring about famine relief should be one part of global policy which also has implications for future population size and our present resource use. These issues are, of course, all related and cannot properly be dealt with in isolation from each other.

VI.a. Peace and War

IMMANUEL KANT

98 Perpetual Peace

A state of peace among men living together is not the same as the state of nature, which is rather a state of war. For even if it does not involve active hostilities, it involves a constant threat of their breaking out. Thus the state of peace must be *formally instituted*, for a suspension of hostilities is not in itself a guarantee of peace. And unless one neighbour gives guarantee to the other at his request (which can happen only in a *lawful* state), the latter may treat him as an enemy.

A republican constitution is founded upon three principles: firstly, the principle of *freedom* for all members of a society (as men); secondly, the principle of the *dependence* of everyone upon a single common legislation (as subjects); and thirdly, the principle of legal *equality* for everyone (as citizens). It is the only constitution which can be derived from the idea of an original contract, upon which all rightful legislation of a people must be founded. Thus as far as right is concerned, republicanism is in itself the original basis of every kind of civil constitution, and it only remains to ask whether it is the only constitution which can lead to a perpetual peace.

The republican constitution is not only pure in its origin (since it springs from the pure concept of right); it also offers a prospect of attaining the desired result, i.e. a perpetual peace, and the reasons for this is as follows.—If, as is inevitably the case under this constitution, the consent of the citizens is required to decide whether or not war is to be declared, it is very natural that they will have great hesitation in embarking on so dangerous an enterprise. For this would mean calling down on themselves all the miseries of war, such as doing the fighting themselves, supplying the costs of the war from their own resources, painfully making good the ensuing devastation, and, as the crowning evil, having to take upon themselves a burden of debt which will embitter peace itself and which can never be paid off on account of the constant threat of new wars. But under a constitution where the subject is not a citizen, and which is therefore not republican, it is the simplest thing in the world to go to war. For the head of state is not a fellow citizen, but the owner of the state, and a war will not force him to make the slightest sacrifice so far as his banquets, hunts, pleasure palaces and court festivals are concerned. He can thus decide on war, without any significant reason, as a kind of amusement, and unconcernedly leave it to the diplomatic corps (who are always ready for such purposes) to justify the war for the sake of propriety. [. . .]

Peoples who have grouped themselves into nation states may be judged in the same way as individual men living in a state of nature, independent of external laws; for they are a standing offence to one another by the very fact that they are neighbours. Each nation, for the sake of its own security, can and ought to demand of the others that they should enter along with it into a constitution, similar to the civil one, within which the rights of each could be secured. This would mean establishing a *federation of peoples*. But a federation of this sort would not be the same thing as an international state. For the idea of an international state is contradictory, since every state involves a relationship between a superior (the legislator) and an inferior (the people obeying the laws), whereas a number of nations forming one state would constitute a single nation. And this contradicts our initial assumption, as we are here considering the right of nations in relation to one another in so far as they are a group of separate states which are not to be welded together as a unit.

We look with profound contempt upon the way in which savages cling to their lawless freedom. They would rather engage in incessant strife than submit to a legal constraint which they might impose upon themselves, for they prefer the freedom of folly to the freedom of reason. We regard this as barbarism, coarseness, and brutish debasement of humanity. We might thus expect that civilised peoples, each united within itself as a state, would hasten to abandon so degrading a condition as soon as possible. But instead of doing so, each *state* sees its own majesty (for it would be absurd to speak of the majesty of a *people*) precisely in not having to submit to any external legal constraint, and the glory of its ruler consists in his power to order thousands of people to immolate themselves for a cause which does not truly concern them, while he need not himself incur any danger whatsoever. And the main difference between the savage nations of Europe and those of America is that while some American tribes have been entirely eaten up by their enemies, the Europeans know how to make better use of those they have defeated than merely by making a meal of them. They would rather use them to increase the number of their own subjects, thereby augmenting their stock of instruments for conducting even more extensive wars. [. . .]

The idea of international right presupposes the separate existence of many independent adjoining states. And such a state of affairs is essentially a state of war, unless there is a federal union to prevent hostilities breaking out. But in the light of the idea of reason, this state is still to be preferred to an amalgamation of the separate nations under a single power which has overruled the rest and created a universal monarchy. For the laws progressively lose their impact as the government increases its range, and a soulless despotism, after crushing the germs of goodness, will finally lapse into anarchy. It is nonetheless the desire of every state (or its ruler) to achieve lasting peace by thus dominating the whole world, if at all possible. But *nature* wills it otherwise, and uses two means to separate the nations and prevent them from intermingling—*linguistic* and *religious* differences. These may certainly occasion mutual hatred and provide pretexts for wars, but as culture grows and men gradually move towards greater agreement over their principles, they lead to mutual understanding and peace. And unlike that universal despotism which saps all man's energies and ends in the graveyard of freedom, this peace is created and guaranteed by an equilibrium of forces and a most vigorous rivalry.

Thus nature wisely separates the nations, although the will of each individual state, even basing its arguments on international right, would gladly unite them under its own sway by force or by cunning. On the other hand, nature also unites nations which the concept of cosmopolitan right would not have protected from violence and war, and does so by means of their mutual self-interest. For the *spirit of commerce* sooner or later takes hold of every people, and it cannot exist side by side with war. And of all the powers (or means) at the disposal of the power of the state, *financial power* can probably be relied on most. Thus states find themselves compelled to promote the noble cause of peace, though not exactly from motives of morality. And wherever in the world there is a threat of war breaking out, they will try to prevent it by mediation, just as if they had entered into a permanent league for this purpose; for by the very nature of things, large military alliances can only rarely be formed, and will even more rarely be successful.

In this way, nature guarantees perpetual peace by the actual mechanism of human inclinations. And while the likelihood of its being attained is not sufficient to enable us to *prophesy* the future theoretically, it is enough for practical purposes. It makes it our duty to work our way towards this goal, which is more than an empty chimera.

> [From *Perpetual Peace,* in *Kant: Political Writings,* ed. Hans Reiss, trans. H.B. Nisbet (Cambridge University Press, Cambridge, 1970, 1991), 98–100, 102–3, 113–14. First published 1795.]

RICHARD COBDEN

99   The Civilizing Influence of Commerce

Nor do we think it would tend less to promote the ulterior benefit of our continental neighbours than our own, were Great Britain to refrain from participating in the conflicts that may arise around here. An onward movement of constitutional liberty must continue to be made by the less advanced nations of Europe, so long as one of its greatest families holds out the example of liberal and enlightened freedom. England, by calmly directing her undivided energies to the purifying of her own internal institutions, to the emancipation of her commerce—above all, to the unfettering of her press from its excise bonds—would, by thus serving as it were for the beacon of other nations, aid more effectually the cause of political progression all over the continent than she could possibly do by plunging herself into the strife of European wars.

For, let it never be forgotten, that it is not by means of war that states are rendered fit for the enjoyment of constitutional freedom; on the contrary, whilst terror and bloodshed reign in the land, involving men's minds in the extremities of hopes and fears, there can be no process of thought, no education going on, by which alone can a people be prepared for the enjoyment of rational liberty. Hence, after a struggle of twenty years, *begun in behalf of freedom*, no sooner had the wars of the French revolution terminated, than all the nations of the continent fell back again into their previous state of political servitude, and from which they have, ever since the peace, been *qualifying* to rescue themselves, by the gradual process of intellectual advancement. Those who, from an eager desire to aid civilisation, wish that Great Britain should interpose in the dissensions of neighbouring states, would do wisely to study, in the history of their own country, how well a people can, by the force and virtue of native elements, and without external assistance of any kind, work out their own political regeneration: they might learn too, by their own annals, that it is only when at peace with other states that a nation finds the leisure for looking within itself, and discovering the means to accomplish great domestic ameliorations.

To those generous spirits we would urge, that, in the present day, commerce is the grand panacea, which, like a beneficent medical discovery, will serve to inoculate with the healthy and saving taste for civilisation all the nations of the world. Not a bale of merchandise leaves our shores, but it bears the seeds of intelligence and fruitful thought to the members of some less enlightened community; not a merchant visits our seats of manufacturing industry, but he returns to his own country the missionary of freedom, peace, and good government—whilst our steam boats, that now visit every port of Europe, and our miraculous railroads, that are the talk of all nations, are the advertisements and vouchers for the value of our enlightened institutions.

[From *England, Ireland and America*, in *The Political Writings of Richard Cobden* (Ridgeway, London, 1887), 356. First published 1835.]

MICHAEL WALZER

100   Just and Unjust War

If states actually do possess rights more or less as individuals do, then it is possible to imagine a society among them more or less like the society of individuals. The comparison of international to civil order is crucial to the theory of aggression. I have already been making it regularly. Every reference to aggression as the international equivalent of armed robbery or murder, and every comparison of home and country or of personal liberty and political independence, relies upon what is called the *domestic analogy*. Our primary perceptions and judgments of aggression are the products of analogical reasoning. When the analogy is made explicit, as it often is among the lawyers, the world of states takes on the shape of a political society the character of which is entirely accessible through such notions as crime and punishment, self-defense, law enforcement, and so on.

These notions, I should stress, are not incompatible with the fact that international society as it exists today is a radically imperfect structure. As we experience it, that society might be likened to a defective building, founded on rights; its superstructure raised, like that of the state itself, through political conflict, cooperative activity, and commercial exchange; the whole thing shaky and unstable because it lacks the rivets of authority. It is like domestic society in that men and women live at peace within it (sometimes), determining the conditions of their own existence, negotiating and bargaining with their neighbors. It is unlike domestic society in that every conflict threatens the structure as a whole with collapse. Aggression challenges it directly and is much more dangerous than domestic crime, because there are no policemen. But that only means that the 'citizens' of international society must rely on themselves and on one another. Police powers are distributed among all the members. And these members have done enough in the exercise of their powers if they merely contain the aggression or bring it to a speedy end—as if the police should stop a murderer after he has killed only one or two people and send him on his way. The rights of the member states must be vindicated, for it is only by virtue of those rights that there is a society at all. If they cannot be upheld (at least sometimes), international society collapses into a state of war or is transformed into a universal tyranny.

From this picture, two presumptions follow. The first, which I have already pointed out, is the presumption in favor of military resistance once aggression has begun. Resistance is important so that rights can be maintained and future aggressors deterred. The theory of aggression restates the old doctrine of the just war: it explains when fighting is a crime and when it is permissible, perhaps even morally desirable. The victim of aggression fights in self-defense, but he isn't only defending himself, for aggression is a crime against society as a whole. He fights in its name and not only in his own. Other states can rightfully join the victim's resistance; their war has the same character as his own, which is to say, they are entitled not only to repel the attack but also to punish it. All resistance is also law enforcement. Hence the second presumption: when fighting breaks out, there must always be some state against which the law can and should be enforced. Someone must be responsible, for someone decided to break the peace of the society of states. No war, as medieval theologians explained, can be just on both sides.

There are, however, wars that are just on neither side, because the idea of justice doesn't pertain to them or because the antagonists are both aggressors, fighting for territory or power where they have no right [. . .]

The theory of aggression first takes shape under the aegis of the domestic analogy. I am going to call that primary form of the theory the *legalist paradigm*, since it consistently reflects the conventions of law and order. It does not necessarily reflect the arguments of the lawyers, though legal as well as moral debate has its starting point here. Later on, I will suggest that our judgments about the justice and injustice of particular wars are not entirely determined by the paradigm. The complex realities of international society drive us toward a revisionist perspective, and the revisions will be significant ones. But the paradigm must first be viewed in its unrevised form; it is our baseline, our model, the fundamental structure for the moral comprehension of war. We begin with the familiar world of individuals and rights, of crimes and punishments. The theory of aggression can then be summed up in six propositions.

1. *There exists an international society of independent states.* States are the members of this society, not private men and women. In the absence of an universal state, men and women are protected and their interests represented only by their own governments. Though states are founded for the sake of life and liberty, they cannot be challenged in the name of life and liberty by any other states. Hence the principle of non-intervention, which I will analyze later on. The rights of private persons can be recognized in international society, as in the UN Charter of Human Rights, but they cannot be enforced without calling into question the dominant values of that society: the survival and independence of the separate political communities.

2. *This international society has a law that establishes the rights of its members— above all, the rights of territorial integrity and political sovereignty.* Once again, these two rest ultimately on the right of men and women to build a common life and to risk their individual lives only when they freely choose to do so. But the relevant law refers only to states, and its details are fixed by the intercourse of states, through complex processes of conflict and consent. Since these processes are continuous, international society has no natural shape; nor are rights within it ever finally or exactly determined. At any given moment, however, one can distinguish the territory of one people from that of another and say something about the scope and limits of sovereignty.

3. *Any use of force of imminent threat of force by one state against the political sovereignty or territorial integrity of another constitutes aggression and is a criminal act.* As with domestic crime, the argument here focuses narrowly on actual or imminent boundary crossings: invasions and physical assaults. Otherwise, it is feared, the notion of resistance to aggression would have no determinate meaning. A state cannot be said to be forced to fight unless the necessity is both obvious and urgent.

4. *Aggression justifies two kinds of violent response: a war of self-defense by the victim and a war of law enforcement by the victim and any other member of international society.* Anyone can come to the aid of a victim, use necessary force against an aggressor, and even make whatever is the international equivalent of a 'citizen's

arrest.' As in domestic society, the obligations of bystanders are not easy to make out, but it is the tendency of the theory to undermine the right of neutrality and to require widespread participation in the business of law enforcement. In the Korean War, this participation was authorized by the United Nations, but even in such cases the actual decision to join the fighting remains a unilateral one, best understood by analogy to the decision of a private citizen who rushes to help a man or woman attacked on the street.

5. *Nothing but aggression can justify war.* The central purpose of the theory is to limit the occasions for war. 'There is a single and only just cause for commencing a war,' wrote Vittoria, 'namely, a wrong received.' There must actually have been a wrong, and it must actually have been received (or its receipt must be, as it were, only minutes away). Nothing else warrants the use of force in international society—above all, not any difference of religion or politics. Domestic heresy and injustice are never actionable in the world of states: hence, again, the principle of nonintervention.

6. *Once the aggressor state has been militarily repulsed, it can also be punished.* The conception of just war as an act of punishment is very old, though neither the procedures nor the forms of punishment have ever been firmly established in customary or positive international law. Nor are its purposes entirely clear: to exact retribution, to deter other states, to restrain or reform this one? All three figure largely in the literature, though it is probably fair to say that deterrence and restraint are most commonly accepted. When people talk of fighting a war against war, this is usually what they have in mind. The domestic maxim is, punish crime to prevent violence; its international analogue is, punish aggression to prevent war. Whether the state as a whole or only particular persons are the proper objects of punishment is a harder question. [...] But the implication of the paradigm is clear: if states are members of international society, the subjects of rights, they must also be (somehow) the objects of punishment.

[From *Just and Unjust Wars* (Basic Books, New York, 1977), 58–63.]

THOMAS NAGEL

101 **The Limits of Warfare**

Many people feel, without being able to say much more about it, that something has gone seriously wrong when certain measures are admitted into consideration in the first place. The fundamental mistake is made there, rather than at the point where the overall benefit of some monstrous measure is judged to outweigh its disadvantages, and it is adopted. An account of absolutism might help us to understand this. If it is not allowable to *do* certain things, such as killing unarmed prisoners or civilians, then no argument about what will happen if one does not do them can show that doing them would be all right.

Absolutism does not, of course, require one to ignore the consequences of one's acts. It operates as a limitation on utilitarian reasoning, not as a substitute for it. An absolutist can be expected to try to maximize good and minimize evil, so long as this does not require him to transgress an absolute prohibition like that against murder. But when such a conflict occurs, the prohibition takes complete precedence over any consideration of consequences. [. . .]

Absolutist restrictions in warfare appear to be of two types: restrictions on the class of persons at whom aggression or violence may be directed and re- strictions on the manner of attack, given that the object falls within that class. These can be combined, however, under the principle that hostile treatment of any person must be justified in terms of something *about that person* which makes the treatment appropriate. Hostility is a personal relation, and it must be suited to its target. One consequence of this condition will be that certain per- sons may not be subjected to hostile treatment in war at all, since nothing about them justifies such treatment. Others will be proper objects of hostility only in certain circumstances, or when they are engaged in certain pursuits. And the appropriate manner and extent of hostile treatment will depend on what is jus- tified by the particular case.

A coherent view of this type will hold that extremely hostile behavior toward another is compatible with treating him as a person—even perhaps as an end in himself. This is possible only if one has not automatically stopped treating him as a person as soon as one starts to fight with him. If hostile, aggressive, or com- bative treatment of others always violated the condition that they be treated as human beings, it would be difficult to make further distinctions on that score *within* the class of hostile actions. That point of view, on the level of interna- tional relations, leads to the position that if complete pacifism is not accepted, no holds need be barred at all, and we may slaughter and massacre to our hearts' content, if it seems advisable. Such a position is often expressed in discussions of war crimes.

But the fact is that ordinary people do not believe this about conflicts, physi- cal or otherwise, between individuals, and there is no more reason why it should be true of conflicts between nations. There seems to be a perfectly nat- ural conception of the distinction between fighting clean and fighting dirty. To fight dirty is to direct one's hostility or aggression not at its proper object, but at a peripheral target which may be more vulnerable, and through which the proper object can be attacked indirectly. This applies in a fist fight, an election campaign, a duel, or a philosophical argument. If the concept is general enough to apply to all these matters, it should apply to war—both to the conduct of in- dividual soldiers and to the conduct of nations. [. . .]

In an altercation with a taxi driver over an excessive fare, it is inappropriate to taunt him about his accent, flatten one of his tires, or smear chewing gum on his windshield; and it remains inappropriate even if he casts aspersions on your race, politics, or religion, or dumps the contents of your suitcase into the street.

The importance of such restrictions may vary with the seriousness of the case; and what is unjustifiable in one case may be justified in a more extreme one. But they all derive from a single principle: that hostility or aggression should be directed at its true object. This means both that it should be directed at the person or persons who provoke it and that it should aim more specifically at what is provocative about them. The second condition will determine what form the hostility may appropriately take.

It is evident that some idea of the relation in which one should stand to other people underlies this principle, but the idea is difficult to state. I believe it is roughly this: whatever one does to another person intentionally must be aimed at him as a subject, with the intention that he receive it as a subject. It should manifest an attitude to *him* rather than just to the situation, and he should be able to recognize it and identify himself as its object. The procedures by which such an attitude is manifested need not be addressed to the person directly. Surgery, for example, is not a form of personal confrontation but part of a medical treatment that can be offered to a patient face to face and received by him as a response to his needs and the natural outcome of an attitude toward *him*. [. . .]

If absolutism is to defend its claim to priority over considerations of utility, it must hold that the maintenance of a direct interpersonal response to the people one deals with is a requirement which no advantages can justify one in abandoning. The requirement is absolute only if it rules out any calculation of what would justify its violation. I have said earlier that there may be circumstances so extreme that they render an absoutist position untenable. One may find then that one has no choice but to do something terrible. Nevertheless, even in such cases absolutism retains its force in that one cannot claim *justification* for the violation. It does not become *all right*.

As a tentative effort to explain this, let me try to connect absolutist limitations with the possibility of justifying *to the victim* what is being done to him. If one abandons a person in the course of rescuing several others from a fire or a sinking ship, one *could* say to him, 'You understand, I have to leave you to save the others.' Similarly, if one subjects an unwilling child to a painful surgical procedure, one can say to him, 'If you could understand, you would realize that I am doing this to help you.' One could *even* say, as one bayonets an enemy soldier, 'It's either you or me.' But one cannot really say while torturing a prisoner, 'You understand, I have to pull out your finger-nails because it is absolutely essential that we have the names of your confederates'; nor can one say to the victims of Hiroshima, 'You understand, we have to incinerate you to provide the Japanese government with an incentive to surrender.'

This does not take us very far, of course, since a utilitarian would presumably be willing to offer justifications of the latter sort to his victims, in cases where he thought they were sufficient. They are really justifications to the world at large, which the victim, as a reasonable man, would be expected to appreciate. However, there seems to me something wrong with this view, for it ignores the possibility that to treat someone else horribly puts you in a special relation to him, which may have to be defended in terms of other features of your relation to him. The suggestion needs much more development; but it may help us to understand how there may be requirements which are absolute in the sense that there can be no justification for violating them. If the justification for what one did to another person had to be such that it could be offered to him specifically, rather than just to the world at large, that would be a significant source of restraint.

If the account is to be deepened, I would hope for some results along the following lines. Absolutism is associated with a view by oneself as a small being interacting with others in a large world. The justifications it requires are primarily interpersonal. Utilitarianism is associated with a view of oneself as a benevolent bureaucrat distributing such benefits as one can control to countless other beings, with whom one may have various relations or none. The justifications it requires are primarily administrative. The argument between the two moral attitudes may depend on the relative priority of these two conceptions.

[From 'War and Massacre', *Philosophy and Public Affairs*, 1 (1972), 128, 133–8.]

VI.b. Nationalism

ISAIAH BERLIN

102 **National Sentiment**

Among the assumptions of rational thinkers of the liberal type in the nineteenth and for some decades in the twentieth century were these: that liberal democracy was the most satisfactory—or at least, the least unsatisfactory—form of human organisation; that the nation-state was, or at least had historically come to be, the normal unit of independent, self-governing human society; and finally, that once the multinational empires (which Herder had denounced as ill-assorted political monstrosities) had been dissolved into their constituent parts, the yearning for union of men with common language, habits, memories, outlooks, would at last be satisfied, and a society of liberated, self-determined nation-states—Mazzini's Young Italy, Young Germany, Young Poland, Young Russia—would come into existence, and, inspired by a patriotism not tainted by aggressive nationalism (itself a symptom of a pathological condition induced by oppression), would live at peace and in harmony with each other, no longer impeded by the irrational survivals of a servile past. The fact that a representative of Mazzini's movement was invited to, and attended, the meeting of the First International Workingmen's Association, however little Marx may have liked it, is significant in this respect. This conviction was shared by the liberal and democratic founders of the succession states after the First World War, and was incorporated in the constitution of the League. As for Marxists, although they regarded nationalism as historically reactionary, even they did not demand the total abolition of national frontiers; provided that class exploitation was abolished by the socialist revolution, it was assumed that free national societies could exist side by side until, and after, the withering away of the state conceived as an instrument of class domination.

Neither of these ideologies anticipated the growth of national sentiment and, more than this, of aggressive nationalism. What, I think, was ignored was the fact which only, perhaps, Durkheim perceived clearly, namely, that the destruction of traditional hierarchies and orders of social life, in which men's loyalties were deeply involved, by the centralisation and bureaucratic 'rationalisation' which industrial progress required and generated, deprived great numbers of men of social and emotional security, produced the notorious phenomena of alienation, spiritual homelessness and growing anomie, and needed the creation, by deliberate social policy, of psychological equivalents for the lost cultural, political, religious values on which the older order rested. The socialists believed that class solidarity, the fraternity of the exploited, and the prospect of a just and rational society which the revolution would bring to birth, would provide this indispensable social cement; and indeed, to a degree it did. Moreover, some among the poor, the displaced, the deprived, emigrated to the New World. But for the majority the vacuum was filled neither by professional associations, nor political parties, nor the revolutionary myths which Sorel sought to provide, but by the old, traditional bonds, language, the soil, historical memories real and imaginary, and by institutions or leaders which functioned as incarnations of men's conceptions of themselves as a community, a *Gemeinschaft*—symbols and agencies which proved far more powerful than either socialists or enlightened liberals wished to believe. The idea, sometimes invested with a mystical or messianic fervour, of the nation as supreme authority, replacing the church or the prince or the rule of law or other sources of ultimate values, relieved the pain of the wound to group consciousness, whoever may have inflicted it—a foreign enemy or native capitalists or imperialist exploiters or an artificially imposed, heartless bureaucracy.

This sentiment was, no doubt, deliberately exploited by parties and politicians, but it was there to be exploited, it was not invented by those who used it for ulterior purposes of their own. It was there, and possessed an independent force of its own, which could be combined with other forces, most effectively with the power of a state bent on modernisation, as a defence against other powers conceived of as alien or hostile, or with particular groups and classes and movements within the state, religious, political and economic, with which the bulk of the society did not instinctively identify itself. It developed, and could be used, in many different directions, as a weapon of secularism, industrialisation, modernisation, the rational use of resources, or in an appeal to a real or imaginary past, some lost, pagan or neo-medieval paradise, a vision of a braver, simpler, purer life, or as the call of the blood or of some ancient faith, against foreigners or cosmopolitans, or 'sophisters, economists and calculators', who did not understand the true soul of the people or the roots from which it sprang, and robbed it of its heritage.

It seems to me that those who, however perceptive in other respects, ignored the explosive power generated by the combination of unhealed mental wounds, however caused, with the image of the nation as a society of the living, the dead and those yet unborn (sinister as this could prove to be when driven to a point of pathological exacerbation), displayed insufficient grasp of social reality. This seems to me to be as true of the present as of the last two hundred years. Modern nationalism was indeed born on German soil, but it developed wherever conditions sufficiently resembled the impact of modernisation on traditional German society. I do not wish to say that this ideology was inevitable: it might, perhaps, not have been born at all. No one has yet convincingly demonstrated that the human imagination obeys discoverable laws, or is able to predict the movement of ideas. If this cluster of ideas had not been born, history might have taken another turn. The wounds inflicted on the Germans would have been there, but the balm which they generated, what Raymond Aron (who applied it to Marxism) has called the opium of the intellectuals, might have been a different one—and if this had happened, things might have fallen out otherwise. But the idea was born: and the consequences were what they were; and it seems to me to show a certain ideological obstinacy not to recognise their nature and importance.

Why was this not seen? Partly, perhaps, because of the 'Whig interpretation' so widely disseminated by enlightened liberal (and socialist) historians; the picture is familiar: on the one side, the powers of darkness: church, capitalism, tradition, authority, hierarchy, exploitation, privilege; on the other, the *lumières*, the struggle for reason, for knowledge and the destruction of barriers between men, for equality, human rights (particularly those of the labouring masses), for individual and social liberty, the reduction of misery, oppression, brutality, the emphasis on what men had in common, not on their differences. Yet, to put it at its simplest, the differences were no less real than the generic identity, than Feuerbach's and Marx's 'species-being'. National sentiment, which sprang from them, fell on both sides of this division between light and darkness, progress and reaction, just as it has within the communist camp of our own day; ignored differences assert themselves, and in the end rise against efforts to ride over them in favour of an assumed, or desired, uniformity. The ideal of a single, scientifically organised world system governed by reason was the heart of the programme of the Enlightenment. When Immanuel Kant, who can scarcely be accused of leanings towards irrationalism, declared, 'From the crooked timber of humanity no straight thing can ever be made', what he said was not absurd.

[From 'Nationalism', in *Against the Current* (Oxford University Press, Oxford, 1981), 351–3.]

ALASDAIR MACINTYRE

103 Is Patriotism a Virtue?

I

One of the central tasks of the moral philosopher is to articulate the convictions of the society in which he or she lives so that these convictions may become available for rational scrutiny. This task is all the more urgent when a variety of conflicting and incompatible beliefs are held within one and the same community, either by rival groups who differ on key moral questions or by one and the same set of individuals who find within themselves competing moral allegiances. In either of these types of case the first task of the moral philosopher is to render explicit what is at issue in the various disagreements and it is a task of this kind that I have set myself in this lecture.

For it is quite clear that there are large disagreements about patriotism in our society. And although it would be a mistake to suppose that there are only two clear, simple and mutually opposed sets of beliefs about patriotism, it is at least plausible to suggest that the range of conflicting views can be placed on a spectrum with two poles. At one end is the view, taken for granted by almost everyone in the nineteenth century, a commonplace in the literary culture of the McGuffey readers, that 'patriotism' names a virtue. At the other end is the contrasting view, expressed with sometimes shocking clarity in the nineteen sixties, that 'patriotism' names a vice. It would be misleading for me to suggest that I am going to be able to offer good reasons for taking one of these views rather than the other. What I do hope to achieve is a clarification of the issues that divide them.

A necessary first step in the direction of any such clarification is to distinguish patriotism properly so-called from two other sets of attitudes that are all too easily assimilated to it. The first is that exhibited by those who are protagonists of their own nation's causes because and only because, so they assert, it is their nation which is *the* champion of some great moral ideal. In the Great War of 1914–18 Max Weber claimed that Imperial Germany should be supported because its was the cause of *Kultur*, while Emile Durkheim claimed with equal vehemence that France should be supported because its was the cause of *civilisation*. And here and now there are those American politicians who claim that the United States deserves our allegiance because it champions the goods of freedom against the evils of communism. What distinguishes their attitude from patriotism is twofold: first it is the ideal and not the nation which is the primary object of their regard; and secondly insofar as their regard for the ideal provides good reasons for allegiance to their country, it provides good reasons for anyone at all to uphold their country's cause, irrespective of their nationality or citizenship.

Patriotism by contrast is defined in terms of a kind of loyalty to a particular nation which only those possessing that particular nationality can exhibit. Only Frenchmen can be patriotic about France, while anyone can make the cause of *civilisation* their own. But it would be all too easy in noticing this to fail to make a second equally important distinction. Patriotism is not to be confused with a mindless loyalty to one's own particular nation which has no regard at all for the characteristics of that particular nation. Patriotism does generally and characteristically involve a peculiar regard not just for one's own nation, but for the particular characteristics and merits and achievements of one's own nation. These latter are indeed valued *as* merits and achievements and their character as merits and achievements provides reasons supportive of the patriot's attitudes. But the patriot does not value in the same way precisely similar merits and achievements when they are the merits and achievements of some nation other than his or hers. For he or she—at least in the role of patriot—values them not just as merits and achievements, but as the merits and achievements of this particular nation.

To say this is to draw attention to the fact that patriotism is one of a class of loyalty-exhibiting virtues (that is, if it *is* a virtue at all), other members of which are marital fidelity, the love of one's own family and kin, friendship, and loyalty to such institutions as schools and cricket or baseball clubs. All these attitudes exhibit a peculiar action-generating regard for particular persons, institutions or groups, a regard founded upon a particular historical relationship of association between the person exhibiting the regard and the relevant person, institution or group. It is often, although not always, the case that associated with this regard will be a felt gratitude for the benefits which the individual takes him or herself to have received from the person, institution or group. But it would be one more mistake to suppose patriotism or other such attitudes of loyalty to be at their core or primarily responses of gratitude. For there are many persons, institutions and groups to which each of us have good reason to feel grateful without this kind of loyalty being involved. What patriotism and other such attitudes involve is not just gratitude, but a particular kind of gratitude; and what those who treat patriotism and other such loyalties as virtues are committed to believing is not that what they owe their nation or whomever or whatever it is is simply a requital for benefits received, based on some relationship of reciprocity of benefits.

So although one may as a patriot love one's country, or as a husband or wife exhibit marital fidelity, and cite as partially supporting reasons one's country's or one's spouse's merits and one's own gratitude to them for benefits received these can be no more than *partially* supporting reasons, just because what is valued is valued precisely as the merits of *my* country or spouse or as the benefits received by *me* from *my* country or spouse. The particularity of the relationship is essential and ineliminable, and in identifying it as such we have already specified one central problem. What *is* the relationship between patriotism as such, the regard for this particular nation, and the regard which the patriot has for the merits and achievements of his or her nation and for the benefits which he or she has received? The answer to this question must be delayed for it will turn out to depend upon the answer to an apparently even more fundamental question, one that can best be framed in terms of the thesis that, if patriotism is understood as I have understood it, then 'patriotism' is not merely not the name of a virtue, but must be the name of a vice, since patriotism thus understood and morality are incompatible.

II

The presupposition of this thesis is an account of morality which has enjoyed high prestige in our culture. According to that account to judge from a moral standpoint is to judge impersonally. It is to judge as any rational person would judge, independently of his or her interests, affections and social position. And to act morally is to act in accordance with such impersonal judgments. Thus to think and to act morally involves the moral agent in abstracting him or herself from all social particularity and partiality. The potential conflict between morality so understood and patriotism is at once clear. For patriotism requires me to exhibit peculiar devotion to my nation and you to yours. It requires me to regard such contingent social facts as where I was born and what government ruled over that place at that time, who my parents were, who my great-great-grandparents were and so on, as deciding for me the question of what virtuous action is—at least insofar as it is the virtue of patriotism which is in question. Hence the moral standpoint and the patriotic standpoint are systematically incompatible.

Yet although this is so, it might be argued that the two standpoints need not be in conflict. For patriotism and all other such particular loyalties can be restricted in their scope so that their exercise is always within the confines imposed by morality. Patriotism need be regarded as nothing more than a perfectly proper devotion to one's own nation which must never be allowed to violate the constraints set by the impersonal moral standpoint. This is indeed the kind of patriotism professed by certain liberal moralists who are often indignant when it is suggested by their critics that they are not patriotic. To those critics however patriotism thus limited in its scope appears to be emasculated, and it does so because in some of the most important situations of actual social life either the patriotic standpoint comes into serious conflict with the standpoint of a genuinely impersonal morality or it amounts to no more than a set of practically empty slogans. What kinds of circumstances are these? They are at least twofold.

The first kind arises from scarcity of essential resources, often historically from the scarcity of land suitable for cultivation and pasture, and perhaps in our own time from that of fossil fuels. What your community requires as the material prerequisites for your survival as a distinctive community and your growth into a distinctive nation may be exclusive use of the same or some of the same natural resources as my community requires for its survival and growth into a distinctive nation. When such a conflict arises, the standpoint of impersonal morality requires an allocation of goods such that each individual person counts for one and no more than one, while the patriotic standpoint requires that I strive to further the interests of my community and you strive to further those of yours, and certainly where the survival of one community is at stake, and sometimes perhaps even when only large interests of one community are at stake, patriotism entails a willingness to go to war on one's community's behalf.

The second type of conflict-engendering circumstance arises from differences between communities about the right way for each to live. Not only competition for scarce natural resources, but incompatibilities arising from such conflict-engendering beliefs may lead to situations in which once again the liberal moral standpoint and the patriotic standpoint are radically at odds.

The administration of the *pax Romana* from time to time required the Roman *imperium* to set its frontiers at the point at which they could be most easily secured, so that the burden of supporting the legions would be reconcilable with the administration of Roman law. And the British empire was no different in its time. But this required infringing upon the territory and the independence of barbarian border peoples. A variety of such peoples—Scottish Gaels, Iroquois Indians, Bedouin—have regarded raiding the territory of their traditional enemies living within the confines of such large empires as an essential constituent of the good life; whereas the settled urban or agricultural communities which provided the target for their depredations have regarded the subjugation of such peoples and their reeducation into peaceful pursuits as one of their central responsibilities. And on such issues once again the impersonal moral standpoint and that of patriotism cannot be reconciled.

For the impersonal moral standpoint, understood as the philosophical protagonists of modern liberalism have understood it, requires neutrality not only between rival and competing interests, but also between rival and competing sets of beliefs about the best way for human beings to live. Each individual is to be left free to pursue in his or her own way that way of life which he or she judges to be best; while morality by contrast consists of rules which, just because they are such that any rational person, independently of his or her interests or point of view on the best way for human beings to live, would assent to them, are equally binding on all persons. Hence in conflicts between nations or other communities over ways of life, the standpoint of morality will once again be that of an impersonal arbiter, adjudicating in ways that give equal weight to each individual person's needs, desires, beliefs about the good and the like, while the patriot is once again required to be partisan.

Notice that in speaking of the standpoint of liberal impersonal morality in the way in which I have done I have been describing a standpoint whose truth is both presupposed by the political actions and utterances of a great many people in our society and explicitly articulated and defended by most modern moral philosophers; and that it has at the level of moral philosophy a number of distinct versions—some with a Kantian flavour, some utilitarian, some contractarian. I do not mean to suggest that the disagreements between these positions are unimportant. Nonetheless the five central positions that I have ascribed to that standpoint appear in all these various philosophical guises: first, that morality is constituted by rules to which any rational person would under certain ideal conditions give assent; secondly, that those rules impose constraints upon and are neutral between rival and competing interests—morality itself is not the expression of any particular interest; thirdly, that those rules are also neutral between rival and competing sets of beliefs about what the best way for human beings to live is; fourthly, that the units which provide the subject-matter of morality as well as its agents are individual human beings and that in moral evaluations each individual is to count for one and nobody for more than one; and fifthly, that the standpoint of the moral agent constituted by allegiance to these rules is one and the same for all moral agents and as such is independent of all social particularity. What morality provides are standards by which all actual social structures may be brought to judgment from a standpoint independent of all of them. It is morality so understood allegiance to which is not only incompatible with treating patriotism as a virtue, but which requires that patriotism—at least in any substantial version—be treated as a vice.

But is this the only possible way to understand morality? As a matter of history, the answer is clearly 'No'. This understanding of morality invaded post Renascence Western culture at a particular point in time as the moral counterpart to political liberalism and social individualism and its polemical stances reflect its history of emergence from the conflicts which those movements engendered and themselves presuppose alternatives against which those polemical stances were and are directed. Let me therefore turn to considering one of those alternative accounts of morality, whose peculiar interest lies in the place that it has to assign to patriotism.

III

According to the liberal account of morality *where* and *from whom* I learn the principles and precepts of morality are and must be irrelevant both to the question of what the content of morality is and to that of the nature of my commitment to it, as irrelevant as *where* and *from whom* I learn the principles and precepts of mathematics are to the content of mathematics and the nature of my commitment to mathematical truths. By contrast on the alternative account of morality which I am going to sketch, the questions of *where* and *from whom* I learn my morality turn out to be crucial for both the content and the nature of moral commitment.

On this view it is an essential characteristic of the morality which each of us acquires that it is learned from, in and through the way of life of some particular community. Of course the moral rules elaborated in one particular historical community will often resemble and sometimes be identical with the rules to which allegiance is given in other particular communities, especially in communities with a shared history or which appeal to the same canonical texts. But there will characteristically be *some* distinctive features of the set of rules considered as a whole, and those distinctive features will often arise from the way in which members of that particular community responded to some earlier situation or series of situations in which particular features of difficult cases led to one or more rules being put in question and reformulated or understood in some new way. Moreover the form of the rules of morality as taught and apprehended will be intimately connected with specific institutional arrangements. The moralities of different societies may agree in having a precept enjoining that a child should honor his or her parents, but what it is so to honour and indeed what a father is and what a mother is will vary greatly between different social orders. So that what I learn as a guide to my actions and as a standard for evaluating them is never morality as such, but always the highly specific morality of some highly specific social order.

To this the reply by the protagonists of modern liberal morality might well be: doubtless this is how a comprehension of the rules of morality is first acquired. But what allows such specific rules, framed in terms of particular social institutions, to be accounted moral rules at all is the fact they are nothing other than applications of universal and general moral rules and individuals acquire genuine morality only because and insofar as they progress from particularised socially specific applications of universal and general moral rules to comprehending them as universal and general. To learn to understand oneself as a moral agent just is to learn to free oneself from social particularity and to adopt a standpoint independent of any particular set of social institutions and the fact that everyone or almost everyone has to learn to do this by starting out from a standpoint deeply infected by social particularity and partiality goes no way towards providing an alternative account of morality. But to this reply a threefold rejoinder can be made.

First, it is not just that I first apprehend the rules of morality in some socially specific and particularised form. It is also and correlatively that the goods by reference to which and for the sake of which any set of rules must be justified are also going to be goods that are socially specific and particular. For central to those goods is the enjoyment of one particular kind of social life, lived out through a particular set of social relationships and thus what I enjoy is the good of *this* particular social life inhabited by me and I enjoy *it* as what *it* is. It may well be that it follows that I would enjoy and benefit equally from similar forms of social life in other communities; but this hypothetical truth in no way diminishes the importance of the contention that my goods are as a matter of fact found *here*, among *these* particular people, in *these* particular relationships. Goods are never encountered except as thus particularised. Hence the abstract general claim, that rules of a certain kind are justified by being productive of and constitutive of goods of a certain kind, is true only if these and these and these particular sets of rules incarnated in the practices of these and these and these particular communities are productive of or constitutive of these and these and these particular goods enjoyed at certain particular times and places by certain specifiable individuals.

It follows that I find *my* justification for allegiance to these rules of morality in *my* particular community; deprived of the life of that community, I would have no reason to be moral. But this is not all. To obey the rules of morality is characteristically and generally a hard task for human beings. Indeed were it not so, our need for morality would not be what it is. It is because we are continually liable to be blinded by immediate desire, to be distracted from our responsibilities, to lapse into backsliding and because even the best of us may at times encounter quite unusual temptations that it is important to morality that *I* can only be a moral agent because *we* are moral agents, that I need those around me to reinforce my moral strengths and assist in remedying my moral weaknesses. It is in general only within a community that individuals become capable of morality, are sustained in their morality and are constituted as moral agents by the way in which other people regard them and what is owed to and by them as well as by the way in which they regard themselves. In requiring much from me morally the other members of my community express a kind of respect for me that has nothing to do with expectations of benefit; and those of whom nothing or little is required in respect of morality are treated with a lack of respect which is, if repeated often enough, damaging to the moral capacities of those individuals. Of course, lonely moral heroism is sometimes required and sometimes achieved. But we must not treat this exceptional type of case as though it were typical. And once we recognise that typically moral agency and continuing moral capacity are engendered and sustained in essential ways by particular institutionalised social ties in particular social groups, it will be difficult to counterpose allegiance to a particular society and allegiance to morality in the way in which the protagonists of liberal morality do.

Indeed the case for treating patriotism as a virtue is now clear. *If* first of all it is the case that I can only apprehend the rules of morality in the version in which they are incarnated in some specific community; and *if* secondly it is the case that the justification of morality must be in terms of particular goods enjoyed within the life of particular communities; and *if* thirdly it is the case that I am characteristically brought into being and maintained as a moral agent only through the particular kinds of moral sustenance afforded by my community, *then* it is clear that deprived of this community, I am unlikely to flourish as a moral agent. Hence my allegiance to the community and what it requires of me—even to the point of requiring me to die to sustain its life—could not meaningfully be contrasted with or counterposed to what morality required of me. Detached from my community, I will be apt to lose my hold upon all genuine standards of judgment. Loyalty to that community, to the hierarchy of particular kinship, particular local community and particular natural community, is on this view a prerequisite for morality. So patriotism and those loyalties cognate to it are not just virtues but central virtues. Everything however turns on the truth or falsity of the claims advanced in the three preceding if-clauses. And the argument so far affords us no resources for delivering a verdict upon that truth or falsity. Nonetheless some progress has been achieved, and not only because the terms of the debate have become clearer. For it has also become clear that this dispute is not adequately characterised if it is understood simply as a disagreement between two rival accounts of morality, as if there were some independently identifiable phenomenon situated somehow or other in the social world waiting to be described more or less accurately by the contending parties.

What we have here are two rival and incompatible moralities, each of which is viewed from within by its adherents as morality-as-such, each of which makes its exclusive claim to our allegiance. How are we to evaluate such claims?

One way to begin is to be learned from Aristotle. Since we possess no stock of clear and distinct first principles or any other such epistemological resource which would provide us with a neutral and independent standard for judging between them, we shall do well to proceed dialectically. And one useful dialectical strategy is to focus attention on those accusations which the adherents of each bring against the rival position which the adherents of that rival position treat as of central importance to rebut. For this will afford at least one indication of the issues about the importance of which both sides agree and about the characterisation of which their very recognition of disagreement suggests that there must also be some shared beliefs. In what areas do such issues arise?

IV

One such area is defined by a charge which it seems reasonable at least *prima facie* for the protagonists of patriotism to bring against morality. The morality for which patriotism is a virtue offers a form of rational justification for moral rules and precepts whose structure is clear and rationally defensible. The rules of morality are justifiable if and only if they are productive of and partially constitutive of a form of shared social life whose goods are directly enjoyed by those inhabiting the particular communities whose social life is of that kind. Hence *qua* member of this or that particular community I can appreciate the justification for what morality requires of me from within the social roles that I live out in my community. By contrast, it may be argued, liberal morality requires of me to assume an abstract and artificial—perhaps even an impossible—stance, that of a rational being as such, responding to the requirements of morality not *qua* parent or farmer or quarterback, but *qua* rational agent who has abstracted him or herself from all social particularity, who has become not merely Adam Smith's impartial spectator, but a correspondingly impartial actor, and one who in his impartiality is doomed to rootlessness, to be a citizen of nowhere. How can I justify to myself performing this act of abstraction and detachment?

The liberal answer is clear: such abstraction and detachment is defensible, because it is a necessary condition of moral freedom, of emancipation from the bondage of the social, political and economic *status quo*. For unless I can stand back from every and any feature of that *status quo*, including the roles within it which I myself presently inhabit, I will be unable to view it critically and to decide for myself what stance it is rational and right for me to adopt towards it. This does not preclude that the outcome of such a critical evaluation may not be an endorsement of all or some of the existing social order; but even such an endorsement will only be free and rational if I have made it for myself in this way. (Making just such an endorsement of much of the economic *status quo* is the distinguishing mark of the contemporary conservative liberal, such as Milton Friedman, who is as much a liberal as the liberal liberal who finds much of the *status quo* wanting—such as J. K. Galbraith or Edward Kennedy—or the radical liberal.) Thus liberal morality does after all appeal to an overriding good, the good of this particular kind of emancipating freedom. And in the name of this good it is able not only to respond to the question about how the rules of morality are to be justified, but also to frame a plausible and potentially damaging objection to the morality of patriotism.

It is of the essence of the morality of liberalism that no limitations are or can be set upon the criticism of the social *status quo*. No institution, no practice, no loyalty can be immune from being put in question and perhaps rejected. Conversely the morality of patriotism is one which precisely because it is framed in terms of the membership of some particular social community with some particular social, political and economic structure, must exempt at least some fundamental structures of that community's life from criticism. Because patriotism has to be a loyalty that is in some respects unconditional, so in just those respects rational criticism is ruled out. But if so the adherents of the morality of patriotism have condemned themselves to a fundamentally irrational attitude—since to refuse to examine some of one's fundamental beliefs and attitudes is to insist on accepting them, whether they are rationally justifiable or not, which is irrational—and have imprisoned themselves within that irrationality. What answer can the adherents of the morality of patriotism make to this kind of accusation? The reply must be threefold.

When the liberal moralist claims that the patriot is bound to treat his or her nation's projects and practices in some measure uncritically, the claim is not only that at any one time certain of these projects and practices will be being treated uncritically; it is that some at least must be permanently exempted from criticism. The patriot is in no position to deny this; but what is crucial to the patriot's case is to identify clearly precisely what it is that is thus exempted. And at this point it becomes extremely important that in outlining the case for the morality of patriotism—as indeed in outlining the case for liberal morality—we should not be dealing with strawmen. Liberalism and patriotism are not positions invented by me or by other external commentators; they have their own distinctive spokesmen and their own distinctive voices. And although I hope that it has been clear throughout that I have only been trying to articulate what those voices would say, it is peculiarly important to the case for patriotic morality at this point that its actual historical protagonists be identified. So what I say next is an attempt to identify the common attitudes on this point of Charles Péguy and Charles de Gaulle, of Bismarck and of Adam von Trott. You will notice that in these pairs one member is someone who was at least for a time a member of his nation's political establishment, the other someone who was always in a radical way outside that establishment and hostile to it, but that even those who were for a time identified with the *status quo* of power, were also at times alienated from it. And this makes it clear that whatever is exempted from the patriot's criticism the *status quo* of power and government and the policies pursued by those exercising power and government never need be so exempted. What then is exempted? The answer is: the nation conceived *as a project*, a project somehow or other brought to birth in the past and carried on so that a morally distinctive community was brought into being which embodied a claim to political autonomy in its various organised and institutionalised expressions. Thus one can be patriotic towards a nation whose political independence is yet to come—as Garibaldi was; or towards a nation which once was and perhaps might be again—like the Polish patriots in the 1860s. What the patriot is committed to is a particular way of linking a past which has conferred a distinctive moral and political identity upon him or her with a future for the project which is his or her nation which it is his or her responsibility to bring into being. Only this allegiance is unconditional and allegiance to particular governments or forms of government or particular leaders will be entirely conditional upon their being devoted to furthering that project rather than frustrating or destroying it. Hence there is nothing inconsistent in a patriot's being deeply opposed to his country's contemporary rulers, as Péguy was, or plotting their overthrow as Adam von Trott did.

Yet although this may go part of the way towards answering the charge of the liberal moralist that the patriot must in certain areas be completely uncritical and therefore irrationalist, it certainly does not go all the way. For everything that I have said on behalf of the morality of patriotism is compatible with it being the case that on occasion patriotism might require me to support and work for the success of some enterprise of my nation as crucial to its overall project, crucial perhaps to its survival, when the success of that enterprise would not be in the best interests of mankind, evaluated from an impartial and impersonal standpoint. The case of Adam von Trott is very much to the point.

Adam von Trott was a German patriot who was executed after the unsuccessful asassination attempt against Hitler's life in 1944. Trott deliberately chose to work inside Germany with the minuscule, but highly placed, conservative opposition to the Nazis with the aim of replacing Hitler from within, rather than to work for an overthrow of Nazi Germany which would result in the destruction of the Germany brought to birth in 1871. But to do this he had to appear to be identified with the cause of Nazi Germany and so strengthened not only his country's cause, as was his intention, but also as an unavoidable consequence the cause of the Nazis. This kind of example is a particularly telling one, because the claim that such and such a course of action 'is to the best interests of mankind' is usually at best disputable, at worst cloudy rhetoric. But there are a very few causes in which so much was at stake—and that this is generally much clearer in retrospect than it was at the time does not alter that fact—that the phrase has clear application: the overthrow of Nazi Germany was one of them.

How ought the patriot then to respond? Perhaps in two ways. The first begins by reemphasising that from the fact that the particularist morality of the patriot is rooted in a particular community and inextricably bound up with the social life of that community, it does not follow that it cannot provide rational grounds for repudiating many features of that country's present organised social life. The conception of justice engendered by the notion of citizenship within a particular community may provide standards by which particular political institutions are found wanting: when Nazi anti-Semitism encountered the phenomena of German Jewish ex-soldiers who had won the Iron Cross, it had to repudiate German particularist standards of excellence (for the award of the Iron Cross symbolised a recognition of devotion to Germany). Moreover the conception of one's own nation having a special mission does not necessitate that this mission may not involve the extension of a justice originally at home only in the particular institutions of the homeland. And clearly particular governments or agencies of government may defect and may be understood to have defected from this mission so radically that the patriot may find that a point comes when he or she has to choose between the claims of the project which constitutes his or her nation and the claims of the morality that he or she has learnt as a member of the community whose life is informed by that project. Yes, the liberal critic of patriotism will respond, this indeed *may* happen; but it may not and if often will not. Patriotism turns out to be a permanent source of moral danger. And this claim, I take it, cannot in fact be successfully rebutted.

A second possible, but very different type of answer on behalf of the patriot would run as follows. I argued earlier that the kind of regard for one's own country which would be compatible with a liberal morality of impersonality and impartiality would be too insubstantial, would be under too many constraints, to be regarded as a version of patriotism in the traditional sense. But it does not follow that some version of traditional patriotism may not be compatible with some other morality of universal moral law, which sets limits to and provides both sanction for and correction of the particularist morality of the patriot. Whether this is so or not is too large and too distinct a question to pursue in this present paper. But we ought to note that even if it is so—and all those who have been both patriots and Christians *or* patriots and believers in Thomistic natural law *or* patriots and believers in the Rights of Man have been committed to claiming that it is so—this would not diminish in any way the force of the liberal claim that patriotism is a morally dangerous phenomenon.

That the rational protagonist of the morality of patriotism is compelled, if my argument is correct, to concede this does not mean that there is not more to be said in the debate. And what needs to be said is that the liberal morality of impartiality and impersonality turns out also to be a morally dangerous phenomenon in an interestingly corresponding way. For suppose the bonds of patriotism to be dissolved: would liberal morality be able to provide anything adequately substantial in its place? What the morality of patriotism at its best provides is a clear account of and justification for the particular bonds and loyalties which form so much of the substance of the moral life. It does so by underlining the moral importance of the different members of a group acknowledging a shared history. Each one of us to some degree or other understands his or her life as an enacted narrative; and because of our relationships with others we have to understand ourselves as characters in the enacted narratives of other people's lives. Moreover the story of each of our lives is characteristically embedded in the story of one or more larger units. I understand the story of my life in such a way that it is part of the history of my family or of this farm or of this university or of this countryside; and I understand the story of the lives of other individuals around me as embedded in the same larger stories, so that I and they share a common stake in the outcome of that story and in what sort of story it both is and is to be: tragic, heroic, comic.

A central contention of the morality of patriotism is that I will obliterate and lose a central dimension of the moral life if I do not understand the enacted narrative of my own individual life as embedded in the history of my country. For if I do not so understand it I will not understand what I owe to others or what others owe to me, for what crimes of my nation I am bound to make reparation, for what benefits to my nation I am bound to feel gratitude. Understanding what is owed to and by me and understanding the history of the communities of which I am a part is on this view one and the same thing.

It is worth stressing that one consequence of this is that patriotism, in the sense in which I am understanding it in this paper, is only possible to certain types of national community under certain conditions. A national community, for example, which systematically disowned its own true history or substituted a largely fictitious history for it or a national community in which the bonds deriving from history were in no way the real bonds of the community (having been replaced for example by the bonds of reciprocal self-interest) would be one towards which patriotism would be—from any point of view—an irrational attitude. For precisely the same reasons that a family whose members all came to regard membership in that family as governed only by reciprocal self-interest would no longer be a family in the traditional sense, so a nation whose members took up a similar attitude would no longer be a nation and this would provide adequate grounds for holding that the project which constituted that nation had simply collapsed. Since all modern bureaucratic states tend towards reducing national communities to this condition, all such states tend towards a condition in which any genuine morality of patriotism would have no place and what paraded itself as patriotism would be an unjustifiable simulacrum.

Why would this matter? In modern communities in which membership is understood only or primarily in terms of reciprocal self-interest, only two resources are generally available when destructive conflicts of interest threaten such reciprocity. One is the arbitrary imposition of some solution by force; the other is appeal to the neutral, impartial and impersonal standards of liberal morality. The importance of this resource is scarcely to be underrated; but how much of a resource is it? The problem is that some motivation has to be provided for allegiance to the standards of impartiality and impersonality which both has rational justification and can outweigh the considerations provided by interest. Since any large need for such allegiance arises precisely and only when and insofar as the possibility of appeals to reciprocity in interests has broken down, such reciprocity can no longer provide the relevant kind of motivation. And it is difficult to identify anything that can take its place. The appeal to moral agents *qua* rational beings to place their allegiance to impersonal rationality above that to their interests has, just because it is an appeal to rationality, to furnish an adequate reason for so doing. And this is a point at which liberal accounts of morality are notoriously vulnerable. This vulnerability becomes a manifest practical liability at one key point in the social order.

Every political community except in the most exceptional conditions requires standing armed forces for its minimal security. Of the members of these armed forces it must require both that they be prepared to sacrifice their own lives for the sake of the community's security and that their willingness to do so be not contingent upon their own individual evaluation of the rightness or wrongness of their country's cause on some specific issue, measured by some standard that is neutral and impartial relative to the interests of their own community and the interests of other communities. And, that is to say, good soldiers may not be liberals and must indeed embody in their actions a good deal at least of the morality of patriotism. So the political survival of any polity in which liberal morality had secured large-scale allegiance would depend upon there still being enough young men and women who rejected that liberal morality. And in this sense liberal morality tends towards the dissolution of social bonds.

Hence the charge that the morality of patriotism can successfully bring against liberal morality is the mirror-image of that which liberal morality can successfully urge against the morality of patriotism. For while the liberal moralist was able to conclude that patriotism is a permanent source of moral danger because of the way it places our ties to our nation beyond rational criticism, the moralist who defends patriotism is able to conclude that liberal morality is a permanent source of moral danger because of the way it renders our social and moral ties too open to dissolution by rational criticism. And each party is in fact in the right against the other.

V

The fundamental task which confronts any moral philosopher who finds this conclusion compelling is clear. It is to enquire whether, although the central claims made on behalf of these two rival modern moralities cannot both be true, we ought perhaps not to move towards the conclusion that both sets of claims are in fact false. And this is an enquiry in which substantial progress has already been made. But history in its impatience does not wait for moral philosophers to complete their tasks, let alone to convince their fellow-citizens. The *polis* ceased to be the key institution in Greek politics even while Aristotle was still restating its rationale and any contemporary philosopher who discusses the key conceptions that have informed modern political life since the eighteenth century is in danger of reliving Aristotle's fate, even if in a rather less impressive way. The owl of Minerva really does seem to fly at dusk.

Does this mean that my argument is therefore devoid of any immediate practical significance? That would be true only if the conclusion that a morality of liberal impersonality and a morality of patriotism must be deeply incompatible itself had no practical significance for our understanding of our everyday politics. But perhaps a systematic recognition of this incompatibility will enable us to diagnose one central flaw in the political life characteristic of modern Western states, or at least of all those modern Western states which look back for their legitimation to the American and the French revolutions. For polities so established have tended to contrast themselves with the older regimes that they displaced by asserting that, while all previous polities had expressed in their lives the partiality and one-sidedness of local customs, institutions and traditions, they have for the first time given expression in their constitutional and institutional forms to the impersonal and impartial rules of morality as such, common to all rational beings. So Robespierre proclaimed that it was an effect of the French Revolution that the cause of France and the cause of the Rights of Man were one and the same cause. And in the nineteenth century the United States produced its own version of this claim, one which at the level of rhetoric provided the content for many Fourth of July orations and at the level of education set the standards for the Americanisation of the late nineteenth century and early twentieth century immigrants, especially those from Europe.

Hegel employs a useful distinction which he marks by his use of words *Sittlichkeit* and *Moralität*. *Sittlichkeit* is the customary morality of each particular society, pretending to be no more than this. *Moralität* reigns in the realm of rational universal, impersonal morality, of liberal morality, as I have defined it. What those immigrants were taught in effect was that they had left behind countries and cultures where *Sittlichkeit* and *Moralität* were certainly distinct and often opposed and arrived in a country and a culture whose *Sittlichkeit* just is *Moralität*. And thus for many Americans the cause of America, understood as the object of patriotic regard, and the cause of morality, understood as the liberal moralist understands it, came to be identified. The history of this identification could not be other than a history of confusion and incoherence, if the argument which I have constructed in this lecture is correct. For a morality of particularist ties and solidarities has been conflated with a morality of universal, impersonal and impartial principles in a way that can never be carried through without incoherence.

One test therefore of whether the argument that I have constructed has or has not empirical application and practical significance would be to discover whether it is or is not genuinely illuminating to write the political and social history of modern America as in key part the living out of a central conceptual confusion, a confusion perhaps required for the survival of a large-scale modern polity which has to exhibit itself as liberal in many institutional settings, but which also has to be able to engage the patriotic regard of enough of its citizens, if it is to continue functioning effectively. To determine whether that is or is not true would be to risk discovering that we inhabit a kind of polity whose moral order requires systematic incoherence in the form of public allegiance to mutually inconsistent sets of principles. But that is a task which—happily—lies beyond the scope of this lecture.

['Is Patriotism a Virtue?', *The Lindley Lecture*, University of Kansas, 1984, copyright Dept of Philosophy, University of Kansas.]

THOMAS HILL

104 **The Message of Affirmative Action**

I suggest that some of the values that give affirmative action its point are best seen as cross-time values that fall outside the exclusively forward-looking and backward-looking perspectives. They include having a history of racial and gender relations governed, so far as possible, by the ideals of mutual respect, trust, and fair opportunity for all.

Our national history provides a context of increasing recognition and broader interpretation of the democratic ideal of the equal dignity of all human beings, an ideal that has been flagrantly abused from the outset, partially affirmed in the bloody Civil War, and increasingly extended in the civil rights movement, but is still far from being fully respected. More specifically, blacks and women were systematically treated in an unfair and demeaning way by public institutions, including universities, until quite recently, and few could confidently claim to have rooted out racism and sexism even now. The historical context is not what grounds or legitimates democratic values, but it is the background of the current problem, the sometimes admirable and often ugly way the chapters up until now have been written.

Consider first the social ideal of mutual respect and trust among citizens. [. . .] the history of our racial and gender relations is obviously not an idyllic story of mutual respect and trust momentarily interrupted by a crisis. Even so, the question to ask is not merely, 'What will promote respectful and trusting racial and gender relations in future generations?' but rather, 'Given our checkered past, how can we appropriately express the social value of mutual respect and trust that we want, so far as possible, to characterize our history?' We cannot change our racist and sexist past, but we also cannot express full respect for those present individuals who live in its aftermath if we ignore it. What is called for is not merely repayment of tangible debts incurred by past injuries, but also a message to counter the deep insult inherent in racism and sexism.

Recognizing that problems of this kind are not amenable to easy solutions deduced from self-evident moral generalizations, we may find it helpful instead to reflect on an analogy. Suppose you return to the hometown you left in childhood, remembering with pride its Fourth of July speeches about the values of community, equality, and fairness for all. You discover, however, that the community was never as perfect as you thought. In fact, for years—until quite recently—certain families, who had been disdainfully labeled 'the Barefeet,' had not only been shunned by most folk but had also been quietly terrorized by a few well-placed citizens. The Barefeet had been arrested on false charges, beaten, raped, and blackmailed into silent submission. The majority, perhaps would never have done these things, but their contempt for the Barefeet was such that most would have regarded these crimes less important than if they had been done to insiders. Fortunately, the worst offenders have died, and so have the victims of the most outrageous crimes. Majority attitudes have changed somewhat, though often merely from open contempt to passive disregard. Some new citizens have come to town, and a few of the Barefeet (now more politely called 'Cross-towners') have managed to become successful. Nonetheless, the older Cross-towners are still fearful and resigned, and the younger generation is openly resentful and distrustful when officials proclaim a new commitment to democratic ideals. It is no surprise, then, that few Cross-towners take full advantage of available opportunities, and that the two groups tend to isolate themselves from each other.

Now suppose you, as one of the majority, could persuade the rest to give a message to the Cross-towners, a message appropriate to the majority's professed value of being a community committed to mutual respect and trust. What would you propose? And, assuming that doing so would violate no one's rights, what means would you think best to convey that message sincerely and effectively? Some would no doubt suggest simply forgetting about the past and hoping that time will heal the wounds. But, whether effective in the future or not, this plan fails to express full respect for the Cross-towners now. Others might suggest a more legalistic approach, trying to determine exactly who has been disadvantaged, the degree of loss, which citizens are most responsible, etc., in order to pay off the debt. But this, taken by itself, faces [. . .] disadvantages. [. . .] If, instead, the value of mutual respect and trust is the governing ideal, the appropriate message would be to acknowledge and deplore the past openly, to affirm a commitment to promote mutual respect and trust in the future, to welcome full interchange and participation with the Cross-towners, and to urge them to undertake the risks of overcoming their understandable suspicions by joining in a common effort to work towards fulfilling the ideal. This would address not merely the injury but also the insult implicit in the town's history.

The more difficult question, however, is how to express such a message effectively and with evident sincerity in an atmosphere already poisoned by the past. Mere words will be taken as mere words, and may in fact turn out to be just that. What is needed is more positive action—concrete steps to prove commitment, to resist backsliding, and to overcome reluctance on both sides. [. . .] The emphasis should be on outreach, increasing awareness of opportunities, accountability and proof of fairness in procedures, and allocating resources (fellowships, release time, etc.) in a way that shows trust that, if given an adequate chance, those formerly excluded would enrich the institution by fully appropriate standards. These seem the most natural way to give force to the message, though arguably other methods may serve the purpose as well.

There is another historical value that is also relevant and seems to favor even more radical steps in affirmative action. The issue is too complex to address adequately here, but it should at least be mentioned. What I have in mind might be called 'fair opportunity.' That is, implicit in our democratic ideals is the idea that our public institutions should be so arranged that they afford to individuals, over time, more or less equal opportunities to develop and make use of their natural talents and to participate and contribute to those institutions. The idea is hard to make precise, but it clearly does not mean that all should have equal chances to have a desirable position, regardless of effort and natural aptitude. The physically handicapped and the mentally retarded suffer from natural misfortunes, and, though society should not ignore them, they cannot expect standards to be rigged to ensure the former equal odds at making the basketball team or the latter equal odds of being appointed to the faculty. Similarly, those who choose not to make the effort to develop their capacities have no right to expect public institutions to include them in a pool from which candidates are selected by lot. But when persons have been disadvantaged by social injustice, having had their initial chances diminished by the network of public institutions themselves, then positive steps are needed to equalize their opportunities over time.

This ideal calls for something more than efforts to ensure that future generations do not suffer from the same disadvantage, for those efforts fail to respond to the unfairness to the present individuals. But, for obvious practical reasons, legal efforts to remedy precisely identifiable disadvantages incurred by individuals are bound to be quite inadequate to address the many subtle losses of opportunity caused by past institutional racism and sexism. Since no perfect solution is possible, we need to choose between this inadequate response and policies that address the problem in a less fine-grained way. Affirmative action programs that employ a working presumption that women and minorities generally have had their opportunities restricted to some degree by institutional racism and sexism will admittedly risk compensating a few who have actually had, on balance, as much opportunity as white males. But the practical alternatives, it seems, are to accept this risk or to refuse to respond at all to the innumerable ways that institutional racism and sexism have undermined opportunities too subtly for the courts to remedy.

Given these options, what would be the message of choosing to limit redress to precisely identifiable losses? This would say, in effect, to women and minorities, 'We cannot find a way to ensure *precisely* that each talented and hard-working person has an equal opportunity over time; and, given our options, we count it more important to see that *none* of you women and minorities are overcompensated than to try to see that the *majority* of you have more nearly equal opportunities over your lifetime. Your grievances are too subtle and difficult to measure, and your group may be harboring some who were not disadvantaged. We would rather let the majority of white males enjoy the advantages of their unfair head-start than to risk compensating one of you who does not deserve it.'

Now *if* it had been established on antecedent grounds that the affirmative action measures in question would violate the *rights* of white male applicants, then one could argue that these coarse-grained efforts to honor the ideal of fair opportunity are illegitimate. But that premise, I think, has not been established. Affirmative action programs would violate the rights of white males only if, all things considered, their guidelines temporarily favoring women and minorities were arbitrary, not serving the legitimate social role of universities or fulfilling the ideals of fairness and respect for all. The considerations offered here, how-ever, point to the conclusion that some affirmative action programs, even those involving a degree of preferential treatment, are legitimated by ideals of mu-tual respect, trust, and fair opportunity.

[From 'The Message of Affirmative Action', *Social Philosophy and Policy* (1991), repr. in Thomas E. Hill Jr., *Autonomy and Self-Respect* (Cambridge University Press, Cambridge, 1991), 205–9.]

AVISHAI MARGALIT and JOSEPH RAZ

105 National Self-Determination

The right to self-determination derives from the value of membership in en-compassing groups. It is a group right, deriving from the value of a collective good, and as such opposed in spirit to contractarian-individualistic approaches to politics or to individual well-being. It rests on an appreciation of the great im-portance that membership in and identification with encompassing groups has in the life of individuals, and the importance of the prosperity and self-respect of such groups to the well-being of their members. That importance makes it reasonable to let the encompassing group that forms a substantial majority in a territory have the right to determine whether that territory shall form an inde-pendent state in order to protect the culture and self-respect of the group, pro-vided that the new state is likely to respect the fundamental interests of its inhabitants, and provided that measures are adopted to prevent its creation from gravely damaging the just interests of other countries. This statement of the argument for the right requires elaboration.

   1. The argument is an instrumental one. It says, essentially, that members of a group are best placed to judge whether their group's prosperity will be jeopar-dized if it does not enjoy political independence. It is in keeping with the view that, even though participation in politics may have intrinsic value to individuals, the shape and boundaries of political units are to be determined by their service to individual well-being, i.e. by their instrumental value. In our world, encom-

passing groups that do not enjoy self-government are not infrequently persecuted, despised, or neglected. Given the importance of their prosperity and self-respect to the well-being of their members, it seems reasonable to entrust their members with the right to determine whether the groups should be self-governing. They may sacrifice their economic or other interests for the sake of group self-respect and prosperity. But such a sacrifice is, given the circumstances of this world, often not unreasonable.

One may ask why such matters should not be entrusted to international adjudication by an international court, or some other international agency. Instead of groups' having a right to self-determination which makes them judges in their own cause, the case for a group's becoming self-governing should be entrusted to the judgment of an impartial tribunal. This would have been a far superior solution to the question 'who is to decide?'. Unfortunately, there simply does not exist any international machinery of enforcement that can be relied upon in preference to a right of self-determination as the right of self-help, nor is there any prospect of one coming into existence in the near future. In the present structure of international relations, the most promising arrangement is one that recognizes group rights to self-determination and entrusts international bodies with the duty to help bring about its realization, and to see to it that the limits and preconditions of the right are observed (these are enumerated in the points 2–5 below).

2. The right belongs to the group. But how should it be exercised? Not necessarily by a simple majority vote. Given the long-term and irreversible nature of the decision (remember that, while independence is up to the group, merger or union is not), the wish for a state must be shared by an overwhelming majority, reflecting deep-seated beliefs and feelings of an enduring nature, and not mere temporary popularity. The precise institutional requirements for the exercise of the right are issues that transcend the topic of this essay. They are liable to vary with the circumstances of different national and ethnic groups. Whatever they are, they should reflect the above principle.

3. The right is over a territory. This simply reflects the territorial organization of our political world. The requirement that the group be a substantial majority of the territory stems from further considerations aimed at balancing the interest in self-government against the interests of nonmembers. First, it is designed to ensure that granting self-government to a territory does not generate a problem as great as it is meant to solve, by ensuring that the independence will not generate a large-scale, new minority problem. That risk cannot be altogether avoided. As was remarked before, numbers count in the end. [. . .]

Do historical ties make a difference? Not to the right if voluntarily abandoned. Suppose that the group was unjustly removed from the country. In that case, the general principle of restitution applies, and the group has a right to self-determination and control over the territory it was expelled from, subject to the general principle of prescription. Prescription protects the interests of the current inhabitants. It is based on several deep-seated concerns. It is meant to prevent the revival of abandoned claims, and to protect those who are not personally to blame from having their life unsettled by claims of ancient wrongs, on the ground that their case now is as good as that of the wronged people or their descendants. Prescription, therefore, may lose the expelled group the right even though its members continue to suffer the effects of the past wrong. Their interest is a consideration to be borne in mind in decisions concerning immigration policies, and the like, but because of prescription they lost the right to self-determination. The outcome is not up to them to decide.

4. The right is conditional on its being exercised for the right reasons, i.e. to secure conditions necessary for the prosperity and self-respect of the group. This is a major protection against abuse. Katanga cannot claim a right to self-determination as a way of securing its exclusive control over uranium mines within its territory. This condition does not negate the nature of a right. The group is still entrusted with the right to decide, and its decision is binding even if wrong, even if the case for self-government does not obtain, provided the reasons that motivate the group's decision are of the right kind.

5. Finally, there are the two broad safeguards on which the exercise of the right is conditional. First, that the group is likely to respect the basic rights of its inhabitants, so that its establishment will do good rather than add to the ills of this world. Secondly, since the establishment of the new state may fundamentally endanger the interests of inhabitants of other countries, its exercise is conditional on measures being taken to prevent or minimize the occurrence of substantial damage of this kind. Such measures, which will vary greatly from case to case, include free-trade agreements, port facilities, granting of air routes, and demilitarization of certain regions.

Two kinds of interest do not call for special protection. One is the interest of a people to regard themselves as part of a larger rather than a smaller grouping or country. The English may have an interest in being part of Great Britain, rather than mere Englanders. But that interest can be justly satisfied only with the willing co-operation of, for example, the Scots. If the other conditions for Scottish independence are met, this interest of the English should not stand in its way. Secondly, unjust economic gains, the product of colonial or other forms of exploitation of one group by another, may be denied to the exploiting group without hesitation or compensation (barring arrangements for a transitory period). But where secession and independence will gravely affect other and legitimate interests of other countries, such interests should be protected by creating free-trade zones, demilitarized areas, etc.

6. A right in one person is sufficient ground to hold some other person(s) to be under a duty. What duties arise out of the right to self-determination? How is this matter to be settled? As the previous discussion makes clear, the right of self-determination is instrumentally justified, as the method of implementing the case for self-government, which itself is based on the fact that in many circumstances

self-government is necessary for the prosperity and dignity of encompassing groups, Hence, in fixing the limits of the right, one has to bear in mind the existing system of international politics, and show that, given other elements in that system, certain duties can be derived from the right to self-determination, whereas others cannot. The first and most important duty arising out of the right is the duty not to impede the exercise of the right, i.e. not to impede groups in their attempts to decide whether appropriate territories should be independent, so long as they do so within the limits of the right. This duty affects in practice first and foremost the state that governs the territory concerned and its inhabitants.

There may be other duties following from the right of self-determination. In particular, there may be a duty on the state governing the territory to provide aid in exercising the right, and a duty on other states to aid the relevant group in realizing its right, and thus to oppose the state governing the territory if it impedes its implementation. But the extent of these duties must be subject to the general principles of international morality, which indicate what methods may and may not be used in pursuit of worthwhile goals and in preventing the violation of rights.

[From 'National Self-Determination', *Journal of Philosophy*, 87 / 8 (Sept. 1990), repr. in Joseph Raz, *Ethics in the Public Domain* (Clarendon Press, Oxford, 1995), 141–5.]

BRIAN BARRY

106 **Justice between Generations**

Suppose that, as a result of using up all the world's resources, human life did come to an end. So what? What is so desirable about an indefinite continuation of the human species, religious convictions apart?[1]

My object in this paper is to ask what if anything those alive at any given time owe their descendants, whether in the form of positive efforts (e.g. investment in capital goods) or in the form of forbearance from possible actions (e.g. those causing irreversible damage to the natural environment). We scan the 'classics' in vain for guidance on this question, and, I think, for understandable reasons. Among human beings, unlike (say) mayflies, generations do not succeed one another in the sense that one is off the scene before the next comes into existence. 'Generations' are an abstraction from a continuous process of population replacement. Prudent provision for the welfare of all those currently alive therefore entails some considerable regard for the future. The way we get into problems that cannot be handled in this way is that there may be 'sleepers' (actions taken at one time that have much more significant effects in the long run than in the short run) or actions that are on balance beneficial in the short run and harmful in the long run (or vice versa).

More precisely the problem arises (as a problem requiring decision) not when actions actually have long-run effects that are different in scale or direction from their short-run effects but when they are *believed* to do so. The increased salience of the problem for us comes about not just because we are more likely to have the opportunity, thanks to technology, of doing things with long-run consequences not mediated by similar short-run consequences but also because there is more chance of our knowing about it. A useful new technology that we have no reason to believe has adverse long-term effects does not present any problem of decision-making for us, even if in fact, unknown to us, it has the most deleterious long-run consequences. Conversely, new knowledge may suggest that things we have been doing for some time have harmful long-term effects. Even if people have been doing something with adverse long-term effects for hundreds or thousands of years, so that we are currently experiencing the ill effects in the form of, say, higher disease rates or lower crop yields than we should otherwise be enjoying, it may still require some break-through in scientific understanding to show that the current situation has been brought about by certain human practices.

In recent years, we have all been made aware by the 'ecological' movement how delicately balanced are the processes that support life on the earth's surface and how easily some disequilibrium may ramify through a variety of processes with cumulative effects. The stage is set for some potentially very awkward decisions by this increased awareness that apparently insignificant impacts on the environment may, by the time they have fully worked themselves through, have serious consequences for human life. We may, any day, be confronted with convincing evidence for believing that something on which we rely heavily—the internal-combustion engine, say—is doing irreversible damage to the ecosystem, even if the effects of our current actions will not build up to a catastrophic deterioration for many years (perhaps centuries) to come.

If we ask what makes our relations with our successors in hundreds of years time so different from our relations with our contemporaries as to challenge the ordinary moral notions that we use in everyday affairs, there are two candidates that come to mind, one concerned with power and one with knowledge. I shall consider these in turn.

A truistic but fundamental difference between our relations with our successors and our relations with our contemporaries, then, is the absolute difference in power. The present inhabitants of Britain may believe that, although they have some discretion in the amount of aid they give to the people of Bangladesh, they have little to hope or fear from the present inhabitants of Bangladesh in return. But they cannot be sure that later geopolitical events may not change this in their own lifetime. We can be quite certain, however, that people alive in several centuries time will not be able to do anything that will make us better off or worse off now, although we can to some degree make them better off or worse off.

Admittedly, our successors have absolute control of something in the future that we may care about now: our reputations. It is up to them to decide what they think of us—or indeed whether they think about us at all. And presumably what, or whether, they think of us is going to be in some way affected by the way that we act towards them. I must confess, however, to doubting that this does much to level up the asymmetry of power between us and our successors, for two reasons. First, although they control a resource which may matter to us, we have no way of negotiating an agreement with them to the effect that they will treat our reputations in a certain way if we behave now in a certain way. We therefore have to guess how they will react to the way we behave, and in the nature of the case such guesses are bound to be inexact. Second, and more important, although individuals are undoubtedly moved by thoughts of posthumous fame for their artistic achievements or political records, it does not seem plausible to suppose that the same motivation would lead a mass electorate to support, say, measures of energy conservation. Altogether, therefore, I do not think that the fact of later generations determining our reputations deserves to be given much weight as an offset to the otherwise completely unilateral power that we have over our successors.

How important is this asymmetry of power between us and our successors—the fact that we can help or hurt them but they can't help or hurt us? It is tempting to say at once that this cannot possibly in itself make any moral difference. Yet it is perhaps surprising to realize that a variety of commonly held views about the basis of morality seem to entail that the absence of reciprocal power relations eliminates the possibility of our having moral obligations (or at any rate obligations of justice) to our successors.

There is a tradition of thought running from Hobbes and Hume to Hart and Warnock according to which the point of morality is that it offers (in Hobbes's terms) 'convenient articles of peace': human beings are sufficiently equal in their capacity to hurt one another, and in their dependence on one another's co-operation to live well, that it is mutually advantageous to all of them to support an institution designed to give people artificial motives for respecting the interests of others.

It seems plain that such a view cannot generate the conclusion that we have moral obligations to those who will not be alive until long after we are dead. Thus, G. J. Warnock, in *The Object of Morality* (Methuen, London, 1967), offers two reasons for saying that moral principles should have universal application rather than being confined to particular groups. 'First, everyone presumably will be a nonmember of some group, and cannot in general have any absolute guarantee that he will encounter no members of groups that are not his own; thus if principles are group-bound, he remains, so to speak, at risk. . . . Second . . . if conduct is to be seen as regulated only *within* groups, we still have the possibility of unrestricted hostility and conflict *between* groups . . .' (p. 150). Obviously, neither of these reasons carries weight in relation to our successors, since we do precisely have an absolute guarantee that we shall never encounter them and cannot conceivably suffer from their hostility to us. It should be added in fairness to Warnock that he himself suggests that morality requires us to take account of the interests of future generations and also of animals. But my point is that I do not see how this squares with his premises.

It is, indeed, possible to get some distance by invoking the fact with which I began this paper, that the notion of 'successive generations' is an artificial one since there is a continuous process of replacement in human populations. Once we have universalized our moral principles to apply to everyone alive now, there are because of this continuity severe practical problems in drawing a neat cut-off point in the future. In the absence of a definite cut-off point, it may seem natural to say that our moral principles hold without temporal limit. But could what is in effect no stronger force than inertia be sufficient to lead us to make big sacrifices for remote generations if these seemed to be called for by atemporal morality? Surely if morality is at basis no more than mutual self-defence, we would (whether or not we made it explicit) agree to ignore the interests of those coming hundreds of years after us.

There is an alternative line of argument about the basis of moral obligations, also involving reciprocity, from which the denial of obligations to future generations follows directly. This view is seldom put forward systematically though it crops up often enough in conversation. This is the idea that by living in a society one gets caught up in a network of interdependencies and from these somehow arise obligations. A recent statement of this view may be found in Burton Zwiebach, *Civility and Disobedience* (Cambridge University Press, London, 1975), who says that 'the basis of our obligation is the common life' (p. 75). The same idea—that obligations to others arise from actual relations with them—underlies Michael Walzer's *Obligations* (Harvard University Press, Cambridge, Mass., 1970). Obviously, this more parochial view, which makes obligations depend on actual rather than potential reciprocal relationships, rules out any obligations to subsequent generations, since there is no reciprocity with them.

As T. D. Weldon recognized when he put forward a similar view in the last chapter of *States and Morals* (John Murray, London, 1946), it is very close to basing obligations on sentiments. This further move is made in one of the very few papers addressed explicitly to the present topic (M. P. Golding, 'Obligations to Future Generations', *Monist* 56 (1972), 85–99) and permits some consideration to be given to future generations—but in a way that I personally find more morally offensive than a blunt disregard of all future interests. According to Golding, obligations rest on a sense of 'moral community'. Whether or not we have any obligations to future generations depends on whether we expect them to live in ways that would lead us to regard them as part of our 'moral community'. If we think they will develop in ways we disapprove of, we have no obligations to them. This view is obviously a diachronic version of the common American view that famine need only be relieved in countries with the right attitude to capitalism.

A third view which appears to leave little room for obligations to future generations is the kind of Lockean philosophy recently revived by Robert Nozick in *Anarchy, State, and Utopia* (Basic Books, New York, 1974). Indeed, it is scarcely accidental that the uniquely short-sighted destruction of trees, animals and soil in the U.S.A. should have been perpetrated by believers in a natural right to property. According to Nozick, any attempt to use the state to redistribute resources among contemporaries in order to bring about some 'end state' is illegitimate, so presumably by the same token any deliberate collective action aimed at distributing resources over time would fall under the same ban. Provided an individual has come by a good justly, he may justly dispose of it any way he likes—by giving it away or bequeathing it, trading it for something else, consuming it, or destroying it. No question of justice arises in all this so long as he does not injure the rights to property and security from physical harm of anyone else. Since we have a right to dispose of our property as we wish, subsequent generations could not charge us with injustice if we were to consume whatever we could in our own lifetimes and direct that what was left should be destroyed at our deaths. (Having one's property destroyed at death has been popular at various times and places and could presumably become so again.) It would clearly be, on Nozick's view, unjust for the survivors to fail to carry out such directions.

Once again, we can see that the problem is the lack of bargaining power in the hands of later generations. Those without bargaining power may appeal to the generous sentiments of others but they cannot make legitimate moral demands, as Nozick's examples of the men on their desert islands vividly illustrates. He asks us to imagine a number of men washed up on desert islands with the possibility of sending goods to each other and transmitting messages by radio transmitter but no means of travelling themselves. Sternly resisting the temptation to comment further on the outlook of a man for whom the paradigm of human relations is a number of adult males on desert islands, let us ask what moral obligations they have to each other. Nozick's answer is simple: none. Even if one has the good fortune to have landed on an island flowing with milk and honey while his neighbour is gradually starving on a barren waste, there is no obligation on one to supply the other's needs. Where could such an obligation possibly come from? To get a parallel with the relations between generations all we have to do is imagine that the islands are situated along the ocean current. Goods can be dispatched in one direction only, down the current. Even if those further down the line could call for help (as later generations in fact cannot) they could make no moral claims on those higher up.

I have so far concentrated on one potentially relevant fact about our relations with our successors: the asymmetry of power. The second one, which is invariably mentioned in this context, is the fact that we have less and less knowledge about the future the more remote the time ahead we are thinking about. Whether or not this is (like the asymmetry of power relations) an absolutely necessary truth derivable from the very concept of the future is a question any attempt to answer which would involve opening the can of worms labelled 'Determinism'. I shall therefore simply accept the basic assertion as true—since it is surely true for us now, anyway—and ask what its implications are.

The answer seems to be fairly clear. As far as I can see, no theory that survives the first consideration and still holds that we have some sort of obligation to take account of the interests of remote future generations would have its conclusions upset by our unavoidable ignorance about the future. Of course, it may be held that we have *no* knowledge of the way in which our present actions will affect the interests of those who come after us in more than *k* years' time—either because we don't know what effects our actions will have on the state of the universe then or because we can have no idea what their interests will be. In that case, it obviously follows that our accepting an obligation to concern ourselves with their interests does not entail our behaving any differently from the way we would behave if we did not accept such an obligation. We can decide what to do without having to bother about any effects it may have beyond *k* years' time. But the obligation still remains latent in the sense that, if at some future date we do come to believe that we have relevant information about the effects of our actions on people living in more than k years' time, we should take account of it in determining our actions. The obligation would have been activated.

Ignorance of the future may be invoked to deny that obligations to remote descendants have any practical implications so that we can ignore them with a good conscience in deciding what to do. Thus John Passmore, in his book on *Man's Responsibility for Nature* (Duckworth, London, 1974), canvasses among other possibilities the rigorous atemporal utilitarianism put forward by Sidgwick, according to which 'the time at which man exists cannot affect the value of his happiness from a universal point of view' (*Methods of Ethics* (Macmillan, London, 1962), p. 414). But he says that, because of the existence of uncertainty, even Sidgwick's approach would lead us to the conclusion that 'our obligations are to *immediate* posterity, we ought to try to improve the world so that we shall be able to hand it over to our immediate successors in a better condition, and that is all' (p. 91, italics in original).

I think this all too convenient conclusion ought to be treated with great mistrust. Of course, we don't know what the precise tastes of our remote descendants will be, but they are unlikely to include a desire for skin cancer, soil erosion, or the inundation of all low-lying areas as a result of the melting of the ice-caps. And, other things being equal, the interests of future generations cannot be harmed by our leaving them more choices rather than fewer.

Even more dubious, it seems to me, is the habit (especially common among economists for some reason) of drawing blank cheques on the future to cover our own deficiencies. The shortages, pollution, over-population, etc., that we leave behind will be no problem for our successors because, it is said, they will invent ways of dealing with them. This Micawberish attitude of expecting something to turn up would be rightly considered imprudent in an individual and I do not see how it is any less so when extended to our successors.

My own view is that, especially in the context of universalistic utilitarianism, the appeal to ignorance normally functions as a smoke-screen, to conceal the fact that we are simply not willing to act in the kind of saintly way that a serious application of the doctrine must entail. Professor Passmore writes (claiming to paraphrase Rawls) that 'the utilitarian principle of impartiality, taken literally, demands too much of us; we cannot reasonably be expected to share our resources with the whole of posterity' (p. 86). He is, I think, more to the point here than when introducing ignorance as a 'fudge factor' to make the answer come out where in any case he feels it should be.

I entirely share the reluctance I have attributed to others to accept the full rigours of universal utilitarianism. Of course, reluctance to accept a theory about our obligations is hardly enough to disqualify it. Presumably the whole idea of talking about obligations is to put to us a motive for doing things that we would (at least sometimes) not be inclined to do otherwise. But the demands of universal utilitarianism—that I should always act in such a way as to maximize the sum of happiness over the future course of human (or maybe sentient) history—are so extreme that I cannot bring myself to believe that there is any such obligation.

At the same time, I find it impossible to believe that it can be right to disregard totally the interests of even remotely future generations, to the extent that we have some idea of the way in which our current actions will affect those interests. If I am correct in saying that it is an implication of the three theories of morality that I briefly considered earlier that there are no obligations to distant future generations, they too have to be rejected.

It may, of course, be argued that good reasons can be given in terms of the interests of actual human beings for not choosing to do something that brings about a substantial risk of ending human life in 500 years' time. The people in the original position would not care to risk the distress at the prospect or the suffering entailed in the process. But human life will presumably come to an end eventually anyway and in a congress at which all potential generations are represented, the risk of being the last generation that actually exists is the same whether that occurs early or late, and the risk of being non-existent (we are saying) is not to count. In any case, I feel fairly sure that my conviction that it would be monstrous to take risks with the existence of future generations in order to secure advantages or avoid hardships for those who will live during the shortened time-span left does not rest on such calculations.

The Hobbesian, Lockean, and Rousseauan theories give only the most tenuous and contingent security to the interests of future generations. It now appears that no theory confining its attention to the states of actual human beings will do. If we say that those who do not get born do not count in the choice of an 'ideal contract', the relatively early end of the human race may be preferred to a longer history at a somewhat lower level. The solution chosen would not be exactly equivalent to average utilitarianism (maximizing the average happiness of those who actually live) if we accept Rawls's arguments that people choosing in the 'original position' would be more concerned to avoid very bad outcomes than to obtain very good ones. But we can certainly say that 'average utilitarianism' where only those who get born count in the denominator runs into the same problem as an 'ideal contract' where only those who get born have a vote. The highest average for those who live may entail not merely a relatively small population at any given time (which seems to me a quite unexceptionable conclusion) but a relatively short time-span for the human race, as those who are alive splurge all the earth's resources with an attitude of 'après nous le deluge'.

The 'total utility' view (that the sum total of happiness should be maximized) in effect enfranchises potential people. (It does not however follow that an 'ideal contract' chosen by all potential people—if we can make sense of that notion—would be for maximizing total happiness. If they were, in Rawlsian fashion, much more concerned to avoid very bad outcomes than to obtain very good ones, it would seem prudent to vote for not bringing the human race into existence. All this would require would be that there should be *some* people of whom Sophocles' 'highest of all is not to be born' would apply.) However, the unpalability of this form of utilitarianism, which I have already remarked upon, seems to me greatly increased when we realize that it would call upon us to make sacrifices merely so that there could be more people, so long as each extra person adds any positive amount to the notional sum total of happiness. It may also be noted that, although the total utility doctrine is biased towards actualizing a lot of potential people, it is not biased towards spreading them over a long time-span. It is consistent with total utilitarianism that we should have a massive population for another two centuries and then nothing. Perhaps it is unlikely that this is the way to maximize total happiness, but the point is that at least as far as I am concerned the continuation of human life into the future is something to be sought (or at least not sabotaged) even if it does not make for the maximum total happiness.

Certainly, if I try to analyse the source of my own strong conviction that we should be wrong to take risks with the continuation of human life, I find that it does not lie in any sense of injury to the interests of people who will not get born but rather in a sense of its cosmic impertinence—that we should be grossly abusing our position by taking it upon ourselves to put a term on human life and its possibilities. I must confess to feeling great intellectual discomfort in moving outside a framework in which ethical principles are related to human interests, but if I am right then these are the terms in which we have to start thinking. In contrast to Passmore, I conclude that those who say we need a 'new ethic' are in fact right. It need not entail the kind of half-baked ideas that Passmore criticizes, but should surely as a minimum include the notion that those alive at any time are custodians rather than owners of the planet, and ought to pass it on in at least no worse shape than they found it in.

[From 'Justice between Generations', in *Law, Society, and Morality: Essays in Honour of H. L. A. Hart* ed. P. M. S. Hacker and J. Raz (Clarendon Press, Oxford, 1977), 268–84.]

PETER SINGER

107 **Famine, Affluence and Morality**

As I write this, in November 1971, people are dying in East Bengal from lack of food, shelter, and medical care. The suffering and death that are occurring there now are not inevitable, not unavoidable in any fatalistic sense of the term. Constant poverty, a cyclone, and a civil war have turned at least nine million people into destitute refugees; nevertheless, it is not beyond the capacity of the richer nations to give enough assistance to reduce any further suffering to very small proportions. The decisions and actions of human beings can prevent this kind of suffering. Unfortunately, human beings have not made the necessary decisions. At the individual level, people have, with very few exceptions, not responded to the situation in any significant way. Generally speaking, people have not given large sums to relief funds; they have not written to their parliamentary representatives demanding increased government assistance; they have not demonstrated in the streets, held symbolic fasts, or done anything else directed toward providing the refugees with the means to satisfy their essential needs. At the government level, no government has given the sort of massive aid that would enable the refugees to survive for more than a few days. Britain, for instance, has given rather more than most countries. It has, to date, given £14,750,000. For comparative purposes, Britain's share of the nonrecoverable development costs of the Anglo-French Concorde project is already in excess of £275,000,000, and on present estimates will reach £440,000,000. The implication is that the British government values a supersonic transport more than thirty times as highly as it values the lives of the nine million refugees. Australia is another country which, on per capita basis, is well up in the 'aid to Bengal' table. Australia's aid, however, amounts to less than one-twelfth of the cost of Sydney's new opera house. The total amount given, from all sources, now stands at about £65,000,000. The estimated cost of keeping the refugees alive for one year is £464,000,000. Most of the refugees have now been in the camps for more than six months. The World Bank has said that India needs a minimum of £300,000,000 in assistance from other countries before the end of the year. It seems obvious that assistance on this scale will not be forthcoming. India will be forced to choose between letting the refugees starve or diverting funds from her own development program, which will mean that more of her own people will starve in the future.[1]

These are the essential facts about the present situation in Bengal. So far as it concerns us here, there is nothing unique about this situation except its magnitude. The Bengal emergency is just the latest and most acute of a series of major emergencies in various parts of the world, arising both from natural and from man-made causes. There are also many parts of the world in which people die from malnutrition and lack of food independent of any special emergency. I take Bengal as my example only because it is the present concern, and because the size of the problem has ensured that it has been given adequate publicity. Neither individuals nor governments can claim to be unaware of what is happening there.

What are the moral implications of a situation like this? In what follows, I shall argue that the way people in relatively affluent countries react to a situation like that in Bengal cannot be justified; indeed, the whole way we look at moral issues—our moral conceptual scheme—needs to be altered, and with it, the way of life that has come to be taken for granted in our society.

In arguing for this conclusion I will not, of course, claim to be morally neutral. I shall, however, try to argue for the moral position that I take, so that anyone who accepts certain assumptions, to be made explicit, will, I hope, accept my conclusion.

I begin with the assumption that suffering and death from lack of food, shelter, and medical care are bad. I think most people will agree about this, although one may reach the same view by different routes. I shall not argue for this view. People can hold all sorts of eccentric positions, and perhaps from some of them it would not follow that death by starvation is in itself bad. It is difficult, perhaps impossible, to refute such positions, and so for brevity I will henceforth take this assumption as accepted. Those who disagree need read no further.

My next point is this: if it is in our power to prevent something bad from happening, without thereby sacrificing anything of comparable moral importance, we ought, morally, to do it. By 'without sacrificing anything of comparable moral importance' I mean without causing anything else comparably bad to happen, or doing something that is wrong in itself, or failing to promote some moral good, comparable in significance to the bad thing that we can prevent. This principle seems almost as uncontroversial as the last one. It requires us only to prevent what is bad, and not to promote what is good, and it requires this of us only when we can do it without sacrificing anything that is, from the moral point of view, comparably important. I could even, so far as the application of my argument to the Bengal emergency is concerned, qualify the point so as to make it: if it is in our power to prevent something very bad from happening, without thereby sacrificing anything morally significant, we ought, morally, to do it. An application of this principle would be as follows: if I am walking past a shallow pond and see a child drowning in it, I ought to wade in and pull the child out. This will mean getting my clothes muddy, but this is insignificant, while the death of the child would presumably be a very bad thing.

The uncontroversial appearance of the principle just stated is deceptive. If it were acted upon, even in its qualified form, our lives, our society, and our world would be fundamentally changed. For the principle takes, firstly, no account of proximity or distance. It makes no moral difference whether the person I can help is a neighbor's child ten yards from me or a Bengali whose name I shall never know, ten thousand miles away. Secondly, the principle makes no distinction between cases in which I am the only person who could possibly do anything and cases in which I am just one among millions in the same position.

I do not think I need to say much in defense of the refusal to take proximity and distance into account. The fact that a person is physically near to us, so that we have personal contract with him, may make it more likely that we *shall* assist him, but this does not show that we *ought* to help him rather than another who happens to be further away. If we accept any principle of impartiality, universalizability, equality, or whatever, we cannot discriminate against someone merely because he is far away from us (or we are far away from him). Admittedly, it is possible that we are in a better position to judge what needs to be done to help a person near to us than one far away, and perhaps also to provide the assistance we judge to be necessary. If this were the case, it would be a reason for helping those near to us first. This may once have been a justification for being more concerned with the poor in one's own town than with famine victims in India. Unfortunately for those who like to keep their moral responsibilities limited, instant communication and swift transportation have changed the situation. From the moral point of view, the development of the world into a 'global village' has made an important, though still unrecognized, difference to our moral situation. Expert observers and supervisors, sent out by famine relief organizations or permanently stationed in famine-prone areas, can direct our aid to a refugee in Bengal almost as effectively as we could get it to someone in our own block. There would seem, therefore, to be no possible justification for discriminating on geographical grounds.

There may be a greater need to defend the second implication of my principle—that the fact that there are millions of other people in the same position, in respect to the Bengali refugees, as I am, does not make the situation significantly different from a situation in which I am the only person who can prevent something very bad from occurring. Again, of course, I admit that there is a psychological difference between the cases; one feels less guilty about doing nothing if one can point to others, similarly placed, who have also done nothing. Yet this can make no real difference to our moral obligations.[2] Should I consider that I am less obliged to pull the drowning child out of the pond if on looking around I see other people, no further away than I am, who have also noticed the child but are doing nothing? One has only to ask this question to see the absurdity of the view that numbers lessen obligation. It is a view that is an ideal excuse for inactivity; unfortunately most of the major evils—poverty, overpopulation, pollution—are problems in which everyone is almost equally involved.

The view that numbers do make a difference can be made plausible if stated in this way: if everyone in circumstances like mine gave £5 to the Bengal Relief Fund, there would be enough to provide food, shelter, and medical care for the refugees; there is no reason why I should give more than anyone else in the same circumstances as I am; therefore I have no obligation to give more than £5. Each premise in this argument is true, and the argument looks sound. It may convince us, unless we notice that it is based on a hypothetical premise, although the conclusion is not stated hypothetically. The argument would be sound if the conclusion were: if everyone in circumstances like mine were to give £5, I would have no obligation to give more than £5. If the conclusion were so stated, however, it would be obvious that the argument has no bearing on a situation in which it is not the case that everyone else gives £5. This, of course, is the actual situation. It is more or less certain that not everyone in circumstances like mine will give £5. So there will not be enough to provide the needed food, shelter, and medical care. Therefore by giving more than £5 I will prevent more suffering that I would if I gave just £5.

It might be thought that this argument has an absurd consequence. Since the situation appears to be that very few people are likely to give substantial amounts, it follows that I and everyone else in similar circumstances ought to give as much as possible, that is, at least up to the point at which by giving more one would begin to cause serious suffering for oneself and one's dependents—perhaps even beyond this point to the point of marginal utility, at which by giving more one would cause oneself and one's dependents as much suffering as one would prevent in Bengal. If everyone does this, however, there will be more than can be used for the benefit of the refugees, and some of the sacrifice will have been unnecessary. Thus, if everyone does what he ought to do, the result will not be as good as it would be if everyone did a little less than he ought to do, or if only some do all that they ought to do.

The paradox here arises only if we assume that the actions in question—sending money to the relief funds—are performed more or less simultaneously, and are also unexpected. For if it is to be expected that everyone is going to contribute something, then clearly each is not obliged to give as much as he would have been obliged to had others not been giving too. And if everyone is not acting more or less simultaneously, then those giving later will know how much more is needed, and will have no obligation to give more than is necessary to reach this amount. To say this is not to deny the principle that people in the same circumstances have the same obligations, but to point out that the fact that others have given, or may be expected to give, is a relevant circumstance: those giving after it has become known that many others are giving and those giving before are not in the same circumstances. So the seemingly absurd consequence of the principle I have put forward can occur only if people are in error about the actual circumstances—that is, if they think they are giving when others are not, but in fact they are giving when others are. The result of everyone doing what he really ought to do cannot be worse than the result of everyone doing less than he ought to do, although the result of everyone doing what he reasonably believes he ought to do could be.

If my argument so far has been sound, neither our distance from a preventable evil nor the number of other people who, in respect to that evil, are in the same situation as we are, lessens our obligation to mitigate or prevent that evil. I shall therefore take as established the principle I asserted earlier. As I have already said, I need to assert it only in its qualified form: if it is in our power to prevent something very bad from happening, without thereby sacrificing anything else morally significant, we ought, morally to do it.

The outcome of this argument is that our traditional moral categories are upset. The traditional distinction between duty and charity cannot be drawn, or at least, not in the place we normally draw it. Giving money to the Bengal Relief Fund is regarded as an act of charity in our society. The bodies which collect money are known as 'charities.' These organisations see themselves in this way—if you send them a check, you will be thanked for your 'generosity.' Because giving money is regarded as an act of charity, it is not thought that there is anything wrong with not giving. The charitable man may be praised, but the man who is not charitable is not condemned. People do not feel in any way ashamed or guilty about spending money on new clothes or a new car instead of giving it to famine relief. (Indeed, the alternative does not occur to them.) This way of looking at the matter cannot be justified. When we buy new clothes not to keep ourselves warm but to look 'well-dressed' we are not providing for any important need. We would not be sacrificing anything significant if we were to continue to wear our old clothes, and give the money to famine relief. By doing so, we would be preventing another person from starving. It follows from what I have said earlier that we ought to give money away, rather than spend it on clothes which we do not need to keep us warm. To do so is not charitable, or generous. Nor is it the kind of act which philosophers and theologians have called 'supererogatory'—an act which it would be good to do, but not wrong not to do. On the contrary, we ought to give the money away, and it is wrong not to do so.

[From 'Famine, Affluence and Morality', in *Philosophy and Public Affairs*, (1) (1972), 229–35.]

ONORA O'NEILL

108 Lifeboat Earth

If in the fairly near future millions of people die of starvation, will those who survive be in any way to blame for those deaths? Is there anything which people ought to do now, and from now on, if they are to be able to avoid responsibility for unjustifiable deaths in famine years? I shall argue from the assumption that persons have a right not to be killed unjustifiably to the claim that we have a duty to try to prevent and postpone famine deaths. A corollary of this claim is that if we do nothing we shall bear some blame for some deaths.

Justifiable Killing

I shall assume that persons have a right not to be killed and a corresponding duty not to kill. I shall make no assumptions about the other rights persons may have. In particular, I shall not assume that persons have a right not to be allowed to die by those who could prevent it or a duty to prevent others' deaths whenever they could do so. Nor will I assume that persons lack this right.

Even if persons have no rights other than a right not to be killed, this right can justifiably be overridden in certain circumstances. Not all killings are unjustifiable. I shall be particularly concerned with two sorts of circumstances in which the right not to be killed is justifiably overridden. The first of these is the case of unavoidable killings; the second is the case of self-defense.

Unavoidable killings occur in situations where a person doing some act causes some death or deaths which he could not avoid. Often such deaths will be unavoidable because of the killer's ignorance of some relevant circumstance at the time of this decision to act. If B is driving a train, and A blunders onto the track and is either unnoticed by B or noticed too late for B to stop the train, and B kills A, then B could not have avoided killing A, given his decision to drive the train. Another sort of case of unavoidable killing occurs when B could avoid killing A or could avoid killing C, but cannot avoid killing one of the two. For example, if B is the carrier of a highly contagious and invariably fatal illness, he might find himself so placed that he cannot avoid meeting and so killing either A or C, though he can choose which of them to meet. In this case the unavoidability of B's killing someone is not relative to some prior decision B made. The cases of unavoidable killings with which I want to deal here are of the latter sort, and I shall argue that in such cases B kills justifiably if certain further conditions are met.

A killing may also be justifiable if it is undertaken in self-defense. I shall not argue here that persons have a right of self-defense which is independent of their right not to be killed, but rather that a minimal right of self-defense is a corollary of a right not to be killed. Hence the notion of self-defense on which I shall rely is in some ways different from, and narrower than, other interpretations of the right of self-defense. I shall also assume that if A has a right to defend himself against B, then third parties ought to defend A's right. If we take seriously the right not to be killed and its corollaries, then we ought to enforce others' rights not to be killed.

The right of self-defense which is a corollary of the right not to be killed is a right to take action to prevent killings. If I have a right not to be killed then I have a right to prevent others from endangering my life, though I may endanger their lives in so doing only if that is the only available way to prevent the danger to my own life. Similarly if another has the right not to be killed then I should, if possible, do something to prevent others from endangering his life, but I may endanger their lives in so doing only if that is the only available way to prevent the danger to his life. This duty to defend others is *not* a general duty of beneficence but a very restricted duty to enforce others' rights not to be killed.

The right to self-defense so construed is quite narrow. It includes no right of action against those who, though they cause or are likely to cause us harm, clearly do not endanger our lives. (However, specific cases are often unclear. The shopkeeper who shoots a person who holds him up with a toy gun was not endangered, but it may have been very reasonable of him to suppose that he was endangered.) And it includes no right to greater than minimal preventive action against a person who endangers one's life. If *B* is chasing *A* with a gun, and *A* could save his life either by closing a bullet-proof door or by shooting *B*, then if people have only a right not to be killed and a minimal corollary right of self-defense, *A* would have no right to shoot *B*. (Again, such cases are often unclear—*A* may not know that the door is bullet-proof or not think of it or may simply reason that shooting *B* is a better guarantee of prevention.) A right of proportionate self-defense which might justify *A* in shooting *B*, even were it clear that closing the door would have been enough to prevent *B*, is not a corollary of the right not to be killed. Perhaps a right of proportionate retaliation might be justified by some claim such as that aggressors lose certain rights, but I shall take no position on this issue.

In one respect the narrow right of self-defense, which is the corollary of a right not to be killed, is more extensive than some other interpretations of the right of self-defense. For it is a right to take action against others who endanger our lives whether or not they do so intentionally. *A*'s right not to be killed entitles him to take action not only against aggressors but also against those 'innocent threats'[1] who endanger lives without being aggressors. If *B* is likely to cause *A*'s death inadvertently or involuntarily, then *A* has, if he has a right not to be killed, a right to take whatever steps are necessary to prevent *B* from doing so, provided that these do not infringe *B*'s right not to be killed unnecessarily. If *B* approaches *A* with a highly contagious and invariably lethal illness, then *A* may try to prevent *B* from getting near him even if *B* knows nothing about the danger he brings. If other means fail, *A* may kill *B* in self-defense, even though *B* was no aggressor.

This construal of the right of self-defense severs the link between aggression and self-defense. When we defend ourselves against innocent threats there is no aggressor, only somebody who endangers life. But it would be misleading to call this right a right of self-preservation. For self-preservation is commonly construed (as by Locke) as including a right to subsistence, and so a right to engage in a large variety of activities whether or not anybody endangers us. But the right which is the corollary of the right not to be killed is a right only to prevent others from endangering our lives, whether or not they intend to do so, and to do so with minimal danger to their lives. Only if one takes a Hobbesian view of human nature and sees others' acts as always completely threatening will the rights of self-defense and self-preservation tend to merge and everything done to maintain life be done to prevent its destruction. Without Hobbesian assumptions the contexts where the minimal right of self-defense can be invoked are fairly special, yet not, I shall argue, rare.

There may be various other circumstances in which persons' rights not to be killed may be overridden. Perhaps, for example, we may justifiably kill those who consent to us doing so. I shall take no position on whether persons can waive their rights not to be killed or on any further situations in which killings might be justifiable.

Justifiable Killings on Lifeboats

The time has come to start imagining lurid situations, which is the standard operating procedure for this type of discussion. I shall begin by looking at some sorts of killings which might occur on a lifeboat and shall consider the sorts of justifications which they might be given.

Let us imagine six survivors on a lifeboat. There are two possible levels of provisions:

(1) Provisions are on all reasonable calculations sufficient to last until rescue. Either the boat is near land, or it is amply provisioned or it has gear for distilling water, catching fish, etc.

(2) Provisions are on all reasonable calculations unlikely to be sufficient for all six to survive until rescue.

We can call situation (1) *the well-equipped lifeboat situation*; situation (2) *the under-equipped lifeboat situation*. There may, of course, be cases where the six survivors are unsure which situation they are in, but for simplicity I shall disregard those here.

On a well-equipped lifeboat it is possible for all to survive until rescue. No killing could be justified as unavoidable, and if someone is killed, then the justification could only be self-defense in special situations. Consider the following examples:

(1A) On a well-equipped lifeboat with six persons, A threatens to jettison the fresh water, without which some or all would not survive till rescue. A may be either hostile or deranged. B reasons with A, but when this fails, shoots him. B can appeal to his own and the others' right of self-defense to justify the killing. 'It was him or us,' he may reasonably say, 'for he would have placed us in an under-equipped lifeboat situation.' He may say this both when A acts to harm the others and when A acts as an innocent threat.

(1B)   On a well-equipped lifeboat with six persons, B, C, D, E, and F decide to withhold food from A, who consequently dies. In this case they cannot appeal to self-defense—for all could have survived. Nor can they claim that they merely let A die—'We didn't *do* anything'—for A would not otherwise have died. This was not a case of violating the problematic right not to be allowed to die but of violating the right not to be killed, and the violation is without justification of self-defense or of unavoidability.

On an under-equipped lifeboat it is not possible for all to survive until rescue. Some deaths are unavoidable, but sometimes there is no particular person whose death is unavoidable. Consider the following examples:

(2A)   On an under-equipped lifeboat with six persons, A is very ill and needs extra water, which is already scarce. The others decide not to let him have any water, and A dies of thirst. If A drinks, then not all will survive. On the other hand it is clear that A was killed rather than allowed to die. If he had received water he might have survived. Though some death was unavoidable, A's was not and selecting him as the victim requires justification.

(2B)   On an under-equipped lifeboat with six persons, water is so scarce that only four can survive (perhaps the distillation unit is designed for supplying four people). But who should go without? Suppose two are chosen to go without, either by lot or by some other method, and consequently die. The others cannot claim that all they did was to allow the two who were deprived of water to die—for these two might otherwise have been among the survivors. Nobody had a greater right to be a survivor, but given that not all could survive, those who did not survive were killed justifiably if the method by which they were chosen was fair. (Of course, a lot needs to be said about what would make a selection procedure fair.)

(2C)   The same situation as in (2B) holds, but the two who are not to drink ask to be shot to ease their deaths. Again the survivors cannot claim that they did not kill but at most that they killed justifiably. Whether they did so is not affected by their shooting rather than dehydrating the victims, but only by the unavoidability of some deaths and the fairness of procedures for selecting victims.

(2D)   Again the basic situation is as in (2B). But the two who are not to drink rebel. The others shoot them and so keep control of the water. Here it is all too clear that those who died were killed, but they too may have been justifiably killed. Whether the survivors kill justifiably depends neither on the method of killing nor on the victims' cooperation, except insofar as cooperation is relevant to the fairness of selection procedures.

Lifeboat situations do not occur very frequently. We are not often confronted starkly with the choice between killing or being killed by the application of a decision to distribute scarce rations in a certain way. Yet this is becoming the situation of the human species on this globe. The current metaphor 'spaceship Earth' suggests more drama and less danger; if we are feeling sober about the situation, 'lifeboat Earth' may be more suggestive.

Some may object to the metaphor 'lifeboat Earth.' A lifeboat is small; all aboard have equal claims to be there and to share equally in the provisions. Whereas the earth is vast and while all may have equal rights to be there, some also have property rights which give them special rights to consume, while others do not. The starving millions are far away and have no right to what is owned by affluent individuals or nations, even if it could prevent their deaths. If they die, it will be said, this is a violation at most of their right not to be allowed to die. And this I have not established or assumed.

I think that this could reasonably have been said in times past. The poverty and consequent deaths of far-off persons was something which the affluent might perhaps have done something to prevent, but which they had (often) done nothing to bring about. Hence they had not violated the right not to be killed of those living far off. But the economic and technological interdependence of today alters this situation.[2] Sometimes deaths are produced by some persons or groups of persons in distant, usually affluent, nations. Sometimes such persons and groups of persons violate not only some persons' alleged right not to be allowed to die but also their more fundamental right not to be killed.

We tend to imagine violations of the right not to be killed in terms of the killings so frequently discussed in the United States today: confrontations between individuals where one directly, violently, and intentionally brings about the other's death. As the lifeboat situations have shown, there are other ways in which we can kill one another. In any case, we do not restrict our vision to the typical mugger or murderer context. B may violate A's right not to be killed even when

(a) B does not act alone.
(b) A's death is not immediate.
(c) It is not certain whether A or another will die in consequence of B's action.
(d) B does not intend A's death.

The following set of examples illustrates these points about killings:

(aa) A is beaten by a gang consisting of B, C, D, etc. No one assailant single-handedly killed him, yet his right not to be killed was violated by all who took part.
(bb) A is poisoned slowly by daily doses. The final dose, like earlier ones, was not, by itself, lethal. But the poisoner still violated A's right not to be killed.

(cc) *B* plays Russian roulette with *A*, *C*, *D*, *E*, *F*, and *G*, firing a revolver at each once, when he knows that one firing in six will be lethal. If *A* is shot and dies, then *B* has violated his right not to be killed.

(dd) Henry II asks who will rid him of the turbulent priest, and his supporters kill Becket. It is reasonably clear that Henry did not intend Becket's death, even though he in part brought it about, as he later admitted.

These explications of the right not to be killed are not too controversial taken individually, and I would suggest that their conjunction is also uncontroversial. Even when *A*'s death is the result of the acts of many persons and is not an immediate consequence of their deeds, nor even a certain consequence, and is not intended by them, *A*'s right not to be killed may be violated.

First Class Versus Steerage on Lifeboat Earth

If we imagine a lifeboat in which special quarters are provided for the (recently) first-class passengers, and on which the food and water for all passengers are stowed in those quarters, then we have a fair, if crude, model of the present human situation on lifeboat Earth. For even on the assumption that there is at present sufficient for all to survive, some have control over the means of survival and so, indirectly, over others' survival. Sometimes the exercise of control can lead, even on a well-equipped lifeboat, to the starvation and death of some of those who lack control. On an ill-equipped lifeboat some must die in any case and, as we have already seen, though some of these deaths may be killings, some of them may be justifiable killings. Corresponding situations can, do, and will arise on lifeboat Earth, and it is to these that we should turn our attention, covering both the presumed present situation of global sufficiency of the means of survival and the expected future situation of global insufficiency.

Sufficiency Situations

Aboard a well-equipped lifeboat any distribution of food and water which leads to a death is a killing and not just a case of permitting a death. For the acts of those who distribute the food and water are the causes of a death which would not have occurred had those agents either had no causal influence or done other acts. By contrast, a person whom they leave in the water to drown is merely allowed to die, for his death would have taken place (other things being equal) had those agents had no causal influence, though it could have been prevented had they rescued him.[3] The distinction between killing and allowing to die, as here construed, does not depend on any claims about the other rights of persons who are killed. The death of the shortchanged passenger of example (1B) violated his property rights as well as his right not to be killed, but the reason the death was classifiable as a killing depended on the part which the acts of the other passengers had in causing it. If we suppose that a stowaway on a lifeboat has no right to food and water and is denied them, then clearly his property rights have not been violated. Even so, by the above definitions he is killed rather than allowed to die. For if the other passengers had either had no causal influence or done otherwise, his death would not have occurred. Their actions—in this case distributing food only to those entitled to it—caused the stowaway's death. Their acts would be justifiable only if property rights can sometimes override the right not to be killed.

Many would claim that the situation on lifeboat Earth is not analogous to that on ordinary lifeboats, since it is not evident that we all have a claim, let alone an equal claim, on the earth's resources. Perhaps some of us are stowaways. I shall not here assume that we do all have some claim on the earth's resources, even though I think it plausible to suppose that we do. I shall assume that even if persons have unequal property rights and some people own nothing, it does not follow that B's exercise of his property rights can override A's right not to be killed.[4] Where our activities lead to others' deaths which would not have occurred had we either done something else or had no causal influence, no claim that the activities were within our economic rights would suffice to show that we did not kill.

It is not far-fetched to think that at present the economic activity of some groups of persons leads to others' deaths. I shall choose a couple of examples of the sort of activity which can do so, but I do not think that these examples do more than begin a list of cases of killing by economic activities. Neither of these examples depends on questioning the existence of unequal property rights; they assume only that such rights do not override a right not to be killed. Neither example is one for which it is plausible to think that the killing could be justified as undertaken in self-defense.

Case one might be called the *foreign investment* situation. A group of investors may form a company which invests abroad—perhaps in a plantation or in a mine—and so manage their affairs that a high level of profits is repatriated, while the wages for the laborers are so minimal that their survival rate is lowered, that is, their expectation of life is lower than it might have been had the company not invested there. In such a case the investors and company management do not act alone, do not cause immediate deaths, and do not know in advance who will die; it is also likely that they intend no deaths. But by their involvement in the economy of an underdeveloped area they cannot claim, as can another company which has no investments there, that they are 'doing nothing.' On the contrary, they are setting the policies which determine the living standards which determine the survival rate. When persons die because of the lowered standard of living established by a firm or a number of firms which dominate a local economy and either limit persons to employment on their terms or lower the other prospects for employment by damaging traditional economic structures, and these firms could either pay higher wages or stay out of the area altogether, then those who establish these policies are violating some persons' rights not to be killed. Foreign investment which *raises* living standards, even to a still abysmal level, could not be held to kill, for it causes no additional deaths, unless there are special circumstances, as in the following example.

Even when a company investing in an underdeveloped country establishes high wages and benefits and raises the expectation of life for its workers, it often manages to combine these payments with high profitability only by having achieved a tax-exempt status. In such cases the company is being subsidized by the general tax revenue of the underdeveloped economy. It makes no contribution to the infrastructure—e.g. roads and harbors and airports—from which it benefits. In this way many underdeveloped economies have come to include developed enclaves whose development is achieved in part at the expense of the poorer majority.[5] In such cases, government and company policy combine to produce a high wage sector at the expense of a low wage sector; in consequence, some of the persons in the low wage sector, who would not otherwise have died, may die; these persons, whoever they may be, are killed and not merely allowed to die. Such killings may sometimes be justifiable—perhaps, if they are outnumbered by lives saved through having a developed sector—but they are killings nonetheless, since the victims might have survived if not burdened by transfer payments to the developed sector.

But, one may say, the management of such a corporation and its investors should be distinguished more sharply. Even if the management may choose a level of wages, and consequently of survival, the investors usually know nothing of this. But the investors, even if ignorant, are responsible for company policy. They may often fail to exercise control, but by law they have control. They choose to invest in a company with certain foreign investments; they profit from it; they can, and others cannot, affect company policy in fundamental ways. To be sure the investors are not murderers—they do not intend to bring about the deaths of any persons; nor do the company managers usually intend any of the deaths company policies cause. Even so, investors and management acting together with the sorts of results just described do violate some persons' rights not to be killed and usually cannot justify such killings either as required for self-defense or as unavoidable.

Case two, where even under sufficiency conditions some persons' economic activities result in the deaths of other persons, might be called the *commodity pricing* case. Underdeveloped countries often depend heavily on the price level of a few commodities. So a sharp drop in the world price of coffee or sugar or cocoa may spell ruin and lowered survival rates for whole regions. Yet such drops in price levels are not in all cases due to factors beyond human control. Where they are the result of action by investors, brokers, or government agencies, these persons and bodies are choosing policies which will kill some people. Once again, to be sure, the killing is not single-handed, it is not instantaneous, the killers cannot foresee exactly who will die, and they may not intend anybody to die.

Because of the economic interdependence of different countries, deaths can also be caused by rises in the prices of various commodities. For example, the present near-famine in the Sahelian region of Africa and in the Indian subcontinent is attributed by agronomists partly to climatic shifts and partly to the increased prices of oil and hence of fertilizer, wheat, and other grains.

The recent doubling in international prices of essential foodstuffs will, of necessity, be reflected in higher death rates among the world's lowest income groups, who lack the income to increase their food expenditures proportionately, but live on diets near the subsistence level to begin with.[6]

Of course, not all of those who die will be killed. Those who die of drought will merely be allowed to die, and some of these who die because less has been grown with less fertilizer will also die because of forces beyond the control of any human agency. But to the extent that the raising of oil prices is an achievement of Arab diplomacy and oil company management rather than a windfall, the consequent deaths are killings. Some of them may perhaps be justifiable killings (perhaps if outnumbered by lives saved within the Arab world by industrialization), but killings nonetheless.

Even on a sufficiently equipped earth some persons are killed by others' distribution decisions. The causal chains leading to death-producing distributions are often extremely complex. Where they can be perceived with reasonable clarity we ought, if we take seriously the right not to be killed and seek not merely to avoid killing others but to prevent third parties from doing so, to support policies which reduce deaths. For example—and these are only examples—we should support certain sorts of aid policies rather than others; we should oppose certain sorts of foreign investment; we should oppose certain sorts of commodity speculation, and perhaps support certain sorts of price support agreements for some commodities (e.g. those which try to maintain high prices for products on whose sale poverty stricken economies depend).

If we take the view that we have no duty to enforce the rights of others, then we cannot draw so general a conclusion about our duty to support various economic policies which might avoid some unjustifiable killings. But we might still find that we should take action of certain sorts either because our own lives are threatened by certain economic activities of others or because our own economic activities threaten others' lives. Only if we knew that we were not part of any system of activities causing unjustifiable deaths could we have no duties to support policies which seek to avoid such deaths. Modern economic causal chains are so complex that it is likely that only those who are economically isolated and self-sufficient could know that they are part of no such systems of activities. Persons who believe that they are involved in some death-producing activities will have some of the same duties as those who think they have a duty to enforce others' rights not to be killed.

Scarcity Situations

The last section showed that sometimes, even in sufficiency situations, some might be killed by the way in which others arranged the distribution of the means of subsistence. Of far more importance in the long run is the true lifeboat situation—the situation of scarcity. We face a situation in which not everyone who is born can live out the normal span of human life and, further, in which we must expect today's normal life-span to be shortened. The date at which serious scarcity will begin is not generally agreed upon, but even the more optimistic prophets place it no more than decades away.[7] Its arrival will depend on factors such as the rate of technological invention and innovation, especially in agriculture and pollution control, and the success of programs to limit human fertility.

Such predictions may be viewed as exonerating us from complicity in famine deaths. If famine is inevitable, then—while we may have to choose whom to save—the deaths of those whom we do not or cannot save cannot be seen as killings for which we bear any responsibility. For these deaths would have occurred even if we had no causal influence. The decisions to be made may be excruciatingly difficult, but at least we can comfort ourselves that we did not produce or contribute to the famine.

However, this comforting view of famine predictions neglects the fact that these predictions are contingent upon certain assumptions about what people will do in the prefamine period. Famine is said to be inevitable *if* people do not curb their fertility, alter their consumption patterns, and avoid pollution and consequent ecological catastrophes. It is the policies of the present which will produce, defer, or avoid famine. Hence if famine comes, the deaths that occur will be results of decisions made earlier. Only if we take no part in systems of activities which lead to famine situations can we view ourselves as choosing whom to save rather than whom to kill when famine comes. In an economically interdependent world there are few people who can look on the approach of famine as a natural disaster from which they may kindly rescue some, but for whose arrival they bear no responsibility. We cannot stoically regard particular famine deaths as unavoidable if we have contributed to the emergence and extent of famine.

If we bear some responsibility for the advent of famine, then any decision on distributing the risk of famine is a decision whom to kill. Even a decision to rely on natural selection as a famine policy is choosing a policy for killing—for under a different famine policy different persons might have survived, and under different prefamine policies there might have been no famine or a less severe famine. The choice of a particular famine policy may be justifiable on the grounds that once we have let it get to that point there is not enough to go around, and somebody must go, as on an ill-equipped lifeboat. Even so, the famine policy chosen will not be a policy of saving some but not all persons from an unavoidable predicament.

Persons cannot, of course, make famine policies individually. Famine and prefamine policies are and will be made by governments individually and collectively and perhaps also by some voluntary organizations. It may even prove politically impossible to have a coherent famine or prefamine policy for the whole world; if so, we shall have to settle for partial and piecemeal policies. But each person who is in a position to support or oppose such policies, whether global or local, has to decide which to support and which to oppose. Even for individual persons, inaction and inattention are often a decision—to support the famine and prefamine policies, which are the status quo whether or not they are 'hands off' policies. There are large numbers of ways in which private citizens may affect such policies. They do so in supporting or opposing legislation affecting aid and foreign investment, in supporting or opposing certain sorts of charities or groups such as Zero Population Growth, in promoting or opposing ecologically conservative technology and lifestyles. Hence we have individually the onus of avoiding killing. For even though we

(a) do not kill single-handedly those who die of famine
(b) do not kill instantaneously those who die of famine
(c) do not know which individuals will die as the result of the prefamine and famine policies we support (unless we support something like a genocidal famine policy)
(d) do not intend any famine deaths

we nonetheless kill and do not merely allow to die. For as the result of our actions in concert with others, some will die who might have survived had we either acted otherwise or had no causal influence.

Famine Policies and Prefamine Policies

Various principles can be suggested on which famine and prefamine policies might reasonably be based. I shall list some of these, more with the aim of setting out the range of possible decisions than with the aim of stating a justification for selecting some people for survival. One very general policy might be that of adopting whichever more specific policies will lead to the fewest deaths. An example would be going along with the consequences of natural selection in the way in which the allocation of medical care in situations of great shortage does, that is, the criteria for relief would be a high chance of survival if relief is given and a low chance otherwise—the worst risks would be abandoned. (This decision is analogous to picking the ill man as the victim on the lifeboat in 2A.) However, the policy of minimizing deaths is indeterminate, unless a certain time horizon is specified. For the policies which maximize survival in the short run—e.g. preventive medicine and minimal living standards—may also maximize population increase and lead to greater ultimate catastrophe.[8]

Another general policy would be to try to find further grounds which can justify overriding a person's right not to be killed. Famine policies adopted on these grounds might permit others to kill those who will forgo their right not to be killed (voluntary euthanasia, including healthy would-be suicides) or to kill those whom others find dependent and exceptionally burdensome, e.g. the unwanted sick or aged or unborn or newborn (involuntary euthanasia, abortion, and infanticide). Such policies might be justified by claims that the right not to be killed may be overridden in famine situations if the owner of the right consents or if securing the right is exceptionally burdensome.

Any combination of such policies is a policy of killing some and protecting others. Those who are killed may not have their right not to be killed violated without reason; those who set and support famine policies and prefamine policies will not be able to claim that they do not kill, but if they reason carefully they may be able to claim that they do not do so without justification.

From this vantage point it can be seen why it is not relevant to restrict the right of self-defense to a right to defend oneself against those who threaten one's life but do not do so innocently. Such a restriction may make a great difference to one's view of abortion in cases where the mother's life is threatened, but it does not make much difference when famine is the issue. Those who might be chosen as likely victims of any famine policy will probably be innocent of contributing to the famine, or at least no more guilty than others; hence the innocence of the victims is an insufficient ground for rejecting a policy. Indeed it is hard to point a finger at the guilty in famine situations. Are they the hoarders of grain? The parents of large families? Inefficient farmers? Our own generation?

In a sense we are all innocent threats to one another's safety in scarcity situations, for the bread one person eats might save another's life. If there were fewer people competing for resources, commodity prices would fall and starvation deaths be reduced. Hence famine deaths in scarcity situations might be justified on grounds of the minimal right of self-defense as well as on grounds of the unavoidability of some deaths and the reasonableness of the policies for selecting victims. For each famine death leaves fewer survivors competing for whatever resources there are, and the most endangered among the survivors might have died—had not others done so. So a policy which kills some may be justified on the grounds that the most endangered survivors could have been defended in no other way.

Global scarcity is not here yet. But its imminence has certain implications for today. If all persons have a right not to be killed and a corollary duty not to kill others, then we are bound to adopt prefamine policies which ensure that famine is postponed as long as possible and is minimized. And a duty to try to postpone the advent and minimize the severity of famine is a duty on the one hand to minimize the number of persons there will be and on the other to maximize the means of subsistence.[9] For if we do not adopt prefamine policies with these aims we shall have to adopt more drastic famine policies sooner.

So if we take the right not to be killed seriously, we should consider and support not only some famine policy for future use but also a population and resources policy for present use. There has been a certain amount of philosophical discussion of population policies.[10] From the point of view of the present argument it has two defects. First, it is for the most part conducted within a utilitarian framework and focuses on problems such as the different population policies required by maximizing the total and the average utility of a population. Secondly this literature tends to look at a scarcity of resources as affecting the quality of lives but not their very possibility. It is more concerned with the question, How many people should we add? than with the question, How few people could we lose? There are, of course, many interesting questions about population policies which are not relevant to famine. But here I shall consider only population and resource policies determined on the principle of postponing and minimizing famine, for these are policies which might be based on the claim that persons have a right not to be killed, so that we have a duty to avoid or postpone situations in which we shall have to override this right.

Such population policies might, depending upon judgments about the likely degree of scarcity, range from the mild to the draconian. I list some examples. A mild population policy might emphasize family planning, perhaps moving in the direction of fiscal incentives or measures which stress not people's rights but their duties to control their bodies. Even a mild policy would require a lot both in terms of invention (e.g. the development of contraceptives suitable for use in poverty-stricken conditions) and innovation (e.g. social policies which reduce the incentives and pressures to have a large family).[11] More draconian policies would enforce population limitation—for example, by mandatory sterilization after a certain number of children were born or by reducing public health expenditures in places with high net reproduction rates to prevent death rates from declining until birth rates do so. A policy of completely eliminating all further births (e.g. by universal sterilization) is also one which would meet the requirement of postponing famine, since extinct species do not suffer famine. I have not in this argument used any premises which show that a complete elimination of births would be wrong, but other premises might give reasons for thinking that it is wrong to enforce sterilization or better to have some persons rather than no persons. In any case the political aspects of introducing famine policies make it likely that this most austere of population policies would not be considered.

There is a corresponding range of resource policies. At the milder end are the various conservation and pollution control measures now being practiced or discussed. At the tougher end of the spectrum are complete rationing of energy and materials consumption. If the aim of a resources policy is to avoid killing those who are born, and adequate policy may require both invention (e.g. solar energy technology and better waste retrieval techniques) and innovation (e.g. introducing new technology in such a way that its benefits are not quickly absorbed by increasing population, as has happened with the green revolution in some places).

At all events, if we think that people have a right not to be killed, we cannot fail to face up to its long range implications. This one right by itself provides ground for activism on many fronts. In scarcity situations which we help produce, the defeasibility of the right not to be killed is important, for there cannot be any absolute duty not to kill persons in such situations but only a commitment to kill only for reasons. Such a commitment requires consideration of the condition or quality of life which is to qualify for survival. Moral philosophers are reluctant to face up to this problem; soon it will be staring us in the face.

['Lifeboat Earth', in *Philosophy and Public Affairs*, 4 (1975), repr. in Charles Beitz, Marshall Cohen, Thomas Scanlon, and A. John Simmons (eds.), *International Ethics* (Princeton University Press, Princeton, 1985), 262–81.]

Section VII

Alternatives to Liberalism

INTRODUCTION

It would not be unfair to say that the general topics selected for discussion, and the particular texts chosen, share, broadly, a liberal outlook. This should not be a surprise. English-language political thought has centred on ideas of freedom, equality, and independence, and has championed democracy and toleration. Although critics have been represented—most notably Plato, Hegel, Marx, and, in some respects, Rousseau—we have largely allowed the concerns of liberalism to set the agenda for this Reader.

In this section we go some way to redressing the balance, sampling some criticisms of liberalism and introducing alternative perspectives. We begin with Jürgen Habermas's argument that bourgeois culture draws on a pre-capitalist moral tradition that it continually undermines and wears out. This prompts what Habermas terms a 'legitimation crisis'. In the first of two extracts from Michael Walzer a similar criticism is aimed more directly at liberalism, while in the second Walzer argues that liberalism cannot provide what we need most: a way of feeling at home in the world.

We turn next to conservatism as an alternative to liberalism. Edmund Burke sets out the case that the present generation should always consider themselves as members of an eternal society, and thus treat the past with the respect it has earned, while being mindful of the legacy it will leave to the future. The poet T. S. Eliot emphasizes the importance of the family and social class in the transmission of culture, which he subtly distinguishes from knowledge of culture. Finally, Michael Oakeshott provides some reflection on what it means to be a conservative, and, in particular, on how a conservative would expect the government to act.

Communitarianism follows; a view of great contemporary interest which defines itself explicitly in opposition to liberalism. Charles Taylor, partly through an exposition of Hegel, argues that contemporary liberalism has a tendency to homogeneity, breaking up traditional communities and ways of life, yet cannot itself generate a form of society to which many will feel able to give strong allegiance. Alasdair MacIntyre argues that both liberals and conservatives have been wrong to contrast reason and tradition: a living tradition will involve exercises of reason and imagination and is essentially connected, he suggests, with the notion of the good life. The final selection in this part is from Michael Sandel who explores what it means to consider oneself as a member of a community.

Selections from the writings of socialists follow, beginning, inevitably, with a selection from Marx and Engels. In this they decry the alienating effect the division of labour has on each individual, and look forward to a future society in which people will take on many different roles. This is followed by a selection from the Communist Manifesto in which Marx and Engels set out in more detail, but no less powerfully, their replies to some objections to communism, and provide an account of some of the transitional measures necessary to bring society closer to their goal. The third selection from Marx briefly presents the view that the 'realm of freedom' will not be achieved until human beings rationalize production by bringing it under collective control. Next Oscar Wilde outlines his own, part-anarchist, part-socialist vision, and the economist Ernest Mandel develops Marx's thought that human beings can find self-realization through an enriched form of labour. Finally in this part G. A. Cohen argues that the distinction, insisted upon by some liberals, between 'equality of opportunity' and 'equality of outcome' is spurious.

The final part of this section introduces 'post-modernism'. This is not an easy current of thought to define succinctly. In general post-modernists are critical of the attempt to give definitive answers to questions of political principle, suspecting that such 'grand narratives' are themselves unconsciously complicit with political authoritarianism. Thus Nietzsche—in many ways the pioneer of post-modernism—argues that behind the apparently anti-authoritarian call for justice on the part of the powerless, lies the far less seemly motive of the desire for revenge. Foucault claims that power and truth stand in a symbiotic relation, so that there is no independent vantage-point from which power relations can be objectively evaluated. Finally, Richard Rorty, in a commentary upon many of the views presented in this section, offers a post-modernist defence of liberalism: although the philosophical defences of liberalism are unsatisfactory, in Rorty's view this does not matter, for liberalism does not, in fact, need any form of philosophical justification.

VII.a. Liberal Theory under Strain

JÜRGEN HABERMAS

109 **Legitimation Crisis**

The Legitimation System. With the appearance of functional weakness in the market and dysfunctional side effects of the steering mechanism, the basic bourgeois ideology of fair exchange collapses. Re-coupling the economic system to the political—which in a way repoliticizes the relations of production—creates an increased need for legitimation. The state apparatus no longer, as in liberal capitalism, merely secures the general conditions of production (in the sense of the prerequisites for the continued existence of the reproduction process), but is now actively engaged in it. It must, therefore—like the pre-capitalist state—be legitimated, although it can no longer rely on residues of tradition that have been undermined and worn out during the development of capitalism. Moreover, through the universalistic value-systems of bourgeois ideology, civil rights—including the right to participate in political elections—have become established; and legitimation can be disassociated from the mechanism of elections only temporarily and under extraordinary conditions. This problem is resolved through a system of formal democracy. Genuine participation of citizens in the processes of political will-formation [*politischen Willens-bildungsprozessen*], that is, substantive democracy, would bring to consciousness the contradiction between administratively socialized production and the continued private appropriation and use of surplus value. In order to keep this contradiction from being thematized, then the administrative system must be sufficiently independent of legitimating will-formation.

The arrangement of formal democratic institutions and procedures permits administrative decisions to be made largely independently of specific motives of the citizens. This takes place through a legitimation process that elicits generalized motives—that is, diffuse mass loyalty—but avoids participation. This structural alteration of the bourgeois public realm [*Öffentlichkeit*] provides for application of institutions and procedures that are democratic in form, while the citizenry, in the midst of an objectively [*an sich*] political society, enjoy the status of passive citizens with only the right to withhold acclamation. Private autonomous investment decisions thus have their necessary complement in the civic privatism of the civil public. [. . .]

Bourgeois culture as a whole was never able to reproduce itself from itself. It was always dependent on motivationally effective supplementation by traditional world-views. Religion, having retreated into the regions of subjective belief, can no longer satisfy neglected communicative needs, even in conjunction with the secular components of bourgeois ideology (that is, an empiricist or rationalist theory of knowledge, the new physics, and the universalistic value systems of modern natural law and utilitarianism). Genuinely bourgeois ideologies, which live only from their own substance,

—offer no support, in the face of the basic risks of existence (guilt, sickness, death) to interpretations that overcome contingency; in the face of individual needs for wholeness [*Heilsbedürfnisse*], they are disconsolate;

—do not make possible human relations with a fundamentally objectivated nature (with either outer nature or one's own body);

—permit no intuitive access to relations of solidarity within groups or between individuals;

—allow no real political ethic; in any case, in political and social life, they accommodate an objectivistic self-interpretation of acting subjects.

Only bourgeois art, which has become autonomous in the face of demands for employment extrinsic to art, has taken up positions on behalf of the victims of bourgeois rationalization. Bourgeois art has become the refuge for a satisfaction, even if only virtual, of those needs that have become, as it were, illegal in the material life-process of bourgeois society. I refer here to the desire for a mimetic relation with nature; the need for living together in solidarity outside the group egoism of the immediate family; the longing for the happiness of a communicative experience exempt from imperatives of purposive rationality and giving scope to imagination as well as spontaneity. Bourgeois art, unlike privatized religion, scientistic philosophy, and strategic-utilitarian morality, did not take on tasks in the economic and political systems. Instead it collected residual needs that could find no satisfaction within the 'system of needs.' Thus, along with moral universalism, art and aesthetics (from Schiller to Marcuse) are explosive ingredients built into the bourgeois ideology. [. . .]

Possessive individualism. Historically, bourgeois society understood itself as an instrumental group that accumulated social wealth only by way of private wealth, that is, which secured economic growth and general welfare through competition between strategically acting private persons. Under these conditions, collective goals could be realized only through possessive-individualistic orientations to gain. This preference system presupposed, naturally,

—that the private economic subjects could, in a subjectively unambiguous way, recognize and calculate needs that remained constant for a given time;

—that these needs could be satisfied with individually demandable goods (as a rule, with monetary rewards conforming to the system).

In developed capitalist societies, neither presupposition is any longer fulfilled as a matter of course. These societies have attained a level of social wealth at which it is no longer a question of averting a few fundamental risks to life and satisfying basic needs. Hence the individualistic preference system is unclear. In the expanded horizon of possible satisfying alternatives, prejudgments that can be monologically ascertained no longer suffice. Socialized upper-class culture, which once provided self-evident orientations for new consumption opportunities, no longer sets the standards (notwithstanding national differences). The constant interpretation and reinterpretation of needs has become a matter of collective will-formation. In this process, free communication can be replaced only by massive manipulation, that is, by strong, indirect control. The more freedom the preference system has, the more pressing become the problems of market policy for the suppliers. This is true, at least, if the appearance that consumers can decide privately and autonomously—that is, according to monologically certain preferences—is to be preserved. Opportunistic adaptation of consumers to market strategies of monopolistic competition is the ironic form of the consumer autonomy that is supposed to be maintained as the façade of possessive individualism. Moreover, collective commodities represent a growing proportion of consumable goods as production is increasingly socialized. Conditions of urban life in complex societies are becoming more and more dependent on an infrastructure (transportation, leisure, health care, education, etc.) that increasingly discards the forms of differential demand and private appropriation.

[From *Legitimation Crisis*, trans. Thomas McCarthy, (Beacon Press, Boston, 1975), 36–7, 77–8, 82–3.]

MICHAEL WALZER

110 Liberalism in Retreat

Liberalism more largely, for all its achievements, or as a kind of necessary constraint on those achievements, has been parasitic not only on older values but also and more importantly on older institutions and communities. And these latter it has progressively undermined. For liberalism is above all a doctrine of liberation. It sets individuals loose from religious and ethnic communities, from guilds, parishes, neighborhoods. It abolishes all sorts of controls and agencies of control: ecclesiastical courts, cultural censorship, sumptuary laws, restraints on mobility, group pressure, family bonds. It creates free men and women, tied together only by their contracts—and ruled, when contracts fail, by a distant and powerful state. It generates a radical individualism and then a radical competition among self-seeking individuals.

What made liberalism endurable for all these years was the fact that the individualism it generated was always imperfect, tempered by older restraints and loyalties, by stable patterns of local, ethnic, religious, or class relationships. An untempered liberalism would be unendurable. [. . .]

If the old 'supporting communities' are in decline or gone forever, then it is necessary to reform them or build new ones. If there are to be new (or renewed) communities, they must have committed members. If marginality and deference are gone too, these members must also be participants, responsible for shaping and sustaining their own institutions. Participation requires a democratic and egalitarian politics—and that is also the only setting, in the modern world, for mutual aid and self-restraint. 'The spirit of a commercial people,' John Stuart Mill wrote almost a century and a half ago, 'will be, we are persuaded, essentially mean and slavish, wherever public spirit is not cultivated by an extensive participation of the people in the business of government in detail. . . .' The argument is as true today as it was when Mill wrote, and far more pressing.

[From *Radical Principles* (Basic Books, New York, 1980), 97–8, 106.]

MICHAEL WALZER

111 The Artificiality of Liberalism

The point of an invented morality is to provide what God and nature do not provide, a universal corrective for all the different social moralities. But why should we bow to universal correction? What exactly is the critical force of the philosopher's invention—assuming, still, that it is the only possible invention? I will try to answer these questions by telling a story of my own, a story meant to parallel and heighten certain features of the Rawlsian account of what happens in the original position: a caricature, I am afraid, for which I apologise in advance; but caricature has its uses.

Imagine, then, that a group of travellers from different countries and different moral cultures, speaking different languages, meet in some neutral space (like outer space). They have to co-operate, at least temporarily, and if they are to co-operate, each of them must refrain from insisting upon his or her own values and practices. Hence we deny them knowledge of their own values and practices; and since that knowledge is not only personal but also social, embodied in language itself, we obliterate their linguistic memories and require them to think and talk (temporarily) in some pidgin language that is equally parasitic on all their natural languages—a more perfect Esperanto. What principles of co-operation would they adopt? I shall assume that there is a single answer to this question and that the principles given in that answer properly govern their life together in the space they now occupy. That seems plausible enough; the design procedure is genuinely useful for the purposes at hand. What is less plausible is that the travellers should be required to carry those same principles with them when they go home. Why should newly invented principles govern the lives of people who already share a moral culture and speak a natural language?

Men and women standing behind the veil of ignorance, deprived of all knowledge of their own way of life, forced to live with other men and women similarly deprived, will perhaps, with whatever difficulties, find a *modus vivendi*—not a way of life but a way of living. But even if this is the only possible *modus vivendi* for these people in these conditions, it does not follow that it is a universally valuable arrangement. (It might, of course, have a kind of heuristic value—many things have heuristic value—but I will not pursue that possibility now.) There seems to be a confusion here: it is as if we were to take a hotel room or an accommodation apartment or a safe house as the ideal model of a human home. Away from home, we are grateful for the shelter and convenience of a hotel room. Deprived of all knowledge of what our own home was like, talking with people similarly deprived, required to design rooms that any one of us might like to live in, we would probably come up with something like, but not quite so culturally specific as, the Hilton Hotel. With this difference: we would not allow luxury suites; all the rooms would be exactly the same; or if there were luxury suites, their only purpose would be to bring more business to the hotel and enable us to improve all the other rooms, starting with those most in need of improvement. But even if the improvements went pretty far, we might still long for the homes we knew we once had but could no longer remember. We would not be morally bound to live in the hotel we had designed.

I have been assuming that my own view of hotels is widely shared, and so I should note one telling dissent—a line from Franz Kafka's journal: 'I like hotel rooms. I always feel immediately at home in hotel rooms, more than at home, really.' Note the irony: there is no other way to convey the sense of being in one's own place except to say 'at home'. It is a hard thing to suggest to men and women that they give up the moral comfort that those words evoke. But what if they do not share that comfort? What if their lives are like that of Kafka's K., or of any twentieth century exile, outcast, refugee, or stateless person? For such people, hotels are very important. They need the protection of the rooms, decent (if bare) human accommodation. They need a universal (if minimal) morality, or at least a morality worked out among strangers. What they commonly *want*, however, is not to be permanently registered in a hotel but to be established in a new home, a dense moral culture within which they can feel some sense of belonging.

[From *Interpretation and Social Criticism* (Harvard University Press, Cambridge, Mass., 1987), 13–15.]

VII.b. Conservatism

EDMUND BURKE

112 **Eternal Society**

But one of the first and most leading principles on which the commonwealth and the laws are consecrated, is lest the temporary possessors and life-renters in it, unmindful of what they have received from their ancestors, or of what is due to their posterity, should act as if they were the entire masters; that they should not think it amongst their rights to cut off the entail, or commit waste on the inheritance, by destroying at their pleasure the whole original fabric of their society; hazarding to leave to those who come after them, a ruin instead of an habitation—and teaching these successors as little to respect their contrivances, as they had themselves respected the institutions of their forefathers. By this unprincipled facility of changing the state as often, and as much, and in as many ways as there are floating fancies or fashions, the whole chain and continuity of the commonwealth would be broken. No one generation could link with the other. Men would become little better than the flies of a summer.

And first of all the science of jurisprudence, the pride of the human intellect, which, with all its defects, redundancies, and errors, is the collected reason of ages, combining the principles of original justice with the infinite variety of human concerns, as a heap of old exploded errors, would be no longer studied. Personal self-sufficiency and arrogance (the certain attendants upon all those who have never experienced a wisdom greater than their own) would usurp the tribunal. Of course, no certain laws, establishing invariably grounds of hope and fear, would keep the actions of men in a certain course, or direct them to a certain end. Nothing stable in the modes of holding property, or exercising function, could form a solid ground on which any parent could speculate in the education of his offspring, or in a choice for their future establishment in the world. No principles would be early worked into the habits. As soon as the most able instructor had completed his laborious course of institution, instead of sending forth his pupil, accomplished in a virtuous discipline, fitted to procure him attention and respect, in his place in society, he would find every thing altered; and that he had turned out a poor creature to the contempt and derision of the world, ignorant of the true grounds of estimation. Who would insure a tender and delicate sense of honour to beat almost with the first pulses of the heart, when no man could know what would be the test of honour in a nation, continually varying the standard of its coin? No part of life would retain its acquisitions. Barbarism with regard to science and literature, unskilfulness with regard to arts and manufactures, would infallibly succeed to the want of a steady education and settled principle; and thus the commonwealth itself would, in a few generations, crumble away, be disconnected into the dust and powder of individuality, and at length dispersed to all the winds of heaven.

To avoid therefore the evils of inconstancy and versatility, ten thousand times worse than those of obstinacy and the blindest prejudice, we have consecrated the state, that no man should approach to look into its defects or corruptions but with due caution; that he should never dream of beginning its reformation by its subversion; that he should approach to the faults of the state as to the wounds of a father, with pious awe and trembling solicitude. By this wise prejudice we are taught to look with horror on those children of their country who are prompt rashly to hack that aged parent in pieces, and put him into the kettle of magicians, in hopes that by their poisonous weeds, and wild incantations, they may regenerate the paternal constitution, and renovate their father's life.

Society is indeed a contract. Subordinate contracts for objects of mere occasional interest may be dissolved at pleasure—but the state ought not to be considered as nothing better than a partnership agreement in a trade of paper and coffee, callico or tobacco, or some other such low concern, to be taken up for a little temporary interest, and to be dissolved by the fancy of the parties. It is to be looked on with other reverence; because it is not a partnership in things subservient only to the gross animal existence of a temporary and perishable nature. It is a partnership in all science; a partnership in all art; a partnership in every virtue, and in all perfection. As the ends of such a partnership cannot be obtained in many generations, it becomes a partnership not only between those who are living, but between those who are living, those who are dead, and those who are to be born. Each contract of each particular state is but a clause in the great primaeval contract of eternal society, linking the lower with the higher natures, connecting the visible and invisible world, according to a fixed compact sanctioned by the inviolable oath which holds all physical and all moral natures, each in their appointed place. This law is not subject to the will of those, who by an obligation above them, and infinitely superior, are bound to submit their will to that law. The municipal corporations of that universal kingdom are not morally at liberty at their pleasure, and on their speculations of a contingent improvement, wholly to separate and tear asunder the bands of their subordinate community, and to dissolve it into an unsocial, uncivil, unconnected chaos of elementary principles. It is the first and supreme necessity only, a necessity that is not chosen but chooses, a necessity paramount to deliberation, that admits no discussion, and demands no evidence, which alone can justify a resort to anarchy. This necessity is no exception to the rule; because this necessity itself is a part too of that moral and physical disposition of things to which man must be obedient by consent or force; but if that which is only submission to necessity should be made the object of choice, the law is broken, nature is disobeyed, and the rebellious are outlawed, cast forth, and exiled, from this world of reason, and order, and peace, and virtue, and fruitful penitence, into the antagonist world of madness, discord, vice, confusion, and unavailing sorrow.

[From *Reflections on the Revolution in France* (Penguin, Harmondsworth, 1968), 192–5. First published 1790.]

T. S. ELIOT

113 The Transmission of Culture

It is obvious, that while in the present state of society there is found the voluntary association of like-minded individuals, and association based upon common material interest, or common occupation or profession, the élites of the future will differ in one important respect from any that we know: they will replace the classes of the past, whose positive functions they will assume. This transformation is not always explicitly stated. There are some philosophers who regard class divisions as intolerable, and others who regard them merely as moribund. The latter may simply ignore class, in their design for an élite-governed society, and say that the élites will 'be drawn from all sections of society'. But it would seem that as we perfect the means for identifying at an early age, educating for their future role, and settling into positions of authority, the individuals who will form the élites, all former class distinctions will become a mere shadow or vestige, and the only social distinction of rank will be between the élites and the rest of the community, unless, as may happen, there is to be an order of precedence and prestige amongst the several élites themselves.

However moderately and unobtrusively the doctrine of élites is put, it implies a radical transformation of society. Superficially, it appears to aim at no more than what we must all desire—that all positions in society should be occupied by those who are best fitted to exercise the functions of the positions. We have all observed individuals occupying situations in life for which neither their character nor their intellect qualified them, and so placed only through nominal education, or birth or consanguinity. No honest man but is vexed by such a spectacle. But the doctrine of élites implies a good deal more than the rectification of such injustice. It posits an *atomic* view of society. [. . .]

What we have to consider is the parts played by the élite and by the class in the transmission of culture from one generation to the next. [. . .]

In an élite composed of individuals who find their way into it solely for their individual pre-eminence, the differences of background will be so great, that they will be united only by their common interests, and separated by everything else. An élite must therefore be attached to *some* class, whether higher or lower: but so long as there are classes at all it is likely to be the dominant class that attracts this élite to itself. What would happen in a classless society—which is much more difficult to envisage than people think—brings us into the area of conjecture. There are, however, some guesses which seem to me worth venturing.

The primary channel of transmission of culture is the family: no man wholly escapes from the kind, or wholly surpasses the degree, of culture which he acquired from his early environment. It would not do to suggest that this can be the *only* channel of transmission: in a society of any complexity it is supplemented and continued by other conduits of tradition. Even in relatively primitive societies this is so. In more civilised communities of specialised activities, in which not all the sons would follow the occupation of their father, the apprentice (ideally, at least) did not merely serve his master, and did not merely learn from him as one would learn at a technical school—he became assimilated into a way of life which went with that particular trade or craft; and perhaps the lost secret of the craft is this, that not merely a skill but an entire way of life was transmitted. Culture—distinguishable from knowledge about culture—was transmitted by the older universities: young men have profited there who have been profitless students, and who have acquired no taste for learning, or for Gothic architecture, or for college ritual and form. I suppose that something of the same sort is transmitted also by societies of the masonic type: for initiation is an introduction into a way of life, of however restricted viability, received from the past and to be perpetuated in the future. But by far the most important channel of transmission of culture remains the family: and when family life fails to play its part, we must expect our culture to deteriorate. Now the family is an institution of which nearly everybody speaks well: but it is advisable to remember that this is a term that may vary in extension. In the present age it means little more than the living members. Even of living members, it is a rare exception when an advertisement depicts a large family or three generations: the usual family on the hoardings consists of two parents and one or two young children. What is held up for admiration is not devotion to a family, but personal affection between the members of it: and the smaller the family, the more easily can this personal affection be sentimentalised. But when I speak of the family, I have in mind a bond which embraces a longer period of time than this: a piety towards the dead, however obscure, and a solicitude for the unborn, however remote. Unless this reverence for past and future is cultivated in the home, it can never be more than a verbal convention in the community. Such an interest in the past is different from the vanities and pretensions of genealogy; such a responsibility for the future is different from that of the builder of social programmes. [. . .]

All that concerns me at the moment is the question whether, by education alone, we can ensure the transmission of culture in a society in which some educationists appear indifferent to class distinctions, and from which some other educationists appear to want to remove class distinctions altogether. There is, in any case, a danger of interpreting 'education' to cover both too much and too little: too little, when it implies that education is limited to what can be taught; too much, when it implies that everything worth preserving can be transmitted by teaching. In the society desired by some reformers, what the family can transmit will be limited to the minimum, especially if the child is to be, as Mr H. C. Dent hopes, manipulated by a unified educational system 'from the cradle to the grave'. And unless the child is classified, by the officials who will have the task of sorting him out, as being just like his father, he will be brought up in a different—not necessarily a better, because all will be equally good, but a different—school environment, and trained on what the official opinion of the moment considers to be 'the genuinely democratic lines'. The élites, in consequence, will consist solely of individuals whose only common bond will be their professional interest: with no social cohesion, with no social continuity. They will be united only by a part, and that the most conscious part, of their personalities; they will meet like committees. The greater part of their 'culture' will be only what they share with all the other individuals composing their nation.

The case for a society with a class structure, the affirmation that it is, in some sense, the 'natural' society, is prejudiced if we allow ourselves to be hypnotised by the two contrasted terms *áristocracy* and *democracy*. The whole problem is falsified if we use these terms antithetically. What I have advanced is not a 'defence of aristocracy'—an emphasis upon the importance of one organ of society. Rather it is a plea on behalf of a form of society in which an aristocracy should have a peculiar and essential function, as peculiar and essential as the function of any other part of society. What is important is a structure of society in which there will be, from 'top' to 'bottom', a continuous gradation of cultural levels: it is important to remember that we should not consider the upper levels as possessing *more* culture than the lower, but as representing a more conscious culture and a greater specialisation of culture. I incline to believe that no true democracy can maintain itself unless it contains these different levels of culture. The levels of culture may also be seen as levels of power, to the extent that a smaller group at a higher level will have equal power with a larger group at a lower level; for it may be argued that complete equality means universal irresponsibility; and in such a society as I envisage, each individual would inherit greater or less responsibility towards the commonwealth, according to the position in society which he inherited—each class would have somewhat different responsibilities. A democracy in which everybody had an equal responsibility in everything would be oppressive for the conscientious and licentious for the rest.

[From *Notes towards the Definition of Culture* (Faber, London, 1948), 36–7, 41, 42–4, 47–8.]

Let us begin at what I believe to be the proper starting-place; not in the empyrean, but with ourselves as we have come to be. I and my neighbours, my associates, my compatriots, my friends, my enemies and those who I am indifferent about, are people engaged in a great variety of activities. We are apt to entertain a multiplicity of opinions on every conceivable subject and are disposed to change these beliefs as we grow tired of them or as they prove unserviceable. Each of us is pursuing a course of his own; and there is no project so unlikely that somebody will not be found to engage in it, no enterprise so foolish that somebody will not undertake it. There are those who spend their lives trying to sell copies of the Anglican Catechism to the Jews. And on half of the world is engaged in trying to make the other half want what it has hitherto never felt the lack of. We are all inclined to be passionate about our own concerns, whether it is making things or selling them, whether it is business or sport, religion or learning, poetry, drink or drugs. Each of us has preferences of his own. For some, the opportunities of making choices (which are numerous) are invitations readily accepted; others welcome them less eagerly or even find them burdensome. Some dream dreams of new and better worlds: others are more inclined to move in familiar paths or even to be idle. Some are apt to deplore the rapidity of change, others delight in it; all recognize it. At times we grow tired and fall asleep: it is blessed relief to gaze in a shop window and see nothing we want; we are grateful for ugliness merely because it repels attention. But, for the most part, we pursue happiness by seeking the satisfaction of desires which spring from one another inexhaustably. We enter into relationships of interest and of emotion, of competition, partnership, guardianship, love, friendship, jealousy and hatred, some of which are more durable than others. We make agreements with one another; we have expectations about one another's conduct; we approve, we are indifferent and we disapprove. This multiplicity of activity and variety of opinion is apt to produce collisions: we pursue courses which cut across those of others, and we do not all approve the same sort of conduct. But, in the main, we get along with one another, sometimes by giving way, sometimes by standing fast, sometimes in a compromise. Our conduct consists of activity assimilated to that of others in small, and for the most part unconsidered and unobtrusive, adjustments.

Why all this should be so, does not matter. It is not necessarily so. A different condition of human circumstance can easily be imagined, and we know that elsewhere and at other times activity is, or has been, far less multifarious and changeful and opinion far less diverse and far less likely to provoke collision; but, by and large, we recognize this to be our condition. It is an acquired condition, though nobody designed or specifically chose it in preference to all others. It is the product, not of 'human nature' let loose, but of human beings impelled by an acquired love of making choices for themselves. And we know as little and as much about where it is leading us as we know about the fashion in hats of twenty years' time or the design of motor-cars.

Surveying the scene, some people are provoked by the absence of order and coherence which appears to them to be its dominant feature; its wastefulness, its frustration, its dissipation of human energy, its lack not merely of a premeditated destination but even of any discernible direction of movement. It provides an excitement similar to that of a stock-car race; but it has none of the satisfaction of a well-conducted business enterprise. Such people are apt to exaggerate the current disorder; the absence of plan is so conspicuous that the small adjustments, and even the more massive arrangements, which restrain the chaos seem to them nugatory; they have no feeling for the warmth of untidiness but only for its inconvenience. But what is significant is not the limitations of their powers of observation, but the turn of their thoughts. They feel that there ought to be something that ought to be done to convert this so-called chaos into order, for this is no way for rational human beings to be spending their lives. Like Apollo when he saw Daphne with her hair hung carelessly about her neck, they sigh and say to themselves: 'What if it were properly arranged.' Moreover, they tell us that they have seen in a dream the glorious, collisionless manner of living proper to all mankind, and this dream they understand as their warrant for seeking to remove the diversities and occasions of conflict which distinguish our current manner of living. Of course, their dreams are not all exactly alike; but they have this in common: each is a vision of a condition of human circumstance from which the occasion of conflict has been removed, a vision of human activity co-ordinated and set going in a single direction and of every resource being used to the full. And such people appropriately understand the office of government to be the imposition upon its subjects of the condition of human circumstances to their dream. To govern is to turn a private dream into a public and compulsory manner of living. Thus, politics becomes an encounter of dreams and the activity in which government is held to this understanding of its office and provided with the appropriate instruments.

I do not propose to criticize this jump to glory style of politics in which governing is understood as a perpetual take-over bid for the purpose of the resources of human energy in order to concentrate them in a single direction; it is not at all unintelligible, and there is much in our circumstances to provoke it. My purpose is merely to point out that there is another quite different understanding of government, and that it is no less intelligible and in some respects perhaps more appropriate to our circumstances.

The spring of this other disposition in respect of governing and the instruments of government—a conservative disposition—is to be found in the acceptance of the current condition of human circumstances as I have described it:

the propensity to make our own choices and to find happiness in doing so, the variety of enterprises each pursued with passion, the diversity of beliefs each held with the conviction of its exclusive truth; the inventiveness, the changefulness and the absence of any large design; the excess, the over-activity and the informal compromise. And the office of government is not to impose other beliefs and activities upon its subjects, not to tutor or to educate them, not to make them better or happier in another way, not to direct them, to galvanize them into action, to lead them or to co-ordinate their activities so that no occasion of conflict shall occur; the office of government is merely to rule. This is a specific and limited activity, easily corrupted when it is combined with any other, and, in the circumstances, indispensable. The image of the ruler is the umpire whose business is to administer the rules of the game, or the chairman who governs the debate according to known rules but does not himself participate in it.

Now people of this disposition commonly defend their belief that the proper attitude of government towards the current condition of human circumstance is one of acceptance by appealing to certain general ideas. They contend that there is absolute value in the free play of human choice, that private property (the emblem of choice) is a natural right, that it is only in the enjoyment of diversity of opinion and activity that true belief and good conduct can be expected to disclose themselves. But I do not think that this disposition requires these or any similar beliefs in order to make it intelligible. Something much smaller and less pretentious will do: the observation that this condition of human circumstance is, in fact, current, and that we have learned to enjoy it and how to manage it; that we are not children in statu pupillari but adults who do not consider themselves under any obligation to justify their preference for making their own choices; and that it is beyond human experience to suppose that those who rule are endowed with a superior wisdom which discloses to them a better range of beliefs and activities and which gives them authority to impose upon their subjects a quite different manner of life. In short, if the man of this disposition is asked: Why ought governments to accept the current diversity of opinion and activity in preference to imposing upon their subjects a dream of their own? it is enough for him to reply: Why not? Their dreams are no different from those of anyone else; and if it is boring to have to listen to dreams of others being recounted, it is insufferable to be forced to re-enact them. We tolerate monomaniacs, it is our habit to do so; but why should we be *ruled* by them? Is it not (the man of conservative disposition asks) an intelligible task for a government to protect its subjects against the nuisance of those who spend their energy and their wealth in the service of some pet indignation, endeavouring to impose it upon everybody, not by suppressing their activities in favour of others of a similar kind, but by setting a limit to the amount of noise anyone may emit?

Nevertheless, if this acceptance is the spring of the conservative's disposition in respect of government, he does not suppose that the office of government is to do nothing. As he understands it, there is work to be done which can be done only in virtue of a genuine acceptance of current beliefs simply because they are current and current activities simply because they are afoot. And, briefly, the office he attributes to government is to resolve some of the collisions which this variety of beliefs and activities generates; to preserve peace, not by placing an interdict upon choice and upon the diversity that springs from the exercise of preference, not by imposing substantive uniformity, but by enforcing general rules of procedure upon all subjects alike.

Government, then, as the conservative in this matter understands it, does not begin with a vision of another, different and better world, but with the observation of the self-government practised even by men of passion in the conduct of their enterprises; it begins in the informal adjustments of interests to one another which are designed to release those who are apt to collide from the mutual frustration of a collision. Sometimes these adjustments are no more than agreements between two parties to keep out of each other's way; sometimes they are of wider application and more durable character, such as the International Rules for the prevention of collisions at sea. In short, the intimations of government are to be found in ritual, not in religion or philosophy; in the enjoyment of orderly and peaceable behaviour, not in the search for truth or perfection.

But the self-government of men of passionate belief and enterprise is apt to break down when it is most needed. It often suffices to resolve minor collisions of interest, but beyond these it is not to be relied upon. A more precise and a less easily corrupted ritual is required to resolve the massive collisions which our manner of living is apt to generate and to release us from the massive frustrations in which we are apt to become locked. The custodian of this ritual is 'the government', and the rules it imposes are 'the law'. One may imagine a government engaged in the activity of an arbiter in cases of collisions of interest but doing its business without the aid of laws, just as one may imagine a game without rules and an umpire who was appealed to in cases of dispute and who on each occasion merely used his judgment to devise *ad hoc* a way of releasing the disputants from their mutual frustration. But the diseconomy of such an arrangement is so obvious that it could only be expected to occur to those inclined to believe the ruler to be supernaturally inspired and to those disposed to attribute to him a quite different office—that of leader, or tutor, or manager. At all events the disposition to be conservative in respect of government is rooted in the belief that where government rests upon the acceptance of the current activities and beliefs of its subjects, the only appropriate manner of ruling is by making and enforcing rules of conduct. In short, to be conservative about government is a reflection of the conservatism we have recognized to be appropriate in respect of rules of conduct.

[From 'On Being Conservative', in *Rationalism in Politics* (Methuen, London, 1962), 184–9.]

VII.c. Communitarianism

CHARLES TAYLOR

115 Identification and Subjectivity

We can see the aspiration to what Hegel calls 'absolute freedom', or universal and total participation, as the attempt to meet an endemic need of modern society. Traditional societies were founded on differentiation: royalty, aristocracy, common folk; priests and laymen; free and serf, and so on. This differentiation was justified as a reflection of a hierarchical order of things. After the revolution of modern, self-defining subjectivity, these conceptions of cosmic order came to be seen as fictions, and were denounced as fraudulent inventions of kings, priests, aristocrats, etc. to keep their subjects submissive. But however much they may have been used, consciously or not, as justifications of the status quo, these conceptions also were the ground of men's identification with the society in which they lived. Man could only be himself in relation to a cosmic order; the state claimed to body forth this order and hence to be one of men's principal channels of contact with it. Hence the power of organic and holistic metaphors: men saw themselves as parts of society in something like the way that a hand, for instance, is part of the body.

The revolution of modern subjectivity gave rise to another type of political theory. Society was justified not by what it was or expressed, but by what it achieved, the fulfilment of men's needs, desires and purposes. Society came to be seen as an instrument and its different modes and structures were to be studied scientifically for their effects on human happiness. Political theory would banish myth and fable. This reached clearest expression in utilitarianism.

But this modern theory has not provided a basis for men's identification with their society. In the intermittent crises of alienation which have followed the breakdown of traditional society, utilitarian theories have been powerless to fill the gap. So that modern societies have actually functioned with a large part of their traditional outlook intact, or only slowly receding, as in the case of Britain, for instance. Or when some radical break is sought, they have had recourse to more powerful stuff, some variant of the general will tradition (Jacobinism, Marxism, anarchism) as a revolutionary ideology. Or modern societies have had recourse either in revolutionary or 'normal' times to the powerful secular religion of nationalism. And even societies which seem to be founded on the utilitarian tradition, or an earlier, Lockeian variant, like the United States, in fact have recourse to 'myth', e.g., the myth of the frontier, of the perpetual new beginning, the future as boundlessly open to self-creation.

This last is the greatest irony of all, in that the utilitarian theory itself leaves no place for myth of this kind, that is, speculative interpretation of the ends of human life in their relation to society, nature and history, as part of the justifying beliefs of a mature society. These are thought to belong to earlier, less evolved ages. Mature men are attached to their society because of what it produces for them. As recently as a decade ago this perspective was widely believed in by the liberal intelligentsia of America and the Western world, who announced an imminent 'end of ideology'. But they turned out to be latter-day, inverted variants of Monsieur Jourdain, who were speaking not prose, but myth without knowing it. It is now clearer that the utilitarian perspective is no less an ideology than its major rivals, and no more plausible. Utilitarian man whose loyalty to his society would be contingent only on the satisfactions it secured for him is a species virtually without members. And the very notion of satisfaction is now not so firmly anchored, once we see that it is interwoven with 'expectations', and beliefs about what is appropriate and just. Some of the richest societies in our day are among the most teeming with dissatisfaction, for instance, the U.S.A.

The aspiration to absolute freedom can be seen as an attempt to fill this lack in modern political theory, to find ground for identification with one's society which are fully in the spirit of modern subjectivity. We have grounds for identifying ourselves with our society and giving our full allegiance to it when it is ours in the strong sense of being our creation, and moreover the creation of what is best in us and mostly truly ourselves: our moral will (Rousseau, Fichte), or our creative activity (Marx). From Rousseau through Marx and the anarchist thinkers to contemporary theories of participatory democracy, there have been recurrent demands to reconstruct society, so as to do away with heteronomy, or overcome alienation, or recover spontaneity. Only a society which was an emanation of free moral will could recover a claim on our allegiance comparable to that of traditional society. For once more society would reflect or embody something of absolute value. Only this would no longer be a cosmic order, but in keeping with the modern revolution, the absolute would be human freedom itself.

The aspiration to absolute freedom is therefore born of a deep dissatisfaction with the utilitarian model of society as an instrument for the furtherance / adjustment of interests. Societies built on this model are experienced as a spiritual desert, or as a machine. They express nothing spiritual, and their regulations and discipline are felt as an intolerable imposition by those who aspire to absolute freedom. It is therefore not surprising that the theorists of absolute freedom have often been close to the reactionary critics of liberal society, and have often themselves expressed admiration for earlier societies. [. . .]

The basic point of this critique is this: absolute freedom requires homogeneity. It cannot brook differences which would prevent everyone participating totally in the decisions of the society. And what is even more, it requires some near unanimity of will to emerge from this deliberation, for otherwise the majority would just be imposing its will on the minority, and freedom would not be universal. But differentiation of some fairly essential kinds are ineradicable. (Let us leave aside for the moment the objection that Hegel did not identify the right ones.) And moreover, they are recognized in our post-Romantic climate as essential to human identity. Men cannot simply identify themselves as men, but they define themselves more immediately by their partial community, cultural, linguistic, confessional, etc. Modern democracy is therefore in a bind.

I think a dilemma of this kind can be seen in contemporary society. Modern societies have moved towards much greater homogeneity and greater interdependence, so that partial communities lose their autonomy and to some extent their identity. But great differences remain; only because of the ideology of homogeneity, these differential characteristics no longer have meaning and value for those who have them. Thus the rural population is taught by the mass media to see itself as just lacking in some of the advantages of a more advanced life style. The poor are seen as marginal to the society, for instance, in America, and in some ways have a worse lot than in more recognizedly class-divided societies.

Homogenization thus increases minority alienation and resentment. And the first response of liberal society is to try even more of the same: programmes to eliminate poverty, or assimilate Indians, move population out of declining regions, bring an urban way of life to the countryside, etc. But the radical response is to convert this sense of alienation into a demand for 'absolute freedom'. The idea is to overcome alienation by creating a society in which everyone, including the present 'out' groups, participate fully in the decisions.

But both these solutions would simply aggravate the problem, which is that homogenization has undermined the communities or characteristics by which people formerly identified themselves and put nothing in their place. What does step into the gap almost everywhere is ethnic or national identity. Nationalism has become the most powerful focus of identity in modern society. The demand for radical freedom can and frequently does join up with nationalism, and is given a definite impetus and direction from this.

But unless this happens, the aspiration to absolute freedom is unable to resolve the dilemma. It attempts to overcome the alienation of a mass society by mass participation. But the very size, complexity and inter-dependence of modern society makes this increasingly difficult on technical grounds alone. What is more serious, the increasing alienation in a society which has eroded its traditional foci of allegiance makes it harder and harder to achieve the basic consensus, to bring everyone to the 'general will', which is essential for radical democracy. As the traditional limits fade with the grounds for accepting them, society tends to fragment, partial groups become increasingly truculent in their demands, as they see less reason to compromise with the 'system'.

But the radical demand for participation can do nothing to stem this fragmentation. Participation of *all* in a decision is only possible if there is a ground of agreement, or of underlying common purpose. Radical participation cannot create this; it presupposes it. [. . .] The demand for absolute freedom by itself is empty. [. . .] For in fact some direction has to be given to society, and hence a group can take over and imprint its own purpose on society claiming to represent the general will. They thus 'solve' the problem of diversity by force. Contemporary communist societies provide examples of this. And whatever can be said for them they can certainly not be thought of as models of freedom. Moreover their solution to the emptiness of absolute freedom is in a sense only provisional. The problem of what social goals to choose or structures to adopt is solved by the exigencies of mobilization and combat towards the free society. Society can be set a definite task because it has to build the *preconditions* of communism, either in defeating class enemies or in constructing a modern economy. Such societies would be in disarray if ever the period of mobilization were to end (which is why it would end only over the dead bodies of the ruling party).

But an ideology of participation which does not want to take this totalitarian road of general mobilization cannot cope with the complexity and fragmentation of a large-scale contemporary society. Many of its protagonists see this, and return to the original Rousseauian idea of a highly decentralized federation of communities. But in the meantime the growth of a large homogeneous society has made this much less feasible. It is not just that with our massive concentrations of population and economic interdependence a lot of decisions have to be taken for the whole society, and decentralization gives us no way of coping with these. More serious is the fact that homogenization has undermined the partial communities which would naturally have been the basis of such a decentralized federation in the past. There is no advantage in an artificial carving up of society into manageable units. If in fact no one identifies strongly with these units, participation will be minimal, as we see in much of our urban politics today.

[From *Hegel* (Cambridge University Press, Cambridge, 1975), 410–14.]

ALASDAIR MACINTYRE

116 Tradition and the Unity of a Life

Any contemporary attempt to envisage each human life as a whole, as a unity, whose character provides the virtues with an adequate *telos* encounters two different kinds of obstacle, one social and one philosophical. The social obstacles derive from the way in which modernity partitions each human life into a variety of segments, each with its own norms and modes of behaviour. So work is divided from leisure, private life from public, the corporate from the personal. So both childhood and old age have been wrenched away from the rest of human life and made over into distinct realms. And all these separations have been achieved so that it is the distinctiveness of each and not the unity of the life of the individual who passes through those parts in terms of which we are taught to think and to feel. [. . .]

In what does the unity of an individual life consist? The answer is that its unity is the unity of a narrative embodied in a single life. To ask 'What is the good for me?' is to ask how best I might live out that unity and bring it to completion. To ask 'What is the good for man?' is to ask what all answers to the former question must have in common. But now it is important to emphasise that it is the systematic asking of these two questions and the attempt to answer them in deed as well as in word which provide the moral life with its unity. The unity of a human life is the unity of a narrative quest. Quests sometimes fail, are frustrated, abandoned or dissipated into distractions; and human lives may in all these ways also fail. But the only criteria for success or failure in a human life as a whole are the criteria of success or failure in a narrated or to-be-narrated quest. A quest for what?

Two key features of the medieval conception of a quest need to be recalled. The first is that without some at least partly determinate conception of the final *telos* there could not be any beginning to a quest. Some conception of the good for man is required. Whence is such a conception to be drawn? Precisely from those questions which led us to attempt to transcend that limited conception of the virtues which is available in and through practices. It is in looking for a conception of *the* good which will enable us to order other goods, for a conception of *the* good which will enable us to extend our understanding of the purpose and content of the virtues, for a conception of *the* good which will enable us to understand the place of integrity and constancy in life, that we initially define the kind of life which is a quest for the good. But secondly it is clear the medieval conception of a quest is not at all that of a search for something already adequately characterised, as miners search for gold or geologists for oil. It is in the course of the quest and only through encountering and coping with the various particular harms, dangers, temptations and distractions which provide any quest with its episodes and incidents that the goal of the quest is finally to be understood. A quest is always an education both as to the character of that which is sought and in self-knowledge.

The virtues therefore are to be understood as those dispositions which will not only sustain practices and enable us to achieve the goods internal to practices, but which will also sustain us in the relevant kind of quest for the good, by enabling us to overcome the harms, dangers, temptations and distractions which we encounter, and which will furnish us with increasing self-knowledge and increasing knowledge of the good. The catalogue of the virtues will therefore include the virtues required to sustain the kind of households and the kind of political communities in which men and women can seek for the good together and the virtues necessary for philosophical enquiry about the character of the good. We have then arrived at a provisional conclusion about the good life for man: the good life for man is the life spent in seeking for the good life for man, and the virtues necessary for the seeking are those which will enable us to understand what more and what else the good life for man is. We have also completed the second stage in our account of the virtues, by situating them in relation to the good life for man and not only in relation to practices. But our enquiry requires a third stage.

For I am never able to seek for the good or exercise the virtues only *qua* individual. This is partly because what it is to live the good life concretely varies from circumstance to circumstance even when it is one and the same conception of the good life and one and the same set of virtues which are being embodied in a human life. What the good life is for a fifth-century Athenian general will not be the same as what it was for a medieval nun or a seventeenth-century farmer. But it is not just that different individuals live in different social circumstances; it is also that we all approach our own circumstances as bearers of a particular social identity. I am someone's son or daughter, someone else's cousin or uncle; I am a citizen of this or that city, a member of this or that guild or profession; I belong to this clan, that tribe, this nation. Hence what is good for me has to be the good for one who inhabits these roles. As such, I inherit from the past of my family, my city, my tribe, my nation, a variety of debts, inheritances, rightful expectations and obligations. These constitute the given of my life, my moral starting point. This is in part what gives my life its own moral particularity.

This thought is likely to appear alien and even surprising from the standpoint of modern individualism. From the standpoint of individualism I am what I myself choose to be. I can always, if I wish to, put in question what are taken to be the merely contingent social features of my existence. I may biologically be my father's son; but I cannot be held responsible for what he did unless I choose implicitly or explicitly to assume such responsibility. I may legally be a citizen of a certain country; but I cannot he held responsible for what my country does or has done unless I choose implicitly or explicitly to assume such responsibility. Such individualism is expressed by those modern Americans who deny any responsibility for the effects of slavery upon black Americans, saying 'I never owned any slaves'. It is more subtly the standpoint of those other modern Americans who accept a nicely calculated responsibility for such effects measured precisely by the benefits they themselves as individuals have indirectly received from slavery. In both cases 'being an American' is not in itself taken to be part of the moral identity of the individual. And of course there is nothing peculiar to modern Americans in this attitude: the Englishman who says, '*I* never did any wrong to Ireland; why bring up that old history as though it had something to do with *me*?' or the young German who believes that being born after 1945 means that what Nazis did to Jews has no moral relevance to his relationship to his Jewish contemporaries, exhibit the same attitude, that according to which the self is detachable from its social and historical roles and statuses. And the self so detached is of course a self very much at home in either Sartre's or

Goffman's perspective, a self that can have no history. The contrast with the narrative view of the self is clear. For the story of my life is always embedded in the story of those communities from which I derive my identity. I am born with a past; and to try to cut myself off from that past, in the individualist mode, is to deform my present relationships. The possession of an historical identity and the possession of a social identity coincide. Notice that rebellion against my identity is always one possible mode of expressing it.

Notice also that the fact that the self has to find its moral identity in and through its membership in communities such as those of the family, the neighbourhood, the city and the tribe does not entail that the self has to accept the moral *limitations* of the particularity of those forms of community. Without those moral particularities to begin from there would never be anywhere to begin; but it is in moving forward from such particularity that the search for the good, for the universal, consists. Yet particularity can never be simply left behind or obliterated. The notion of escaping from it into a realm of entirely universal maxims which belong to man as such, whether in its eighteenth-century Kantian form or in the presentation of some modern analytical moral philosophies, is an illusion and an illusion with painful consequences. When men and women identify what are in fact their partial and particular causes too easily and too completely with the cause of some universal principle, they usually behave worse than they would otherwise do.

What I am, therefore, is in key part what I inherit, a specific past that is present to some degree in my present. I find myself part of a history and that is generally to say, whether I like it or not, whether I recognise it or not, one of the bearers of a tradition. It was important when I characterised the concept of a practice to notice that practices always have histories and that at any given moment what a practice is depends on a mode of understanding it which has been transmitted often through many generations. And thus, insofar as the virtues sustain the relationships required for practices, they have to sustain relationships to the past—and to the future—as well as in the present. But the traditions through which particular practices are transmitted and reshaped never exist in isolation for larger social traditions. What constitutes such traditions?

We are apt to be misled here by the ideological uses to which the concept of a tradition has been put by conservative political theorists. Characteristically such theorists have followed Burke in contrasting tradition with reason and the stability of tradition with conflict. Both contrasts obfuscate. For all reasoning takes place within the context of some traditional mode of thought, transcending through criticism and invention the limitations of what had hitherto been reasoned in that tradition; this is as true of modern physics as of medieval logic. Moreover when a tradition is in good order it is always partially constituted by an argument about the goods the pursuit of which gives to that tradition its particular point and purpose.

So when an institution—a university, say, or a farm, or a hospital—is the bearer of a tradition of practice or practices, its common life will be partly, but in a centrally important way, constituted by a continuous argument as to what a university is and ought to be or what good farming is or what good medicine is. Traditions, when vital, embody continuities of conflict. Indeed when a tradition becomes Burkean, it is always dying or dead.

The individualism of modernity could of course find no use for the notion of tradition within its own conceptual scheme except as an adversary notion; it therefore all too willingly abandoned it to the Burkeans, who, faithful to Burke's own allegiance, tried to combine adherence in politics to a conception of tradition which would vindicate the oligarchical revolution of property of 1688 and adherence in economics to the doctrine and institutions of the free market. The theoretical incoherence of this mismatch did not deprive it of ideological usefulness. But the outcome has been that modern conservatives are for the most part engaged in conserving only older rather than later versions of liberal individualism. Their own core doctrine is as liberal and as individualist as that of self-avowed liberals.

A living tradition then is an historically extended, socially embodied argument, and an argument precisely in part about the goods which constitute that tradition.

[From *After Virtue* (Duckworth, London, 1981), 190, 203–6.]

MICHAEL SANDEL
....

117   Conceptions of Community

A theory of community whose province extended to the subject as well as the object of motivations would be individualistic in neither the conventional sense nor in Rawls'. It would resemble Rawls' conception in that the sense of community would be manifest in the aims and values of the participants—as fraternal sentiments and fellow-feeling, for example—but would differ from Rawls' conception in that community would describe not just a *feeling* but a mode of self-understanding partly constitutive of the agent's identity. On this strong view, to say that the members of a society are bound by a sense of community is not simply to say that a great many of them profess communitarian sentiments and pursue communitarian aims, but rather that they conceive their identity—the subject and not just the object of their feelings and aspirations—as defined to some extent by the community of which they are a part. For them, community describes not just what they *have* as fellow citizens but also what they *are*, not a relationship they choose (as in a voluntary association) but an attachment they discover, not merely an attribute but a constituent of their identity. In contrast to the instrumental and sentimental conceptions of community, we might describe this strong view as the constitutive conception.

Despite Rawls' resistance to the constitutive conception of community and the theory of the subject it requires, we have already seen how his language seems at times to carry him beyond the sentimental conception, as if implicitly to acknowledge what we have argued is the case, that his theory of justice depends ultimately for its coherence on precisely the intersubjective dimension he officially rejects. In the account of the difference principle we are told that the distribution of natural talents is best described as a 'common asset', and that in justice as fairness men agree to 'share one another's fate'. In the account of social union, the bounds between empirical, bodily persons seem more attenuated still. Human beings are said to have 'shared final ends', and to participate through community 'in the total sum of the realized natural assets of the others'. We are thus led 'to the notion of the community of humankind', whose boundaries can be imagined to extend even across time and space, 'for those widely separated by history and circumstance can nevertheless co-operate in realizing their common nature'. 'Only in social union is the individual complete', for it is here that 'we cease to be mere fragments'. The members of community 'participate in one another's nature', and 'the self is realized in the activities of many selves'.

It is difficult to know how seriously to take these 'intersubjective-sounding' passages, for much is couched in metaphor, and often the metaphor is mixed. Intersubjective and individualistic images appear in uneasy, sometime infelicitous combination, as if to betray the incompatible commitments contending within. Assets described as 'common' in one passage turn 'collective' in another. A conception in which men 'share one another's fate' is later re-described as a principle of 'reciprocity' and 'mutual benefit'. Those who 'participate in one another's nature' at the one point are said elsewhere more distantly to engage in 'associative activities'. And those who at one moment can overcome their partiality and realize their nature only in community later find their communitarian imperative reduced to the mere likelihood that they will join one or more associations and 'have at least some collective ends in this sense'. In perhaps the most conspicuously unsettled imagery of all, community is said at one point to consist in the fact that 'different persons with *similar* or *complementary* capacities may *co-operate so to speak* in *realizing* their *common* or *matching* nature' [emphasis added].

But as the distinction between the sentimental and constitutive conceptions of community suggests, the moral vocabulary of community in the strong sense cannot in all cases be captured by a conception that 'in its theoretical basis is individualistic'. Thus a 'community' cannot always be translated without loss to an 'association', nor an 'attachment' to a 'relationship', nor 'sharing' to 'reciprocating', nor 'participation' to 'co-operation', nor what is 'common' to what is 'collective'. Though Rawls' argument for the priority of plurality over unity may normally apply to the second of each of these pairs, it does not necessarily hold for the first. Where 'collective' assets imply endowments once separately held, now ceded to society as a whole, 'common' assets do not necessarily; they need not logically presuppose a prior individuation. And while 'reciprocity' implies a principle of exchange and hence a plurality of agents, the notion of 'sharing' may suggest a solidarity such that no exchange need be involved, as in sharing a joke, or an aspiration, or an understanding. And while 'association' and 'co-operation' typically presuppose the antecedent plurality of those who join together to associate or co-operate, 'community' and 'participation' may describe a form of life in which the members find themselves commonly situated 'to begin with', their commonality consisting less in relationships they have entered than in attachments they have found. [. . .]

Not egoists but strangers, sometimes benevolent, make for citizens of the deontological republic; justice finds its occasion because we cannot know each other, or our ends, well enough to govern by the common good alone. This condition is not likely to fade altogether, and so long as it does not, justice will be necessary. But neither is it guaranteed always to predominate, and in so far as it does not, community will be possible, and an unsettling presence for justice.

Liberalism teaches respect for the distance of self and ends, and when this distance is lost, we are submerged in a circumstance that ceases to be ours. But by seeking to secure this distance too completely, liberalism undermines its own insight. By putting the self beyond the reach of politics, it makes human agency an article of faith rather than an object of continuing attention and concern, a premise of politics rather than its precarious achievement. This misses the pathos of politics and also its most inspiring possibilities. It overlooks the danger that when politics goes badly, not only disappointments but also dislocations are likely to result. And it forgets the possibility that when politics goes well, we can know a good in common that we cannot know alone.

[From *Liberalism and the Limits of Justice* (Cambridge University Press, Cambridge, 1982), 150–2, 183.]

KARL MARX

118 **Work in Communist Society**

And finally, the division of labour offers us the first example of how, as long as man remains in natural society, that is, as long as a cleavage exists between the particular and the common interest, as long, therefore, as activity is not voluntarily, but naturally, divided, man's own deed becomes an alien power opposed to him, which enslaves him instead of being controlled by him. For as soon as the distribution of labour comes into being, each man has a particular, exclusive sphere of activity, which is forced upon him and from which he cannot escape. He is a hunter, a fisherman, a herdsman, or a critical critic, and must remain so if he does not want to lose his means of livelihood; while in communist society, where nobody has one exclusive sphere of activity but each can become accomplished in any branch he wishes, society regulates the general production and thus makes it possible for me to do one thing today and another tomorrow, to hunt in the morning, fish in the afternoon, rear cattle in the evening, criticise after dinner, just as I have a mind, without ever becoming hunter, fisherman, herdsman or critic. [. . .]

[From *The German Ideology*, ed. and introd. C. J. Arthur, (Lawrence & Wishart, London, 1970), 54. Written 1845–6.]

KARL MARX

119 **The Communist Manifesto**

Communism deprives no man of the power to appropriate the products of society; all that it does is to deprive him of the power to subjugate the labour of others by means of such appropriation.

It has been objected that upon the abolition of private property all work will cease, and universal laziness will overtake us.

According to this, bourgeois society ought long ago to have gone to the dogs through sheer idleness; for those of its members who work, acquire nothing, and those who acquire anything, do not work. The whole of this objection is but another expression of the tautology that there can no longer be any wage labour when there is no longer any capital. [. . .]

The charges against communism made from a religious, a philosophical, and, generally, from an ideological standpoint, are not deserving of serious examination.

Does it require deep intuition to comprehend that man's ideas, views and conceptions, in one word, man's consciousness, changes with every change in the conditions of his material existence, in his social relations and in his social life?

What else does the history of ideas prove, than that intellectual production changes its character in proportion as material production is changed? The ruling ideas of each age have ever been the ideas of its ruling class.

When people speak of ideas that revolutionize society, they do but express the fact that within the old society, the elements of a new one have been created, and that the dissolution of the old ideas keeps even pace with the dissolution of the old conditions of existence.

When the ancient world was in its last throes, the ancient religions were overcome by Christianity. When Christian ideas succumbed in the eighteenth century to rationalist ideas, feudal society fought its death battle with the then revolutionary bourgeoisie. The ideas of religious liberty and freedom of conscience merely gave expression to the sway of free competition within the domain of knowledge.

'Undoubtedly,' it will be said, 'religious, moral, philosophical and juridical ideas have been modified in the course of historical development. But religion, morality, philosophy, political science and law constantly survived this change.'

There are, besides, eternal truths, such as freedom, justice, etc., that are common to all states of society. But communism abolishes eternal truths, it abolishes all religions and all morality, instead of constituting them on a new basis; it therefore acts in contradiction to all past historical experiences.'

What does this accusation reduce itself to? The history of all past society has consisted in the development of class antagonisms, antagonisms that assumed different forms at different epochs.

But whatever form they may have taken, one fact is common to all past ages, viz., the exploitation of one part of society by the other. No wonder, then, that the social consciousness of past ages, despite all the multiplicity and variety it displays, moves within certain common forms, or general ideas, which cannot completely vanish except with the total disappearance of class antagonisms.

The communist revolution is the most radical rupture with traditional property relations; no wonder that its development involves the most radical rupture with traditional ideas.

But let us have done with the bourgeois objections to communism.

We have seen above, that the first step in the revolution by the working class is to raise the proletariat to the position of ruling class, to win the battle of democracy.

The proletariat will use its political supremacy to wrest, by degrees, all capital from the bourgeoisie, to centralize all instruments of production in the hands of the state, i.e., of the proletariat organized as the ruling class, and to increase the total of productive forces as rapidly as possible.

Of course, in the beginning, this cannot be effected except by means of despotic inroads on the rights of property, and on the conditions of bourgeois production; by means of measures, therefore, which appear economically insufficient and untenable, but which, in the course of the movement, outstrip themselves, necessitate further inroads upon the old social order, and are unavoidable as a means of entirely revolutionizing the mode of production.

These measures will of course be different in different countries.

Nevertheless, in the most advanced countries, the following will be pretty generally applicable.

1. Abolition of property in land and application of all rents of land to public purposes.

2. A heavy progressive or graduated income tax.

3. Abolition of all right of inheritance.

4. Confiscation of the property of all emigrants and rebels.

5. Centralization of credit in the hands of the state, by means of a national bank with state capital and an exclusive monopoly.

6. Centralization of the means of communication and transport in the hands of the state.

7. Extension of factories and instruments of production owned by the state; the bringing into cultivation of waste lands, and the improvement of the soil generally in accordance with a common plan.

8. Equal liability of all to labour. Establishment of industrial armies, especially for agriculture.

9. Combination of agriculture with manufacturing industries; gradual abolition of the distinction between town and country, by a more equable distribution of the population over the country.

10. Free education for all children in public schools. Abolition of children's factory labour in its present form. Combination of children's factory labour in its present form. Combination of education with industrial production, etc.

When, in the course of development, class distinctions have disappeared, and all production has been concentrated in the hands of a vast association of the whole nation, the public power will lose its political character. Political power, properly so called, is merely the organized power of one class for oppressing another. If the proletariat during its contest with the bourgeoisie is compelled, by the force of circumstances, to organize itself as a class; if, by means of a revolution, it makes itself the ruling class, and, as such, sweeps away by force the old conditions of production, then it will, along with these conditions, have swept away the conditions for the existence of class antagonisms and of classes generally, and will thereby have abolished its own supremacy as a class.

In place of the old bourgeois society, with its classes and class antagonisms, we shall have an association, in which the free development of each is the condition for the free development of all.

[From Karl Marx and Friedrich Engels, *Manifesto of the Communist Party*, in *The Revolutions of 1848* (Penguin, Harmondsworth 1973), 82, 85–7. First published 1848; first published in this translation 1888.]

KARL MARX

120   The Realm of Freedom

The realm of freedom really begins only where labour determined by necessity and external expediency ends; it lies by its very nature beyond the sphere of material production proper. Just as the savage must wrestle with nature to satisfy his needs, to maintain and reproduce his life, so must civilized man, and he must do so in all forms of society and under all possible modes of production. This realm of natural necessity expands with his development, because his needs do too; but the productive forces to satisfy these expand at the same time. Freedom, in this sphere, can consist only in this, that socialized man, the associated producers, govern the human metabolism with nature in a rational way, bringing it under their collective control instead of being dominated by it as a blind power; accomplishing it with the least expenditure of energy and in conditions most worthy and appropriate for their human nature. But this always remains a realm of necessity. The true realm of freedom, the development of human powers as an end in itself, begins beyond it, though it can only flourish with this realm of necessity as its basis. The reduction of the working day is the basic prerequisite.

[From *Capital*, vol. iii, trans. David Fernbach (Penguin, Harmondsworth, 1981) 958–9. First published 1894.]

OSCAR WILDE

121   The Soul of Man under Socialism

Individualism, then, is what through Socialism we are to attain. As a natural result, the State must give up all idea of government. It must give it up because, as a wise man once said many centuries before Christ, there is such a thing as leaving mankind alone; there is no such thing as governing mankind. All modes of government are failures. Despotism is unjust to everybody, including the despot, who was probably made for better things. Oligarchies are unjust to the many, and ochlocracies are unjust to the few. High hopes were once formed of democracy; but democracy means simply the bludgeoning of the people by the people for the people. It has been found out. I must say that it was high time, for all authority is quite degrading. It degrades those who exercise it, and degrades those over whom it is exercised. When it is violently, grossly, and cruelly used, it produces a good effect, by creating, or at any rate bringing out, the spirit of revolt and individualism that is to kill it. When it is used with a certain amount of kindness, and accompanied by prizes and rewards, it is dreadfully demoralizing. People, in that case, are less conscious of the horrible pressure that is being put on them, and so go through their lives in a sort of coarse comfort, like petted animals, without ever realizing that they are probably thinking other people's thoughts, living by other people's standards, wearing practically what one may call other people's second-hand clothes, and never being themselves for a single moment. 'He who would be free', says a fine thinker, 'must not conform.' And authority, by bribing people to conform, produces a very gross kind of overfed barbarism amongst us.

With authority, punishment will pass away. This will be a great gain—a gain, in fact, of incalculable value. As one reads history, not in the expurgated editions written for schoolboys and passmen, but in the original authorities of each time, one is absolutely sickened, not by the crimes that the wicked have committed, but by the punishments that the good have inflicted; and a community is infinitely more brutalized by the habitual employment of punishment than it is by the occasional occurrence of crime. It obviously follows that the more punishment is inflicted the more crime is produced, and most modern legislation has clearly recognized this, and has made it its task to diminish punishment as far as it thinks it can. Wherever it has really diminished it, the results have always been extremely good. The less punishment, the less crime. When there is no punishment at all, crime will either cease to exist, or, if it occurs, will be treated by physicians as a very distressing form of dementia, to be cured by care and kindness. For what are called criminals nowadays are not criminals at all. Starvation, and not sin, is the parent of modern crime. That indeed is the reason why our criminals are, as a class, so absolutely uninteresting from any psychological point of view. They are not marvellous Macbeths and terrible Vautrins. They are merely what ordinary respectable, commonplace people would be if they had not got enough to eat. When private property is abolished there will be no necessity for crime, no demand for it; it will cease to exist. Of course, all crimes are not crimes against property, though such are the crimes that the English law, valuing what a man has more than what a man is, punishes with the harshest and most horrible severity (if we except the crime of murder, and regard death as worse than penal servitude, a point on which our criminals, I believe, disagree). But though a crime may not be against property, it may spring from the misery and rage and depression produced by our wrong system of property-holding, and so, when that system is abolished, will disappear. When each member of the community has sufficient for his wants, and is not interfered with by his neighbour, it will not be an object of any interest to him to interfere with anyone else. Jealousy, which is an extraordinary source of crime in modern life, is an emotion closely bound up with our conceptions of property, and under Socialism and Individualism will die out. It is remarkable that in communistic tribes jealousy is entirely unknown.

Now as the State is not to govern, it may be asked what the State is to do. The State is to be a voluntary association that will organize labour, and be the manufacturer and distributor of necessary commodities. The State is to make what is useful. The individual is to make what is beautiful. And as I have mentioned the word labour. I cannot help saying that a great deal of nonsense is being written and talked nowadays about the dignity of manual labour. There is nothing necessarily dignified about manual labour at all, and most of it is absolutely degrading. It is mentally and morally injurious to man to do anything in which he does not find pleasure, and many forms of labour are quite pleasureless activities, and should be regarded as such. To sweep a slushy crossing for eight hours on a day when the east wind is blowing is a disgusting occupation. To sweep it with mental, moral, or physical dignity seems to me to be impossible. To sweep it with joy would be appalling. Man is made for something better than disturbing dirt. All work of that kind should be done by a machine.

And I have no doubt that it will be so. Up to the present, man has been, to a certain extent, the slave of machinery, and there is something tragic in the fact that as soon as man had invented a machine to do his work he began to starve. This, however, is, of course, the result of our property system and our system of competition. One man owns a machine which does the work of five hundred men. Five hundred men are, in consequence, thrown out of employment, and, having no work to do, become hungry and take to thieving. The one man secures the produce of the machine and keeps it, and has five hundred times as much as he should have, and probably, which is of much more importance, a great deal more than he really wants. Were that machine the property of all, everybody would benefit by it. It would be an immense advantage to the community. All unintellectual labour, all monotonous, dull labour, all labour that deals with dreadful things, and involves unpleasant conditions, must be done by machinery. Machinery must work for us in coal mines, and do all sanitary services, and be the stoker of steamers, and clean the streets, and run messages on wet days, and do anything that is tedious or distressing. At present machinery competes against man. Under proper conditions machinery will serve man. There is no doubt at all that this is the future of machinery; and just as trees grow while the country gentlemen is asleep, so while Humanity will be amusing itself, or enjoying cultivated leisure—which, and not labour, is the aim of man—or making beautiful things, or reading beautiful things, or simply contemplating the world with admiration and delight, machinery will be doing all the necessary and unpleasant work. The fact is, that civilization requires slaves. The Greeks were quite right there. Unless there are slaves to do the ugly, horrible, uninteresting work, culture and contemplation become almost impossible.

Human slavery is wrong, insecure, and demoralizing. On mechanical slavery, on the slavery of the machine, the future of the world depends. And when scientific men are no longer called upon to go down to a depressing East End and distribute bad cocoa and worse blankets to starving people, they will have delightful leisure in which to devise wonderful and marvellous things for their own joy and the joy of everyone else. There will be great storages of force for every city, and for every house if required, and this force man will concert into heat, light, or motion, according to his needs. Is this Utopian? A map of the world that does not include Utopia is not worth even glancing at, for it leaves out the one country at which Humanity is always landing. And when Humanity lands there, it looks out, and, seeing a better country, sets sail. Progress is the realization of Utopias.

[From 'The Soul of Man under Socialism', in *De Profundis and Other Writings* (Penguin, Harmondsworth, 1954), 30–4. First published 1891.]

ERNEST MANDEL

122 Productive Activity

But will this creative human activity, integrating theory and practice, leaving all mechanical and routine work to machines, passing from research to production and from the painter's studio to the site where a new town is being built amid the woods—will it still be 'labour'? This basic category of Maxist sociology and economics must in its turn be subjected to a critical analysis.

Labour is the fundamental characteristic of man. It is through labour that the human race appropriates its necessary means of life; it is labour which is at once the primary reason for, the product of and the cement of social relationships. Man does not become a social being in the anthropological sense of the word, does not acquire his normal physiological equipment, without a phase of 'active socialisation' which extends from his birth until puberty, if not until his physical and intellectual maturity.

But when the *need* to work in order to produce the means of life has gone, because machines by themselves carry out this work, what remains of labour as man's fundamental characteristic? Anthropology defines the concept of labour. What is, in fact, characteristic of man is *praxis*, action: 'Man is a creature so constituted physically that he can survive only by acting.'

Labour in the historical sense of the word, labour as it has been practised up to now by suffering and miserable mankind, condemned to earn their bread in the sweat of their brows, is only the most wretched, the most 'inhuman', the most 'animal' form of human *praxis*. Just as for Frederick Engels the entire history of class-divided humanity is only the pre-history of mankind, so labour in its traditional form is only the prehistoric form of *creative, all-sided human praxis*,

which no longer produces things but harmoniously developed human personalities.
After the withering away of the commodity, of value, money, classes, the state
and the social division of labour, fully-developed socialist society will bring
about the *withering-away of labour* in the traditional sense of the word.

The final purpose of socialism cannot be the humanisation of labour, any
more than it can be the improvement of wages or of the wage relationship;
there are only transitional stages, expedients and palliatives. A modern factory
will never constitute a 'normal' or 'human' setting for human life, no matter
how much the working day is shortened or the place and its machinery are
adapted to man's needs. The process of the humanisation of man will not be
completed until labour has withered away and given place to creative *praxis*
which is solely directed to the creation of human beings of all-round development.

For a long time, *homo faber*, man as producer of the instruments of labour,
has been put before us as the real creator of civilisation and of human culture.
Recently, writers have tried to show that science, and even philosophy itself, has
emerged progressively from productive labour in the strict sense, constantly
nourishing itself from practice. The Dutch historian Huizinga has, however,
sharply opposed this tradition, with his contrary conception, of *homo ludens*,
'man at play', as the real creator of culture.

Marxism, brilliantly confirmed by all present-day anthropology, and to a
large extent even by Freudian psychology, enables us to integrate these two currents of thought, each of which reflects a fundamental aspect of human history.
At the start, man was both *faber* and *ludens*. Scientific and artistic techniques
progressively separated off from production techniques; but, with their specialisation, a social division of labour became indispensable for an initial phase of
further progress. *Homo faber*, banished to outer darkness, has neither the resources nor the leisure for play, free creation, the spontaneous and disinterested
exercise of his faculties, which is the specific aspect of human *praxis*. *Homo ludens* has become, more and more, man of the privileged classes, that is, of the
possessing classes and those dependent on them.

But thereby he has in turn suffered a special kind of alienation: his play becomes increasing *sad play*, and to continues so even during the great centuries of
social optimism (for instance, the sixteenth and nineteenth centuries). Freed
from the constraint of routine work, reintegrated in the collective community,
socialist man will once again become both *faber* and *ludens*, increasingly *ludens*
and at the same time *faber*. Already today, attempts are being made to introduce
more and more 'play' into certain forms of work, and more and more 'serious
work' into play. The abolition of labour in the traditional sense of the word implies at the same time a new flowering of the chief productive force, the creative
energy of man himself. Material disinterestedness is crowned by the creative
spontaneity which brings together in the same eternal youth the playfulness of
children, the enthusiasm of the artist, and the '*eureka*' of the scientist.

For the bourgeoisie, property means freedom. In an 'atomised' society of commodity owners, this definition is broadly true; only a sufficient amount of property releases a man from the slavery of selling his labour-power to get the means of existence, from this condemnation to forced labour. This is why bourgeois philanthropists, no less than demagogues, ceaselessly call for the impossible 'deproletarisation' of the proletariat through the 'diffusion of property'.

Vulgar Marxists have taken out of its context a famous phrase of Hegel's, quoted by Engels, according to which freedom is merely 'the recognition of necessity.' They interpret it in the sense that socialist man will be the subject to the same 'iron economic laws' as capitalist man with the sole difference that, having become conscious of these laws, he will endeavour to 'use them to his advantage'.

This positivist variant of Marxism has nothing in common with the real humanist tradition of Marxist and Engels, with the boldness of their analysis and the profundity of their vision of the future. Marx and Engels both repeated more than once that the realm of freedom begins *where necessity ends*. Even in a socialist society, factory work would continue to be a *sad necessity*, which was felt as such; it is in one's leisure hours that real freedom unfolds itself. The more that labour in the traditional sense of the word withers away, the more it is replaced by a creative *praxis* of all-round-developed and socially integrated personalities. The more man frees himself from his needs by satisfying them, the more does 'the realm of necessity give place to the realm of freedom'.

Human freedom is not a 'freely accepted' constraint, nor is it a mass of instinctive and disorderly activities such as would degrade the individual. It is self-realisation of man which is an eternal becoming and an eternal surpassing, a continual enrichment of everything human, an all-round development of all facets of humanity. It is neither absolute rest nor 'perfect happiness', but, after thousands of years of conflicts unworthy of man, the beginning of the real 'human drama'. It is a hymn sung to the glory of man by men aware of their limitations who draw from this awareness the courage to overcome them. To the man of today it seems impossible to be both doctor and architect, machine-builder and atom-smasher. But who can speak of limitations that man will *never* be able to break through, man who is stretching out his arms towards the stars, who is on the brink of producing life in test-tubes, and who tomorrow will embrace the entire family of mankind in a spirit of universal brotherhood?

[From *Marxist Economic Theory*, trans. Brian Pearce, (Merlin, London, 1962), 683–6.]

1. Equality of opportunity removes obstacles to opportunity from which some people suffer and others don't. We can distinguish three forms of equality of opportunity, corresponding to three obstacles to opportunity which the three forms remove.

First, there is what might be called *bourgeois*, or *right-liberal*, equality of opportunity, the rock-bottom equality of opportunity of the modern liberal age. Bourgeois equality of opportunity removes socially constructed status restrictions on life chances, such as those under which a serf labours in a feudal society, and those from which a black person suffers in a racist society. This first equality of opportunity widens people's feasible sets by removing constraints caused by rights assignments and by social perceptions, of the illustrated kind.

Left liberal equality of opportunity, which goes beyond bourgeois equality of opportunity. For it sets itself against the constraining effect of social circumstances by which bourgeois equality of opportunity is undisturbed, namely, those circumstances of birth and upbringing that constrain not by assigning an inferior status to their victims, but by casting them into poverty and cognate types of deprivation. The deprivation target by left-liberal equality of opportunity derives immediately from a person's circumstances and does not depend for its constraining power on social perceptions or on assignments of superior and inferior rights. Policies promoting left-liberal equality of opportunity include head-start education for children from deprived backgrounds. When left-liberal equality of opportunity is fully achieved, people's fates are determined by their native talent and their choices, and, therefore, not at all by their social backgrounds.

Left-liberal equality of opportunity corrects for *social* disadvantage, but not for native, or *inborn*, disadvantage. Left-liberal equality of opportunity is therefore consistent with considerable inequality of outcome. *Socialist* equality of opportunity treats the inequality induced by native differences as no less unjust than that imposed by unchosen social backgrounds. Socialist equality of opportunity seeks to correct for *all* unchosen disadvantages, disadvantages, that is, for which the agent cannot herself reasonably be held responsible, whether they be disadvantages that reflect social misfortune or disadvantages that reflect natural misfortune. When socialist equality of opportunity prevails, differences of outcome reflect nothing but differences of taste and choice, not differences in natural and social capacities and powers.

So, for example, under socialist equality of opportunity income differences are acceptable when they reflect nothing but different income/leisure preferences. People differ in their tastes, not only across consumer items, but also between working only a few hours and consuming rather little on the one hand,

and working long hours and consuming rather more on the other. Preferences across income and leisure are not in principle different from preferences across apples and oranges, and there can be no objection to differences in people's benefits and burdens that reflect nothing but different preferences.

Let me spell out the analogy at which I have just gestured. A table is laden with apples and oranges. Each of us is entitled to take six pieces of fruit, with apples and oranges appearing in any combination to make up that six. Suppose, now, I complain that Sheila has five apples whereas I have only three. Then you extinguish my sense of grievance by pointing out that Sheila has only one orange whereas I have three, and that I could have had a bundle just like Sheila's had I sacrificed a couple of oranges. So, similarly, under a system where each gets the same income per hour, but can choose how many hours she works, the income/leisure trade-off is relevently like the apples/oranges trade-off: inequality of income no more represents inequality, as such, than having four apples rather than two represents inequality, as such.

Notice, then, that socialist equality of opportunity amounts to equality of outcome: no egalitarian could object to differences of outcome that reflect uses of equality of opportunity in this third sense, because these differences do not constitute inequalities in the benefits people get in life, save where those are truly their own responsibility. Accordingly, if the ideal of equality of opportunity is fully realised, equality of result ensues: 'inequalities' within the result would be ones that even the most radical egalitarian could accept. One regrettable aspect of New Labour's present stance is its pretence that there is a defensibly *socialist* conception of equality of opportunity which *doesn't* induce equality of outcome. I return to this point in section 4 below.

Now, you might think that, in light of what I have used the phrase 'socialist equality of opportunity' to denote, that phrase is a misnomer, and you *will* think it is a misnomer if, as a result of its customary employment in political rhetoric, the phrase 'equality of opportunity' has become riveted in your mind to the idea of (in some sense) fair competition for *unequal* outcomes. But while socialist equality of opportunity is not, *ex hypothesi*, equality of opportunity to get more than others can get, it is quite evidently equality of opportunity to live as one wants. Socialist equality of opportunity induces equality of result with respect to benefits and burdens in just the sense that apple-and-orange-tickets, which are sets of opportunities, induce equality of result with respect to the distribution of apples and oranges. Equality of opportunity for *unequal* positions gives way to equality of opportunity for *different but equal* positions when the unfairness objection to inequality of opportunity caused by social disadvantage is thought to generalise into an objection to inequality of opportunity caused by *any* disadvantage for which the agent is not herself responsible.

2. You and I and a whole bunch of other people go on a camping trip. We are friends. There is no hierarchy among us; our common aim is that each of us

should have a good time, doing whatever he or she likes best. Somebody fishes, somebody else prepares the food, and another person cooks it. People who hate cooking may do all the washing up, and so on. There are plenty of differences, but no inequalities to which anyone can have a principled objection.

On camping trips, and on certain small scale projects of other kinds, we cooperate within a concern that everybody has the same opportunity to flourish, insofar as the activity in question permits: in these contexts most people, even most anti-egalitarians, accept, indeed, take for granted, a norm of equality. The socialist aspiration is to realise that sort of equality and community in society as a whole. The difficulties facing achievement of that socialist ideal are awesome, but the negative epithets that are hurled at the ideal by New Labour, epithets like 'mechanical equality', or 'sameness of outcome', represent a semi-deliberate attempt to replace argument by rhetoric. There isn't sameness of outcome here in the relevant sense of a bland uniformity that is boring because everybody is wearing a Mao jacket.

The effort to realise the socialist ideal runs up against entrenched power and individual selfishness. Politically serious people must take those obstacles seriously. But they are not reasons to disparage the ideal itself. Disparaging the ideal leads to confusion, and confusion generates disorientation: there are contexts where the ideal *can* be pushed forward in education, in health, in housing, but is pushed forward less resolutely than it might be, because of a lack of clarity about what the ideal is.

3. Gordon Brown says that we *can't* deliver equality, or even move towards it. That infeasibility thesis depends on claims about the position of our society in relation to the international market that have been challenged. It also depends on claims about the taxability, in political terms, of better off people, even when problems of the international market have been set aside—and those claims about taxability have *also* been challenged. If, moreover, the claims about taxability are true, then they reflect an anti-egalitarian selfishness on the part of the better off that Labour Chancellors should challenge.

To be sure, politics is politics, and Labour's rhetoric has to offer something to middle class people, if it is going to be elected. But it doesn't have to offer to them what suits their own unreflective self-interest without qualification: being human beings, they are open to a degree of moral appeal.

Brown also says that we *shouldn't* seek equality, that it's not 'desirable'. The stance of Brown's *Guardian* article is thoroughly left-liberal. He says that 'Everyone should have the chance to bridge the gap between what they are and what they have it in them to become'; that we should 'get the best out of people'; that there is an 'equal right to realise potential'. As Brown intends these phrases, they foresee those with greater potential ending up better off than those with less. There might be more radical ways of interpreting Brown's phrases, but that is their only possible interpretation under the endorsement of inequality of outcome that Brown defends.

Is equality desirable? It is indeed undesirable when it is so construed that it contradicts socialist equality of opportunity, when, for example, it demands equal income regardless of different preferences about work and life-style. But socialist equality of opportunity *is* equality, and the position Brown counter-poses to that is unstable.

4. I say it is unstable because, so I believe, the only way to resist the move from left-liberal to socialist equality of opportunity, and, therefore, from left-liberal equality of opportunity to equality itself, is by affirming a principle which Brown and his allies are still too socialist to want to embrace. For consider. Brown endorses left-liberal equality of opportunity because be thinks it unfair that unchosen social disadvantage should operate to hold people back. But what, exactly, renders unchosen social disadvantage unjust? If it is the unchosen character of unchosen social disadvantage that renders it unjust, then, since natural disadvantage is equally unchosen, no one who affirms left-liberal equal-ity of opportunity on the stated basis (that is: unchosen social disadvantage is unjust because it is unchosen) can resist the move to socialist equality of oppor-tunity and, therefore and therefrom, to equality itself. That move can be re-sisted only by those who so distinguish between social and natural disadvantage that they can say that it is not *merely* its unchosen character that constitutes the injustice of social disadvantage. But what might the required distinction be? It must be that, while socially advantaged people have no right to the benefits of their good *social* fortune, naturally advantaged people do have a right to the benefits of *their* good *natural* fortune. Now that is certainly not unbelievable: it formulates something like the principle of self-ownership, which is a staple of right-wing thought. But a socialist of even a rather residual kind cannot happily invoke it in explanation of his resistance to socialist equality of opportunity. And that is why Brown's position is, so I claim, unstable.

5. Brown's policies, moreover, fall leagues short of the left-liberal ideal that he professes: he is not doing what he could do to promote left-liberal equality of opportunity. He has, for example, no intention of touching private schooling, which preserves and reinforces social disadvantage. Even common schooling for all, without special measures for the socially deprived, would contradict left-liberal equality of opportunity. Private healthcare would be attacked by a more courageously left-liberal regime. Inheritance would need to be curtailed. To claim to favour equality of opportunity in more than a merely bourgeois sense while countenancing all the facilities that enable relatively wealthy people to perpetuate their advantages down the generations is to display stupidity and / or dishonesty and / or self-deception.

It is evasive to say, as New Labourites do: 'We don't believe in redistribution of wealth, but we do believe in overcoming social exclusion', since it costs money to defeat social exclusion, and that money can't be got from the excluded. When sink schools create socially excluded people, you need programmes like New Directions in Lewisham which gives racially disadvantaged people who have had a terrible education a kind of bridge that leads to further education. It is fantastically expensive but very effective.

6. It is entirely Utopian to aspire to achieve socialist equality of opportunity within the foreseeable future, or even to aspire to achieve, soon, full left-liberal equality of opportunity. But much more could be done on behalf of both if Brown and company had half the courage with respect to attacking the better off that Margaret Thatcher showed in her attack on the badly off. There is little sign that Labour intends serious moves in reversal of the regressive redistribution of the Thatcher/Major years.

Suppose we settle for left-liberal equality of opportunity. Thereby forswearing equality itself, we might nevertheless look critically at the structure of the ladder of positions on which left-liberal equality of opportunity distributes people to higher and lower places. That ladder's rungs can be more or less distant from one another, and its top rung can be more or less distant from its bottom one. A socialist who professes herself against equality but for equality of opportunity believes in a ladder of outcomes, but she might nevertheless seek to reduce the length of that ladder, since, even though she thinks that there should be a ladder, she might recognise that there are many reasons for not accepting the ladder that the market produces. But no ladder-contracting intention is discernible in a Labour government whose leader smiles at millionaires, and who declares that 'consistent with the high quality of public services we need, you should be able to keep as much money as you have earned and spend it on what you like'.

[From 'Socialism and Equality of Opportunity', expanded version of 'Equality, Equality of Opportunity and the Labour Party', *Red Pepper* (Nov. 1997).]

FRIEDRICH NIETZSCHE

124 **The Impulse towards Justice**

The preponderance of an altruistic mode of valuation is the consequence of an instinct that one is ill-constituted. The value judgment here is at bottom: 'I am not worth much': a merely physiological value judgement; even more clearly: the feeling of impotence, the absence of the great affirmative feelings of power (in muscles, nerves, ganglia). This value judgment is translated into a moral or a religious judgment, according to the culture of this class (—the predominance of religious and moral judgments is always a sign of a lower culture—): it seeks to establish itself by relating to spheres in which it recognizes the concept 'value' in general. The interpretation by means of which the Christian sinner believes he understands himself is an attempt to justify his lack of power and self-confidence: he would rather consider himself guilty than feel bad for no reason: it is a symptom of decay to require interpretations of this sort at all.

In other cases, the underprivileged man seeks the reason not in his 'guilt' (as the Christian does), but in society: the socialist, the anarchist, the nihilist—in as much as they find their existence something of which someone must be *guilty*, they are still the closest relations of the Christian, who also believes he can better endure his sense of sickness and ill-constitutedness by finding someone whom he can make responsible for it. The instinct of revenge and *ressentiment* appears here in both cases as a means of enduring, as the instinct of self-preservation: just as is the preference for altruistic theory and practice.

Hatred of egoism, whether it be one's own (as with Christians) or another's (as with socialists), is thus revealed as a value judgment under the predominating influence of revenge; on the other hand, as an act of prudence for the self-preservation of the suffering by an enhancement of their feelings of cooperation and solidarity—

Finally, even that release of *ressentiment* in the judging, rejecting, punishing of egoism (one's own or another's) is also, as already indicated, an instinct of self-preservation on the part of the underprivileged. *In summa*: the cult of altruism is a specific form of egoism that regularly appears under certain physiological conditions.

When the socialist with a fine indignation demands 'justice,' 'right,' 'equal rights,' he is merely acting under the impress of his inadequate culture that cannot explain why he is suffering: on the other hand, he enjoys himself; if he felt better he would refrain from crying out: he would then find pleasure in other things. The same applies to the Christian: he condemns, disparages, curses the 'world'—himself not excluded. But that is no reason for taking his clamor seriously. In both cases we are in the presence of invalids who feel better for crying out, for whom defamation is a relief. [. . .]

One speaks of the 'profound unjustice' of the social pact; as if the fact that this man is born in favourable circumstances, that in unfavourable ones, were in itself an injustice; or even that it is unjust that this man should be born with these qualities, that man with those. Among the most honest of these opponents of society it is asserted: 'we ourselves, with all our bad, sick, criminal qualities, which we admit to, are only the inescapable *consequences* of a long suppression of the weak by the strong'; they make the ruling classes responsible for their characters. And they threaten, they rage, they curse; they become virtuous from indignation—they do not want to have become bad men, *canaille*, for nothing.

This pose, an invention of the last few decades, is also called pessimism, as I hear; the pessimism of indignation. Here the claim is made to judge history, to divest it of its fatality, to discover responsibility behind it, guilty men in it. For this is the rub: one needs guilty men. The underprivileged, the decadents of all kinds are in revolt on account of themselves and need victims so as not to quench their thirst for destruction by destroying themselves (—which would perhaps be reasonable). To this end, they need an appearance of justice, i.e., a theory through which they can shift the responsibility for their existence, for their being thus and thus, on to some sort of scapegoat. This scapegoat can be God—in Russian there is no lack of such atheists from *ressentiment*—or the social order, or education and training, or the Jews, or the nobility, or those who have turned out well in any way. 'It is a crime to be born in favorable circumstances; for thus one has disinherited the others, pushed them aside, condemned them to vice, even to *work*—How can I help it that I am wretched! But somebody must be responsible, *otherwise it would be unbearable!*'

In short, the pessimism of indignation invents responsibility in order to create a *pleasant* feeling for itself—revenge—'Sweeter than honey' old Homer called it.—

[From *The Will to Power*, trans. Walter Kaufmann and R. J. Hollingdale (Vintage, New York, 1967), 201–2, 400]

MICHEL FOUCAULT

125 Power/Knowledge

Schematically, we can formulate the traditional question of political philosophy in the following terms: how is the discourse of truth, or quite simply, philosophy as that discourse which *par excellence* is concerned with truth, able to fix limits to the rights of power? That is the traditional question. The one I would prefer to pose is rather different. Compared to the traditional, noble and philosophic question it is much more down to earth and concrete. My problem is rather this: what rules of right are implemented by the relations of power in the production of discourses of truth? Or alternatively, what type of power is susceptible of producing discourses of truth that in a society such as ours are endowed with such potent effects? What I mean is this: in a society such as ours, but basically in any society, there are manifold relations of power which permeate, characterise and constitute the social body, and these relations of power cannot themselves be established, consolidated nor implemented without the production, accumulation, circulation and functioning of a discourse. There can be no possible exercise of power without a certain economy of discourses of truth which operates through and on the basis of this association. We are subjected to the production of truth through power and we cannot exercise power except through the production of truth. This is the case for every society, but I believe that in ours the relationship between power, right and truth is organised in a highly specific fashion. If I were to characterise, not its mechanism itself, but its intensity and constancy, I would say that we are forced to produce the truth of power that our society demands, of which it has need, in order to function: we *must* speak the truth; we are constrained or condemned to confess or to discover the truth. Power never ceases its interrogation, its inquisition, its registration of truth: it institutionalises, professionalises and rewards its pursuit. In the last analysis, we must produce truth as we must produce wealth, indeed we must produce truth in order to produce wealth in the first place. In another way, we are also subjected to truth in the sense in which it is truth that makes the laws, that produces the true discourse which, at least partially, decides, transmits and itself extends upon the effects of power. In the end, we are judged, condemned, classified, determined in our undertakings, destined to a certain mode of living or dying, as a function of the true discourses which are the bearers of the specific effects of power.

So, it is the rules of right, the mechanisms of power, the effects of truth or if you like, the rules of power and the powers of true discourses, that can be said more or less to have formed the general terrain of my concern, even if, as I know full well, I have traversed it only partially and in a very zig-zag fashion. I should like to speak briefly about this course of research, about what I have considered as being its guiding principle and about the methodological imperatives and precautions which I have sought to adopt. As regards the general principle involved in a study of the relations between right and power, it seems to me that in Western societies since Medieval times it has been royal power that has provided the essential focus around which legal thought has been elaborated. It is in response to the demands of royal power, for its profit and to serve as its instrument or justification, that the juridical edifice of our own society has been developed. Right in the West is the King's right. Naturally everyone is familiar with the famous, celebrated, repeatedly emphasised role of the jurists in the organisation of royal power. We must not forget that the re-vitalisation of Roman Law in the twelfth century was the major event around which, and on whose basis, the juridical edifice which had collapsed after the fall of the Roman Empire was reconstructed. This resurrection of Roman Law had in effect a technical and constitutive role to play in the establishment of the authoritarian, administrative, and, in the final analysis, absolute power of the monarchy. And when this legal edifice escapes in later centuries from the control of the monarch, when, more accurately, it is turned against that control, it is always the limits of this sovereign power that are put in question, its prerogatives that are challenged. In other words, I believe that the King remains the central personage in the whole legal edifice of the West. When it comes to the general organisation of the legal system in the West, it is essentially with the King, his rights, his power and its eventual limitations, that one is dealing. Whether the jurists were the King's henchmen or his adversaries, it is of royal power that we are speaking in every case when we speak of these grandiose edifices of legal thought and knowledge.

There are two ways in which we do so speak. Either we do so in order to show the nature of the juridical armoury that invested royal power, to reveal the monarch as the effective embodiment of sovereignty, to demonstrate that his power, for all that it was absolute, was exactly that which befitted his fundamental right. Or, by contrast, we do so in order to show the necessity of imposing limits upon this sovereign power, of submitting it to certain rules of right, within whose confines it had to be exercised in order for it to remain legitimate. The essential role of the theory of right, from medieval times onwards, was to fix the legitimacy of power; that is the major problem around which the whole theory of right and sovereignty is organised.

[From 'Two Lectures', in *Power/Knowledge*, ed. Colin Gordon (Harvester Press, Brighton, 1980), 93–5.]

RICHARD RORTY

126 The Priority of Democracy to Philosophy

In our century, the rationalist justification of the Enlightenment compromise has been discredited. Contemporary intellectuals have given up the Enlightenment assumption that religion, myth, and tradition can be opposed to something ahistorical, something common to all human beings qua human. Anthropologists and historians of science have blurred the distinction between innate rationality and the products of acculturation. Philosophers such as Heidegger and Gadamer have given us ways of seeing human beings as historical all the way through. Other philosophers, such as Quine and Davidson, have blurred the distinction between permanent truths of reason and temporary truths of fact. Psychoanalysis has blurred the distinction between conscience and the emotions of love, hate, and fear, and thus the distinction between morality and prudence. The result is to erase the picture of the self common to Greek metaphysics, Christian theology, and Enlightenment rationalism: the picture of an ahistorical natural center, the locus of human dignity, surrounded by an adventitious and inessential periphery.

The effect of erasing this picture is to break the link between truth and justifiability. This, in turn, breaks down the bridge between the two sides of the Enlightenment compromise. The effect is to polarize liberal social theory. If we stay on the absolutist side, we shall talk about inalienable 'human rights' and about 'one right answer' to moral and political dilemmas without trying to back up such talk with a theory of human nature. We shall abandon metaphysical accounts of what a right is while nevertheless insisting that everywhere, in all times and cultures, members of our species have had the same rights. But if we swing to the pragmatist side, and consider talk of 'rights' an attempt to enjoy the benefits of metaphysics without assuming the appropriate responsibilities, we shall still need something to distinguish the sort of individual conscience we respect from the sort we condemn as 'fanatical.' This can only be something relatively local and ethnocentric—the tradition of a particular community, the consensus of a particular culture. According to this view, what counts as rational or as fanatical is relative to the group to which we think it necessary to justify ourselves—to the body of shared belief that determines the reference of the word 'we.' The Kantian identification with a central transcultural and ahistorical self is thus replaced by a quasi-Hegelian identification with our own community, thought of as a historical product. For pragmatist social theory, the question of whether justifiability to the community with which we identify entails truth is simply irrelevant.

Ronald Dworkin and others who take the notion of ahistorical human 'rights' seriously serve as examples of the first, absolutist, pole. John Dewey and, as I shall shortly be arguing, John Rawls serve as examples of the second pole. But there is a third type of social theory—often dubbed 'communitarianism'—which is less easy to place. Roughly speaking, the writers tagged with this label are those who reject both the individualistic rationalism of the Enlightenment and the idea of 'rights,' but, unlike the pragmatists, see this rejection as throwing doubt on the institutions and culture of the surviving democratic states. Such theorists include Robert Bellah, Alasdair MacIntyre, Michael Sandel, Charles Taylor, early Roberto Unger, and many others. These writers share some measure of agreement with a view found in an extreme form both in Heidegger and in Horkheimer and Adorno's *Dialectic of Enlightenment*. This is the view that liberal institutions and culture either should not or cannot survive the collapse of the philosophical justification that the Enlightenment provided for them.

There are three strands in communitarianism that need to be disentangled. First, there is the empirical prediction that no society that sets aside the idea of ahistorical moral truth in the insouciant way that Dewey recommended can survive. Horkheimer and Adorno, for example, suspect that you cannot have a moral community in a disenchanted world because toleration leads to pragmatism, and it is not clear how we can prevent, 'blindly pragmatized thought' from losing 'its transcending quality and its relation to truth.' They think that pragmatism was the inevitable outcome of Enlightenment rationalism and that pragmatism is not a strong enough philosophy to make moral community possible. Second, there is the moral judgment that the sort of human being who is produced by liberal institutions and culture is undesirable. MacIntyre, for example, thinks that our culture—a culture he says is dominated by 'the Rich Aesthete, the Manager, and the Therapist'—is a *reductio ad absurdum* both of the philosophical views that helped create it and of those now invoked in its defense. Third, there is the claim that political institutions 'presuppose' a doctrine about the nature of human beings and that such a doctrine must, unlike Enlightenment rationalism, make clear the essentially historical character of the self. So we find writers like Taylor and Sandel saying that we need a theory of the self that incorporates Hegel's and Heidegger's sense of the self's historicity.

The first claim is a straightforward empirical, sociological-historical one about the sort of glue that is required to hold a community together. The second is a straightforward moral judgment that the advantages of contemporary liberal democracy are outweighed by the disadvantages, by the ignoble and sordid character of the culture and the individual human beings that it produces. The third claim, however, is the most puzzling and complex. [. . .]

To evaluate this third claim, we need to ask two questions. The first is whether there is any sense in which liberal democracy 'needs' philosophical justification at all. Those who share Dewey's pragmatism will say that although it may need philosophical articulation, it does not need philosophical backup. On this view, the philosopher of liberal democracy may wish to develop a theory of the human self that comports with the institutions he or she admires. But such a philosopher is not thereby justifying these institutions by reference to more fundamental premises, but the reverse: He or she is putting politics first and tailoring a philosophy to suit. Communitarians, by contrast, often speak as though political institutions were no better than their philosophical foundations.

The second question is one that we can ask even if we put the opposition between justification and articulation to one side. It is the question of whether a conception of the self that, as Taylor says, makes 'the community constitutive of the individual' does in fact comport better with liberal democracy than does the Enlightenment conception of the self. Taylor summarizes the latter as 'an ideal of disengagement' that defines a 'typically modern notion' of human dignity: 'the ability to act on one's own, without outside interference or subordination to outside authority.' On Taylor's view, as on Heidegger's, these

Enlightenment notions are closely linked with characteristically modern ideas of 'efficacy, power, unperturbability.' They are also closely linked with the contemporary form of the doctrine of the sacredness of the individual conscience—Dworkin's claim that appeals to rights 'trump' all other appeals. Taylor, like Heidegger, would like to substitute a less individualistic conception of what it is to be properly human—one that makes less of autonomy and more of interdependence.

I answer 'no' to the first question about the communitarians' third claim and 'yes' to the second. Rawls, following up on Dewey, shows us how liberal democracy can get along without philosophical presuppositions. He has thus shown us how we can disregard the third communitarian claim. But communitarians like Taylor are right in saying that a conception of the self that makes the community constitutive of the self does comport well with liberal democracy. That is, if we *want* to flesh out our self-image as citizens of such a democracy with a philosophical view of the self, Taylor gives us pretty much the right view. But this sort of philosophical fleshing-out does not have the importance that writers like Horkheimer and Adorno, or Heidegger, have attributed to it.

[From 'The Priority of Democracy to Philosophy', in *Objectivity, Relativism and Truth: Philosophical Papers*, vol. i (Cambridge University Press, Cambridge, 1991), 176–9 (repr. from *The Virginia Statute for Religious Freedom*, ed. Merrill D. Peterson and Robert C. Vaughn (Cambridge University Press, Cambridge, 1988).]

Section VIII

Progress and Civilization

INTRODUCTION

The final section of the Reader takes up a pair of themes implicit in many of the earlier discussions: are human beings and civilization fit for each other, and in what ways do we make progress and at what cost? Rousseau, against the spirit of his own age, argues that progress in the arts and sciences has created a society of happy slaves. Civilization, despite its advantages, has produced a servile conformity. Adam Smith lays a more specific charge. While, without doubt, the division of labour has contributed enormously to human productive power and produced wealth undreamed of in earlier eras, it has had a diminishing effect on those who find themselves on a production line, performing just a few repetitive and simple tasks. The stimulation of the challenges of earlier, 'barbarous' times created a more inventive and alive human being. Schiller again develops a similar point. Compared to the Ancient Greeks, modern man is fragmented, lacking all-round development. But Schiller proposes a remedy: aesthetic education and the enjoyment of high art.

Karl Marx, greatly influenced by each of Rousseau, Smith, and Schiller, believes that only revolutionary economic and political change can restore human beings to the 'wholeness' for which we yearn. In this extract he lays out what he sees as the underlying forces of history which will eventually bring about the changes desired. Dostoevsky provides an interesting contrast in arguing that our one true instinct is to disrupt whatever patterns and systems are laid down for us: for this reason we will never achieve the high levels of civilization to which we aspire. Nevertheless, Engels continues Marx's project, explaining how our repressive capitalist society will transform itself into a liberating communist one. Weber resumes the theme of Schiller, poignantly terming our modern world a 'disenchanted' one.

Popper argues that Marx and Engels (as well as Plato and Hegel) are enemies of the open society, and in this selection he accuses the great majority of political thinkers of a form of utopianism, which will lead to violence if followed. The section ends with Fukuyama's reflection upon the thought that the increasing achievement and domination of liberal democracy throughout the globe has, in a sense, brought about the end of history.

127 The Effect of the Arts and Sciences

The mind, as well as the body, has its needs: those of the body are the basis of society, those of the mind its ornaments.

So long as government and law provide for the security and well-being of men in their common life, the arts, literature, and the sciences, less despotic though perhaps more powerful, fling garlands of flowers over the chains which weigh them down. They stifle in men's breasts that sense of original liberty, for which they seem to have been born; cause them to love their own slavery, and so make of them what is called a civilized people.

Necessity raised up thrones; the arts and sciences have made them strong. Powers of the earth, cherish all talents and protect those who cultivate them. Civilized peoples, cultivate such pursuits: to them, happy slaves, you owe that delicacy and exquisiteness of taste, which is so much your boast, that sweetness of disposition and urbanity of manners which make intercourse so easy and agreeable among you—in a word, the appearance of all the virtues, without being in possession of one of them.

It was this sort of refined civilization, all the more attractive for its apparent lack of ostentation, which distinguished Athens and Rome in those most celebrated days of their splendour and magnificence: and it is doubtless in the same respect that our own age and nation will excel all periods and peoples. An air of philosophy without pedantry; an address at once natural and engaging, distant equally from Teutonic rusticity and Italian pantomime; these are the effects of a taste acquired by liberal studies and improved by conversation with the world. What happiness would it be for those who live among us, if our external appearance were always a true mirror of our hearts; if decorum were but virtue; if the maxims we professed were the rules of our conduct; and if real philosophy were inseparable from the title of a philosopher! But so many good qualities too seldom go together; virtue rarely appears in so much pomp and state.

Richness of apparel may proclaim the man of fortune, and elegance the man of taste; but true health and manliness are known by different signs. It is under the homespun of the labourer, and not beneath the gilt and tinsel of the courtier, that we should look for strength and vigour of body.

External ornaments are no less foreign to virtue, which is the strength and activity of the mind. The honest man is an athlete, who loves to wrestle stark naked; he scorns all those vile trappings, which prevent the exertion of his strength, and were, for the most part, invented only to conceal some deformity.

Before art had moulded our behaviour, and taught our passions to speak an artificial language, our morals were rude but natural; and the different ways in which we behaved proclaimed at the first glance the difference of our dispositions. Human nature was not at bottom better then than now; but men found their security in the ease with which they could see through one another, and this advantage, of which we no longer feel the value, prevented their having many vices.

In our day, now that more subtle study and a more refined taste have reduced the art of pleasing to a system, there prevails in modern manners a servile and deceptive conformity; so that one would think every mind had been cast in the same mould. Politeness requires this thing; decorum that; ceremony has its forms, and fashion its laws, and these we must always follow, never the promptings of our own nature.

We no longer dare seem what we really are, but lie under a perpetual restraint; in the meantime the herd of men, which we call society, all act under the same circumstances exactly alike, unless very particular and powerful motives prevent them. Thus we never know with whom we have to deal; and even to know our friends we must wait for some critical and pressing occasion; that is, till it is too late; for it is on those very occasions that such knowledge is of use to us.

What a train of vices must attend this uncertainty! Sincere friendship, real esteem, and perfect confidence are banished from among men. Jealousy, suspicion, fear, coldness, reserve, hate, and fraud lie constantly concealed under that uniform and deceitful veil of politeness; that boasted candour and urbanity, for which we are indebted to the enlightened spirit of this age. We shall no longer take in vain by our oaths the name of our Creator; but we shall insult Him with our blasphemies, and our scrupulous ears will take no offence. We have grown too modest to brag of our own merits; but we do not scruple to decry those of others. We do not grossly outrage even our enemies, but artfully calumniate them. Our hatred of other nations diminishes, but patriotism dies with it. Ignorance is held in contempt; but a dangerous scepticism has succeeded it. Some vices indeed are condemned and others grown dishonourable; but we have still many that are honoured with the names of virtues, and it is become necessary that we should either have, or at least pretend to have them. Let who will extol the moderation of our modern sages, I see nothing in it but a refinement of intemperance as unworthy of my commendation as their deceitful simplicity.

Such is the purity to which our morals have attained; this is the virtue we have made our own. Let the arts and sciences claim the share they have had in this salutary work. I shall add but one reflection more; suppose an inhabitant of some distant country should endeavour to form an idea of European morals from the state of the sciences, the perfection of the arts, the propriety of our public entertainments, the politeness of our behaviour, the affability of our conversation, our constant professions of benevolence, and from those tumultuous assemblies of people of all ranks, who seem, from morning till night, to have no other care than to oblige one another. Such a stranger, I maintain, would arrive at a totally false view of our morality.

Where there is no effect, it is idle to look for a cause: but here the effect is certain and the depravity actual; our minds have been corrupted in proportion as the arts and sciences have improved. Will it be said, that this is a misfortune peculiar to the present age? No, gentlemen, the evils resulting from our vain curiosity are as old as the world. The daily ebb and flow of the tides are not more regularly influenced by the moon than the morals of a people by the progress of the arts and sciences. As their light has risen above our horizon, virtue has taken flight, and the same phenomenon has been constantly observed in all times and places. [. . .]

A wise man does not go in chase of fortune; but he is by no means insensible to glory, and when he sees it so ill distributed, his virtue, which might have been animated by a little emulation, and turned to the advantage of society, droops and dies away in obscurity and indigence. Preferring the agreeable arts to the useful ones must, in the long run, inevitably result in this; and this truth has been but too much confirmed since the revival of the arts and sciences. We have physicists, geometricians, chemists, astronomers, poets, musicians, and painters in plenty; but we have no longer a citizen among us; or if there be found a few scattered over our abandoned countryside, they are left to perish there unnoticed and neglected. Such is the condition to which those who give us our daily bread, and our children milk, are reduced, and such are our feelings towards them.

[From *A Discourse on the Arts and Sciences*, in *The Social Contract and Discourses*, trans. and introd. G. D. H. Cole (J. M. Dent, London, 1973), 4–8, 24. First published 1750.]

ADAM SMITH

128 Division of Labour

In the progress of the division of labour, the employment of the far greater part of those who live by labour, that is, of the great body of the people, comes to be confined to a few very simple operations; frequently to one or two. But the understandings of the greater part of men are necessarily formed by their ordinary employments. The man whose whole life is spent in performing a few simple operations, of which the effects too are, perhaps, always the same, or very nearly the same, has no occasion to exert his understanding, or to exercise his invention in finding out expedients for removing difficulties which never occur. He naturally loses, therefore, the habit of such exertion, and generally becomes as stupid and ignorant as it is possible for a human creature to become. The torpor of his mind renders him, not only incapable of relishing or bearing a part in any rational conversation, but of conceiving any generous, noble, or tender sentiment, and consequently of forming any just judgment concerning many even of the ordinary duties of private life. Of the great and extensive interests of his country he is altogether incapable of judging; and unless very particular pains have been taken to render him otherwise, he is equally incapable of defending his country in war. The uniformity of his stationary life naturally corrupts the courage of his mind, and makes him regard with abhorrence the irregular, uncertain, and adventurous life of a soldier. It corrupts even the activity of his body, and renders him incapable of exerting his strength with vigour and perseverance, in any other employment than that to which he has been bred. His dexterity at his own particular trade seems, in this manner, to be acquired at the expence of his intellectual, social, and martial virtues. But in every improved and civilized society this is the state into which the labouring poor, that is, the great body of the people, must necessarily fall, unless government takes some pains to prevent it.

It is otherwise in the barbarous societies, as they are commonly called, of hunters, of shepherds, and even of husbandmen in that rude state of husbandry which precedes the improvement of manufactures, and the extension of foreign commerce. In such societies the varied occupations of every man oblige every man to exert his capacity, and to invent expedients for removing difficulties which are continually occurring. Invention is kept alive, and the mind is not suffered to fall into that drowsy stupidity, which, in a civilized society, seems to benumb the understanding of almost all the inferior ranks of people. In those barbarous societies, as they are called, every man, it has already been observed, is a warrior. Every man too is in some measure a statesman, and can form a tolerable judgment concerning the interest of the society, and the conduct of those who govern it. How far their chiefs are good judges in peace, or good leaders in war, is obvious to the observation of almost every single man among them. In such a society indeed, no man can well acquire that improved and refined understanding, which a few men sometimes possess in a more civilized state. Though in a rude society there is a good deal of variety in the occupations of every individual, there is not a great deal in those of the whole society. Every man does, or is capable of doing, almost every thing which any other man does, or is capable of doing. Every man has a considerable degree of knowledge, ingenuity, and invention; but scarce any man has a great degree. The degree, however, which is commonly possessed, is generally sufficient for conducting the whole simple business of the society. In a civilized state, on the contrary, though there is little variety in the occupations of the greater part of individuals, there is an almost infinite variety in those of the whole society. These varied occupations present an almost infinite variety of objects to the contemplation of those few, who, being attached to no particular occupation themselves, have leisure and inclination to examine the occupations of other people. The contemplation of so great a variety of objects necessarily exercises their minds in endless comparisons and combinations and renders their understandings, in an extraordinary degree, both acute and comprehensive. Unless those few, however, happen to be placed in some very particular situations, their great abilities, though honourable to themselves, may contribute very little to the good government or happiness of their society. Notwithstanding the great abilities of those few, all the nobler parts of the human character may be, in a great measure, obliterated and extinguished in the great body of the people.

[From *An Inquiry into the Nature and Causes of the Wealth of Nations*, ed. Edwin Cannan (The Modern Library, New York, 1937), 302–4. First published 1776.]

FRIEDRICH SCHILLER

129 **Fragmentation and Aesthetic Education**

1. Have I not perhaps been too hard on our age in the picture I have just drawn? That is scarcely the reproach I anticipate. Rather a different one: that I have tried to make it prove too much. Such a portrait, you will tell me, does indeed resemble mankind as it is today; but does it not also resemble any people caught up in the process of civilization, since all of them, without exception, must fall away from Nature by the abuse of Reason before they can return to her by the use of Reason?

2. Closer attention to the character of our age will, however, reveal an astonishing contrast between contemporary forms of humanity and earlier ones, especially the Greek. The reputation for culture and refinement, on which we otherwise rightly pride ourselves *vis-à-vis* humanity in its merely natural state, can avail us nothing against the natural humanity of the Greeks. For they were wedded to all the delights of art and all the dignity of wisdom, without however, like us, falling a prey to their seduction. The Greeks put us to shame not only by simplicity to which our age is a stranger; they are at the same time our rivals, indeed often our models, in those very excellences with which we are wont to console ourselves for the unnaturalness of our manners. In fullness of form no less than of content, at once philosophic and creative, sensitive and energetic, the Greeks combined the first youth of imagination with the manhood of reason in a glorious manifestation of humanity.

3. At that first fair awakening of the powers of the mind, sense and intellect did not as yet rule over strictly separate domains; for no dissension had as yet provoked them into hostile partition and mutual demarcation of their frontiers. Poetry had not as yet coquetted with wit, nor speculation prostituted itself to sophistry. Both of them could, when need arose, exchange functions, since each in its own fashion paid honour to truth. However high the mind might soar, it always drew matter lovingly along with it; and however fine and sharp the distinctions it might make, it never proceeded to mutilate. It did indeed divide human nature into its several aspects, and project these in magnified form into the divinities of its glorious pantheon; but not by tearing it to pieces; rather by combining its aspects in different proportions, for in no single one of their deities was humanity in its entirety ever lacking. How different with us

Moderns! With us too the image of the human species is projected in magnified form into separate individuals—but as fragments, not in different combinations, with the result that one has to go the rounds from one individual to another in order to be able to piece together a complete image of the species. With us, one might almost be tempted to assert, the various faculties appear as separate in practice as they are distinguished by the psychologist in theory, and we see not merely individuals, but whole classes of men, developing but one part of their potentialities, while of the rest, as in stunted growths, only vestigial traces remain.

4. I do not underrate the advantages which the human race today, considered as a whole and weighed in the balance of intellect, can boast in the face of what is best in the ancient world. But it has to take up the challenge in serried ranks, and let whole measure itself against whole. What individual Modern could sally forth and engage, man against man, with an individual Athenian for the prize of humanity?

5. Whence this disadvantage among individuals when the species as a whole is at such an advantage? Why was the individual Greek qualified to be the representative of his age, and why can no single Modern venture as much? Because it was from all-unifying Nature that the former, and from the all-dividing Intellect that the latter, received their respective forms.

6. It was civilization itself which inflicted this wound upon modern man. Once the increase of empirical knowledge, and more exact modes of thought, made sharper divisions between the sciences inevitable, and once the increasingly complex machinery of State necessitated a more rigorous separation of ranks and occupations, then the inner unity of human nature was severed too, and a disastrous conflict set its harmonious powers at variance. The intuitive and the speculative understanding now withdrew in hostility to take up positions in their respective fields, whose frontiers they now began to guard with jealous mistrust; and with this confining of our activity to a particular sphere we have given ourselves a master within, who not infrequently ends by suppressing the rest of our potentialities. While in the one a riotous imagination ravages the hard-won fruits of the intellect, in another the spirit of abstraction stifles the fire at which the heart should have warmed itself and the imagination been kindled.

7. This disorganization, which was first started within man by civilization and learning, was made complete and universal by the new spirit of government. It was scarcely to be expected that the simple organization of the early republics should have survived the simplicity of early manners and conditions; but instead of rising to a higher form of organic existence it degenerated into a crude and clumsy mechanism. That polypoid character of the Greek States, in which every individual enjoyed an independent existence but could when need arose, grow into the whole organism, now made way for an ingenious clock-work, in

which, out of the piecing together of innumerable but lifeless parts, a mechanical kind of collective life ensued. State and Church, laws and customs, were now torn asunder; enjoyment was divorced from labour, the means from the end, the effort from the reward. Everlastingly chained to a single little fragment of the Whole, man himself develops into nothing but a fragment; everlastingly in his ear the monotonous sound of the wheel that he turns, he never develops the harmony of his being, and instead of putting the stamp of humanity upon his own nature, he becomes nothing more than the imprint of his occupation or of his specialized knowledge. But even that meagre, fragmentary participation, by which individual members of the State are still linked to the Whole, does not depend upon forms which they spontaneously prescribe for themselves (for how could one entrust to their freedom of action a mechanism so intricate and so fearful of light and enlightenment?); it is dictated to them with meticulous exactitude by means of a formulary which inhibits all freedom of thought. The dead letter takes the place of living understanding, and a good memory is a safer guide than imagination and feeling.

8. When the community makes his office the measure of the man; when in one of its citizens it prizes nothing but memory, in another a mere tabularizing intelligence, in a third only mechanical skill; when, in the one case, indifferent to character, it insists exclusively on knowledge, yet is, in another, ready to condone any amount of obscurantist thinking as long as it is accompanied by a spirit of order and law-abiding behaviour; when, moreover, it insists on special skills being developed with a degree of intensity which is only commensurate with its readiness to absolve the individual citizen from developing himself in extensity—can we wonder that the remaining aptitudes of the psyche are neglected in order to give undivided attention to the one which will bring honour and profit? True, we know that the outstanding individual will never let the limits of his occupation dictate the limits of his activity. But a mediocre talent will consume in the office assigned him the whole meagre sum of his powers, and a man has to have a mind above the ordinary if, without detriment to his calling, he is still to have time for the chosen pursuits of his leisure. Moreover, it is rarely a recommendation in the eyes of the State if a man's powers exceed the tasks he is set, or if the higher needs of the man of parts constitute a rival to the duties of his office. So jealously does the State insist on being the sole proprietor of its servants that it will more easily bring itself (and who can blame it?) to share its man with the Cytherean, than with the Uranian, Venus.

9. Thus little by little the concrete life of the Individual is destroyed in order that the abstract idea of the Whole may drag out its sorry existence, and the State remains for ever a stranger to its citizens since at no point does it ever make contact with their feeling. Forced to resort to classification in order to cope with the variety of its citizens, and never to get an impression of humanity except through representation at second hand, the governing section ends up by losing

sight of them altogether, confusing their concrete reality with a mere construct of the intellect; while the governed cannot but receive with indifference laws which are scarcely, if at all, directed to them as persons. Weary at last of sustaining bonds which the State does so little to facilitate, positive society begins (this has long been the fate of most European States) to disintegrate into a state of primitive morality, in which public authority has become but one party more, to be hated and circumvented by those who make authority necessary, and only obeyed by such as are capable of doing without it.

10. With this twofold pressure upon it, from within and from without, could humanity well have taken any other course than the one it actually took? In its striving after inalienable possessions in the realm of ideas, the spirit of speculation could do no other than become a stranger to the world of sense, and lose sight of matter for the sake of form. The practical spirit, by contrast, enclosed within a monotonous sphere of material objects, and within this uniformity still further confined by formulas, was bound to find the idea of an unconditioned Whole receding from sight, and to become just as impoverished as its own poor sphere of activity. If the former was tempted to model the actual world on a world conceivable by the mind, and to exalt the subjective conditions of its own perceptual and conceptual faculty into laws constitutive of the existence of things, the latter plunged into the opposite extreme of judging all experience whatsoever by one particular fragment of experience, and of wanting to make the rules of its own occupation apply indiscriminately to all others. The one was bound to become the victim of empty subtitles, the other of narrow pedantry; for the former stood too high to discern the particular, the latter too low to survey the Whole. But the damaging effects of the turn which mind thus took were not confined to knowledge and production; it affected feeling and action no less. We know that the sensibility of the psyche depends for its intensity upon the liveliness, for its scope upon the richness, of the imagination. The preponderance of the analytical faculty must, however, of necessity, deprive the imagination of its energy and warmth, while a more restricted sphere of objects must reduce its wealth. Hence the abstract thinker very often has a cold heart, since he dissects his impressions, and impressions can move the soul only as long as they remain whole; while the man of practical affairs often has a narrow heart, since his imagination, imprisoned within the unvarying confines of his own calling, is incapable of extending itself to appreciate other ways of seeing and knowing.

11. It was part of my procedure to uncover the disadvantageous trends in the character of our age and the reasons for them, not to point out the advantages which Nature offers by way of compensation. I readily concede that, little as individuals might benefit from this fragmentation of their being, there was no other way in which the species as a whole could have progressed. With the Greeks, humanity undoubtedly reached a maximum of excellence, which

could neither be maintained at that level nor rise any higher. Not maintained, because the intellect was unavoidably compelled by the store of knowledge it already possessed to dissociate itself from feeling and intuition in an attempt to arrive at exact discursive understanding; not rise any higher, because only a specific degree of clarity is compatible with a specific fullness and warmth. This degree the Greeks had attained; and had they wished to proceed to a higher stage of development, they would, like us, have had to surrender their wholeness of being and pursue truth along separate paths.

12. If the manifold potentialities in man were ever to be developed, there was no other way but to pit them one against the other. This antagonism of faculties and functions is the great instrument of civilization—but it is only the instrument; for as long as it persists, we are only on the way to becoming civilized. Only through individual powers in man becoming isolated, and arrogating to themselves exclusive authority, do they come into conflict with the truth of things, and force the Common Sense, which is otherwise content to linger with indolent complacency on outward appearance, to penetrate phenomena in depth. By pure thought usurping authority in the world of sense, while empirical thought is concerned to subject the usurper to the conditions of experience, both these powers develop to their fullest potential, and exhaust the whole range of their proper sphere. And by the very boldness with which, in the one case, imagination allows her caprice to dissolve the existing world-order, she does, in the other, compel Reason to rise to the ultimate sources of knowing, and invoke the law of Necessity against her.

13. One-sidedness in the exercise of his powers must, it is true, inevitably lead the individual into error; but the species as a whole to truth. Only by concentrating the whole energy of our mind into a single focal point, contracting our whole being into a single power, do we, as it were, lend wings to this individual power and lead it, by artificial means, far beyond the limits which Nature seems to have assigned to it. Even as it is certain that all individuals taken together would never, with the powers of vision granted them by Nature alone, have managed to detect a satellite of Jupiter which the telescope reveals to the astronomer, so it is beyond question that human powers of reflection would never have produced an analysis of the Infinite or a Critique of Pure Reason, unless, in the individuals called to perform such feats, Reason had separated itself off, disentangled itself, as it were, from all matter, and by the most intense effort of abstraction armed their eyes with a glass for peering into the Absolute. But will such a mind, dissolved as it were into pure intellect and pure contemplation, ever be capable of exchanging the rigorous bonds of logic for the free movement of the poetic faculty, or of grasping the concrete individuality of things with a sense innocent of preconceptions and faithful to the object? At this point Nature sets limits even to the most universal genius, limits which he cannot transcend; and as long as philosophy has to make its prime

business the provision of safeguards against error, truth will be bound to have its martyrs.

14. Thus, however much the world as a whole may benefit through this fragmentary specialization of human powers, it cannot be denied that the individuals affected by it suffer under the curse of this cosmic purpose. Athletic bodies can, it is true, be developed by gymnastic exercises; beauty only through the free and harmonious play of the limbs. In the same way the keying up of individual functions of the mind can indeed produce extraordinary human beings; but only the equal tempering of them all, happy and complete human beings. And in what kind of relation would we stand to either past or future ages, if the development of human nature were to make such sacrifice necessary? We would have been the serfs of mankind; for several millenia we would have done slaves' work for them, and our mutilated nature would bear impressed upon it the shameful marks of this servitude. And all this in order that a future generation might in blissful indolence attend to the care of its moral health, and foster the free growth of its humanity!

15. But can Man really be destined to miss himself for the sake of any purpose whatsoever? Should Nature, for the sake of her own purposes, be able to rob us of a completeness which Reason, for the sake of hers, enjoins upon us? It must, therefore, be wrong if the cultivation of individual powers involves the sacrifice of wholeness. Or rather, however much the law of Nature tends in that direction, it must be open to us to restore by means of a higher Art the totality of our nature which the arts themselves have destroyed.

[From *On the Aesthetic Education of Man: Sixth Letter*, trans. Elizabeth Wilkinson and L. A. Willoughby (Clarendon Press, Oxford, 1967), 31, 33, 35, 37, 39, 41, 43. First published 1795.]

KARL MARX

130 Development of the Productive Forces

What is society, whatever its form may be? The product of men's reciprocal action. Are men free to choose this or that form of society for themselves? By no means. Assume a particular state of development in the productive forces of man and you will get a particular form of commerce and consumption. Assume particular stages of development in production, commerce and consumption and you will have a corresponding social constitution, a corresponding organisation of the family, of orders or of classes, in a word, a corresponding civil society. Assume a particular civil society and you will get particular political conditions which are only the official expression of civil society.

It is superfluous to add that men are not free to choose their *productive forces*—which are the basis of all their history—for every productive force is an acquired force, the product of former activity. The productive forces are therefore the result of practical human energy; but this energy is itself conditioned by the circumstances in which men find themselves, by the productive forces already acquired, by the social form which exists before they do, which they do not create, which is the product of the preceding generation. Because of this simple fact that every succeeding generation finds itself in possession of the productive forces acquired by the previous generation, which serve it as the raw material for new production, a coherence arises in human history, a history of humanity takes shape which is all the more a history of humanity as the productive forces of man and therefore his social relations have been more developed. Hence it necessarily follows that the social history of men is never anything but the history of their individual development, whether they are conscious of it or not. Their material relations are the basis of all their relations. These material relations are only the necessary forms in which their material and individual activity is realised.

Men never relinquish what they have won, but this does not mean that they never relinquish the social form in which they have acquired certain productive forces. On the contrary, in order that they may not be deprived of the result attained, and forfeit the fruits of civilisation, they are obliged, from the moment when the form of their commerce no longer corresponds to the productive forces acquired, to change all their traditional social forms. I am using the word 'commerce' here in its widest sense, as we use *Verkehr* in German. For example: the privileges, the institution of guilds and corporations, the regulatory regime of the Middle Ages, were social relations that alone corresponded to the acquired productive forces and to the social condition which had previously existed and from which these institutions had arisen. Under the protection of the regime of corporations and regulations, capital was accumulated, overseas trade was developed, colonies were founded. But the fruits of this men would have forfeited if they had tried to retain the forms under whose shelter these fruits had ripened. Hence burst two thunderclaps—the Revolutions of 1640 and 1688. All the old economic forms, the social relations corresponding to them, the political conditions which were the official expression of the old civil society, were destroyed in England. Thus the economic forms in which men produce, consume, and exchange, are *transitory and historical*. With the acquisition of new productive faculties, men change their mode of production and with the mode of production all the economic relations which are merely the necessary relations of this particular mode of production.

[From 'Letter to Annenkov', in *The Poverty of Philosophy* (Progress Publishers, Moscow, 1955), 156–8. Written 1846.]

131 Our Self-Destructive Impulse

The point, gentlemen, is this: doesn't there, in fact, exist something that is dearer to almost every man than his own very best interests, or—not to violate logic—some best good (the one that is always omitted from the lists, of which we were speaking just now) which is more important and higher than any other good, and for the sake of which man is prepared if necessary to go against all the laws, against, that is, reason, honour, peace and quiet, prosperity—in short against all those fine and advantageous things—only to attain that primary, best good which is dearer to him than all else?

'Well, but then it is still a good,' you interrupt. By your leave, we will explain further, and the point is not in a play on words, but in the fact that this good is distinguished precisely by upsetting all our classifications and always destroying the systems established by lovers of humanity for the happiness of mankind. In short, it interferes with everything. But before I name this good, I want to compromise myself personally, and so I roundly declare that all these beautiful systems—these theories of explaining his best interests to man with the idea that in his inevitable striving to attain those interests he will immediately become virtuous and noble—are, in my opinion, nothing but sophistry! Really, to maintain the theory of the regeneration of the whole of mankind by means of a tabulation of his own best interests is in my opinion the same as . . . well, as to affirm with T. H. Buckle that civilization renders man milder and so less bloodthirsty and addicted to warfare. Logically, it appears that that ought to be the result. But man is so partial to systems and abstract deduction that in order to justify his logic he is prepared to distort the truth intentionally. This is why I take this example, because it is an extremely striking one. Look round you: everywhere blood flows in torrents, and what's more, as merrily as if it was champagne. There's our nineteenth century—and it was Buckle's century too. There's your Napoleon—both the great Napoleon and the present-day one. There's your North America—the everlasting Union. There is finally your grotesque Schleswig-Holstein. . . . And what softening effect has civilization had on us? Civilization develops in man only a many-sided sensitivity to sensations, and . . . definitely nothing more. And through the development of that many-sidedness man may perhaps progress to the point where he finds pleasure in blood. In fact, it has already happened. Have you noticed that the most refined shedders of blood have been almost always the most highly civilized gentlemen, to whom all the various Attilas and Stenka Razins could not have held a candle?—and if they are not so outstanding as Attila and Stenka Razin, it is because they are too often met with, too ordinary, too familiar. At least, if civilization has not made man more bloodthirsty, it has certainly made him viler in his thirst for blood than he was before. Before, he saw justice in bloodshed and massacred, if he had to, with a quiet conscience; now, although we consider bloodshed an abomination, we engage in it more than ever. Which is worse? Decide for yourselves. They say that Cleopatra (excuse my taking an example from Roman history) liked to stick golden pins into the breasts of her slaves, and took pleasure in their screams and writhings. You will say that that was in barbarous times, comparatively speaking; that even today the times are barbarous because (again speaking comparatively) pins are still being thrust into people; and that even now man, although he has learnt to see more clearly than in the days of barbarism, is still far from having grown accustomed to acting as reason and science direct. But all the same you are quite sure that he will inevitably acquire the habit, when certain bad old habits have altogether passed away, and common sense and science have completely re-educated and normally direct human nature. You are convinced that then men will of their own accord cease to make mistakes and refuse, in spite of themselves, as it were, to make a difference between their volition and their normal interests. Furthermore, you say, science will teach men (although in my opinion this is a superfluity) that they have not, in fact, and never have had, either will or fancy, and are no more than a sort of piano keyboard or barrel-organ cylinder; and that the laws of nature still exist on the earth, so that whatever man does he does not of his own volition but, as really goes without saying, by the laws of nature. Consequently, these laws of nature have only to be discovered, and man will no longer be responsible for his actions, and it will become extremely easy for him to live his life. All human actions, of course, will then have to be worked out by those laws, mathematically, like a table of logarithms, and entered in the almanac; or better still, there will appear orthodox publications, something like our encyclopaedic dictionaries, in which everything will be so accurately calculated and plotted that there will no longer be any individual deeds or adventures left in the world.

'Then,' (this is all of you speaking), 'a new political economy will come into existence, all complete, and also calculated with mathematical accuracy, so that all problems will vanish in the twinkling of an eye, simply because all possible answers to them will have been supplied. Then the Palace of Crystal will arise. Then. . . .' Well, in short, the golden age will come again. Of course it is quite impossible (here I am speaking myself) to guarantee that it won't be terribly boring then (because what can one do if everything has been plotted out and tabulated?), but on the other hand everything will be eminently sensible. Of course, boredom leads to every possible kind of ingenuity. After all, it is out of boredom that golden pins get stuck into people, but all this would not matter. What is bad (again this is me speaking) is that for all I know people may then find pleasure even in golden pins. Man, after all, is stupid, phenomenally stupid. That is to say, although he is not in the least stupid, he is so ungrateful that it is useless to expect anything else from him. Really I shall not be in the least surprised if, for example, in the midst of the future universal good sense, some gentleman with an ignoble, or rather a derisive and reactionary air, springs up suddenly out of nowhere, puts his arms akimbo and says to all of us, 'Come on, gentlemen, why shouldn't we get rid of all this calm reasonableness with one kick, just so as to send all these logarithms to the devil and be able to live our own lives at our own sweet will?' That wouldn't matter either, but what is really mortifying is that he would certainly find followers: that's the way men are made. And all this for the most frivolous of reasons, hardly worth mentioning, one would think: namely that a man, whoever he is, always and everywhere likes to act as he chooses, and not at all according to the dictates of reason and self-interest; it is indeed possible, and sometimes *positively imperative* (in my view), to act directly contrary to one's own best interests. One's own free and unfettered volition, one's own caprice, however wild, one's own fancy, inflamed sometimes to the point of madness—that is the one best and greatest good, which is never taken into consideration because it will not fit into any classification, and the omission of which always sends all systems and theories to the devil. Where did all the sages get the idea that a man's desires must be normal and virtuous? Why did they imagine that he must inevitably will what is reasonable and profitable? What a man needs is simply and solely *independent* volition, whatever that independence may cost and wherever it may lead. Well, but the devil only knows what volition . . .

[From *Notes from the Underground*, trans. Jessie Coulson (Penguin Books, Harmondsworth 1972), 30–4. First published 1864.]

FRIEDRICH ENGELS

132 Transition to Communism

If the crises demonstrate the incapacity of the bourgeoisie for managing any longer modern productive forces, the transformation of the great establishments for production and distribution into joint-stock companies, trusts and state property show how unnecessary the bourgeoisie are for that purpose. All the social functions of the capitalist are now performed by salaried employees. The capitalist has no further social function than that of pocketing dividends, tearing off coupons, and gambling on the Stock Exchange, where the different capitalists despoil one another of their capital. At first the capitalistic mode of production forces out the workers. Now it forces out the capitalists, and reduces them, just as it reduced the workers, to the ranks of the surplus population, although not immediately into those of the industrial reserve army.

But the transformation, either into joint-stock companies and trusts, or into state ownership, does not do away with the capitalistic nature of the productive forces. In the joint-stock companies and trusts this is obvious. And the modern state, again, is only the organisation that bourgeois society takes on in order to support the external conditions of the capitalist mode of production against the encroachments as well of the workers as of individual capitalists. The modern state, no matter what its form, is essentially a capitalist machine, the state of the capitalists, the ideal personification of the total national capital. The more it proceeds to the taking over of productive forces, the more does it actually become the national capitalist, the more citizens does it exploit. The workers remain wage-workers—proletarians. The capitalist relation is not done away with. It is rather brought to a head. But, brought to a head, it topples over. State ownership of the productive forces is not the solution of the conflict, but concealed within it are the technical conditions that form the elements of that solution.

This solution can only consist in the practical recognition of the social nature of the modern forces of production, and therefore in the harmonising of the modes of production, appropriation, and exchange with the socialised character of the means of production. And this can only come about by society openly and directly taking possession of the productive forces which have outgrown all control except that of society as a whole. The social character of the means of production and of the products to-day reacts against the producers, periodically disrupts all production and exchange, acts only like a law of Nature working blindly, forcibly, destructively. But with the taking over by society of the productive forces, the social character of the means of production and of the products will be utilised by the producers with a perfect understanding of its nature, and instead of being a source of disturbance and periodical collapse, will become the most powerful lever of production itself.

Active social forces work exactly like natural forces: blindly, forcibly, destructively, so long as we do not understand, and reckon with them. But when once we understand them, when once we grasp their action, their direction, their effects, it depends only upon ourselves to subject them more and more to our own will, and by means of them to reach our own ends. And this holds quite especially of the mighty productive forces of to-day. As long as we obstinately refuse to understand the nature and the character of these social means of action—and this understanding goes against the grain of the capitalist mode of production and its defenders—so long these forces are at work in spite of us, in opposition to us, so long they master us, as we have shown above in detail.

But when once their nature is understood, they can, in the hands of the producers working together, be transformed from master demons into willing servants. The difference is as that between the destructive force of electricity in the lighting of the storm, and electricity under command in the telegraph and the voltaic arc; the difference between a conflagration, and fire working in the service of man. With this recognition, at last, of the real nature of the productive forces of to-day, the social anarchy of production gives place to a social regulation of production upon a definite plan, according to the needs of the community and of each individual. Then the capitalist mode of appropriation, in which the product enslaves first the producer and then the appropriator, is replaced by the mode of appropriation of the products that is based upon the nature of the modern means of production; upon the one hand, direct social appropriation, as means to the maintenance and extension of production—on the other, direct individual appropriation, as means of subsistence and of enjoyment.

Whilst the capitalist mode of production more and more completely transforms the great majority of the population into proletarians, it creates the power which, under penalty of its own destruction, is forced to accomplish this revolution. Whilst it forces on more and more the transformation of the vast means of production, already socialised, into state property, it shows itself the way to accomplishing this revolution. *The proletariat seizes political power and turns the means of production into state property.*

But, in doing this, it abolishes itself as proletariat, abolishes all class distinctions and class antagonisms, abolishes also the state as state. Society thus far, based upon class antagonisms had need of the state. That is, of an organisation of the particular class which was *pro tempore* the exploiting class, an organisation for the purpose of preventing any interference from without with the existing conditions of production, and, therefore, especially, for the purpose of forcibly keeping the exploited classes in the condition of oppression corresponding with the given mode of production (slavery, serfdom, wage-labour). The state was the official representative of society as a whole; the gathering of it together into a visible embodiment. But it was this only in so far as it was the state of that class which itself represented, for the time being, society as a whole: in ancient times, the state of slave-owning citizens; in the Middle Ages, the feudal lords; in our own time, the bourgeoisie. When at last it becomes the real representative of the whole of society, it renders itself unnecessary. As soon as there is no longer any social class to be held in subjection; as soon as class rule, and the individual struggle for existence based upon our present anarchy in production, with the collisions and excesses arising from these, are removed, nothing more remains to be repressed, and a special repressive force, a state, is no longer necessary. The first act by virtue of which the state really constitutes itself the representative of the whole of society—the taking possession of the means of production in the name of society—this is, at the same time, its last independent act as a state. State interference in social relations becomes, in one domain after another, superfluous, and then dies out of itself; the government of persons is replaced by the administration of things, and by the conduct of processes of production. The state is not 'abolished'. *It dies out.* This gives the measure of the value of the phrase 'a free state', both as to its justifiable use at times by agitators, and as to its ultimate scientific insufficiency; and also of the demands of the so-called anarchists for the abolition of the state out of hand.

[From *Socialism Utopian and Scientific* (Progress Publishers, Moscow, 1954), 71–4. First published 1880, English translation 1892.]

133 **Disenchantment**

Scientific progress is a fraction, the most important fraction, of the process of intellectualization which we have been undergoing for thousands of years and which nowadays is usually judged in such an extremely negative way. Let us first clarify what this intellectualist rationalization, created by science and by scientifically oriented technology, means practically.

Does it mean that we, today, for instance, everyone sitting in this hall, have a greater knowledge of the conditions of life under which we exist than has an American Indian or a Hottentot? Hardly. Unless he is a physicist, one who rides on the streetcar has no idea how the car happened to get into motion. And he does not need to know. He is satisfied that he may 'count' on the behavior of the streetcar, and he orients his conduct according to this expectation; but he knows nothing about what it takes to produce such a car so that it can move. The savage knows incomparably more about his tools. When we spend money today I bet that even if there are colleagues of political economy here in the hall, almost every one of them will hold a different answer in readiness to the question: How does it happen that one can buy something for money—sometimes more and sometimes less? The savage knows what he does in order to get his daily food and which institutions serve him in this pursuit. The increasing intellectualization and rationalization do *not*, therefore, indicate an increased and general knowledge of the conditions under which one lives.

It means something else, namely, the knowledge or belief that if one but wished one *could* learn it at any time. Hence, it means that principally there are no mysterious incalculable forces that come into play, but rather that one can, in principle, master all things by calculation. This means that the world is disenchanted. One need no longer have recourse to magical means in order to master or implore the spirits, as did the savage, for whom such mysterious powers existed. Technical means and calculations perform the service. This above all is what intellectualization means.

Now, this process of disenchantment, which has continued to exist in Occidental culture for millennia, and, in general, this 'progress', to which science belongs as a link and motive force, do they have any meanings that go beyond the purely practical and technical? You will find this question raised in the most principled form in the works of Leo Tolstoi. He came to raise the question in a peculiar way. All his broodings increasingly revolved around the problem of whether or not death is a meaningful phenomenon. And his answer was: for civilized man death has no meaning. It has none because the individual life of civilized man, placed into an infinite 'progress,' according to its own imminent meaning should never come to an end; for there is always a further step ahead of one who stands in the march of progress. And no man who comes to die stands upon the peak which lies in infinity. Abraham, or some peasant of the past, died 'old and satiated with life' because he stood in the organic cycle of life; because his life, in terms of its meaning and on the eve of his days, had given to him what life had to offer; because for him there remained no puzzles he might wish to solve; and therefore he could have had 'enough' of life. Whereas civilized man, placed in the midst of the continuous enrichment of culture by ideas, knowledge, and problems, may become 'tired of life' but not 'satiated with life.' He catches only the most minute part of what the life of the spirit brings forth ever anew, and what he seizes is always something provisional and not definitive, and therefore death for him is a meaningless occurrence. And because death is meaningless, civilized life as such is meaningless; by its very 'progressiveness' it gives death the imprint of meaninglessness. Throughout his late novels one meets with this thought as the keynote of the Tolstoyan art.

What stand should one take. Has 'progress' as such a recognizable meaning that goes beyond the technical, so that to serve it is a meaningful vocation? The question must be raised. But this is no longer merely the question of man's calling *for* science, hence, the problem of what science as a vocation means to its devoted disciples. To raise this question is to ask for the vocation of science within the total life of humanity. What is the value of science? [. . .]

'Scientific' pleading is meaningless in principle because the various value spheres of the world stand in irreconcilable conflict with each other. The elder Mill, whose philosophy I will not praise otherwise, was on this point right when he said: If one proceeds from pure experience, one arrives at polytheism. This is shallow in formulation and sounds paradoxical, and yet there is truth in it. If anything, we realize again today that something can be sacred not only in spite of its not being beautiful, but rather because and in so far as it is not beautiful. You will find this documented in the fifty-third chapter of the book of Isaiah and in the twenty-first Psalm. And, since Nietzsche, we realize that something can be beautiful, not only in spite of the aspect in which it is not good, but rather in that very aspect. You will find this expressed earlier in the *Fleurs du mal*, as Baudelaire named his volume of poems. It is commonplace to observe that something may be true although it is not beautiful and not holy and not good. Indeed it may be true in precisely those aspects. But all these are only the most elementary cases of the struggle that the gods of the various orders and values are engaged in. I do not know how one might wish to decide 'scientifically' the value of French and German culture; for here, too, different gods struggle with one another, now and for all times to come.

We live as did the ancients when their world was not yet disenchanted of its gods and demons, only we live in a different sense. As Hellenic man at times sacrificed to Aphrodite and at other times to Apollo, and, above all, as everybody sacrificed to the gods of his city, so do we still nowadays, only the bearing of man has been disenchanted and denuded of its mystical but inwardly genuine plasticity. Fate, and certainly not 'science,' holds sway over these gods and their struggles. One can only understand what the godhead is for the one order or for the other, or better, what godhead is in the one or in the other order. With this understanding, however, the matter has reached its limit so far as it can be discussed in a lecture-room and by a professor. Yet the great and vital problem that is contained therein is, of course, very far from being concluded. But forces other than university chairs have their say in this matter.

[From 'Science as a Vocation' in *From Max Weber*, trans. and ed. H. H. Gerth and C. Wright Mills (Routledge & Kegan Paul, London, 1948), 138–40, 147–8. First published 1919.]

KARL POPPER

134 The Utopian Method

As far as I can see, Utopianism is the result of a way of reasoning which is accepted by many who would be astonished to hear that this apparently quite inescapable and self-evident way of reasoning leads to Utopian results. This specious reasoning can perhaps be presented in the following manner.

An action, it may be argued, is rational if it makes the best use of the available means in order to achieve a certain end. The end, admittedly, may be incapable of being determined rationally. However this may be, we can judge an action rationally, and describe it as rational or adequate, only relative to some given end. Only if we have an end in mind, and only relative to such an end, can we say that we are acting rationally.

Now let us apply this argument to politics. All politics consists of actions; and these actions will be rational only if they pursue some end. The end of a man's political actions may be the increase of his own power or wealth. Or it may perhaps be the improvement of the laws of the state, a change in the structure of the state.

In the latter case political action will be rational only if we first determine the final ends of the political changes which we intend to bring about. It will be rational only relative to certain ideas of what a state ought to be like. Thus it appears that as a preliminary to any rational political action we must first attempt to become as clear as possible about our ultimate political ends; for example the kind of state which we should consider the best; and only afterwards can we begin to determine the means which may best help us to realize this state, or to move slowly towards it, taking it as the aim of a historical process which we may to some extent influence and steer towards the goal selected.

Now it is precisely this view which I call Utopianism. Any rational and non-selfish political action, on this view, must be preceded by a determination of our ultimate ends, not merely of intermediate or partial aims which are only steps towards our ultimate end, and which therefore should be considered as means rather than as ends; therefore rational political action must be based upon a more or less clear and detailed description or blueprint of our ideal state, and also upon a plan or blueprint of the historical path that leads towards this goal.

I consider what I call Utopianism an attractive and, indeed, an all too attractive theory; for I also consider it dangerous and pernicious. It is, I believe, self-defeating, and it leads to violence.

That it is self-defeating is connected with the fact that it is impossible to determine ends scientifically. There is no scientific way of choosing between two ends. Some people, for example, love and venerate violence. For them a life without violence would be shallow and trivial. Many others, of whom I am one, hate violence. This is a quarrel about ends. It cannot be decided by science. This does not mean that the attempt to argue against violence is necessarily a waste of time. It only means that you may not be able to argue with the admirer of violence. He has a way of answering an argument with a bullet if he is not kept under control by the threat of counter-violence. If he is willing to listen to your arguments without shooting you, then he is at least infected by rationalism, and you may, perhaps win him over. This is why arguing is no waste of time—as long as people listen to you. But you cannot, by means of argument, make people listen to argument; you cannot, by means of argument, convert those who suspect all argument, and who prefer violent decisions to rational decisions. You cannot prove to them that they are wrong. And this is only a particular case, which can be generalized. No decision about aims can be established by *purely* rational or scientific means. Nevertheless argument may prove extremely helpful in reaching a decision about aims.

Applying all this to the problem of Utopianism, we must first be quite clear that the problem of constructing a Utopian blueprint cannot possibly be solved by science alone. Its aims, at least, must be given before the social scientist can begin to sketch his blueprint. We find the same situation in the natural sciences. No amount of physics will tell a scientist that it is the right thing for him to construct a plough, or an aeroplane, or an atomic bomb. Ends must be adopted by him, or given to him; and what he does *qua* scientist is only to construct means by which these ends can be realized. [. . .]

That the Utopian method, which chooses an ideal state of society as the aim which all our political actions should serve, is likely to produce violence can be shown thus. Since we cannot determine the ultimate ends of political actions scientifically, or by purely rational methods, differences of opinion concerning what the ideal state should be like cannot always be smoothed out by the method of argument. They will at least partly have the character of religious differences. And there can be no tolerance between these different Utopian religions. Utopian aims are designed to serve as a basis for rational political action and discussion, and such action appears to be possible only if the aim is definitely decided upon. Thus the Utopianist must win over, or else crush, his Utopianist competitors who do not share his own Utopian aims and who do not profess his own Utopianist religion.

[From *Conjectures and Refutations* (Routledge & Kegan Paul, London, 1963), 358–60.]

It is safe to say that the enormous historical pessimism engendered by the twentieth century has discredited most Universal Histories. The use of Marx's concept of 'History' to justify terror in the Soviet Union, China, and other communist countries has given that word a particularly sinister connotation in the eyes of many. The notion that history is directional, meaningful, progressive, or even comprehensible is very foreign to the main currents of thought of our time. To speak as Hegel did of World History is to invite sneers and bemused condescension from intellectuals who believe they grasp the world in all its complexity and tragedy. It is no accident that the only writers of Universal Histories who have achieved any degree of popular success in this century were those like Spengler and Toynbee who described the decline and decay of Western values and institutions.

But while our pessimism is understandable, it is contradicted by the empirical flow of events in the second half of the century. We need to ask whether our pessimism is not becoming something of a pose, adopted as lightly as was the optimism of the nineteenth century. For a naive optimist whose expectations are belied appears foolish, while a pessimist proven wrong maintains an aura of profundity and seriousness. It is therefore safer to follow the second course. But the appearance of democratic forces in parts of the world where they were never expected to exist, the instability of authoritarian forms of government, and the complete absence of coherent *theoretical* alternatives to liberal democracy force us to raise Kant's old question anew: Is there such a thing as a Universal History of mankind, taken from a point of view far more cosmopolitan than was possible in Kant's day? [. . .]

It is possible that if events continue to unfold as they have done over the past few decades, that the idea of a universal and directional history leading up to liberal democracy may become more plausible to people, and that the relativist impasse of modern thought will in a sense solve itself. That is, cultural relativism (a European invention) has seemed plausible to our century because for the first time Europe found itself forced to confront non-European cultures in a serious way through the experience of colonialism and de-colonization. Many of the developments of the past century—the decline of the moral self-confidence of European civilization, the rise of the Third World, and the emergence of new ideologies—tended to reinforce belief in relativism. But if, over time, more and more societies with diverse cultures and histories exhibit similar long-term patterns of development; if there is a continuing convergence in the types of institutions governing most advanced societies; and if the homogenization of mankind continues as a result of economic development, then the idea of relativism may seem much stranger than it does now. For the apparent differences between peoples' 'languages of good and evil' will appear to be an artifact of their particular stage of historical development.

Rather than a thousand shoots blossoming into as many different flowering plants, mankind will come to seem like a long wagon train strung out along a road. Some wagons will be pulling into town sharply and crisply, while others will be bivouacked back in the desert, or else stuck in ruts in the final pass over the mountains. Several wagons, attacked by Indians, will have been set aflame and abandoned along the way. There will be a few wagoneers who, stunned by the battle, will have lost their sense of direction and are temporarily heading in the wrong direction, while one or two wagons will get tired of the journey and decide to set up permanent camps at particular points back along the road. Others will have found alternative routes to the main road, though they will discover that to get through the final mountain range they all must use the same pass. But the great majority of wagons will be making the slow journey into town, and most will eventually arrive there. The wagons are all similar to one another: while they are painted different colors and are constructed of varied materials, each has four wheels and is drawn by horses, while inside sits a family hoping and praying that their journey will be a safe one. The apparent differences in the situations of the wagons will not be seen as reflecting permanent and necessary differences between the people riding in the wagons, but simply a product of their different positions along the road.

Alexandre Kojève believed that ultimately history itself would vindicate its own rationality. That is, enough wagons would pull into town such that any reasonable person looking at the situation would be forced to agree that there had been only one journey and one destination. It is doubtful that we are at that point now, for despite the recent worldwide liberal revolution, the evidence available to us now concerning the direction of the wagons' wanderings must remain provisionally inconclusive. Nor can we in the final analysis know, provided a majority of the wagons eventually reach the same town, whether their occupants, having looked around a bit at their new surroundings, will not find them inadequate and set their eyes on a new and more distant journey.

[From *The End of History and the Last Man* (Penguin, Harmondsworth, 1992), 69–70, 338–9.]

Appendix

Fundamental Political Documents

We end this book with an appendix containing a small number of funda-mental political documents. The five items selected here have each be-come cultural reference points; codifying the aims and aspirations of a people—or even all people. They have a particular resonance which remains undiminished.

The first is the US Declaration of Independence, in which the United States asserted its independence from Great Britain. It is a work of high literary, as well as political, power, adopted in Congress in 1776 unanimously by the then thir-teen states. The document was drafted by Thomas Jefferson, although slightly modified by Benjamin Franklin and John Adams, two other members of the 'committee of five' who had been instructed by Congress to draw up the decla-ration.

Jefferson also had a minor hand in the second document, the Declaration of the Rights of Man and of the Citizen, approved by the National Assembly of France in 1789, and signed under duress by King Louis XVI, very shortly before the French Revolution. It was drafted by The Marquis de Lafayette, with the help of Jefferson, then envoy to France. It did not, however, meet with universal approval, even among those sympathetic to the ideas of the revolutionaries. It is explicitly criticized in two of the earlier selections here: the selections from Bentham and Marx in the discussion of rights in Section IV.

The Bill of Rights, proposed to Congress in 1789 and ratified in 1791, consists of the first ten amendments to the US Constitution, and has, strangely enough, become a far more powerful expression of American constitutional expecta-tions than the Constitution itself. The amendments famously protect freedom of speech and the right to bear arms, among other legal protections and immu-nities. They are a constant reference point in American legal and political argu-ment. Later amendments include provisions for the abolition of slavery (1865), the prohibition of alcoholic drink (1919), votes for women (1920), and the repeal of prohibition (1933).

The Gettysburg Address, of 1863, is President Abraham Lincoln's speech at the dedication of the Gettysburg National Cemetery, which was provided to bury the Union victims of the battle of Gettysburg during the US Civil War. Al-though just two or three minutes in length, the speech has come to symbolize the pursuit of equality, freedom, and democracy.

We end with the more recent, and, arguably rather less stylishly written, Uni-versal Declaration of Human Rights, adopted by the United Nations in 1948, shortly after the Second World War. It differs from the earlier declarations in two main respects: first, it is intended to be global in scope, applying to all peoples on the earth; second, rather than merely concentrating on the attempt to protect individuals from the arbitrary intrusion of government, it offers a very wide range of rights. Article 15 gives everyone a right to a nationality; Article 23 the right to work and to free choice of employment; and Article 28 entitles everyone to a suitable social and international order to protect the other rights and freedoms. The degree to which the United Nations has been able to deliver to the people what their rights apparently entitle them to varies considerably between country and country, but nevertheless there remains work to be done almost everywhere.

The Unanimous Declaration of the Thirteen United States of America

When, in the course of human events, it becomes necessary for one people to dissolve the political bonds which have connected them with another, and to assume among the powers of the earth, the separate and equal station to which the laws of nature and of nature's God entitle them, a decent respect to the opinions of mankind requires that they should declare the causes which impel them to the separation.

We hold these truths to be self-evident, that all men are created equal, that they are endowed by their Creator with certain unalienable rights, that among these are life, liberty and the pursuit of happiness. That to secure these rights, governments are instituted among men, deriving their just powers from the consent of the governed. That whenever any form of government becomes destructive to these ends, it is the right of the people to alter or to abolish it, and to institute new government, laying its foundation on such principles and organizing its powers in such form, as to them shall seem most likely to effect their safety and happiness. Prudence, indeed, will dictate that governments long established should not be changed for light and transient causes; and accordingly all experience hath shown that mankind are more disposed to suffer, while evils are sufferable, than to right themselves by abolishing the forms to which they are accustomed. But when a long train of abuses and usurpations, pursuing invariably the same object evinces a design to reduce them under absolute despotism, it is their right, it is their duty, to throw off such government, and to provide new guards for their future security.—Such has been the patient sufferance of these colonies; and such is now the necessity which constrains them to alter their former systems of government. The history of the present King of Great Britain is a history of repeated injuries and usurpations, all having in direct object the establishment of an absolute tyranny over these states. To prove this, let facts be submitted to a candid world.

He has refused his assent to laws, the most wholesome and necessary for the public good.

He has forbidden his governors to pass laws of immediate and pressing importance, unless suspended in their operation till his assent should be obtained; and when so suspended, he has utterly neglected to attend to them.

He has refused to pass other laws for the accommodation of large districts of people, unless those people would relinquish the right of representation in the legislature, a right inestimable to them and formidable to tyrants only.

He has called together legislative bodies at places unusual, uncomfortable, and distant from the depository of their public records, for the sole purpose of fatiguing them into compliance with his measures.

He has dissolved representative houses repeatedly, for opposing with manly firmness his invasions on the rights of the people.

He has refused for a long time, after such dissolutions, to cause others to be elected; whereby the legislative powers, incapable of annihilation, have returned to the people at large for their exercise; the state remaining in the meantime exposed to all the dangers of invasion from without, and convulsions within.

He has endeavored to prevent the population of these states; for that purpose obstructing the laws for naturalization of foreigners; refusing to pass others to encourage their migration hither, and raising the conditions of new appropriations of lands.

He has obstructed the administration of justice, by refusing his assent to laws for establishing judiciary powers.

He has made judges dependent on his will alone, for the tenure of their offices, and the amount and payment of their salaries.

He has erected a multitude of new offices, and sent hither swarms of officers to harass our people, and eat out their substance.

He has kept among us, in times of peace, standing armies without the consent of our legislature.

He has affected to render the military independent of and superior to civil power.

He has combined with others to subject us to a jurisdiction foreign to our constitution, and unacknowledged by our laws; giving his assent to their acts of pretended legislation:

For quartering large bodies of armed troops among us:

For protecting them, by mock trial, from punishment for any murders which they should commit on the inhabitants of these states:

For cutting off our trade with all parts of the world:

For imposing taxes on us without our consent:

For depriving us in many cases, of the benefits of trial by jury:

For transporting us beyond seas to be tried for pretended offenses:

For abolishing the free system of English laws in a neighboring province, establishing therein an arbitrary government, and enlarging its boundaries so as to render it at once an example and fit instrument for introducing the same absolute rule in these colonies:

For taking away our charters, abolishing our most valuable laws, and altering fundamentally the forms of our governments:

For suspending our own legislatures, and declaring themselves invested with power to legislate for us in all cases whatsoever.

He has abdicated government here, by declaring us out of his protection and waging war against us.

He has plundered our seas, ravaged our coasts, burned our towns, and destroyed the lives of our people.

He is at this time transporting large armies of foreign mercenaries to complete the works of death, desolation and tyranny, already begun with circumstances of cruelty and perfidy scarcely paralleled in the most barbarous ages, and totally unworth the head of a civilized nation.

He has constrained our fellow citizens taken captive on the high seas to bear arms against their country, to become the executioners of their friends and brethren, or to fall themselves by their hands.

He has excited domestic insurrections amongst us, and has endeavoured to bring on the inhabitants of our frontiers, the merciless Indian savages, whose known rule of warfare, is undistinguished destruction of all ages, sexes and conditions.

In every stage of these oppressions we have petitioned for redress in the most humble terms: our repeated petitions have been answered only by repeated injury. A prince, whose character is thus marked by every act which may define a tyrant, is unfit to be the ruler of a free people.

Nor have we been wanting in attention to our British brethren. We have warned them from time to time of attempts by their legislature to extend an unwarranted jurisdiction over us. We have reminded them of the circumstances of our emigration and settlement here. We have appealed to their native justice and magnanimity, and we have conjured them by the ties of our common kindred to disavow these usurpations, which, would inevitably interrupt our connections and correspondence. We must, therefore, acquiesce in the necessity, which denounces our separation, and hold them, as we hold the rest of mankind, enemies in war, in peace friends.

We, therefore, the representatives of the United States of America, in General Congress, assembled, appealing to the Supreme Judge of the world for the rectitude of our intentions, do, in the name, and by the authority of the good people of these colonies, solemnly publish and declare, that these united colonies are, and of right ought to be free and independent states; that they are absolved from all allegiance to the British Crown, and that all political connection between them and the state of Great Britain, is and ought to be totally dissolved; and that as free and independent states, they have full power to levey war, conclude peace, contract alliances, establish commerce, and to do all other acts and things which independent states may of right do. And for the support of this declaration, with a firm reliance on the protection of Divine Providence, we mutually pledge to each other our lives, our fortunes and our sacred honor.

The representatives of the French people, organized as a National Assembly, believing that the ignorance, neglect, or contempt of the rights of man are the sole cause of public calamities and of the corruption of governments, have determined to set forth in a solemn declaration the natural, unalienable, and sacred rights of man, in order that this declaration, being constantly before all the members of the Social body, shall remind them continually of their rights and duties; in order that the acts of the legislative power, as well as those of the executive power, may be compared at any moment with the objects and purposes of all political institutions and may thus be more respected, and, lastly, in order that the grievances of the citizens, based hereafter upon simple and incontestable principles, shall tend to the maintenance of the constitution and redound to the happiness of all. Therefore the National Assembly recognizes and proclaims, in the presence and under the auspices of the Supreme Being, the following rights of man and of the citizen:

Articles

1. Men are born and remain free and equal in rights. Social distinctions may be founded only upon the general good.

2. The aim of all political association is the preservation of the natural and imprescriptible rights of man. These rights are liberty, property, security, and resistance to oppression.

3. The principle of all sovereignty resides essentially in the nation. No body nor individual may exercise any authority which does not proceed directly from the nation.

4. Liberty consists in the freedom to do everything which injures no one else; hence the exercise of the natural rights of each man has no limits except those which assure to the other members of the society the enjoyment of the same rights. These limits can only be determined by law.

5. Law can only prohibit such actions as are hurtful to society. Nothing may be prevented which is not forbidden by law, and no one may be forced to do anything not provided for by law.

6. Law is the expression of the general will. Every citizen has a right to participate personally, or through his representative, in its foundation. It must be the same for all, whether it protects or punishes. All citizens, being equal in the eyes of the law, are equally eligible to all dignities and to all public positions and occupations, according to their abilities, and without distinction except that of their virtues and talents.

7. No person shall be accused, arrested, or imprisoned except in the cases and according to the forms prescribed by law. Any one soliciting, transmitting, executing, or causing to be executed, any arbitrary order, shall be punished. But any citizen summoned or arrested in virtue of the law shall submit without delay, as resistance constitutes an offense.

8. The law shall provide for such punishments only as are strictly and obviously necessary, and no one shall suffer punishment except it be legally inflicted in virtue of a law passed and promulgated before the commission of the offense.

9. As all persons are held innocent until they shall have been declared guilty, if arrest shall be deemed indispensable, all harshness not essential to the securing of the prisoner's person shall be severely repressed by law.

10. No one shall be disquieted on account of his opinions, including his religious views, provided their manifestation does not disturb the public order established by law.

11. The free communication of ideas and opinions is one of the most precious of the rights of man. Every citizen may, accordingly, speak, write, and print with freedom, but shall be responsible for such abuses of this freedom as shall be defined by law.

12. The security of the rights of man and of the citizen requires public military forces. These forces are, therefore, established for the good of all and not for the personal advantage of those to whom they shall be intrusted.

13. A common contribution is essential for the maintenance of the public forces and for the cost of administration. This should be equitably distributed among all the citizens in proportion to their means.

14. All the citizens have a right to decide, either personally or by their representatives, as to the necessity of the public contribution; to grant this freely; to know to what uses it is put; and to fix the proportion, the mode of assessment and of collection and the duration of the taxes.

15. Society has the right to require of every public agent an account of his administration.

16. A society in which the observance of the law is not assured, nor the separation of powers defined, has no constitution at all.

17. Since property is an inviolable and sacred right, no one shall be deprived thereof except where public necessity, legally determined, shall clearly demand it, and then only on condition that the owner shall have been previously and equitably indemnified.

[Prepared by Gerald Murphy (The Cleveland Fee-Net aa300). Distributed by the Cybercasting Services Division of the National Public Telecomputing Network.]

138 **The Bill of Rights (1789)**

Amendment I

Congress shall make no law respecting an establishment of religion, or pro-hibiting the free exercise thereof; or abridging the freedom of speech, or of the press; or the right of the people peaceably to assemble, and to petition the government for a redress of grievances.

Amendment II

A well regulated militia, being necessary to the security of a free state, the right of the people to keep and bear arms, shall not be infringed.

Amendment III

No soldier shall, in time of peace be quartered in any house, without the consent of the owner, nor in time of war, but in a manner to be prescribed by law.

Amendment IV

The right of the people to be secure in their persons, houses, papers, and ef-fects, against unreasonable searches and seizures, shall not be violated, and no warrants shall issue, but upon probable cause, supported by oath or affir-mation, and particularly describing the place to be searched and the persons or things to be seized.

Amendment V

No person shall be held to answer for a capital, or otherwise infamous crime, unless on a presentment or indictment of a grand jury, except in cases arising in the land or naval forces, or in the militia, when in actual service in time of war or public danger; nor shall any person be subject for the same offense to be twice put in jeopardy of life or limb; nor shall be compelled in any crimi-nal case to be a witness against himself nor be deprived of life, liberty, or property, without due process of law; nor shall private property be taken for public use without just compensation.

Amendment VI

In all criminal prosecutions, the accused shall enjoy the right to a speedy and public trial, by an impartial jury of the state and district wherein the crime shall have been committed, which district shall have been previously ascer-tained by law, and to be informed of the nature and cause of the accusation; to be confronted with the witnesses against him; to have compulsory process for obtaining witnesses in his favor, and to have the assistance of counsel for his defense.

Amendment VII

In suits at common law, where the value in controversy shall exceed twenty dollars, the right of trial by jury shall be preserved, and no fact tried by a jury shall be otherwise re-examined in any court of the United States, than according to the rules of the common law.

Amendment VIII

Excessive bail shall not be required, nor excessive fines imposed, nor cruel and unusual punishments inflicted.

Amendment IX

The enumeration in the Constitution of certain rights shall not be construed to deny or disparage others retained by the people.

Amendment X

The powers not delegated to the United States by the Constitution, nor prohibited by it to the states, are reserved to the states respectively, or to the people.

139 The Gettysburg Address (1863)

Four score and seven years ago our fathers brought forth on this continent a new nation, conceived in liberty and dedicated to the proposition that all men are created equal. Now we are engaged in a great civil war, testing whether that nation or any nation so conceived and so dedicated can long endure. We are met on a great battlefield of that war. We have come to dedicate a portion of that field as a final resting-place for those who here gave their lives that that nation might live. It is altogether fitting and proper that we should do this. But in a larger sense, we cannot dedicate, we cannot consecrate, we cannot hallow this ground. The brave men, living and dead who struggled here have consecrated it far above our poor power to add or detract. The world will little note nor long remember what we say here, but it can never forget what they did here. It is for us the living rather to be dedicated here to the unfinished work which they who fought here have thus far so nobly advanced. It is rather for us to be here dedicated to the great task remaining before us—that from these honored dead we take increased devotion to that cause for which they gave the last full measure of devotion—that we here highly resolve that these dead shall not have died in vain, that this nation under God shall have a new birth of freedom, and that government of the people, by the people, for the people shall not perish from the earth.

[Prepared by Gerald Murphy (The Cleveland Fee-Net aa300). Distributed by the Cybercasting Services Division of the National Public Telecomputing Network.]

140   United Nations Universal Declaration of Human Rights (1948)

Preamble

Whereas recognition of the inherent dignity and of the equal and inalienable rights of all members of the human family is the foundation of freedom, justice and peace in the world,

Whereas disregard and contempt for human rights have resulted in barbarous acts which have outraged the conscience of mankind, and the advent of a world in which human beings shall enjoy freedom of speech and belief and freedom from fear and want has been proclaimed as the highest aspiration of the common people,

Whereas it is essential, if man is not to be compelled to have recourse, as a last resort, to rebellion against tyranny and oppression, that human rights should be protected by the rule of law,

Whereas it is essential to promote the development of friendly relations between nations,

Whereas the peoples of the *United Nations* have in the *Charter* reaffirmed their faith in fundamental human rights, in the dignity and worth of the human person and in the equal rights of men and women and have determined to promote social progress and better standards of life in larger freedom,

Whereas *Member States* have pledged themselves to achieve, in co-operation with the United Nations, the promotion of universal respect for and observance of human rights and fundamental freedoms,

Whereas a common understanding of these rights and freedoms is of the greatest importance for the full realization of this pledge,

Now, Therefore,

The General Assembly

proclaims

THIS UNIVERSAL DECLARATION OF HUMAN RIGHTS as a common standard of achievement for all peoples and all nations, to the end that every individual and every organ of society, keeping this Declaration constantly in mind, shall strive by teaching and education to promote respect for these rights and freedoms and by progressive measures, national and international, to secure their universal and effective recognition and observance, both among the peoples of Member States themselves and among the peoples of territories under their jurisdiction.

Article 1. All human beings are born free and equal in dignity and rights. They are endowed with reason and conscience and should act towards one another in a spirit of brotherhood.

Article 2. Everyone is entitled to all the rights and freedoms set forth in this Declaration, without distinction of any kind, such as race, colour, sex, language, religion, political or other opinion, national or social origin, property, birth or other status.

Furthermore, no distinction shall be made on the basis of the political, jurisdictional or international status of the country or territory to which a person belongs, whether it be independent, trust, non-self-governing or under any other limitation of sovereignty.

Article 3. Everyone has the right to life, liberty and security of person.

Article 4. No one shall be held in slavery or servitude; slavery and the slave trade shall be prohibited in all their forms.

Article 5. No one shall be subjected to torture or to cruel, inhuman or degrading treatment or punishment.

Article 6. Everyone has the right to recognition everywhere as a person before the law.

Article 7. All are equal before the law and are entitled without any discrimination to equal protection of the law. All are entitled to equal protection against any discrimination in violation of this Declaration and against any incitement to such discrimination.

Article 8. Everyone has the right to an effective remedy by the competent national tribunals for acts violating the fundamental rights granted him by the constitution or by law.

Article 9. No one shall be subjected to arbitrary arrest, detention or exile.

Article 10. Everyone is entitled in full equality to a fair and public hearing by an independent and impartial tribunal, in the determination of his rights and obligations and of any criminal charge against him.

Article 11. (1) Everyone charged with a penal offence has the right to be presumed innocent until proved guilty according to law in a public trial at which he has had all the guarantees necessary for his defence.

(2) No one shall be held guilty of any penal offence on account of any act or omission which did not constitute a penal offence, under national or international law, at the time when it was committed. Nor shall a heavier penalty be imposed than the one that was applicable at the time the penal offence was committed.

Article 12. No one shall be subjected to arbitrary interference with his privacy, family, home or correspondence, nor to attacks upon his honour and reputation. Everyone has the right to the protection of the law against such interference or attacks.

Article 13. (1) Everyone has the right to freedom of movement and residence within the borders of each state.

(2) Everyone has the right to leave any country, including his own, and to return to his country.

Article 14. (1) Everyone has the right to seek and to enjoy in other countries asylum from persecution.

(2) This right may not be invoked in the case of prosecutions genuinely arising from non-political crimes or from acts contrary to the purposes and principles of the United Nations.

Article 15. (1) Everyone has the right to a nationality.

(2) No one shall be arbitrarily deprived of his nationality nor denied the right to change his nationality.

Article 16. (1) Men and women at full age, without any limitation due to race, nationality or religion, have the right to marry and to found a family. They are entitled to equal rights as to marriage, during marriage and at its dissolution.

(2) Marriage shall be entered into only with the free and full consent of the intending spouses.

(3) The family is the natural and fundamental group unit of society and is entitled to protection by society and the State.

Article 17. (1) Everyone has the right to own property alone as well as in association with others.

(2) No one shall be arbitrarily deprived of his property.

Article 18. Everyone has the right to freedom of thought, conscience and religion; this right includes freedom to change his religion or belief, and freedom, either alone or in community with others and in public or private, to manifest his religion or belief in teaching, practice, worship and observance.

Article 19. Everyone has the right to freedom of opinion and expression; this right includes freedom to hold opinions without interference and to seek, receive and impart information and ideas through any media and regardless of frontiers.

Article 20. (1) Everyone has the right to freedom of peaceful assembly and association.

(2) No one may be compelled to belong to an association.

Article 21. (1) Everyone has the right to take part in the government of his country, directly or through freely chosen representatives.

(2) Everyone has the right of equal access to public service in his country.

(3) The will of the people shall be the basis of the authority of government; this will shall be expressed in periodic and genuine elections which shall be by

universal and equal suffrage and shall be held by secret vote or by equivalent free voting procedures.

Article 22. Everyone, as a member of society, has the right to social security and is entitled to realization, through national effort and international cooperation and in accordance with the organization and resources of each State, of the economic, social and cultural rights indispensable for his dignity and the free development of his personality.

Article 23. (1) Everyone has the right to work, to free choice of employment, to just and favourable conditions of work and to protection against unemployment.

(2) Everyone, without any discrimination, has the right to equal pay for equal work.

(3) Everyone who works has the right to just and favourable remuneration ensuring for himself and his family an existence worthy of human dignity, and supplemented, if necessary, by other means of social protection.

(4) Everyone has the right to form and to join trade unions for the protection of his interests.

Article 24. Everyone has the right to rest and leisure, including reasonable limitation of working hours and periodic holidays with pay.

Article 25. (1) Everyone has the right to a standard of living adequate for the health and well-being of himself and of his family, including food, clothing, housing and medical care and necessary social services, and the right to security in the event of unemployment, sickness, disability, widowhood, old age or other lack of livelihood in circumstances beyond his control.

(2) Motherhood and childhood are entitled to special care and assistance. All children, whether born in or out of wedlock, shall enjoy the same social protection.

Article 26. (1) Everyone has the right to education. Education shall be free, at least in the elementary and fundamental stages. Elementary education shall be compulsory. Technical and professional education shall be made generally available and higher education shall be equally accessible to all on the basis of merit.

(2) Education shall be directed to the full development of the human personality and to the strengthening of respect for human rights and fundamental freedoms. It shall promote understanding, tolerance and friendship among all nations, racial or religious groups, and shall further the activities of the United Nations for the maintenance of peace.

(3) Parents have a prior right to choose the kind of education that shall be given to their children.

Article 27. (1) Everyone has the right freely to participate in the cultural life of the community, to enjoy the arts and to share in scientific advancement and its benefits.

(2) Everyone has the right to the protection of the moral and material interests resulting from any scientific, literary or artistic production of which he is the author.

Article 28. Everyone is entitled to a social and international order in which the rights and freedoms set forth in this Declaration can be fully realized.

Article 29. (1) Everyone has duties to the community in which alone the free and full development of his personality is possible.

(2) In the exercise of his rights and freedoms, everyone shall be subject only to such limitations as are determined by law solely for the purpose of securing due recognition and respect for the rights and freedoms of others and of meeting the just requirements of morality, public order and the general welfare in a democratic society.

(3) These rights and freedoms may in no case he exercised contrary to the purposes and principles of the United Nations.

Article 30. Nothing in this Declaration may be interpreted as implying for any State, group or person any right to engage in any activity or to perform any act aimed at the destruction of any of the rights and freedoms set forth herein.

Adopted December 10, 1948

Notes

Extract 65

QUENTIN SKINNER: *The Republican Ideal of Political Liberty*

1. Alasdair MacIntyre, *After Virtue* (London, 1981), p. 241.
2. The ensuing argument constitutes an adapted and extended version of my article 'The paradoxes of political liberty' in *The Tanner Lectures on Human Values*, vol. vii, 1986, ed. Sterling M. McMurrin (Cambridge, 1986), pp. 225–50.
3. See Douglas G. Long, *Bentham on Liberty* (Toronto, 1977), p. 74, for Bentham speaking of liberty as 'an idea purely negative.' Berlin uses the formula in his classic essay, 'Two concepts of liberty', in *Four Essays on Liberty* (Oxford, 1969), at p. 121 and *passim*.
4. For freedom as the non-restriction of options, see, for example, S.I. Benn and W. Weinstein, 'Being free to act, and being a free man', *Mind*, 80 (1971), 194–211. Cf. also John N. Gray, 'On negative and positive liberty', *Political Studies*, 28 (1980), 507–26, who argues (esp. p. 519) that this is how Berlin's argument in his 'Two concepts' essay (cited in note 3 above) is best understood. For the stricter suggestion that we should speak only of freedom to choose between alternatives, see, for example, Felix Oppenheim, *Political Concepts: A Reconstruction* (Oxford, 1981), ch. 4, pp. 53–81. For a defence of the even narrower Hobbesian claim that freedom consists in the mere absence of external impediments, see Hillel Steiner, 'Individual liberty', *Proceedings of the Aristotelian Society*, 75 (1975), 33–50. This interpretation of the concept of constraint is partly endorsed by Michael Taylor, *Community, Anarchy and Liberty* (Cambridge, 1982), pp. 142–6, but is criticised both by Oppenheim and by Benn and Weinstein in the works cited above.
5. Thomas Hobbes, *Leviathan*, ed. C.B. Macpherson (Harmondsworth, 1968), Bk. ii, ch. 21, p. 261. (Here and elsewhere in citing from seventeenth-century sources I have modernised spelling and punctuation.)
6. John Locke, *An Essay Concerning Human Understanding*, ed. Peter H. Nidditch (Oxford, 1975), ii.21.56.
7. Gerald C. MacCallum, Jr., 'Negative and positive freedom' in *Philosophy, Politics and Society*, Peter Laslett, W.G. Runciman, and Quentin Skinner, eds., 4th ser. (Oxford, 1972), pp. 174–93.
8. This is the main implication of the article by MacCallum cited in note 7 above. For a recent and explicit statement to this effect, see for example J.P. Day, 'Individual liberty' in A. Phillips Griffiths, ed., *Of Liberty* (Cambridge, 1983), who claims (p. 18) 'that "free" is univocal and that the negative concept is the only concept of liberty'.
9. This formulation derives from the article by MacCallum cited in note 7 above. For recent discussions in which the same approach has been used to analyse the concept of political liberty, see, for example, Joel Feinberg, *Social Philosophy* (Englewood Cliffs, NJ, 1973), esp. pp. 12, 16, and J. Roland Pennock, *Democratic Political Theory* (Princeton, NJ, 1979), esp. pp. 18–24.
10. Charles Taylor, 'What's wrong with negative liberty' in *The Idea of Freedom*, Alan Ryan, ed. (Oxford, 1979), pp. 175–93, at p. 181.

11. For a discussion that moves in this Kantian direction, connecting freedom with rationality and concluding that it cannot therefore 'be identified with absence of impediments,' see, for example, C.I. Lewis, 'The meaning of liberty', in *Values and Imperatives*, John Lange, ed. (Stanford, 1969), pp. 145–55, at p. 147. For a valuable recent exposition of the same Kantian perspective, see the section 'Rationality and freedom' in Martin Hollis, *Invitation to Philosophy* (Oxford, 1985), pp. 144–51.

12. Hobbes, *Leviathan*, Bk. 11, ch. 21, p. 266.

13. *Ibid.*

14. Oppenheim, *Political Concepts*, p. 92.

15. *Ibid.*, p. 162. For a recent endorsement of the claim that, since liberty requires no action, it can hardly require virtuous or valuable action, see Lincoln Allison, *Right Principles* (Oxford, 1984), pp. 134–5.

16. D.D. Raphael, *Problems of Political Philosophy*, rev. edn (London, 1976), p. 139.

17. *Ibid.*, p. 137.

18. Oppenheim, *Political Concepts*, p. 164.

19. See, for example, Thomas Aquinas, *De Regimine Principum*, Bk. 1, ch. 1, in *Aquinas: Selected Political Writings*, A.P. D'Entrèves, ed. (Oxford, 1959), p. 2.

20. For a fuller exploration of this point see the important article by Tom Baldwin, 'MacCallum and the two concepts of freedom', *Ratio*, 26 (1984), 125–42, esp. at 135–6.

21. Taylor, 'Negative liberty', p. 177.

22. *Ibid.*

23. See, for example, the conclusions in W. Parent, 'Some recent work on the concept of liberty', *American Philosophical Quarterly*, 11 (1974), 149–67, esp. 152, 166.

24. Anthony Flew, '"Freedom is slavery": a slogan for our new philosopher kings' in *Of Liberty*, Griffiths, ed., pp. 45–59, esp. at pp. 46, 48, 52.

25. At this point I am greatly indebted once more to Baldwin, 'Two concepts', esp. pp. 139–40.

26. Jean-Jacques Rousseau, *The Social Contract*, tr. Maurice Cranston (Harmondsworth, 1968), p. 64.

27. This is how Berlin expresses the point in the title of his essay, although he shifts in the course of it to speaking instead of the different 'senses' of the term. See *Four Essays*, esp. p. 121.

28. *Ibid.*, esp. p. 152.

29. *Ibid.*, pp. 160–2.

30. Taylor, 'Negative liberty', p. 193.

31. See Taylor, *ibid.*, insisting (p. 193) that this is 'altogether too quick a way with them'.

32. I cannot hope to give anything like a complete account of this ideology here, nor even of the recent historical literature devoted to it. Suffice it to point to the earlier chapters of the present volume [*Machiavelli and Republicanism*], and to add that the classic general study is J. G. A. Pocock, *The Machiavellian Moment* (Princeton, NJ, 1975), a work to which I am much indebted. I have tried to give a fuller account of my own view in two earlier articles: 'Machiavelli on the maintenance of liberty', *Politics*, 18 (1983), 3–15, and 'The idea of negative liberty: philosophical and historical perspectives', *Philosophy in History*, Richard Rorty, J. B. Schneewind, and Quentin Skinner, eds. (Cambridge, 1984), pp. 193, 221. The present essay may be regarded as an attempt to bring out the implications of those earlier studies, although at the same time I have considerably modified and I hope strengthened my earlier arguments.

33. All citations from the *Discorsi* refer to the version in Niccolò Machiavelli, *Il Principe e Discoursi*, ed. Sergio Bertelli (Milan, 1960). All translations are my own.
34. *Ibid.*, I.ii, p. 129.
35. *Ibid.*, II.ii, p. 280.
36. *Ibid.*, II.ii, p. 284.
37. *Ibid.*, I.xvi. p. 176.
38. *Ibid.*, I.xvi, p. 176; cf. also II.ii, pp. 284–85.
39. See Z.S. Fink, *The Classical Republicans*, 2nd edn (Evanston, 1962), esp. pp. 103–7, on Milton and Harrington. For Machiavelli's equivocations on the point see Marcia Colish, 'The idea of liberty in Machiavelli', *Journal of the History of Ideas*, 32 (1971), 323–50.
40. This constitutes a leading theme of Book II of Machiavelli's *Discorsi*.
41. Book III of Machiavelli's *Discorsi* is much concerned with the role played by great men—defined as those possessing exceptional *virtù*—in Rome's rise to greatness.
42. For a classic discussion of 'corruption' see Machiavelli, *Discorsi*, I.xvii–xix, pp. 177–85.
43. *Ibid.*, I.liii, p. 249.
44. See, for example, the way in which the concept of 'the common good' is discussed in John Rawls, *A Theory of Justice* (Cambridge, MA, 1971), pp. 243, 246.
45. Machiavelli, *Discorsi*, I.iii, p. 136.

Extract 106

BRIAN BARRY: *Justice between Generations*

1. Wilfred Beckerman, 'The Myth of "Finite" Resources', *Business and Society Review* 12 (Winter 1974–5), 22.

Extract 107

PETER SINGER: *Famine, Affluence and Morality*

1. There was also a third possibility: that India would go to war to enable the refugees to return to their lands. Since I wrote this paper, India has taken this way out. The situation is no longer that described above, but this does not affect my argument, as the next paragraph indicates.
2. In view of the special sense philosophers often give to the term, I should say that I use 'obligation' simply as the abstract noun derived from 'ought,' so that 'I have an obligation to' means no more, and no less, than 'I ought to.' This usage is in accordance with the definition of 'ought' given by the *Shorter Oxford English Dictionary*: 'the general verb to express duty or obligation.' I do not think any issue of substance hangs on the way the term is used; sentences in which I use 'obligation' could all be rewritten, although somewhat clumsily as sentences in which a clause containing 'ought' replaces the term 'obligation.'

Extract 108

ONORA O'NEILL: *Lifeboat Earth*

1. Cf. Robert Nozick, *Anarchy, State, and Utopia* (New York, 1974), p. 34. Nozick defines an innocent threat as 'someone who is innocently a causal agent in a process such that he would be an aggressor had he chosen to become such an agent.'

2. Cf. Peter Singer, 'Famine, Affluence, and Morality,' *Philosophy & Public Affairs* 1, no. 3 (Spring 1972): 229–243, 232. I am in agreement with many of the points which Singer makes, but am interested in arguing that we must have some famine policy from a much weaker set of premises. Singer uses some consequentialist premises: starvation is bad; we ought to prevent bad things when we can do so without worse consequences; hence we ought to prevent starvation whether it is nearby or far off and whether others are doing so or not. The argument of this article does not depend on a particular theory about the grounds of obligation, but should be a corollary of any nonbizarre ethical theory which has any room for a notion of rights.

3. This way of distinguishing killing from allowing to die does not rely on distinguishing 'negative' from 'positive' acts. Such attempts seem unpromising since any act has multiple descriptions of which some will be negative and others positive. If a clear distinction is to be made between killing and letting die, it must hinge on the *difference* which an act makes for a person's survival, rather than on the description under which the agent acts.

4. The point may appear rather arbitrary, given that I have not rested my case on one theory of the grounds of obligation. But I believe that almost any such theory will show a right not to be killed to override a property right. Perhaps this is why Locke's theory can seem so odd—in moving from a right of self-preservation to a justification of unequal property rights, he finds himself gradually having to reinterpret all rights as property rights, thus coming to see us as the owners of our persons.

5. Cf. P. A. Baron, *The Political Economy of Growth* (New York, 1957), especially chap. 5, 'On the Roots of Backwardness'; or A. G. Frank, *Capitalism and Underdevelopment in Latin America* (New York, 1967). Both works argue that underdeveloped economies are among the products of developed ones.

6. Lester R. Brown and Erik P. Eckholm, 'The Empty Breadbasket,' *Ceres* (F.A.O. Review on Development), March–April 1974, p. 59. See also N. Borlaug and R. Ewell, 'The Shrinking Margin,' in the same issue.

7. For discussions of the time and extent of famine see, for example, P. R. Ehrlich, *The Population Bomb*, rev. ed. (New York, 1971); R.L. Heilbroner, *An Inquiry into the Human Prospect* (New York, 1974); *Scientific American*, September 1974, especially R. Freedman and B. Berelson, 'The Human Population'; P. Demeny, 'The Populations of the Underdeveloped Countries'; R. Revelle, 'Food and Population.'

8. See *Scientific American*, September 1974, especially A. J. Coale, 'The History of the Human Population.'

9. The failure of 'right to life' groups to pursue these goals seriously casts doubt upon their commitment to the preservation of human lives. Why are they active in so few of the contexts where human lives are endangered?

10. For example, J. C. C. Smart, *An Outline of a System of Utilitarian Ethics* (Melbourne, 1961), pp. 18, 44ff.; Jan Narveson, 'Moral Problems of Population,' *Monist* 57 (1973): 62–86; 'Utilitarianism and New Generations,' *Mind* 76 (1967): 62–72.

11. Cf. Mahmood Mamdani, *The Myth of Population Control* (New York, 1972), for evidence that high fertility can be based on rational choice rather than ignorance or incompetence.

Select Bibliography

GENERAL TEXTS

GOODIN, R. E., and PETTIT, P., *A Companion to Contemporary Political Philosophy* (Blackwell: Oxford, 1993).

HAMPSHER-MONK, IAIN, *A History of Modern Political Thought* (Blackwell: Oxford, 1992).

HAMPTON, JEAN, *Political Philosophy* (Westview: Boulder, Colo., 1997).

KYMLICKA, WILL, *Contemporary Political Philosophy: An Introduction* (Oxford University Press: Oxford, 1990).

WOLFF, JONATHAN, *An Introduction to Political Philosophy* (Oxford University Press: Oxford, 1996).

CLASSIC WORKS

ARISTOTLE, *The Politics* (Cambridge University Press: Cambridge, 1988).

BENTHAM, JEREMY, *A Fragment on Government* (Cambridge University Press: Cambridge, 1988).

——'Anarchical Fallacies', in *Nonsense on Stilts*, ed. Jeremy Waldron (Methuen: London, 1987).

BURKE, EDMUND, *Reflections on the Revolution in France* (Penguin: Harmondsworth, 1968).

ENGELS, FREDERICK, *Socialism Utopian and Scientific* (Progress Publishers: Moscow, 1954).

HAMILTON, ALEXANDER, MADISON, JAMES, and JAY, JOHN, *The Federalist Papers* (New American Library: New York, 1961).

HEGEL, G. W. F., *Philosophy of Right* (Clarendon Press: Oxford, 1952).

HOBBES, THOMAS, *Leviathan* (Penguin: Harmondsworth, 1968).

HUME, DAVID, 'Of the Original Contract', in his *Essays Moral Political and Literary*, ed. E. F. Miller (Liberty Press: Indianapolis, 1985).

——*A Treatise of Human Nature*, ed. L. A. Selby-Bigge, 2nd edition (Oxford University Press: Oxford, 1978), Book III.

KANT, IMMANUEL, *Political Writings* (Cambridge University Press: Cambridge, 1991).

KROPOTKIN, PETER, *Mutual Aid* (Black Rose Books: Montreal, 1989).

LOCKE, JOHN, *Two Treatises of Government*, ed. Peter Laslett (Cambridge University Press: Cambridge, 1988).

MACHIAVELLI, NICCOLÒ, *The Discourses* (Penguin: Harmondsworth, 1970).

——*The Prince* (Penguin: Harmondsworth, 1961).

MILL, JOHN STUART, *On Liberty* and *The Subjection of Women* in *On Liberty and Other Writings* (Cambridge University Press: Cambridge, 1989).

——*Considerations on Representative Government*, in *Utilitarianism* etc. (Dent: London, 1972).

MARX, KARL, *Selected Writings*, ed. D. McLellan (Oxford University Press: Oxford, 1977).

PAINE, THOMAS, *The Rights of Man* (Oxford University Press: Oxford, 1995).

PLATO, *The Republic*, ed. H. D. P. Lee (Penguin: Harmondsworth, 1955).

——*Crito* in *The Last Days of Socrates*, ed. H. Tredennick (Penguin: Harmondsworth, 1954).

ROUSSEAU, JEAN-JACQUES, *The Social Contract and Discourses*, ed. G. D. H. Cole, J. H. Brumfitt, and John C. Hall (Dent: London, 1973).
——*Émile* (Dent: London, 1974).
WOLLSTONECRAFT, MARY, *Vindication of the Rights of Women* (Penguin: Harmondsworth, 1982).

CONTEMPORARY WORKS

BARRY, BRIAN, *Justice as Impartiality* (Oxford University Press: Oxford, 1995).
BERLIN, ISAIAH, 'Two Concepts of Liberty', in his *Four Essays on Liberty* (Oxford University Press: Oxford, 1969).
COHEN, G. A., *Karl Marx's Theory of History: A Defence* (Oxford University Press: Oxford, 1978).
DEVLIN, PATRICK, *The Enforcement of Morals* (Oxford University Press: Oxford, 1965).
DWORKIN, RONALD, *Taking Rights Seriously* (Duckworth: London, 1978).
ELSTER, JON, *Sour Grapes* (Cambridge University Press: Cambridge, 1983).
FRIEDMAN, MILTON, *Capitalism and Freedom* (Chicago University Press: Chicago, 1962).
GILLIGAN, CAROL, *In A Different Voice* (Harvard University Press: Cambridge, Mass., 1982).
HABERMAS, JÜRGEN, *Legitimation Crisis* (Beacon Press: Boston, 1975).
HART, H. L. A., 'Are There Any Natural Rights?', *Philosophical Review* 1955, repr. in *Theories of Rights*, ed. J. Waldron (Oxford University Press: Oxford, 1984).
——*Law Liberty and Morality* (Oxford University Press: London, 1963).
HAYEK, F. A. VON, *The Constitution of Liberty* (Routledge & Kegan Paul: London, 1960).
——*The Road to Serfdom* (Routledge & Kegan Paul: London, 1944).
JAGGAR, ALISON M., *Feminist Politics and Human Nature* (Rowman & Littlefied: Atlantic Highlands, NJ, 1983).
KYMLICKA, WILL, *Multicultural Citizenship* (Oxford University Press: Oxford, 1995).
MACINTYRE, ALASDAIR, *After Virtue* (Duckworth: London, 1981).
MACKINNON, CATHARINE, *Feminism Unmodified* (Harvard University Press: Cambridge, Mass., 1987).
NOZICK, ROBERT, *Anarchy, State, and Utopia* (Blackwell: Oxford, 1974).
OAKESHOTT, MICHAEL, *Rationalism in Politics* (Methuen: London, 1962).
OKIN, SUSAN MOLLER, *Justice, Gender and the Family* (Basic Books: New York, 1989).
——*Women in Western Political Thought* (Princeton University Press: Princeton, 1979).
PATEMAN, CAROLE, *The Sexual Contract* (Stanford University Press: Stanford, Calif., 1988).
RAWLS, JOHN, *A Theory of Justice* (Oxford University Press: Oxford, 1971).
——*Political Liberalism* (Columbia University Press: New York, 1993).
RORTY, RICHARD, *Contingency, Irony and Solidarity* (Cambridge University Press: Cambridge, 1989).
SANDEL, MICHAEL, *Liberalism and The Limits of Justice* (Cambridge University Press: Cambridge, 1982).
SIMMONS, A. JOHN, *Moral Principles and Political Obligations* (Princeton University Press: Princeton, 1979).
TAYLOR, CHARLES, *Hegel* (Cambridge University Press: Cambridge, 1975).
WALZER, MICHAEL, *Spheres of Justice* (Blackwell: Oxford, 1983).
WOLFF, R. P., *In Defense of Anarchism* (Harper: New York, 1973).

Biographical Notes

AESOP (*c.*620–560 BC) Said to have been an Ancient Greek slave from Phrygia who later became a free man. How many of the fables collected under his name were actually composed by him is unknown.

ARISTOTLE (384–322 BC) Athenian philosopher, native of Stagyra. A pupil of Plato, Aristotle went on to found his own school, the Lyceum. Aristotle's works span a vast range of philosophical and scientific subjects. His principal works of relevance to political thought are the *Nichomachean Ethics* (dedicated to his son Nicomachus) and the *Politics*.

BAKUNIN, MICHAEL (1814–76) Russian anarchist and political activist who spent many years in prison for sedition. He led the opposition to Marx within the First International, from which he was expelled in 1872. He died in poverty.

BARRY, BRIAN British political philosopher. Currently Professor of Philosophy and Political Science at Columbia University, New York. His many books include *Political Argument* (1965) and *Justice as Impartiality* (1995)

BELLAMY, EDWARD (1850–98) American utopian novelist, best known for his romance *Looking Backward* (1888), which continues to influence contemporary thought on questions of economic justice.

BENTHAM, JEREMY (1748–1832) English founder of Utilitarianism. Bentham was an incredibly prolific writer on philosophical, legal, political, and practical matters and played an active role in social reform. His *Introduction to the Principles of Moral and Legislation* (1789) is his best-known philosophical work.

BERLIN, ISAIAH (1909–97) Born in Riga, Berlin was brought up in England. He was Chichele professor of Social and Political Theory at Oxford and the first President of Wolfson College. Known as a leading defender of liberalism, much of his writing was devoted to understanding the appeal of illiberal forms of thought. Of his many works, the most important for political thought is probably his *Four Essays on Liberty* (1969).

BURKE, EDMUND (1729–97) Irish-born parliamentarian and political theorist. Burke, with Charles James Fox, was the leading orator of the late eighteenth-century English parliament. His best-known work, *Reflections on the Revolution in France* (1790), was written in protest at the excessive radicalism of the French Revolutionaries. Burke is regarded as the father of modern conservatism.

COBDEN, RICHARD (1804–65) English economist, politician, and businessman. A staunch advocate of free trade, Cobden was the most prominent member of the Anti-Corn-Law League, which was instrumental in the repeal of the tariffs on imported corn in 1846. He made out the case for free trade in his 1835 work *England, Ireland, and America*.

COHEN, GERALD ALAN Canadian political philosopher. Currently Chichele Professor of Social and Political Theory at Oxford University, Cohen is the author of *Karl Marx's Theory of History: A Defence* (1978) and of many other writings in political philosophy which defend egalitarian principles.

CONSTANT, BENJAMIN (Henri Benjamin Constant de Rebecque) (1767–1830) Constant was born in Lausanne of French Huguenot ancestry. He travelled widely before settling in Paris. Constant became a member of the Chamber of Deputies in 1819 and for a time was leader of the opposition. Apart from his political writings, Constant was also the author of a celebrated psychological novel, *Adolphe* (1816).

DARWIN, CHARLES (1809–92) English biologist, founder of the theory of evolution. Darwin developed his revolutionary ideas in the course of a five-year scientific voyage undertaken as a young man aboard the survey ship HMS Beagle. His major work, *The Origin of Species by Means of Natural Selection* (1859), sold out on the day of its publication.

DEVLIN, PATRICK (1905–92) English Judge of the Queen's Bench 1948–60, created Lord of Appeal in 1961. Author of many works, including *The Enforcement of Morals* (1965).

DOSTOEVSKY, FYODOR (1821–81) Russian novelist whose famous works such as *Notes from the Underground* (1864), *Crime and Punishment* (1865–6), and *The Brothers Karamazov* (1880) are noted, amongst other things, for their psychological insight and exploration of philosophical themes.

DWORKIN, RONALD American legal and political theorist, currently Professor of Law at New York University and Professor of Jurisprudence at University College London, formerly Professor of Jurisprudence at Oxford University. His works include *Taking Rights Seriously* (1977), *Law's Empire* (1986), and *Life's Dominion* (1993).

ELIOT, T(HOMAS) S(TEARNS) (1888–1965) US-born poet, one of the most influential literary figures of the twentieth century. Eliot studied philosophy at Harvard and Oxford and began a doctoral dissertation on the philosopher F. H. Bradley. Two of his most notable poems are *The Waste Land* (1922) and *Four Quartets* (1944). *Notes Towards a Definition of Culture* (1948) is the most comprehensive published account of his conservative social views.

ENGELS, FRIEDRICH (1820–95) Karl Marx's devoted friend and collaborator. Engels was originally responsible for introducing Marx to the study of economics. After Marx's death, Engels edited Marx's works and wrote extensive works of his own to popularize and interpret Marx's thought. Engels's *Dialectics of Nature* is an attempt to develop a dialectical philosophy which goes considerably beyond anything Marx committed himself to.

FOUCAULT, MICHEL (1926–84) French historian of ideas with philosophical interests who also played an active role in left-wing politics. Foucault was especially noted for his studies of power and sexuality in such works as *Discipline and Punish* (1975) and *The History of Sexuality* (1976). Regarded as one of the founders of post-modernist thought.

FREDERICK THE GREAT (Frederick II of Prussia) (1712–86) Frederick became King of Prussia in 1740. He was an enlightened despot who introduced many domestic reforms and allowed his subjects a degree of toleration that was unusual in the eighteenth century. Frederick's political intrigues and military prowess made Prussia into a leading military power. A patron of the arts, who enjoyed the company of intellectuals, his works, written entirely in French, were published in 31 volumes by the Berlin Academy (1846–57).

FREUD, SIGMUND (1856–1939) Austrian founder of psychoanalysis. A prolific writer of immense influence, his magnum opus, *The Interpretation of Dreams*, was published in 1900. Freud's most explicitly political work is *Civilization and Its Discontents* (1930). He died in exile in London.

FRIEDMAN, MILTON American Nobel Prize-winning economist, working primarily at the University of Chicago, best known for his advocacy of 'monetarism' in opposition to Keynesian macro-economics. In addition to many works on economics, Friedman's defence of laissez-faire capitalism, *Capitalism and Freedom* (1962), was followed by *Free to Choose* (1980), written in collaboration with his wife, Rose Friedman.

FRIEDMAN, ROSE Wife of Milton Friedman and co-author of their *Free to Choose* (1980). Also assisted with the preparation of Milton Friedman's *Capitalism and Freedom* (1962).

FUKUYAMA, FRANCIS American political scientist. Fukuyama received his Ph.D. from Harvard University and was a member of the Policy Planning Staff on the US State Department. His article 'The End of History?' (1989) generated enormous controversy. It was followed by a book, *The End of History and the Last Man* (1992).

GILLIGAN, CAROL American psychologist, Professor at Harvard University, whose particular interest is in the psychology of moral development. Her *In a Different Voice* (1982), which drew attention to apparent differences in the structure of moral thought between girls and boys, has been extremely influential on feminist thought.

HABERMAS, JÜRGEN German philosopher and sociologist, Professor at the University of Frankfurt, considered to be the leading living representative of the Frankfurt School, one of the most original currents in twentieth-century Marxism. His most important works include *Knowledge and Human Interests* (1968), *Legitimation Crisis* (1976), and *The Theory of Communicative Action* (two volumes, 1984 and 1987).

HART, HERBERT (1907–92) English barrister who became Professor of Jurisprudence at Oxford. An editor of the works of Jeremy Bentham, Hart was also a major legal theorist in his own right. His *Concept of Law* (1961) is taken to be the classic modern statement of legal positivism.

HAYEK, F. A. VON (1899–1992) Nobel Prize-winning Austrian economist, who taught at the London School of Economics, The University of Chicago, and the University of Freibur. A fervent opponent of central economic planning, Hayek argued for the indispensability of markets under conditions of imperfect knowledge. His political writings, such as *The Road to Serfdom* (1944) and *The Constitution of Liberty* (1960), have had a profound effect on the development of neo-conservative thought in the UK and USA.

HEGEL, GEORG WILHELM FRIEDRICH (1770–1831) Systematic and often obscure German idealist philosopher, who has exerted an enormous influence over subsequent German philosophy. *The Phenomenology of Mind* (1807) is his most widely admired work. *The Philosophy of Right* (1821)—his major contribution to political thought—defends a form of constitutional monarchy.

HILL, THOMAS American philosopher, Professor of Philosophy at the University of North Carolina, Chapel Hill, and the author of *Autonomy and Self-Respect* (1989) among other works.

HOBBES, THOMAS (1588–1679) Hobbes produced works on metaphysics and general philosophy as well as political philosophy. He argued that passive obedience on the part of subjects was necessary for civil peace. He was deeply disturbed by the English Civil War and fled to France in 1640, returning only in 1651 on the publication of his great masterpiece, *Leviathan*.

HUME, DAVID (1711–76) Scottish philosopher. Hume's *Treatise on Human Nature* (1739–40), published when he was still in his twenties, set out revolutionary new views on many philosophical topics, pushing the empiricism of John Locke to its limits. Its value was not immediately appreciated, however, and in his lifetime Hume was known primarily as an essayist and as a historian, following the success of his six-volume *History of England* (1754–62).

JAGGAR, ALISON, M. American feminist philosopher, Professor of Philosophy at the University of Colorado, Boulder. Jaggar is the author of *Feminist Politics and Human Nature* (1983) and *Feminist Frameworks* (1993) amongst other works.

KANT, IMMANUEL (1724–1804) Although Kant never left the region around his home town of Königsberg in East Prussia, he was arguably the most influential philosopher since Aristotle. Kant is celebrated above all for his three Critiques: *The Critique of Pure Reason* (1781); *The Critique of Practical Reason* (1788); and *The Critique of Judgement* (1790). Political philosophy is a relatively minor part of his corpus. Nevertheless, his ideas helped lay the foundations for an individualistic form of liberalism.

KING, MARTIN LUTHER (1929–68) The leading figure of the American Civil Rights movement, King was awarded the Nobel Peace Prize in 1964. An advocate of non-violent forms of political protest, he was assassinated in Memphis, Tennessee, while trying to organize a march against poverty.

KROPOTKIN, PETER (1842–1921) Russian anarchist and member of the royal family, Kropotkin was imprisoned for his political activities, and subsequently fled to England. He returned to Russia after the Russian Revolution of 1917. Author of *Memoirs of a Revolutionist* (1899), and *Mutual Aid* (1900).

LENIN, VLADIMIR ILICH (1870–1924) Founder of the Bolshevik Party and chief architect of the Russian Revolution. After the Revolution, as Chairman of the Council of People's Commissars, Lenin became virtual dictator of the USSR. Lenin was a prolific political writer, as a follower, interpreter, and developer of the ideas of Karl Marx.

LOCKE, JOHN (1632–1704) Locke was a central figure in English philosophy, equally important for his *Essay Concerning Human Understanding* (1690), a work dealing with metaphysics and epistemology, as for his political philosophy. His *Two Treatises on Government* (1690) were written in support of the movement which was to lead to the 'Glorious Revolution' of 1688, although they were only published later, anonymously. Locke always publicly denied authorship of them.

MACHIAVELLI, NICCOLÒ (1469–1527) Italian diplomat and historian, commonly regarded as the founder of political science. His best-known work, *The Prince* (written around 1513) takes the form of advice to a ruler as to how to obtain and ruthlessly retain power. *The Discourses on the First Ten Books of Titus Livius* (also written around 1513) show Machiavelli's sympathies for republican principles.

MacIntyre, Alasdair Scottish-born moral and political philosopher who has spent much of his working life in the USA. He is currently Professor of Philosophy at Duke University. MacIntyre's early work was sympathetic to Marxism, but he is best known for *After Virtue* (1981) and such subsequent writings as *Whose Justice? Which Rationality?* (1988) which combine criticism of liberal individualism with a defence of a form of Christian-Aristotelian moral theory.

MacKinnon, Catharine American feminist legal scholar and activist, Professor of Law at the University of Chicago and the University of Michigan, who has argued against the consequences of liberal rights (particularly with regard to the freedom of expression) in a world of pervasive sexual inequality. Her works include *Feminism Unmodified* (1987) and *Only Words* (1993).

Madison, James (1751–1836) Fourth President of the United States of America, known as the 'father of the Constitution' for his central role in the Constitutional Convention. Madison wrote the *Federalist Papers* (1788) with John Jay and Alexander Hamilton in the effort to have the Constitution adopted. He also strongly supported the Bill of Rights.

Mandel, Ernest (1923–95) Marxist economist and author of *Late Capitalism* (1975), *The Second Slump* (1978), and *The Long Waves of Capitalist Development* (1980), among many other works. His influential pamphlet, *An Introduction to Marxist Economics* (2nd English edition 1975), sold over half a million copies and was translated into thirty languages.

Margalit, Avishai Israeli political philosopher, Professor of Philosophy at the Hebrew University, Jerusalem. Author of *The Decent Society* (1996).

Marx, Karl (1818–83) Without doubt, Marx is the single political thinker whose ideas have had most impact—for better or worse—on world history. Born and educated in Germany, Marx dedicated his life to the active promotion of socialist revolution and he was forced to live largely in exile in Paris, Brussels, and, finally, London. His greatest work, *Capital*, attempts to lay bare the workings of capitalism. Only Volume I (1867) was published in his lifetime, while Volume II (1885) and Volume III (1895) were later edited and collated by Engels.

Mill, John Stuart (1806–73) English liberal philosopher who wrote on a vast range of philosophical and political topics, best known for two works of moral and political philosophy, *On Liberty* (1859) and *Utilitarianism* (1863). His intellectual life embodies the struggle to supplement Benthamite utilitarianism, of which he had been a devoted follower in his youth, with a more sensitive regard for the value of individuality.

Montesquieu (Charles Louis de Secondat, Baron de) (1689–1755) Philosopher and jurist of the French Enlightenment. Montesquieu became famous for his satire on French society and institutions, the *Persian Letters* (1721), while his work *The Spirit of the Laws* (1748) is one of the earliest attempts to study the way in which physical and cultural circumstances shape the character of political institutions.

Nagel, Thomas American philosopher of wide interests who has made contributions to the philosophy of mind, epistemology, and moral philosophy as well as political philosophy. Formerly at Princeton University, Nagel is currently Professor of Law and Philosophy at New York University. His works include *The Possibility of Altruism* (1963), *Mortal Questions* (1979), *The View from Nowhere* (1986), and *Equality and Partiality* (1991).

NIETZSCHE, FRIEDRICH (1844–1900) German classicist and philosopher, who argued against the 'slave morality' of Christianity in favour of a 'transvaluation of all values'. A brilliant, aphoristic writer, Nietzsche considered himself to be the harbinger of a new epoch of thought and feeling. His writings have been interpreted in many conflicting ways and he has inspired thinkers on both the far left and the radical right. His major works include *The Birth of Tragedy* (1872), *Beyond Good and Evil* (1886), and *The Genealogy of Morals* (1887).

NOZICK, ROBERT Professor of Philosophy at Harvard University. Best known for his classic work of libertarian political philosophy, *Anarchy, State, and Utopia* (1974). However, political philosophy has occupied only a small part of Nozick's philosophical career, and, in works such as *Philosophical Explanations* (1981), he has dealt with many of the central questions of metaphysics and epistemology.

OAKESHOTT, MICHAEL (1901–90) English conservative political philosopher, noted for his insistence that human experience cannot be reduced to science or captured in any complete set of rational principles. His works include *Experience and its Modes* (1933) and *Rationalism in Politics* (1962).

O'NEILL, ONORA (Baroness O'Neill of Bengarve) British moral philosopher in the Kantian tradition, formerly Professor of Philosophy at the University of Essex, currently Principal of Newnham College, Cambridge. Her books include *Acting on Principle* (1975), *Faces of Hunger* (1986), *Constructions of Reason* (1989), and *Towards Justice and Virtue* (1996).

OWEN, ROBERT (1771–1858) Socialist and social reformer, born in Wales. As owner-manager of a cotton mill in New Lanark, Scotland, Owen had a chance to put his utopian theories into practice, with spectacular success both with regard to productivity and the well-being of his workforce. Further experiments, in the United Kingdom, Ireland, and the United States, were much less successful. *A New View of Society* (1813) is his major work.

PARETO, VILFREDO (1848–1923) Italian economist and sociologist, especially interested in failures of human rationality and in the formation of elites. *Mind and Society* (1917–18) is his main work of social theory.

PATEMAN, CAROLE Professor of Political Science at the University of California, Berkeley. In such works as *Participation and Democratic Theory* (1970), *The Problem of Political Obligation* (1985), and *The Sexual Contract* (1988), Pateman develops a critique of liberal theory, initially from a radical democratic, latterly much more of a feminist, standpoint.

PERICLES (c.495–429 BC) Athenian statesman, leader of Athens at the height of its glory. His 'funeral oration', recorded, some thirty years after it was delivered, by Thucydides (c.460–c.400 BC) in his *History of the Peloponnesian War*, may well have been Thucydides' own composition.

PLATO (427–347 BC) Athenian philosopher. Alongside his teacher, Socrates, who left no written work, Plato is the first major figure in the western philosophical tradition. Even now very many philosophical debates take place within the framework first established by Plato. Although the best-known of his political works is the *Republic*, with its advocacy of the idea of 'philosopher-rulers', his political views underwent considerable modification in the later works, *The Statesman*, and the *Laws*.

POPPER, KARL (1902–94) Austrian philosopher of science and social science who emigrated to New Zealand in 1938, moving to London in 1946. An opponent of pseudo-science, totalitarianism, and the totalitarian tendencies he perceived in the works of certain other political philosophers (especially Plato, Hegel, and Marx), his best-known political works are *The Open Society and Its Enemies* (1945) and *The Poverty of Historicism* (1957).

RAWLS, JOHN American political philosopher, arguably the most important moral or political philosopher working in English in the twentieth century, whose writing revitalized the subject after the Second World War. Rawls's work presents a detailed and systematic argument for a form of liberal equality. His main work, *A Theory of Justice* (1971), was followed by *Political Liberalism* (1993).

RAZ, JOSEPH Professor of the Philosophy of Law at Oxford University. His major works include *The Morality of Freedom* (1986) and *Ethics in the Public Domain* (1994).

RORTY, RICHARD American philosopher, Professor of Philosophy at the University of Virginia. In *Philosophy and the Mirror of Nature* (1980) Rorty argued that philosophers have sought foundations for their views where none are available. He himself adopts a pragmatist approach to philosophy and in later works, such as *Contingency, Irony and Solidarity* (1989), this is extended to a defence of liberalism on relativist grounds.

ROUSSEAU, JEAN-JACQUES (1712–78) Born in Geneva, Rousseau first found fame with his *Discourse on the Arts and Sciences* (1750), in which he argued that the progress of the arts and sciences had done more to corrupt morals than to improve them. His major works, *Émile* (1762) and *The Social Contract* (1762), have had enormous influence on the philosophy of education and political philosophy respectively, while his remarkable *Confessions* (1781) is an early example of a wholly candid, revelatory autobiography.

SANDEL, MICHAEL American political philosopher, Professor of Government at Harvard University. His early work, *Liberalism and the Limits of Justice* (1982), criticized Rawls's *A Theory of Justice* from a communitarian point of view and helped establish communitarianism at the centre of debate in contemporary political philosophy.

SCANLON, THOMAS American moral and political philosopher, Professor of Philosophy at Harvard University. Scanlon has published numerous papers defending liberal egalitarianism and arguing for a contractualist approach to moral philosophy. His *What We Owe to Each Other* (1998) builds on this earlier work.

SCHILLER, FRIEDRICH VON (1759–1805) German poet, dramatist, historian, and philosopher of art. His poem 'Ode to Joy' (1785) was set by Beethoven in his Ninth Symphony. Schiller's many works include *On the Aesthetic Education of Man* (1795) and the historical drama *Wallenstein* (1798–1800).

SINGER, PETER Australian moral and political philosopher whose work *Animal Liberation* (1975) has been among the most influential sources for the animal rights movement. Singer's other works include *Practical Ethics* (1979), *The Expanding Circle* (1981), and *How Should We Live?* (1993).

SKINNER, QUENTIN English historian and political philosopher, Regius Professor of History at Cambridge University. Skinner has a particular interest in early modern political thought which he has explored in his books *The Foundations of Modern Political*

Thought (1978), *Machiavelli* (1981), and *Reason and Rhetoric in the Philosophy of Hobbes* (1996).

SMITH, ADAM (1723–90) Scottish economist and moral philosopher, regarded as the greatest of the classical economists. A fierce opponent of monopolies, both state and private, and theorist of the division of labour, his major works are the *Theory of Moral Sentiments* (1759) and his masterpiece, *An Inquiry into the Nature and Causes of the Wealth of Nations* (1776).

SPENCER, HERBERT (1820–1903) English author who wrote prolifically on ethics, biology, psychology, and sociology. Coined the phrase 'survival of the fittest', which was later to be used by Darwin. His political works include *Social Statics* (1851) and *The Principles of Sociology* (1876).

STEPHEN, JAMES FITZJAMES (1829–94) English lawyer and journalist whose best-known work, *Liberty, Equality and Fraternity* (1873), gave a conservative rejoinder to contemporary radical utilitarianism. According to the entry on Stephen in the *Dictionary of National Biography*, 'in mind as in body [Stephen] showed much more strength than flexibility'. (The entry was written by the editor of the *Dictionary*, Stephen's son, Leslie.)

TAWNEY, RICHARD HENRY (1880–1962) Historian and political philosopher whose ideas were influential on the British Labour Party. His works include *The Acquisitive Society* (1920), *Religion and the Rise of Capitalism* (1926), and *Equality* (1931).

TAYLOR, CHARLES Canadian philosopher, Professor of Philosophy at McGill University. A critic of liberal individualism, his major works include the studies *Hegel* (1976) and *Sources of the Self* (1989).

THOREAU, HENRY DAVID (1817–62) American thinker and writer. His work *Walden* (1854) records the period he spent living in a cabin near Walden Pond, living out his philosophy of individual responsibility.

TOCQUEVILLE, ALEXIS DE (1805–59) French political philosopher and historian. His two-volume *Democracy in America* (1835) is a classic account of American society and politics and an extended argument on the advantages and dangers of democracy.

WALDRON, JEREMY New Zealand-born liberal political philosopher and philosopher of law, Professor of Law at Columbia University. His works include *The Right to Private Property* (1988), and *Liberal Rights* (1993).

WALZER, MICHAEL American radical political philosopher and historian of ideas. He is currently a member of the Institute for Advanced Study, Princeton University, having previously taught at Harvard University. He is the author of *The Revolution of the Saints* (1966), *Just and Unjust Wars* (1977), and *Spheres of Justice* (1983) among many other works.

WEBER, MAX (1864–1920) German sociologist whose *Protestant Ethic and the Spirit of Capitalism* (1904–5) and the posthumously published *Economy and Society* have had a profound influence on the development of sociological thought.

WILDE, OSCAR (1854–1900) Irish-born writer. His plays *Lady Windermere's Fan* (1892), *A Woman of No Importance* (1893), *An Ideal Husband* (1895), and *The Importance of Being Earnest* (1895) are classic comedies of the English upper classes. He also wrote poetry, short stories, and more serious drama. His essay 'The Soul of Man under Socialism' (1895) contradicts the popular image of Wilde as merely a superficial society wit.

WINSTANLEY, G. (1609?–?) English radical. Little is known about Winstanley's life. In 1649, a group of 'Diggers' led by Winstanley occupied a patch of waste land near Cobham in Surrey and established a communist colony. The colony survived until 1650 and Winstanley published a number of pamphlets on its behalf. He disappeared into obscurity after 1660.

WOLFF, ROBERT PAUL American philosopher, Professor of Philosophy at the University of Massachusetts, Amherst. Wolff is the author of works on Kant and many writings on political philosophy including *The Poverty of Liberalism* (1968) and *In Defence of Anarchism* (1970).

WOLLSTONECRAFT, MARY (1759–1797) English writer and pioneer feminist, author of *A Vindication of the Rights of Woman* (1792). She was a member of the radical circle around William Blake in London and married the political theorist William Godwin. Their daughter was the writer Mary Shelley.

Source acknowledgements

Aesop, 'The Grasshopper and the Ants', in Aesop's Fables, translated by V.S. Vernon Jones (Wordsworth Classics: Hertfordshire, 1994), reprinted by permission of Wordsworth Editions.

Aristotle, Nicomachean Ethics, translated by J. A. K. Thomson (Penguin Books: London, 1953), reprinted by permission of Routledge.

Aristotle, Politics Books I and II, translated with a commentary by Trevor J. Saunders (Clarendon Press: Oxford, 1995).

Aristotle, Politics Books III and IV, translated with comments by Richard Robinson (Clarendon Press: Oxford, 1995).

Michael Bakunin, Statism and Anarchy, translated and edited by Marshall S. Shatz (Cambridge University Press: Cambridge, 1990), reprinted by permission of Cambridge University Press.

Brian Barry, 'Justice Between Generations', in Law, Society, and Morality: Essays in Honour of H. L. A. Hart (Clarendon Press: Oxford, 1977).

Isaiah Berlin, 'Nationalism', in Against the Current, (Oxford University Press: Oxford, 1981).

Isaiah Berlin, 'Two Concepts of Liberty', in Four Essays on Liberty (Oxford University Press: Oxford, 1969).

G. A. Cohen, 'Justice, Freedom and Market Transactions', in Self-Ownership, Freedom and Equality (Cambridge University Press: Cambridge, 1995), reprinted by permission of Cambridge University Press.

G. A. Cohen, 'Socialism and Equality of Opportunity', expanded version of 'Equality, Equality of Opportunity and the Labour Party', Red Pepper, November 1997, reprinted by permission of Red Pepper Manchester.

Benjamin Constant, Political Writings, translated and edited by Biancamaria Fontana (Cambridge University Press: Cambridge, 1988), reprinted by permission of Cambridge University Press.

Charles Darwin, The Origin of Species, edited by Gillian Beer (Oxford University Press: Oxford, 1996).

Patrick Devlin, 'Morals and the Criminal Law', in The Enforcement of Morals (Oxford University Press: Oxford, 1965).

Fyodor Dostoyevsky, Notes from the Underground, translated by Jessie Coulson (Penguin Books: London, 1972).

Ronald Dworkin, 'What Rights Do We Have?' in Taking Rights Seriously, (London: Duckworth, 1977, 1978), reprinted by permission of Gerald Duckworth & Co. Ltd.

Ronald Dworkin, 'Taking Rights Seriously', in Taking Rights Seriously, (Duckworth: London, 1977, 1978), reprinted by permission of Gerald Duckworth & Co. Ltd.

Ronald Dworkin, 'What is Equality? Part 2: Equality of Resources', Philosophy and Public Affairs 10 (1981) pp. 285-7, 289, 292-4, 296-8, 304-7, 314-5, 331, copyright © 1981 The Johns Hopkins University Press, reprinted by permission of The Johns Hopkins University Press.

T. S. Eliot, Notes Towards the Definition of Culture (Faber and Faber: London, 1948), copyright © 1949 by T. S. Eliot and renewed 1977 by Esme Valerie Eliot, reprinted by permission of Faber and Faber Ltd and Harcourt Brace & Company.

Michel Foucault, 'Two Lectures', in Power/Knowledge, edited by Colin Gordon (Harvester Press, 1980).

Sigmund Freud, Civilization and Its Discontents, from The Standard Edition of the Complete Psychological Works of Sigmund Freud, edited and translated by James Strachey, reprinted by permission of Sigmund Freud © Copyrights, the Institute of Psycho-Analysis, the Hogarth Press, and W. W. Norton and Company, Inc.

Milton Friedman and Rose Friedman, Free to Choose (Secker & Warburg: London), copyright © 1980 by Milton Friedman and Rose D. Friedman, reprinted by permission of Random House UK Limited and Harcourt, Inc.

Francis Fukuyama, The End of History and the Last Man (Penguin Books: London, 1992).

Carol Gilligan, In a Different Voice (Harvard University Press: Cambridge Mass, 1982), copyright © 1982, 1993 by Carol Gilligan, reprinted by permission of the publisher.

Goethe, Faust - Mephistopheles, Part 1 Scene 4, translated by P. Wayne (Penguin Books: London, 1949).

Jurgen Habermas, Legitimation Crisis, translated by Thomas McCarthy (Beacon Press: Boston, 1975), introduction and English translation © 1975 by Beacon Press, reprinted by permission of Beacon Press, Boston and Suhrkamp Verlag, Frankfurt.

H. L. A. Hart, 'Are There Any Natural Rights?', Philosophical Review (64) 1955, reprinted in Anthony Quinton (ed.), Political Philosophy (Oxford University Press: Oxford, 1967).

H. L. A. Hart, Law, Liberty and Morality, (Oxford University Press: Oxford, 1963).

H. L. A. Hart, Punishment and Responsibility (Oxford University Press: Oxford, 1968).

F. A. Hayek, Law, Legislation and Liberty, Vol II (Routledge: London, 1982), reprinted by permission of Routledge.

F. A. Hayek, The Road To Serfdom, (Routledge and Kegan Paul: London, 1944), reprinted by permission of Routledge.

G. W. F. Hegel, Philosophy of Right, translated by T. M. Knox (Clarendon Press: Oxford, 1952).

Thomas Hill, 'The Message of Affirmative Action', Social Philosophy and Policy, 1991, reprinted in Thomas E. Hill Jr., Autonomy and Self-Respect (Cambridge University Press: Cambridge, 1991), reprinted by permission of Cambridge University Press.

Thomas Hobbes, Leviathan, edited with an introduction by J. C. A. Gaskin, (Oxford University Press: Oxford, 1996).

David Hume, Enquiry Concerning the Principles of Morals, in Enquiries, edited by L. A. Selby-Bigge, Third Edition (Clarendon Press: Oxford, 1975).

Alison M. Jaggar, Feminist Politics and Human Nature (Rowman and Littlefield: Atlantic Highlands, New Jersey, 1983), reprinted by permission of Rowman & Littlefield.

Immanuel Kant, On the Common Saying 'This May Be True in Theory, But it Does Not Apply in Practice' and Perpetual Peace in Hans Reiss (ed.), Kant: Political Writings, translated by H. B. Nisbet (Cambridge University Press: Cambridge, 1970, 1991), reprinted by permission of Cambridge University Press.

Martin Luther King, Letter from Birmingham City Jail, in Civil Disobedience in Focus, edited by Hugo Bedau, (Routledge: London, 1991), reprinted by permission of Routledge.

Niccolò Machiavelli, The Discourses, translated by Father L. J. Walker (Routledge: London, 1950), reprinted by permission of Routledge.

Alasdair MacIntyre, After Virtue, (Duckworth: London, 1981), © 1981 by University of Notre Dame Press, reprinted by permission of Gerald Duckworth & Co. Ltd. and the University of Notre Dame Press.

Alasdair MacIntyre, 'Is Patriotism a Virtue?' The Lindley Lecture, University of Kansas, 1984, copyright Department of Philosophy, University of Kansas, reprinted by permission of the University of Kansas and the author.

Catharine A. MacKinnon, Only Words (Harvard University Press: Cambridge Mass, 1993), reprinted by permission of the author.

Ernest Mandel, Marxist Economic Theory, translated by Brian Pearce, (Merlin: London, 1962), reprinted by permission of The Merlin Press Ltd.

Avishai Margalit and Joseph Raz, 'National Self-Determination', Journal of Philosophy 87/8 Sept 1990, reprinted in Joseph Raz, Ethics in the Public Domain (Clarendon Press, Oxford 1994).

Marx, 'On The Jewish Question', in Early Writings, edited by L. Colletti, translated by Rodney Livingstone and Gregor Benton (Penguin Books: London, 1975), reprinted by permission of Verso.

Karl Marx, 'On Money', from Economic and Philosophical Manuscripts, in Early Writings, edited by L. Colletti, translated by Rodney Livingstone and Gregor Benton, (Penguin Books: London, 1975), reprinted by permission of Verso.

Karl Marx, Capital Volume 1, translated by Ben Fowkes (Penguin Books: London, 1976), reprinted by permission of Verso.

Karl Marx, Capital Volume 3, translated by David Fernbach (Penguin Books: London, 1981), reprinted by permission of Verso.

Karl Marx, 'Critique of the Gotha Programme', translated by Joris de Bres, in The First International and After (Penguin Books: London, 1974), reprinted by permission of Verso.

John Stuart Mill, 'Speech in Favour of Capital Punishment', in Applied Ethics, edited by Peter Singer (Oxford University Press: Oxford, 1986).

Charles Louis de Secondat, Baron de Montesquieu, The Spirit of Laws, translated by Thomas Nugent (Hafner Press: New York and Collier Macmillan: London, 1949).

Thomas Nagel, 'War and Massacre', Philosophy and Public Affairs (1) 1972, pp. 128, 133-8, copyright © 1972 The Johns Hopkins University Press, reprinted by permission of The Johns Hopkins University Press.

Friedrich Nietzsche, The Will to Power, translated by Walter Kaufman and R.J. Hollingdale (Vintage: New York, 1967), copyright © 1967 by Walter Kaufman, reprinted by permission of Random House, Inc.

Robert Nozick, Anarchy, State, and Utopia (Basic Books: New York, 1974), copyright © 1974 by Basic Books, Inc., reprinted by permission of Basic Books, a member of Perseus Books, L. L. C.

Michael Oakeshott, 'On Being Conservative', in Rationalism in Politics, (Methuen: London, 1962), reprinted by permission of Routledge.

Onora O'Neill, 'Lifeboat Earth', in Philosophy and Public Affairs (4), 1975, reprinted in Charles Beitz, Marshall Cohen, Thomas Scanlon, and A. John Simmons (eds.),

International Ethics (Princeton University Press, Princeton N. J., 1985) pp. 262-81, copyright © 1975 The Johns Hopkins University Press, reprinted by permission of The Johns Hopkins University Press.

Carole Pateman, Participation and Democratic Theory (Cambridge University Press: Cambridge, 1970), reprinted by permission of Cambridge University Press.

Plato, Crito, in The Last Days of Socrates, translated by Hugh Tredennick (Penguin Books: London, 1954).

Plato, The Republic, translated by H. D. P. Lee (Penguin, 1955).

Karl Popper, Conjectures and Refutations (Routledge and Kegan Paul: London, 1963), reprinted by permission of Melitta and Alfred Raymond Mew.

John Rawls, A Theory of Justice, (Clarendon Press: Oxford, 1972).

Richard Rorty, 'The Priority of Democracy to Philosophy', in Objectivity, Relativism and Truth: Philosphical Papers Volume 1, (Cambridge University Press, Cambridge, 1991), reprinted in Merrill D. Peterson and Robert C. Vaughn (eds.), The Virginia Statute for Religious Freedom (Cambridge University Press: Cambridge, 1988), reprinted by permission of Cambridge University Press.

Jean-Jacques Rousseau, A Discourse on the Arts and Sciences, A Discourse on the Origin of Inequality, and The Social Contract in The Social Contract and Discourses, translated and introduced by G. D. H. Cole (J. M. Dent: London, 1973), reprinted by permission of Everyman's Library, David Campbell Publishers Ltd.

Jean-Jacques Rousseau, Émile, translated by Barbara Foxley (Dent: London, 1911), reprinted by permission of Everyman's Library, David Campbell Publishers Ltd.

Michael Sandel, Liberalism and the Limits of Justice (Cambridge University Press: Cambridge, 1982), reprinted by permission of Cambridge University Press.

Thomas Scanlon, 'A Theory of Freedom of Expression', Philosophy and Public Affairs (1) 1972, pp. 212-3, 215-8, copyright © 1972 The Johns Hopkins University Press, reprinted by permission of The Johns Hopkins University Press.

Friedrich Schiller, On the Aesthetic Education of Man: Sixth Letter, translated by Elizabeth Wilkinson and L. A. Willoughby (Clarendon Press, Oxford, 1967).

Peter Singer, 'Famine, Affluence and Morality', in Philosophy and Public Affairs (1) 1972, pp. 229-235, copyright © 1975 The Johns Hopkins University Press, reprinted by permission of The Johns Hopkins University Press.

Quentin Skinner, 'The Republican Ideal of Political Liberty', in G. Bock, Q. Skinner and M. Viroli (eds.), Machiavelli and Republicanism (Cambridge University Press: Cambridge, 1990), reprinted by permission of Cambridge University Press and the author.

James Fitzjames Stephen, Liberty, Equality, Fraternity, Second Edition, edited by R. J. White (Cambridge University Press: Cambridge, 1967), reprinted by permission of Cambridge University Press.

R.H. Tawney, The Acquisitive Society (Fontana: London, 1966).

Charles Taylor, Hegel (Cambridge University Press: Cambridge, 1975), reprinted by permission of Cambridge University Press.

Charles Taylor, 'What's Wrong With Negative Liberty', in The Idea of Freedom, edited by Alan Ryan (Oxford University Press: Oxford, 1979).

Thucydides, Pericles' Funeral Oration, in History of the Peloponnesian War, translated by Rex Warner with an introduction by M. I. Finley, (Penguin, 1972).

Jeremy Waldron, 'Rushdie and Religion', in Liberal Rights (Cambridge University

Press: Cambridge, 1993) originally published in Times Literary Supplement, March 10-16, 1989, reprinted by permission of the author.

Michael Walzer, Interpretation and Social Criticism (Harvard University Press: Cambridge Mass, 1987), delivered as a Tanner Lecture on Human Values at Brasenose College, Oxford, 1988. Printed with permission of the Tanner Lectures on Human Values, a Corporation, University of Utah, Salt Lake City, Utah.

Michael Walzer, Just and Unjust Wars: A Moral Argument with Historical Illustrations (Basic Books: New York, 1977) copyright © 1977 by Basic Books, Inc., reprinted by permission of Basic Books, a member of Perseus Books, L. L. C.

Michael Walzer, Radical Principles: Reflections of an Unreconstructed Democrat (Basic Books: New York, 1980) copyright © 1980 by Basic Books, Inc., reprinted by permission of Basic Books, a member of Perseus Books, L. L. C.

Max Weber, 'Bureaucracy' pp. 224-226, 'Politics as a Vocation' pp. 77-78, 'Science as a Vocation' pp. 138-140, 147-148, in H. H. Gerth and C. Wright Mills (eds.), From Max Weber: Essays in Sociology, translated by H. H. Gerth and C. Wright Mills (Routledge and Kegan Paul: London, 1948), translation copyright 1946, 1958 by H. H. Gerth and C. Wright Mills, reprinted by permission of Oxford University Press, Inc.

Oscar Wilde, 'The Soul of Man Under Socialism', in De Profundis and Other Writings (Penguin Books: London, 1954), reprinted by permission of Routledge.

Gerald Winstanley, The Law of Freedom, edited by Christopher Hill (Penguin Books: London, 1973), reprinted by permission of Christopher Hill.

Robert Paul Wolff, In Defence of Anarchism (University of California Press, 1970), copyright © 1970, reprinted by permission of the University of California Press.

Declaration of the Rights of Man and Citizen (1789), prepared by Gerald Murphy (The Cleveland Fee-Net aa300), distributed by the Cybercasting Services Division of the National Public Telecomputing Network, reprinted by permission.

The Gettysburg Address (1863), prepared by Gerald Murphy (The Cleveland Fee-Net aa300), distributed by the Cybercasting Services Division of the National Public Telecomputing Network, reprinted by permission.

Index

Page references in *italics* indicate entries in the biographical notes.